Finance Act 1997

Alan Melville
FCA BSc Cert. Ed.

London · Hong Kong · Johannesburg · Melbourne · Singapore · Washington DC

PITMAN PUBLISHING
128 Long Acre, London WC2E 9AN
Tel: +44 (0)171 447 2000
Fax: +44 (0)171 240 5771

A Division of Pearson Professional Limited

First published in Great Britain 1997

ISBN 0 273 62699 X

British Library Cataloguing in Publication Data
A CIP catalogue record for this book can be obtained from the British Library.

10 9 8 7 6 5 4 3 2 1

Printed and bound in Great Britain by Clays Ltd, St Ives plc

The Publishers' policy is to use paper manufactured from sustainable forests.

Contents

Preface

The main aim of this book is to describe the UK taxation system in sufficient depth and with sufficient clarity to meet the needs of those undertaking a first course of study in taxation. The book has not been written with any specific syllabus in mind but is suitable for students who are preparing for any of the following examinations :

Examining body	*Level*	*Examination title*
Institute of Chartered Accountants in England and Wales	Intermediate	Taxation
Association of Chartered Certified Accountants	Certificate Stage	The Tax Framework
Chartered Institute of Management Accountants	Stage 3	Business Taxation
Association of Taxation Technicians	Associateship	Personal and Business Taxation
Association of Accounting Technicians	Technician Stage	Preparing Taxation Computations
Association of Chartered Certified Accountants (Technician qualification)	Level C	Preparing Taxation Computations and Returns
Association of International Accountants	Foundation Stage	Auditing and Taxation
Institute of Company Accountants	Level 2	Taxation 1
Chartered Institute of Bankers	Associateship	Taxation

The book will also be of value to those studying taxation as part of a university or college course in accounting, finance or business studies and may be used as an introductory text for a study of taxation at an advanced level.

Every effort has been made to explain the tax system as clearly as possible. There are numerous worked examples and each chapter (except Chapter 1) concludes with a set of exercises which thoroughly test the reader's grasp of the new topics introduced in that chapter. The book also contains four sets of review questions which are drawn from the past examination papers of the professional accounting bodies. The solutions to most of the exercises and review questions are to be found at the back of the book but the solutions to those exercises and questions marked with an asterisk (*) are provided in a separate Instructor's Manual.

This third edition incorporates the provisions of the Finance Act 1997.

Alan Melville
April 1997

Acknowledgements

I would like to thank the following accounting bodies for granting me permission to use their past examination questions :

- Institute of Chartered Accountants in England and Wales (ICAEW)
- Association of Chartered Certified Accountants (ACCA)
- Chartered Institute of Management Accountants (CIMA)
- Association of Accounting Technicians (AAT).

I must point out that the answers provided to these questions are entirely my own and are not the responsibility of the accounting body concerned.

I would also like to thank the Central Statistical Office for granting me permission to reproduce the table of Retail Price Indexes given in Chapter 17.

Alan Melville

Summary of Tax Data

Income tax

Rates			1997/98 £		1996/97 £
Lower rate	20%	first	4,100	first	3,900
Basic rate	23% (*24% in 1996/97*)	next	22,000	next	21,600
Higher rate	40%	over	26,100	over	25,500

A special rate of 34% (*also 34% in 1996/97*) applies to discretionary trusts.

Allowances	*1997/98* £	*1996/97* £
Personal allowance		
Age 0 to 64	4,045	3,765
Age 65 to 74	5,220	4,910
Age 75 or over	5,400	5,090
Blind person's allowance	1,280	1,250
Married couple's allowance†		
Age 0 to 64	1,830	1,790
Age 65 to 74	3,185	3,115
Age 75 or over	3,225	3,155
Additional personal allowance†	1,830	1,790
Widow's bereavement allowance†	1,830	1,790
Income limit for age-related allowances	15,600	15,200

Allowances marked† are restricted to 15% relief.

Car fuel benefit	£	£
Petrol-driven cars		
up to 1,400 cc	800	710
1,401 cc to 2,000 cc	1,010	890
2,001 cc and above	1,490	1,320
Diesel-driven cars		
up to 2,000 cc	740	640
2,001 cc and above	940	820

Personal pensions		
Earnings cap	84,000	82,200

National Insurance contributions

		1997/98	*1996/97*
Class 1 (not contracted out)			
Lower earnings limit (weekly)		£62	£61
Upper earnings limit (weekly)		£465	£455
Employee contributions			
Lower rate		2%	2%
Standard rate		10%	10%
Employer contributions on all earnings (weekly)			
Earnings less than £62	(*1996/97 £61*)	0%	0%
Earnings less than £110	(*1996/97 £110*)	3%	3%
Earnings less than £155	(*1996/97 £155*)	5%	5%
Earnings less than £210	(*1996/97 £210*)	7%	7%
Earnings £210 or more	(*1996/97 £210*)	10%	10.2%
Class 2			
Weekly contribution		£6.15	£6.05
Small earnings exemption limit		£3,480	£3,430
Class 3			
Weekly contribution		£6.05	£5.95
Class 4			
Rate		6%	6%
Lower profits limit		£7,010	£6,860
Upper profits limit		£24,180	£23,660

Capital gains tax

	1997/98	*1996/97*
	£	£
Annual exemption	6,500	6,300
Retirement relief		
upper limit for 100% relief	250,000	250,000
upper limit for 50% relief	1,000,000	1,000,000

Corporation tax

Financial Year	*Full rate*	*Small company rate*	*Marginal relief fraction*	*Lower limit*	*Upper limit*	*ACT rate*
				£	£	
FY91	33%	25%	1/50	250,000	1,250,000	25%
FY92	33%	25%	1/50	250,000	1,250,000	25%
FY93	33%	25%	1/50	250,000	1,250,000	22.5%
FY94	33%	25%	1/50	300,000	1,500,000	20%
FY95	33%	25%	1/50	300,000	1,500,000	20%
FY96	33%	24%	9/400	300,000	1,500,000	20%
FY97	33%	23%	1/40	300,000	1,500,000	20%

Inheritance tax

Date of transfer	**0% Band**	**Rate on chargeable lifetime transfers**	**Rate on death**
6 April 1990 to 5 April 1991	0 - £128,000	20%	40%
6 April 1991 to 9 March 1992	0 - £140,000	20%	40%
10 March 1992 to 5 April 1995	0 - £150,000	20%	40%
6 April 1995 to 5 April 1996	0 - £154,000	20%	40%
6 April 1996 to 5 April 1997	0 - £200,000	20%	40%
On or after 6 April 1997	0 - £215,000	20%	40%

Value added tax

Standard rate (from 1 April 1991)	17.5%
Registration threshold (from 27 November 1996)	£48,000
Deregistration threshold (from 27 November 1996)	£46,000

PART 1
INCOME TAX AND NATIONAL INSURANCE

Chapter 1

Introduction to the UK tax system

Introduction

The purpose of this first chapter is to provide an overview of the UK tax system. The main taxes are introduced, the principal sources of tax law are explained and the structure of the Inland Revenue (which is the main body concerned with the assessment and collection of tax in the UK) is described. This chapter also outlines the administration system which is used to assess the tax liability of an individual.

UK taxes

The UK taxation system is composed of a number of different taxes, some of which are *direct* taxes and some of which are *indirect* taxes.

Direct taxes are charged on a taxpayer's income, profits or other gains and are often paid by the taxpayer directly to the tax authorities. The main direct taxes are income tax, capital gains tax and inheritance tax (which are paid by individuals) and corporation tax (which is paid by companies). All of these taxes are administered by the Inland Revenue. National insurance contributions are, in effect, a form of direct taxation administered by the Department of Social Security.

Indirect taxes are taxes on spending. They are charged when a taxpayer buys an item and are paid to the vendor as part of the purchase price of the item. It is then the vendor's duty to pass the tax on to the tax authorities. The main indirect taxes are value added tax, customs duties and excise duties (e.g. the duties on alcohol, tobacco and petrol). The only indirect tax considered in this book is value added tax, which is administered by the Customs and Excise.

Sources of tax law

There is no single source of UK tax law. The basic rules are laid down in Acts of Parliament but it is left to the courts to interpret these Acts and to provide much of the fine detail of the tax system. In addition, the Inland Revenue, the Department of Social Security and the Customs and Excise issue a variety of statements, notices and leaflets which explain how the law is implemented in practice. These statements have no legal backing but they do provide information on the tax authorities' interpretation of the law and will be adhered to unless successfully challenged in the courts.

Statute law

The basic rules of the UK tax system are embodied in a number of tax *statutes* or Acts of Parliament. The main statutes which are currently in force are as follows :

Tax	*Statute*	*Abbreviation*
Income tax & }	Income and Corporation Taxes Act 1988	ICTA 1988
Corporation Tax }	Capital Allowances Act 1990	CAA 1990
Capital gains tax	Taxation of Chargeable Gains Act 1992	TCGA 1992
Inheritance tax	Inheritance Tax Act 1984	IHTA 1984
National insurance	Social Security Contributions & Benefits Act 1992	SSCBA 1992
Value added tax	Value Added Tax Act 1994	VATA 1994
Administration of direct taxation	Taxes Management Act 1970	TMA 1970
Administration of indirect taxation	Customs and Excise Management Act, 1979	CEMA 1979

These statutes are amended and supplemented each year by the annual Finance Act, which usually receives Royal Assent in early May and is based upon the Budget proposals put forward by the Chancellor of the Exchequer in the previous November or December. From time to time, all the statute law relating to a particular tax is consolidated into a new statute. In 1994, for example, the law relating to value added tax (which was previously embodied in VATA 1983, as modified and extended by subsequent Finance Acts) was consolidated into the new VATA 1994.

Some of the statutes (especially VATA 1994) provide for the making of detailed regulations by *statutory instrument.* A statutory instrument (SI) is a document which is laid before Parliament and which automatically becomes law within a stated period unless any objections are raised to it.

It is also worth noting that membership of the European Union involves adherence to EU law and that if there is a conflict between EU law and the law of a member state then EU law will take priority. This applies as much to tax law as to any other category of law and the European influence on UK tax law is likely to increase over time. At present, the main impact is on value added tax, where the prevailing legislation takes the form of EU Directives. These Directives are binding on the UK and dictate the results which the internal legislation of the UK must bring about.

Case law

Over the years, many thousands of tax cases have been brought before the courts and the decisions made by judges in order to resolve these cases form an important part of the tax law of the UK. Some of the more significant cases are referred to in this book.

Statements made by the tax authorities

The main statements and other documents produced by the Inland Revenue as a guide to the law on direct taxation are as follows :

(a) **Statements of practice (SP's)**. A statement of practice explains the Inland Revenue's interpretation of tax legislation and clarifies the way in which the law will be applied in practice. For example, SP 1/94 (the first SP issued in 1994) deals with the taxation of non-statutory redundancy payments.

(b) **Extra-statutory concessions (ESC's)**. An extra-statutory concession is a relaxation which gives taxpayers a reduction in liability to which they are not entitled under the strict letter of the law. Most ESC's are made so as to resolve anomalies or to relieve hardship. For example, ESC B10 is concerned with the income of contemplative religious communities.

(c) **Press releases**. These are issued throughout the year on a wide variety of tax-related subjects. Of especial interest are the Budget press releases which are issued on Budget day and which provide a detailed explanation of the Budget proposals.

(d) **Manuals**. The Inland Revenue produces a very comprehensive set of internal tax manuals for the guidance of its own staff. These manuals may be inspected at tax offices and are also available for sale.

(e) **Pamphlets**. These are aimed at the general public and explain the tax system in non-technical language. For example, pamphlet IR95 is a guide to profit sharing schemes (see Chapter 7).

Similarly, the Department of Social Security and the Customs and Excise issue a range of explanatory notices and leaflets on matters relating to national insurance contributions and value added tax respectively.

The tax year

The proposed amendments to the tax system which are put forward in the annual Budget speech are usually intended to take effect as from the beginning of the next tax year, though some of the proposals may have a more immediate effect.

A "tax year" (which is also known as a "fiscal year" or a "year of assessment") runs from 6 April in one year to 5 April in the following year so that the tax year referred to as 1996/97 ran from 6 April 1996 to 5 April 1997 inclusive. This book takes into account the provisions of the Finance Act 1997 (based on the November 1996 Budget proposals) and describes the UK tax system for tax year 1997/98.

It is worth noting that the tax year for corporation tax purposes is slightly different from the usual tax year. A corporation tax "financial year" runs from 1 April in one year to 31 March in the following year and is identified by the year in which it begins. This book describes the corporation tax system for Financial Year 1997, which runs from 1 April 1997 to 31 March 1998 inclusive.

Structure of the Inland Revenue

The structure of the Inland Revenue, which is responsible for the administration of the direct tax system, is described below. The structure of the Customs and Excise, which is responsible for the administration of the indirect tax system, is described in Chapter 30.

The Inland Revenue is a body of civil servants which is headed by the *Commissioners of Inland Revenue* (CIR), known collectively as the *Board of Inland Revenue*. The Commissioners are appointed by the *Treasury*, which is the Government department with overall responsibility for the public finances and which is managed by the *Chancellor of the Exchequer*. The main duties of the Commissioners of Inland Revenue are :

(a) to implement the statute law relating to direct taxation

(b) to provide advice to the Chancellor of the Exchequer on direct tax matters

(c) to administer the many divisions and offices into which the Inland Revenue is organised.

The Inland Revenue has specialist offices which deal with such matters as pension schemes, oil taxation, share valuations etc. but most of the day-to-day work of the Inland Revenue is carried out by *Inspectors of Taxes*, whose function is to calculate or "assess" a taxpayer's tax liability, and *Collectors of Taxes*, whose function is to collect the tax due. Under the Self Assessment system (see below) each taxpayer is given the opportunity of calculating his or her own tax liability, in which case it is the Inspector's responsibility to check the taxpayer's "self-assessment".

Her Majesty's Inspectors of Taxes (HMIT) are organised into several hundred local district offices, each managed by a district Inspector with the assistance of other Inspectors and clerical staff. The Collectors of Taxes also have district offices but much of the routine collection work is performed by centralised accounts offices, which are highly computerised.

This separation of assessment and collection is traditional but inevitably gives rise to communication problems and seems to possess few virtues. As a consequence, a programme of reorganisation is currently underway which will eventually replace the existing district offices by :

(a) Taxpayer Assistance Offices, which will deal with taxpayers' general queries and issue tax forms and pamphlets
(b) Taxpayer Service Offices, which will deal with much routine assessment and collection work
(c) Taxpayer District Offices, which will concentrate on compliance work (i.e. checking that taxpayers have complied with tax regulations).

When this programme of reorganisation is complete, the functions of assessment and collection will merge and the term "Officer of the Board" will replace the traditional terms "Inspector" and "Collector". By April 1996, the reorganisation programme was approximately one-third complete.

Administration of the tax system

This chapter concludes with a description of the administration system which is used to assess an individual's liability to income tax and capital gains tax. Later chapters explain the equivalent systems used for corporation tax, inheritance tax and value added tax.

For tax years up to and including 1995/96, the assessment of an individual's tax liability was entirely the responsibility of the Inland Revenue and it was possible for taxpayers to delay the assessment and payment of tax by withholding information from the Inland Revenue for as long as possible. The introduction of the Self Assessment system in 1996/97 has shifted responsibility from the Inland Revenue to the taxpayer and makes it much more likely that tax is assessed and paid on time.

The Self Assessment system is explained below. The pre-Self Assessment system is no longer in use and is not described here.

Self Assessment

If an individual's tax liability for a tax year cannot be collected entirely by deduction at source (see Chapter 2) or via the PAYE system (see Chapter 7), then the tax liability must be the subject of a formal tax assessment. The amount of tax due for the year may be assessed by the taxpayer (a "self-assessment") and then checked by the Inland Revenue. Alternatively, if the taxpayer chooses not to make a self-assessment, the amount due will be assessed by the Inland Revenue. In either case, the first step is the completion of an annual *tax return*. The procedure is as follows :

(a) In early April each year, the Inland Revenue issues tax returns to those taxpayers who are likely to need them. The tax return consists of a basic 8-page form together with a number of accompanying "supplementary pages", each dealing with a different type of income or gains (e.g. income from self-employment, foreign income etc). Taxpayers are sent only those supplementary pages which are thought to be relevant to their particular circumstances, but can request further supplementary pages if necessary. A disk version of the tax return is available for those who wish to complete their tax return with the aid of a personal computer and submit the completed return electronically (the "Electronic Lodgement Service").

(b) The information requested in a tax return relates to the tax year just ended. For example, the tax returns issued in April 1998 require taxpayers to declare their income and gains for the year to 5 April 1998 and to claim allowances and reliefs (see Chapters 3 and 4) for the same year.

(c) The tax return must be completed in full. It is not permissible to omit figures or to make entries such as "see accounts" or "as submitted by employer". Unless asked to submit accounts or other supporting documentation with the return, a taxpayer is under no obligation to do so. However, it is necessary to retain all supporting documentation in case the Inland Revenue enquires into the accuracy of a return.

(d) The tax return includes an optional tax calculation section in which the taxpayer can calculate his or her own tax liability. If this section is left blank, the Inland Revenue will assess the tax liability on the taxpayer's behalf and send a copy of this assessment to the taxpayer. In either case, the resulting assessment is referred to as a "self-assessment".

(e) The tax return must be "filed" i.e. sent back to the Inspector of Taxes on or before the following dates :

   (i) 31 January following the end of the year to which the return relates (or within 3 months of the date of issue of the return, if later), for taxpayers who have calculated their own tax liability, or

   (ii) 30 September following the end of the year to which the return relates (or within 2 months of the date of issue of the return, if later), for taxpayers who wish the Inland Revenue to calculate their tax liability.

   The 31 January following the end of a tax year is known as the "annual filing date" for that year. For example, the annual filing date for tax year 1997/98 is 31 January 1999. A regime of automatic penalties (see Chapter 14) applies if a return is filed late.

(f) Strictly speaking, taxpayers who fail to submit a tax return by the 30 September deadline have lost the opportunity to ignore the optional tax calculation section of the return and the Inland Revenue are entitled to reject (as incomplete) any return received after 30 September unless this section has been filled in. If a return is rejected in these circumstances and the taxpayer is then obliged to complete the tax calculation section, it is possible that eventual submission of the completed return will be delayed beyond the annual filing date and an automatic penalty will be incurred (see Chapter 14).

However, it seems likely that the Inland Revenue will usually assess the tax due if a return is submitted not long after 30 September, but the taxpayer then runs the risk that the assessment might not be made until after the date on which the assessed tax is due for payment. In such cases, surcharges and interest will be charged on any tax paid late (see Chapter 14).

(g) The Inland Revenue has the right to "repair" a taxpayer's self-assessment (i.e. to correct any obvious mistakes) within 9 months of the date on which the return is filed by the taxpayer.

(h) The taxpayer has the right to amend his or her tax return and self-assessment within 12 months of the annual filing date for that return. Taxpayers who believe that an error or mistake in their tax return has resulted in an excessive self-assessment may make an "error or mistake" claim within five years of the annual filing date for the year to which the claim relates.

(i) The tax due in relation to a self-assessment is normally payable as follows :

   (i) A first payment on account (POA) is due on 31 January in the tax year to which the self-assessment relates.

   (ii) A second POA is due on the following 31 July.

   (iii) A final balancing payment is due on the annual filing date i.e. on 31 January following the end of the tax year.

   For example, the tax due in relation to a 1997/98 self-assessment would be payable on 31 January 1998 (first POA), 31 July 1998 (second POA) and 31 January 1999 (balancing payment). Further information regarding the payment of tax is given in Chapter 14.

Notification of chargeability to tax

Individuals who have not received a tax return, but have taxable income or capital gains of which the Inland Revenue is not aware, must notify the Revenue of their chargeability to tax within 6 months of the end of the tax year in which the income arises. Penalties are imposed for non-compliance with this requirement (see Chapter 14). Notification of chargeability to tax is *not* required if :

(a) the taxpayer has no capital gains, and

(b) the taxpayer is not a higher rate taxpayer (see Chapter 2), and

(c) all of the taxpayer's income has been subject to deduction of tax at source (see Chapter 2) or has been dealt with via the PAYE system (see Chapter 7).

Enquiries

The Inland Revenue adopts a "process now - check later" approach to tax returns filed under the Self Assessment system. The information supplied in tax returns is processed when the returns are filed and any obvious errors in taxpayers' self-assessments are repaired (see above) but no attempt is made at that time to check that the correct amount of income and gains has been declared. However, all returns are eventually checked and some are selected for detailed enquiry. Note that :

(a) The majority of enquiries arise because the Inspector wishes to ask questions about the information given in a specific tax return, but it is not necessary for the Inspector to justify an enquiry and some enquiry cases are chosen entirely at random.

(b) In most cases, enquiries must begin within 12 months of the annual filing date for the year to which the enquiry relates. This means that a taxpayer who has made full disclosure of all relevant facts in a tax return can be sure that the corresponding self-assessment is final if no enquiry has begun within 12 months of the annual filing date. However, the Inspector may raise a "discovery assessment" after these 12 months have elapsed if it is discovered that full disclosure has not been made. The time limits for discovery assessments under the Self Assessment system are :

   (i) 31 January in the sixth tax year following the year to which the assessment relates, in the case of incomplete disclosure of facts without negligence or fraud

   (ii) 31 January in the twenty-first tax year following the year to which the assessment relates, in the case of negligence or fraud.

Determinations

If a taxpayer fails to file a tax return by the required date, the Inspector of Taxes may make a "determination" of the tax due, calculated according to "the best of his information and belief". The taxpayer cannot appeal against this determination and cannot apply for the tax due to be postponed (see below). A determination can be displaced only if the taxpayer files the required return.

Appeals

Under Self Assessment, taxpayers have the right of appeal in relation to certain Inland Revenue decisions. The main classes of appeal are :

(a) an appeal against the imposition of a fixed penalty (see Chapter 14)

(b) an appeal against the imposition of a surcharge (see Chapter 14)

(c) an appeal against a request by the Inland Revenue that the taxpayer should submit documents, records etc. in the course of an Inland Revenue enquiry

(d) an appeal against amendments made to a self-assessment as a consequence of an Inland Revenue enquiry

(e) an appeal to the effect that the relevant conditions for the making of a discovery assessment do not exist

(f) an appeal against a discovery assessment.

The appeals procedure

In general, appeals must be made in writing to the Inspector of Taxes and must be made within 30 days of the relevant Inland Revenue decision. In the case of disputed amendments to self-assessments and disputed discovery assessments, the taxpayer may also apply to postpone payment of all or part of the tax assessed, pending settlement of the appeal. Note that :

(a) Postponement applications are subject to the agreement of the Inspector of Taxes. Applications which cannot be accepted by the Inspector may be referred to the appeal Commissioners (see below).

(b) Any non-postponed part of the tax due on a disputed assessment is payable on the due date in the usual way. If the appeal is subsequently determined in the taxpayer's favour, any overpaid tax is refunded.

(c) Most appeals are settled by an informal process of discussion between the Inspector and the taxpayer (or the taxpayer's accountant), culminating in agreement of the amount of tax due. Appeals which cannot be resolved amicably in this way are referred to the appeal Commissioners (who should not be confused with the Commissioners of Inland Revenue mentioned earlier in this chapter). Appeal Commissioners fall into two categories, the *General Commissioners* and the *Special Commissioners.*

(d) The General Commissioners are appointed by the Lord Chancellor to hear appeals locally. They do not usually possess any formal tax qualifications and are similar in many ways to magistrates, being part-time and unpaid. They are assisted by a paid clerk who is normally a local solicitor or accountant. The appeals brought before the General Commissioners are usually of a fairly straightforward nature.

(e) The Special Commissioners, who are also appointed by the Lord Chancellor, are similar to circuit judges and travel the country hearing appeals which involve complex matters of tax law. They are full-time tax professionals and they are paid for their services.

(f) The appeal Commissioners may either confirm, reduce or increase a disputed assessment and their decision on a matter of fact is final. But either the Inspector of Taxes or the taxpayer may express dissatisfaction with the Commissioners' decision on a point of law and take the appeal further, first to the High Court, then to the Court of Appeal and ultimately to the House of Lords.

(g) The costs of bringing an appeal before the appeal Commissioners are usually fairly modest. Each party to the appeal bears their own costs and the Commissioners cannot normally require the losing party to pay the costs of the victor (though the Special Commissioners may do so if they believe that a taxpayer has acted wholly unreasonably). The costs of taking an appeal to the High Court and beyond can be extremely high and an unsuccessful taxpayer may be required to pay the costs of the Inland Revenue in defending the appeal as well as his or her own costs.

Record keeping

It is compulsory for taxpayers to keep proper records so that they can make a correct tax return. Business records relating to a given tax year must be retained for 5 years after the annual filing date for that year. Personal records must be retained for 12 months after the annual filing date.

Inland Revenue Adjudicator

The Inland Revenue Adjudicator acts independently of the Inland Revenue and considers complaints made by taxpayers who are not satisfied with the quality of the service which they have received from the Inland Revenue. The Adjudicator produces an annual report and makes recommendations for improvements to Inland Revenue procedures and practices. To date, all of these recommendations have been accepted by the Inland Revenue. The Adjudicator is not empowered to hear appeals.

The Inland Revenue Adjudicator also acts as Adjudicator for the Customs and Excise and for the Contributions Agency of the Department of Social Security. As a result, complainants have a single point of contact for complaints about any tax matter.

Taxpayer's Charter

The Taxpayer's Charter (which was produced jointly by the Inland Revenue and the Customs and Excise) sets out the standards of service which a taxpayer has the right to expect from the tax authorities. The Charter also describes the tax authorities' expectations of the taxpayer. In summary, a taxpayer has the right to expect that the tax authorities will be fair, helpful and efficient, whilst the authorities expect the taxpayer to be honest, to provide accurate information and to pay tax on the due date.

A series of codes of practice is being published by the Inland Revenue in support of the Taxpayer's Charter, each relating to a specific aspect of the Revenue's work.

Tax evasion and tax avoidance

As stated above, the Inland Revenue expects a taxpayer to be honest. Dishonest behaviour, such as deliberately concealing a source of income, is known as *tax evasion* and is punishable by law.

On the other hand, taxpayers are entitled to organise their financial affairs in such a way that their tax burden is minimised. This perfectly legal activity is known as *tax avoidance.*

Summary

- Direct taxes are charged on income, profits and other gains and are often paid directly to the tax authorities. The main direct taxes are income tax, capital gains tax, inheritance tax and corporation tax. National insurance contributions are also a form of direct taxation.
- Indirect taxes are taxes on spending and are paid as part of the price of a bought item. The main indirect taxes are VAT, customs duties and excise duties.
- Taxation law is a combination of statute law and case law. Statements made by the tax authorities have no legal force but provide information on the authorities' interpretation of the law.
- The fiscal year runs from 6 April to the following 5 April. The corporation tax financial year runs from 1 April to the following 31 March.
- The Inland Revenue is headed by the Commissioners of Inland Revenue.
- The duty of the Inspector of Taxes is to calculate a taxpayer's tax liability (or to check the taxpayer's own calculation of that liability) based upon information provided in the annual tax return. The tax due is then collected by the Collector of Taxes.
- The system of Self Assessment applies as from tax year 1996/97. Under this system, taxpayers are given the option to calculate their own tax liabilities.
- Tax returns must normally be filed by 30 September following the end of the tax year if the taxpayer wishes the Inland Revenue to calculate the amount of tax due, or by 31 January following the end of the tax year if the taxpayer performs the calculation.
- A taxpayer who has not received a tax return, but has taxable income or capital gains of which the Inland Revenue is not aware, must notify the Revenue of his or her chargeability to tax within 6 months of the end of the tax year in which the income arises.

- The Inspector of Taxes may initiate an enquiry within 12 months of the annual filing date for the year to which the enquiry relates. Discovery assessments may be made after these 12 months have elapsed if it is discovered that the taxpayer has not made full disclosure of all relevant facts.
- In certain circumstances, taxpayers have the right of appeal against Inland Revenue decisions. Appeals are heard initially by the General Commissioners or the Special Commissioners but may progress to the Courts.
- Tax evasion should be distinguished from tax avoidance. The former involves dishonest conduct by the taxpayer and is illegal. The latter involves the sensible arrangement of the taxpayer's affairs so as to minimise the liability to tax and is perfectly legal.

Chapter 2

Introduction to income tax

Introduction

Income tax assessments are computed for a tax year (or "year of assessment") and are based on the taxpayer's aggregate income for that year from all sources, ignoring any income which is exempt from income tax. The computation takes into account any tax-deductible payments made by the taxpayer during the year and the taxpayer's entitlement to personal allowances and reliefs. This chapter explains the main features of an income tax computation, in preparation for the much more detailed information which is provided in subsequent chapters.

As stated in Chapter 1, current income tax legislation is to be found in the Income and Corporation Taxes Act 1988, as amended by subsequent Finance Acts.

Taxable persons

In general, an individual who is resident in the UK for a tax year is liable to pay income tax on all of his or her income for that year, including both income arising in the UK and income which is derived from an overseas source. However, there are two main exceptions to this general rule :

(a) Certain forms of income are exempt from income tax altogether (see later in this chapter).

(b) Income derived from an overseas source by a UK resident who is not domiciled in the UK (i.e. whose natural home is not the UK) is only subject to income tax to the extent that the income is remitted to the UK.

Individuals who are not UK residents are liable to pay income tax on their UK income only. (Chapter 32 provides a detailed explanation of "residence" and its application to income tax). Income tax is payable by :

(a) adults, on their own personal income and on their share of the income of a partnership

(b) children, if they have sufficient income to pay tax

(c) trustees, on the income of a trust or settlement
(d) personal representatives, on the income arising from the estate of a deceased person.

The following persons and organisations are *not* liable to pay income tax, whether or not they are resident in the UK :

(a) companies (which pay corporation tax on their income instead of income tax)
(b) registered charities
(c) scientific research associations
(d) approved pension funds
(e) representatives of foreign countries (e.g. ambassadors)
(f) visiting members of foreign armed forces (on their service pay only)
(g) local authorities
(h) trade unions (on certain types of income).

The schedular system

Some types of income are *taxed at source* (i.e. tax is deducted from the income before the taxpayer receives it). Typical examples are dividends, building society interest and most forms of bank interest. Other types of income are received in full, without deduction of any tax at source. Typical examples are the profits of a self-employed person and the rents received by a landlord. The tax due on these types of income has to be assessed by the Inspector of Taxes (or self-assessed by the taxpayer) and therefore such income is often referred to as income which is *taxed by direct assessment*. Income which is taxed by direct assessment is classified into three main categories or "schedules", each identified by a letter of the alphabet. Two of the schedules are subdivided into further categories known as "cases". The main types of income assessed under each schedule and case are as follows :

Schedule A		-	Income from property (e.g. rents)
Schedule D	Case I	-	Profits of a trade
	Case II	-	Profits of a profession or vocation
	Case III	-	Interest received "gross" (i.e. without deduction of tax at source)
	Case IV	-	Interest on overseas securities
	Case V	-	Income from overseas possessions
	Case VI	-	Income not assessed under any other schedule or case
Schedule E	Case I	-	} Emoluments of an office or employment (the applicable
	Case II	-	} case depends upon the employee's residence status and
	Case III	-	} whether the work is performed in the UK or abroad).

Each schedule and case has its own rules for determining the amount of income arising in a given tax year. Since the rules differ from one schedule and case to another it is vitally important to allocate income to the correct schedule and case.

Note that the tax due under Schedule E is usually deducted from employees' wages and salaries by their employers and then paid over to the Inland Revenue. In general, therefore, employees receive their emoluments net of tax. However, the amount of tax deducted from an employee depends upon that employee's tax code (see Chapter 7), which has to be determined for each employee individually by the Inspector of Taxes. Consequently, this type of income is regarded as assessed income rather than as income which is taxed at source.

The missing Schedules B and C have been abolished. There is also a Schedule F but this has no impact on individual taxpayers. Schedule F relates to companies which effectively pay dividends net of tax and account for this tax to the Inland Revenue (see Chapter 25 for a more detailed explanation).

Non-taxable income

Schedule D Case VI seems to catch any income not already caught by the other schedules and cases. However, certain types of income are specifically exempt from income tax. Some of the most important sources of non-taxable income are :

(a) the first £70 of interest received on a National Savings Bank (NSB) Ordinary account (see Chapter 6)

(b) interest on National Savings Certificates

(c) interest on Tax Exempt Special Savings Accounts (see Chapter 6)

(d) income from Personal Equity Plans (see Chapter 6)

(e) dividends received on ordinary shares in a Venture Capital Trust, so long as certain conditions are satisfied (see Chapter 6)

(f) winnings from betting, competition prizes and premium bond prizes

(g) certain social security benefits (e.g. family credit, housing benefit, child benefit, attendance allowance, mobility allowance) though others are taxable (e.g. the state retirement pension)

(h) wound and disability pensions.

(i) statutory redundancy pay and the first £30,000 of compensation received for loss of employment (see Chapter 7)

(j) income of up to £4,250 p.a. received under the "rent-a-room" scheme (see Chapter 5)

(k) income from scholarships.

Structure of an income tax computation

In order to calculate a taxpayer's income tax liability for a tax year it is necessary to bring together *all* of the taxpayer's income into a single tax computation. For reasons which are explained below, income which has already been taxed at source must also be included in this computation. A typical income tax computation for the year 1997/98 might appear as follows :

		£
Schedule A (Income from property)		2,500
Schedule D Case I (Income from self-employment)		34,500
Schedule D Case III (Interest received gross)		2,300
Building society interest taxed at source (pre-tax equivalent)		700
Total income		40,000
Less : Charges on income		1,000
Statutory total income		39,000
Less : Personal allowance		4,045
Taxable Income		34,955
Income tax		
4,100	@ 20%	820.00
22,000	@ 23%	5,060.00
8,855	@ 40%	3,542.00
34,955		9,422.00
Less : Tax reducers		274.50
Tax borne		9,147.50
Add : Tax withheld on charges		230.00
Tax liability for the year		9,377.50
Less : Tax paid by deduction at source		140.00
Tax payable		9,237.50

All of the terms used in this computation are explained in great detail in this chapter and in later chapters. For the time being it is sufficient to understand the main features of the computation, which are as follows :

(a) The taxpayer's total income for the year is calculated by adding together income from all sources, including the pre-tax equivalent of any income which has already been taxed but excluding any income which is exempt from income tax.

(b) Certain payments made by the taxpayer known as "charges on income" are deducted from total income, giving statutory total income (STI).

(c) The taxpayer's personal allowance is deducted from STI, giving taxable income. The personal allowance (£4,045 in 1997/98) acts as a tax threshold, ensuring that those on very low incomes do not have to pay income tax.

(d) Income tax is charged on the taxable income, using the rates of tax in force for the year in question. The amount of tax calculated in this way is then subject to a number of adjustments and the result is the tax payable to the Inland Revenue.

(e) The *tax borne* by the taxpayer is the amount of tax suffered for the year. This may be different from the *tax liability*, which is the amount of tax which the taxpayer must account for to the Inland Revenue and the *tax payable* which is the tax remaining to be paid after deducting any tax already paid for the year. These distinctions will become clearer in the course of this chapter and the next two chapters.

A tax computation is not required for every taxpayer. For example, a computation is not usually required for an individual whose income consists entirely of remuneration from employment, since the correct amount of tax is deducted automatically by the PAYE system (see Chapter 7). However, the only way to calculate the tax liability in more complex cases (e.g. for taxpayers with several sources of income) is to prepare a computation and this approach should always be adopted when answering examination questions.

Married couples

At one time, a wife's income was aggregated with that of her husband into a single joint assessment but this arrangement ceased in tax year 1989/90. Married couples are now taxed independently, which means that the husband's income and the wife's income are taxed completely separately. If a married couple receive joint income (e.g. interest received on a joint bank account) then the income is normally divided between them equally. However, if the source of the income is genuinely held between them in some other proportion, the couple may make a declaration to that effect and the income will then be divided between them as appropriate.

The rates of income tax

An individual's taxable income is taxed according to the rates of income tax in force for the year in question. For 1997/98, the rates of income tax are as follows :

First £4,100 of taxable income	20% (the "lower rate")
Next £22,000 of taxable income	23% (the "basic rate")
Remainder of taxable income after first £26,100	40% (the "higher rate")

Note that :

(a) The first £4,100 of taxable income is referred to as the "lower rate band" and the next £22,000 of taxable income is referred to as the "basic rate band".

(b) Calculations are normally made to the nearest pound when calculating a taxpayer's taxable income but the tax due is calculated to the nearest penny.

(c) Income from savings is treated specially, as explained below.

EXAMPLE 1

Calculate the income tax payable in 1997/98 on a taxable income (i.e. income after deducting charges and the personal allowance) of :

(a) £1,750

(b) £19,600

(c) £36,804

(Assume that none of the income is derived from savings).

SOLUTION

(a) 1,750 @ 20% = £350.00.

(b) 4,100 @ 20% + 15,500 @ 23% = £4,385.00.

(c) 4,100 @ 20% + 22,000 @ 23% + 10,704 @ 40% = £10,161.60.

Income taxed at source

If tax has already been deducted from a source of income (e.g. wages and salaries received after deduction of tax, or dividends and interest received net of tax) such income must still be included in the taxpayer's computation. This may seem to be unnecessary (since tax has already been paid) but there are two good reasons for including the income in the computation :

(a) It is important to derive the correct figures for total income and statutory total income, as will become clearer in later chapters.

(b) The amount of tax which has already been deducted might not be the correct amount. The only way to check this is to aggregate the income concerned with all of the taxpayer's other income in a single tax computation.

In any tax computation, all income must be shown "gross" (i.e. before any deduction of tax). When the tax liability has been calculated, the taxpayer is given credit for any tax already paid and is required to pay only the balance of the liability. A tax refund is given if tax credits exceed the tax liability for the year.

If wages and salaries are received net of income tax, the gross pay and the tax deducted can easily be found by examining the end-of-year certificate supplied by the taxpayer's employer. But in the case of dividends, interest etc. it is normally necessary to deduce the gross figure from the net figure, as follows :

(a) Certain forms of income are received net of income tax deducted at the lower rate of 20%. In this case, the gross income is equal to the net income multiplied by 100/80 and the tax credit is equal to the net income multiplied by 20/80 (or 20% of the gross income). The main classes of income which are received net of lower rate tax are :

    (i) building society interest and most types of bank interest
    (ii) interest on most UK Government securities ("gilt edged" securities)
    (iii) debenture and other loan interest paid by UK companies
    (iv) the income element of purchased life annuities.

    In effect, dividends from UK companies are also received net of lower rate income tax. (The tax treatment of dividends paid by UK companies is fully described in Chapter 25).

(b) Other forms of income (e.g. patent royalties) are received net of income tax deducted at the basic rate of 23%. In this case, the gross income is equal to the net income multiplied by 100/77 and the tax credit is equal to the net income multiplied by 23/77 (or 23% of the gross income).

EXAMPLE 2

In 1997/98, an individual receives net income of £1,232. Compute the equivalent gross income and the accompanying tax credit if the income consists entirely of :

(a) building society interest
(b) patent royalties.

SOLUTION

(a) If the income consists of building society interest then the equivalent gross income is £1,232 x 100/80 = £1,540 and the tax credit is £1,232 x 20/80 = £308.

(b) If the income consists of patent royalties then the equivalent gross income is £1,232 x 100/77 = £1,600 and the tax credit is £1,232 x 23/77 = £368.

Savings income

As from tax year 1996/97, the tax due on income derived from savings is calculated differently from the tax due on non-savings income. The main categories of savings income are :

(a) interest from banks and building societies
(b) interest from gilt-edged securities and corporate bonds (i.e. debentures)
(c) dividends
(d) the income element of purchased life annuities.

The crucial difference between savings income and non-savings income is that savings income falling into the basic rate band is taxed at only 20% (*not* 23%). It is therefore necessary to split taxable income into savings income and non-savings income before calculating the tax due. Note that :

(a) This split is necessary only if the taxpayer concerned has both savings income and non-savings income.
(b) Charges on income and the personal allowance are set against non-savings income first. Any excess is set against savings income.
(c) Savings income is regarded as the "top slice" of taxable income, which means that the lower rate band and the basic rate band are made available to non-savings income in priority to savings income.
(d) The effect of these rules is that the tax due on savings income is generally calculated at 20%, sometimes at 40% but *never* at 23%.

EXAMPLE 3

In 1997/98, Robert has business profits of £13,920, net dividends of £360 and no charges on income. He claims the personal allowance of £4,045. Calculate the income tax payable for the year.

SOLUTION

	Non-savings	*Savings*	*Tax credits*
	£	£	£
Schedule D Case I/II	13,920		
Dividends £360 x 100/80		450	90.00
Statutory total income	13,920	450	
Less : Personal allowance	4,045		
Taxable income	9,875	450	

Income tax due				
Lower rate band		4,100	@ 20%	820.00
Basic rate band	: Non-savings	5,775	@ 23%	1,328.25
	: Savings	450	@ 20%	90.00
		10,325		
Tax borne				2,238.25
Less : Tax credits				90.00
Tax payable				2,148.25

Non-savings income occupies the whole of the lower rate band and the first £5,775 (£9,875 - £4,100) of the basic rate band. Savings income falls entirely into the basic rate band and is taxed at only 20%, not 23%.

EXAMPLE 4

In 1997/98, Roberta has rents of £19,045, net bank interest of £5,280, net dividends of £4,000 and no charges on income. She claims the personal allowance of £4,045. Calculate the income tax payable for the year.

SOLUTION

	Non-savings £	*Savings* £	*Tax credits* £
Schedule A	19,045		
Bank interest £5,280 x 100/80		6,600	1,320.00
Dividends £4,000 x 100/80		5,000	1,000.00
Statutory total income	19,045	11,600	
Less : Personal allowance	4,045		
Taxable income	15,000	11,600	

Income tax due				
Lower rate band		4,100	@ 20%	820.00
Basic rate band	: Non-savings	10,900	@ 23%	2,507.00
	: Savings	11,100	@ 20%	2,220.00
Higher rate band		500	@ 40%	200.00
		26,600		
Tax borne				5,747.00
Less : Tax credits				2,320.00
Tax payable				3,427.00

Non-savings income occupies the whole of the lower rate band and the first £10,900 (£15,000 - £4,100) of the basic rate band. This leaves £11,100 (£22,000 - £10,900) of the basic rate band for savings income. The remaining £500 is taxed at the higher rate.

EXAMPLE 5

In 1997/98, Philip has business profits of £33,980, net dividends of £4,000 and no charges on income. He claims the personal allowance of £4,045. Calculate the income tax payable for the year.

SOLUTION

			Non-savings	Savings	Tax credits
			£	£	£
Schedule D Case I/II			33,980		
Dividends £4,000 x 100/80				5,000	1,000.00
Statutory total income			33,980	5,000	
Less : Personal allowance			4,045		
Taxable income			29,935	5,000	
Income tax due					
Lower rate band	4,100	@ 20%		820.00	
Basic rate band : Non-savings	22,000	@ 23%		5,060.00	
Higher rate band	8,835	@ 40%		3,534.00	
	34,935				
Tax borne				9,414.00	
Less : Tax credits				1,000.00	
Tax payable				8,414.00	

Non-savings income occupies the whole of the lower rate and basic rate bands so savings income (and the balance of non-savings income) is taxed entirely at the higher rate.

EXAMPLE 6

In 1997/98, Philippa has net dividends of £35,504, National Savings Bank investment account interest (received gross) of £1,500 and no charges on income. She claims the personal allowance of £4,045. Calculate the income tax payable for the year.

SOLUTION

	Savings	Tax credits
	£	£
Schedule D Case III	1,500	
Dividends £35,504 x 100/80	44,380	8,876.00
Statutory total income	45,880	
Less : Personal allowance	4,045	
Taxable income	41,835	

Income tax due			
Lower rate band	4,100	@ 20%	820.00
Basic rate band : Savings	22,000	@ 20%	4,400.00
Higher rate band	15,735	@ 40%	6,294.00
	41,835		
Tax borne			11,514.00
Less : Tax credits			8,876.00
Tax payable			2,638.00

NSB interest received gross (see Chapter 6) is savings income. In the absence of non-savings income, the personal allowance is set against savings income and the whole of the lower rate and basic rate bands are available in full to savings income.

Summary

- In general, income tax is chargeable on all the income of UK residents and on the UK income of non-residents.
- Income is classified into a number of schedules and cases, each of which has its own rules for determining the amount of assessable income in a tax year.
- Certain types of income are specifically exempt from income tax.
- To calculate a taxpayer's income tax liability it is necessary to bring together all of the taxpayer's income into a single computation.
- Husband and wife are assessed to income tax independently.
- In 1997/98 there are 3 rates of income tax. These are the lower rate (20%), the basic rate (23%) and the higher rate (40%).
- The gross equivalent of income which is received net of income tax must be included in the taxpayer's computation.
- The tax due on savings income is generally calculated at 20%, sometimes at 40% but never at 23%.

Exercises

2.1 Calculate the income tax payable in 1997/98 on a taxable income (i.e. income after deducting charges and the personal allowance) of :

(a) £11,900 (b) £33,800 (c) £59,803.

(Assume in each case that none of the income is derived from savings).

2.2 Calculate the income tax payable in 1997/98 on the following income, assuming no charges on income and a personal allowance of £4,045 :

(a) Business profits of £18,920 and net dividends of £720.

(b) Business profits of £18,880, net bank interest of £1,500 and net dividends of £8,000.

(c) Net dividends of £24,800.

2.3 Stephanie has the following income in 1997/98 :

	£
Income from employment	17,750
Rents received	12,000
Bank interest (net)	160
NSB interest, ordinary account, received gross	63
Dividends (net)	200

(a) Identify the schedules or cases under which each of the above sources of income is assessed, assuming that the rents received are not within the "rent-a-room" scheme.

(b) Compute the income tax payable by Stephanie for the year, assuming that there are no charges on income and that Stephanie is entitled to the personal allowance of £4,045.

2.4 Ernest has a retirement pension in 1997/98 of £3,030. He also receives net dividends of £420. Compute his tax rebate for the year, assuming a personal allowance of £4,045 and no charges on income.

***2.5** Ivan's income for the tax year 1997/98 is as follows :

	£
Salary	15,680
Building society interest (net)	560
Premium bond prize	50
NSB interest, investment account, received gross	60

Compute the income tax payable by Ivan for the year, assuming a personal allowance of £4,045 and no charges on income.

***2.6** Mary's income for the tax year 1997/98 is as follows :

	£
Business profits	26,570
Rents received	2,600
Dividends (net)	880

Compute the income tax payable by Mary for the year, assuming that the rents received are not within the "rent-a-room" scheme. Mary is entitled to a personal allowance of £4,045 and has no charges on income.

Chapter 3

Personal allowances

Introduction

Personal allowances are intended to adjust a taxpayer's income tax liability so as to take account of his or her personal circumstances. There are several different personal allowances and the way in which tax relief is given depends upon the allowance which is being claimed. Either :

(a) the allowance is deducted from the taxpayer's STI, decreasing taxable income and therefore decreasing the taxpayer's income tax liability, or

(b) the allowance is ignored until taxable income has been calculated but is then relieved by reducing the amount of tax due on the taxable income.

The purpose of this chapter is to describe each of the available allowances and to explain the way in which relief is given for each allowance.

In general, personal allowances are indeed "personal". If an allowance cannot be used (in full or in part) by the person to whom it is available, then any unused part of the allowance is lost. Excess allowances cannot usually be transferred to anyone else and cannot be carried back to previous years or carried forward to future years. However, some very limited provisions exist for transferring excess allowances between husband and wife (see later in this chapter).

Personal allowances for 1997/98

Personal allowances may be claimed by UK residents and by some non-residents. The main classes of non-resident who may claim personal allowances are :

(a) citizens of the Commonwealth or of the European Economic Area (EEA), which comprises all EU states plus Norway, Iceland and Liechtenstein

(b) residents in the Isle of Man or the Channel Islands and persons who used to reside in the UK but now reside abroad for health reasons

(c) Crown servants, ex-Crown servants, their widows/widowers and missionaries.

The personal allowances for 1997/98 are as follows :

Allowances which are deducted from STI :	£
Personal allowance (age 0-64)	4,045
Personal allowance (age 65-74)	5,220
Personal allowance (age 75 and over)	5,400
Blind person's allowance	1,280
Income limit for age-related allowances	15,600
Allowances which are "tax reducers" :	£
Married couple's allowance (age 0-64)	1,830
Married couple's allowance (age 65-74)	3,185
Married couple's allowance (age 75 and over)	3,225
Additional personal allowance	1,830
Widow's bereavement allowance	1,830
Income limit for age-related allowances	15,600

The personal allowance (PA)

Anyone who is entitled to claim personal allowances is entitled to at least the basic personal allowance (£4,045 in 1997/98). The allowance is given in full in the tax year in which a taxpayer is born or dies.

The personal allowance is available to adults and children alike, though the income of most children is insufficient to enable them to make full use of the allowance. If an unmarried minor child receives investment income which is derived from a parent then this income is treated for tax purposes as the income of the parent, not the child, unless the amount involved does not exceed £100. This prevents parents (but not other relatives e.g. grandparents) from transferring income-bearing assets to a child so as to utilise the child's personal allowance.

Older taxpayers

As can be seen from the list of allowances given above, the amount of the personal allowance depends upon the taxpayer's age :

(a) A taxpayer who is over 65 years old, or who reaches the age of 65 during the tax year, is entitled to an increased personal allowance (£5,220 in 1997/98), and

(b) the allowance is higher still (£5,400 in 1997/98) for taxpayers who are over 75 years old or who reach the age of 75 during the tax year.

These higher age-related personal allowances are granted *instead* of the usual personal allowance, not in addition to it. A taxpayer who dies in the tax year in which he or she would have reached the age of 65 or 75 is granted the higher allowance for the year of death.

The age-related personal allowances are reduced if the taxpayer's statutory total income exceeds a specified limit (£15,600 in 1997/98). If STI exceeds this limit, then the personal allowance is reduced by one-half of the excess. However, the allowance is never reduced to less than the personal allowance for those aged 0-64.

EXAMPLE 1

Calculate the personal allowance due in 1997/98 to each of the following taxpayers :

(a) Born on 31 July 1932, STI £7,500

(b) Born on 31 July 1922, STI £6,850

(c) Born 22 November 1929, STI £16,200

(d) Born 2 May 1928, STI £18,200

(e) Born 22 November 1919, STI £16,200

(f) Born 2 May 1918, STI £18,950.

SOLUTION

(a) This taxpayer reaches the age of 65 during 1997/98 and is therefore entitled to a PA of £5,220 for the year.

(b) This taxpayer reaches the age of 75 during 1997/98 and is therefore entitled to a PA of £5,400 for the year.

(c) This taxpayer is in the 65-74 age group and has an STI which exceeds the limit by £600, giving a PA of £4,920 (£5,220 - 1/2 x £600).

(d) This taxpayer is in the 65-74 age group and has an STI which exceeds the income limit by £2,600. This would give a PA of £3,920 (£5,220 - 1/2 x £2,600) but the allowance is never reduced to less than the PA for those aged 0-64 so the taxpayer will claim £4,045.

(e) This taxpayer is over 75 and has an STI which exceeds the limit by £600, giving a PA of £5,100 (£5,400 - 1/2 x £600).

(f) This taxpayer is over 75 and has an STI which exceeds the limit by £3,350. This would give a PA of £3,725 (£5,400 - 1/2 x £3,350) so the taxpayer will claim £4,045.

Blind person's allowance (BPA)

This allowance (£1,280 in 1997/98) is granted to registered blind persons. If both a husband and wife are registered blind persons they can each claim the allowance. The allowance is given in full in the tax year in which the taxpayer is first registered as a blind person.

If a husband or a wife who is granted the blind person's allowance cannot make full use of it, then the unused part can be transferred to the other spouse, even if that spouse is not a registered blind person.

Tax reducers

As noted above, the personal allowance and the blind person's allowance are the only allowances which are deducted from STI when calculating taxable income. All of the other allowances are relieved by reducing the amount of tax due on the taxpayer's taxable income. For this reason, these allowances are often referred to as "tax reducers". Note the following points :

(a) In 1997/98, the amount of the tax reduction is calculated as 15% of the amount of the allowance.

(b) Tax reductions are made in the following order :

   (i) tax reduction relating to the additional personal allowance
   (ii) tax reduction relating to the widow's bereavement allowance
   (iii) tax reduction relating to the married couple's allowance.

(c) The amount of tax borne can never be reduced to less than zero as a result of this tax reduction process. If the available tax reductions exceed the tax due on taxable income, there is no repayment of the excess. Any unused part of a tax reduction is simply lost (though the tax reduction relating to the married couple's allowance can sometimes be transferred between spouses, as explained below).

EXAMPLE 2

In 1997/98, a married man (aged 45) claims only the personal allowance and the married couple's allowance. Calculate the tax borne if the man's STI (none of which is derived from savings) is equal to :

(a) £32,000 (b) £10,000 (c) £4,280.

SOLUTION

	(a)	(b)	(c)
	£	£	£
Statutory total income	32,000	10,000	4,280
<u>Less</u> : Personal allowance	4,045	4,045	4,045
Taxable income	27,955	5,955	235

				£	£	£
Income tax						
(a)	(b)	(c)				
4,100	4,100	235	@ 20%	820.00	820.00	47.00
22,000	1,855		@ 23%	5,060.00	426.65	
1,855			@ 40%	742.00		
27,955	5,955	235		6,622.00	1,246.65	47.00
Less : MCA £1,830 @ 15%				274.50	274.50	47.00
Tax borne				6,347.50	972.15	0.00

Note :

In case (c), £227.50 (£274.50 - £47.00) of the tax reduction relating to the MCA cannot be used. There can be no refund of this £227.50, but it may be transferred to the wife's computation if she has sufficient income to use it (see below).

Married couple's allowance (MCA)

The married couple's allowance (£1,830 in 1997/98) is granted to a legally married couple who live together for at least part of the tax year. The allowance is not available to a married couple who are separated for the whole of the year. (A couple are regarded as "separated" for tax purposes if they are legally separated or if they are separated in circumstances which make it likely that separation will be permanent).

The tax reduction relating to the MCA is normally set against the husband's tax, but there are three exceptions to this general rule :

(a) The husband and wife may make a joint election to the effect that the whole of the tax reduction relating to the MCA should be set against the wife's tax.

(b) The wife may make a unilateral election to the effect that 50% of the tax reduction relating to the MCA should be set against her tax.

(c) If either spouse is unable to use their MCA-related tax reduction in full or in part, the unused part may be transferred to the other spouse (assuming that the other spouse can use it).

The elections described in (a) and (b) must normally be made before the start of the tax year to which they apply, but the elections can be made during the tax year if this is the year of marriage. These elections apply only to the basic MCA and not to any age-related increase in the MCA to which a married couple might be entitled (see "older taxpayers" below).

The transfer described in (c) may be claimed at any time up to 31 January in the sixth tax year following the tax year to which the transfer relates and applies to both the basic MCA and to any age-related increase.

Year of marriage

In the tax year in which a marriage takes place the MCA is reduced by one-twelfth for each full tax month which elapses between the start of the year and the date of the marriage. (A tax month runs from the 6th of one month to the 5th of the next month, inclusive).

EXAMPLE 3

Calculate the personal allowances available in 1997/98 to a husband and wife (both aged 0-64) who marry on each of the following dates :

(a) 5 April 1997 (b) 9 April 1997 (c) 23 June 1997 (d) 4 April 1998

SOLUTION

Husband and wife are each entitled to the personal allowance of £4,045. As regards the married couple's allowance :

(a) A couple who marry on 5 April 1997 are already married by the start of tax year 1997/98. Therefore the MCA of £1,830 is available in full.

(b) A couple who marry on 9 April 1997 are not married for the whole of 1997/98 but no full tax months have passed between the start of the tax year and the date of the marriage. Therefore the full MCA of £1,830 is available.

(c) If the marriage takes place on 23 June 1997 then two full tax months have passed since the start of the tax year (i.e. 6 April 1997 to 5 May 1997 and 6 May 1997 to 5 June 1997). Therefore the MCA is reduced by two twelfths, giving an MCA of £1,830 x 10/12 = £1,525.

(d) If the marriage takes place on 4 April 1998 then eleven full tax months have passed since the start of the tax year. Therefore the MCA is reduced by eleven twelfths, giving an MCA of £1,830 x 1/12 = £153.

Year of divorce, separation or death

The MCA is available in full in the tax year in which a couple divorce or separate or in which one of them dies. But if an election has been made to transfer all or 50% of the MCA to the wife then, in the tax year in which the husband dies, this election is ignored and the tax reduction relating to the MCA is set first against the husband's tax. Any unused part of this tax reduction can be transferred to the wife in the usual way.

EXAMPLE 4

Calculate the tax borne in 1997/98 by a husband and wife (both aged 0-64), given the information shown below. In each case, an election has been made for 50% of the tax reduction relating to the MCA to be set against the wife's tax and none of the income shown is derived from savings.

(a) Married all year, husband's STI £17,920, wife's STI £17,610.

(b) Married 1 March 1998, husband's STI £5,020, wife's STI £19,870.

(c) Husband dies on 12 October 1997, husband's STI to date of death £9,120, wife's STI for the year £14,870.

SOLUTION

					(a)	(b)	(c)
					£	£	£
HUSBAND							
Statutory total income					17,920	5,020	9,120
Less : Personal allowance					4,045	4,045	4,045
Taxable income					13,875	975	5,075
Income tax							
	(a)	(b)	(c)				
	4,100	975	4,100	@ 20%	820.00	195.00	820.00
	9,775		975	@ 23%	2,248.25		224.25
	13,875	975	5,075		3,068.25	195.00	1,044.25
Less : MCA £915 @ 15%					137.25		
MCA £915 x 2/12 @ 15%						22.88	
MCA £1,830 @ 15%							274.50
Tax borne					2,931.00	172.12	769.75
WIFE							
Statutory total income					17,610	19,870	14,870
Less : Personal allowance					4,045	4,045	4,045
Taxable income					13,565	15,825	10,825
Income tax							
	(a)	(b)	(c)				
	4,100	4,100	4,100	@ 20%	820.00	820.00	820.00
	9,465	11,725	6,725	@ 23%	2,176.95	2,696.75	1,546.75
	13,565	15,825	10,825		2,996.95	3,516.75	2,366.75
Less : MCA £915 @ 15%					137.25		
MCA £915 x 2/12 @ 15%						22.87	
WBA £1,830 @ 15%							274.50
Tax borne					2,859.70	3,493.88	2,092.25

Note : A wife is entitled to WBA in the year of her husband's death (see below).

Older taxpayers and the MCA

An increased MCA is granted to an older married couple, according to the age of the older spouse. The allowance rises (to £3,185 in 1997/98) if one or both of the spouses is at least 65 years old and rises again (to £3,225 in 1997/98) if one or both of the spouses is at least 75 years old.

In the same way as the age-related personal allowance is reduced for taxpayers whose STI exceeds a specified limit, the age-related MCA is reduced if the *husband's* STI exceeds the same limit (£15,600 in 1997/98). However, the allowance is never reduced to less than the MCA for couples aged 0-64. It is noteworthy that the *wife's* STI is never taken into account when calculating the amount of the age-related MCA, even if :

(a) the higher MCA is being given because of her age rather than because of her husband's age, or

(b) all or part of the tax reduction relating to the MCA is set against her tax.

The amount of the husband's STI is therefore used in calculating both his own personal allowance and the MCA. The method of calculation is as follows :

(a) The excess of the husband's STI over the income limit is divided by two, giving the required reduction in allowances.

(b) The husband's own personal allowance is reduced first, but never to an amount which is less than the personal allowance for those aged 0-64.

(c) If the reduction made in the husband's own personal allowance has not fully achieved the reduction required at (a) then the MCA is reduced next, but never to an amount which is less than the MCA for those aged 0-64.

If the age-related MCA is due in the year of marriage, the amount of the allowance is calculated as above and then reduced by one-twelfth for each full tax month which has elapsed between the start of the tax year and the date of the marriage.

EXAMPLE 5

Calculate the allowances available to a husband and wife in 1997/98, given the following information :

(a) Husband aged 67 STI £11,500 , wife aged 72 STI £6,500.

(b) Husband aged 63 STI £nil , wife aged 67 STI £21,400.

(c) Husband aged 77 STI £15,750, wife aged 68 STI £nil.

(d) Husband aged 73 STI £19,600, wife aged 78 STI £7,000.

SOLUTION

Assuming that the couple have not elected for the MCA to be set against the wife's income and that the wife has not elected to receive 50% of the MCA, allowances will be given as follows :

(a) Husband and wife are both over 65 and are each entitled to a PA of £5,220. The husband will claim an MCA of £3,185.

(b) The husband is under 65 and is therefore entitled to a PA of £4,045, all of which is unused. His wife is over 65 but her STI exceeds the income limit by £5,800. This would give her a PA of only £2,320 (£5,220 - 1/2 x £5,800) but the allowance is never reduced to less than the PA for those aged 0-64 so she will claim a PA of £4,045.

An MCA of £3,185 is available by virtue of the wife's age and the tax reduction relating to this MCA may be set against the wife's tax. The MCA is not reduced at all since the husband's STI does not exceed the income limit.

(c) The husband is over 75 but his STI exceeds the limit by £150. This gives him a PA of £5,325 (£5,400 - 1/2 x £150). His wife is over 65 and she is entitled to a PA of £5,220, all of which is unused.

An MCA of £3,225 is available by virtue of the husband's age. This is not reduced at all since the reduction required because of the size of his STI has already been made in full against his own PA.

(d) The husband is over 65 but his STI exceeds the limit by £4,000. Therefore he must lose a total of £2,000 in allowances. His own PA is first reduced from £5,220 to the minimum of £4,045 (a reduction of £1,175). The remaining £825 is deducted from the MCA of £3,225 (available by virtue of the wife's age) giving an MCA of £2,400.

His wife is over 75 and she is entitled to a PA of £5,400.

Additional personal allowance (APA)

The additional personal allowance (£1,830 in 1997/98) may be claimed by certain taxpayers who have a "qualifying child" resident with them for at least part of the tax year. A "qualifying child" is one who is born during the tax year, or is under 16 at the start of the year, or is over 16 but is in full-time education. The child must either be the child of the taxpayer or must be under 18 at the start of the tax year.

The additional personal allowance is intended primarily to help single-parent families. To be eligible to claim APA, the taxpayer must be either :

(a) a man or woman who is single for the entire tax year

(b) a married man or woman who is separated from his or her spouse for the entire tax year

(c) a married man whose wife is totally incapacitated for the entire tax year

(d) a woman who marries during the year and has a qualifying child living with her prior to the date of marriage

(e) a married woman whose husband dies during the tax year and who has a qualifying child living with her after the death of her husband

(f) a married man or woman who separates from his or her spouse during the tax year and who has a qualifying child living with him or her after the date of separation (but the APA available in these circumstances is reduced by any MCA also claimed for the year, ignoring any MCA which has been transferred to a spouse because the other spouse's income is insufficient to use it).

In the year of marriage, a man who would have been entitled to claim APA if he had not married is entitled to elect that his marriage should be disregarded for tax purposes for that year. This will usually be beneficial, since the man will then be able to claim the full APA rather than the MCA, which is usually reduced in the year of marriage.

A taxpayer may claim only one APA per year, regardless of the number of children. If more than one person is entitled to claim APA in respect of the same child then the APA is divided between them. If an unmarried couple live together and have two or more children living with them, relief is given only for the youngest child.

EXAMPLE 6

Tom was divorced some years ago and has two children of his former marriage living with him, aged 12 and 9. His annual income is approximately £30,000. On 27 July 1997 he marries Joanne, who has no income for tax purposes. Tom and Joanne are both aged 38.

(a) What personal allowances may Tom claim in 1997/98 ?

(b) Would the situation be any different if Tom had no income and Joanne had income of £30,000 per annum ?

SOLUTION

(a) Tom should elect that his marriage should be disregarded for tax purposes in 1997/98. If he does this he will be entitled to claim the full APA of £1,830 (as well as his PA of £4,045). If he does not make the election he will not be entitled to APA and will receive instead an MCA of only £1,830 x 9/12 = £1,373.

(b) If Tom has no income there is no point in claiming APA (which cannot be transferred between spouses). He should claim the MCA of £1,373 and then elect for the tax reduction relating to this MCA to be set against his wife's tax.

EXAMPLE 7

A married couple (both under 65) separate permanently on 1 December 1997. What personal allowances may each of them claim for 1997/98 in the following circumstances ?

(a) The couple's children reside with the wife for the remainder of the tax year.
(b) The couple's children reside with the husband for the remainder of the tax year.
(c) The couple's children reside with the wife for the remainder of the tax year and the wife has elected to receive 50% of the MCA for the year.

SOLUTION

(a) Husband : PA £4,045, MCA £1,830
Wife : PA £4,045, APA £1,830

(b) Husband : PA £4,045, MCA £1,830, APA £nil (reduced to £nil because he claims the full MCA)
Wife : PA £4,045

(c) Husband : PA £4,045, MCA £915
Wife : PA £4,045, MCA £915, APA £915 (£1,830 - MCA £915).

Widow's bereavement allowance (WBA)

The widow's bereavement allowance (£1,830 in 1997/98) is granted to a woman whose husband dies during the tax year. The allowance is also available in the following year, so long as the woman does not remarry before it begins. There is no equivalent allowance for widowers.

Summary

- Everyone is entitled to at least the basic personal allowance.
- The married couple's allowance is available to a legally married couple who live together for at least part of the tax year.
- Older taxpayers are entitled to a higher personal allowance and a higher married couple's allowance, but these allowances are reduced if income exceeds a specified limit.
- The additional personal allowance is available mainly to single-parent families.
- The widow's bereavement allowance is given to a woman in the year of her husband's death and in the following year, unless she remarries before it begins.
- The blind person's allowance is granted to registered blind persons.
- Tax relief for the personal allowance and the blind person's allowance is given by deducting the amount of the allowance from the taxpayer's STI. All of the other allowances reduce tax borne by 15% of the amount of the allowance.

- If all or part of an allowance cannot be used by the person to whom it is available, then any unused part of the allowance is lost (except that the married couple's allowance and the blind person's allowance can sometimes be transferred between husband and wife).

Exercises

3.1 Calculate the married couple's allowance available in 1997/98 to a married couple who marry on each of the following dates :

(a) 4 May 1997 (both aged 0-64)

(b) 25 December 1997 (both aged 0-64)

(c) 14 February 1998 (husband aged 63, wife aged 67, each with an income of less than £15,600).

3.2 Calculate the tax borne in 1997/98 by a husband and wife (both aged 0-64), given the information shown below. No elections have been made in relation to the married couple's allowance and none of the income shown is derived from savings.

(a) Married all year, husband's STI £11,420, wife's STI £12,720.

(b) Married 17 August 1997, husband's STI £3,500, wife's STI £8,480.

(c) Husband dies on 16 September 1997, husband's STI to date of death £4,380, wife's STI for the year £10,920.

3.3 Calculate the personal allowance due in 1997/98 to each of the following taxpayers :

(a) Born on 28 August 1930, STI £10,500

(b) Born on 25 May 1921, STI £16,600

(c) Born on 2 February 1933, STI £19,200.

3.4 Calculate the allowances available to a husband and wife in 1997/98, given the following information :

(a) Husband aged 76 STI £13,300 , wife aged 73 STI £15,900.

(b) Husband aged 70 STI £16,300, wife aged 70 STI £3,500.

(c) Husband aged 66 STI £20,160, wife aged 64 STI £17,000.

3.5 Toby is a widower. He was born in August 1921 and his income for 1997/98 is as follows :

	£
Retirement pension	4,380
Bank interest (net)	912

Calculate his tax refund for 1997/98.

3.6 What personal allowances may be claimed by each of the following taxpayers in 1997/98 ?

(a) John is single, 45 years old and registered blind.

(b) June is 28 years old. Her husband died in September 1997, leaving her with two young children.

(c) James is 14 years old. He earns about £10 per week from his paper round.

(d) Jeremy is 68 years old and has a total income of £25,000. His wife died in May 1996.

3.7 Richard was born on 5 February 1935. His wife, Patricia, was born on 5 April 1933. They were married in 1962. Their income for 1997/98 is as follows :

	£
Richard :	
Business profits	17,480
Patricia :	
Building society interest (net)	1,600

Calculate their tax borne and tax payable in 1997/98.

***3.8** A married man (aged 53) dies on 8 July 1997, leaving a widow and three young children. He had earnings from employment of £5,275 between 6 April 1997 and the date of his death. His wife (aged 52) had no income whilst her husband was alive but received a pension of £10,300 between 8 July 1997 and 5 April 1998.

Calculate their tax borne in 1997/98.

***3.9** Bill and Hilary (both aged under 65) have been married for many years but agree to separate permanently on 31 December 1997. The couple's two small children stay with their father.

In 1997/98, Bill received a salary of £34,820 and Hilary received a salary of £17,280. They have no other income. Calculate their tax borne in 1997/98, assuming that Hilary has elected to receive 50% of the married couple's allowance.

Chapter 4

Charges on income and other payments

Introduction

Certain types of payment made by a taxpayer are eligible for tax relief. Some of these payments, known as "charges on income", are relieved by deducting them from the taxpayer's total income when calculating STI. Other payments act as tax reducers and are relieved by reducing the tax due on the taxpayer's taxable income.

The purpose of this chapter is to describe the main types of payment which attract tax relief and to explain how relief is given for each type of payment.

Charges on income

The following payments made by a taxpayer during the tax year are treated as charges on income and are deducted from total income when calculating STI for the year :

(a) payments made to charities under a deed of covenant

(b) payments made to charities under the "gift aid" scheme

(c) eligible interest payments

(d) payments made by individuals for their own vocational training

(e) patent royalties and copyright royalties

(Each of these types of payment is described in detail later in this chapter).

Tax relief for charges on income is given at the highest rates of tax to which the taxpayer is liable. Deducting charges from total income automatically gives the right amount of relief, since the effect of the deduction is to reduce the amount of taxable income falling into the upper tax bands.

Charges paid gross or net

Some charges are paid "gross" (without deduction of tax) whilst other charges are paid "net" (after deduction of basic rate tax). Charges paid gross are deducted from the taxpayer's total income when computing STI, but it is tempting to ignore any charges paid net since the taxpayer has already taken tax relief at source. However, the tax deducted at source is always calculated at the basic rate and this will not give the right amount of relief to a taxpayer whose highest rate of tax is not the basic rate. The only way to be sure that the right amount of tax relief is given for a charge paid net is to :

(a) calculate the gross amount of the charge (net payment x 100/77)

(b) subtract the gross figure from total income when calculating STI (thus giving the correct amount of tax relief)

(c) increase the taxpayer's income tax liability by the amount of basic rate tax which was deducted from the payment when it was made. (In effect, the person making the payment is regarded as having collected basic rate income tax from the recipient on behalf of the Inland Revenue and must therefore account to the Inland Revenue for this tax as part of his or her income tax liability).

It is worth noting that this treatment of payments made net is entirely consistent with the treatment of income received net (see Chapter 2). Income received net is shown gross in the taxpayer's computation and the taxpayer then receives a tax credit for the tax suffered at source. Similarly, payments made net are shown gross in the taxpayer's computation and the taxpayer is then charged with a "tax debit" for the tax deducted at source.

EXAMPLE 1

Bob is single and has income in 1997/98 of £13,060. None of the income is derived from savings. He is subject to an annual charge of £200, which he pays gross. Cathy's circumstances are precisely the same as Bob's in all respects except that she pays her charge net (i.e. she pays a net £154 in the year).

Compute Bob and Cathy's tax liabilities for 1997/98. Does it seem to be better to pay charges gross or net ?

SOLUTION

	Bob	*Cathy*
	£	£
Total income	13,060	13,060
Less : Charge on income	200	
Charge on income £154 x 100/77		200
Statutory total income c/f	12,860	12,860

			Bob	Cathy
			£	£
Statutory total income b/f			12,860	12,860
Less : Personal allowance			4,045	4,045
Taxable income			8,815	8,815
Income tax				
Bob	*Cathy*			
4,100	4,100	@ 20%	820.00	820.00
4,715	4,715	@ 23%	1,084.45	1,084.45
8,815	8,815			
Tax borne			1,904.45	1,904.45
Add : Tax deducted from charge			0.00	46.00
Tax liability			1,904.45	1,950.45

Note :

Bob has paid a charge of £200 and has a tax liability of £1,904.45, a total of £2,104.45. Cathy has paid a charge of £154 and has a tax liability of £1,950.45, again a total of £2,104.45. It makes no difference whether the charge is paid gross or net and this is evidenced by the fact that tax borne is the same for both taxpayers.

Higher rate taxpayers

A charge on income costs a higher rate taxpayer less than it costs a basic rate taxpayer, since relief is automatically given at the highest rate of tax to which the taxpayer is liable. There is no need to adjust the method of computation in order to deal specially with higher rate taxpayers since, as stated earlier, the method gives the correct result for all taxpayers.

EXAMPLE 2

Derek is single and has income in 1997/98 of £20,460 (all non-savings). He pays a net annual charge of £231. Show his income tax computation :

(a) with the annual charge

(b) as it would have been without the annual charge.

How much has the annual charge effectively cost him ? How much would it have cost him if his income for the year had been £30,460 ?

SOLUTION

				Income £20,460		Income £30,460	
				(a)	(b)	(a)	(b)
				£	£	£	£
Total income				20,460	20,460	30,460	30,460
Less : Charge £231 x 100/77				300		300	
Statutory total income				20,160	20,460	30,160	30,460
Less : Personal allowance				4,045	4,045	4,045	4,045
Taxable income				16,115	16,415	26,115	26,415
Income tax							
(a)	(b)						
4,100	4,100	@ 20%		820.00	820.00		
12,015	12,315	@ 23%		2,763.45	2,832.45		
16,115	16,415						
(a)	(b)						
4,100	4,100	@ 20%				820.00	820.00
22,000	22,000	@ 23%				5,060.00	5,060.00
15	315	@ 40%				6.00	126.00
26,115	26,415						
Tax borne				3,583.45	3,652.45	5,886.00	6,006.00
Add : Tax deducted from charge				69.00		69.00	
Tax liability				3,652.45	3,652.45	5,955.00	6,006.00

Notes :

(i) With income of £20,460, Derek's tax liability is the same whether or not he pays the annual charge. This is to be expected since he is a basic rate taxpayer and he has paid the charge net of basic rate tax (giving him the right amount of tax relief at source). The cost of the charge to him is therefore just £231.

(ii) With income of £30,460, Derek becomes a higher rate taxpayer and his tax liability is reduced by £51 if he pays the annual charge. The cost of the charge to him is only £180 (payment £231 less reduction in tax liability £51). In effect, the gross charge of £300 is reduced by tax relief at 40% (£120), leaving £180 as the cost to Derek. An alternative way of looking at the situation is to say that Derek takes 23% tax relief when making the payment but is entitled to 40% tax relief. Therefore the extra 17% is given via Derek's tax computation (17% of £300 = £51).

Lower rate taxpayers

The lower rate taxpayer is entitled to tax relief on charges at the lower rate only (20% for 1997/98). But, as was the case with higher rate taxpayers, there is no need to adjust the method of computation in order to deal specially with lower rate taxpayers. The method described above will automatically ensure that relief is given at the lower rate.

EXAMPLE 3

Esmé is single and has income in 1997/98 of £6,600 (all non-savings). She is subject to a net annual charge of £123.20. Show her income tax computation :

(a) with the annual charge

(b) as it would have been without the annual charge.

How much has the annual charge effectively cost her ?

SOLUTION

	(a)	(b)
	£	£
Total income	6,600	6,600
Less : Charge £123.20 x 100/77	160	
Statutory total income	6,440	6,600
Less : Personal allowance	4,045	4,045
Taxable income	2,395	2,555
Income tax		
Tax borne £2,395/£2,555 @ 20%	479.00	511.00
Add : Tax deducted from charge	36.80	
Tax liability	515.80	511.00

Notes :

(i) As a lower rate taxpayer, Esmé's tax liability is increased by £4.80 if she pays the annual charge. This is logical since she takes 23% tax relief when making the payment but is entitled to only 20% tax relief. Therefore the difference of 3% is "clawed back" by the tax system (3% of £160 = £4.80).

(ii) The cost of the charge to her is therefore £128 (payment £123.20 plus increase in tax liability £4.80). In effect, the gross charge of £160 is reduced by tax relief at 20% (£32), leaving £128 as the cost to Esmé.

Non-taxpayers

Non-taxpayers (i.e. those whose income after deduction of personal allowances is zero) are not entitled to any tax relief at all on the charges that they pay. But, once again, there is no need to adjust the method of computation in order to deal specially with non-taxpayers. The method described above will automatically ensure that no relief is given.

It should be noted that if charges exceed a taxpayer's total income, then the opportunity for tax relief on the excess charges is permanently lost. There is no provision for carrying unrelieved charges back to previous years or forward to future years (unless they are unrelieved trade charges - see Chapter 11).

EXAMPLE 4

Glenda is single and has income in 1997/98 of £4,000. She is subject to a net annual charge of £38.50. Show her income tax computation :

(a) with the annual charge

(b) as it would have been without the annual charge.

How much has the annual charge effectively cost her ?

SOLUTION

	(a)	(b)
	£	£
Total income	4,000	4,000
Less : Charge £38.50 x 100/77	50	
Statutory total income	3,950	4,000
Less : Personal allowance (restricted)	3,950	4,000
Taxable income	0	0
Income tax		
Tax borne	0.00	0.00
Add : Tax deducted from charge	11.50	
Tax liability	11.50	0.00

Notes :

(i) As a non-taxpayer, Glenda's tax liability is increased by £11.50 if she pays the annual charge. This is logical since she takes 23% tax relief when making the payment but is entitled to no tax relief. Therefore the tax relief which she deducts at source is clawed back by the tax system. The £11.50 assessment would be raised under Section 350 of ICTA 1988 and assessments of this type are often referred to as "Section 350 assessments".

(ii) The cost of the charge to her is £50 (payment £38.50 plus increase in tax liability £11.50). In effect, she pays the full gross amount of the charge, with no reduction for tax relief.

Payments to charity

There are two ways of making charitable donations which are relieved as charges on income. These are :

(a) a deed of covenant
(b) the "gift aid" scheme.

Deeds of covenant

A deed of covenant to a charity is a legally binding agreement, under the terms of which the taxpayer agrees to pay a certain amount to the charity annually. In order to attract tax relief the deed of covenant must be :

(a) capable of lasting for more than 3 years, and
(b) irrevocable within the first 3 years, and
(c) not made for valuable consideration (i.e. the covenantor must receive nothing in return).

Payments made under such a deed of covenant are made net of basic rate income tax. For a married couple, tax relief is given to the spouse in whose name the covenant is made and tax relief on joint covenants is shared equally between the spouses.

Gift aid

Tax relief is available on one-off gifts to charity of at least £250 (net). This provides a means of obtaining tax relief on a charitable donation without the taxpayer having to agree to make regular payments over a number of years (as would be the case with a deed of covenant). Gifts qualifying for tax relief under this provision are made net of basic rate tax.

Eligible interest payments

The interest paid on certain loans is treated as a charge on income. This interest is paid gross. The main types of eligible loan are :

(a) A loan to buy equipment used in the taxpayer's employment. The interest paid on such a loan is eligible for relief in the tax year in which the loan is taken out and for the next three years.

(b) A loan to purchase an interest in a partnership.

(c) A loan to buy shares in an employee-controlled company.

(d) A loan to purchase ordinary shares in a close company (see Chapter 28), so long as the taxpayer has a material interest in the company or works for the greater part of his or her time in the management of the company.

(e) A loan to pay inheritance tax. The interest paid on such a loan is eligible for tax relief for 12 months only.

Interest paid wholly and exclusively for business purposes is generally treated as an allowable business expense and is deducted from the business profits assessed under Schedule D Case I or II (see Chapter 8). In this case, the interest is not regarded as a charge on income and it is not necessary for the loan to fall into one of the above categories for relief to be given.

Payments for vocational training

Tax relief is given in relation to course fees and examination fees paid by an individual for his or her own vocational training, provided that :

(a) the training leads to a National Vocational Qualification, or

(b) the trainee is 30 or over and the course :

  (i) is full-time, and

  (ii) lasts for more than four weeks but for no more than a year, and

  (iii) is wholly aimed at acquiring knowledge or skills for gainful employment.

The fees are paid net of basic rate income tax. Note that the tax deducted from such payments is *not* clawed back from individuals who are non-taxpayers or who are liable to tax at the lower rate only.

Royalties

Patent royalties are paid net but copyright royalties are paid gross. These types of payment are most likely to be made in the course of business and are considered in Chapter 8.

Payments which are tax reducers

The following payments are granted tax relief by means of a reduction in the tax due on the taxpayer's taxable income :

(a) private medical insurance payments made for those aged 60 and over
(b) maintenance payments
(c) mortgage interest
(d) interest on a loan used to purchase an annuity and secured on the taxpayer's main residence.

Some of these payments are made gross; others are paid net of the appropriate tax reduction (see below). If a payment is made gross, the tax reduction relating to the payment is shown in the taxpayer's computation. Such tax reductions are given in priority to the tax reductions relating to personal allowances (see Chapter 3) and no tax refund is available if the available tax reductions exceed the tax due on the payer's taxable income.

If a payment which ranks as a tax reducer is made net, then it can be (and should be) *entirely omitted* from the payer's tax computation. This is because precisely the correct amount of tax relief has been given at source and the Inland Revenue do *not* claw back excess relief from individuals whose tax liability is less than the tax reduction deducted at source.

Private medical insurance

Tax relief is available on premiums paid for private medical insurance for those aged 60 and over. The following points relate to this relief :

(a) The relief is available to the person who pays the premiums (who need not be the insured person).
(b) Premiums are usually paid net of basic rate income tax but some premiums are paid gross.
(c) The amount of the tax reduction is calculated as 23% of the gross amount of the premiums.

If premiums are paid gross, 23% of the amount paid should be deducted from the tax due on the payer's taxable income. If premiums are paid net (which is normally the case) they should be entirely omitted from the tax computation, as explained above.

Maintenance payments

Maintenance payments consist of payments made by one spouse to the other after they have separated (or divorced) for the maintenance of a spouse or child. The system whereby such maintenance payments attract tax relief was radically altered by the Finance Act 1988. The new system (for payments made under agreements dated after 15 March 1988) is as follows :

(a) Maintenance payments are made gross, without any deduction of tax at source.

(b) The recipient of maintenance payments is not liable to pay income tax on them.

(c) Tax relief is available to the person making the payments only if the payments are made under a court order or a legally binding agreement, or if the payments have been assessed by the Child Support Agency.

(d) Maintenance payments made directly to children do not attract tax relief.

(e) A taxpayer making qualifying maintenance payments in 1997/98 is entitled to a tax reduction equal to 15% of the *lower* of :

    (i) the payments made in the tax year, and

    (ii) the married couple's allowance (£1,830 in 1997/98).

Mortgage interest

In order that mortgage interest should qualify for tax relief, the mortgage loan must be for the purchase of land and buildings which are the borrower's only or main residence, located in the UK or the Republic of Ireland. The following points relate to this relief :

(a) The term "land and buildings" includes, for this purpose, houseboats and permanently-sited caravans.

(b) If the taxpayer is required to live in "job-related" accommodation (see Chapter 7), tax relief will be given on the mortgage interest paid in relation to a property which the taxpayer intends to make his or her main residence at some future time.

(c) Relief continues to be given if the taxpayer is absent from the property for up to one year (or up to four years if the absence is caused by the needs of the taxpayer's employment).

(d) If only one taxpayer (or a married couple) has taken out a mortgage on a given residence there is a limit of £30,000 on the amount of the loan which can qualify for tax relief. If the mortgage exceeds £30,000 tax relief is given on the interest on the first £30,000 of the loan.

(e) If two or more taxpayers share a main residence and jointly take out mortgage loans on that residence, the £30,000 limit mentioned above is apportioned between them.

(f) Tax relief is also available (for up to 12 months) on bridging loans of up to £30,000.

(g) The amount of the tax reduction is calculated (in 1997/98) as 15% of the gross amount of qualifying interest.

Mortgage interest paid within the MIRAS scheme

In the majority of cases, mortgage interest is paid within the MIRAS (Mortgage Interest Relief At Source) scheme. This means that qualifying interest is paid net of tax at the appropriate rate (15% for 1997/98). As explained earlier, mortgage interest paid net can be (and should be) completely ignored when preparing income tax computations.

Mortgage interest paid gross

If mortgage interest is paid gross, a tax reduction equal to 15% of the qualifying interest must be shown in the taxpayer's income tax computation.

EXAMPLE 5

Owen is a married man and has a £35,000 mortgage on his main residence. In 1997/98, he pays gross interest on this mortgage at an annual rate of 5.9%. Show his tax computation for 1997/98 if his STI for the year (all non-savings) is :

(a) £25,480
(b) £5,780.

SOLUTION

	(a)	(b)
	£	£
Statutory total income	25,480	5,780
Less : Personal allowance	4,045	4,045
Taxable income	21,435	1,735

			£	£
Income tax				
(a)	(b)			
4,100	1,735	@ 20%	820.00	347.00
17,335		@ 23%	3,987.05	
21,435	1,735			
			4,807.05	347.00
Less : MI £1,770 @ 15%			(265.50)	(265.50)
MCA £1,830 @ 15%			(274.50)	(81.50)
Tax borne and tax liability			4,267.05	0.00

Notes :

(i) Tax relief on the mortgage interest is limited to the interest paid on the first £30,000 of the loan i.e. 5.9% of £30,000 = £1,770.

(ii) If STI is only £5,780, full relief can be given for the mortgage interest but this leaves a tax liability of only £81.50 which is insufficient to provide full relief for the married couple's allowance. The unused tax reduction of £193.00 (£274.50 - £81.50) relating to the MCA might be transferred to Owen's wife.

Allocation of interest election

If a married couple pay gross mortgage interest jointly, the available relief is normally shared between them equally. If the mortgage is in the name of only one of the spouses relief is normally given to that spouse. However, a married couple may elect to share mortgage interest relief between them in any way they choose and this "allocation of interest" election may produce a tax saving in certain circumstances.

EXAMPLE 6

A married couple have a joint mortgage on which interest is paid gross. The qualifying interest payable in 1997/98 is £2,000. Should allocation of interest elections be made in each of the following cases ?

(a) Husband's income £18,500, Wife's income £16,500

(b) Husband's income £17,200, Wife's income £4,100

(c) Husband's income nil , Wife's income £15,000

SOLUTION

(a) There is no point in making an allocation of interest election. The total relief available is £300 (£2,000 @ 15%) and, without an election, relief of £150 will be available to each spouse. Clearly, they each have an income tax liability which is sufficient to make use of this amount of relief.

(b) The wife's income tax liability, before deducting mortgage interest relief, is only £11 (£4,100 - £4,045 = £55 @ 20%). Therefore an election should be made to allocate no more than £11 of the relief to the wife. The remaining £289 of relief will then be deducted from the husband's income tax liability.

(c) The husband has no income tax liability and so cannot make use of any mortgage interest tax relief. The whole £300 should be allocated to the wife.

Loans used to purchase an annuity

Tax relief is given in relation to the interest paid on the first £30,000 of a loan which :

(a) is made to a taxpayer aged 65 or over, and

(b) is used to purchase a life annuity, and

(c) is secured on the taxpayer's main residence.

Relief takes the form of a tax reduction equal to 23% of the qualifying interest. If the interest is paid gross, this relief should be given in the payer's tax computation. As explained earlier, interest paid net should be completely ignored when preparing the payer's tax computation.

Summary

- ► Certain payments made by a taxpayer attract tax relief either as charges on income or as tax reducers.
- ► Charges must always be shown gross in the tax computation. Any tax deducted when the payment was made is added to the tax liability of the payer.
- ► Payments to charity made by deed of covenant or made within the gift aid scheme qualify as charges on income.
- ► Certain interest payments qualify as charges on income, as do patent royalties and copyright royalties.
- ► Payments for the taxpayer's own vocational training qualify as charges on income and non-taxpayers are allowed to retain the tax deducted when making such payments.
- ► If a payment which ranks as a tax reducer is made gross, the appropriate tax reduction is given in the payer's income tax computation. But payments made net should be omitted from the computation entirely.

- Payments for private medical insurance for those aged 60 or over are relieved at the basic rate of tax.
- Qualifying maintenance payments of up to the amount of the married couple's allowance are relieved at 15%.
- Subject to certain conditions, mortgage interest payments are relieved at 15%.

Exercises

4.1 Mabel is single and has income in 1997/98 of £17,820, none of which is derived from savings. During the year she pays £192.50 (net) to a charity under the terms of a deed of covenant. Show her income tax computation for the year.

4.2 Paul is single and has income in 1997/98 of £34,250, none of which is derived from savings. During the year he makes a charitable donation (within the gift aid scheme) of £1,232 (net). Show his income tax computation :

(a) with the charitable donation

(b) as it would have been without the charitable donation.

How much has the charitable donation effectively cost him ?

4.3 Rose is single and has income in 1997/98 of £3,985. During the year she pays £19.25 (net) to a charity under the terms of a deed of covenant.. Show her income tax computation for the year.

4.4 At what rate of income tax is each of the following types of payment relieved in 1997/98 ?

(a) payments made for the taxpayer's own vocational training

(b) payments made for private medical insurance for those aged 60 and over

(c) qualifying maintenance payments

(d) mortgage interest.

4.5 A married couple, each of whom earns a high salary, pay a joint deed of covenant to a charity. In May 1997 the wife is made redundant and expects to have little or no taxable income for the foreseeable future. What steps should the couple take to maximise tax relief on the deed of covenant from now on ?

4.6 Raj is a married man with a statutory total income in 1997/98 of £21,200, none of which is derived from savings. He has a £40,000 mortgage on his main residence and pays gross interest on this mortgage at a rate of 7.2% per annum. Show his 1997/98 income tax computation.

4.7 Geoffrey is married, aged 48 and has two children under the age of 16. His income for 1997/98 consists of a salary of £28,820 and net dividends of £2,400. He pays £77 (net) per annum to a charity under the terms of a deed of covenant. Show his 1997/98 income tax computation.

***4.8** Pauline marries Adrian on 17 October 1997. Their income for 1997/98 is as follows :

	£
Pauline :	
Salary	7,609
Net building society interest	20
Adrian :	
Salary	19,450
Net dividends	1,400

Adrian has a £32,000 mortgage on their main residence. Interest on this mortgage is charged at 6.7% per annum and tax is deducted at source under MIRAS. Adrian also pays maintenance of £2,400 per annum to his former wife, as required by a court order.

Show Pauline and Adrian's income tax computations for 1997/98.

***4.9** Matthew dies on 23 December 1997, leaving a widow and two small children. His only income in 1997/98 is his salary between 6 April 1997 and 23 December 1997 of £15,620. His wife has income from property of £12,980 and no other income. She makes a charitable donation of £385 (net) during the year.

Calculate their tax liability in 1997/98.

Chapter 5

Income from property

Introduction

For tax years up to and including 1994/95, income from property was assessed under either Schedule A or Schedule D Case VI, depending upon whether the property in question was let unfurnished or furnished. But the Finance Act 1995 introduced major changes to the assessment of income from property. With effect from tax year 1995/96 :

(a) all of an individual's income from property (including income from furnished lettings) is assessed under Schedule A, and

(b) new rules are used to calculate the amount of an individual's Schedule A assessment.

These changes apply only to individuals, *not* to companies. Even though a company's income is normally assessed to corporation tax in accordance with current income tax principles (see Chapter 23), a company's property income will continue to be assessed according to the old pre-FA1995 rules.

This chapter describes only the new regime, which applies to individuals in 1995/96 and subsequent years. The old regime (which used to apply to individuals but which now applies only to companies) is described in Chapter 23.

Schedule A income and expenditure

As from 1995/96, an individual is charged to income tax under Schedule A on the "profits of a business of letting property" situated in the UK. The main types of income assessed under Schedule A are :

(a) rents (regardless of whether the property is let furnished or unfurnished)

(b) lease premiums, if the length of the lease does not exceed 50 years

(c) amounts receivable in respect of rights of way and sporting rights.

Despite the use of the word "business" above, it is important to realise that income from property is almost always *unearned* income. The only occasion on which income from property is treated as earned income is when the income derives from the commercial letting of furnished holiday accommodation (see later in this chapter). The distinction between earned and unearned income is especially important if the owner of the property is hoping to obtain tax relief on premiums paid into a personal pension scheme (see Chapter 13).

Basis of assessment and allowable expenditure

The income assessable under Schedule A for a tax year is calculated on the accruals basis, using ordinary accounting principles. An exception to this rule occurs in the case of short lease premiums, which are dealt with in a special way (see later in this chapter).

Expenditure which is incurred wholly and exclusively for the purposes of the property letting business is deducted from the assessable income, giving the Schedule A assessment for the year. This "wholly and exclusively" rule is copied directly from Schedule D Case I and is considered fully in Chapter 8, but the types of expenditure which are likely to be deductible in a Schedule A assessment include the following :

(a) repairs and maintenance to the property (excluding improvements)

(b) insurance of the property and/or its contents

(c) the cost of providing services to tenants

(d) administrative and management costs, including bad debts incurred

(e) rent paid to a superior landlord (if the property is sub-let)

(f) business rates, water rates or council tax (these are the responsibility of the occupier of premises, not the owner, but may be paid by a landlord on behalf of a tenant and then recouped via an increased rent)

(g) interest paid on a loan to buy or improve the property concerned.

If a property is partly let and partly owner-occupied, it will be necessary to apportion expenditure accordingly.

EXAMPLE 1

Ryan owns a house which he lets to a tenant. Rent is payable monthly in advance on the 6th day of each month. For some years the rent has been fixed at £2,400 per annum but this was increased to £3,000 per annum with effect from 6 December 1997. The rent due on 6 March 1998 was not paid until 7 April 1998.

Compute Ryan's 1997/98 Schedule A assessment, given that his allowable expenditure for the year is £800.

SOLUTION

The rent relating to 1997/98 (calculated on a daily basis) is £2,599 (£2,400 x 244/365 + £3,000 x 121/365), so the Schedule A assessment for the year is £1,799 (£2,599 - £800). The fact that some of the rent was not received until early 1998/99 is irrelevant, since the accruals basis takes into account accrued rent as well as rent actually received.

Capital expenditure

Capital expenditure is never deductible in a Schedule A assessment but tax relief may be obtained on certain types of capital expenditure as follows :

(a) Capital allowances (see Chapter 10) are available in relation to expenditure on :

  (i) plant and machinery used in the repair, maintenance or management of let property, and

  (ii) qualifying industrial buildings let for industrial use.

  Capital allowances are standardised depreciation allowances which are deductible when computing the Schedule A assessment.

(b) A "wear and tear allowance" may be available in relation to expenditure on furniture and other equipment let to a tenant (which does not usually qualify for capital allowances). The wear and tear allowance is commonly calculated as 10% of the rent for the year, net of any council tax or rates borne by the landlord on behalf of the tenant.

(c) An alternative to the wear and tear allowance is the "renewals basis". If this basis applies, no tax relief is available in relation to the initial cost of providing furniture etc., but subsequent expenditure on replacements (not improvements) is allowed as a deduction in the Schedule A assessment for the year in which the expenditure is incurred.

EXAMPLE 2

Ursula owns a flat which she lets furnished. In 1997/98 the flat was let for 46 weeks at £40 per week. For the remaining 6 weeks of the year, Ursula occupied the flat herself. Her expenditure during the year was as follows :

	£
Council tax	380
Water rates	240
Minor repairs	135
Advertising for tenants	38
Cleaning (only when the property was let)	296
Painting and decorating	250
Insurance	120

Compute Ursula's Schedule A assessment for 1997/98, assuming that the wear and tear allowance is claimed.

SOLUTION

	£	£	£
Rents for the year £40 x 46			1,840
Less : Expenses allowed in full :			
Advertising for tenants		38	
Cleaning		296	
Apportioned expenses :			
Council tax	380		
Water rates	240		
Minor repairs	135		
Painting and decorating	250		
Insurance	120		
	$\frac{46}{52}$ x 1,125	995	
Wear and tear allowance (see note)		129	1,458
Schedule A assessment			382

Note :

The wear and tear allowance is calculated at 10% of the rents, less any part of those rents which are deemed to reimburse Ursula for expenses incurred by her which are legally the tenants' responsibility (i.e. council tax and water rates). The tenants were in occupation for 46 weeks, so 46/52th of the council tax and water rates were their responsibility. The wear and tear allowance is therefore 10% of (£1,840 - 46/52th of (£380 + £240)) = £129.

Schedule A losses

If a taxpayer's total income from property for a year is exceeded by the allowable expenditure, the taxpayer has incurred a loss and the Schedule A assessment for the year is £nil. The loss is carried forward and relieved against the first available Schedule A income in subsequent years.

EXAMPLE 3

Sandra's entire income is derived from the letting of property. She has the following income and expenditure in tax years 1996/97 through to 1998/99 :

	1996/97	*1997/98*	*1998/99*
	£	£	£
Income from property	19,320	19,650	20,100
Allowable expenditure	27,410	15,430	11,540

Compute her Schedule A assessment for each year.

SOLUTION

	1996/97	*1997/98*	*1998/99*
	£	£	£
Income from property	19,320	19,650	20,100
Allowable expenditure	27,410	15,430	11,540
Profit/(loss)	(8,090)	4,220	8,560
Assessment before loss relief	0	4,220	8,560
Less : Losses b/f	-	(4,220)	(3,870)
Schedule A assessment	0	0	4,690

Note :

The 1996/97 loss must be set against the first available Schedule A income in subsequent years. This means that Sandra's Schedule A income for 1997/98 is reduced to £nil and (since this is her only source of income) her personal allowance for that year is wasted. However, it is not possible to conserve personal allowances by restricting the amount of loss relief claimed in 1997/98.

Lease premiums

A premium is a lump sum payable to a landlord by a tenant on the grant of a lease. The way in which such premiums are taxed depends upon the length of the lease :

(a) If the lease is for more than 50 years, any premium payable to the landlord is not subject to income tax but to capital gains tax (see Chapter 18).

(b) If the lease is for 50 years or less, any premium payable to the landlord on the grant of the lease is assessed to income tax under Schedule A in the tax year in which the lease is granted. The amount assessed is equal to the amount of the premium, reduced by 2% for each year of the lease except for the first year.

It should be noted that the above provisions relate only to the *grant* of a lease not to the *assignment* of a lease. The grant of a lease occurs when a new lease is created, under the terms of which the property will eventually revert to the landlord. The assignment of a lease occurs when an existing lease is sold to a new owner. This distinction is discussed further in Chapter 18.

EXAMPLE 4

In 1997/98, a landlord receives a premium of £36,000 when granting a 25 year lease to a tenant. What is the Schedule A assessment on this premium ?

SOLUTION

The assessable premium is reduced by 2% for each year of the lease except for the first year. Therefore 48% (24 x 2%) of the premium is not taxable and the remaining 52% is taxable. The Schedule A assessment on the premium is therefore £18,720 (52% of £36,000).

Relief for premiums paid

A tenant who pays a premium on being granted a short lease may obtain tax relief on the premium paid in one of two ways :

(a) If the tenant uses the property for business purposes then, throughout the duration of the lease, the tenant may claim an annual deduction from his or her trading profits assessed under Schedule D Case I or II (see Chapter 8). This annual deduction is equal to the amount of the landlord's Schedule A assessment on the premium, divided by the number of years of the lease.

(b) If the tenant sublets the property to someone else and receives a premium from the sub-lessee then the assessable amount of the premium received is reduced by virtue of the premium paid. The reduction is equal to :

$$\text{Landlord's Sch. A assessment on premium paid} \times \frac{\text{Duration of sub-lease}}{\text{Duration of head-lease}}$$

If full relief cannot be given in this way for the premium paid (either because the premium received is too small or because no premium was received at all) the excess may be set against the rents due from the sub-lessee.

EXAMPLE 5

Susan is granted a 20-year lease on a property, paying a premium of £76,000. To what extent will she be allowed tax relief in relation to this premium if :

(a) she uses the property for trading purposes, or

(b) she grants a sub-lease to Timothy for 5 years, receiving a premium of :

  (i) £25,000

  (ii) £10,000.

SOLUTION

(a) The amount assessable on Susan's landlord is £47,120 (£76,000 less 38% of £76,000). If Susan uses the premises for trading purposes she will be able to claim an annual deduction of £2,356 from her trading profits for each of the next 20 years. (£47,120 divided by 20 = £2,356).

(b)

	(i)	(ii)
	£	£
Premium received	25,000	10,000
Less : 2% x 4 x £25,000	2,000	
2% x 4 x £10,000		800
	23,000	9,200
Less : Premium paid £47,120 x $\frac{5}{20}$	11,780	11,780
Assessable premium	11,220	nil

In case (ii) it is not possible to relieve the whole of the part of the premium paid which relates to the sub-letting period against the premium received for the sub-let. The amount unrelieved is £2,580 (£11,780 - £9,200). No assessment will be raised on the premium received and an annual deduction of £516 will be made from Susan's Schedule A assessment on the rents falling due from the sub-lessee. (£2,580 divided by 5 = £516).

"Rent-a-room" relief

If an individual lets furnished accommodation which is part of his or her only or main residence, gross annual rents of up to £4,250 (for 1997/98) are exempt from income tax. If such rents exceed £4,250, the taxpayer may choose between :

(a) being assessed on the excess of the rents over £4,250, with no deduction for expenses of any kind, or

(b) being assessed on the total rents received, less expenses, in the usual way.

EXAMPLE 6

In 1997/98, Victor rents out two rooms in his house and receives rents totalling £4,900. He incurs allowable expenses of £820. How should he choose to be assessed under Schedule A for the year ?

SOLUTION

If Victor chooses method (a) above, he will be assessed on £650 (£4,900 - £4,250), with no deduction for expenses. If he chooses method (b) he will be assessed on £4,080 (£4,900 - £820). Therefore he should choose method (a).

Furnished holiday lettings

If the letting of furnished property satisfies certain conditions, it qualifies as income from the "commercial letting of furnished holiday accommodation". Such income is still assessed under Schedule A but is regarded as trading income. The main beneficial effects of this are as follows :

(a) The income is regarded as earned income and personal pension premiums may therefore be relieved against it (see Chapter 13).

(b) Losses are treated as trading losses and may be relieved as such under the rules of Schedule D Case I (see Chapter 11).

(c) Business-related capital gains tax reliefs may be available (see Chapter 22).

The conditions which must be satisfied in order that the letting of property should qualify as the commercial letting of furnished holiday accommodation are :

(a) The property must be let commercially i.e. with a view to profit.

(b) The property must be let furnished.

(c) The property must be :

    (i) available for letting for at least 140 days in the tax year, and

    (ii) actually let for at least 70 days in the tax year, and

    (iii) not normally in the same occupation for more than 31 consecutive days.

If a taxpayer owns two or more properties each of which satisfy the 140-day rule but which do not all satisfy the 70-day rule, these properties will all be regarded as satisfying the 70-day rule so long as their average number of days let is at least 70.

EXAMPLE 7

Yvonne owns four cottages, all of which she lets furnished with a view to profit. None of the cottages is normally in the same occupation for more than 31 consecutive days. In 1997/98 the number of days for which each cottage was available for letting, and the number of days actually let, were :

	Days available	*Days actually let*
Cottage A	150	80
Cottage B	170	56
Cottage C	120	113
Cottage D	180	68

Show Yvonne's potential averaging claims.

SOLUTION

Cottage C cannot be regarded as furnished holiday accommodation since it does not pass the 140-day test. Cottages A, B and D all pass this test but only Cottage A also passes the 70-day test. Without any averaging claims, therefore, only Cottage A will be regarded as furnished holiday accommodation. Possible averaging claims are :

(a) Average Cottage A with Cottage B. This is no use since the average number of days let is only 68.

(b) Average Cottage B with Cottage D. This is no use since the average number of days let is only 62.

(c) Average Cottage A with Cottage D. This would be beneficial since the average number of days let is 74.

(d) Average Cottage A with Cottage B and Cottage D. This is no use since the average number of days let is only 68.

Therefore, Yvonne should claim that Cottage A should be averaged with Cottage D, in which case both cottages would qualify as furnished holiday accommodation.

Summary

- As from 1995/96, income tax is charged under Schedule A on the profits of a business of letting property situated in the UK.
- Schedule A income is treated as unearned unless it arises from the commercial letting of furnished holiday accommodation.
- The Schedule A assessment for a tax year is equal to the income for that year, calculated according to ordinary accounting principles, less any expenditure incurred wholly and exclusively for the purposes of the property letting business.
- Capital allowances are available in relation to certain types of capital expenditure incurred in relation to a property letting business.
- Schedule A losses are carried forward and set against the first available Schedule A income in subsequent years.
- A premium received on the grant of a lease is assessable if the lease does not exceed 50 years. The amount assessed is the amount of the premium less 2% for each year of the lease except the first.

- A person paying a lease premium will receive tax relief on the premium if the property is sublet or is used for the purposes of a trade.
- Rent-a-room relief is available if a taxpayer receives rents of up to £4,250 p.a. from the letting of furnished rooms in his or her main residence.
- Under certain conditions, the letting of furnished property qualifies as the commercial letting of furnished holiday accommodation. This offers a number of benefits to the taxpayer.

Exercises

5.1 Andrew owns a house which he lets to tenants. Rent is payable quarterly in advance on 1 January, 1 April, 1 July and 1 October. The rent was £4,000 per annum until it was increased to £4,400 per annum with effect from 1 January 1998. Rent received by Andrew during 1997/98 was as follows :

	£
2 July 1997	1,000
30 September 1997	1,000
3 January 1998	1,100
	3,100

Andrew did not receive the payment due on 1 April 1998 until 7 April 1998. Compute the income assessable under Schedule A in 1997/98.

5.2 Simon owns a country cottage which he uses as a holiday home for 4 weeks per year and lets furnished at £120 per week for the remaining 48 weeks of the year. Simon's expenses in relation to the cottage in 1997/98 were as follows :

	£
Council tax	400
Accountant's fee	35
Repairs to furniture (damaged by tenant)	50
Gardener's wages (£10 per week)	520
Insurance	230

Compute Simon's Schedule A assessment for 1997/98.

5.3 In 1997/98, a landlord receives a premium of £12,000 when granting a lease to a tenant. What is the Schedule A assessment on this premium if the length of the lease is :

(a) 60 years

(b) 50 years

(c) 20 years.

5.4 In 1997/98, Jasper is granted a 10-year lease on a property, paying a premium of £15,000. He uses the property for trading purposes. Compute the tax relief which he will be allowed in respect of the lease premium.

5.5 Georgina owns three holiday flats, all of which she lets furnished with a view to profit. None of the flats is normally in the same occupation for more than 31 consecutive days. In 1997/98 the number of days for which each flat was available for letting, and the number of days actually let, were :

	Days available	*Days actually let*
Flat 1	140	64
Flat 2	150	72
Flat 3	182	74

Show Georgina 's potential averaging claims.

***5.6** In 1997/98, Peter is granted a 12-year lease on a property, paying a premium of £40,000. He immediately grants a 4-year sub-lease to Paula, receiving a premium of £14,000. Calculate the Schedule A assessment on the premium received by Peter.

***5.7** Melissa is single and was born in 1928. She owns a house which she lets unfurnished at a rent of £100 per week. Her allowable expenditure in 1997/98 was £4,100 and she had Schedule A losses brought forward from 1996/97 of £1,350. Her other income in 1997/98 was as follows :

	£
Retirement pension	5,184
Dividends received (net)	9,200

Compute the income tax payable by Melissa for the year.

Chapter 6

Investment income and miscellaneous income

Introduction

This chapter deals with the tax treatment of income arising from investments other than property. The main options available to a taxpayer who wishes to make an investment are to invest in stocks and shares or to save money in bank and building society accounts. Each of these types of investment has its taxation implications and the purpose of this chapter is to explain those implications.

The chapter also considers the taxation of income from trusts and settlements and the tax treatment of some miscellaneous sources of income.

Dividends received

In effect, dividends from shares held in UK companies are received net of lower rate income tax (20% in 1997/98). The gross equivalent of the dividends actually received during the tax year is included in the taxpayer's total income for that year and a tax credit is given for the tax deducted at source. Since dividends rank as savings income (see Chapter 2) any amount falling into the basic rate band is taxed at the lower rate only. Note also that :

(a) No expenses are allowed against this form of income.

(b) Dividends from overseas companies are taxed under Schedule D Case V (see Chapter 32).

Personal Equity Plans

If a taxpayer buys shares directly in a UK company then any dividends received are subject to income tax (see above) and any capital gain arising on the disposal of the shares is subject to capital gains tax (see Chapter 19). A Personal Equity Plan (PEP) provides an alternative, tax-efficient means of investing in stocks and shares. The main features of PEP's are as follows :

(a) An individual who is 18 or over and resident in the UK may invest up to £6000 p.a. in one "general" PEP and a further £3000 p.a. in one "corporate" or "single company" PEP (which invests in the shares of only one company).

(b) The money invested in a PEP must be used to acquire "qualifying investments". The main classes of qualifying investments are :
   (i) ordinary shares in UK companies
   (ii) ordinary shares in companies incorporated elsewhere in the EU
   (iii) preference shares in UK companies and in companies incorporated elsewhere in the EU
   (iv) certain corporate bonds
   (v) units in an authorised unit trust, so long as at least 50% of the investments held by the unit trust are qualifying investments.

(c) PEP's are administered by a plan manager (often a bank), and must be approved by the Inland Revenue. The plan manager will undoubtedly make a charge for administering the plan, and this charge must be taken into consideration when weighing up the advantages and disadvantages of investing in a PEP.

(d) Dividends and interest paid on PEP investments are not subject to income tax.

(e) Disposals of investments in a PEP are exempt from capital gains tax. This means that investors in a PEP will not have to pay any CGT when selling investments which have increased in value but also means that no loss relief will be available if investments are sold which have declined in value (see Chapter 16).

Enterprise Investment Scheme

The Enterprise Investment Scheme (EIS) was established in 1994 to provide a means of encouraging investment in industry. It replaced a previous scheme known as the Business Expansion Scheme (BES). The main features of the EIS are as follows :

(a) Income tax relief is available for those subscribing for newly-issued shares in certain "qualifying" companies. Essentially these are unlisted UK trading companies.

(b) Relief takes the form of a reduction in the amount of tax due on the taxpayer's taxable income and is equal to 20% of the amount invested in qualifying companies during the tax year. This reduction takes priority over the tax reductions relating to certain payments made by the taxpayer (see Chapter 4) and the tax reductions relating to certain personal allowances (see Chapter 3).

(c) A minimum of £500 and a maximum of £100,000 may be invested per tax year.

(d) The taxpayer must not be "connected" with the company at any time during the two years prior to the date of the investment or during the five years after that date. Broadly speaking, an individual is connected with a company for this purpose if he or she is an employee of the company or, together with associates, owns more than 30% of the company's ordinary shares.

(e) The taxpayer must retain the shares for at least 5 years or the EIS relief is lost.

(f) Dividends received on the shares are subject to income tax in the usual way.

(g) Any capital gain arising on the eventual disposal of the shares is exempt from capital gains tax but any loss arising on the disposal is eligible for relief. A loss may be relieved either :

    (i) as a capital loss, in the usual way (see Chapter 16), or

    (ii) under Section 574 of ICTA 1988, against the taxpayer's income of the year in which the loss is incurred or the previous year (see Chapter 11).

    When calculating the gain or loss arising on disposal, the shares are deemed to have been acquired for their issue price, less the tax reduction obtained by the taxpayer when the shares were purchased.

Venture Capital Trusts

A Venture Capital Trust (VCT) is a company approved as such by the Board of Inland Revenue. The main conditions which must be satisfied before Board approval can be obtained are :

(a) The company's ordinary shares must be listed on the Stock Exchange.

(b) Its income must be derived wholly or mainly from shares or securities.

(c) At least 70% of its investments must consist of "qualifying holdings". Shares or securities owned by a VCT are regarded as qualifying holdings if they were first issued to the VCT and if they consist of shares etc. in unlisted companies carrying on a qualifying trade in the UK.

(d) No holding in any one company (other than in another VCT) can represent more than 15% of a VCT's investments.

An individual who is at least 18 years old can obtain income tax relief in respect of an investment in newly-issued shares of a VCT. The relief is equal to 20% of the amount invested (subject to a maximum of £100,000 per tax year) providing that the shares are held for at least 5 years. Dividends received from the VCT are exempt from income tax and any gain or loss arising on disposal of shares in a VCT is exempt from capital gains tax (i.e. gains are not chargeable and losses are not allowable).

Interest taxed at source

If a taxpayer receives interest on an investment, then it is likely that the interest will be taxed at source and received by the taxpayer net of lower rate income tax (20% in 1997/98). Some types of investment do pay gross interest but these are comparatively few (see later in this chapter). The main categories of interest taxed at source are :

(a) building society interest

(b) bank interest (other than interest from the National Savings Bank)

(c) debenture and other loan interest from UK companies

(d) interest from most Government securities (or "gilts"), with the notable exception of 3.5% War Loan which pays gross interest.

The gross equivalent of the interest received during a tax year is included in the taxpayer's total income for that year and a tax credit is given for the tax suffered by deduction at source. All of the above types of interest rank as savings income so that any amounts falling into the basic rate band are taxed at the lower rate only. No expenses are allowed against this form of income.

Self-certification

Individuals resident in the UK who are unlikely to be liable to income tax for a given tax year may supply a certificate to this effect to their bank or building society. Interest is then paid to such individuals without deduction of tax at source, so avoiding the need for repayment claims at the end of the year. As might be expected, there are penalties for supplying such certificates fraudulently or negligently.

EXAMPLE 1

Alfred is single and 66 years old. He receives the following income in 1997/98 :

	£
Retirement pension	4,450
Building society interest (net)	352

(a) Calculate the amount of income tax reclaimed by Alfred at the end of 1997/98.

(b) Could the need to make a repayment claim have been avoided ?

SOLUTION

(a) Alfred's total income for the year is £4,890 (£4,450 + £352 x 100/80). This is less than his personal allowance of £5,220 (over 65), resulting in a zero income tax liability for the year. He may reclaim the £88 tax deducted at source from the building society interest.

(b) Since it was probably evident at the beginning of the year that Alfred was going to be a non-taxpayer in 1997/98, he could have supplied his building society with a certificate to that effect. He would then have received his interest without deduction of tax (i.e. he would have received £440).

Tax Exempt Special Savings Accounts

As from 1 January 1991, banks and building societies have been able to offer tax exempt special savings accounts (TESSA's) to their investors. These accounts offer tax advantages and are designed to encourage saving. The main features of TESSA's are as follows :

(a) An individual may have only one TESSA at a time and the account must be with a UK building society or bank or with a credit institution which is classed as a "European authorised institution".

(b) The account holder must be at least 18 years old.

(c) Interest received on a TESSA is exempt from income tax, whether or not the interest is withdrawn from the account.

(d) A TESSA retains its tax exempt status for five years, so long as no capital is withdrawn from the account. If any capital is withdrawn during the five-year period the account loses its tax exempt status and all interest credited to the account since it was opened becomes taxable.

(e) At the end of five years the account ceases to be a TESSA, and any interest subsequently received on the account is taxed in the usual way. However, there is nothing to prevent the account holder from then opening a new TESSA.

(f) Up to £9,000 in total may be invested in a TESSA, but no more than £3,000 may be invested in the first year and no more than £1,800 per annum may be invested in each of the remaining four years.

(g) An investor who has held a TESSA until maturity may open a "follow-up" TESSA with the full amount of capital deposited in the original TESSA, even if this exceeds the usual £3,000 limit on deposits made in the first year. This provision applies only if the new TESSA is opened within 6 months of the maturity date of the original TESSA. If the amount transferred from the mature TESSA to the follow-up TESSA is less than £9,000, the investor is able to continue saving within the usual limits.

Interest not taxed at source

Interest not taxed at source is assessed under Schedule D Case III and ranks as savings income (see Chapter 2). No expenses are allowed against this form of income. The main sources of Schedule D Case III income are :

(a) National Savings Bank (NSB) ordinary account interest (apart from the first £70 per annum which is exempt from income tax)

(b) National Savings Bank investment account interest

(c) 3.5% War Loan interest and interest on some other Government securities

(d) Interest which would normally be taxed at source but which has been received gross by an individual who is self-certificated as a non-taxpayer. Such interest will only be taxable if it transpires that the individual is a taxpayer after all.

In tax year 1997/98 and in subsequent years, Schedule D Case III income is assessed on the "current year basis" (also known as the "actual basis"). On this basis, the income assessed in a tax year is simply the income arising in that year. Interest "arises" when it is paid to the taxpayer or credited to the taxpayer's account. Any interest accrued at the end of a tax year but not yet paid or credited to the taxpayer is ignored when computing the Schedule D Case III assessment for that year.

Prior to 1997/98, the basis of assessment used in relation to a source of Schedule D Case III income depended upon the age of the source. New sources (defined as those with income first arising after 5 April 1994) were assessed on the current year basis but older sources (i.e. those with income first arising before 6 April 1994) were assessed in the following way :

(a) For tax years up to and including 1995/96, the income assessed was the income which arose in the *preceding* tax year (the "preceding year basis"), with special rules in the opening and closing years of the source.

(b For tax year 1996/97 (a transitional year) the assessment was usually equal to 50% of the income arising during the two years from 6 April 1995 to 5 April 1997.

EXAMPLE 2

Charles opened an NSB ordinary account on 1 January 1995. Interest credited to the account since it was opened has been as follows :

	£
credited 31 December 1995	376
credited 31 December 1996	399
credited 31 December 1997	405

Compute Charles' Schedule D Case III assessment for 1995/96, 1996/97 and 1997/98.

SOLUTION

Interest first arose on the account after 5 April 1994 so this is a new source of Schedule D Case III income and the current year basis applies throughout. The income assessed in 1995/96 is therefore the income arising in the year to 5 April 1996, giving an assessment of £306 (£376 less the first £70 which is exempt). Similarly, the 1996/97 assessment is £329 and the 1997/98 assessment is £335.

EXAMPLE 3

Diana opened a National Savings Bank investment account in 1986. Interest credited to the account in recent years has been as follows :

	£
year ended 5 April 1995	131
year ended 5 April 1996	135
year ended 5 April 1997	143
year ended 5 April 1998	145

Compute Diana's Schedule D Case III assessment for 1995/96, 1996/97 and 1997/98.

SOLUTION

Interest first arose on the account before 6 April 1994 so this is an old source of Schedule D Case III income. The preceding year basis applies in 1995/96, the transitional basis applies in 1996/97 and the current year basis applies as from 1997/98. The income assessed in 1995/96 is the income arising in the preceding year (i.e. the year ended 5 April 1995) giving an assessment of £131. The income assessed in 1996/97 is £139 i.e. 50% x (£135 + £143). The income assessed in 1997/98 is £145.

Opening years rules for old sources

As mentioned above, special "commencement rules" used to apply to the opening years of an old source of Schedule D Case III income. These rules have no relevance after 1996/97 and are not considered here.

Closing years rules for old sources

Special "cessation rules" are used to determine assessments in the closing years of an old source of Schedule D Case III income. These rules are still important since they apply to cessations occurring in any year up to and including 1997/98. The rules are :

(a) In the final tax year in which the source exists (e.g. the year in which an NSB account is closed), the assessment is based on the actual income arising in that year.

(b) In the penultimate year, the assessment is normally made on the preceding year basis but the Inland Revenue may revise the assessment for that year to the actual basis.

If an old source ceases in 1996/97 or 1997/98, these cessation rules override the rules of assessment which would normally apply to an old source in those years.

EXAMPLE 4

Sarah opened an NSB investment account in 1987 and interest has been credited to the account annually since it was opened. Interest in recent years has been as follows :

	£
31 December 1994	225
31 December 1995	195
31 December 1996	207
31 December 1997	217

Compute her Schedule D Case III assessments for 1995/96, 1996/97 and 1997/98, assuming that :

(a) the account remains open beyond 5 April 1998

(b) Sarah closed the account on 31 December 1997.

SOLUTION

(a) There is no cessation and therefore the assessments will be as follows :

		£	
1995/96	preceding year basis	225	
1996/97	transitional basis	201	(50% of the sum of £195 and £207)
1997/98	current year basis	217	

(b) The account is closed during 1997/98, so this is the year for which the final assessment is raised. The assessments for the final three tax years will be as follows :

		£	
1995/96	preceding year basis	225	
1996/97	actual basis	207	(revised by the Inland Revenue)
1997/98	actual basis	217	

Note :

One effect of the special cessation rules is that the £195 received on 31 December 1995 does not form the basis of any assessment. The rules make it inevitable that one year's income will escape tax in this way.

Income from trusts and settlements

A trust or settlement is an arrangement whereby property is held by persons known as *trustees*, for the benefit of other persons known as *beneficiaries*. Trusts fall into two main categories, as follows :

(a) If one or more persons are entitled to receive all of the income generated by the trust property, those persons are "life tenants" and the trust is a "trust with an interest in possession".

(b) If there is no life tenant and the trustees have the discretion to distribute as much or as little of the trust income to the beneficiaries as they see fit, the trust is a "discretionary trust".

Trusts with an interest in possession

The trustees must account to the Inland Revenue for lower rate tax on the trust's savings income and basic rate tax on all of its other income. Note that :

(a) The tax liability of the trustees is never calculated at the higher rate, no matter how large the amount of income involved.

(b) The expenses of administering the trust are *not* allowed when computing the trustees' tax liability but expenses which relate to specific items of trust income (e.g. expenses normally deductible from property income) are set against that income.

(c) The trustees' tax liability is calculated without deduction of personal allowances.

(d) If trust income has suffered tax by deduction at source, then tax credits are given in the usual way.

The income which remains after tax and expenses have been deducted is paid to the life tenants and is treated in their personal tax computations as income received net of either lower rate tax (to the extent that the income is derived from savings) or basic rate tax (to the extent that the income is derived from non-savings). The administration expenses of the trust are deemed to have been paid out of savings income in priority to non-savings income.

EXAMPLE 5

An interest in possession trust with a single life tenant has the following income in 1997/98 :

	£
Rents received	30,200
Bank deposit interest (net)	7,200
Dividends (net)	8,400

Expenses were incurred in the year as follows :

	£
Property expenses	6,900
Administration expenses	2,000

(a) Compute the trustees' income tax liability for 1997/98.

(b) How much income does the life tenant receive from the trust in 1997/98 and how will this be treated in his or her personal tax computation ?

SOLUTION

	Non-Savings	*Savings*	*Tax credit*
	£	£	£
Schedule A £30,200 - £6,900	23,300		
Bank deposit interest £7,200 x 100/80		9,000	1,800
Dividends £8,400 x 100/80		10,500	2,100
	23,300	19,500	3,900
			Tax due
Income tax @ 20%		3,900	3,900
Income tax @ 23%	5,359		5,359
Income after tax	17,941	15,600	9,259
Administration expenses		2,000	
Income after tax and expenses	17,941	13,600	

(a) The trustees' tax liability for the year is £9,259. Credit is given for the £3,900 of tax deducted at source from trust income, leaving tax payable by the trustees of £5,359.

(b) The income of the life tenant is :

	Gross	*Tax credit*
	£	£
Non-savings £17,941 x 100/77	23,300	5,359
Savings £13,600 x 100/80	17,000	3,400
Total	40,300	8,759

This income will be included in the life tenant's income tax computation for 1997/98, presumably giving rise to a higher rate tax liability. The tax credit of £8,759 will be given when calculating tax payable for the year but the life tenant is not entitled to reclaim the difference between this tax credit and the amount of the trustees' tax liability (£9,259).

Discretionary trusts

Discretionary trusts are taxed in much the same way as trusts with an interest in possession, except that the tax liability of a discretionary trust is calculated *at the special rate of 34%.* This rate applies to all income except income which has been used to fund the expenses of administering the trust (such income is taxed at 20% if it is savings income and 23% otherwise). Any payments made to beneficiaries are deemed to have been made net of 34% tax and must therefore be grossed-up at 100/66 in their personal income tax computations.

EXAMPLE 6

Assume that a discretionary trust has the same income and expenses in 1997/98 as the trust described in the above example. Assume also that a payment of £9,900 was made to a beneficiary during the year.

(a) Compute the trustees' income tax liability for 1997/98.

(b) Show how the £9,900 received by the beneficiary will be treated in his or her personal tax computation.

SOLUTION

	Non-Savings	*Savings*		*Tax credit*
	£	£	£	£
Schedule A £30,200 - £6,900	23,300			
Bank interest £7,200 x 100/80		6,500	2,500	1,800
Dividends £8,400 x 100/80		10,500		2,100
	23,300	17,000	2,500	3,900
				Tax due
Income tax @ 20%			500	500
Income tax @ 34%	7,922	5,780		13,702
Income after tax	15,378	11,220	2,000	14,202
Administration expenses			2,000	
Income after tax and expenses	15,378	11,220	0	

Note :

The administration expenses of £2,000 are deemed to have been paid out of net savings income. Therefore gross savings income of £2,500 is taxed at only 20% and not at the special rate of 34%.

(a) The trustees' tax liability for the year is £14,202. Credit is given for the £3,900 of tax deducted at source from trust income, leaving tax payable by the trustees of £10,302.

(b) The payment of £9,900 will be grossed-up at 100/66, giving gross income of £15,000 and a tax credit of £5,100.

Miscellaneous income

Miscellaneous income (i.e. income which does not fall within any of the other schedules and cases) is assessed under Schedule D Case VI. Some examples of income assessed under Schedule D Case VI are :

(a) receipts from casual authorship
(b) casual commissions
(c) post-cessation receipts (i.e. income received after a business has ceased trading)
(d) receipts from the sale of patent rights.

The basis of assessment is the income actually arising in the tax year, less any allowable expenses.

Summary

- ► A Personal Equity Plan provides a tax-efficient means of investing in stocks and shares.
- ► The Enterprise Investment Scheme provides tax incentives for those subscribing for the shares of unlisted UK trading companies.
- ► Subject to certain conditions, tax relief is available in relation to an investment in a Venture Capital Trust.
- ► Most interest received is taxed at source. Non-taxpayers may receive interest gross if they certify that they are non-taxpayers.
- ► A Tax Exempt Special Savings Account provides a tax-efficient means of saving money with a bank or building society.
- ► Interest not taxed at source is taxed under Schedule D Case III.
- ► As from tax year 1997/98, all sources of Schedule D Case III income are assessed on the current year basis.
- ► Trustees must account to the Inland Revenue for income tax on the income of a trust. The administration expenses of the trust are not allowed when computing the trustees' tax liability.
- ► A special tax rate of 34% applies to the income of a discretionary trust.
- ► Miscellaneous income is taxed under Schedule D Case VI.

Exercises

6.1 Edward has the following income in 1997/98 :

	£
Building society interest (net)	5,600
UK dividends (net)	24,400

Compute the income tax payable by Edward for the year, assuming that there are no charges on income and that he claims only the personal allowance.

6.2 Anne is single and aged 76. She has the following income in 1997/98 :

	£
Bank interest :	
Interest on deposit account (net)	384
Interest credited to TESSA	210
UK dividends received (net)	520
Retirement pension	4,786

Compute the income tax payable by Anne for the year, assuming that there are no charges on income and that no capital has been withdrawn from the TESSA.

6.3 Tony opened an NSB ordinary account on 1 January 1981 and an NSB investment account on 1 June 1995. Interest credited to these accounts in recent years has been :

	Ordinary a/c	*Investment a/c*
	£	£
year ended 5 April 1996	88	49
year ended 5 April 1997	92	53
year ended 5 April 1998	95	56

Compute Tony's Schedule D Case III assessment for 1996/97 and 1997/98.

6.4 Outline the income tax advantages of investing in :

(a) a Personal Equity Plan

(b) the Enterprise Investment Scheme

(c) a Venture Capital Trust.

6.5 Bernice was born on 1 March 1923 and is a widow (her husband died in February 1997). Her income for the years ended 5 April 1997 and 5 April 1998 is as follows :

	1997	*1998*
	£	£
Pension	5,960	6,670
NSB ordinary account interest	74	68
NSB investment account interest	53	52
Building society interest	50	48

The NSB ordinary account was opened in 1966. The NSB investment account was opened in July 1995. Compute Bernice's income tax liability for 1997/98.

***6.6** Brenda opened an NSB investment account in 1991. Interest credited to the account in recent years has been :

	30 June	*31 December*
	£	£
1994	72	75
1995	69	69
1996	71	73
1997	75	77

Compute Brenda's Schedule D Case III assessments for 1995/96, 1996/97 and 1997/98, assuming that :

(a) the account remains open beyond 5 April 1998

(b) the account was closed on 31 December 1997.

***6.7** An interest in possession trust with two life tenants has the following income in 1997/98 :

	£
Rents received	12,620
Bank deposit interest (net)	992
Interest received gross	1,800
Dividends (net)	11,200

Property expenses incurred in the year were £2,220 and general administration expenses amounted to £3,000.

(a) Compute the trustees' income tax liability for 1997/98.

(b) Assuming that the trust income is divided equally between the two life tenants, calculate each life tenant's income from the trust in 1997/98.

Chapter 7

Income from employment

Introduction

Income from employment is taxed under Schedule E. This chapter explains the way in which employment income is assessed and considers the expenses which may be deducted when computing a Schedule E assessment. There is also a brief description of the Pay As You Earn system, through which most employees pay their income tax.

This chapter is concerned primarily with those employees whose duties are performed within the UK. The taxation of overseas earnings is considered in Chapter 32.

Employment and self-employment

As will become clear in the next few chapters, self-employed people (assessed under Schedule D Case I or II) enjoy considerable tax advantages when compared with employees (assessed under Schedule E). Two of the main advantages of being self-employed are :

(a) A much wider range of expenses is allowed against the income of self-employed people than is allowed against the income of employees (see this chapter and Chapter 8).

(b) Self-employed people pay their income tax by instalments (see Chapter 14) and effectively pay their tax much later than employees, who normally pay income tax under the PAYE system (see later in this chapter).

It is usually quite obvious whether someone is employed or self-employed but sometimes there are borderline cases. For example, it may be difficult to distinguish between an employee with several part-time jobs and a self-employed person with several clients. In such cases, the taxpayer (mindful of the tax advantages of being self-employed) will usually wish to claim self-employed status whilst the Inland Revenue will often feel that the taxpayer should be treated as an employee.

The key test to be applied when trying to establish a taxpayer's status is concerned with the nature of the contract between the taxpayer and the person who is paying for the work done by that taxpayer :

(a) If it can be shown that a *contract of service* exists, then the taxpayer is regarded as an employee who is in service to an employer.

(b) If it can be shown that a *contract for services* exists, then the taxpayer is regarded as a self-employed person who is rendering services to a client.

A great deal of case law has accumulated on this subject over the years and, as a consequence, several criteria have been established which may be used to distinguish between the two types of contract (and, therefore, between employment and self-employment). The main criteria are as follows :

(a) **Control**. The more control that the person paying for the work has over the person doing the work, the more likely it is that a contract of service exists. Employees are usually unable to choose whether or not to do certain work, how to do the work, when to do the work or where to do the work. Self-employed people are usually able to decide these matters for themselves.

(b) **Financial risk**. Employees do not usually risk their own capital in the business for which they work and they receive their remuneration regularly, whether or not their employer in making a profit. Self-employed people may make losses as well as profits and may lose their capital if the business fails.

(c) **Equipment**. In general, employees do not provide their own equipment but self-employed people do.

(d) **Work performance and correction**. Employees are usually expected to do their work themselves. If they make mistakes they usually correct the work during working hours and so get paid both for the original work and for the corrections. Self-employed people often delegate their work to staff or to subcontractors. If the work done is unsatisfactory the client will not expect to have to pay again for it to be corrected.

(e) **Holidays and sickness**. Employees are likely to receive holiday pay and sick pay from their employers. Self-employed people are paid by their clients only for the work that they do and do not get paid when on holiday or when ill.

(f) **Exclusivity**. Employees (on the whole) work for a single employer. Self-employed people normally have a number of clients to whom they provide services.

There are exceptions to all of the general statements given above and therefore these criteria should be applied with caution. Nonetheless, they usually provide enough clues to decide whether a taxpayer should be regarded as employed or self-employed in all but the most difficult of cases.

Basis of assessment

The income taxed under Schedule E for a tax year is the income actually received in that year (the "receipts basis"). Income is deemed to be received on the *earliest* of the following dates :

(a) the date that the income is actually received by the employee

(b) the date that the employee becomes entitled to receive the income

and, for a company director only :

(c) the date that the income is credited to the director in the company's records

(d) the end of an accounting period, if the amount of the director's income for that period is decided before it ends

(e) the date that the amount of the director's income for an accounting period is decided, if this falls after the end of that accounting period.

Note that the income received in a tax year is not necessarily the same as the income earned during that year.

EXAMPLE 1

Barry is a sales manager. He receives a basic salary plus an annual bonus (received in February), based on the sales achieved in the previous calendar year. Compute his total Schedule E income in 1997/98, given that his basic salary for the year was £25,000 and that bonuses for calendar years 1996, 1997 and 1998 are as follows :

	£
year ended 31 December 1996 (received February 1997)	6,250
year ended 31 December 1997 (received February 1998)	7,350
year ended 31 December 1998 (received February 1999)	7,900

SOLUTION

Barry's Schedule E income for 1997/98 is £32,350 (£25,000 + £7,350). The bonus received in February 1998 is assessed in 1997/98, regardless of the fact that some of it relates to sales achieved in 1996/97. For tax purposes, all that matters is the date on which the bonus was received.

Income assessable under Schedule E

Income tax under Schedule E is chargeable on the "emoluments" of an office or employment. The term "emoluments" includes practically anything of value that could conceivably be received by an employee in respect of an employment e.g. wages, salaries, commissions, bonuses, fees, expenses allowances, payments on the termination of an employment, pensions arising from an employment and benefits in kind. Also, certain social security benefits are taxable under Schedule E, including :

(a) the retirement pension and the widow's pension
(b) the job seeker's allowance
(c) statutory sick pay and maternity pay
(d) incapacity benefit (except for short-term benefit paid in the first 28 weeks of incapacity)
(e) the invalid care allowance
(f) industrial death benefit.

Note that it is not necessary for the employee to receive the emoluments directly from the employer. So long as the emoluments are received as a result of the office or employment they are taxable under Schedule E, no matter who has paid them. For example, a waiter's tips are taxable under Schedule E, even though these are paid by customers rather than by the waiter's employer.

Non-taxable emoluments

Although the above definition of "emoluments" seems to be all-embracing, certain forms of income from employment are in fact exempt from income tax. The main types of exempt income are as follows :

(a) luncheon vouchers provided by an employer of up to 15p per day in value
(b) free or subsidised meals in a staff canteen, if available to all employees
(c) an annual Christmas party or similar function paid for by the employer, so long as the function is open to staff generally and the cost does not exceed £75 per head, but note that :
    (i) if a function costs over £75 per head, the whole cost of the function is taxable
    (ii) if there is more than one function during the year and their total cost exceeds £75 per head, the functions which total £75 per head or less are exempt from tax but any other functions are taxed in full
(d) reasonable mileage allowances (see "fixed profit car scheme" below)
(e) the provision by an employer of a car parking space at or near the employee's place of work
(f) the payment by an employer of an employee's personal incidental expenses (e.g. the cost of telephone calls home) when the employee is staying away from home overnight on business, of up to £5 per night for stays within the UK or £10 per night for stays outside the UK

(g) reasonable removal expenses (up to a maximum of £8,000) paid for by an employer when an employee first takes up an employment or transfers to a new location within the organisation

(h) reasonable gifts made by an employer to an employee on special occasions (e.g. marriage, exam success)

(i) non-cash long service awards (e.g. a gold watch on retirement) so long as the award is in respect of at least 20 years of service and does not cost the employer more than £20 per year of service

(j) non-cash gifts received by virtue of the employment from someone other than the employer (so long as the value of the gifts from any one source amounts to no more than £150 in the tax year and the gifts are not made in recognition of the performance of particular services in the course of the employment)

(k) awards made under a staff suggestion scheme

(l) the cost of training courses for an employee, borne by the employer

(m) the provision by an employer of workplace child care facilities

(n) the provision by an employer of workplace sports and recreation facilities.

Fixed profit car scheme (FPCS)

Employees who use their own cars on business may receive mileage allowances from their employers, calculated at some number of pence per mile travelled.

Strictly speaking, these allowances should be regarded as part of an employee's income for tax purposes and the employee should then claim tax relief for the motor expenses actually incurred by him or her on business trips. This would require the employee to keep fairly extensive records of business and private mileage, fuel costs, car maintenance costs etc.

An alternative (but optional) approach, which is available to all employees and which avoids the need for extensive record-keeping, is the "fixed profit car scheme". Under this scheme, reasonable mileage allowances are not regarded as part of an employee's income for tax purposes. The definition of a "reasonable" allowance per mile of business travel is embodied in a standard table of tax-free mileage rates, as follows :

Engine size	*first 4,000 miles in 1997/98*	*miles in excess of 4,000 in 1997/98*
up to 1,000 cc	28p	17p
1,001 - 1,500 cc	35p	20p
1,501 - 2,000 cc	45p	25p
over 2,000 cc	63p	36p

Note that :

(a) If the mileage allowances paid to an employee exceed the sum calculated using the above rates, the excess is taxable.

(b) If the mileage allowances paid to an employee are less than the sum calculated using the above rates, the difference is an allowable expense (see below).

EXAMPLE 2

Julie uses her own 1,800 cc car when travelling on her employer's business. In 1997/98 she drives 5,000 business miles. Explain the taxation implications of each of the following :

(a) Her employer pays her a mileage allowance of 42p per mile.

(b) Her employer pays her a mileage allowance of 32p per mile.

(c) Her employer does not reimburse her at all for using her car for business journeys.

SOLUTION

(a) Having driven 5,000 business miles in an 1,800 cc car, Julie may receive a tax-free mileage allowance of up to £2,050 (4,000 @ 45p + 1,000 @ 25p) for the year. She actually receives £2,100 (5,000 @ 42p) so her taxable mileage allowance is £50 (£2,100 - £2,050).

(b) If the mileage allowance is only 32p per mile, Julie receives only £1,600 from her employer. Therefore she has incurred an allowable Schedule E expense of £450 (£2,050 - £1,600) which may be set against her income from employment.

(c) If Julie receives no reimbursement for business mileage, she has an allowable Schedule E expense of £2,050.

Allowable expenses

If an employee incurs expenses by virtue of his or her employment, then one of two situations may arise :

(a) The employer does not reimburse the employee for the expenses incurred. In this case the expenses (if allowable) will be deducted from the employee's income for Schedule E purposes.

(b) The employer reimburses the employee. In this case the amount reimbursed by the employer will be treated as part of the employee's emoluments and the expenses (if allowable) will be deducted from the employee's income for Schedule E purposes.

Expenses incurred by an employee are allowable for tax purposes only if they are :

(a) contributions to an approved occupational pension scheme or premiums paid to secure a personal pension or retirement annuity (see Chapter 13)

(b) subscriptions to relevant professional bodies

(c) donations made under a payroll giving scheme (see later in this chapter)

(d) travelling expenses necessarily incurred in the performance of the duties of the employment (but travel between home and work is not allowable)

(e) other expenses incurred "wholly, exclusively and necessarily in the performance of the duties of the employment".

The "wholly, exclusively and necessarily" rule is applied with great stringency and this means that only absolutely essential expenses can be allowed.

EXAMPLE 3

Lee incurs travelling expenses of £500 in connection with his employment. His employer reimburses him the whole £500. Can the expenses and the reimbursement be ignored for tax purposes ?

SOLUTION

The answer to the question is "No". The expenses and the reimbursement cannot simply be cancelled out with each other. The £500 paid to Lee by his employer will be regarded as part of Lee's Schedule E income for the year. It will then be up to Lee to show that the expenses he has incurred are allowable against that income.

EXAMPLE 4

In which of the following cases will the expenses described be allowable against the employee's income for tax purposes ?

(a) A bank manager voluntarily pays an annual subscription to a London club (he uses the club only for the purpose of meeting the bank's clients).

(b) A workman is required to provide his own tools and protective clothing.

(c) A clerk pays to attend a college course in the evenings, so as to gain qualifications and improve her career prospects.

(d) The finance director of a company pays an annual subscription to the Institute of Chartered Accountants.

(e) A college lecturer teaches at one of the college's sites and then drives to another of the college's sites to take his next class. He pays his own costs of travel between the two sites.

(f) A barrister living and practising in London is appointed Recorder of Portsmouth. He pays his own travel costs between London and Portsmouth.

SOLUTION

(a) The bank manager uses the club wholly and exclusively for business purposes, but it is not necessary for him to be a member of the club in order to perform his duties. Therefore the cost of the subscription will be disallowed. The facts of this case are similar to those of *Brown* v *Bullock* (1961).

(b) The cost of necessary tools and protective clothing will be allowed. In some cases, the Inland Revenue have agreed standard tax allowances for tools and protective clothing with the relevant trade union.

(c) Whilst attending college, the clerk is not performing the duties of her employment. Therefore the cost of the college course will be disallowed, even if college attendance is a condition of her employment. The facts of this case are similar to those of *Blackwell* v *Mills* (1945).

(d) Relevant professional subscriptions of this nature are specifically allowed by statute. Therefore the cost of the subscription will be allowed.

(e) Travel between the two sites will be allowed, since the travel is necessary and is incurred in the performance of the duties of the employment.

(f) The duties of the employment are carried out entirely in Portsmouth. Whilst travelling from London, the barrister is not performing those duties so the expense will be disallowed. The facts of this case are similar to those of *Ricketts* v *Colquhoun* (1935).

Entertaining expenses

In general, entertaining expenses (e.g. expenses incurred when entertaining clients) are not allowable under Schedule E and an employee who is obliged to defray such expenses personally cannot claim them as a deduction from income. However, if an employer either :

(a) reimburses an employee for entertaining expenses incurred, or

(b) pays an employee an allowance which is specifically intended for entertaining purposes

then the entertaining expenses incurred by the employee may be set against the sums received from the employer. This rule is subject to the overriding rule that the entertaining expenses must be incurred wholly, exclusively and necessarily in the performance of the duties of the employment.

Payroll giving scheme

Employees whose employers operate a "payroll giving scheme" may make charitable donations of up to £1,200 per annum by requesting that the donations should be deducted from their gross earnings. Income tax is payable on the earnings remaining *after* the charitable donations have been deducted, thus providing tax relief. The employer, who must gain Inland Revenue approval to operate the scheme, passes the donations on to an approved charity or charity agency.

Benefits in kind

The definition of "emoluments" given above includes benefits in kind i.e. income received by an employee in the form of goods or services, rather than money. For the purpose of assessing benefits in kind, employees are divided into "P11D employees" and "non-P11D employees" :

(a) P11D employees comprise those earning at least £8,500 per annum and most company directors. The only exceptions are full-time working directors who earn less than £8,500 per annum and who do not control more than 5% of their company's ordinary share capital. Employers are required to submit a form P11D to the Inland Revenue for each such employee each year, listing the employee's benefits in kind.

(b) All other employees (i.e. those earning less than £8,500 per annum) are non-P11D employees or "lower-paid employees".

As a general rule, lower-paid employees are taxed only on benefits in kind that are convertible into money, and then only on the amount of money that the employee could obtain in this way. In other words, lower-paid employees are taxed on the *second-hand value* of their benefits in kind. P11D employees are taxed on the *cost to the employer* of providing the benefits in kind, whether or not these benefits are convertible into money.

The cost of providing a benefit is to be taken as the marginal cost incurred by the employer i.e. the additional cost borne by the employer as a consequence of providing the benefit. This rule was established in the case of *Pepper* v *Hart* (1992), which concerned the provision of school places for the children of masters at the school. It was held that the cost of this provision for Schedule E purposes should consist only of the additional costs borne by the school (e.g. extra food and laundry costs) rather than the average cost per pupil which would be obtained by dividing the total running costs of the school by the total number of pupils.

When comparing an employee's emoluments with the watershed figure of £8,500, it is necessary to take into account all of the employee's emoluments including benefits in kind *valued as if the employee were* a *P11D employee*. No expenses may be deducted from the employee's emoluments for this purpose, except for contributions made by the employee to an approved superannuation scheme.

If an employee works for more than one employer and the employers are connected in some way (e.g. they are both subsidiaries of the same holding company) the employee's emoluments from all connected employers must be aggregated for the purpose of deciding the employee's classification for benefits in kind purposes.

EXAMPLE 5

Classify each of the following employees for benefits in kind purposes :

(a) Joan has a salary of £7,300 p.a. She also receives benefits in kind which cost her employer £900 but which have a second-hand value of £500.

(b) Kate has a salary of £8,320 p.a. She also receives benefits in kind which cost her employer £600 with a second-hand value of £300. She has allowable expenses of £535, including contributions of £416 to her employer's approved superannuation scheme.

(c) Lawrence is a company director. He has 10% of the company's share capital, works one day per week on company business and receives an annual director's fee of £8,000. Benefits in kind cost his company £250 with a second-hand value of £150.

SOLUTION

(a) Joan's salary, plus the cost of her benefits in kind, total £8,200. This is less than £8,500 and therefore she is a lower-paid employee. She will be taxed on her salary and on the second-hand value of her benefits, a total of £7,800.

(b) Kate's salary, plus the cost of her benefits, total £8,920. Her superannuation contributions of £416 reduce this total to £8,504 but this is not less than £8,500 so she is a P11D employee. She will be taxed on her salary, plus the full cost of her benefits, less her allowable expenses i.e. £8,385 (£8,320 + £600 - £535).

(c) Lawrence is a P11D employee by virtue of being a company director who does not work full-time and who owns more than 5% of his company's share capital. He will be taxed on his fees, plus the full cost of his benefits i.e. £8,250.

Benefits assessable on all employees

In general, the tax treatment of benefits in kind depends upon the employee's classification, as explained above. But certain types of benefit form exceptions to the general rule and are assessable in the same way on all employees, regardless of their classification. The two main types of benefit which are assessable in the same way on all employees are :

(a) vouchers which may be exchanged for goods or services

(b) living accommodation.

Vouchers for goods or services

All employees are taxed on the cost to their employer of providing vouchers which may be exchanged for goods or services (e.g. gift vouchers, season tickets). However, the first 15p per day of luncheon vouchers is exempt from income tax and vouchers for a car parking space at or near the employee's workplace are also exempt. Note that :

(a) entertainment and hospitality vouchers provided by a person other than the employer or someone connected with the employer are exempt from income tax unless provided as a reward for specific services rendered by the employee

(b) the provision of a cash voucher (i.e. a voucher which may be converted directly into cash) results in an assessable benefit equal to the amount of cash into which the voucher can be converted.

Living accommodation

All employees are taxed in the same way on the value of any living accommodation provided for them by their employer. The employee is assessed on either :

(a) the rateable value of the accommodation (if the employer owns the accommodation), or

(b) the rent that the employer pays for the accommodation (if the employer rents the accommodation and the rent paid exceeds its rateable value).

The abolition of domestic rates in 1990 means that the rateable value of newer properties has to be estimated. In either case, the assessable benefit is reduced by any contribution made by the employee.

Accommodation costing the employer more than £75,000 is regarded as "expensive" and gives rise to an increase in the assessable benefit. This increase is calculated by applying an appropriate percentage to the amount by which the cost of the accommodation exceeds £75,000. Note the following points :

(a) The "appropriate percentage" used for this purpose is the same as the official rate of interest used in beneficial loan calculations (see below), as it stood at the beginning of the tax year.

(b) The cost of providing accommodation is equal to the purchase price of the property, plus the cost of any improvements made to the property before the start of the tax year, less any capital contribution made by the employee.

(c) If the property was acquired by the employer more than 6 years before it was made available to the employee, then the purchase price of the property may be replaced for benefits in kind purposes by its market value on the date that it was first occupied by the employee.

EXAMPLE 6

As from 1 January 1997, an employee is provided with the use of a house which has a rateable value of £2,300. The employer bought the house in 1994 for £70,000 and spent £35,000 on improvements in 1996. A further £10,000 is spent on improvements in July

1997. The employee pays £1,000 per annum to his employer in relation to this benefit. Calculate the taxable benefit in 1997/98 (assuming an official rate of interest of 6.75% per annum).

SOLUTION

	£
Rateable value	2,300
Add : 6.75% x (£70,000 + £35,000 - £75,000)	2,025
	4,325
Less : Employee contribution	1,000
Assessable benefit	3,325

Job-related accommodation

If accommodation provided by an employer is "job-related" then no taxable benefit arises. Accommodation is job-related if :

(a) it is necessary for the employee to reside in the accommodation for the proper performance of his or her duties (e.g. a caretaker who is required to live in a caretaker's flat on an employer's premises)

(b) the accommodation is provided for the better performance of the employee's duties and it is customary for such accommodation to be provided (e.g. a clergyman living in a vicarage provided by an employer)

(c) the accommodation is provided as part of security arrangements (if there is a special threat to the employee's security).

Special rules for P11D employees

Certain types of benefits in kind are assessed on P11D employees according to special rules. The main benefits for which special rules exist are :

(a) assets loaned to the employee for private use

(b) ancillary services connected with living accommodation

(c) cars provided for private use

(d) fuel provided for private use

(e) vans provided for private use

(f) mobile telephones

(g) beneficial loans.

Lower-paid employees would be taxed on these benefits only if they were capable of being converted into cash in some way, and then only on the amount of cash obtainable.

Assets loaned to the employee for private use

If an employer loans an asset to a P11D employee for his or her private use, the employee is assessed annually on 20% of the asset's market value on the date of the loan. If the period of the loan exceeds five years, the total of the annual assessments will exceed the total value of the asset. If the asset is subsequently sold or given to the employee, the employee is additionally assessed on the greater of :

(a) the market value of the asset when sold or given to the employee, less any amount paid for the asset by the employee, and

(b) the market value of the asset when first loaned to the employee, less the amounts already assessed during the period of the loan, less any amount paid for the asset by the employee.

EXAMPLE 7

On 6 April 1995, an employer purchases a stereo system for £400 and immediately lends the system to a P11D employee for his private use. The system remains in the employee's possession until 6 October 1997 when the employee buys it from his employer for £50, its market value on that day being £120. Calculate the assessable benefit for the years 1995/96 to 1997/98 inclusive.

SOLUTION

			£
1995/96	20% of £400		80
1996/97	20% of £400		80
1997/98	20% of £400 x 6/12	40	
	plus, the greater of :		
	(i) £120 - £50 = £70		
	(ii) £400 - £80 - £80 - £40 - £50 = £150	150	190
Total benefit in kind assessed over period of the loan			350

Ancillary services connected with living accommodation

If an employer provides living accommodation for a P11D employee, the employee is taxed not only on the accommodation itself but also on the cost to the employer of providing ancillary services in connection with the accommodation. Such services include cleaning, heating and lighting, repairs and maintenance etc. The provision of furniture for the employee's use is also included under the heading of ancillary services and is assessed as an asset loaned for private use (see above). The assessable benefit is reduced by any contribution made by the employee.

However, if the accommodation is job-related, the assessment with regard to these ancillary services is limited to no more than 10% of the employee's net emoluments for the year (i.e. total emoluments, excluding the ancillary services, less all allowable expenses), less any contribution made by the employee.

EXAMPLE 8

In 1997/98, an employer provides living accommodation for a P11D employee and also provides the following services in connection with this accommodation :

	£
Cleaning	520
Heating and lighting	850
Repairs and maintenance	235
Loan of furniture, cost to the employer	12,000

The employee contributes £100 per month towards the cost of these services. Compute the assessable benefit in kind, given that the employee has net emoluments for the year of £37,500 (excluding the ancillary services).

SOLUTION

If the accommodation is not job-related then the assessable benefit is £2,805 (i.e. £520 + £850 + £235 + 20% of £12,000, less £1,200). If the accommodation is job-related then the assessment is limited to 10% of £37,500, less £1,200 = £2,550.

Cars provided for private use

A P11D employee is assessed on the provision of a car unless the car is totally unavailable for the employee's private use. The assessable benefit for a given tax year is based upon the price of the car when new (even if the employer bought it second-hand) but is adjusted to reflect the car's age and the number of business miles driven in the year. The method of computation is as follows :

(a) The price of a car for benefits in kind purposes is found by taking the lower of £80,000 and :

  (i) the list price of the car when new, including standard accessories and delivery charges, plus

  (ii) the cost of all optional accessories (other than mobile telephones), fitted to the car before it is made available to the employee, plus

  (iii) the cost of any optional accessories (other than mobile telephones) costing £100 or more and fitted to the car after it is made available to the employee.

(b) Accessories which are designed for use only by disabled persons are ignored when calculating the price of the car. If the employee holds a disabled person's "Orange Badge", this exemption extends to any accessories required because of the employee's disability (e.g. power steering) and is not limited to accessories designed for use solely by the disabled.

(c) If the car is a "classic car", defined as a car which :

  (i) is over 15 years old at the end of the tax year, and

  (ii) has a market value at the end of the year exceeding £15,000 and exceeding the price calculated at (a) above

then the car's market value (or £80,000 if lower) is substituted for the car's price when calculating the assessable benefit.

(d) The price calculated at (a) or (c) above is reduced by any capital contribution made by the employee towards the cost of the car or its accessories, up to a maximum of £5,000. If the employee makes a capital contribution exceeding £5,000, the excess over £5,000 is ignored.

(e) The assessable benefit in kind is calculated by applying a factor of 35% to the price of the car, less capital contributions. This figure may be subject to a number of reductions, as explained below.

(f) If the employee drives at least 2,500 but less than 18,000 business miles in the year, the assessed benefit is reduced by one-third. If the employee drives at least 18,000 business miles in the year, the assessed benefit is reduced by two-thirds. But if the employee has two or more cars simultaneously, these reductions apply only to the car with the greatest business mileage.

(g) A one-third reduction is given in relation to a second or subsequent car if it is driven for at least 18,000 business miles in the year.

(h) If the car is available to the employee for only part of the year, the assessed benefit in that year is reduced proportionately, depending upon the number of days for which the car is available. This applies if the car is not made available to the employee for the whole of the year or if the car is unusable for a continuous period of at least 30 days during the year. The mileage thresholds of 2,500 and 18,000 miles are also reduced proportionately in these circumstances.

(i) The assessable benefit is reduced by a further one-third if the car is 4 years old (or more) at the end of the tax year.

(j) Finally, the assessable benefit is reduced by any contribution which the employee pays to the employer towards the running costs of the car.

EXAMPLE 9

(a) Throughout the whole of 1997/98, Lucy (a P11D employee) is provided by her employer with the use of a car first registered on 1 February 1996, costing £12,400 new. She contributed £1,000 towards the cost of the car. Her mileage for the year is 26,100 miles, of which 70% is business mileage. She contributes £300 per annum to her employer in relation to the car's running costs. Calculate the benefit assessable in 1997/98.

(b) During 1997/98, Luke (a P11D employee) is provided by his employer with the use of a car first registered in 1993, with a list price at that time of £20,000. His employer bought the car for £15,700 in 1995. Luke's mileage in the car is 40% business and 60% private. Calculate the benefit assessable in 1997/98 if :

(i) the car is available to Luke throughout the entire year and he drives a total of 6,000 miles during the year

(ii) the car is made available to Luke only from 1 October 1997 and he drives 6,000 miles between that date and 5 April 1998.

SOLUTION

(a) Lucy has driven 18,270 business miles (70% of 26,100) and is therefore entitled to a two-thirds reduction in the assessable benefit. The calculation is as follows :

	£
35% of (£12,400 - £1,000)	3,990
Less : two-thirds reduction (business mileage)	2,660
	1,330
Less : contribution to running costs	300
Assessable benefit	1,030

(b) The fact that Luke's employer bought the car for £15,700 is irrelevant. The assessable benefit is based on the original list price of the car. The calculation is :

(i) *Car available all year*

Luke's business mileage of 2,400 during the year (40% of 6,000) is insufficient to give a reduction in the assessable benefit since it is less than 2,500 miles per year. The benefit is therefore £4,667 (i.e. 35% of £20,000, less one-third because of the age of the car).

(ii) *Car available from 6 October 1997*

Luke has the car for only 187 days during the tax year and is therefore assessed on only 187/365ths of the usual benefit. The mileage thresholds are reduced proportionately to 1,281 and 9,222 miles respectively, so his 2,400 business miles entitle him to a one-third reduction. The assessable benefit is :

	£
35% of £20,000 x 187/365	3,586
Less : one-third reduction (business mileage)	1,195
	2,391
Less : further one-third reduction (age of car)	797
Assessable benefit	1,594

Pool cars

The above provisions do not apply to "pool cars". A pool car is one which satisfies all of the following criteria :

(a) It is available for use by more than one employee and is not ordinarily used by one employee exclusively.

(b) It is not normally kept at an employee's residence overnight.

(c) It is used for private purposes only incidentally to its use for business purposes.

If all these criteria are satisfied, no assessable benefit will arise.

Fuel provided for private use

The assessable benefit described above is intended to cover the cost of providing the car itself, together with the costs of road fund licence, insurance and maintenance. But a separate assessable benefit arises if any fuel at all is supplied by the employer to the employee for private purposes during the year. The assessable benefit in 1997/98 is calculated by reference to the following table.

	Petrol engines	*Diesel engines*
	£	£
up to 1,400 cc	800	740
up to 2,000 cc	1,010	740
2,001 cc or more	1,490	940

It is important to note that the assessed benefit is *not* reduced by any contribution which the employee makes towards the cost of private fuel. Employees either pay the full cost of all private fuel (in which case there is no assessable benefit) or pay less than the full cost of all private fuel (in which case they are assessed according to the above table). However, the assessed benefit *is* reduced proportionately if the car is not made available to the employee for the entire tax year.

EXAMPLE 10

Miranda (a P11D employee) is supplied with a 1,600cc petrol-engined company car for both business and private use and her employer pays all running costs. Calculate her assessable fuel benefit in 1997/98 if :

(a) she contributes nothing towards private fuel

(b) she reimburses her employer for the cost of all private fuel

(c) she reimburses her employer £1,000 per year towards the cost of private fuel.

SOLUTION

(a) £1,010, taken from the standard table.

(b) £nil (since the employer pays for no private fuel at all).

(c) £1,010, taken from the standard table. Miranda's contribution is less than 100% and so has no effect on the assessed benefit.

Vans provided for private use

If an employee is provided with a van (weighing 3.5 tonnes or less) for private use then the assessable benefit in 1997/98 is as follows :

	£
Under 4 years old at end of the tax year	500
Over 4 years old at end of the tax year	350

There is no separate assessable benefit in respect of van fuel provided for private use. If the van weighs more than 3.5 tonnes no assessable benefit will arise unless the van is used wholly or mainly for private purposes.

Mobile telephones

P11D employees are taxed on a flat rate charge of £200 per annum if provided with a mobile telephone by their employer. The charge also applies to fixed car telephones. No charge arises if there is no private use of the telephone, or if the employee repays the full cost of private use.

Beneficial loans

A beneficial loan is one that is granted by an employer to an employee (or to a member of the employee's family) either interest-free or at a low rate of interest. A loan is deemed to be at a low rate of interest if the rate charged is less than the "official rate" which is set by the Treasury and which is changed from time to time. P11D employees are taxed on the difference between the interest actually payable to the employer and the interest that would have been payable at the official rate. Note that :

(a) Loans made in the ordinary course of the employer's money-lending business and made on the same terms and conditions as loans made to the general public are ignored when calculating the assessable benefit arising in connection with low-interest loans.

(b) If an assessable benefit arises in connection with a "qualifying loan" (i.e. a loan which attracts tax relief, such as a mortgage) the employee is given tax relief in relation to the loan as if interest had been paid at the official rate.

(c) No assessable benefit arises in relation to a low-interest loan if either :

   (i) the total amount outstanding on all loans made by the employer to the employee does not exceed £5,000 at any time during the tax year, or

   (ii) the loan is not a qualifying loan and the total amount outstanding on all non-qualifying loans does not exceed £5,000 at any time during the tax year.

If a loan is wholly or partly written off by the employer, the amount written off is assessed on the employee in the tax year in which the write-off takes place. This provision applies to all loans, including those made in the ordinary course of a money-lending business. However, no assessable benefit will arise if the loan is written off on the death of the employee or if the loan is to a relative of the employee and it can be shown that the employee has derived no benefit from the write-off.

EXAMPLE 11

Adam (a P11D employee) has the following three loans from his employer :

(a) A £36,000 loan at 3% p.a. interest to enable Adam to buy his own home.

(b) An interest-free season ticket loan of £2,000.

(c) A £2,500 personal loan at 4% p.a. interest.

The full amount of each loan was outstanding at 6 April 1997 and no repayments were made during 1997/98.

Calculate Adam's assessable benefit in 1997/98 (assuming an official rate of interest of 6.75% per annum). Also calculate the tax reduction which will be given in relation to the home purchase loan in Adam's 1997/98 tax computation. (Assume that the loan is outside the MIRAS system).

SOLUTION

Non-qualifying loans (the season ticket loan and the personal loan) total less than £5,000 and so these loans do not give rise to an assessable benefit. As regards the home loan :

(i) The interest actually paid is £1,080 (3% of £36,000). Interest at the official rate would be £2,430 (6.75% of £36,000). Therefore Adam is assessed on the difference of £1,350.

(ii) Interest on the first £30,000 of a mortgage attracts tax relief, so the tax reduction will be £30,000 x 6.75% x 15% = £303.75.

In the above example, it was assumed that the amount of the loans did not vary during the tax year. However, if the amount of a beneficial loan does vary during the year, the assessable benefit can be calculated in one of two ways :

(a) The amount of the loan outstanding at the start of the tax year and at the end of the tax year are averaged and then multiplied by the average official rate in force during the year. Interest actually paid to the employer is then subtracted, giving the assessable benefit.

(b) Interest at the official rate is calculated precisely on the day-to-day outstanding balance. Interest actually paid is then subtracted, giving the assessable benefit.

Clearly, the first method will be quicker and easier and is generally used. However, either the employee or the Inland Revenue may insist that the precise method should be used. The employee will presumably do so if this results in a lower assessment and the Inland Revenue may do so if it appears that the "average" method is being deliberately exploited for tax avoidance purposes.

Payments made on termination of employment

Payments received by an employee on the termination of employment fall into three distinct categories :

(a) **Fully exempt**. The following types of termination payment are fully exempt from income tax :

   (i) payments made on the death of the employee

   (ii) payments made to the employee because of injury or disability

   (iii) lump sum payments under approved superannuation schemes

   (iv) statutory redundancy pay.

(b) **Fully taxable**. If an employee receives a termination payment which does not fall into any of the categories listed above and which is made by way of reward for the employee's services, then the payment is fully taxable. This applies if the employee was contractually entitled to the payment or if there was a reasonable expectation that the payment would be made.

(c) **Partially exempt**. Payments made at the employer's discretion so to compensate an employee for loss of employment are exempt up to £30,000. Any excess over £30,000 is taxable. If the employee also receives statutory redundancy pay then the amount of statutory redundancy pay received reduces the £30,000 exemption.

The taxable part of a partially exempt termination payment is regarded as the top slice of the employee's income, ranking even above income from savings. This provision ensures that savings income is not moved from the basic rate band (where it is taxed at only 20%) into the higher rate band as a consequence of receiving a partially exempt termination payment.

EXAMPLE 12

Henrietta is made redundant in March 1998. She receives statutory redundancy pay of £2,500 and an ex gratia payment of £40,000 from her employer as compensation for loss of office. Her only other income in 1997/98 consists of her salary of £24,320 and net dividends of £4,000. Calculate her tax liability for 1997/98, assuming that she claims only the personal allowance.

SOLUTION

	Non-savings	*Savings*	*Compensation*	*Tax credits*
	£	£	£	
Salary	24,320			
Compensation £40,000 - £27,500			12,500	
Dividends £4,000 x 100/80		5,000		1,000.00
Statutory total income	24,320	5,000	12,500	
Less : Personal allowance	4,045			
Taxable income	20,275	5,000	12,500	

Non-savings income occupies the whole of the lower rate band and the first £16,175 of the basic rate band. Savings income falls entirely into the basic rate band, leaving £825 of this band for the compensation. The remainder of the compensation is taxed at the higher rate.

Income tax due

Lower rate band		4,100	@ 20%	820.00
Basic rate band	: Non-savings	16,175	@ 23%	3,720.25
	: Savings	5,000	@ 20%	1,000.00
	: Compensation	825	@ 23%	189.75
Higher rate band		11,675	@ 40%	4,670.00
		37,775		
Tax borne				10,400.00
Less : Tax credits				1,000.00
Tax payable				9,400.00

Note :

The statutory redundancy pay of £2,500 is exempt from income tax but reduces the £30,000 exemption to £27,500.

The PAYE system

Under the "Pay As You Earn" (PAYE) system, employers deduct income tax and national insurance contributions from their employees when paying them their wages and salaries. The amounts deducted, together with the employer's secondary National Insurance contributions (see Chapter 15), must be accounted for to the Collector of Taxes within 14 days of the end of the tax month in which the employees are paid. A tax month runs from the 6th of one month to the 5th of the next month, so employers generally make a payment to the Collector of Taxes on or before the 19th of each month. But employers whose payments to the Collector do not exceed an average of £600 per month are allowed to make these payments quarterly instead of monthly.

The PAYE system applies to all payments assessable under Schedule E. This includes payments which take the form of tradeable assets such as shares, gold bars and coffee beans but excludes "own company" shares provided under an Inland Revenue approved share scheme (see later in this chapter). PAYE also applies to vouchers exchangeable for cash or for tradeable assets.

Tax codes

The PAYE system is based upon the concept of "tax codes". It is the responsibility of the Inspector of Taxes to issue a tax code for each employee for each tax year, representing the amount which the employee may earn in that year before becoming liable to tax. The tax code takes into account a number of factors affecting the employee's income tax liability, including :

(a) the personal allowances to which the employee is entitled

(b) the employee's charges on income

(c) the employee's allowable expenses

(d) adjustments made in order to collect tax on benefits in kind

(e) adjustments for tax overpaid or underpaid in previous years.

The tax code allocated to an employee is equal to one-tenth of the aggregate of the above items, rounded down to a whole number.

EXAMPLE 13

Henry is single and claims only the personal allowance. He pays gross interest of £100 per year (eligible as a charge on income) and he also pays a professional subscription (allowable under Schedule E rules) of £80 per year. In 1997/98 he has assessable benefits in kind of £500. Compute his 1997/98 tax code.

SOLUTION

By virtue of his personal allowance, his charges on income and his allowable expenses, Henry is entitled to earn £4,225 (£4,045 + £100 + £80) in the year before paying tax. However, some of this must be set against his benefits in kind of £500, leaving only £3,725 to set against his salary. Therefore Henry's tax code for the year would be 372, which is one-tenth of £3,725, rounded down to a whole number.

Note that the same result would be obtained if the aggregate figure of £3,725 were anywhere in the range £3,720 - £3,729, so tax codes are not absolutely precise. But dividing the aggregate figure by ten results in only one-tenth as many different tax codes as would be obtained otherwise and cuts down the size of the tax tables used by employers (see below).

Tax code suffixes

A tax code also has a suffix, which is generally a letter of the alphabet. The most common suffixes are "L" (which stands for "low" and indicates that the employee is entitled to the personal allowance) and "H" (which stands for "high" and indicates that the employee is entitled to the personal allowance plus either the MCA or the APA). So Henry's full tax code in the above example would be 372L.

The purpose of the suffix is to facilitate the recoding exercise which is needed whenever personal allowances are increased. When this happens, the Inspector of Taxes simply instructs employers to increase all "L" codes by the amount required to reflect the increase in the personal allowance and to increase all "H" codes by the amount required to reflect the increase in both the personal allowance and the MCA/APA. This avoids the need to individually recode every employee in the country. Other suffixes in general use include :

P - the employee is entitled to the personal allowance for those aged 65-74

V - the employee is entitled to the personal allowance and age-related MCA for those aged 65-74

BR - which instructs the employer to deduct tax at the basic rate from all payments made to the employee

NT - which instructs the employer not to deduct tax from the employee at all.

A fairly recent innovation is the "K" code which is, in effect, a negative code. "K" codes are used mainly for employees whose benefits in kind exceed their personal allowances and allow tax on the excess benefits to be collected by increasing the amount of tax charged on the employee's wage or salary.

Operation of the PAYE system

Employers are issued with sets of tax tables which enable them to calculate the amount of income tax that should be deducted from an employee in a given week or month. The main tables used are :

Table A This table (also known as the Pay Adjustment Table) contains pages for each week or month of the year and shows, for every possible tax code, the amount of tax-free pay to which the employee is entitled for the year to date. In effect, the table spreads an employee's allowances evenly over the year, giving 1/12th of the allowances per month or 1/52th of the allowances per week.

Table B This table (also known as the Taxable Pay Table) is used to look up an employee's income tax liability for the year to date, after the entitlement to tax-free pay has been taken into account.

In outline, the procedure followed for each employee in each week or month is as follows :

(a) The employee's tax code is looked up in Table A, which shows the amount of tax-free pay to which the employee is entitled for the year to date.

(b) This is then subtracted from the employee's gross pay for the year to date giving the employee's taxable pay for the year to date.

(c) The employee's taxable pay for the year to date is then looked up in Table B, which shows the tax due for the year to date. Tables C and D are used if the employee is a 40% taxpayer.

(d) Finally, the tax paid to date by the employee in previous weeks or months is subtracted from the tax due for the year to date, giving the employee's income tax liability for the current week or month.

The entire system is cumulative and requires the employer to keep track of an employee's gross pay and tax paid "to date" (i.e. since the beginning of the tax year on 6 April). Employers are provided with deductions working sheets (form P11) which facilitate the accumulation of the necessary "to date" figures.

PAYE forms

Some of the main forms used by the PAYE system are as follows :

P6 An employee's notice of coding, sent to the employer by the Inspector of Taxes.

P9D An end of year return showing the benefits in kind and expenses of a lower-paid employee. P9D's must be submitted to the Inland Revenue by 6 July following the end of the tax year and the employees concerned must be provided with copies by the same date.

P11D An end of year return showing the benefits in kind and expenses of a director or employee earning at least £8,500. P11D's must be submitted to the Inland Revenue by 6 July following the end of the tax year and the employees concerned must be provided with copies by the same date.

P11 Deductions working sheet (see above).

P14 An end of year return, sent to the Inspector of Taxes by the employer, showing an individual employee's gross pay, tax paid and national insurance paid for the year.

P35 An end of year return, sent to the Inspector of Taxes by the employer, summarising all employees' gross pay, tax paid and national insurance paid for the year. The P35, together with the P14's, must be submitted to the Inland Revenue by 19 May following the end of the tax year.

P45 A 4-part form used when an employee leaves an employment, showing the employee's tax code, gross pay to date and tax paid to date. Part 1 is sent to the Inspector of Taxes by the employer and Parts 2, 3 & 4 are given to the leaving employee. The employee gives Parts 2 & 3 of the form to his or her new employer who retains Part 2 (using it to fill in a deductions working sheet for the employee) and sends Part 3 to the Inspector of Taxes. The employee retains Part 4.

P60 Certificate of gross pay and tax deducted, given to employees by employers at the end of the tax year. P60's must be provided to employees by 31 May following the end of the tax year.

Construction industry tax deduction scheme

The construction industry tax deduction scheme applies to payments made by a contractor to a subcontractor under a contract relating to construction operations. Such payments must be made net of 23% income tax (24% before 1 July 1997) unless the subcontractor holds a subcontractor's 714 tax certificate. Any part of a payment which represents a reimbursement of the cost of materials supplied by the subcontractor may be excluded from the amount which is subject to deduction of tax.

714 certificates are issued only to subcontractors carrying on a genuine construction business in the UK with proper premises, equipment etc. The business must have its own bank account and proper accounting records must be maintained. A further requirement is that the subcontractor has complied with all tax and National Insurance obligations throughout the three years prior to the application for a 714 certificate.

With effect from a date yet to be determined (but probably 1 August 1998) some changes are to be made to the construction industry tax deduction scheme. The most important changes are :

(a) Deduction of tax at the basic rate is to be replaced by deduction at a percentage determined by the Treasury (but not exceeding basic rate).

(b) 714 certificates will be issued only to those subcontractors with an annual turnover of not less than a minimum figure (which is to be prescribed by regulations).

Employee incentive schemes

An employee incentive scheme provides financial incentives for employees to improve their work performance. The main types of scheme which have income tax implications are :

(a) approved profit-related pay schemes
(b) approved profit-sharing schemes
(c) approved share option schemes.

A brief description of each of these types of scheme is given below.

Profit-related pay schemes

Subject to certain conditions, that part of an employee's pay which derives from an approved profit-related pay (PRP) scheme is exempt from income tax (though not from National Insurance contributions). The main conditions that must be satisfied by a PRP scheme in order to gain approval are as follows :

(a) There must be a clear relationship between the employer's profits and the amount of PRP paid to employees.
(b) At least 80% of employees must be included in the scheme.
(c) The scheme must treat all eligible employees in a similar way, though it is permitted for the amount of PRP paid to an employee to depend upon his or her remuneration or length of service.

The amount of tax-free PRP payable to any employee cannot exceed the lower of £4,000 p.a. and 20% of the employee's total pay (including PRP but excluding benefits in kind) in the profit period to which the PRP relates. If the employee receives more PRP than this, the excess is subject to income tax. A "profit period" is the employer's accounting period, usually of 12 months' duration.

It has been announced, however, that income tax relief for PRP is to be phased out over the next few years. The £4,000 ceiling will be reduced to £2,000 for profit periods beginning during 1998 and to £1,000 for profit periods beginning during 1999. No relief at all will be available in relation to profit periods beginning on or after 1 January 2000.

Profit-sharing schemes

If an employee works for a company and is given shares in that company as part of his or her emoluments then, in normal circumstances, income tax is charged on the market value of the shares on the date of the gift. A profit-sharing scheme is a means by which employees can be given shares in the company for which they work without incurring an income tax liability. The main features of a profit-sharing scheme are :

(a) The company sets up a trust and gives the trust money which is used to purchase shares in the company. These shares are allocated to employees but are held in trust on their behalf.

(b) The shares allocated to an employee must be held in trust for a minimum of two years (the "period of retention") unless the employee dies, retires or is made redundant within the two-year period. At the end of the period of retention, the shares may be transferred into the employee's name or sold on the employee's behalf.

(c) There is an annual maximum on the value of shares which may be allocated to an employee under such a scheme, equal to the greater of £3,000 and 10% of the employee's salary (excluding benefits in kind). If the employee's salary exceeds £80,000, it is deemed to be £80,000 for the purpose of calculating this maximum.

No income tax is chargeable if shares are held in trust for at least three years. But an income tax liability may arise if shares are transferred into an employee's name or sold on the employee's behalf before three years have expired. The following situations are possible :

(a) The shares allocated to an employee are sold within three years of being acquired by the trust and this sale is caused by the death of the employee. No income tax is chargeable in this case.

(b) Shares are transferred to the employee or sold within the three-year period because the employee retires or is made redundant. In this case, income tax is chargeable on 50% of the market value of the shares when they were acquired by the trust (or, if lower, on 50% of the disposal proceeds of the shares).

(c) Shares are transferred to the employee or sold during the third year and this is not caused by death, retirement or redundancy. In this case the employee is charged to income tax on 100% of the market value of the shares when they were acquired by the trust (or, if lower, on 100% of the disposal proceeds of the shares).

When an employee disposes of shares acquired under a profit-sharing scheme, the allowable cost of the shares for capital gains tax purposes (see Chapter 17) is deemed to be their market value on the day that they were allocated to the employee.

Share option schemes

If an employee works for a company and is granted an option to buy shares in that company (usually at a favourable price) then income tax is charged on the difference between the market value of the shares on the date that the option is exercised and the amount that the employee pays for the shares. This income tax liability can be avoided if the option falls within an approved share option scheme. Approved schemes are of two types :

(a) **Savings-related share option schemes**. Under such a scheme employees are granted an option to buy shares and then save through a Save As You Earn (or "sharesave") scheme in order to raise funds to exercise the option. The amount saved must be between £5 and £250 per month and the savings contract may last for 3, 5 or 7 years. The scheme must be open to all employees who have worked for the company for a specified qualifying period (which cannot exceed 5 years). The price at which employees are given the option to buy shares must be at least 80% of the shares' market value at the time that the option is granted.

(b) **Company share option plans**. These schemes are less restrictive than savings-related schemes. The company can select the employees to which it would like to offer share options and can set these employees performance targets which must be achieved before the options are made available. The price at which an option may be exercised must not be manifestly less than the market value of the shares at the time that the option is granted and options must be exercised no earlier than 3 years and no later than 10 years after they are granted. There is an upper limit of £30,000 on the value of the shares for which an employee may hold options at any one time.

If a share option is granted under an approved scheme of either type and all necessary conditions are satisfied, then no income tax is payable on either the grant or the exercise of the option. For capital gains tax purposes (see Chapter 17) the allowable cost of shares acquired under an approved share option scheme is the price actually paid for the shares by the employee.

Summary

- ► Several criteria have been established which may be used to distinguish employment from self-employment.
- ► The basis of assessment for income taxed under Schedule E is the income actually received in the year.
- ► Income tax is payable on all the income received in respect of an employment, including benefits in kind. Certain social security benefits are also taxable.
- ► In general, an employee's expenses are allowed only if they are incurred wholly, exclusively and necessarily in the performance of the duties of the employment.
- ► The way in which an employee's benefits in kind are taxed depends upon whether or not the employee is a P11D employee, though some benefits are taxable in the same way on all employees.
- ► Any amount to which an employee is contractually entitled on the termination of employment is fully taxable. Certain termination payments (e.g. on death or injury) are fully exempt and ex gratia termination payments are partially exempt.

- ► The PAYE system is used to deduct income tax and National Insurance contributions from employees' wages and salaries.
- ► Certain employee incentive schemes offer tax advantages. Common schemes include profit-related pay schemes, profit-sharing schemes and share option schemes.

Exercises

7.1 List the criteria which might be used to distinguish employment from self-employment.

7.2 Malcolm earns a basic salary of £17,500 in 1997/98. He also receives an annual bonus based on his employer's profits for the accounting year, which ends on 31 March. The bonus for the year ended 31 March 1997 (received 1 June 1997) was £2,350 and the bonus for the year ended 31 March 1998 (received 1 June 1998) was £2,570. Compute Malcolm's 1997/98 Schedule E assessment.

7.3 Which of the following forms of income from employment would be exempt from income tax ?

(a) Luncheon vouchers of £2 per working day.

(b) Free meals in the company canteen.

(c) Removal expenses of £4,500.

(d) A cheque for £1,000 given to an employee on reaching 25 years of service with his employer.

(e) A canteen of cutlery given to an employee on her marriage.

(f) A mileage allowance of 25p per mile given to an employee who drives his own 1,300 cc car on 2,500 business miles per year.

7.4 Which of the following expenses incurred by an employee would be allowable under Schedule E ?

(a) Travel costs between work and home.

(b) Travel costs between employment sites.

(c) Subscriptions to professional bodies.

(d) The cost of protective clothing.

(e) The cost of a suit to wear at the office.

(f) The cost of textbooks purchased in relation to a college course.

7.5 Kim is an employee earning a salary of £7,000 per annum, out of which she pays 5% to her employer's superannuation scheme. She has allowable expenses of £1,000, all of which are reimbursed by her employer and is provided with a company car on which the assessable benefit if she were a P11D employee would be £1,800. Is she a P11D employee or a lower-paid employee ?

7.6 Niall (a P11D employee) is provided with a diesel-engined 2,800 cc company car which had a list price of £18,500 when it was new on 1 April 1994. His employer pays for all running expenses including fuel for private use. In 1997/98 Niall drove 27,000 miles of which 25% was private mileage. Compute the assessable benefit in 1997/98.

7.7 On being made redundant by her employer, Penny received statutory redundancy pay of £1,750 and an ex gratia payment from her employer as compensation for the loss of employment. Compute the amount assessable if the ex gratia payment was :

(a) £12,000

(b) £29,000.

***7.8** Emma is the sales director of a company. She earns an annual salary of £40,000 together with a bonus (received in September each year) based on the company's profits for the accounting year ending on the previous 30 June. She also receives a general expenses allowance of £5,000 per annum, which she uses for business travel and entertaining. The company provides her with a new BMW motor car every two years and pays all running costs. She has an interest-free loan from the company of £20,000 and the company pays her annual subscription to a private medical insurance scheme, costing £300. Explain the taxation implications of each of the elements of Emma's remuneration package.

***7.9** Jim is the managing director of a company and earns a basic salary in 1997/98 of £100,000. He receives benefits in kind from the company during the year as follows :

(a) He is provided with the use of a company house which has a rateable value of £4,750 and which cost his employer £250,000. Jim makes no contribution towards the cost of the house or towards its running costs which cost the company £2,300 in 1997/98. The company has also furnished the house at a cost of £8,500. Jim's occupation of the house is not job-related.

(b) He is provided with a petrol-engined company car which is one year old and had a list price when purchased of £45,000. The company pays all running costs and Jim drove 20,000 miles in 1997/98, of which one-quarter was business mileage. The car is equipped with a telephone.

(c) He is provided with a company loan of £50,000 on which he pays interest at 2% per annum.

Calculate Jim's assessable benefits in 1997/98 (assuming an official rate of interest of 6.75%).

Chapter 8

Income from self-employment : Computation of income

Introduction

This is the first of five chapters concerned with the assessment of self-employed people under the rules of Schedule D Cases I and II.

The profits of a trade are assessed under Schedule D Case I whilst the profits of a profession or a vocation are assessed under Schedule D Case II. As there are no significant differences between the two cases, references to Case I in this chapter and in subsequent chapters should be taken to include Case II unless the context indicates otherwise. Similarly, the terms "trader" and "sole trader" will be used to refer to any self-employed person, regardless of whether the person in question is actually conducting a trade, a profession or a vocation.

The badges of trade

When deciding whether or not a person's activities make that person liable to income tax under Schedule D Case I or II, two important distinctions must be drawn. These are :

(a) the distinction between employment and self-employment (which is discussed in Chapter 7), and

(b) for a taxpayer who sells goods or assets, the distinction between :

  (i) trading activities, giving rise to trading profits which are charged to income tax under Schedule D Case I, and

  (ii) non-trading activities, giving rise either to profits charged to income tax under Schedule D Case VI (see Chapter 6) or to capital gains which may be charged to capital gains tax (see Chapter 16).

The Income and Corporation Taxes Act 1988 states that the term "trade" includes "every trade, manufacture, adventure or concern in the nature of trade". This circular definition is of little real help and it has been left largely to the courts to decide whether or not a given activity constitutes trading.

In 1955, a Royal Commission summarised the guidance provided by case law up to that time and produced a list of the main criteria which may be used to distinguish between trading and non-trading activities. These criteria (which are known as the "badges of trade") are as follows :

(a) **Subject matter of the transaction**

If the assets which the taxpayer has sold are of a type which might normally be acquired for personal enjoyment or as an investment (e.g. works of art, stocks and shares), this may suggest that any profit arising on their sale should be treated as a capital gain rather than a trading profit.

But if the assets concerned do not provide personal enjoyment and would not normally be held as an investment, any profit arising on their sale is more likely to be treated as a trading profit assessable to income tax. In *Martin* v *Lowry* (1927) the taxpayer bought and sold 44 million yards of aircraft linen and in *Rutledge* v *CIR* (1929) the taxpayer bought and sold 1 million toilet rolls. In both of these cases, it was held that the subject matter of the transaction was such that the activity must be construed as trading.

(b) **Length of the period of ownership**

Trading stocks are normally retained for only a short period before being sold, whereas assets acquired for personal use or as an investment are generally retained for much longer. Therefore, if assets are bought and sold within a short space of time it is likely that any profit made will be treated as a trading profit.

(c) **Frequency of transactions**

The more often that a taxpayer repeats a certain type of transaction, the more likely it is that the activity will be construed as trading. In *Pickford* v *Quirke* (1927) the taxpayer bought a cotton mill and sold off its assets at a profit. This was the fourth time that the taxpayer had carried out this particular type of transaction and therefore he was held to be trading.

(d) **Supplementary work**

A taxpayer who buys an asset, performs work on that asset so as to make it more saleable and then sells the asset at a profit is more likely to be regarded as trading than someone who simply buys and sells without performing any supplementary work. In *Cape Brandy Syndicate* v *CIR* (1921) a group of individuals bought a large quantity of brandy which they first blended and then sold. They were held to be trading.

(e) **Reason for the sale**

The circumstances which have prompted the sale of an asset might be taken into account when deciding whether trading has occurred. A sale necessitated by a sudden urgent need for cash is less likely to be regarded as a trading activity than a sale made in the normal course of events.

(f) **Motive**

The presence of a profit motive in the mind of the taxpayer when acquiring the asset provides strong evidence of trading. In *Wisdom* v *Chamberlain* (1969) the taxpayer acquired silver bullion with the intention of selling it at a profit and eventually did so. He was held to be trading.

However, this test is not always conclusive. After all, many investments are bought at least partially with a view to their long-term sale at a profit and yet such profits are generally treated as capital gains. This point emphasises the need to consider the evidence provided by *all* of the badges of trade (not just one) when trying to decide whether or not trading has occurred.

Since trading requires the presence of a profit motive in the mind of the taxpayer when the asset was acquired, the sale of an asset originally acquired by inheritance or by gift (or in any way otherwise than by purchase) is very unlikely to be construed as trading.

The calculation of adjusted profits

The computation of a self-employed person's Schedule D Case I assessment begins with the net profit shown by that person's accounts. Business accounts are normally drawn up on the accruals basis and this is also the basis used by Schedule D Case I. However, it is usually necessary to make a number of adjustments to the net profit shown by the accounts in order to arrive at the taxable profit. These adjustments can be summarised as follows :

		£	£
Net profit shown by the accounts			x
Add :	Expenditure shown in the accounts but not deductible under Schedule D Case I	x	
	Income assessable under Schedule D Case I but not shown in the accounts	x	x
			x
Less :	Income shown in the accounts but not assessable under Schedule D Case I	x	
	Expenditure deductible under Schedule D Case I but not shown in the accounts	x	x
Profit adjusted for tax purposes			x

Each of these adjustments is explained below.

Deductibility of expenditure

In general, expenditure is deductible (or "allowable") under Schedule D Case I only if it is incurred *wholly and exclusively for the purposes of the trade*. This rule is not as restrictive as the "wholly, exclusively and necessarily" rule applied under Schedule E (see Chapter 7), but it does have the following implications :

(a) Expenditure which has no connection with the trade will be disallowed (the "remoteness test"). In *Strong & Co of Romsey Ltd* v *Woodifield* (1906), damages paid by a brewery to a hotel guest injured by a falling chimney were disallowed. The damages were incurred by the brewery in its capacity as a property owner, not in its capacity as a trader, and therefore failed the remoteness test.

(b) Expenditure which serves both a business purpose and a private purpose should, in principle, be entirely disallowed (the "duality test"). In practice, however, it is usual to disallow only the private element so long as the expenditure can be apportioned with reasonable accuracy. In *Mallalieu* v *Drummond* (1983) the cost of black clothing worn in court by a lady barrister was disallowed. The clothing provided warmth and decency as well as satisfying professional standards of dress and therefore failed the duality test.

Even if expenditure passes both the remoteness test and the duality test it may still be disallowed by statute.

Disallowed expenditure

The main categories of expenditure which are disallowed in a Schedule D Case I computation (either by statute or as a consequence of case law decisions) are as follows :

Capital expenditure

Capital expenditure is specifically disallowed by ICTA 1988 but the Act does not provide a definition of the term "capital". Consequently, there is a great deal of case law on this subject, much of which is concerned with distinguishing between repairs (which are allowed as revenue expenditure) and improvements (which are disallowed as capital expenditure). In *Atherton* v *British Insulated & Helsby Cables Ltd* (1926), it was stated that capital expenditure is such that it brings an "enduring benefit" to the business, and this test is still widely used. The following capital-related expenses are also disallowed :

(a) legal or professional fees incurred in relation to an item of capital expenditure

(b) depreciation and amortisation charges (but capital allowances may be available instead, see Chapter 10)

(c) losses on the disposal of fixed assets.

Even repairs may be disallowed if they relate to a newly acquired asset and are required in order to put the asset into usable condition. In *Law Shipping Co Ltd* v *CIR* (1923) the cost of putting a newly acquired ship into seaworthy condition was disallowed for this reason. However, repairs to a newly acquired asset which was usable before the repairs were carried out are generally allowed. In *Odeon Associated Theatres Ltd* v *Jones* (1971) repairs to cinemas which had been bought in a state of disrepair (but were nonetheless usable) were allowed.

Appropriations of profit

Any appropriations of profit made by the owner of a business (whether described as drawings, proprietor's salary, interest on capital or anything else) are disallowed, as are the owner's personal income tax payments and personal National Insurance contributions.

Transfers to reserves or to general provisions (e.g. a general provision for bad debts) are regarded as appropriations of profit and are also disallowed.

Charges on income

Payments which are treated as a charge on income (e.g. patent royalties) are relieved against the taxpayer's total income (see Chapter 4) and must therefore be disallowed in the Schedule D Case I computation. It should be noted that :

(a) the amount disallowed is the amount shown in the accounts (usually the amount *accrued* in the accounting period), but

(b) the amount relieved as a charge on income for a given tax year is the amount actually *paid* in that year.

Entertainment and gifts

Entertaining expenses are disallowed unless they relate to staff entertaining (in which case the employees concerned may incur a Schedule E liability if the amount involved is excessive, as explained in Chapter 7). The cost of gifts is also disallowed, other than :

(a) gifts to employees (but again, the employees may incur a Schedule E liability)

(b) gifts to customers costing no more than £10 per head, displaying a prominent advertisement for the business and not consisting of food, drink or tobacco

(c) gifts to educational establishments of items manufactured, sold or used in the trade

(d) reasonably small gifts to local charities, so long as the "wholly and exclusively" test is satisfied (e.g. if the gift attracts favourable publicity and enhances the firm's public image).

It should be noted that charitable donations made under the terms of a deed of covenant or under the gift aid scheme are treated as charges on income and are therefore disallowed in the Schedule D Case I computation.

In general, political donations (and subscriptions) are not allowed. But political donations which result in a definite benefit to the trade being carried on may be allowed. In *Morgan* v *Tate & Lyle Ltd* (1955) the costs of a political campaign against nationalisation were allowed on the grounds that the campaign was waged for the survival of the trade.

Non-trade bad debts

Bad debts incurred in the course of trade are allowable. But employee loans written off are not allowable unless :

(a) the loan was made in the course of trade (i.e. the firm is in the business of lending money), or

(b) it can be shown that the written-off loan formed part of the employee's remuneration (and was therefore taxable under Schedule E).

Transfers to a *specific* bad debts provision are allowable but transfers to a general provision are disallowed, as stated earlier. Bad debts recovered and reductions in a specific bad debts provision are both treated as trading income.

EXAMPLE 1

A sole trader's nominal ledger contains the following bad and doubtful debts account for the year ended 30 June :

	£	£		£	£
Trade debts w/o		812	Provisions b/f at 1 July :		
Staff loan w/o		50	General	432	
			Specific	312	744
Provisions c/f at 30 June :					
General	459		Trade debt recovered		42
Specific	288	747	P & L Account		823
		1,609			1,609

How much of the £823 charged to the profit and loss account for the year should be added back when calculating the Schedule D Case I adjusted profit ?

SOLUTION

The figure of £823 charged to the profit and loss account can be analysed as follows :

	£
Trade debts written off, less trade debts recovered (£812 - £42)	770
Staff loan written off	50
Increase in general provision for bad debts (£459 - £432)	27
Decrease in specific provision for bad debts (£312 - £288)	(24)
	823

The £50 staff loan written off and the £27 increase in the general provision are disallowed, so a total of £77 should be added back when calculating the adjusted profit.

Criminal payments

A payment will be disallowed if the making of the payment in itself constitutes a criminal offence (e.g. the payment of a bribe). Payments to a blackmailer or extortionist are also disallowed.

Fines and penalties

Fines or penalties incurred because of infringements of the law are not regarded as trading expenses and are disallowed. An exception occurs if an employer pays parking fines incurred by employees whilst on their employer's business. Such payments are usually allowed under Schedule D Case I but may then be assessed under Schedule E as emoluments of the employee.

Allowable expenditure

As explained earlier, expenditure is allowable under Schedule D Case I if it has been incurred wholly and exclusively for the purposes of the trade and is not specifically disallowed by statute. Other than the disallowed items listed above, most of the expenditure shown in a typical profit and loss account will probably be allowable but the following points should be noted :

(a) **Interest**. Interest of all types, including credit card and overdraft interest, is allowable if incurred for the purposes of the trade. But interest which constitutes a charge on income is disallowed (see above) and interest paid on overdue tax is also disallowed.

(b) **Legal and professional fees**. Legal and professional fees relating to capital expenditure are specifically disallowed (see above) but fees incurred for other trading purposes are normally allowable. For example, fees are allowed if incurred in connection with such matters as the collection of trade debts, the raising of long-term loan finance, the renewal of a short lease (i.e. a lease of up to 50 years), an action for breach of contract or the preservation of trading rights.

Audit and accountancy fees incurred in relation to the preparation of accounts and the agreement of tax liabilities are normally allowed. Fees incurred in relation to tax appeals and investigations are incurred in the role of taxpayer rather than trader and should be disallowed.

(c) **Short lease premiums**. As explained in Chapter 5, if a premium is paid for the grant of a short lease of business premises, part of this premium will be allowable in equal annual instalments over the period of the lease.

(d) **Damages**. Damages and compensation payments are allowed if incurred for the purposes of the trade.

(e) **Value Added Tax**. If a trader suffers VAT in relation to an item of expenditure and is unable to reclaim that VAT (see Chapter 30), the amount of VAT suffered will be allowable so long as the item of expenditure is itself allowable.

(f) **Trade subscriptions**. Subscriptions payable to professional and trade associations are generally regarded as having been incurred for the purposes of the trade and are allowable. Political subscriptions are generally disallowed (see above).

(g) **Employees' remuneration**. Remuneration paid to employees is allowable so long as it is genuinely expended for business purposes. In *Copeman* v *Flood (William) & Sons Ltd* (1941) it was held that large salaries paid to family members could be allowed only to the extent that they were expended for trading purposes.

Remuneration which is not actually paid to employees within 9 months of the end of the accounting period in which it is accrued is disallowed in that period but allowed in the period of payment.

Employers' contributions to approved occupational pension schemes (see Chapter 13) are allowable in the *accounting period in which they are paid.*

Redundancy payments and compensation payments for loss of office are normally allowable, as are lump sum payments made to employees on retirement. When a firm ceases trading, statutory redundancy payments made to staff are allowed, together with further compensation payments of up to three times the statutory payments.

The cost of educational courses provided for employees is allowable if incurred for trade purposes. The cost of retraining employees who are about to leave (or have recently left) is allowable subject to certain conditions.

The cost of temporarily seconding an employee to a charity is also allowable.

(h) **Staff defalcations**. Losses caused by the dishonesty of an employee are normally allowable. But, following the decision in *Curtis* v *J & G Oldfield Ltd* (1925), the defalcations of a person having control over the business (e.g. the proprietor or a senior employee) are disallowed.

(i) **Travel expenses**. The cost of travelling in the course of business is allowable but the cost of travelling between home and work is not allowable. In *Newsom* v *Robertson* (1952) the travelling expenses of a barrister between his home and his chambers were disallowed. But in *Horton* v *Young* (1971) the travelling expenses of a self-employed bricklayer between his home and the building sites at which he worked was allowed, on the grounds that his business was conducted from his home.

(j) **Car leasing and rental costs**. The costs of hiring, leasing or renting plant and equipment are normally allowable. However, in the case of "expensive" cars (defined as those with an original cost of more than £12,000), the allowable amount is restricted to :

$$\text{Hire charge} \times \frac{\pounds 12{,}000 + 1/2(\text{Cost of car} - \pounds 12{,}000)}{\text{Cost of car}}$$

For example, if a car costing £18,000 is rented at a cost of £3,600 per annum, then the amount allowed is restricted to :

$$\pounds 3{,}600 \times \frac{\pounds 12{,}000 + 1/2(\pounds 18{,}000 - \pounds 12{,}000)}{\pounds 18{,}000} = \pounds 3{,}000.$$

(k) **Pre-trading expenditure**. Expenditure incurred during the seven years before starting to trade is treated as if it had been incurred on the first day of trading and is allowable so long as the expenditure is of a type which would normally be allowable under the rules of Schedule D Case I.

(l) **Registration of patents and trademarks**. The cost of registering a patent or trademark is allowable.

Trading income not shown in the accounts

The most common example of trading income not being shown in the accounts of a business occurs when the owner takes goods from the business for personal use, either without paying for them or paying less than their full value. This is often known as "own consumption".

If own consumption occurs, then an amount equal to the normal *selling price* of the goods (less any amount paid for the goods by the owner) must be added to the net profit shown by the accounts when computing the adjusted profit. This rule stems from the case of *Sharkey* v *Wernher* (1955) in which horses were transferred from a stud farm to the owner's private stables. It was held that the profits of the stud farm should be increased, for tax purposes, by the full market value of the horses.

Non-trading income shown in the accounts

Any non-trading income shown in the accounts of a business must be deducted when computing the adjusted profit for Schedule D Case I purposes. The main categories of non-trading income which might be found in the accounts of a business are :

(a) income which is taxed under other schedules and cases of income tax or which has been taxed at source (e.g. income from property, interest received, dividends received)

(b) profits on the disposal of fixed assets (these are usually depreciation adjustments but a genuine gain may be chargeable to capital gains tax)

(c) interest received from the Inland Revenue in connection with a repayment of income tax (see Chapter 14)

(d) any transfers from reserves or decreases in general provisions.

Expenditure not shown in the accounts

The most common example of allowable expenditure not shown in the accounts of a business is a premium paid for the grant of a short lease of business premises. As explained in Chapter 5 (and as mentioned earlier in this chapter) part of such a premium is deductible from trading income in equal annual instalments over the period of the lease.

If a premium is being amortised in the business accounts, computation of the adjusted profit involves adding back the amortisation charges and deducting instead the amount of the premium which is allowable under the rules given in Chapter 5.

Summary

- ► A set of criteria known as the "badges of trade" may be used to distinguish between trading activities and non-trading activities.
- ► The net profit shown in the accounts of a self-employed person needs adjusting for tax purposes.
- ► Expenditure is allowable under Schedule D Case I if it is wholly and exclusively incurred for the purposes of the trade. Expenditure which is not so incurred will be disallowed. Certain categories of expenditure are disallowed by statute.
- ► If the owner of a business takes goods for personal use, an amount equal to the full market value of the goods (less any amount paid by the owner) must be added to the net profit shown by the accounts when computing the adjusted profit.

- ► Non-trading income included in the accounts of a business must be deducted from the net profit shown by those accounts when computing the adjusted profit.
- ► Any allowable expenditure not shown in the accounts (e.g. the deductible part of a premium paid for the grant of a short lease) must be deducted from the net profit shown by the accounts when computing the adjusted profit.

Exercises

8.1 List the six badges of trade.

8.2 State the general rule which governs whether or not expenditure is deductible under the rules of Schedule D Case I.

8.3 Which of the following items of expenditure would be allowed under the rules of Schedule D Case I ?

(a) the salary paid to a sole trader's wife

(b) a deed of covenant to charity

(c) a new lathe bought by an engineering business

(d) diaries costing £3 each given to customers

(e) the cost of the annual staff outing to Blackpool

(f) the black suit worn at work by a self-employed undertaker

(g) the legal costs of acquiring new freehold premises

(h) a subscription to the local chamber of commerce

(i) bottles of whisky costing £9.99 each given to customers at Christmas

(j) the legal costs of suing a trade debtor for non-payment.

8.4 Julian, a self-employed shopkeeper, takes goods costing £30 from his business stock for his own personal use. If he had sold the stock to a customer he would have charged £45. What adjustment would need to be made for tax purposes to his net profit if :

(a) he pays nothing for the goods

(b) he puts £30 of his own money into the till so as to pay for the goods

(c) he puts £45 of his own money into the till.

8.5 (a) A motor car with an original cost of £21,000 is leased for an annual rental of £5,670. How much of the £5,670 should be added back each year when calculating the Schedule D Case I adjusted profit ?

(b) A sole trader is granted a 15 year lease on premises which he uses for business purposes. He pays a premium of £15,000 and writes off £1,000 per year in his business accounts. How much of the £1,000 should be added back each year when calculating the Schedule D Case I adjusted profit ?

8.6 Linda's profit and loss account for the year ended 31 March 1998 is as follows :

		£	£
Sales			82,500
Less :	Cost of sales		37,200
Gross profit			45,300
Add :	Rents receivable	1,200	
	Bank interest receivable	80	
	Profit on sale of fixed assets	310	1,590
			46,890
Less :	Wages and salaries	22,620	
	Business rates and insurance	1,750	
	Heating and lighting	2,170	
	Repairs and renewals	4,280	
	Telephone	880	
	Motor expenses	3,250	
	Sundry expenses	1,650	
	Bad and doubtful debts	640	
	Credit card interest	120	
	Loss on sale of fixed asset	70	
	Depreciation	2,500	39,930
Net profit for the year			6,960

Notes :

(a) Linda draws a salary of £200 per week from the business. This is included in the wages and salaries figure.

(b) Repairs and renewals are as follows :

	£
Decoration of business premises	400
Installation of new improved heating system	3,800
Minor repair	80
	4,280

(c) It has been agreed with the Inspector of Taxes that one-quarter of telephone costs and one-fifth of motor expenses relate to private use.

(d) Sundry expenses include business entertaining of £520.

(e) Trade debts written off in the year amount to £440 and £200 has been set aside as a general provision for bad and doubtful debts.

Compute the adjusted profit for Schedule D Case I purposes for the year ended 31 March 1998.

***8.7** A sole trader's bad and doubtful debts account for the year ended 31 March 1998 is as follows :

	£	£		£	£
Trade debts written off		638	Provisions b/f		
Provisions c/f			General	200	
General	150		Specific	231	431
Specific	317	467			
			Staff loan recovered		500
			P & L Account		174
		1,105			1,105

How much of the £174 charged to the profit and loss account for the year should be added back when calculating the Schedule D Case I adjusted profit ?

***8.8** Imran owns a wholesaling business which operates from rented premises. He has a 10-year lease on the premises and paid a premium of £7,000 in order to obtain the lease. His profit and loss account for the year ended 31 December 1997 is as follows :

		£	£
Gross profit for the year			52,618
Add :	Interest receivable	212	
	Surplus on sale of office equipment	300	512
			53,130
Less :	Wages (see Note 1)	19,280	
	Rent, rates and insurance (see Note 2)	6,915	
	Electricity	4,328	
	Telephone (see Note 3)	1,650	
	Repairs (see Note 4)	2,286	
	Printing and advertising	1,250	
	Motor expenses (see Note 5)	5,712	
	Legal and professional expenses (see Note 6)	3,000	
	Sundry expenses (see Note 7)	4,777	
	Bad and doubtful debts (see Note 8)	860	
	Bank charges and interest	2,765	
	Lease premium amortisation	700	
	Depreciation	8,749	62,272
Net loss for the year			(9,142)

Notes :

1. Wages include £5,800 for Imran's wife (who works full-time for the business) and £1,000 for his son (a student who does not work for the business at all). Also included is Imran's personal Schedule D Case I income tax of £3,229 and personal National Insurance contributions of £286.

2. Rent, rates and insurance includes Imran's private medical insurance premium of £414.

3. It has been agreed that one-sixth of telephone costs relate to private use.

4. Repairs include £750 for the cost of essential repairs to a newly-acquired second-hand forklift truck which could not be used until the repairs had been carried out.

5. Motor expenses are as follows :

	£
Vehicle servicing and repairs	1,165
Fuel and oil	2,815
Loss on disposal of motor vehicle	422
Road fund licences and insurance	610
Fine for speeding by Imran	700
	5,712

   It has been agreed that one-tenth of motor expenses relate to private use.

6. Legal and professional expenses consist of :

	£
Fees relating to renewal of lease	500
Debt collection	1,500
Accountancy fees	1,000
	3,000

7. Sundry expenses are :

	£
Entertaining UK customers	630
Entertaining overseas customer	150
Staff Christmas dinner	312
Gift to employee on examination success	100
Patent royalties	2,540
Subscription to trade association	250
Donation to political party	200
Miscellaneous small items (all allowable)	595
	4,777

8. Trade debts of £500 were written off during the year. The general provision for bad debts was reduced by £100 and the specific provision for bad debts was increased by £460.

9. During the year, Imran took goods costing £220 from stock for personal use, paying £220 of his own money into the business bank account. His gross profit percentage on turnover is 20%.

Compute the adjusted profit for Schedule D Case I purposes for the year ended 31 December 1997.

Chapter 9

Income from self-employment : Basis periods

Introduction

Income tax assessments are raised for tax years or "years of assessment", which run from 6 April to the following 5 April. It would be convenient, therefore, if all traders were required to choose 5 April as their annual accounting date, so that the profits for a given tax year could be readily identified. However, traders are free to choose any accounting date they wish and so it is necessary to devise some means of establishing a link between the accounting periods for which profits are calculated and the tax years in which those profits are charged to tax.

The profits charged to tax in a tax year are the profits earned during the *basis period* for that tax year, and the purpose of this chapter is to explain the rules which are used to determine the basis period for any given tax year.

The impact of Finance Act 1994

The Finance Act 1994 (FA1994) introduced major changes to the rules which are used to determine Schedule D Case I basis periods. These changes have been phased in over a number of years, as follows :

(a) If a business commenced trading before 6 April 1994, the old (pre-FA1994) rules were used for tax years up to and including 1995/96, special transitional rules apply in 1996/97 and the new (post-FA1994) rules apply as from 1997/98.

(b) For businesses commencing to trade on or after 6 April 1994, the new (post-FA1994) rules apply in all years.

This chapter is mainly concerned with the *new* basis period rules, which are generally applicable to all businesses in tax year 1997/98 and in subsequent years. However, certain aspects of the old rules and transitional rules are still relevant and are considered later in this chapter. Note that the term "new business" is often used to refer to a business which commences on or after 6 April 1994 and the term "old business" refers to a business which commenced before that date.

Basis periods (post-FA1994 rules)

The main principle of the new basis period rules is that the basis period for a year of assessment is *the accounting year ending in that year of assessment.* This is known as the current year basis (CYB). However, special rules apply when a business starts trading, ceases trading or changes its accounting date. These special rules are considered later in this chapter.

EXAMPLE 1

(a) A trader prepares accounts annually to 31 December. Identify the basis period for the 1998/99 Schedule D Case I assessment.

(b) A trader prepares accounts annually to 30 April. For which tax year will the accounting year to 30 April 1997 form the basis period ?

SOLUTION

(a) The accounting year to 31 December 1998 ends during 1998/99 and therefore forms the basis period for the 1998/99 assessment.

(b) The accounting year to 30 April 1997 ends during 1997/98 and therefore forms the basis period for the 1997/98 assessment.

Commencement of trade

The Finance Act 1994 provides special rules for determining basis periods when a new business commences trading. The basis periods for the opening years of assessment for a new business are as follows :

Year of assessment	*Basis period*
1	Date of commencement to the following 5 April (the "actual basis")
2	(a) 12 months to the accounting date in year 2 (if possible), or (b) First 12 months of trading (if the accounting date in year 2 is less than 12 months after commencement), or (c) Actual i.e. 6 April to 5 April (if there is no accounting date in year 2)
3	(a) Current year basis (if possible), or (b) 12 months to the accounting date in year 3
4 etc.	Current year basis.

Note the following points :

(a) Basis periods for the opening tax years may overlap to some extent and therefore some of the profits made in the early years of trading may be the subject of more than one assessment (see below).

(b) If necessary, the adjusted profits for early accounting periods are apportioned on a time basis in order to compute the assessments in the opening years.

(c) Strictly speaking, all apportionments required for the purposes of Schedule D Case I or II should be made exactly, according to the number of days in the relevant basis period. This is the approach adopted in this book (although, for the sake of simplicity, the existence of February 29th has been ignored and all tax years have been assumed to contain 365 days). However, *some examining bodies may be prepared to accept approximate apportionments, calculated to the nearest month.* Therefore the reader is advised to find out whether his or her examining body requires apportionments to be made in days or months and then to proceed accordingly when answering examination questions.

EXAMPLE 2

(a) Vera commences trading on 1 January 1997, preparing accounts annually to 31 December. Identify the basis periods for the first four tax years.

(b) Wilbur commences trading on 1 October 1997. He chooses 30 June as his annual accounting date and prepares his first accounts for the 9 months to 30 June 1998. Identify the basis periods for the first four tax years.

(c) Yasmin commences trading on 1 February 1996 and chooses 30 April as her annual accounting date. She prepares her first accounts for the 15 months to 30 April 1997. Identify the basis periods for the first four tax years.

SOLUTION

(a)	1996/97	Actual	1 January 1997 to 5 April 1997
	1997/98	12 months to a/c date in year 2	1 January 1997 to 31 December 1997
	1998/99	CYB	year to 31 December 1998
	1999/00	CYB	year to 31 December 1999
(b)	1997/98	Actual	1 October 1997 to 5 April 1998
	1998/99	First 12 months	1 October 1997 to 30 September 1998
	1999/00	CYB	year to 30 June 1999
	2000/01	CYB	year to 30 June 2000
(c)	1995/96	Actual	1 February 1996 to 5 April 1996
	1996/97	Actual	6 April 1996 to 5 April 1997
	1997/98	12 months to a/c date in year 3	1 May 1996 to 30 April 1997
	1998/99	CYB	year to 30 April 1998

Overlap profits

If a new business prepares accounts to 5 April in all years, the basis periods used in the opening tax years will not overlap at all. In most cases, however, the opening basis periods will overlap and some profits will form the basis of more than one assessment. Such profits are known as "overlap profits".

EXAMPLE 3

Albert begins trading on 1 May 1997 and has the following results :

	Adjusted profit
	£
15 months to 31 July 1998	16,800
year to 31 July 1999	21,600

Compute Albert's Schedule D Case I assessments for the first three tax years and calculate the amount of any overlap profits.

SOLUTION

Albert's first accounting period contains 457 days and his first assessment is based on the profits of the 340 days from 1 May 1997 to 5 April 1998. The assessments for the first three tax years are as follows :

Year	*Basis*	*Basis period*	*Workings*	*Assessment*
				£
1997/98	Actual	1/5/97 to 5/4/98	£16,800 x 340/457	12,499
1998/99	12 months to a/c date in year 2	1/8/97 to 31/7/98	£16,800 x 365/457	13,418
1999/00	CYB	y/e 31/7/99		21,600

The overlap period consists of the 248 days from 1 August 1997 to 5 April 1998, which are common to the basis periods for 1997/98 and 1998/99. The overlap profits are therefore £9,117 (£16,800 x 248/457).

Overlap relief

In general, any overlap profits arising in the opening tax years of a new business are deducted from the assessment raised for the final year when the business ceases trading. Note the following points regarding "overlap relief" :

(a) Overlap relief ensures that, over the entire lifetime of a new business, the total of all the assessments raised is equal to the total adjusted profits.

(b) Overlap profits are not index-linked. The real value of overlap relief will therefore be eroded by inflation, especially in the case of businesses which trade for many years.

(c) If overlap profits exceed the final year's assessment, the resulting loss is dealt with in the usual way (see Chapter 11).

However, if a business changes its accounting date at some point during its lifetime, it is possible that some of the overlap profits arising in the opening years may be relieved by deduction from the assessment raised for the year of the change. It is also possible that further overlap profits might arise on a change of accounting date (see below).

Cessation of trade

A cessation of trade occurs when the owner of a business retires, sells the business or dies and the final tax year in which the trader is assessed under Schedule D Case I is the tax year in which the cessation occurs. Under the post-FA1994 basis period rules, the basis period for this final tax year is determined as follows :

(a) If a business commences trading and ceases trading in the same tax year, the basis period for that year consists of the entire lifespan of the business.

(b) If a business ceases trading in its second tax year, the basis period for that year runs from 6 April at the start of the year up to the date of cessation. (This rule overrides the usual commencement rules for the second year of assessment).

(c) Otherwise, the basis period for the final tax year runs from the end of the basis period for the previous tax year up to the date of the cessation. This basis period may be less than, equal to or more than 12 months in length. (The usual commencement rules for the third year are overridden if a business ceases trading in its third tax year).

If the final set of accounts prepared for a business covers a period of more than 12 months, it is possible that no accounting date at all falls into the penultimate tax year (i.e. the last year but one). This makes it impossible to apply the usual current year basis in that year. In these circumstances, the basis period for the penultimate tax year is the 12 months up to the normal accounting date falling in that year. Special rules apply if an old business ceases trading in 1997/98 or in 1998/99 (see "transitional rules" later in this chapter).

It is important to appreciate that Schedule D Case I assessments are raised on the owner of a business and not on the business itself, so that a change in the ownership of a business is treated for tax purposes as a cessation of one business followed by the commencement of another.

EXAMPLE 4

Carmen starts trading on 1 July 1997 and chooses 30 June as her annual accounting date. Identify the basis periods for her last two tax years if she ceases trading as follows :

	Date of cessation	*Final set of accounts*
(a)	31 March 1998	9 months to 31 March 1998
(b)	30 June 1998	year to 30 June 1998
(c)	30 June 2005	year to 30 June 2005
(d)	31 May 2005	11 months to 31 May 2005
(e)	30 April 2005	22 months to 30 April 2005

SOLUTION

(a) Trade both commences and ceases in 1997/98. The basis period for this single tax year is the entire lifespan of the business i.e. 1 July 1997 to 31 March 1998.

(b) The cessation occurs in 1998/99, which is the second year of assessment. The basis periods are :

	1997/98	Actual	1 July 1997 to 5 April 1998
	1998/99	6 April to date of cessation	6 April 1998 to 30 June 1998
(c)	2004/05	CYB	y/e 30 June 2004
	2005/06	End of previous basis period up to date of cessation	1 July 2004 to 30 June 2005
(d)	2004/05	CYB	y/e 30 June 2004
	2005/06	End of previous basis period up to date of cessation	1 July 2004 to 31 May 2005
(e)	2004/05	12 months to normal a/c date	1 July 2003 to 30 June 2004
	2005/06	End of previous basis period up to date of cessation	1 July 2004 to 30 April 2005

EXAMPLE 5

Damien starts trading on 1 July 1994 and chooses 31 December as his annual accounting date. He ceases trading on 30 September 1999 and has the following results :

	Adjusted profit
	£
6 months to 31 December 1994	8,400
year to 31 December 1995	9,200
year to 31 December 1996	10,500
year to 31 December 1997	7,500
year to 31 December 1998	6,400
9 months to 30 September 1999	5,800

Compute the Schedule D Case I assessments for all years. Show that the total of these assessments is equal to the total of the adjusted profits.

SOLUTION

Year	*Basis period*	*Workings*	*Assessment*
			£
1994/95	1/7/94 to 5/4/95	£8,400 + £9,200 x 95/365	10,795
1995/96	y/e 31/12/95		9,200
1996/97	y/e 31/12/96		10,500
1997/98	y/e 31/12/97		7,500
1998/99	y/e 31/12/98		6,400
1999/00	1/1/99 to 30/9/99	£5,800 - overlap relief £2,395	3,405
			47,800

Notes :

(a) The overlap period is from 1 January 1995 to 5 April 1995 (95 days) and the overlap profits are £2,395 (£9,200 x 95/365).

(b) The total of the assessments is £47,800, the same as the total of the adjusted profits.

Change of accounting date

If a business changes its accounting date from one date (the "old date") to another (the "new date") special rules are used to determine the basis period for the year of the change. The "year of change" is defined as the first year of assessment in which accounts are *not* made up to the old date or *are* made up to the new date (or both). There will be a change of basis period for a year of change so long as all of the following conditions are satisfied :

(a) The first set of accounts made up to the new date does not cover a period of more than 18 months.

(b) Notice of the change of accounting date is given to the Inland Revenue in a tax return on or before the due filing date for that return.

(c) Either :

  (i) None of the previous five years of assessment has been a year of change resulting in a change of basis period, or

  (ii) The Inland Revenue is satisfied that the change of date has been made for genuine commercial reasons and not for tax avoidance purposes.

If all of these conditions are satisfied, the basis period for the year of change is determined as follows :

(a) The "relevant period" is identified as the period beginning immediately after the end of the basis period for the previous year of assessment and ending with the new date in the year of change.

(b) If the length of the relevant period is less than 12 months, the basis period for the year of change is the 12 months to the new date in the year of change.

(c) If the length of the relevant period is not less than 12 months, the basis period for the year of change is the relevant period itself.

(d) In consequence, the basis period for a year of change will always be of at least 12 months' duration.

If all of the required conditions are *not* satisfied, the basis period for the year of change is the 12 months to the old date in that year. However, the following year of assessment is then regarded as a year of change (the taxpayer being treated as though this were the first year in which the new date had been used) and a change of basis period will occur in that year if all of the conditions are satisfied in relation to that year. A change of accounting date can be carried forward indefinitely in this way until such time as the necessary conditions for a change of basis period are satisfied.

EXAMPLE 6

(a) Frank began trading on 1 October 1995, preparing accounts to 30 September each year. He decided to change his accounting date to 30 June and the first accounts made up to the new date were for the period from 1 October 1997 to 30 June 1998. The conditions necessary for a change of basis period were all satisfied. Identify the basis periods for years 1995/96 to 1999/00 inclusive.

(b) Audrey began trading on 1 January 1995, preparing accounts to 31 December each year. She decided to change her accounting date to 31 March and the first accounts made up to the new date were for the period from 1 January 1997 to 31 March 1998. The conditions necessary for a change of basis period were all satisfied. Identify the basis periods for years 1994/95 to 1999/00 inclusive.

(c) Grant began trading on 1 July 1995, preparing accounts to 30 June each year. He decided to change his accounting date to 31 December and the first accounts made up to the new date were for the period from 1 July 1998 to 31 December 1998. The conditions necessary for a change of basis period were all satisfied. Identify the basis periods for years 1995/96 to 2000/01 inclusive.

(d) Clare began trading on 1 March 1995, preparing accounts to 31 January each year. Her first accounts were for the period to 31 January 1996. She decided to change her accounting date to 30 April and the first accounts made up to the new date were for the period from 1 February 1998 to 30 April 1999. The conditions necessary for a change of basis period were all satisfied. Identify the basis periods for years 1994/95 to 2000/01 inclusive.

SOLUTION

(a) The year of change is 1998/99 (the first year in which the old date was not used and the new date was used). The basis period for 1997/98 ended on 30 September 1997, so the relevant period is from 1 October 1997 to 30 June 1998. This is less than 12 months in length so the basis period for 1998/99 is the 12 months to 30 June 1998. Basis periods for 1995/96 to 1999/00 are :

1995/96 1 October 1995 to 5 April 1996
1996/97 year to 30 September 1996
1997/98 year to 30 September 1997
1998/99 year to 30 June 1998
1999/00 year to 30 June 1999

Note that there is an overlap between the basis periods for 1997/98 and 1998/99 (as well as the usual overlap arising on the commencement of trade). The treatment of overlap profits on a change of accounting date is described below.

(b) The year of change is 1997/98 (the first year in which the old date was not used and the new date was used). The basis period for 1996/97 ended on 31 December 1996, so the relevant period is from 1 January 1997 to 31 March 1998. This is not less than 12 months in length so the basis period for 1997/98 is the same as the relevant period. Basis periods for 1994/95 to 1999/00 are :

1994/95 1 January 1995 to 5 April 1995
1995/96 year to 31 December 1995
1996/97 year to 31 December 1996
1997/98 1 January 1997 to 31 March 1998
1998/99 year to 31 March 1999
1999/00 year to 31 March 2000

(c) The year of change is 1998/99 (the first year in which the new date was used). The basis period for 1997/98 ended on 30 June 1997, so the relevant period is from 1 July 1997 to 31 December 1998. This is not less than 12 months in length so the basis period for 1998/99 is the same as the relevant period. Basis periods are :

1995/96 1 July 1995 to 5 April 1996
1996/97 year to 30 June 1996
1997/98 year to 30 June 1997
1998/99 1 July 1997 to 31 December 1998
1999/00 year to 31 December 1999
2000/01 year to 31 December 2000

(d) The year of change is 1998/99 (the first year in which the old date was not used). The basis period for 1997/98 ended on 31 January 1998, so the relevant period is from 1 February 1998 to 30 April 1998. This is less than 12 months in length so the basis period for 1998/99 is the 12 months to 30 April 1998 (even though this accounting date was not used in 1998/99). Basis periods for 1994/95 to 2000/01 are :

1994/95 1 March 1995 to 5 April 1995
1995/96 1 March 1995 to 28 February 1996
1996/97 year to 31 January 1997
1997/98 year to 31 January 1998
1998/99 year to 30 April 1998
1999/00 year to 30 April 1999
2000/01 year to 30 April 2000

There is an overlap between the basis periods for 1997/98 and 1998/99 (as well as the usual overlap arising on the commencement of trade).

Overlap profits on a change of accounting date

If a change of accounting date results in profits being assessed more than once, these overlap profits are added to any earlier overlap profits (which arose in the opening years or on a previous change of accounting date) and the total is carried forward for relief on cessation or on a subsequent change of accounting date.

Alternatively, if the basis period for a year of change exceeds 12 months, a part of the overlap profits brought forward from previous years may be relieved in the year of change. The amount to be relieved is calculated according to the following formula :

$$\text{Amount relieved} = A \times \frac{(B - C)}{D}$$

where : A = Total overlap profits brought forward and not yet relieved

B = Length of the relevant period (in days)

C = 365 (or, strictly, 366 if the relevant period includes a 29 February)

D = Total length of the overlap period(s) to which the total overlap profits brought forward relate.

EXAMPLE 7

(a) Byron began trading on 1 November 1995, preparing accounts to 31 October each year. He decided to change his accounting date to 31 August and the first accounts made up to the new date were for the period from 1 November 1997 to 31 August 1998. The conditions necessary for a change of basis period were all satisfied. The adjusted profits for Byron's first five accounting periods were as follows :

	£
Year to 31 October 1996	12,000
Year to 31 October 1997	18,000
Period to 31 August 1998	16,000
Year to 31 August 1999	21,000
Year to 31 August 2000	24,000

Compute Byron's Schedule D Case I assessments for years 1995/96 to 2000/01.

(b) Michelle began trading on 1 January 1995, preparing accounts to 31 December each year. She decided to change her accounting date to 28 February and the first accounts made up to the new date were for the period from 1 January 1998 to 28 February 1999. The conditions necessary for a change of basis period were all satisfied. The adjusted profits for Michelle's first five accounting periods were :

	£
Year to 31 December 1995	4,530
Year to 31 December 1996	5,250
Year to 31 December 1997	11,680
Period to 28 February 1999	14,390
Year to 28 February 2000	16,270

Compute Michelle's Schedule D Case I assessments for years 1994/95 to 1999/00.

SOLUTION

(a) The year of change is 1998/99 (the first year in which the old date was not used and the new date was used). The basis period for 1997/98 ended on 31 October 1997, so the relevant period is from 1 November 1997 to 31 August 1998. This is less than 12 months in length so the basis period for 1998/99 is the 12 months to 31 August 1998. The assessments for 1995/96 to 2000/01 are :

Year	*Basis period*	*Workings*	*Assessment*
			£
1995/96	1/11/95 to 5/4/96	£12,000 x 156/365	5,129
1996/97	y/e 31/10/96		12,000
1997/98	y/e 31/10/97		18,000
1998/99	y/e 31/8/98	£18,000 x 61/365 + £16,000	19,008
1999/00	y/e 31/8/99		21,000
2000/01	y/e 31/8/00		24,000

There are overlap profits of £5,129 (156 days) on the commencement of trade and a further £3,008 (61 days) on the change of accounting date. Total overlap profits carried forward are £8,137 (217 days).

(b) The year of change is 1998/99 (the first year in which the old date was not used and the new date was used). The basis period for 1997/98 ended on 31 December 1997, so the relevant period is from 1 January 1998 to 28 February 1999. This is not less than 12 months in length so the basis period for 1998/99 is the relevant period itself. The assessments for 1994/95 to 1999/00 are :

Year	*Basis period*	*Workings*	*Assessment*
			£
1994/95	1/1/95 to 5/4/95	£4,530 x 95/365	1,179
1995/96	y/e 31/12/95		4,530
1996/97	y/e 31/12/96		5,250
1997/98	y/e 31/12/97		11,680
1998/99	1/1/98 to 28/2/99	£14,390 - overlap relief £732	13,658
1999/00	y/e 28/2/00		16,270

There are overlap profits of £1,179 (95 days) on the commencement of trade. The relevant period is 424 days long, which exceeds 365 days by 59 days. Overlap relief in the year of change is calculated as £1,179 x 59/95 = £732. Overlap profits carried forward are £447 (36 days).

Basis periods (pre-FA1994 rules)

The basis of assessment used for old businesses for tax years up to and including 1995/96 was known as the "preceding year basis" (PYB). The general rule was that the basis period for a year of assessment was *the accounting year ending in the preceding year of assessment.* For example, if an old business prepared accounts to 31 December each year, then the basis period for 1995/96 would be the year to 31 December 1994.

Special rules applied on a commencement of trade but these rules have now fallen into disuse and are not considered here. Special rules also applied on a cessation of trade and these rules were used for old businesses ceasing to trade in years up to and including 1996/97. In summary, the cessation rules were as follows :

(a) The basis period for the final year of assessment ran from 6 April at the start of the year up to the date of the cessation.

(b) The Inland Revenue were empowered to revise the assessments for *both* the penultimate and ante-penultimate years to the actual basis if this increased the total of the assessments for those two years.

(c) There was inevitably a gap between basis periods in the closing years and profits earned during this gap were not assessed to tax at all.

As from 1997/98, the post-FA1994 cessation rules described earlier in this chapter are used for all businesses but these rules may be modified if an old business ceases trading in 1997/98 or in 1998/99 (see "transitional rules" below).

EXAMPLE 8

Sean began trading in 1972, preparing accounts annually to 30 September. He ceased trading on 30 September 1996.

(a) Identify the basis periods for the final four tax years if the Inland Revenue *do not* revise the assessments for the penultimate and ante-penultimate years.

(b) Identify the basis periods for the final four tax years if the Inland Revenue *do* revise the assessments for the penultimate and ante-penultimate years.

(c) Identify the gaps between basis periods in each case.

SOLUTION

(a) If the assessments for the penultimate and ante-penultimate years are not revised to the actual basis, the basis periods for Sean's final four tax years will be :

1996/97	Actual	6 April 1996 to 30 September 1996
1995/96	PYB	year to 30 September 1994
1994/95	PYB	year to 30 September 1993
1993/94	PYB	year to 30 September 1992

(b) If the assessments for the penultimate and ante-penultimate years are revised to the actual basis, the basis periods for Sean's final four tax years will be :

1996/97	Actual	6 April 1996 to 30 September 1996
1995/96	Actual	6 April 1995 to 5 April 1996
1994/95	Actual	6 April 1994 to 5 April 1995
1993/94	PYB	year to 30 September 1992

(c) In case (a) there is a gap between the basis periods for 1995/96 and 1996/97. Profits earned between 1 October 1994 and 5 April 1996 inclusive will not be taxed.

In case (b) there is a gap between the basis periods for 1993/94 and 1994/95. Profits earned between 1 October 1992 and 5 April 1994 inclusive will not be taxed.

Transitional rules

As stated earlier, old businesses are assessed on the current year basis with effect from 1997/98. The preceding year basis was used for years up to and including 1995/96 and transitional rules of assessment apply in 1996/97. Broadly speaking, the 1996/97 assessment on an old business is equal to the *average* of :

(a) the profit of the accounting year that would have been the basis period for 1996/97 under the preceding year basis, and

(b) the profit of the accounting year that would have been the basis period for 1996/97 under the current year basis.

If a loss is incurred in either of these two accounting years, the loss counts as zero in the averaging calculation and is then eligible for the usual loss reliefs (see Chapter 11).

EXAMPLE 9

Edna began trading many years ago, making up accounts annually to 31 March. Recent adjusted profits have been as follows :

	£
year to 31 March 1995	13,200
year to 31 March 1996	15,640
year to 31 March 1997	16,180
year to 31 March 1998	18,230

Compute Edna's Schedule D Case I assessments for years 1995/96 to 1997/98 inclusive.

SOLUTION

Year	*Basis*	*Basis period*	*Workings*	*Assessment*
				£
1995/96	PYB	y/e 31/3/95		13,200
1996/97	Transitional	24 mths to 31/3/97	50% of (£15,640 + £16,180)	15,910
1997/98	CYB	y/e 31/3/98		18,230

Transitional overlap relief

Under the old cessation rules there was always a gap between basis periods in the closing tax years. Profits earned during this gap escaped tax. But the switch to the CYB has deprived old businesses of this advantage, since the CYB cessation rules do not give rise to such a gap.

To some extent, the averaging process used in 1996/97 compensates old businesses for this deprivation but further compensation, known as "transitional overlap relief" is also available. Under the transitional rules, the period between :

(a) the end of the basis period for 1996/97, and

(b) 5 April 1997

is treated as an overlap period and the profits of this overlap period are then eligible for overlap relief on a subsequent cessation of trade or change of accounting date.

EXAMPLE 10

Norman began trading many years ago. Recent adjusted profits have been as follows :

	£
year to 31 October 1994	22,500
year to 31 October 1995	25,460
year to 31 October 1996	26,820
year to 31 October 1997	28,550

Compute Norman's Schedule D Case I assessments for years 1995/96 to 1997/98 and calculate the amount of any transitional overlap relief.

SOLUTION

Year	*Basis*	*Basis period*	*Workings*	*Assessment* £
1995/96	PYB	y/e 31/10/94		22,500
1996/97	Transitional	24 mths to 31/10/96	50% of (£25,460 + £26,820)	26,140
1997/98	CYB	y/e 31/10/97		28,550

Transitional overlap relief is available in relation to the profits of the period from 1 November 1996 to 5 April 1997 i.e. £28,550 x 156/365 = £12,202.

Cessation of an old business after 6 April 1997

The pre-FA1994 cessation rules described earlier in this chapter apply to old businesses ceasing to trade in tax years up to and including 1996/97. For cessations on or after 6 April 1997 :

(a) If an old business ceases trading in tax year 1997/98, the new (post-FA1994) cessation rules are normally used. However, the Inland Revenue may direct that tax years 1995/96, 1996/97 and 1997/98 should instead be assessed on the actual basis. This direction will be made if the amount of tax assessed increases as a result.

(b) If an old business ceases trading in tax year 1998/99, the new cessation rules are used but the Inland Revenue may direct that the assessment for 1996/97 should be revised from the transitional basis (see above) to the actual basis.

(c) If an old business ceases trading on or after 6 April 1999, the new cessation rules are used without modification.

Averaging of agricultural profits

More than any other trade, the trade of farming and market gardening is at the mercy of the weather. As a consequence, farming profits may fluctuate considerably from one year to the next, leading to corresponding fluctuations in Schedule D Case I assessments. Such fluctuations may be smoothed out by a claim for *averaging*.

The Schedule D Case I assessments of two consecutive tax years may be averaged if the difference between them is at least 30% of the higher assessment. The effect of an averaging claim is to replace the normal assessment in each of the two years concerned by the average of the two assessments which would otherwise be raised.

EXAMPLE 11

The recent tax-adjusted profits of a self-employed farmer who began trading on 1 December 1994 are as follows :

	£
year to 30 November 1996	36,200
year to 30 November 1997	10,640

(a) May an averaging claim be made ?

(b) Would the farmer benefit from an averaging claim ?

SOLUTION

(a) This is a new business, assessed on the current year basis, so the tax years in question are 1996/97 and 1997/98. The difference between the two profit figures is £25,560, which is far more than 30% of £36,200 so an averaging claim may be made.

(b) If an averaging claim is made, the 1996/97 and 1997/98 assessments are each revised to £23,420 (the average of £36,200 and £10,640). The farmer benefits from this claim in two ways :

   (i) the likelihood of paying 40% tax for 1996/97 is removed, so reducing the total tax liability for the two years, and

   (ii) the farmer's cash flow situation is improved, since the 1996/97 tax liability is reduced and the 1997/98 tax liability is increased.

Note the following points in relation to the averaging of agricultural profits :

(a) If a loss has been incurred in either of the two years involved in an averaging claim, the loss counts as zero in the averaging calculation. (The loss is then relieved in the usual way, as described in Chapter 11).

(b) An averaging claim may not be made for the tax year in which trade commences or for the tax year in which trade ceases.

(c) If an averaging claim has been made for two tax years, then the revised assessment for the second year may subsequently be used in another averaging claim. For example, if a claim has already been made for 1996/97 and 1997/98, then another claim may be made for 1997/98 and 1998/99. Overlapping claims of this nature must be made in chronological order.

(d) An averaging claim which does not involve tax years subsequent to 1995/96 must be made within two years of the end of the second tax year to which the claim relates. Claims which involve 1996/97 or subsequent years must be made by 31 January in the next tax year but one following the end of the second tax year to which the claim relates.

EXAMPLE 12

A market gardener who began trading on 1 January 1995 has the following recent results :

	Adjusted profit (loss)
	£
year to 31 December 1997	21,500
year to 31 December 1998	14,200
year to 31 December 1999	(5,400)
year to 31 December 2000	6,900
year to 31 December 2001	10,800

Compute the assessments for 1997/98 to 2001/02 inclusive, assuming that all possible averaging claims are made.

SOLUTION

1997/98 and 1998/99

	£	
Original assessment for 1997/98 (y/e 31/12/97)	21,500	
Original assessment for 1998/99 (y/e 31/12/98)	14,200	
Difference	7,300	(more than 30% of £21,500)

Averaging gives revised assessments of £17,850 in 1997/98 & 1998/99.

1998/99 and 1999/00

	£	
Revised assessment for 1998/99	17,850	
Original assessment for 1999/00 (y/e 31/12/99)	0	
Difference	17,850	(more than 30% of £17,850)

Averaging gives revised assessments of £8,925 in 1998/99 & 1999/00.

1999/00 and 2000/01

	£	
Revised assessment for 1999/00	8,925	
Original assessment for 2000/01 (y/e 31/12/00)	6,900	
Difference	2,025	(less than 30% of £8,925)

No averaging is possible so assessments are unaltered.

2000/01 and 2001/02

	£	
Original assessment for 2000/01 (y/e 31/12/00)	6,900	
Original assessment for 2001/02 (y/e 31/12/01)	10,800	
Difference	3,900	(more than 30% of £10,800)

Averaging gives revised assessments of £8,850 in 2000/01 & 2001/02. The final assessments for all years concerned are as follows :

	£	
1997/98	17,850	
1998/99	8,925	
1999/00	8,925	
2000/01	8,850	
2001/02	8,850	(which may perhaps be averaged with 2002/03).

Marginal relief

As explained above, an averaging claim may not be made if the difference between the assessments for the two years concerned is less than 30% of the higher assessment. If, however, this difference is at least 25% of the higher assessment, then a form of averaging known as the "marginal relief" may be claimed.

The effect of the marginal relief is to reduce the higher assessment (H) and to increase the lower assessment (L) by an amount given by the following formula :

$$3 \times (H - L) - 0.75 \times H$$

If the difference between H and L is exactly 30% of H, this formula has the same effect as an ordinary averaging claim. If the difference between H and L is exactly 25% of H, this formula has no effect at all.

EXAMPLE 13

A farmer's Schedule D Case I assessment for 1997/98 is £12,000. What averaging claims (if any) can he make if his Schedule D Case I assessment for 1998/99 is :

(a) £7,600

(b) £8,600

(c) £9,600.

SOLUTION

(a) The difference between the two assessments is £4,400, which is more than 30% of £12,000 so a normal averaging claim can be made, revising both assessments to £9,800 (the average of £12,000 and £7,600).

(b) The difference between the two assessments is £3,400, which is between 25% and 30% of £12,000 so a marginal relief claim can be made. The adjustment to each assessment is :

$$3 \times (£12{,}000 - £8{,}600) \; - \; 0.75 \times £12{,}000 = £1{,}200.$$

The assessment for 1997/98 is reduced to £10,800 and the assessment for 1998/99 is increased to £9,800.

(c) The difference between the two assessments is £2,400, which is less than 25% of £12,000 so no averaging is possible at all.

Summary

- The new post-FA1994 basis period rules apply in all years of assessment to businesses which commence trading on or after 6 April 1994.
- Under the new rules, Schedule D Case I assessments are made on the current year basis. Special rules apply in the opening and closing years of a business and on a change of accounting date.
- Overlap profits arising in the opening years of a new business are relieved either on the cessation of trade or on a change of accounting date.
- Businesses which commenced trading before 6 April 1994 were assessed on the preceding year basis for the last time in 1995/96 and are assessed on the current year basis as from 1997/98. Special transitional rules apply in 1996/97.
- Transitional overlap relief compensates old businesses for the effects of the switch from the preceding year basis to the current year basis.
- In certain circumstances, farmers and market gardeners may claim that the profits of two consecutive tax years should be averaged.

Exercises

9.1 Under the *current year basis*, for which tax years would the following accounting years form the basis period ?

(a) year to 31 October 1997
(b) year to 31 March 1998
(c) year to 30 April 1999
(d) year to 5 April 1999.

9.2 Frank began trading on 1 July 1997. Identify the basis periods for his first 4 years of assessment if he :

(a) chooses 30 June as his annual accounting date and prepares his first accounts for the year to 30 June 1998
(b) chooses 30 April as his annual accounting date and prepares his first accounts for the 22 months to 30 April 1999
(c) chooses 30 April as his annual accounting date and prepares his first accounts for the 10 months to 30 April 1998.

Also identify any overlap periods which arise in each case.

9.3 Greta commences trading on 1 January 1997 and chooses 30 June as her annual accounting date. Her first accounts are made up for the 18 months to 30 June 1998 and show an adjusted profit of £27,300. Compute Greta's assessments for the first three tax years and calculate the amount of any overlap profits.

9.4 Hitesh begins trading in 1995 and chooses 31 January as his annual accounting date. His last full year of trading is the year to 31 January 2002. Identify the basis periods for the last three tax years in each of the following cases :

	Date of cessation	*Final set of accounts*
(a)	31 May 2002	4 months to 31 May 2002
(b)	31 March 2003	14 months to 31 March 2003
(c)	30 April 2003	15 months to 30 April 2003

9.5 Larry began trading in 1980, preparing accounts to 31 July each year. He ceases trading on 31 July 1998 and his adjusted profits in the closing years are as follows :

	£
year to 31 July 1994	12,700
year to 31 July 1995	21,500
year to 31 July 1996	14,300
year to 31 July 1997	15,900
year to 31 July 1998	12,800

Compute the Schedule D Case I assessments for 1995/96 to 1998/99 inclusive. (Assume that the Inland Revenue makes no direction regarding the 1996/97 assessment).

***9.6** Ivy begins trading as a market gardener on 1 January 1997, making up annual accounts to 31 December. Her adjusted profits in the opening years are as follows :

	£
year to 31 December 1997	7,200
year to 31 December 1998	5,010
year to 31 December 1999	4,570

(a) Compute the Schedule D Case I assessments for the first four tax years, assuming that no averaging claims are made.

(b) Compute the revised Schedule D Case I assessments for the first four tax years, assuming that all possible averaging claims are made.

***9.7** Ken starts trading on 1 October 1994 and chooses 30 April as his annual accounting date. He ceases trading on 31 January 2000 and has the following results :

	Adjusted profit £
7 months to 30 April 1995	3,500
year to 30 April 1996	6,480
year to 30 April 1997	7,700
year to 30 April 1998	7,900
year to 30 April 1999	8,200
9 months to 31 January 2000	7,300

Compute the Schedule D Case I assessments for all years.

***9.8** Belinda began trading on 1 March 1995 and chose 31 December as her accounting date. Her first accounts were for the period to 31 December 1995. She eventually decided to change her accounting date to 31 May and the first accounts made up to the new date were for the 17 months to 31 May 1999. The conditions necessary for a change of basis period were all satisfied. The adjusted profits for her first five accounting periods were as follows :

	Adjusted profit £
1 March 1995 to 31 December 1995	43,700
year to 31 December 1996	52,600
year to 31 December 1997	54,300
1 January 1998 to 31 May 1999	71,100
year to 31 May 2000	68,200

Compute the Schedule D Case I assessments for 1994/95 to 2000/01 inclusive.

***9.9** Roger began trading on 1 January 1996, preparing accounts to 30 April each year. His first accounts were for the 16 months to 30 April 1997. In 1999 he decided to change his accounting date to 30 June. The first accounts made up to the new date were for the 14 months to 30 June 1999 and the conditions necessary for a change of basis period were all satisfied. Roger ceased trading on 31 May 2002. His adjusted profits were as follows :

	Adjusted profit
	£
1 January 1996 to 30 April 1997	33,950
year to 30 April 1998	29,700
1 May 1998 to 30 June 1999	33,300
year to 30 June 2000	41,600
year to 30 June 2001	37,900
1 July 2001 to 31 May 2002	23,500

Compute the Schedule D Case I assessments for all years.

Chapter 10

Income from self-employment : Capital allowances

Introduction

Capital expenditure is not in itself deductible under the rules of Schedule D Case I, but certain types of capital expenditure do attract tax relief in the form of standardised depreciation allowances known as *capital allowances*. The purpose of this chapter is to define the categories of capital expenditure which are eligible for capital allowances and to explain how capital allowances are calculated.

Eligible expenditure

In order to be eligible for capital allowances, expenditure must fall into one of the following categories :

(a) plant and machinery

(b) industrial buildings

(c) agricultural buildings

(d) patents, know-how and scientific research

(e) mineral extraction, dredging and crematoria.

Each of these categories (other than the last, which is of limited application) is considered in this chapter.

Chargeable periods

Capital allowances are granted in respect of *chargeable periods*. Prior to 1997/98, the meaning of the term "chargeable period" depended upon whether the business in question was a "new" business or an "old" business (see Chapter 9). As from 1997/98, chargeable periods are determined in the same way for both new and old businesses.

Determining chargeable periods - the new rules

For new businesses (and for old businesses as from 1997/98), each *accounting period* normally ranks as a chargeable period for capital allowances purposes. There is one capital allowances computation per accounting period and the computation takes into account acquisitions and disposals of capital assets made during that period. The only exception to this rule occurs if an accounting period lasts for more than 18 months, in which case it is divided into one or more 12-month chargeable periods with (possibly) a short chargeable period at the end.

When the capital allowances due for an accounting period have been calculated, they are *treated as a trading expense* of that accounting period and are deducted when calculating the adjusted profit assessable under Schedule D Case I. The basis period rules described in Chapter 9 are then applied to the profit *after* deduction of capital allowances.

EXAMPLE 1

A trade commences on 1 January 1998 and accounts are made up annually to 31 December. The adjusted profits for the year to 31 December 1998 (before deduction of capital allowances) are £9,000 and capital allowances of £1,200 are claimed for that year. Compute the first two Schedule D Case I assessments.

SOLUTION

The adjusted profits (after deduction of capital allowances) are £7,800. Therefore the assessments for the first two tax years are :

Year	*Basis*	*Basis period*	*Workings*	*Assessment*
				£
1997/98	Actual	1/1/98 to 5/4/98	£7,800 x 95/365	2,030
1998/99	12 months to a/c date in year 2	1/1/98 to 31/12/98		7,800

Determining chargeable periods - the old rules

For old businesses (up to and including 1996/97), each *tax year* ranked as a chargeable period for capital allowances purposes. There was one capital allowances computation per tax year and the computation took into account acquisitions and disposals of capital assets made during the basis period for that tax year. The pre-1997/98 basis period rules for old businesses (see Chapter 9) applied to the profit *before* deduction of capital allowances. The capital allowances due for a tax year were then deducted from the Schedule D Case I assessment for that year.

Plant and machinery

The Capital Allowances Act 1990, which is the main statute concerned with capital allowances, does not provide a definition of the term "plant and machinery". Therefore it has been left mainly to case law to decide whether or not any given item should qualify as plant and machinery and so attract capital allowances.

In *Yarmouth* v *France* (1887) it was stated that plant and machinery includes "whatever apparatus is used by a businessman for carrying on his business, not his stock in trade which he buys or makes for sale, but all goods and chattels, fixed or moveable, live or dead, which he keeps for permanent employment in his business".

It is clear that machinery of all types, motor vehicles and office furniture and equipment all qualify as plant and machinery but difficulties arise in connection with expenditure on buildings and fixtures to buildings. Much case law has been concerned with the distinction between :

(a) assets which perform an *active function* in the carrying on of the business i.e. the apparatus *with which* the business is carried on, and

(b) assets which perform a *passive function* in the carrying on of the business i.e. the setting *in which* the business is carried on.

Assets in the first of these categories qualify as plant and machinery whilst assets in the second category do not, but the distinction between the categories can be a very fine one. Some of the more important case law decisions have been as follows :

Held to be plant and machinery :

(a) a dry dock built for the repair and maintenance of ships, in *CIR* v *Barclay Curle & Co Ltd* (1969)

(b) a swimming and paddling pool, in *Cooke* v *Beach Station Caravans Ltd* (1974)

(c) a concrete grain silo, in *Schofield* v *R & H Hall Ltd* (1975)

(d) decorative screens placed in the window of a building society's offices and incorporating the name of the building society, in *Leeds Permanent Building Society* v *Proctor* (1982)

(e) moveable office partitions, in *Jarrold* v *John Good & Sons Ltd* (1963)

(f) display lighting in a store window, in *Cole Brothers* v *Phillips* (1982)

(g) light fittings, plaques and pictures on the walls of an hotel, in *IRC* v *Scottish and Newcastle Breweries Ltd* (1982)

(h) storage platforms built in a warehouse, in *Hunt* v *Henry Quick Ltd* (1992)

(i) a barrister's law books, in *Munby* v *Furlong* (1977).

Held *not* to be plant and machinery :

(a) prefabricated school buildings, in *St John's School* v *Ward* (1974)

(b) a moored ship used as a restaurant, in *Benson* v *The Yard Arm Club Ltd* (1979)

(c) a petrol station forecourt canopy, in *Dixon* v *Fitch's Garage Ltd* (1975)
(d) a football stand, in *Brown* v *Burnley Football and Athletic Club* (1980)
(e) a false ceiling built to hide electrical conduits, in *Hampton* v *Fortes Autogrill Ltd* (1979)
(f) a false ceiling, mezzanine floors, staircases, decorative floor and wall tiles all used to create ambience in a restaurant, in *Wimpey International Ltd* v *Warland* (1988).

In an attempt to clarify the distinction between buildings and plant, the Finance Act 1994 provides a detailed list of types of expenditure on buildings (or structures) which are statutorily excluded from qualifying as plant. The Act also provides a detailed list of types of expenditure on buildings (or structures) which are not statutorily excluded from qualifying as plant, and may therefore qualify if permitted by case law.

Expenditure statutorily deemed to be plant and machinery

By statute, expenditure of the following types always qualifies as plant and machinery :

(a) expenditure incurred so as to comply with fire regulations
(b) expenditure on the thermal insulation of industrial buildings
(c) expenditure incurred so as to comply with safety regulations at sports grounds
(d) expenditure on assets necessary to safeguard personal security
(e) expenditure on computer software
(f) expenditure incurred on building alterations, incidental to the installation of plant and machinery.

Capital allowances on plant and machinery

Capital allowances are available to a person who incurs capital expenditure on plant and machinery which is provided :

(a) for the purposes of a trade, profession or vocation carried on by that person, or
(b) for the purposes of a Schedule A business carried on by that person (excluding plant which is let for use in a dwelling house e.g. furniture let to a tenant).

To qualify for capital allowances, plant and machinery must be owned by the claimant and the expenditure must be notified to the Inland Revenue. As from 1996/97, this notification must be made by 31 January in the second year of assessment following the year of assessment in which the relevant chargeable period ends.

Note that an item of plant and machinery acquired by hire purchase is treated as if bought for its cash price on the date of the HP agreement. HP interest is an allowable expense under Schedule D Case I and may be written off over the life of the HP contract.

Writing down allowance (WDA)

With some exceptions (see later in this chapter) capital allowances are not calculated individually for each item of plant and machinery acquired by a business. Instead, expenditure on plant and machinery is pooled and capital allowances are calculated with reference to the value of the pool. The basic procedure for each chargeable period is as follows :

(a) The written down value (WDV) of the pool at the end of the previous chargeable period is brought forward.

(b) The cost of any items of plant and machinery acquired during the chargeable period (or basis period for old businesses prior to 1997/98) is added into the pool. Items of plant and machinery originally owned personally by the trader, and then brought into the business at a later date, are treated as if purchased at their market value on the date when brought into the business.

(c) If any items have been disposed of during the chargeable period (or basis period for old businesses prior to 1997/98) a disposal value is subtracted from the pool, equal to :

    (i) the sale proceeds, if the asset is sold in the open market

    (ii) the market value on the date of disposal, if the asset is given away or sold for less than market value (unless the new owner will be claiming capital allowances, in which case the sale proceeds are used)

    (iii) the scrap value or any compensation received, if the asset is scrapped or destroyed.

    But if the disposal value exceeds the original cost of the item, only the original cost is subtracted from the pool. The profit on the disposal may give rise to a capital gains tax liability (see Chapter 18).

(d) A *writing down allowance* (WDA) is then given, calculated at 25% per annum.

(e) The WDA given for the chargeable period is subtracted from the pool, leaving a WDV which is carried forward to the next chargeable period. This WDV will then attract WDA's in future chargeable periods (even if all the plant and machinery has now been sold).

(f) It is not mandatory to claim the maximum allowances available for a chargeable period and a trader with low profits (or a loss) may wish to claim less than the maximum amount, usually so as to avoid wasting personal allowances. This is discussed further in Chapter 11. Any unclaimed allowances are added onto the WDV carried forward, so increasing the allowances available in future chargeable periods.

Note that WDA is calculated at a rate of 25% per annum. For new businesses (and for old businesses as from 1997/98) the "per annum" refers to the length of the chargeable period for which capital allowances are being claimed. For old businesses prior to 1997/98, the "per annum" referred to the length of the basis period for the tax year for which capital allowances were being claimed (but only 25% WDA was given in transitional year 1996/97, even though the basis period for this tax year for an old business was usually 24 months long).

EXAMPLE 2

(a) Sharon began trading on 1 February 1996 and chose 30 April as her annual accounting date. Her first accounts covered the period from 1 February 1996 to 30 April 1997 and showed an adjusted profit (before capital allowances) of £28,500. During this period she bought and sold plant and machinery as follows :

		£
1 February 1996	Bought plant	10,000
1 March 1997	Bought plant	8,000
15 April 1997	Sold plant (original cost £2,160)	2,500

Compute the first three Schedule D Case I assessments.

(b) Sharon's accounts for the year to 30 April 1998 showed an adjusted profit (before capital allowances) of £31,720. Her purchases and sales of plant and machinery during this year were :

		£
1 June 1997	Bought plant	4,750
30 June 1997	Sold plant (original cost £3,500)	2,600
28 February 1998	Bought plant	1,240

Compute Sharon's Schedule D Case I assessment for 1998/99.

SOLUTION

(a) The computation for the 454-day period from 1 February 1996 to 30 April 1997 is as follows :

	Pool £	*Allowances* £
1/2/96 - 30/4/97		
Additions (£10,000 + £8,000)	18,000	
Disposals (limited to original cost)	(2,160)	
	15,840	
WDA @ 25% x 454/365	4,926	4,926
WDV c/f	10,914	

Capital allowances due for the period are £4,926, reducing the adjusted profit to £23,574. The first three Schedule D Case I assessments are therefore :

Year	*Basis period*	*Workings*	*Assessment*
			£
1995/96	1/2/96 to 5/4/96	£23,574 x 64/454	3,323
1996/97	6/4/96 to 5/4/97	£23,574 x 365/454	18,953
1997/98	1/5/96 to 30/4/97	£23,574 x 365/454	18,953

There is an overlap period from 1 May 1996 to 5 April 1997 (340 days) and overlap profits are £23,574 x 340/454 = £17,655.

(b) The capital allowances computation for the year to 30 April 1998 is as follows :

	Pool	*Allowances*
	£	£
y/e 30/4/98		
WDV b/f	10,914	
Additions (£4,750 + £1,240)	5,990	
	16,904	
Disposals	(2,600)	
	14,304	
WDA @ 25%	3,576	3,576
WDV c/f	10,728	

Capital allowances available in the year to 30 April 1998 are £3,576, reducing the adjusted profit for the year to £28,144 (£31,720 - £3,576). Therefore the 1998/99 Schedule D Case I assessment is £28,144.

EXAMPLE 3

Ian began trading on 1 September 1996, preparing accounts to 31 March each year. His first accounts covered the period from 1 September 1996 to 31 March 1998 and showed an adjusted profit (before deduction of capital allowances) of £72,600. Ian bought and sold plant and machinery as follows :

		£
1 September 1996	Bought plant and machinery	16,000
21 August 1997	Bought plant and machinery	12,000
5 September 1997	Bought plant and machinery	8,000
1 January 1998	Sold plant (original cost £3,700)	3,000
31 March 1998	Bought plant and machinery	4,000

Compute Ian's Schedule D Case I assessments for the first two years of assessment.

SOLUTION

Ian's first accounting period covers 19 months. Since this exceeds 18 months it must be divided into two chargeable periods for capital allowances purposes. The first chargeable period is the year to 31 August 1997. The second chargeable period runs from 1 September 1997 to 31 March 1998. The capital allowances computation is as follows :

	Pool	Allowances
	£	£
y/e 31/8/97		
Additions (£16,000 + £12,000)	28,000	
WDA @ 25%	7,000	7,000
	21,000	
1/9/97 - 31/3/98		
Additions (£8,000 + £4,000)	12,000	
	33,000	
Disposals	(3,000)	
	30,000	
WDA @ 25% x 212/365	4,356	4,356
WDV c/f	25,644	
Total allowances		11,356

Ian's profit after deduction of capital allowances is £61,244 (£72,600 - £11,356). His first two Schedule D Case I assessments are :

Year	*Basis*	*Basis period*	*Workings*	*Assessment*
				£
1996/97	Actual	1/9/96 to 5/4/97	£61,244 x 217/577	23,033
1997/98	12 months to a/c date in year 2	1/4/97 to 31/3/98	£61,244 x 365/577	38,742

There is an overlap period from 1 April 1997 to 5 April 1997 (5 days) and overlap profits are £61,244 x 5/577 = £531.

First year allowance (FYA)

At various times in the past, expenditure on plant and machinery has qualified for a *first year allowance* (FYA). If FYA is available in relation to an item of plant and machinery, it is given instead of WDA in the chargeable period in which the item first attracts capital allowances. The remainder of the cost of the asset (after deducting FYA) then enters the pool and is eligible for WDA in subsequent chargeable periods.

FYA was most recently available (at a rate of 40%) in relation to expenditure on plant and machinery (other than motor cars) incurred between 1 November 1992 and 31 October 1993 inclusive.

Balancing allowances and charges

If the total disposal value of the disposals for a chargeable period exceeds the balance of expenditure in the pool (before disposals are deducted) then this is evidence that the capital allowances given to date are greater than the true amount of depreciation suffered by the business. In these circumstances the written down value of the pool is set to zero and a *balancing charge* (a negative capital allowance) is made, equal to the amount of the excess. Balancing adjustments may also be required in the following circumstances :

(a) when a business ceases trading (see later in this chapter)

(b) when a non-pooled asset is disposed of.

Non-pooled assets are those assets which are treated individually for capital allowances purposes and not brought into a pool (see below). When a non-pooled asset is sold, a balancing adjustment is required to ensure that the total capital allowances granted in relation to the asset are exactly equal to the depreciation of the asset whilst owned by the business. The balancing adjustment is calculated as follows :

(a) if the disposal value of the asset exceeds its written down value, a *balancing charge* is made, equal to the excess

(b) if the written down value of the asset exceeds its disposal value, a *balancing allowance* is given, equal to the excess.

Non-pooled assets

The following types of plant and machinery are not brought into the general pool :

(a) motor cars

(b) assets with some private use

(c) short-life assets

(d) long-life assets (for certain businesses).

The treatment of each of these types of asset is explained below.

Motor cars

The general pool of plant and machinery includes motor vans and lorries but does not include motor cars. Cars costing £12,000 or less are pooled together but are kept in a *separate* pool from the general pool. Cars costing more than £12,000 are dealt with on an individual basis and attract a maximum WDA of £3,000 per annum. For cars bought before 11 March 1992, these limits are £8,000 and £2,000 respectively.

EXAMPLE 4

Bianca began trading on 1 September 1995 and chose 31 December as her annual accounting date. Her first accounts covered the 16 months to 31 December 1996. On 21 October 1995 she bought a motor car costing £17,600. Compute the capital allowances available on this car for the first three chargeable periods.

SOLUTION

Bianca's first accounts cover a 487-day period. The capital allowances computation is as follows :

	Expensive Car	*Allowances*
	£	£
1/9/95 - 31/12/96		
Addition	17,600	
WDA restricted to £3,000 x 487/365	4,003	4,003
WDV c/f	13,597	
y/e 31/12/97		
WDA restricted to £3,000	3,000	3,000
WDV c/f	10,597	
y/e 31/12/98		
WDA @ 25% (no restriction necessary)	2,649	2,649
WDV c/f	7,948	

Assets with some private use

An asset which is used partly for private purposes by the *owner* of a business is not pooled but is treated on an individual basis. The capital allowances calculation is carried out in the usual way but the owner of the business may then claim only the business proportion of the allowances which have been calculated.

Note that capital allowances are available in full on assets used partly for private purposes by an *employee* of the business (but the employee may then be assessed on a benefit in kind under Schedule E).

EXAMPLE 5

Allan began trading on 1 June 1996 , making up accounts to 31 May each year. On 1 July 1996 he bought a motor car costing £14,000. Compute the capital allowances available on this car for the first two chargeable periods, assuming 30% private use of the car by Allan.

SOLUTION

	Expensive car (30% private)		*Allowances*
	£		£
y/e 31/5/97			
Addition	14,000		
WDA restricted to £3,000	3,000	x 70% =	2,100
WDV c/f	11,000		

	Expensive car (30% private)		*Allowances*
	£		£
y/e 31/5/98			
WDV b/f	11,000		
WDA @ 25%	2,750	x 70% =	1,925
WDV c/f	8,250		

Short-life assets

A trader may elect that an asset should be treated as a "short-life asset". Such an election has the following consequences :

(a) The asset does not join any pool but is treated on an individual basis (for this reason, the election is known as a "de-pooling" election).

(b) Capital allowances are calculated in the usual way.

(c) If the asset is not disposed of within four years of the end of the chargeable period in which it is acquired (or basis period for old businesses prior to 1997/98) it joins the general pool at its written down value and the de-pooling election will have had no effect.

(d) If the asset is disposed of within the four-year period, a balancing allowance will be given (or a balancing charge will be made).

The election is usually made for assets such as computers, which are likely to be sold or scrapped within the stated four-year period for less than their written down values. De-pooling such assets generates balancing allowances on their disposal, so ensuring that capital allowances are given as quickly as possible. If such assets are not de-pooled, the capital allowances given in relation to them are spread out over a much longer period. A de-pooling election cannot be made for a motor car.

As from 1996/97, a de-pooling election in relation to expenditure incurred during a chargeable period must be made by 31 January in the second year of assessment following the year of assessment in which the chargeable period ends.

EXAMPLE 6

Anita begins trading on 1 July 1996, making up accounts to 30 June each year. On 1 July 1996 she buys general plant and machinery costing £20,000 and a computer costing £4,000. She sells the computer on 31 March 1999 for £1,300. Compute her capital allowances for the first three accounting periods if :

(a) she makes a de-pooling election with regard to the computer

(b) she does not make the de-pooling election.

SOLUTION

(a)	General Pool	Short-life asset	Allowances
	£	£	£
y/e 30/6/97			
Additions	20,000	4,000	
WDA @ 25%	5,000	1,000	6,000
WDV c/f	15,000	3,000	
y/e 30/6/98			
WDA @ 25%	3,750	750	4,500
WDV c/f	11,250	2,250	
y/e 30/6/99			
Disposal		(1,300)	
Balancing allowance		950	950
WDA @ 25%	2,813		2,813
WDV c/f	8,437		
Total allowances			3,763

(b)	General Pool	Allowances
	£	£
y/e 30/6/97		
Additions	24,000	
WDA @ 25%	6,000	6,000
WDV c/f	18,000	
y/e 30/6/98		
WDA @ 25%	4,500	4,500
WDV c/f	13,500	
y/e 30/6/99		
Disposal	(1,300)	
	12,200	
WDA @ 25%	3,050	3,050
WDV c/f	9,150	

Note :

The de-pooling election increases the capital allowances in the year to 30 June 1999 by £713, at the expense of reducing the WDV c/f (and therefore future capital allowances) by the same amount.

Long-life assets

A long-life asset is defined as one with a working life of 25 years or more. As from 26 November 1996, the rate of WDA available in relation to long-life assets acquired by businesses *spending more than £100,000 a year on such assets* is reduced from 25% per annum to 6% per annum. Businesses affected by this rule maintain a separate pool of long-life assets and calculate WDA at 6% per annum on the balance of expenditure in this pool.

Allowances on cessation of trade

When a business ceases trading and all the plant and machinery is disposed of, capital allowances for the final chargeable period are computed as follows :

(a) Items acquired in the final chargeable period (or basis period for old businesses prior to 1997/98) are added onto the WDV brought forward.

(b) No WDA's are given for the final chargeable period.

(c) The disposal value of each pool (and each non-pooled asset) is subtracted from the balance of unrelieved expenditure, giving rise to balancing allowances or balancing charges. Assets taken over personally by the trader are treated as if sold for their market value on the date taken over.

The balancing adjustments normally made on a cessation of trade can be avoided if the business is being taken over by a "connected person" (e.g. the trader's spouse or other relative or a company which the trader controls) so long as an election to this effect is made by both parties. In this case, the final chargeable period is treated in exactly the same way as any other chargeable period (with WDA's as appropriate) and the assets are then transferred to the new owner at their WDV's.

EXAMPLE 7

Jake, who began trading on 1 October 1994, prepares accounts to 30 September each year. The written down value of his plant and machinery at 30 September 1997 was :

	£
General pool	11,350
Expensive motor car (20% private use by Jake)	13,200

Jake ceased trading on 30 June 1998. His purchases and sales of plant and machinery in the 9 months to 30 June 1998 were :

		£
15 October 1997	Bought plant	1,150
30 June 1998	Sold all pool items (all for less than original cost)	12,850
30 June 1998	Sold car	12,000

Prepare the capital allowances computation for the 9 months to 30 June 1998.

SOLUTION

	General Pool	Expensive car (20% private)	Allowances
	£	£	£
1/10/97 - 30/6/98			
WDV b/f	11,350	13,200	
Additions	1,150		
	12,500		
Disposals	(12,850)	(12,000)	
Balancing allowance/(charge)	(350)	1,200 x 80% = 960	610

Old businesses ceasing to trade prior to 1997/98

If an old business ceased trading in 1996/97 or earlier, there was always a gap between the basis periods used on cessation (see Chapter 9). Items of plant and machinery acquired or disposed of during this gap were allocated to the basis period *before* the gap for capital allowances purposes, unless the Inland Revenue revised assessments for the penultimate and ante-penultimate years, in which case such items were allocated to the basis period *after* the gap.

Industrial buildings allowances

Capital allowances known as *industrial buildings allowances* (IBA's) are available in relation to "qualifying buildings", which consist of :

(a) industrial buildings

(b) certain hotels.

Industrial buildings

The term "industrial buildings" includes such buildings as :

(a) factories used for manufacturing purposes, or for processing goods and materials in some way

(b) ancillary buildings associated with such factories e.g. warehouses for the storage of raw materials or finished goods

(c) staff welfare buildings (e.g. canteens) provided for the welfare of those working in factories and ancillary buildings

(d) sports pavilions provided for the welfare of employees in any trade.

The term does *not* include buildings such as dwelling houses, shops, showrooms and offices (other than drawing offices attached to an industrial building). If a building is used partly as a qualifying industrial building and partly for a non-qualifying purpose, then the whole building will qualify for IBA's if the cost of the non-qualifying part does not exceed 25% of the cost of the entire building. If the 25% limit is exceeded only the qualifying part of the building attracts IBA's.

Hotels

IBA's may be claimed in relation to an hotel which satisfies the following conditions :

(a) it offers sleeping accommodation consisting wholly or mainly of "letting bedrooms", available to the general public and not normally occupied by the same person for more than one month

(b) it has at least 10 letting bedrooms

(c) it offers ancillary services including (at least) breakfast, evening meals, cleaning of rooms and bed-making

(d) it is open for at least four months between April and October.

Accommodation for hotel staff (either in a separate building or forming part of the hotel itself) is regarded as part of the hotel but accommodation for the proprietor's own use is not. For the remainder of this chapter, references to industrial buildings should be taken to include qualifying hotels.

Qualifying expenditure

IBA's are based on the "qualifying expenditure" of the trader who first uses the building for industrial purposes. This is either :

(a) the construction cost of the building, if constructed by the trader

(b) the price paid for the building, if bought unused from a builder

(c) the lower of the price paid for the building and the original cost incurred by the building's first owner, if bought unused from someone other than a builder.

In all cases, the cost of land is excluded but the costs of land preparation are allowed, as are professional fees such as those paid to an architect.

EXAMPLE 8

(a) Smith (who does not trade as a builder) buys a building site for £100,000 and then incurs the following costs on the erection of an industrial building on that site :

	£
Levelling the site and preparing foundations	95,000
Architect's fees	50,000
Building costs	650,000

What is Smith's qualifying expenditure for IBA's purposes ?

(b) If the building is sold unused to Brown for £1,000,000 (including £120,000 for the land), what is Brown's qualifying expenditure ?

(c) If instead of buying Smith's building, Brown buys a similar unused building for the same price from a firm of builders, what is Brown's qualifying expenditure ?

SOLUTION

(a) The costs of construction (excluding land) amount to £795,000. This is Smith's qualifying expenditure.

(b) Brown's qualifying expenditure is also £795,000 (i.e. the lower of Smith's original construction cost and £880,000, the price paid by Brown).

(c) If Brown purchases an industrial building from a firm of builders, then the price paid to that builder (which will, of course, include the builder's profit) is fully eligible for IBA's. Therefore Brown's qualifying expenditure is £1,000,000 less the part of that price which is allocated to the land.

Initial allowance

At various times in the past, expenditure on industrial buildings has qualified for an *initial allowance* (IA). IA was most recently available (at a rate of 20%) in relation to expenditure incurred between 1 November 1992 and 31 October 1993 inclusive on the construction of an industrial building or the purchase of an unused industrial building, However, IA was not available if the building was not brought into industrial use by the end of 1994. The chargeable period in which IA was given depended upon the date of the expenditure rather than the date that the building was first brought into use.

Writing down allowance

A *writing down allowance* (WDA) is available in relation to an industrial building so long as the building is in industrial use at the end of the chargeable period (or basis period for old businesses prior to 1997/98) in which IBA's are being claimed. The annual WDA is calculated as 4% of qualifying expenditure (2% if the expenditure was incurred before 6 November 1962). Note that :

(a) WDA is given to the holder of the "relevant interest" in a building. This is the interest of the person who first acquired the building (e.g. a freehold) and is transferred to the new owner (along with the right to claim WDA) when the building is sold.

(b) The relevant interest is *not* transferred when a building is leased, so that WDA is normally given to the landlord of a leased building rather than to the tenant. However, the landlord and tenant may jointly elect that the grant of a long lease (i.e. a lease of more than 50 years) should be treated as a sale for capital allowances purposes, in which case WDA will be given to the tenant.

(c) Industrial buildings are always treated on an individual basis and are never pooled.

(d) WDA is calculated on a straight line basis (as opposed to the reducing balance basis used for plant and machinery).

(e) For new businesses (and for old businesses as from 1997/98) WDA is given in proportion to the length of the chargeable period for which allowances are claimed. For old businesses prior to 1997/98, WDA was always calculated at 4% (or 2%) regardless of the length of the basis period.

(f) WDA in relation to an industrial building may not be disclaimed.

(g) IA (if available) and WDA can both be claimed in the same chargeable period.

(h) The total allowances given can never exceed the qualifying expenditure. If IA is not claimed, WDA will be given at 4% p.a. for 25 years (or 2% p.a. for 50 years). But WDA will cease earlier if initial allowance is claimed.

(i) A building has a "tax life" of 25 years, as from the date on which it is first brought into use (50 years for pre-November 1962 buildings). The tax life is always regarded as 25 years (or 50 years), even if IA is claimed so that WDA stops earlier.

EXAMPLE 9

Brian began trading on 1 April 1996, preparing accounts annually to 31 December. His first accounts were for the 9 months to 31 December 1996. On 12 May 1996, he bought a new factory building for £250,000 (excluding the cost of land) and immediately put the building to industrial use. Calculate the IBA's available for Brian's first three chargeable periods.

SOLUTION

	Factory £	*Allowances* £
1/4/96 - 31/12/96		
Cost	250,000	
WDA @ 4% of £250,000 x 275/365	7,534	7,534
WDV c/f	242,466	
y/e 31/12/97		
WDA @ 4% of £250,000	10,000	10,000
WDV c/f	232,466	
y/e 31/12/98		
WDA @ 4% of £250,000	10,000	10,000
WDV c/f	222,466	

If Brian keeps the building and uses it for industrial purposes throughout its entire tax life, a WDA of £10,000 per annum will be available up to and including the year to 31 December 2020, with a final WDA of £2,466 in the year to 31 December 2021.

Non-industrial use

WDA's cannot be claimed for a chargeable period if, at the end of the chargeable period (or basis period for old businesses prior to 1997/98), the building is being used for a non-industrial purpose. A "notional WDA" is still calculated for such a chargeable period and deducted from the WDV of the building in the usual way, but the notional WDA is not available to the trader.

EXAMPLE 10

Carole begins trading on 1 April 1995, producing annual accounts to 31 March. On 1 July 1995, she buys a new building for £200,000 (excluding the cost of land) and immediately puts it to industrial use. This use continues until 1 July 1998, when she starts using the building for a non-industrial purpose. On 1 July 2000, the building reverts to industrial use. Show the capital allowances computation for all years up to and including the year ended 31 March 2001.

SOLUTION

	Building £	*Allowances* £
y/e 31/3/96, 97 & 98		
Cost	200,000	
WDA @ 4% of £200,000 for 3 years	24,000	24,000
WDV c/f	176,000	
y/e 31/3/99 & y/e 31/3/00		
Notional WDA @ 4% of £200,000 for 2 years	16,000	
WDV c/f	160,000	
y/e 31/3/01		
WDA @ 4% of £200,000	8,000	8,000
WDV c/f	152,000	

Note :

The notional WDA's of £16,000 given in the years to 31 March 1999 and 31 March 2000 serve to reduce the building's WDV but are not available to Carole.

Sale of a building after continual industrial use

If an industrial building which has been in continual industrial use is sold during its tax life of 25 (or 50) years, then :

(a) No WDA is given in the final chargeable period and a balancing adjustment is made in the usual way, calculated by comparing the building's WDV with the disposal proceeds (or original cost, if lower).

(b) The second-hand buyer of the building takes over the right to claim a WDA for the remainder of the building's tax life, calculated by dividing the "residue of expenditure" by the number of years remaining of the tax life. The residue of expenditure is equal to the WDV of the building before the sale, plus any balancing charge and less any balancing allowance made on the sale. In effect, the second-hand buyer's WDA's are calculated on the lower of the original cost of the building and the price for which it was sold.

If a building is sold after the expiry of its tax life then no balancing adjustments are made and the second-hand buyer is unable to claim any WDA.

EXAMPLE 11

Christopher has been trading since 1 January 1995 and produces accounts annually to 31 December. On 1 January 1995 he bought a new building for £150,000 (excluding land) and started using it immediately for an industrial purpose. Show the capital allowances computation for all affected years if he sells the building to Dean on 1 July 1998 for :

(a) £110,000 (b) £175,000

Also calculate the WDA's available to Dean, assuming that he started business on 1 April 1998 and makes up accounts to 31 March each year.

SOLUTION

(a)	*Building* £	*Allowances* £
y/e 31/12/95, 96 & 97		
Cost	150,000	
WDA @ 4% of £150,000 for 3 years	18,000	18,000
WDV c/f	132,000	
y/e 31/12/98		
Disposal value	110,000	
Balancing allowance	22,000	22,000

The residue of expenditure is £110,000 (£132,000 - £22,000). The tax life of the building ends on 31 December 2019, giving an unexpired life of 21 years 184 days (21.504 years) on the date of the second-hand purchase by Dean. Dean may therefore claim an annual

WDA of £110,000/21.504 = £5,115 for each of the 21 years to 31 March 2019 and a final WDA of £2,585 (to bring the total to £110,000) in the year to 31 March 2020.

(b)	*Building* £	*Allowances* £
y/e 31/12/98		
WDV b/f	132,000	
Disposal value (limited to original cost)	150,000	
Balancing charge	(18,000)	(18,000)

The residue of expenditure is £150,000 (£132,000 + £18,000). Therefore Dean may claim an annual WDA of £150,000/21.504 = £6,975 for each of the 21 years to 31 March 2019 and a final WDA of £3,525 in the year to 31 March 2020.

Sale of a building after non-industrial use

As explained above, an industrial building is written down by notional WDA's during a period of non-industrial use. If the building is then sold (within its tax life) the balancing adjustments made on the sale depend upon whether the building is sold for more or less than its original cost.

(a) If the building is sold for *more* than original cost, the balancing charge made on the sale is restricted to the actual allowances given to date (i.e. excluding the notional WDA's).

(b) If the building is sold for *less* than original cost, the required balancing adjustment is calculated as follows :

  (i) "Net cost" = original cost - sale proceeds

  (ii) "Adjusted net cost" = net cost x $\frac{\text{period of industrial use}}{\text{period of total use}}$

  (iii) Balancing adjustment = adjusted net cost - actual allowances given.

(c) The second-hand buyer's WDA's are based on the lower of the residue of expenditure (calculated as before) and the second-hand price paid.

EXAMPLE 12

Rework the above example, assuming that Christopher used the building for non-industrial purposes between 1 July 1996 and 30 June 1997.

SOLUTION

(a) The period of total use by Christopher is 3 years 181 days (3.496 years), of which 1 year comprises non-industrial use and the remainder comprises industrial use. The building was not in industrial use on 31 December 1996, so only notional WDA's would be calculated for the year to 31 December 1996. The actual allowances given (in the other 2 chargeable periods) are 4% of £150,000 for 2 years = £12,000.

Net cost is £40,000 (£150,000 - £110,000) and adjusted net cost is £28,558 (£40,000 x 2.496/3.496). A balancing allowance of £16,558 (£28,558 - £12,000) would be made.

The residue of expenditure is now £115,442 (£132,000 - £16,558). This exceeds the price paid by Dean so Dean's annual WDA's are equal to £110,000 divided by 21.504.

(b) The balancing charge is limited to the actual allowances given i.e. £12,000. The residue of expenditure is £144,000 (£132,000 + £12,000) and Dean's annual WDA's are equal to this figure divided by 21.504.

Commercial buildings in enterprise zones

Certain areas of the country are designated as "enterprise zones". IBA's are available in relation to *any* commercial building constructed in an enterprise zone (including shops, showrooms and offices, but not dwellings) so long as the construction expenditure :

(a) is contracted for within 10 years of the zone's designation, and

(b) is actually incurred within 20 years of the zone's designation.

An initial allowance of 100% is available for the chargeable period in which the expenditure is incurred. If the full allowance is not claimed, the remaining expenditure is eligible for an annual WDA of 25%, calculated straight-line on the cost of the building and beginning when the building is first brought into use. For example, if an initial allowance of only 30% is claimed, the remaining 70% of the expenditure is eligible for WDA's equal to 25% of the cost of the building in each of the first two years of use and 20% of the cost in the third year.

Agricultural buildings

Agricultural buildings allowances (ABA's) are available in relation to capital expenditure on the construction of farmhouses, farm cottages, farm buildings, fences, drainage works etc. However, no more than one-third of the expenditure on a farmhouse is eligible for ABA's. The cost of land is always excluded. The system of granting allowances is similar (but not identical) to that used for industrial buildings :

(a) An annual WDA, calculated at 4% per annum on the straight line basis, is given in relation to qualifying expenditure. WDA begins in the chargeable period (or basis period for old businesses prior to 1997/98) in which the expenditure is incurred.

(b) Qualifying expenditure incurred between 1 November 1992 and 31 October 1993 attracted an initial allowance of 20%, so long as the building was brought into use by the end of 1994.

(c) The 25-year tax life of an agricultural building begins on the first day of the chargeable period in which ABA's are first given.

Sale of an agricultural building

If an agricultural building is sold during its tax life, and the vendor and buyer do not elect for a balancing adjustment to be made (see below), then the buyer simply takes over the right to receive the WDA's that the vendor would have received if the sale had not occurred. The procedure is as follows :

(a) No balancing adjustments are made on the sale and the price paid by the second-hand buyer is totally ignored.

(b) For the chargeable period in which the sale is dealt with, the vendor receives WDA on the building for the last time, calculated at 4% per annum from the start of the chargeable period (basis period for old businesses prior to 1997/98) to the date of the sale.

(c) For the chargeable period in which the purchase is dealt with, the buyer receives WDA for the first time, calculated (on the original cost of the building) at 4% per annum from the date of purchase to the end of the chargeable period (basis period for old businesses prior to 1997/98).

(d) The buyer then receives WDA of 4% p.a. until the building is fully written off.

If vendor and buyer both elect for the sale of an agricultural building to be treated as a balancing event, then the capital allowances computation is exactly the same as that performed on the sale of an industrial building (see above).

EXAMPLE 13

Bill began trading as a farmer on 1 January 1995 making up accounts to 31 December. On 1 December 1995 he constructed a barn at a cost of £50,000 (excluding land). On 1 August 1997 he sold the barn to Ben for £47,000. Ben started trading as a farmer on 1 July 1994, making up accounts to 30 June annually. No election is made for the sale to be treated as a balancing event. Calculate the ABA's available to Bill and Ben.

SOLUTION

Bill's allowances are :		£
y/e 31/12/95	£50,000 x 4%	2,000
y/e 31/12/96	£50,000 x 4%	2,000
y/e 31/12/97	£50,000 x 4% x 212/365	1,162

Ben's allowances are :		£
y/e 30/6/98	£50,000 x 4% x 334/365	1,830
y/e 30/6/99 etc.	£50,000 x 4%	2,000

Notes :

(a) Bill's sale is made after 212 days of the accounting period have elapsed, so his final WDA is calculated at 212/365th of 4%.

(b) Ben's purchase is made with 334 days of the accounting period remaining, so his first WDA is calculated at 334/365th of 4%.

(c) Ben will continue to receive WDA's of £2,000 per annum until the barn's WDV reaches zero.

EXAMPLE 14

Rework the Bill and Ben example above, given that an election is made for the sale to be treated as a balancing event.

SOLUTION

Bill's allowances in the years to 31 December 1995 and 1996 total £4,000, reducing the WDV of the barn to £46,000. The barn is sold for £47,000, so a balancing charge of £1,000 is made in the year to 31 December 1997.

The tax life of the building began on 1 January 1995 (the first day of the chargeable period in which ABA's were first given) and ends on 31 December 2019, giving an unexpired life of 22 years and 153 days (22.419 years) on the date of the second-hand purchase by Ben. The residue of expenditure is £47,000 (£46,000 + £1,000). Therefore Ben's annual WDA is £2,096 (£47,000 ÷ 22.419).

Miscellaneous capital allowances

Capital allowances are available in relation to some miscellaneous categories of capital expenditure, including expenditure on patent rights, know-how and scientific research.

Patent rights

Purchased patent rights are treated in a similar way to plant and machinery for capital allowances purposes.

(a) All patent rights are pooled together.

(b) The pool is adjusted in each chargeable period for acquisitions and disposals and a WDA is then given calculated at 25% per annum on the reducing balance.

(c) As with plant and machinery, disposal value is limited to original cost. But whereas a sale of plant and machinery for more than original cost may give rise to a capital gains tax liability (see Chapter 18), a sale of patent rights for more than original cost gives rise to a Schedule D Case VI income tax liability (see Chapter 6).

(d) If the disposal value of a patent exceeds the balance of unrelieved expenditure in the pool, a balancing charge is made and the pool value is set to zero.

(e) A balancing allowance will arise if :

  (i) there is a cessation of trade and the patents are sold for less than the balance of unrelieved expenditure in the pool, or

  (ii) there is no cessation of trade but the last patent in the pool is sold (or comes to the end of its term) and the disposal value is less than the balance of unrelieved expenditure in the pool. (This treatment is different from that used for plant and machinery).

EXAMPLE 15

Gemma began trading on 1 August 1994, making up accounts to 31 July each year. At the end of the capital allowances computation for the year to 31 July 1996, the WDV of her patents pool was £3,800.

(a) Calculate the capital allowances due for the year to 31 July 1997 if she acquires no further patents during the year but sells for £1,500 a patent which had cost her £2,000.

(b) Rework the computation given that the sold patent is Gemma's last remaining patent.

SOLUTION

(a)

	Patents pool	*Allowances*
	£	£
y/e 31/7/97		
WDV b/f	3,800	
Disposals	(1,500)	
	2,300	
WDA @ 25%	575	575
WDV c/f	1,725	

(b) If the last patent has been sold, then a balancing allowance of £2,300 will be given instead of the £575 WDA and the pool will be closed.

Know-how

"Know-how" is defined as industrial information and techniques, of use in either :

(a) manufacturing, or

(b) the processing of goods or materials, or

(c) the working of mineral deposits, or

(d) agricultural, fishing or forestry operations.

All expenditure on know-how is pooled and, in general, capital allowances are calculated as for patent rights. However, if know-how is sold for more than original cost, the disposal value used in the capital allowances computation is the *full sale proceeds*. Depending upon the balance of unrelieved expenditure in the pool prior to the disposal, this will either create a balancing charge or restrict the value of subsequent WDA's. In either case, the profit made on the disposal is, in effect, taxed under Schedule D Case I, thus avoiding the need for a Schedule D Case VI assessment (which would be required if the sale had been of patent rights).

Scientific research

Capital expenditure on scientific research related to the claimant's trade attracts a first year allowance of 100%. Any proceeds subsequently received on the disposal of a scientific research asset are treated as a trading receipt.

Summary

- Capital allowances are granted for chargeable periods. For new businesses (and for old businesses as from 1997/98) each accounting period ranks as a chargeable period, except that accounting periods exceeding 18 months in length are divided into two or more chargeable periods. For old businesses prior to 1997/98, each tax year ranked as a chargeable period.
- In order to qualify as plant and machinery, an asset must perform an active function in the trade, not merely provide the setting in which the trade is carried on.
- Writing down allowances on plant and machinery are granted at 25% per annum, calculated on the reducing balance basis.
- In general, expenditure on plant and machinery is pooled and capital allowances are calculated by reference to the value of the pool. Inexpensive motor cars are held in a separate pool from the general pool. Expensive motor cars are treated individually, as are assets with private use and short-life assets. Long-life assets acquired by certain businesses are pooled separately and attract an annual WDA of 6%, calculated on the reducing balance basis.

- On the cessation of a business, the disposal value of each pool (and of each non-pooled asset) is subtracted from the balance of unrelieved expenditure, giving rise to balancing adjustments.
- Writing down allowances are available on qualifying industrial buildings, hotels and agricultural buildings at a rate of 4% per annum, calculated on the straight line basis. Notional WDA's are deducted if an industrial building is put to non-industrial use.
- Commercial buildings constructed in enterprise zones are granted an initial allowance of 100%.
- Capital allowances are also available in relation to patent rights, know-how and scientific research expenditure.

Exercises

10.1 Laura began trading on 1 January 1997 and chose 31 January as her annual accounting date. Her first accounts covered the period from 1 January 1997 to 31 January 1998 and showed an adjusted profit (before capital allowances) of £41,800. During this period she bought and sold plant and machinery as follows :

		£
1 January 1997	Bought machinery	12,000
1 January 1997	Bought motor car	15,000
31 October 1997	Bought machinery	6,000
1 January 1998	Sold machinery (original cost £2,800)	1,500

Compute the first two Schedule D Case I assessments, assuming 40% private use of the car by Laura. Also compute the amount of any overlap profits.

10.2 Maurice began trading on 1 May 1994, producing annual accounts to 31 March. The tax written down values of his plant and machinery at 31 March 1997 were :

	£
General pool	2,700
Motor cars pool	7,600

He had the following transactions during the year to 31 March 1998 :

		£
1 May 1997	Bought plant	600
11 July 1997	Sold motor car (original cost £7,000)	3,000
11 July 1997	Bought motor car	8,000
1 November 1997	Bought machinery	400
12 January 1998	Sold machinery (original cost £4,000)	4,200

Compute the capital allowances claimable for the year to 31 March 1998, assuming no private use of any of the assets.

10.3 Norma began trading on 1 November 1995 and chose 30 June as her annual accounting date. Her first accounts covered the period to 30 June 1997 and showed an adjusted profit (before deduction of capital allowances) of £56,200. Her accounts for the year to 30 June 1998 showed an adjusted profit (before deduction of capital allowances) of £59,900. Plant and machinery was bought and sold as follows :

		£
1 November 1995	Bought plant	10,000
17 May 1996	Bought plant	17,400
12 October 1996	Bought car (40% private use by Norma)	8,800
3 November 1996	Sold plant (original cost £2,000)	1,750
3 November 1996	Bought plant	4,600
1 February 1997	Bought car	7,200
8 August 1997	Sold plant (original cost £1,500)	1,600
8 August 1997	Bought plant	11,500
31 March 1998	Sold car bought on 12 October 1996	6,300
31 March 1998	Bought car (40% private use by Norma)	14,100

Compute Norma's Schedule D Case I assessments for her first four years of assessment. and calculate the amount of any overlap profits.

10.4 Oliver has been trading since 1 July 1994, producing annual accounts to 30 June. On 1 May 1997 he acquired a brand new factory for £100,000 and put the factory to immediate industrial use. The cost of £100,000 included land of £20,000 and offices of £22,500. Calculate the IBA's available for the years to 30 June 1997 and 1998.

10.5 Francesco begins trading on 1 January 1996, producing annual accounts to 31 December. On 1 December 1996 he buys a new workshop for £56,000 (including land £11,000). He begins using the workshop on 1 January 1997 and it is in continual industrial use until 1 July 2004, when he sells it to Maria for £45,000 (including land £15,000). Maria immediately begins to use the workshop for an industrial purpose.

(a) Compute the IBA's available to Francesco for all affected years.

(b) Compute the IBA's available to Maria, who starts trading on 1 May 2004, making her first accounts up to 30 November 2004, and then producing accounts annually to 30 November thereafter.

10.6 Giles has been trading as a farmer since 1 April 1996, producing accounts to 31 March annually, and on 1 July 1996 he constructed a barn at a cost (excluding land) of £30,000. On 1 October 1997, he sold the barn to Pam for £35,000 (excluding land). Pam also trades as a farmer and began trading on 1 May 1997. She made up her first accounts for the period from 1 May 1997 to 31 December 1997 and intends to produce accounts for calendar years thereafter. Calculate the ABA's available to Giles and to Pam :

(a) if no election is made for the sale to be treated as a balancing event

(b) if such an election is made.

***10.7** David has been trading for many years and produces accounts annually to 31 March. On 1 July 1998 he buys a new industrial building for £80,000 (excluding land) and puts the building to immediate industrial use. Throughout David's ownership, the building is always in industrial use apart from the period between 1 January 2001 and 31 December 2003 when it is used for a non-industrial purpose. On 1 February 2006, he sells the building to Sanjay, who started business on 1 July 2005 and makes up accounts to 30 June each year. Calculate the IBA's available to David and to Sanjay, if the building was sold for :

(a) £60,000 (excluding land) (b) £120,000 (excluding land).

***10.8** Talat has been trading for many years, producing accounts to 31 October each year. The written down value of his plant and machinery after deducting capital allowances for the year to 31 October 1997 was as follows :

	£
General pool	8,290
Motor cars pool	4,900
Motor car (30% private use by Talat)	14,500

He had the following transactions during the next three years :

		£
y/e 31/10/98		
10 November 1997	Bought plant	2,000
1 January 1998	Sold plant (original cost £4,200)	1,310
y/e 31/10/99		
5 May 1999	Sold pool car (original cost £7,500)	3,000
5 May 1999	Bought pool car	8,200
12 June 1999	Bought plant	600
y/e 31/10/00		
5 April 2000	Sold plant (original cost £1,000)	1,150
6 April 2000	Bought plant	900

There were no capital transactions between 1 November 2000 and 31 March 2001, when Talat ceased trading. On 31 March 2001, the plant and machinery was disposed of as follows :

(i) All the general pool items were sold for £4,000.

(ii) There was only one car in the motor cars pool and Talat gave this to his brother, who will be using it for private purposes. The market value of the car on 31 March 2001 was £5,900.

(iii) Talat took over his own car. Its market value on 31 March 2001 was £8,000.

Prepare the capital allowances computations for the years to 31 October 1998, 1999 and 2000 and for the period from 1 November 2000 to 31 March 2001.

Chapter 11

Income from self-employment : Trading losses

Introduction

If the computation of a trader's adjusted profit for an accounting period produces a negative result, then a trading loss has been incurred. Such a loss has two main consequences :

(a) the Schedule D Case I assessment for the relevant tax year is set to £nil, and

(b) the trader may be able to claim tax relief in respect of the loss.

Several forms of relief are available and each involves offsetting the trading loss against other income or gains of the trader, so reducing the tax payable on that income or on those gains. The purpose of this chapter is to explain the main features of each form of relief.

Relief for trading losses

In general, trading losses may be relieved in one of two ways :

(a) Under Section 385 of ICTA 1988, a trading loss may be carried forward and relieved against future profits of the same trade.

(b) Under Section 380 of ICTA 1988, trading losses may be relieved against the statutory total income of the trader. A claim under Section 380 may also be extended by a further claim, under Section 72 of the Finance Act 1991, that unrelieved trading losses should be relieved against the trader's capital gains.

Each of these forms of loss relief is described below. The loss reliefs are usually referred to by their section numbers in ICTA 1988 or Finance Act 1991 and this practice is followed for the remainder of this chapter.

Section 385 relief

Unless a trader claims any other form of loss relief, a trading loss is automatically carried forward under Section 385 and relieved against future trading profits. It is important to note the following points :

(a) Relief under Section 385 is given only against future *trading* profits, not against any other form of income.

(b) Furthermore, relief is given only against future trading profits arising from *the same trade* as that in which the loss was incurred. Therefore, if a trader ceases one trade and commences another, the losses of the old trade cannot be carried forward and relieved against the future profits of the new trade. Similarly, if a trader carries on two trades simultaneously, a loss incurred in one of the trades cannot be carried forward and relieved against the future profits of the other trade.

(c) Relief must be given against the *first available* trading profits arising in the future. The maximum possible amount of relief must be taken in each future year until the loss is fully relieved, even if this leaves insufficient income to absorb personal allowances.

EXAMPLE 1

Carla began trading on 1 July 1994, preparing accounts to 30 June each year. In the year to 30 June 1997 she incurred a trading loss of £7,500. Her projected trading profits for the next three years are as follows :

	£
year to 30 June 1998	2,600
year to 30 June 1999	4,200
year to 30 June 2000	18,500

Carla's only other income consists of rents receivable of £500 per annum. Assuming that the trading loss is carried forward under Section 385, calculate her total income for 1997/98 to 2000/01 inclusive.

SOLUTION

	1997/98	*1998/99*	*1999/00*	*2000/01*
	£	£	£	£
Schedule D Case I	nil	2,600	4,200	18,500
Less : S385 relief	-	(2,600)	(4,200)	(700)
	-	-	-	17,800
Schedule A	500	500	500	500
Total income	500	500	500	18,300

Notes :

(a) The Schedule D Case I assessment in 1997/98 is £nil since there is a loss in the basis period for that year.

(b) The trading loss carried forward is relieved only against future trading profits (not against the rents) and the maximum relief must be given in each year. This results in a waste of personal allowances in 1998/99 and 1999/00. Carla would probably prefer to carry forward the loss in its entirety to 2000/01, where it can be put to good use, but this is not possible.

Capital allowances

For new businesses (and for old businesses as from 1997/98) any capital allowances claimed for an accounting period are treated as a trading expense of that period and are therefore automatically included in any trading loss which is carried forward under Section 385. For old businesses prior to 1997/98, unrelieved capital allowances were carried forward separately from trading losses and were set against subsequent trading profits in priority to trading losses carried forward.

It is important to remember that there is no compulsion to claim the maximum plant and machinery capital allowances available for a chargeable period. If a trading loss has been incurred it may be advisable to claim less than the maximum capital allowances (or even none at all) so as to avoid wasting personal allowances. Any unclaimed capital allowances are added to the WDV's carried forward, so increasing capital allowances in future years.

EXAMPLE 2

Colin began trading on 1 September 1994, preparing annual accounts to 31 August. His profits/(losses) for the years to 31 August 1996 and 1997 are as follows :

	Before capital allowances	*Capital allowances available*	*After capital allowances*
	£	£	£
year to 31 August 1996	(8,300)	1,900	(10,200)
year to 31 August 1997	11,800	1,400	10,400

Colin is single and has no other income. If the trading loss is carried forward under Section 385, should Colin claim maximum capital allowances in these two years ?

SOLUTION

If Colin claims maximum capital allowances in both years, S385 relief in 1997/98 will be £10,200. This will almost entirely absorb the trading profit of £10,400 assessed in that year, leaving only £200 against which to set personal allowances, most of which will therefore be wasted.

It would be better to claim no capital allowances at all for the two years concerned. The loss carried forward under S385 would then be only £8,300 and this would be relieved in 1997/98 against the trading profit of £11,800, leaving income of £3,500 against which to set personal allowances. There would be minimal waste of personal allowances and the capital allowances available to Colin in future years would be increased.

Section 380 relief

As illustrated earlier, carrying losses forward under Section 385 does not always provide the most satisfactory form of loss relief. Problems associated with Section 385 relief include :

(a) Relief is delayed until sufficient profits arise from the same trade in future years (if, indeed, they ever do).

(b) The trader has no control over the amount of relief given in each year and therefore personal allowances may be wasted.

(c) If tax rates are falling, relief may be given at a lower rate than the rates which were in force when the loss was incurred.

An alternative form of loss relief, which overcomes some of these problems, is provided by Section 380, under which trading losses may be set against the trader's *statutory total income* (i.e. the total income from all sources, less charges on income) for a period of up to two years. It is important to note that :

(a) The trader is under no obligation to make a Section 380 claim. If no such claim is made, trading losses are automatically carried forward under Section 385.

(b) Any unrelieved losses remaining after a Section 380 claim has been made are automatically carried forward under Section 385.

(c) Section 380 relief is available only if the business is being carried on on a commercial basis with a view to making profits. If this is not the case then only Section 385 relief is available.

(d) In the case of farmers and market gardeners (see Chapter 9), a loss is not eligible for Section 380 relief if losses have also been incurred in each of the previous 5 tax years. In these circumstances only Section 385 relief is available.

(e) Section 380 relief is set against non-savings income in priority to savings income.

The way in which Section 380 operates for new businesses (and for old businesses as from 1997/98) is explained below. The operation of Section 380 for old businesses in years prior to 1997/98 is also briefly explained.

Section 380 relief - the new rules

Section 380 relief is available in respect of the trading loss "incurred in a year of assessment" i.e. the loss incurred in a tax year. For new businesses (and old businesses as from 1997/98) the loss incurred in a tax year is simply the loss incurred in the basis period for that year. The only exception to this rule occurs if a trading loss occurs in an overlap period (see later in this chapter). As mentioned earlier, any capital allowances claimed by the business are included automatically in the calculation of a trading loss. A trading loss incurred in a tax year may be set against the statutory total income of either :

(a) the tax year in which the loss is incurred, or

(b) the previous tax year, or

(c) both of these years.

A claim for Section 380 relief must be made by 31 January in the second tax year following the tax year in which the loss was incurred. For example, a Section 380 claim in relation to a loss incurred in 1997/98 must be made by 31 January 2000.

The trader can decide whether to make a Section 380 claim for one of the available years, for both years, or for neither of them. But partial claims are not allowed. A Section 380 claim must be for the whole of the trading loss, even if this leaves insufficient income to absorb personal allowances. However, if a claim is made for both available years, and the combined STI of the two years exceeds the amount of the loss, then the trader can decide whether to claim maximum relief in the year of the loss, relieving the remainder of the loss in the previous year, or vice versa.

If two Section 380 claims are made for the same year (one for a trading loss incurred in the current year and one for a trading loss incurred in the subsequent year) the claim in respect of the current year's loss takes priority.

EXAMPLE 3

Ashok begins trading on 1 July 1995, making up accounts to 30 June each year. His trading profits/(losses), after deduction of the capital allowances claimed, are as follows :

	£
year to 30 June 1996	8,900
year to 30 June 1997	(9,500)

He has other income amounting to £4,000 per annum and claims only the personal allowance. Show his Schedule D Case I assessments (before deduction of any loss relief) and his possible Section 380 claims. Should any of these claims be recommended ?

SOLUTION

The Schedule D Case I assessments are :

Year	*Basis period*	*Workings*	*Assessment*
			£
1995/96	1/7/95 to 5/4/96	£8,900 x 279/365	6,803
1996/97	1/7/95 to 30/6/96		8,900
1997/98	y/e 30/6/97		nil

Ashok could make a Section 380 claim for 1997/98, or for 1996/97, or for both years, or for neither year :

(a) A claim for 1997/98 only would relieve £4,000 of the loss against his other income, leaving no tax liability for the year and losses of £5,500 to carry forward under Section 385. This would be a waste, since the other income of £4,000 would have been covered by personal allowances anyway.

(b) A claim for 1996/97 only would relieve the entire loss against that year's STI of £12,900 (£8,900 + £4,000), leaving income of £3,400 (£12,900 - £9,500) against which to set personal allowances. There would be a small wastage of personal allowances but the tax liability for 1996/97 would become zero. This seems to be a fairly efficient way of relieving the loss.

(c) A claim for both years is pointless, since :

    (i) a claim giving maximum relief in 1996/97 would leave no losses to relieve in 1997/98, and

    (ii) a claim giving maximum relief in 1997/98 leads to a waste of personal allowances in that year (see above).

(d) A claim for neither year would result in the entire loss being carried forward under Section 385. This would mean that loss relief would be delayed until such time as sufficient profits of the same trade arose in future years.

On balance, a Section 380 claim for 1996/97 might be recommended. This claim combines early relief of the loss with minimal wastage of personal allowances. The claim would have to be made by 31 January 2000.

Section 380 relief - the old rules

In the case of old businesses prior to 1997/98, strict interpretation of the phrase "incurred in a year of assessment" required calculation of the *actual* loss for a tax year (from 6 April to the following 5 April) and this "statutory basis" could be insisted upon either by the Inland Revenue or by the taxpayer. In practice, however, a loss incurred in the accounting year ending in a tax year was normally treated as a loss incurred in that tax year. This was known as the "concessionary basis". Note that :

(a) The strict statutory basis had to be used when calculating losses incurred in the opening tax years on a commencement of trade and in the final tax year on a cessation.

(b) Any unrelieved capital allowances for a tax year could be used to augment the amount of a trading loss eligible for Section 380 relief

Having determined the amount of a loss eligible for a Section 380 claim, the loss could then be relieved against the statutory total income of either :

(a) the tax year in which the loss was incurred, or
(b) the following tax year (if the trade was still being carried on in that year), or
(c) both of these years.

The trader could decide whether to make a claim for one of the available years, for both years, or for neither of them. If claims were made for both years, then relief was given in the order in which the claims were made. If the claims were made simultaneously, the trader could specify the order in which relief was to be given. If two Section 380 claims were made for the same year (one for a trading loss incurred in the current year and one for a trading loss incurred in the previous year) the claim in respect of the previous year's loss took priority.

Section 72 relief

If a Section 380 claim is made for a tax year and the effect of that claim is to reduce the trader's total income for the year to nil, a claim may also be made under Section 72 of the Finance Act 1991 for any unrelieved part of the loss to be set against the trader's capital gains for the year. The time limit for making such a claim is the same as for Section 380 relief. Section 72 relief is considered further in Chapter 16.

Relief for trade charges

If a trading loss is incurred in the basis period for a tax year, or if a loss is brought forward under Section 385 and set against the year's trading profit, then it is quite possible that the trader's total income for the year in question will be minimal or even zero. As a consequence, there may be insufficient income to relieve the year's charges and the Inland Revenue may then raise a Section 350 assessment (see Chapter 4) to claw back the tax deducted at source when the charges were paid.

In these circumstances, Section 387 of ICTA 1988 allows any unrelieved *trade* charges (i.e. those incurred wholly and exclusively for business purposes) to be carried forward and set against future trading profits in the same way as trading losses carried forward under Section 385. Unrelieved non-trade charges may *not* be carried forward in this way and may be relieved only in the year in which they occur. Therefore non-trade charges (which cannot be carried forward) should be set against income in priority to trade charges (which can, if necessary, be carried forward).

EXAMPLE 4

Joyce has been self-employed since 1 January 1995, producing annual accounts to 31 December. Her recent profits/(losses) are :

	£
year to 31 December 1997	(3,000)
year to 31 December 1998	18,000

Each year she pays patent royalties (net) of £1,540 and a charitable covenant (net) of £770. She has other income amounting to £800 per annum. Calculate Joyce's STI in 1997/98 and 1998/99, assuming that no Section 380 claim is made and that the basic rate of income tax is 23% throughout.

SOLUTION

	1997/98	*1998/99*
	£	£
Schedule D Case I	nil	18,000
Less : S385 relief	-	(3,000)
S387 relief	-	(2,000)
	-	13,000
Other income	800	800
	800	13,800
Less : Non-trade charges (£770 x 100/77 = £1,000)	(800)	(1,000)
Trade charges (£1,540 x 100/77 = £2,000)	-	(2,000)
Statutory total income	-	10,800
Unrelieved non-trade charges	200	-
Trade charges c/f under S387	2,000	-

Losses on commencement of trade

Losses incurred in the opening years of trading may, just like any other trading losses, be carried forward under Section 385 or set against statutory total income under Section 380. But, in addition to these forms of relief, Section 381 of ICTA 1988 allows trading losses incurred in any of the first 4 tax years to be set against the statutory total income of the three previous years. Note that :

(a) Section 381 relieves the trading loss incurred in a tax year against the STI of the three previous tax years, beginning with the earliest year. For example, a trading loss incurred in 1997/98 could be set against the STI of 1994/95, 1995/96 and 1996/97, in that order.

(b) A Section 381 claim, if made, applies to *all* of the three years previous to the loss-making year. The trader cannot specify the years in which relief is to be given or the amount of relief to be given in each year. The maximum possible relief is given in each year and this may result in a wastage of personal allowances.

(c) Relief is given against non-savings income in priority to savings income.

(d) Claims under Section 381 must be made by 31 January in the second tax year following the loss-making tax year.

(e) Unlike a Section 380 claim, a claim under Section 381 cannot be extended so as to set unrelieved trading losses against capital gains.

(f) A loss incurred in an overlap period is treated as a loss of the earlier tax year only. This rule ensures that a loss is relieved only once.

EXAMPLE 5

Carl begins trading on 1 July 1996 and chooses 30 June as his accounting date. His adjusted profits/(losses) for the first two accounting years are as follows :

	£
year to 30 June 1997	(31,200)
year to 30 June 1998	(12,400)

Now that he is self-employed, Carl has no other income. Prior to becoming self-employed his only income was from employment, as follows :

	£
1993/94	14,900
1994/95	15,760
1995/96	16,120
1996/97 (to 30 June 1996)	4,180

Assuming that Carl makes all possible Section 381 claims, calculate his total income for years 1993/94 to 1996/97 inclusive.

SOLUTION

The losses which are eligible for Section 381 relief are :

Year	*Basis period*	*Workings*	*Loss*	*Years for S381 claim*
			£	
1996/97	1/7/96 to 5/4/97	£(31,200) x 279/365	(23,849)	93/94-95/96
1997/98	1/7/96 to 30/6/97	£(31,200) - overlap £(23,849)	(7,351)	94/95-96/97
1998/99	y/e 30/6/98		(12,400)	95/96-97/98

The Schedule D Case I assessments for 1996/97 through to 1998/99 will of course be £nil. If all possible Section 381 claims are made, total income for years 1993/94 to 1996/97 is :

	1993/94	1994/95	1995/96	1996/97
	£	£	£	£
Schedule E	14,900	15,760	16,120	4,180
Less : Section 381 relief :				
1996/97 loss	(14,900)	(8,949)		
1997/98 loss		(6,811)	(540)	
1998/99 loss			(12,400)	
Total income (after loss reliefs)	-	-	3,180	4,180

Losses on cessation of trade

In normal circumstances, a trader has a choice between carrying forward trading losses under Section 385 or relieving such losses against total income under Section 380. But if a loss is incurred in the final year of trading the first of these alternatives is unavailable since there can be no future profits against which to set the loss. In order to remedy this situation, Section 388 of ICTA 1988 provides a relief known as "terminal loss relief" which allows a trading loss incurred in the last 12 months of trading to be set against the trading profits of :

(a) for new businesses (and old businesses as from 1997/98) the tax year in which the cessation occurs and the previous three tax years

(b) for old businesses prior to 1997/98, the three tax years preceding the year of the cessation.

In effect, terminal loss relief is a form of Section 385 relief which works backwards rather than forwards.

Calculating the terminal loss

The "terminal loss" eligible for relief is the trading loss incurred in the final 12 months of trading, excluding any part of the loss which is relieved under Section 380. The terminal loss is calculated by adding together the following components :

(a) *Losses* :

(i) the actual trading loss incurred in the year of cessation, from 6 April to the date of the cessation

(ii) the actual trading loss incurred from a date 12 months before the cessation up to the following 5 April

(if either (i) or (ii) yields a profit rather than a loss, this profit counts as zero in the calculation of the terminal loss)

(b) *Capital allowances* (for old businesses prior to 1997/98 only) :

(i) the capital allowances of the final tax year

(ii) any unrelieved capital allowances of the penultimate tax year (but restricted so that only capital allowances of the final 12 months are included in the calculation altogether)

(c) *Trade charges* :

(i) any unrelieved trade charges of the final tax year

(ii) any unrelieved trade charges of the penultimate tax year (but restricted so that only trade charges of the final 12 months are included in the calculation altogether).

If overlap relief is available, it is added on to the loss shown above at (a) (i).

EXAMPLE 6

Andrea has been trading since 1995, making up accounts to 31 December annually. On 31 October 2001 she ceases trading. Her adjusted profits/(losses) net of capital allowances for the closing accounting periods are as follows :

	£
year to 31 December 1999	6,600
year to 31 December 2000	2,400
10 months to 31 October 2001	(22,500)

Her trade charges and her other income are as follows :

	2000/01	*2001/02*
	£	£
Trade charges	5,000	3,000
Other income	nil	nil

Overlap profits of £3,200 arose when Andrea began trading. Calculate the amount of the terminal loss, assuming that no Section 380 claims are made.

SOLUTION

			£
(a) *Losses* :			
(i) 6/4/01 to 31/10/01		£(22,500) x 209/304	(15,469)
Overlap relief			(3,200)
(ii) 1/11/00 to 5/4/01		£2,400 x 61/365 + £(22,500) x 95/304	(6,630)
(b) *Trade charges* :			
(i) unrelieved in 2001/02			(3,000)
(ii) unrelieved in 2000/01		£2,600, but restrict to £5,000 x 156/365	(2,137)
Terminal loss			(30,436)

Notes :

1. The Schedule D Case I assessment for 2000/01 (basis period y/e 31/12/00) is £2,400. The assessment for 2001/02 is £nil. Unrelieved trade charges in 2000/01 are £2,600 (£5,000 - £2,400). Unrelieved trade charges in 2001/02 are £3,000.
2. The 10 months to 31/10/01 is a 304-day period, of which 209 days fall into 2001/02.
3. Trade charges for 2001/02 cover 209 days (6 April 2001 to 31 October 2001) so no more than 156 days' worth of the trade charges for 2000/01 can be taken into account when calculating the terminal loss.

Relieving the terminal loss

As stated above, the terminal loss may be relieved against the trading profits of the year of cessation (for new businesses and for old businesses as from 1997/98) and against the trading profits of the three tax years preceding the year of the cessation. Note that :

(a) Relief is given in later years first. For example, a terminal loss arising as a consequence of a business ceasing to trade during 1998/99 would be set against the trading profits of 1998/99, 1997/98, 1996/97 and 1995/96, in that order.

(b) The trader cannot specify how much relief is given in each year. The maximum possible relief must be given in each year even if this results in a wastage of personal allowances.

(c) Relief is given after the deduction from trading profits of any charges paid net which are not covered by other income.

EXAMPLE 7

Brendan, who has been trading since 1995, ceases trading on 30 June 2000. His recent profits/(losses) after deduction of capital allowances are as follows :

	£
year to 31 January 1998	24,700
year to 31 January 1999	12,500
year to 31 January 2000	6,600
5 months to 30 June 2000 (150 days)	(27,300)

He pays charges (net of income tax) and receives other income as follows :

	1997/98	*1998/99*	*1999/00*	*2000/01*
	£	£	£	£
Trade charges (gross amounts)	2,000	2,000	2,000	2,000
Non-trade charges(gross amounts)	500	500	500	500
Other income	nil	nil	nil	nil

Overlap profits of £2,700 arose when Brendan began trading. Calculate the amount of the terminal loss (assuming that no Section 380 claims are made) and show how this may be relieved.

SOLUTION

The calculation of the terminal loss is as follows :

			£
(a)	*Losses* :		
	(i) 6/4/00 to 30/6/00	£(27,300) x 86/150	(15,652)
	Overlap relief		(2,700)
	(ii) 1/7/99 to 5/4/00	£6,600 x 215/365 + £(27,300) x 64/150	(7,760)
(b)	*Trade charges* :		
	(i) unrelieved in 2000/01		(2,000)
	(ii) unrelieved in 1999/00		nil
Terminal loss			(28,112)

The loss may be relieved as follows :

	1997/98	*1998/99*	*1999/00*	*2000/01*
	£	£	£	£
Adjusted profit	24,700	12,500	6,600	nil
Less : Non-trade charges	(500)	(500)	(500)	-
Trade charges	(2,000)	(2,000)	(2,000)	-
	22,200	10,000	4,100	-
Less : Terminal loss relief :				
(i) 1999/00			(4,100)	
(ii) 1998/99		(10,000)		
(iii) 1997/98	(14,012)			
Total income	8,188	-	-	-

Post-cessation expenditure

As a general rule, post-cessation expenditure which was not provided for in the final accounts of a business is relieved against any post-cessation receipts assessed under Schedule D Case VI. If post-cessation receipts are insufficient to absorb post-cessation expenditure, the excess expenditure is normally unrelieved.

However, certain categories of unrelieved post-cessation expenditure may be set against the taxpayer's income and capital gains for the year of assessment in which the expenditure is incurred. The main categories of post-cessation expenditure which may be relieved in this way are :

(a) the costs of remedying defective work done whilst the business was operating, together with associated legal costs and insurance premiums

(b) bad debts which were not provided for in the accounts of the business, together with associated debt collection costs.

Transfer of a business to a company

If the owner of a business transfers that business to a limited company, there is a change in the legal ownership of the business and the vendor is deemed to have ceased trading. As a consequence, any trading losses sustained by the vendor before the date of the transfer cannot be carried forward and set against the company's trading profits.

Relief for these losses might be sought under Section 380 or (if the losses were incurred in the final 12 months of trading) in the form of terminal loss relief, but an alternative is provided by Section 386 of ICTA 1988. Section 386 provides that :

(a) if a business is transferred wholly or mainly in exchange for shares in a company, and

(b) the vendor of the business continues to hold those shares, and

(c) the company continues to carry on the transferred business, then

(d) the vendor may set his or her unrelieved trading losses against the first available income that he or she receives from the company.

The offset is against earned income (e.g. salaries and directors' fees) in priority to dividends.

Losses on shares in unlisted trading companies

An individual who subscribes for shares in an unlisted UK trading company and then incurs a capital loss on the disposal of those shares may claim that this loss should be set against his or her total income as if it were a trading loss being relieved under Section 380. This relief is provided by Section 574 of ICTA 1988 and a Section 574 claim in a year of assessment takes priority over any Section 380 or Section 381 claims made for the same year.

Summary

- ► Under Section 385 of ICTA 1988, a trading loss may be carried forward and relieved against future profits of the same trade.
- ► Under Section 380 of ICTA 1988, trading losses may be relieved against the statutory total income of the trader for a specified two-year period.
- ► Under Section 72 of the Finance Act 1991, any losses remaining unrelieved after a Section 380 claim has been made for a tax year may be set against the trader's capital gains for that year.

- For new businesses (and for old businesses as from 1997/98) capital allowances are automatically included in the calculation of a trading loss.
- Unrelieved trade charges may be carried forward as if they were trading losses.
- On a commencement of trade, a loss incurred in any of the first four tax years may be set against the STI of the previous three tax years.
- On a cessation of trade, a trading loss incurred during the final 12 months of trading may be set against the trading profits of the year in which trade ceases and the previous 3 years.
- If a business is transferred to a company, the unrelieved trading losses of the vendor may (subject to certain conditions) be set against the first available income which the vendor receives from the company.

Exercises

11.1 Sally, who has been trading since 1 January 1995, incurs an adjusted trading loss of £10,000 in the year to 31 December 1997.

(a) What is her Schedule D Case I assessment for 1997/98 ?

(b) If she makes no claim under Section 380, how will the loss be relieved ?

(c) How will the loss be relieved if she does make a Section 380 claim ?

11.2 Jane is single and has been self-employed since 1 June 1994. Her recent adjusted trading profits/(losses) are :

	£
year to 31 May 1997	(18,860)
year to 31 May 1998	4,710
year to 31 May 1999	6,210
year to 31 May 2000	14,810

Jane has other income of £5,000 per annum. Assuming that no claims are made under Section 380, calculate her total income for years 1997/98 through to 2000/01.

11.3 Marcus is married and self-employed. He begins trading on 1 January 1996 and has the following results :

	Profits/(losses) before capital allces	*Capital allowances claimed*
	£	£
year to 31 December 1996	12,720	2,460
year to 31 December 1997	(7,680)	2,120

(a) Compute the Schedule D Case I assessments (before any loss relief) for 1995/96 to 1997/98.

(b) Assuming that Marcus has no other income, show his possible Section 380 claims. Which (if any) of these claims should be recommended ?

11.4 Nathan begins trading on 1 October 1995, making up accounts to 31 December each year. His first two sets of accounts show the following adjusted losses (after deduction of capital allowances) :

	£
15 months to 31 December 1996	(11,850)
year to 31 December 1997	(9,660)

He has had no other income since becoming self-employed but his income before he started trading was as follows :

	£
1992/93	6,100
1993/94	6,250
1994/95	6,400
1995/96 (to 30 September 1995)	3,450

Assuming that all possible Section 381 claims are made, calculate Nathan's total income for years 1992/93 to 1995/96.

***11.5** Olive, who has been trading since 1 July 1994, ceases trading on 31 May 2001. Her recent adjusted profits/(losses) after deduction of capital allowances are :

	£
year to 30 June 1997	37,450
year to 30 June 1998	39,190
year to 30 June 1999	22,870
year to 30 June 2000	6,840
11 months to 31 May 2001	(36,300)

Her charges (paid net) are as follows :

	1998/99	*1999/00*	*2000/01*	*2001/02*
	£	£	£	£
Trade charges (gross amounts)	1,500	1,500	1,500	1,500
Non-trade charges (gross amounts)	6,750	6,750	6,750	6,750

She had no other income in any of these years. Overlap relief of £4,390 is available. Calculate the terminal loss and show how this would be relieved.

***11.6** Craig is married and self-employed. His wife has no income. He began trading on 1 August 1995 and has the following results :

	Profits/(losses) before capital allces	*Capital allowances claimed*
	£	£
year to 31 July 1996	5,460	1,140
year to 31 July 1997	(17,400)	1,920

Before commencing to trade, Craig lived entirely on investment income but he sold all his investments in July 1996 (realising a large capital gain) so as to raise extra working capital for his own business. His income from investments in recent years has been :

	£
1993/94	3,150
1994/95	4,040
1995/96	2,390
1996/97 (to July 1996)	1,110

(a) Compute the Schedule D Case I assessments for 1995/96 to 1997/98.

(b) Explain the loss reliefs available to Craig. Which would you recommend ?

Chapter 12

Income from self-employment : Partnerships

Introduction

The purpose of this chapter is to explain the taxation treatment of partnerships. In many ways, a partnership is treated for tax purposes in much the same way as a sole trader, and the rules given in Chapters 8 to 11 as regards computation of the adjusted profit, basis periods, capital allowances and losses apply to partnerships as well as to sole traders. The important new problem which arises when considering partnership taxation is the division of the partnership's tax liability between the partners, and much of this chapter is devoted to that problem.

New partnerships and old partnerships

The Finance Act 1994, which introduced new basis period rules for sole traders taxed under Schedule D Case I (see Chapter 9), also introduced new rules for the taxation of partnerships. It is now necessary to distinguish between "new partnerships" and "old partnerships", as follows :

(a) A "new partnership" is one which commences trading on or after 6 April 1994. A new partnership uses the new basis period rules and the new partnership rules in all tax years.

(b) An "old partnership" is one which commenced trading before 6 April 1994. An old partnership (like any other old business) used the old basis period rules for tax years up to and including 1995/96 with special transitional rules in 1996/97. The old partnership rules apply to 1996/97 and earlier years. The new partnership rules apply as from 1997/98.

This chapter is mainly concerned with the new partnership rules but a summary of the old rules and the transitional rules is given at the end of the chapter.

New partnership rules

Under the new partnership rules, a partnership is not regarded as a separate entity for taxation purposes and assessments are not raised on the partnership itself. Instead, the profits of the partnership are allocated between the partners and assessments are then raised on the partners as individuals. In detail, the procedure for each tax year is as follows :

(a) The partnership submits a return to the Inland Revenue. This return provides information on the profit (or loss) for the accounting period ending in the tax year and gives details of the profit-sharing agreement in force during that accounting period. The return is also used to :

 (i) claim capital allowances for the accounting period (both on partnership assets and on individual partners' assets)

 (ii) claim relief for any business expenses incurred personally by partners.

(b) The adjusted trading profit (or loss) of the partnership is calculated in the usual way. Any drawings or appropriations of profit made by the partners are disallowed. Capital allowances on partnership assets are treated as a trading expense.

(c) The adjusted trading profit (or loss) is then allocated between the partners according to the profit-sharing agreement in force during the accounting period. If the agreement changes during the accounting period, it is necessary to time-apportion the profit (or loss) for the period, applying the old agreement to the pre-change profit (or loss) and the new agreement to the post-change profit (or loss).

(d) Any capital allowances claimed on an individual partner's assets and any expenses incurred personally by a partner are deducted from the relevant partner's share of the adjusted profit or added to that partner's share of the adjusted loss.

(e) Partners are then assessed to tax individually, as if each partner's share of the partnership profit or loss had arisen from a trade carried on by that partner alone. In effect, each partner is treated as a sole trader who began trading when joining the partnership, has the same accounting dates as the partnership, and will cease trading when leaving the partnership.

(f) Each partner is solely responsible for the tax due on his or her share of the partnership profit. As from tax year 1996/97, partners must include their share of the partnership profit (or loss) in their own tax returns and in their self-assessment calculations.

EXAMPLE 1

Ferdinand, Beardsley and Lee begin trading as a partnership on 1 January 1996, sharing profits in the ratio 3:2:1. With effect from 1 January 1997, they agree that Lee should receive a salary of £4,000 p.a., that partners should be entitled to 4% p.a. interest on capital and that remaining profits should be shared in the ratio 5:3:2. The adjusted profits of the partnership are :

	£
y/e 31/12/96	18,000
y/e 31/12/97	22,000

Fixed capitals are Ferdinand £10,000, Beardsley £12,000, Lee £16,000. Compute each partner's Schedule D Case I assessment for 1995/96, 1996/97 and 1997/98.

SOLUTION

The allocation of profit for each accounting period is :

	Ferdinand £	*Beardsley* £	*Lee* £	*Total* £
y/e 31/12/96				
Profit (shared 3:2:1)	9,000	6,000	3,000	18,000
y/e 31/12/97				
Salary	-	-	4,000	4,000
Interest on capital	400	480	640	1,520
Remainder of profit (shared 5:3:2)	8,240	4,944	3,296	16,480
	8,640	5,424	7,936	22,000

Each partner is treated as a sole trader, commencing trade on 1 January 1996, making up accounts to 31 December and with profits for the first two accounting years as shown above. The assessments on each partner are :

Ferdinand

Year	*Basis period*	*Workings*	*Assessment* £
1995/96	1/1/96 to 5/4/96	£9,000 x 95/365	2,342
1996/97	y/e 31/12/96		9,000
1997/98	y/e 31/12/97		8,640

Beardsley

Year	*Basis period*	*Workings*	*Assessment* £
1995/96	1/1/96 to 5/4/96	£6,000 x 95/365	1,561
1996/97	y/e 31/12/96		6,000
1997/98	y/e 31/12/97		5,424

Lee

Year	*Basis period*	*Workings*	*Assessment*
			£
1995/96	1/1/96 to 5/4/96	£3,000 x 95/365	781
1996/97	y/e 31/12/96		3,000
1997/98	y/e 31/12/97		7,936

Note :

In each case, the overlap period is from 1 January 1996 to 5 April 1996. Overlap profits are Ferdinand £2,342, Beardsley £1,561 and Lee £781. These overlap profits will be relieved when the relevant partner leaves the partnership (or on a change of accounting date).

Notional profits and losses (new partnership rules)

Occasionally, the effect of taking into account partners' salaries and/or interest on capital is to allocate a loss to an individual partner, even though the partnership as a whole has made a profit. In these circumstances, that partner's share of the partnership assessment is set to £nil and then his or her "notional loss" is allocated between the remaining partners in proportion to their original profit allocations. A similar procedure is followed if a partner is allocated a "notional profit" in a year in which the partnership as a whole has sustained a loss.

EXAMPLE 2

(a) Cantona, Irwin and Giggs have been in partnership since 1 July 1994, making up accounts to 30 June. Their profit-sharing agreement specifies that Cantona and Giggs should receive annual salaries of £20,000 and £24,000 respectively and that the remaining profits should be divided equally. The partnership has an adjusted profit of £26,000 in the year to 30 June 1997. Show how this profit will be allocated between the partners.

(b) Beckham, Keane and Ferguson have also been in partnership since 1 July 1994, making up accounts to 30 June. Their profit-sharing agreement specifies that Ferguson should receive an annual salary of £25,000 and that remaining profits should be shared in the ratio 3:2:1. The partnership has an adjusted loss of £5,000 in the year to 30 June 1997. Show how this loss will be allocated between the partners.

SOLUTION

(a)

	Cantona	*Irwin*	*Giggs*	*Total*
	£	£	£	£
Salaries	20,000	-	24,000	44,000
Remainder (£26,000 - £44,000)	(6,000)	(6,000)	(6,000)	(18,000)
c/f	14,000	(6,000)	18,000	26,000

	Cantona	*Irwin*	*Giggs*	*Total*
	£	£	£	£
b/f	14,000	(6,000)	18,000	26,000
Irwin's notional loss divided in the ratio 14,000 : 18,000	(2,625)	6,000	(3,375)	-
Allocation of profit for the year	11,375	-	14,625	26,000

(b)

	Beckham	*Keane*	*Ferguson*	*Total*
	£	£	£	£
Salaries	-	-	25,000	25,000
Remainder (£5,000 + £25,000)	(15,000)	(10,000)	(5,000)	(30,000)
	(15,000)	(10,000)	20,000	(5,000)
Ferguson's notional profit divided 15,000 : 10,000	12,000	8,000	(20,000)	-
Allocation of loss for the year	(3,000)	(2,000)	-	(5,000)

Change in partnership composition (new partnership rules)

A change in partnership composition occurs if a new partner joins the partnership or if an existing partner dies or leaves the partnership. Such a change has no effect on those persons who were carrying on the trade before the change (either alone or in partnership) and who continue to carry on the trade after the change (either alone or in partnership). Such persons are taxed on the current year basis as if the change had not taken place. But new partners have commenced trading and are subject to the commencement rules, whilst leaving partners have ceased trading and are subject to the cessation rules.

EXAMPLE 3

Wright and Merson begin trading as a partnership on 1 October 1995, sharing profits equally. On 1 January 1997, they agree to admit Platt as a partner and to share profits in the ratio 3:2:1. The adjusted profits of the partnership are :

	£
y/e 30/9/96	21,000
y/e 30/9/97	24,000
y/e 30/9/98	27,000

Compute each partner's Schedule D Case I assessment for the years 1995/96 through to 1998/99.

SOLUTION

The allocation of profit for each accounting period is :

	Wright	*Merson*	*Platt*	*Total*
	£	£	£	£
y/e 30/9/96 (shared equally)	10,500	10,500	-	21,000
y/e 30/9/97				
1/10/96 - 31/12/96				
£24,000 x 92/365 (shared equally)	3,025	3,024	-	6,049
1/1/97 - 30/9/97				
£24,000 x 273/365 (shared 3:2:1)	8,975	5,984	2,992	17,951
	12,000	9,008	2,992	24,000
y/e 30/9/98 (shared 3:2:1)	13,500	9,000	4,500	27,000

Wright and Merson both started trading on 1 October 1995, with an accounting date of 30 September. Platt started trading on 1 January 1997, also with an accounting date of 30 September. None of the partners have ceased to trade. The assessments on each partner are therefore :

Wright

Year	*Basis period*	*Workings*	*Assessment*
			£
1995/96	1/10/95 to 5/4/96	£10,500 x 187/365	5,379
1996/97	y/e 30/9/96		10,500
1997/98	y/e 30/9/97		12,000
1998/99	y/e 30/9/98		13,500

Merson

Year	*Basis period*	*Workings*	*Assessment*
			£
1995/96	1/10/95 to 5/4/96	£10,500 x 187/365	5,379
1996/97	y/e 30/9/96		10,500
1997/98	y/e 30/9/97		9,008
1998/99	y/e 30/9/98		9,000

Platt

Year	*Basis period*	*Workings*	*Assessment*
			£
1996/97	1/1/97 to 5/4/97	£2,992 x 95/273	1,041
1997/98	1/1/97 to 31/12/97	£2,992 + £4,500 x 92/365	4,126
1998/99	y/e 30/9/98		4,500

Note :

In the case of Wright and Merson, the overlap period is from 1 October 1995 to 5 April 1996 and each partner has overlap profits of £5,379. In the case of Platt, there is an overlap period from 1 January 1997 to 5 April 1997 and another overlap period from 1

October 1997 to 31 December 1997. Platt's overlap profits are £1,041 + £4,500 x 92/365 = £2,175.

Non-trading income (new partnership rules)

A partnership which has trading income may also have non-trading income. For assessment purposes, non-trading income falls into two categories :

(a) **Non-trading income which is not taxed at source**

Income of this type (e.g. income from property or interest received gross) is dealt with separately from the partnership's trading income but is assessed using *the same basis periods as those used for the trading income.* The basis periods that would normally be applied if the income were received by an individual rather than a partnership are totally ignored. If this treatment results in non-trading income being taxed twice when a partner starts trading, overlap relief is available.

(b) **Non-trading income which is taxed at source**

Income of this type (e.g. dividends and most bank interest) is also dealt with separately from the partnership's trading income but is assessed on the actual basis. The income arising in a period of account is allocated between the partners in the usual way but each partner's share is then apportioned between tax years.

If a partnership does not carry on a trade or profession, the treatment described at (b) above applies to *all* of the partnership's non-trading income (whether taxed at source or not).

EXAMPLE 4

Redknapp, Fowler and McAteer begin trading as a partnership on 1 July 1995, sharing profits equally. The chosen accounting date is 30 June and the first accounts are made up for the year to 30 June 1996. In addition to its trading income, the partnership has non-trading income as follows :

	y/e 30/6/96	*y/e 30/6/97*
	£	£
Income from property	1,500	1,800
Net dividends	2,400	3,600

(a) Compute each partner's Schedule A assessment for 1995/96, 1996/97 and 1997/98.

(b) Compute the gross amount of dividends assessed on each partner in 1995/96 and 1996/97.

SOLUTION

(a) Each partner is allocated property income of £500 in the year to 30 June 1996 and £600 in the year to 30 June 1997. The Schedule A assessments on each partner are as follows :

Year	*Basis period*	*Workings*	*Assessment*
			£
1995/96	1/7/95 to 5/4/96	£500 x 279/365	382
1996/97	y/e 30/6/96		500
1997/98	y/e 30/6/97		600

Each partner is entitled to overlap relief of £382.

(b) Each partner is allocated gross dividends of £1,000 (£2,400 x 100/80 x 1/3) in the year to 30 June 1996 and £1,500 (£3,600 x 100/80 x 1/3) in the year to 30 June 1997. The gross dividends assessed on each partner are as follows :

Year	*Workings*	*Assessment*
		£
1995/96	£1,000 x 279/365	764
1996/97	£1,000 x 86/365 + £1,500 x 279/365	1,382

The remaining 86/365th of the dividends received during the year to 30 June 1997 will be assessed in 1997/98, along with the first 279/365th of any dividends received in the year to 30 June 1998.

Losses (new partnership rules)

An adjusted loss is allocated between the partners in the same way as an adjusted profit. Each partner is then entitled to precisely the same loss reliefs as a sole trader.

Old partnership rules

A partnership is not a legal "person" in its own right and therefore cannot be liable to tax. Nonetheless, in the case of old partnerships prior to 1997/98, Schedule D Case I assessments were raised on the partnership itself rather than on the individual partners. The procedure was as follows :

(a) The adjusted trading profit of the partnership for Schedule D Case I purposes was calculated in the usual way. The profit was then assessed on the preceding year basis (for years up to 1995/96) or on the transitional basis (for 1996/97). Capital allowances claimed on partnership assets were deducted.

(b) The trading profit, less capital allowances, for a given tax year was allocated between the partners according to the profit-sharing agreement in force *during that tax year* (see below). Notional profits and losses were dealt with in the same way as by the new partnership rules (see above).

(c) Partners could claim capital allowances in relation to the business use of privately-owned assets and relief for business expenses incurred personally. Such individual capital allowances and expenses, if claimed, were deducted from the relevant partner's allocation of profit.

(d) The individual tax liability of each partner was then calculated, taking into account the partner's share of any business charges on income and the partner's personal allowances.

(e) The partnership's tax liability was simply the sum of the individual partners' tax liabilities. The partners had joint and several responsibility for this liability and therefore any one of the partners could be required to pay the entire amount due in the case of default by the other partners.

Any non-trading income of the partnership (e.g. rents received, interest received, dividends etc.) did not form part of the partnership assessment. The non-trading income for a tax year was allocated between the partners in profit-sharing ratio and then assessed individually on each partner. Similarly, non-trade charges were dealt with in the partner's individual tax assessments.

Allocation of the trading profit (old partnership rules)

As stated above, the trading profit for a tax year was allocated between the partners according to the profit-sharing agreement in force during that tax year. The profit-sharing agreement in force during the basis period for the year was irrelevant and this could lead to anomalies when the profit sharing agreement changed.

EXAMPLE 5

Best, Law and Charlton have been in business since 1966, making up accounts to 31 December annually. Their profit-sharing agreement, which has been in force for many years, specifies that each partner should receive 5% interest on fixed capital, that Best should receive an annual salary of £5,000 and that the remaining profits should be divided equally. Fixed capitals are Best £20,000, Law £25,000 and Charlton £18,000. The adjusted trading profit is £31,000 for the year to 31 December 1995 and £33,000 for the year to 31 December 1996.

(a) Compute each partner's share of the 1996/97 Schedule D Case I assessment.

(b) On 6 April 1996, the partners agree to change the profit-sharing agreement so that all profits will be shared in the ratio 5:2:1 with no salaries or interest on capital. How will this affect the allocation of the 1996/97 Schedule D Case I assessment ?

SOLUTION

The 1996/97 assessment is £32,000 i.e. 50% x (£31,000 + £33,000).

(a)

	Best	*Law*	*Charlton*	*Total*
	£	£	£	£
Interest on capital	1,000	1,250	900	3,150
Salaries	5,000	-	-	5,000
Remainder (shared equally)	7,950	7,950	7,950	23,850
	13,950	9,200	8,850	32,000

(b) Even though the change in profit-sharing agreement did not take place until part way through the 24 months to 31 December 1996, which forms the basis for 1996/97, the new agreement is in force throughout 1996/97 and therefore dictates how the entire assessment for the year should be allocated. The revised allocation would be:

	Best	*Law*	*Charlton*	*Total*
	£	£	£	£
Profit (shared 5:2:1)	20,000	8,000	4,000	32,000

Change in profit-sharing agreement (old partnership rules)

If the profit-sharing agreement changed during a tax year, it was necessary to time-apportion the profit assessed in that year. The old profit-sharing arrangements were applied to the profit arising between 6 April and the date of the change. The new profit-sharing arrangements were applied to the remainder of the profit.

Change in partnership composition (old partnership rules)

Unless an election was made for the "continuation basis" (see below) a change in the composition of an old partnership prior to 1997/98 was treated as the cessation of one business followed by the immediate commencement of a new business. The cessation triggered the usual cessation rules for an old business. The commencement was dealt with as follows :

(a) If the change occurred on or after 6 April 1994, the newly-composed partnership was treated as a "new partnership", subject both to the commencement rules for new businesses and to the new partnership rules.

(b) If the change occurred before 6 April 1994, a set of special commencement rules was used in relation to the newly-composed partnership. These special rules are no longer in use and are not considered here.

The continuation basis (old partnership rules)

If a change occurred in the composition of an old partnership prior to 1997/98, the partners could avoid the cessation and commencement provisions described above by electing for the "continuation basis" to apply. In this case, the partnership was assessed as a continuing business and the same basis periods were used as would have been used if the change in composition had not taken place. Note that :

(a) The continuation basis election could not be made unless at least one person was a partner both before and after the change in composition.

(b) The election had to be made within two years of the date of the change in composition.

(c) All the partners, both before and after the change, had to sign the election. (A deceased partner's personal representative could sign on his or her behalf).

(d) Partnerships with more than 50 members (usually firms of accountants or lawyers) could make a blanket election for the continuation basis to apply on all changes in the partnership composition. This had effect so long as all new members added their names to the election.

EXAMPLE 6

Clark and Clough have been in partnership for many years, sharing profits equally. On 1 January 1996 they admitted Pearce as a partner and agreed to share profits in the ratio 3:2:1. Adjusted trading profits are as follows :

	£
year to 31 December 1993	54,000
year to 31 December 1994	33,000
year to 31 December 1995	44,000
year to 31 December 1996	46,000

Calculate the Schedule D Case I assessments for 1994/95 to 1996/97 inclusive and show how these assessments are divided between the partners, assuming that an election is made for the continuation basis to apply.

SOLUTION

Election for the continuation basis ensures that is no need to deal with a cessation or a commencement. However, it is necessary to apportion the 1995/96 assessment since the profit-sharing agreement changed on 1 January 1996. The assessments are as follows :

	Clark	*Clough*	*Pearce*	*Total*
	£	£	£	£
1994/95 (y/e 31/12/93)	27,000	27,000	-	54,000

	Clark £	*Clough* £	*Pearce* £	*Total* £
1995/96 (y/e 31/12/94)				
6/4/95 - 31/12/95 (£33,000 x 270/365 = £24,411)	12,206	12,205	-	24,411
1/1/96 - 5/4/96 (£33,000 x 95/365 = £8,589)	4,295	2,863	1,431	8,589
	16,501	15,068	1,431	33,000
1996/97 (24 mths to 31/12/96)	22,500	15,000	7,500	45,000

Note that Pearce is assessed on profits earned before he became a partner.

Losses (old partnership rules)

If an old partnership incurred a loss prior to 1997/98, each partner could decide individually whether to claim loss relief under Section 380 or to carry forward his or her share of the loss under Section 385 (see Chapter 11). The way in which the loss was allocated between the partners depended upon the form of loss relief chosen, as explained below :

(a) If *all* the partners chose to carry forward their losses under Section 385, the loss was allocated between the partners according to the profit-sharing agreement in force *during the loss-making accounting period.*

(b) If *all* the partners chose to claim loss relief under Section 380, the loss was allocated between the partners according to the profit-sharing agreement in force *during the tax year in which the loss-making accounting period ended.*

(c) There was no statutory ruling on the allocation of the loss if some partners made Section 380 claims whilst others did not. In practice :

    (i) a partner who made a Section 380 claim was allocated a share of the loss calculated as if all the partners had made Section 380 claims, and

    (ii) a partner who carried forward losses under Section 385 was allocated a share of the loss calculated as if all the partners had carried forward losses under Section 385.

    In some circumstances, this practice gave the partners loss relief totalling more than the actual loss sustained by the partnership.

Transition to the new partnership rules

As from 1997/98, all partnerships are assessed according to the new partnership rules. For old partnerships, this entails the identification of appropriate basis periods for 1997/98 and subsequent years. The procedure for each partner is as follows :

(a) Identify the date on which the partner joined the partnership and identify the basis periods which would have been used for that partner if the new partnership rules had applied throughout.

(b) To the extent that the basis periods identified at (a) relate to 1997/98 or to later years, these basis periods are used for the partner concerned.

EXAMPLE 7

Smith and Jones have been in equal partnership for many years, preparing accounts to 31 December each year. Brown was admitted as an equal partner on 1 March 1997 and an election was made for the continuation basis to apply. Profits in recent years have been :

	£
year to 31 December 1994	17,000
year to 31 December 1995	21,000
year to 31 December 1996	15,000
year to 31 December 1997	24,000
year to 31 December 1998	27,000

Calculate each partner's assessment for years 1995/96 to 1997/98 inclusive.

SOLUTION

	Smith	*Jones*	*Brown*	*Total*
	£	£	£	£
1995/96 (y/e 31/12/94)	8,500	8,500	-	17,000
1996/97 (24 mths to 31/12/96)				
6/4/96 - 28/2/97				
(£18,000 x 329/365 = £16,225)	8,113	8,112	-	16,225
1/3/97 - 5/4/97				
(£18,000 x 36/365 = £1,775)	592	592	591	1,775
Totals	8,705	8,704	591	18,000
1997/98				
Smith, Jones (y/e 31/12/97)				
1/1/97 - 28/2/97				
(£24,000 x 59/365 = £3,879)	1,940	1,939	-	3,879
1/3/97 - 31/12/97				
(£24,000 x 306/365 = £20,121)	6,707	6,707	-	13,414
c/f	8,647	8,646	-	17,293

	Smith	*Jones*	*Brown*	*Total*
	£	£	£	£
1997/98				
b/f	8,647	8,646	-	17,293
Brown (1/3/97 to 28/2/98)				
1/3/97 - 31/12/97				
(1/3 x £24,000 x 306/365)	-	-	6,707	6,707
1/1/98 - 28/2/98				
(1/3 x £27,000 x 59/365)	-	-	1,455	1,455
Totals	8,647	8,646	8,162	25,455

Notes :

(i) Smith and Jones have been in business for many years and are therefore well outside the scope of the commencement rules. They are assessed on the current year basis in 1997/98 and beyond.

(ii) Brown began trading on 1 March 1997. The basis period for 1997/98 if the new rules applied throughout would be the first 12 months i.e. 1 March 1997 to 28 February 1998, so this is the basis period used for Brown. Brown's basis period for 1998/99 will be the year to 31/12/98.

(iii) The partners are entitled to transitional overlap relief relating to the period from 1 January 1997 to 5 April 1997. This is calculated as follows :

	Smith	*Jones*	*Brown*
	£	£	£
1/1/97 - 28/2/97			
(£24,000 x 59/365 = £3,875)	1,940	1,939	-
1/3/97 - 5/4/97			
(£24,000 x 36/365 = £2,367)	789	789	789
Totals	2,729	2,728	789

(iv) Brown has overlap profits relating to the period from 1 January 1998 to 28 February 1998 of £1,455.

Summary

- Under the new partnership rules, Schedule D Case I assessments are raised on each partner individually and each partner is solely responsible for his or her tax liability.
- The trading income of a new partnership (and of an old partnership as from 1997/98) is allocated between the partners according to the profit-sharing agreement for the accounting period in which the income arises. Notional profits and losses allocated to a partner are redistributed among the remaining partners.
- The effect of the new partnership rules is that each partner is treated as a sole trader who begins trading when joining the partnership, has the same accounting dates as the partnership and ceases trading when leaving the partnership.
- The tax treatment of the non-trading income of a new partnership (and of an old partnership as from 1997/98) depends upon whether or not the partnership also has trading income and whether or not the non-trading income is taxed at source.
- Under the old partnership rules, a Schedule D Case I assessment was raised at the partnership level and the partners shared joint and several responsibility for the partnership tax liability.
- The trading income of an old partnership prior to 1997/98 was allocated between the partners according to the profit-sharing agreement for the tax year in which the income was assessed.
- A change in the composition of an old partnership prior to 1997/98 was treated as a cessation followed by a commencement (with special commencement rules if this occurred before 6 April 1994) unless an election was made for the continuation basis.
- If an old partnership incurred an adjusted loss prior to 1997/98, the way in which this loss was allocated between the partners depended upon the form of loss relief chosen by each partner.

Exercises

12.1 Nickleby, Copperfield and Drood began trading as equal partners on 1 January 1995, making up accounts to 31 December each year. As from 1 April 1997 they agreed to share profits in the ratio 1:2:2. The adjusted profit for the year to 31 December 1997 is £18,250. Show how this profit is allocated between the partners.

12.2 Pickwick, Snodgrass and Tupman have been in partnership since 1 April 1995, making up accounts to 31 March annually. Each partner receives 6% interest on fixed capital, Pickwick and Tupman each receive an annual salary of £8,000 and remaining profits are divided equally. Fixed capitals are Pickwick £12,000, Snodgrass £20,000 and Tupman £10,000. The adjusted trading profit for the year to 31 March 1998 is £14,500. Show how this profit is allocated between the partners.

12.3 Dodson and Fogg began trading in equal partnership on 1 July 1994. On 1 July 1995, they admitted Jackson as a partner and agreed to share profits in the ratio 5:4:1. The adjusted profits of the partnership are :

	£
year to 30 June 1995	17,000
year to 30 June 1996	22,000
year to 30 June 1997	29,000

Compute each partner's Schedule D Case I assessment for 1994/95 through to 1997/98.

12.4 Wardle, Jingle and Trotter began trading on 1 October 1995, preparing accounts to 30 September each year and sharing profits in the ratio 7:2:1. Results for the first two years of trading are as follows :

	y/e 30/9/96	*y/e 30/9/97*
	£	£
Trading profit	23,490	27,310
Interest received gross	2,000	2,200
Interest received net (net amount received)	1,000	1,088

(a) Compute each partner's Schedule D Case I assessment for 1995/96, 1996/97 and 1997/98.

(b) Compute each partner's Schedule D Case III assessment for 1995/96, 1996/97 and 1997/98.

(c) Compute the gross amount of taxed interest assessed on each partner in 1996/97.

***12.5** Cluppins and Raddle form a partnership on 1 November 1994, preparing accounts to 31 May each year. Bardell is admitted as a partner on 1 January 1996. Cluppins leaves the partnership on 28 February 1997 and Winkle is admitted as a partner on 1 March 1997.

Profits and losses are shared as follows :

Cluppins and Raddle	1:2
Cluppins, Raddle and Bardell	7:8:5
Raddle, Bardell and Winkle	4:3:1

Adjusted trading profits are :

	£
1 November 1994 to 31 May 1995	6,000
year to 31 May 1996	12,000
year to 31 May 1997	3,000
year to 31 May 1998	8,000

Calculate each partner's Schedule D Case I assessments for 1994/95 through to 1998/99, identifying any overlap periods and profits.

***12.6** Sawyer and Allen have been in partnership for many years, sharing profits equally. On 1 January 1997 they admit Pell as a partner and agree to share profits in the ratio 3:2:1. An election is made for the continuation basis to apply. Adjusted trading profits are as follows :

	£
year to 30 September 1994	29,500
year to 30 September 1995	17,700
year to 30 September 1996	14,800
year to 30 September 1997	24,240
year to 30 September 1998	36,360

Calculate each partner's Schedule D Case I assessments for 1995/96 to 1997/98 inclusive.

Chapter 13

Pension schemes

Introduction

The most tax-efficient way of providing for a retirement pension is to make contributions into an approved pension scheme. Employees may join their employer's pension scheme or take out a personal pension plan. Self-employed people may have a personal pension plan or a retirement annuity contract. The purpose of this chapter is to describe the tax reliefs available in relation to each of these types of pension scheme.

Occupational pension schemes

An occupational pension scheme (or superannuation scheme) is a pension scheme set up by an employer for the benefit of employees. Employees normally contribute a percentage of their earnings each week or month into the scheme (though some employers operate non-contributory schemes) and the employer also makes contributions. In order for such a scheme to be "approved" by the Inland Revenue it is necessary that the following main conditions are satisfied :

(a) The sole purpose of the scheme must be to provide benefits on retirement (or death) to employees (or their widows, widowers and dependants).

(b) The employer must make contributions into the scheme.

(c) Any contributions made by employees must be non-returnable.

(d) Employees' pensions must start at some time between the ages of 60 and 75, with no distinction made between men and women.

(e) The maximum pension payable to an employee under the terms of the scheme must not exceed the product of :

   (i) the number of years of service worked by the employee (up to a maximum of 40 years), and

(ii) 1/60th of the employee's "final remuneration" (i.e. the average annual remuneration of the employee over the final 3 years of service),

giving a maximum pension of 2/3rds of the employee's final remuneration.

(f) A lump sum may be payable on retirement of no greater than 3/80th of final remuneration for each year of service up to 40 years, giving a maximum lump sum of 1.5 x final remuneration.

If a scheme satisfies these criteria then :

(a) Any contributions made by an employee (up to a maximum of 15% of remuneration) are allowable against the employee's income from employment assessed under Schedule E (see Chapter 7).

(b) The contributions actually paid by the employer during an accounting period are allowable when computing the employer's profit assessed to income tax under Schedule D Case I or II (see Chapter 8) or to corporation tax (see Chapter 23).

(c) The employer's contributions on behalf of an employee are not treated as part of the employee's emoluments.

(d) Subject to further conditions, the scheme may enable employees to be "contracted-out" of the State Earnings-Related Pension Scheme (SERPS). In this case, both the employee's and the employer's National Insurance contributions are reduced (see Chapter 15).

For approved schemes established after 13 March 1989, or for employees joining older schemes on or after 1 June 1989, the employee's contributions and benefits are restricted by reference to an "earnings cap" of (for 1997/98) £84,000 per annum. Employees' contributions and benefits are calculated according to their actual remuneration or the earnings cap, whichever is the lower.

EXAMPLE 1

Gordon joined his employer's approved occupational pension scheme in 1990. Calculate the maximum pension contributions which he could make in 1997/98 if his earnings for the year were :

(a) £50,000

(b) £90,000.

SOLUTION

(a) Gordon could contribute no more than 15% of £50,000 = £7,500.

(b) Gordon could contribute no more than 15% of £84,000 = £12,600.

Retirement annuities and personal pensions

Subject to certain restrictions which are explained later in this chapter, tax relief is available in respect of premiums paid by an individual in relation to :

(a) a retirement annuity contract, or

(b) a personal pension plan.

Retirement annuity contracts

Retirement annuities were for many years the main means by which the self-employed and certain employees were able to provide for their retirement. The following persons were eligible to take out a retirement annuity contract :

(a) the self-employed

(b) employees in non-pensionable employment

(c) employees who chose to opt out of their employer's occupational pension scheme (if this was permitted by the employer).

Individuals taking out a retirement annuity contract agreed to pay regular premiums in order to provide for a pension (which would commence at some time between the ages of 60 and 75) and the premiums paid attracted tax relief.

With effect from 1 July 1988 (the date on which personal pension plans were introduced) no new retirement annuity contracts can be taken out. However, there are many such contracts still in existence which were taken out on or before 30 June 1988 and the premiums paid in relation to such contracts continue to attract tax relief.

Personal pension plans

Personal pension plans were introduced on 1 July 1988 and are similar in many ways to retirement annuities. As before, premiums are paid by the self-employed or by employees in order to provide for a pension in later life and these premiums attract tax relief. The main differences between retirement annuities and personal pension plans are as follows :

(a) Benefits under a personal pension plan may be taken by the individual at any time from the age of 50.

(b) Employees are now legally entitled to opt out of their employer's occupational scheme if they so wish (whether or not the employer approves) and take out a personal pension plan instead.

(c) If a personal pension plan is taken out by an employee, the employer may also make contributions to the plan and these contributions do not rank as part of the employee's taxable emoluments. (It was not possible for employers to make contributions towards an employee's retirement annuity).

Relief for premiums paid

If a taxpayer pays premiums under an approved retirement annuity contract or personal pension plan, then :

(a) The premiums paid during a tax year are allowed against the taxpayer's "net relevant earnings" (see below) for that year.

(b) Self-employed taxpayers pay their premiums gross (whether for a retirement annuity or a personal pension) and obtain tax relief by the premiums being deducted in their Schedule D Case I or II assessment.

(c) Employees pay retirement annuity premiums gross and generally obtain tax relief by means of an adjustment to their tax code.

(d) Employees pay personal pension premiums net of basic rate tax. Further relief for employees who are higher rate taxpayers is given by adjusting the employee's tax code or by making a tax rebate at the end of the year. The basic rate tax relief taken at source is not clawed back from lower-rate taxpayers or non-taxpayers.

Net relevant earnings

An employee's "net relevant earnings" (NRE) for a tax year are equal to the employee's earnings from non-pensionable employment for that year, including benefits in kind, less allowable expenses.

A self-employed taxpayer's net relevant earnings for a tax year are defined as the taxpayer's earnings from self-employment for that year as assessed under Schedule D Case I or II (net of capital allowances), plus any income arising from furnished holiday lettings (see Chapter 5), and less :

(a) loss reliefs claimed in the year and set against trading income

(b) trade charges paid in the year, to the extent that they cannot be set against the taxpayer's unearned income. An example of a trade charge would be patent royalties paid to an inventor by a self-employed person.

If, in a given tax year, a trading loss is relieved against non-trading income (e.g. by virtue of a Section 380 claim) then the amount relieved against non-trading income has no effect on that year's NRE but reduces the NRE of the following year instead. If the following year's earnings are insufficient to absorb the whole of the loss, any balance is carried forward to subsequent years.

EXAMPLE 2

Wesley is self-employed. His tax-adjusted profit assessed in 1997/98 is £32,700 (net of capital allowances of £2,300). He has losses brought forward under Section 385 of £15,200 and pays trade charges during the year amounting to £500. His only other income for 1997/98 is £200 of interest arising on a National Savings Bank investment account. Calculate his net relevant earnings for 1997/98.

SOLUTION

	£	£
Profits assessed under Sch. D Case I or II		32,700
Less : Loss relief	15,200	
Excess of trade charges over unearned income (£500 - £200)	300	15,500
Net relevant earnings for 1997/98		17,200

Maximum premiums allowable

There is an upper limit on the amount of personal pension or retirement annuity premiums which can attract tax relief in a given tax year. This upper limit depends upon the age of the taxpayer at the start of the tax year and is expressed as a percentage of NRE. The maximum allowable percentages are as follows :

Age at start of tax year	*Personal Pensions*	*Retirement Annuities*
Up to 35	17.5%	17.5%
36-45	20%	17.5%
46-50	25%	17.5%
51-55	30%	20%
56-60	35%	22.5%
61 or more	40%	27.5%

In the case of personal pension plans, the maximum NRE in 1997/98 to which the appropriate percentage can be applied is £84,000 (the "earnings cap"). There is no such maximum in the case of retirement annuity contracts.

EXAMPLE 3

Calculate the maximum relief available to each of the following taxpayers in respect of their retirement annuity or personal pension premiums in 1997/98 :

(a) Alana was born on 4 May 1961. She has a personal pension plan and her net relevant earnings for 1997/98 are £27,000.

(b) Bruce was born on 14 August 1939. He has a retirement annuity contract and his net relevant earnings for 1997/98 are £52,000.

(c) Charlotte was born on 24 December 1935. She has a personal pension plan and her net relevant earnings for 1997/98 are £85,000.

(d) Diane was born on 12 January 1945. She has a retirement annuity contract and her net relevant earnings for 1997/98 are £100,000.

SOLUTION

(a) Alana is aged 35 at the start of tax year 1997/98. The maximum relief to which she is entitled is £4,725 (17.5% of £27,000).

(b) Bruce is aged 57 at the start of tax year 1997/98. The maximum relief to which he is entitled is £11,700 (22.5% of £52,000).

(c) Charlotte is aged 61 at the start of tax year 1997/98. Her net relevant earnings exceed the earnings cap, so the maximum relief to which she is entitled is £33,600 (40% of £84,000).

(d) Diane is aged 52 at the start of tax year 1997/98. The earnings cap does not apply to retirement annuities so the maximum relief to which she is entitled is £20,000 (20% of £100,000).

Excess premiums carried back

If the retirement annuity or personal pension premiums paid by a taxpayer exceed the allowable maximum for the year, the excess premiums cannot be relieved in that year. However, the taxpayer may elect that excess premiums should be treated as if they had been paid in the previous tax year, or (if there are no net relevant earnings in that year) in the year before that. This "carry-back" election may be of use if the net relevant earnings of the previous tax year were higher than those of the current year and can absorb the current year's excess premiums.

EXAMPLE 4

Jill is self-employed, 29 years old and a member of a personal pension scheme into which she pays £1,000 per annum. Her net relevant earnings for 1996/97 were £12,400 but 1997/98 is a poor year and her net relevant earnings for that year are only £5,000. Can she use the carry-back election to obtain relief on her 1997/98 personal pension premiums ?

SOLUTION

In 1996/97 Jill's maximum allowable premiums were £2,170 (17.5% of £12,400) and so her premiums paid in that year of only £1,000 were allowable in full.

But in 1997/98 her maximum allowable premiums drop to only £875 (17.5% of £5,000) and she has excess premiums of £125, which cannot be relieved in 1997/98. However, she can elect to treat the £125 as if it had been paid in 1996/97. This would give relief on £1,125 in 1996/97 (still within the maximum allowable for that year) and on £875 in 1997/98. In this way tax relief can be obtained on the entire £2,000 of premiums paid in 1996/97 and 1997/98.

In fact, all or part of *any* premium paid in a year (not just excess premiums) can be carried back in this way and the taxpayer would obviously elect to do this if a tax saving would result (e.g. if the taxpayer's marginal rate of tax was higher in the previous tax year than the current year).

The election to carry premiums back must be made by 31 January following the end of the tax year in which the premiums were paid.

EXAMPLE 5

Eric was born on 1 January 1964. He has net relevant earnings of £50,000 in 1996/97 and £18,000 in 1997/98. He pays £1,800 per annum into a personal pension plan. Show the alternative ways in which tax relief may be given on the premiums paid in 1996/97 and 1997/98.

SOLUTION

Eric's allowable percentage in both 1996/97 and 1997/98 is 17.5%. The maximum premiums allowable are therefore £8,750 in 1996/97 (17.5% of £50,000) and £3,150 in 1997/98 (17.5% of £18,000). The premiums of £1,800 paid in each year are beneath these maxima, so Eric could relieve each year's premiums in full against that year's NRE.

However, an alternative is to elect that the 1997/98 premiums should be treated as if they were paid in 1996/97 and to offset both the 1996/97 premiums and the 1997/98 premiums against the NRE of 1996/97. Since Eric is presumably a 40% taxpayer in 1996/97 (but not in 1997/98) this would provide a greater tax saving than relieving each year's premiums against the NRE of the year in which the premiums were paid.

Unused relief carried forward

If the retirement annuity or personal pension premiums paid by a taxpayer are less than the maximum allowed for the year, then the premiums paid in the year are allowed in full and there is "unused relief" equal to the difference between the premiums actually paid and the maximum premiums that would have been allowed.

EXAMPLE 6

Freda is aged 30 and has net relevant earnings in 1997/98 of £15,000. She belongs to an approved personal pension scheme. Calculate the amount of Freda's unused relief in 1997/98 if the premiums paid in the year are :

(a) £1,500

(b) £2,625

(c) £3,000.

SOLUTION

Freda's allowable percentage in 1997/98 is 17.5%. The maximum premiums allowable in 1997/98 are therefore £2,625 (17.5% of £15,000).

(a) If Freda pays premiums of £1,500 then the entire £1,500 is allowable for tax purposes and she has unused relief of £1,125 (£2,625 - £1,500).

(b) If Freda pays premiums of £2,625 then she has paid precisely the maximum amount allowed. The entire £2,625 is allowable for tax purposes and she has no unused relief.

(c) If Freda pays premiums of £3,000 then she has paid more than the allowable maximum. Only £2,625 is allowable and she has no unused relief for the year. (She may elect to carry back the excess premiums of £375 to 1996/97).

Unused relief represents a wasted opportunity to obtain tax relief but it may not be lost irretrievably. Unused relief can be carried forward for up to 6 tax years and used to relieve excess premiums paid during those 6 years. It should be noted that :

(a) unused relief brought forward from previous years can only be used if the current year's maximum relief has already been used in full, and

(b) unused relief is used on a first-in, first-out basis i.e. unused relief brought forward from earlier years in used in preference to unused relief brought forward from later years.

EXAMPLE 7

Sharon is 32 years old and pays personal pension premiums of £1,900 in 1997/98. Her net relevant earnings for the year are £9,600. She has unused relief of £250 brought forward from 1991/92 and £400 brought forward from 1994/95. Compute the allowable premiums in 1997/98.

SOLUTION

Sharon's maximum allowable premiums would normally be £1,680 (17.5% of £9,600). Since the premiums paid exceed this maximum by £220 she would normally have excess premiums of £220 which would not attract tax relief (unless they could be carried back to the previous year).

However, £220 of the unused relief brought forward from 1991/92 (used in preference to the more recent unused relief from 1994/95) may be used to relieve this shortfall, so ensuring that the full £1,900 is allowed in 1997/98.

The remaining £30 of the 1991/92 unused relief is now too old to carry forward to 1998/99 and the opportunity to use this relief is lost forever. The £400 of unused relief arising in 1994/95 may carried forward for 3 further years before being lost.

Choice between carry-back and carry-forward

Sometimes, a taxpayer is confronted with a choice between :

(a) carrying excess premiums back to the previous year, or

(b) relieving excess premiums with unused relief brought forward from the previous 6 years.

In this situation it is necessary to consider the consequences of each choice and to select the most tax-effective alternative.

EXAMPLE 8

Stuart is single, aged 40 and has net relevant earnings of £36,000 in 1996/97 (he has no other income). He pays personal pension premiums of £2,350 in the year and he has no unused relief brought forward from previous years.

(a) How much unused relief does Stuart have in 1996/97 ?

(b) If his net relevant earnings for 1997/98 decrease to £6,700 and the premiums paid remain the same as in 1996/97, calculate his allowable premiums in that year (ignore for a moment the possibility of carrying back premiums from 1997/98 to 1996/97).

(c) Would the carry-back provisions described earlier be of any use to Stuart ?

SOLUTION

(a) Maximum allowable premiums for a taxpayer of Stuart's age are 20% of NRE i.e. £7,200. He has paid only £2,350 in 1996/97, so the full £2,350 is allowable and there is unused relief of £4,850. This unused relief may be carried forward for up to 6 tax years (i.e. up to and including 2002/03) and used to relieve excess premiums paid in those 6 years.

(b) 20% of Stuart's NRE in 1997/98 amounts to only £1,340, leaving excess premiums of £1,010. However, he has unused relief of £4,850 to bring forward from 1996/97 so £1,010 of this can be used to relieve the excess premiums. The remainder of the unused relief (£3,840) can be carried forward for a further 5 years. The situation in 1996/97 and 1997/98 is as follows :

	1996/97	*1997/98*
NRE	36,000	6,700
Less : allowable premiums	2,350	2,350
Taxable earnings	33,650	4,350

(c) As an alternative to carrying forward unused relief from 1996/97 and using it to relieve excess premiums paid in 1997/98, Stuart could elect to treat £1,010 of his premiums paid in 1997/98 as if they had been paid in 1996/97. If he did this, the situation would be as follows :

	1996/97	*1997/98*
NRE	36,000	6,700
Less : allowable premiums	3,360	1,340
Taxable earnings	32,640	5,360

As before, the total of the taxable earnings in the two years is £38,000. However, the way in which the £38,000 is split between the two years is different and, in particular, the carry-back alternative reduces Stuart's taxable earnings in 1996/97, a year in which he is probably a higher-rate taxpayer. In fact it would be beneficial for Stuart to carry back the whole of the £2,350 paid in 1997/98, not just the excess premium of £1,010.

Additional voluntary contributions

Employees who already belong to an occupational pension scheme can obtain tax relief on contributions made to a form of personal pension scheme known as a "free standing additional voluntary contributions" (FSAVC) scheme. An employee would contribute to such a scheme in order to provide for an extra pension, additional to the pension payable from the employer's scheme.

Contributions are limited to a maximum of 15% of earnings up to the earnings cap (£84,000 for 1997/98), less any contributions made to the occupational pension scheme.

EXAMPLE 9

Darren belongs to his employer's superannuation scheme and contributes 6% of his gross pay into the scheme each month. In 1997/98 his total gross pay was £12,500. Calculate the maximum amount which Darren could pay into an FSAVC scheme in 1997/98 if he so wished.

SOLUTION

Darren has contributed 6% of his earnings to the occupational scheme and may therefore contribute a further 9% to an FSAVC scheme. His maximum contributions in 1997/98 are £1,125 (9% of £12,500).

Summary

- Contributions of up to 15% of earnings made by an employee to an approved occupational pension scheme are allowable under Schedule E.

- Subject to certain conditions, tax relief is available on premiums paid by the self-employed and by certain employees in order to secure a retirement annuity or personal pension. The maximum allowable premium in any tax year depends upon the taxpayer's age at the start of the year and earnings during the year.
- A taxpayer may elect that retirement annuity or personal pension premiums paid in a tax year should be treated as if paid in the previous year.
- If retirement annuity or personal pension premiums paid in a tax year are less than the maximum amount that could have been relieved, the unused relief may be carried forward and used to relieve excess premiums for up to 6 years.
- An employee belonging to an occupational pension scheme may obtain tax relief on premiums paid to a free standing additional voluntary contributions scheme.

Exercises

13.1 List the main conditions which must be satisfied in order for an occupational pension scheme to be approved by the Inland Revenue and explain the taxation consequences of a scheme being approved.

13.2 Calculate the maximum contribution which could be made to an occupational pension scheme in 1997/98 by an employee with remuneration in the year of :

(a) £20,000

(b) £95,000.

13.3 Explain the meaning of the term "net relevant earnings" for a self-employed person and for an employee.

13.4 Karen is self-employed and was born on 7 April 1936. Her 1997/98 Schedule D Case I assessment is £22,450 (net of capital allowances of £800). She has losses brought forward under Section 385 of £1,200 and trade charges for the year of £250. She has no other income. Calculate the maximum allowable personal pension premium which Karen could pay in 1997/98.

13.5 Damon is self-employed and was born on 10 July 1960. He has net relevant earnings and personal pension premiums as follows :

	NRE	*Premiums paid*
1995/96	17,200	2,500
1996/97	18,400	2,600
1997/98	5,600	2,600

He has unused relief brought forward from 1990/91 of £400. Assuming that no carry-back elections are made, show how relief would be given for Damon's personal pension premiums.

***13.6** Irma is self-employed and single. She was born in 1939. The following information relates to 1997/98 :

(a) Irma's profits assessed under Schedule D Case I (net of capital allowances) are £21,700. She has no other income.

(b) She pays a trade charge on income of £300.

(c) She pays personal pension premiums of £7,521 and has unused relief brought forward from 1991/92 of £220.

Calculate Irma's 1997/98 income tax liability.

***13.7** Tony is self-employed, aged 31 and has net relevant earnings of £67,200 in 1996/97 and £24,400 in 1997/98. He pays an annual premium of £5,000 into a personal pension scheme. Show how relief would be given for the personal pension premiums in 1996/97 and 1997/98 if :

(a) Tony elects to carry back the 1997/98 premiums to 1996/97, or

(b) Tony does not make a carry-back election.

Which of these alternatives is preferable ?

Chapter 14

Interest and penalties

Introduction

Interest is charged on income tax which is paid late. Conversely, interest may be added to repayments of income tax. The main purpose of this chapter is to describe the circumstances in which a taxpayer is charged or paid interest and to explain how the amount of interest is calculated. This chapter also considers various financial penalties to which a taxpayer may become liable as a consequence of non-compliance with the tax law.

The introduction of the Self Assessment system in 1996/97 (see Chapter 1) made extensive changes to the dates on which income tax is due for payment and to the way in which interest and penalties are calculated. This chapter describes only the new system. The old (pre-Self Assessment) system is no longer in use and is not considered here.

Payment of income tax

For tax year 1996/97 and subsequent years, income tax which is not deducted at source or collected via the PAYE system is payable as follows :

(a) The taxpayer's liability in relation to all Schedules and Cases of income tax is aggregated into a single tax liability.

(b) Payments on account of this liability (POA's) are due on 31 January in the tax year and on 31 July following the end of the tax year. For example, the POA's for 1997/98 are due on 31 January 1998 and 31 July 1998. Each POA is normally equal to 50% of the taxpayer's income tax liability for the previous year (less any tax paid by deduction at source). For this purpose, the term "deduction at source" includes tax paid via the PAYE system as well as tax deducted at source from bank interest, building society interest, dividends etc. Note that :

(i) POA's are not required at all if the taxpayer's total income tax liability for the preceding year (less tax deducted at source) was beneath a specified "de minimis" limit, currently set at £500.

(ii) POA's are also not required if more than 80% of the taxpayer's income tax liability for the previous year was satisfied by deduction of tax at source.

(iii) The taxpayer may make a claim to reduce or cancel POA's by writing to the Inland Revenue stating the grounds for the claim. Suitable grounds would be the taxpayer's belief that the income tax liability for the year in question will be less than in the previous year. The Inland Revenue cannot reject such a claim but there are penalties for making such a claim fraudulently or negligently (see below).

(c) A balancing payment (or repayment) is due on 31 January following the end of the tax year. For example, the balancing payment for 1997/98 is due on 31 January 1999. But note that :

(i) If a tax return is issued late (i.e. after 31 October following the end of the tax year to which it relates) and this has not been caused by the taxpayer's failure to notify his or her chargeability to tax, the balancing payment is due 3 months after the issue date of the return.

(ii) If a self-assessment is amended (either by the taxpayer or by the Inland Revenue) or if a discovery assessment is raised, any additional tax payable is due 30 days after the date of its notification to the taxpayer or on 31 January following the end of the tax year, whichever is the later.

It is important to note that POA's and balancing payments are automatically payable on the due dates and that interest and surcharges (see below) are charged in the case of late payment. At least once per year (usually in November or December) taxpayers are sent a statement showing the state of their account with the Inland Revenue and informing them of the payments which (according to Inland Revenue calculations) are due on the following 31 January and 31 July.

EXAMPLE 1

Warren's income tax liability for 1996/97 was £17,200, of which £14,500 was paid by deduction at source. His liability for 1997/98 is £19,300, of which £16,100 is paid by deduction at source. State the dates on which Warren is required to pay his 1997/98 income tax and compute the amount payable on each date.

SOLUTION

Over 80% of Warren's income tax liability for 1996/97 was paid by deduction at source and therefore no POA's are required for 1997/98. His liability of £3,200 (£19,300 - £16,100) is payable on 31 January 1999.

EXAMPLE 2

In 1996/97, Barbara paid income tax of £4,000 by deduction at source and £22,000 by self-assessment. Her total 1997/98 income tax liability is £34,000, of which £5,000 is paid by deduction at source. State the dates on which Barbara is required to pay her 1997/98 income tax and compute the amount payable on each date.

SOLUTION

(i) 31 January 1998, POA of £11,000 (50% of 1996/97 tax, excluding tax paid at source)

(ii) 31 July 1998, POA of £11,000

(iii) 31 January 1999, balancing payment of £7,000 (£34,000 - £5,000 - POA's £22,000).

Surcharges on income tax paid late

In addition to any interest due on income tax paid late (see below), the taxpayer may also be required to pay a "surcharge". The surcharges scheme operates as follows :

(a) If all or part of a balancing payment remains unpaid more than 28 days after the due date, a surcharge arises equal to 5% of the tax unpaid.

(b) If all or part of any additional tax payable because a self-assessment has been amended (or because a discovery assessment has been raised) remains unpaid more than 28 days after the due date, a surcharge arises equal to 5% of the tax unpaid.

(c) Any tax that remains unpaid more than 6 months after the due date is subject to a further 5% surcharge.

(d) Surcharges are payable 30 days after the date on which they are imposed.

The surcharges scheme does not apply to POA's. The scheme does apply, however, to any assessments for 1995/96 or earlier years which are raised on or after 6 April 1998.

EXAMPLE 3

Continuing the above example, Barbara paid income tax for 1997/98 as follows :

	£
31 January 1998	11,000
1 September 1998	11,000
31 January 1999	6,000
1 September 1999	1,000

Compute the surcharges (if any) which would be imposed.

SOLUTION

(i) The first POA is paid in full and on time.

(ii) The second POA is paid in full but 32 days late. However, late POA's do not attract surcharges.

(iii) £1,000 of the balancing payment is paid over 6 months late. A first surcharge of £50 (£1,000 x 5%) will be imposed on 1 March 1999 (payable 31 March 1999) and a further surcharge of £50 will be imposed on 1 August 1999 (payable 31 August 1999).

Interest on income tax

Under the Self Assessment system, interest is charged on all late payments of income tax, surcharges and penalties. Conversely, interest is paid to the taxpayer when repayments of overpaid tax are made.

Interest on overdue income tax

Interest charged on overdue income tax is calculated as follows :

(a) In the case of late POA's and balancing payments, interest runs from the due date of payment up to the date on which the tax is actually paid.

(b) In the case of discovery assessments and amendments to self-assessments, interest normally runs from the *annual filing date* for the relevant tax year (i.e. 31 January following the tax year) even though the tax itself might not be due for payment until a later date.

(c) Interest on a surcharge runs from the due date of payment of the surcharge (i.e. 30 days after its imposition).

(d) If a taxpayer submits a tax return by the 30 September deadline (see Chapter 1) and asks the Inland Revenue to calculate the tax due, but the Inland Revenue fail to issue a statement of account in time for the first POA to be made on 31 January, then interest on this POA starts to run 30 days after the issue date of the statement of account.

These interest rules also apply to any assessments for 1995/96 or earlier years which are raised on or after 6 April 1998.

EXAMPLE 4

Again continuing the above example, calculate the total interest payable by Barbara for 1997/98, assuming that the two surcharges are both paid on 29 September 1999 and that interest is charged at 8.5% per annum.

SOLUTION

(i) Interest on the second POA is £81.97 (£11,000 x 8.5% x 32/365).

(ii) Interest on the final £1,000 of the balancing payment (paid 213 days late) is £49.60 (£1,000 x 8.5% x 213/365).

(iii) Interest on the first surcharge (paid 182 days late) is £2.12 (£50 x 8.5% x 182/365).

(iv) Interest on the second surcharge (paid 29 days late) is £0.34 (£50 x 8.5% x 29/365).

Total interest due is £134.03 (£81.97 + £49.60 + £2.12 + £0.34).

Interest on overpaid income tax

Repayments of overpaid income tax attract interest, but this interest is calculated at a lower rate than the rate charged on overdue income tax. Interest on overpaid income tax (sometimes referred to as "repayment supplement") usually runs from the date on which the tax was originally paid up to the date on which it is repaid to the taxpayer.

However, if a repayment is caused by the carry back of a relief to an earlier year (e.g. by carrying back trading losses or personal pension premiums) the repayment is regarded as a repayment of tax for the year in which the claim is established (i.e. the year in which the loss occurs or in which the premiums are paid). Interest will arise in connection with a repayment of this type only if the tax concerned is repaid to the taxpayer later than 31 January following the end of the tax year in which the claim is established.

Penalties

A taxpayer who fails to comply with statutory requirements may become liable to a number of financial penalties, the most important of which are listed below. Some of these penalties are fixed in amount but, in most cases, the law specifies only a *maximum* amount for the penalty and the Board of Inland Revenue has the power to "mitigate" (i.e. reduce) the amount charged if it sees fit to do so. Whether or not a penalty is mitigated will usually depend upon the seriousness of the taxpayer's offence and the degree to which the taxpayer has co-operated with the Inland Revenue.

(a) **Failure to notify chargeability to tax**. An individual must notify the Inland Revenue if he or she is liable to tax for a tax year, even if a return has not been issued for that year. Failure to do so within 6 months of the end of the tax year could render the individual liable to a maximum penalty equal in amount to the tax remaining unpaid on 31 January following the end of the tax year.

(b) **Late submission of a tax return**. A £100 fixed penalty is imposed if a tax return is submitted late and a further £100 fixed penalty is imposed if the return is more than 6 months late. If the return is more than 12 months late, an additional penalty may be imposed of up to 100% of the tax liability for the year.

Furthermore, the General or Special Commissioners may direct that a penalty of up to £60 per day should be imposed, running from the date of the Commissioners' direction to the date on which the tax return is finally submitted.

(c) **Submission of an incorrect tax return**. If a taxpayer, either negligently or fraudulently, submits an incorrect tax return (or submits incorrect information in support of a tax return) a penalty may be imposed of up to 100% of the amount of tax underpaid as a consequence of the incorrect return.

(d) **Fraud or negligence when claiming reduced POA's**. A taxpayer who makes a claim for reduced POA's and does so fraudulently or negligently may be subject to a maximum penalty equal to the difference between the POA's actually made and the POA's that would have been made if the claim had not been made.

(e) **Failure to keep required records**. A taxpayer who fails to maintain or retain adequate records in support of the year's tax return may be subject to a penalty of up to £3,000.

In every case, the penalty is in addition both to the tax itself and to any surcharges or interest charged in relation to that tax.

Summary

- The introduction of Self Assessment has made extensive changes to the dates on which tax is payable and to the system for calculating interest and penalties.
- Under the Self Assessment system, income tax not collected at source or via the PAYE system is usually payable by means of two payments on account, followed by a balancing payment.
- Surcharges may be levied if a balancing payment is paid late and interest is payable on any tax paid late. Interest usually runs from the due date of payment up the actual date of payment.
- Repayments of overpaid tax also attract interest, usually running from the date on which the tax was paid up to the date of repayment.
- Financial penalties may be imposed for various breaches of the tax law.

Exercises

14.1 For each of the following taxpayers, state the dates on which the taxpayer is due to pay his or her 1997/98 income tax and calculate the amount payable on each date.

(a) Guy's 1996/97 income tax liability was £1,600, of which £1,150 was paid via the PAYE system and £50 was deducted at source from investment income. His 1997/98 liability is £1,750, of which £1,250 is paid via PAYE and £60 is deducted at source.

(b) Marie's 1996/97 income tax liability was £6,730, of which £4,370 was paid via PAYE and £20 was deducted at source. Her 1997/98 liability is £6,580, of which £4,810 is paid via PAYE and £35 is deducted at source.

(c) Majid's 1996/97 income tax liability was £14,850, of which £11,990 was paid via PAYE and £110 was deducted at source. His 1997/98 liability is £16,110, of which £12,370 is paid via PAYE and £140 is deducted at source.

14.2 Dorothy's 1996/97 income tax liability was £30,000, of which £6,000 was deducted at source. Her liability for 1997/98 is £35,000, of which £7,000 is deducted at source. She made a first POA for 1997/98 on 27 February 1998 and a second POA on 12 September 1998. She also made a balancing payment for the year on 21 February 1999. All of her payments were for the correct amount.

(a) Calculate the amount of any surcharges payable by Dorothy in relation to 1997/98.

(b) Assuming an interest rate of 8.5% per annum, calculate the amount of any interest payable by Dorothy in relation to 1997/98.

14.3 Jabran did not receive a tax return for 1997/98 but he was aware that he had income which had not been assessed to tax. He notified the Inland Revenue of this fact on 2 October 1998 and a return was issued to him on 15 November 1998. He completed the return and sent it back with the necessary payment on 7 April 1999.

Explain the penalties, surcharges and interest which Jabran might be required to pay.

***14.4** Frances paid income tax of £43,000 in 1996/97, of which £19,000 was deducted at source. Her liability for 1997/98 is £63,000, of which £21,000 is deducted at source. Her payments of income tax for 1997/98 are as follows :

	£
15 February 1998	12,000
14 September 1998	12,000
3 February 1999	14,000
15 December 1999	4,000

Calculate the surcharges and interest payable for the year, assuming that any surcharges are paid on 15 December 1999 and that interest is charged at 8.5% per annum.

Chapter 15

National Insurance contributions

Introduction

National Insurance contributions (NIC's) are payable by the self-employed, by employers and by employees. Contributions are collected by the Department of Social Security (or by the Inland Revenue acting on behalf of the DSS) and paid into a National Insurance Fund. This fund, supplemented by a grant from the Treasury, is then used to provide "contributory" social security benefits such as the state retirement pension. The purpose of this chapter is to explain the circumstances in which NIC's are payable and the way in which NIC's are calculated.

Class 1 National Insurance contributions

Class 1 NIC's are payable in relation to employees aged 16 or over. The employees themselves pay "primary" Class 1 NIC's whilst employers pay "secondary" Class 1 NIC's on their employees' behalf. Employees who continue to work after reaching pensionable age pay no further primary contributions but employers must still pay secondary contributions for such employees.

The amount of Class 1 NIC's payable in relation to an employee depend upon that employee's earnings. For this purpose, an employee's earnings consist of his or her gross pay (including any profit related pay) *before* deducting contributions made to an occupational pension scheme, charitable donations made under the terms of a payroll giving scheme or any expenses borne by the employee. An employee's earnings for this purpose do *not* include :

(a) tips received directly from customers

(b) personal incidental expenses paid by the employer, if exempt from Schedule E income tax (see Chapter 7)

(c) mileage allowances received (see Chapter 7) if calculated at a rate which is less than or equal to the FPCS rate for the first 4,000 miles driven, regardless of the number of miles actually driven by the employee (but any excess forms part of the employee's earnings chargeable to Class 1 NIC's)

(d) business expenses paid for by the employer or reimbursed by the employer.

Benefits in kind which are not convertible into money are not subject to Class 1 NIC's, but a Class 1A liability may arise in connection with a car provided for an employee's private use (see later in this chapter). If remuneration is paid in the form of non-cash assets such as gold bars, coffee beans, fine wines etc, then a liability to Class 1 NIC's arises if the assets can be turned into cash. Payments made in shares are also liable to Class 1 NIC's unless they consist of "own company" shares provided under an approved profit sharing scheme or share option scheme (see Chapter 7).

Contribution periods

The main principles of the Class 1 National Insurance system are as follows :

(a) Primary and secondary Class 1 NIC's are calculated according to an employee's earnings in a "contribution period". For those paid weekly, each week constitutes a contribution period and for those paid monthly, each month constitutes a contribution period (but see later in this chapter for special rules concerning company directors).

(b) The liability to Class 1 NIC's in a given contribution period is governed solely by the employee's earnings in that contribution period and is unaffected by earnings in other contribution periods. This is in contrast to the income tax PAYE system (see Chapter 7) which accumulates an employee's earnings over the year and calculates a tax liability each week or month based on the employee's total earnings for the tax year to date.

(c) If an employee has two or more employments in a contribution period then each employment is normally considered quite separately for the purposes of calculating the liability to Class 1 NIC's. Earnings from two or more employments are aggregated only if those employments are with the same employer or with associated employers.

(d) The rate at which Class 1 NIC's are calculated depends upon whether or not the employee is contracted out of the State Earnings Related Pension Scheme (SERPS). Those who are not contracted out of SERPS pay higher Class 1 NIC's in return for an earnings-related increase in some of their social security benefits (e.g. the retirement pension).

    Most contracted-out employees are members of their employer's contracted-out salary-related (COSR) occupational pension scheme. Others belong to contracted-out money-purchase (COMP) schemes or pay contributions into an appropriate personal pension scheme. The primary and secondary Class 1 NIC's payable in relation to a contracted-out employee depend upon the type of scheme to which the employee belongs. Only members of COSR schemes are considered here.

Primary Class 1 NIC's

The primary Class 1 NIC's payable by an employee in a contribution period are calculated as follows :

(a) The employee's earnings are compared with the "lower earnings limit". For 1997/98, the lower earnings limit is £62 for weekly paid employees and £269 for monthly paid employees. If earnings in the contribution period are less than the lower earnings limit, no primary Class 1 NIC's are payable.

(b) For employees whose earnings are at least equal to the lower earnings limit, primary Class 1 NIC's are payable on *all* of the employee's earnings up to the "upper earnings limit". For 1997/98, the upper earnings limit is £465 for weekly paid employees and £2,015 for monthly paid employees. No primary contributions are payable on the excess of an employee's earnings over the upper earnings limit.

(c) The rates (for 1997/98) at which primary Class 1 NIC's are calculated for employees whose earnings are not less than the lower earnings limit are as follows :

	Not contracted out	*Contracted out (COSR)*
Weekly paid :		
On the first £62	2%	2%
On remaining earnings up to £465	10%	8.4%
Monthly paid :		
On the first £269	2%	2%
On remaining earnings up to £2,015	10%	8.4%

EXAMPLE 1

(a) Compute the primary Class 1 NIC's payable by the following weekly paid employees for the week ending 4 August 1997 :

- (i) Employee A has earnings for the week of £60 and is not contracted out.
- (ii) Employee B has earnings for the week of £194 and is not contracted out.
- (iii) Employee C has earnings for the week of £470 and is contracted out.

(b) Compute the primary Class 1 NIC's payable by the following monthly paid employees for the month of August 1997 :

- (i) Employee D has earnings for the month of £269 and is not contracted out.
- (ii) Employee E has earnings for the month of £1,017 and is contracted out.
- (iii) Employee F has earnings for the month of £2,200 and is contracted out.

SOLUTION

(a) (i) £nil (earnings are less than the lower limit).

(ii) 2% x £62 + 10% x £132 = £14.44.

(iii) 2% x £62 + 8.4% x £403 = £35.09. The earnings beyond the first £465 do not attract primary contributions.

(b) (i) 2% x £269 = £5.38. If earnings had been only one penny less, no contributions would have been payable at all.

(ii) 2% x £269 + 8.4% x £748 = £68.21.

(iii) 2% x £269 + 8.4% x £1,746 = £152.04.

Secondary Class 1 NIC's

Secondary Class 1 NIC's are those payable by employers in relation to their employees. No secondary contributions are payable in relation to an employee whose earnings are less than the lower earnings limit. For employees whose earnings are not less than the lower earnings limit, secondary contributions (in 1997/98) are calculated as follows :

	Not contracted out (on all earnings)	*Contracted out (COSR)*	
		On first £62 or £269	*On remainder*
Earnings (weekly paid) :			
£62 to £109.99	3%	3%	0%
£110 to £154.99	5%	5%	2%
£155 to £209.99	7%	7%	4%
£210 to £465	10%	10%	7%
over £465	10%	10%	7% to upper limit and 10% on remainder
Earnings (monthly paid) :			
£269 to £476.99	3%	3%	0%
£477 to £671.99	5%	5%	2%
£672 to £909.99	7%	7%	4%
£910 to £2,015	10%	10%	7%
over £2,015	10%	10%	7% to upper limit and 10% on remainder

It is important to appreciate that secondary Class 1 NIC's are payable on the *whole* of an employee's earnings (so long as these are not less than the lower earnings limit). Primary contributions are payable only on earnings up to the upper earnings limit, so there is a maximum to the amount of primary contributions which an employee could pay in a contribution period. But there is no such maximum on the amount of secondary contributions payable by an employer.

EXAMPLE 2

Refer back to the previous example in this chapter and compute the secondary Class 1 NIC's payable in relation to each employee.

SOLUTION

(a) (i) £nil (earnings are less than the lower limit).

(ii) 7% x £194 = £13.58.

(iii) 10% x £62 + 7% x £403 + 10% x £5 = £34.91.

(b) (i) 3% x £269 = £8.07.

(ii) 10% x £269 + 7% x £748 = £79.26.

(iii) 10% x £269 + 7% x £1,746 + 10% x £185 = £167.62.

Directors' Class 1 NIC's

The fact that there is a maximum to the amount of primary contributions which an employee can pay in a contribution period means that employees with identical annual earnings may pay very different amounts of primary contributions in the year, depending upon the distribution of their earnings over the year. Consider the following (rather extreme) example :

EXAMPLE 3

During 1997/98, an employee (not contracted out) earns a total of £27,000, paid at the rate of £2,250 each month.

(a) Calculate the total primary and secondary Class 1 NIC's payable for the year.

(b) What would the total primary and secondary contributions be for the year if the employee received £27,000 in one month and nothing in the remaining 11 months ?

SOLUTION

(a) Primary contributions each month are £179.98 (2% x £269 + 10% x £1,746), giving £2,159.76 for the year. Secondary contributions each month are £225 (10% x £2,250), giving £2,700 for the year.

(b) Primary contributions for the month in which the employee was paid £27,000 would be £179.98, with nothing payable for the rest of the year. Secondary contributions in that month would be £2,700, again with nothing payable for the rest of the year.

The total secondary contributions are the same in both cases but the employee would save £1,979.78 in primary contributions (£2,159.76 - £179.98) if the entire year's salary were received in a single month.

Employees are not normally able to arrange for all their year's earnings to be paid in one contribution period so as to avoid primary Class 1 NIC's, but company directors may well have sufficient influence to make such an arrangement. To counter this, the Class 1 NIC's of company directors are always calculated on an *annual* basis, regardless of the distribution of their earnings over the tax year. For 1997/98, the calculation is as follows :

(a) The lower earnings limit is £3,224 for the year.

(b) The upper earnings limit is £24,180 for the year.

(c) The total primary contributions payable for the tax year by directors with earnings of at least the lower earnings limit are calculated as 2% of the first £3,224 plus 10% of the remaining earnings up to £24,180 (or 8.4% for a director who is contracted out).

(d) The total secondary contributions payable for the tax year in relation to directors with earnings of at least the lower earnings limit are calculated according to the following table :

	Not contracted out	*Contracted out (COSR)*	
	(on all earnings)	*On first £3,224*	*On remainder*
Annual earnings :			
£3,224 to £5,719.99	3%	3%	0%
£5,720 to £8,059.99	5%	5%	2%
£8,060 to £10,919.99	7%	7%	4%
£10,920 to £24,180	10%	10%	7%
over £24,180	10%	10%	7% to upper limit and 10% on remainder

EXAMPLE 4

Rework the above example given that the employee in question is a company director.

SOLUTION

Regardless of the distribution of the director's earnings over the tax year, primary contributions would be £2,160.08 (2% x £3,224 + 10% x £20,956) and secondary contributions would be £2,700 (10% x £27,000).

Class 1a National Insurance contributions

As stated above, benefits in kind which are not convertible into cash are generally not subject to Class 1 NIC's. However, an exception arises in the case of motor cars and fuel provided by an employer for an employee's private use. In this case, a Class 1A contribution is payable *by the employer only* (not by the employee), calculated in 1997/98 at 10% of the benefit in kind assessed on the employee under Schedule E (see Chapter 7).

EXAMPLE 5

In 1997/98, George is provided with a 1,600cc petrol-engined car by his employer who pays for all fuel and other running costs. George's annual mileage is 20,000 of which 75% relates to business travel. The car had a list price of £11,700 when it was purchased new in late 1996. Calculate George's employer's Class 1A contribution for the year.

SOLUTION

The car benefit assessed under Schedule E is £2,730 (35% of £11,700, less one-third). The assessable fuel benefit is £1,010. Therefore the Class 1A contribution payable by George's employer is £374.00 (10% of (£2,730 + £1,010)).

Class 2 National Insurance contributions

Class 2 NIC's are payable by self-employed people at a flat rate (for 1997/98) of £6.15 per week. A self-employed person whose earnings from self-employment in a tax year are less than the "small earnings exemption limit" (£3,480 for 1997/98) is not required to pay Class 2 NIC's that year but may do so voluntarily in order to maintain a full contributions record.

For Class 2 purposes, a self-employed person's earnings in a tax year are equal to the net profits, *before* adjustment for tax purposes, shown by that person's accounts for the year (i.e. the actual net profits from 6 April to the following 5 April). Unless accounts are drawn up to 5 April each year, it will be necessary to apportion the net profits shown in two years' accounts in order to obtain the required figure.

If a self-employed person has two or more businesses then the profits of all of them are aggregated and a Class 2 liability arises unless the aggregate profits are less than the exemption limit.

EXAMPLE 6

(a) Alison is self-employed. Her accounts for the year ended 5 April 1998 show a net profit of £3,450. Is she liable to pay Class 2 NIC's in 1997/98 ?

(b) Amanda is also self-employed. Her accounts for the year ended 31 December 1997 show a net profit of £3,370 and her accounts for the year ended 31 December 1998 show a net profit of £3,840. Is she liable to pay Class 2 NIC's in 1997/98 ?

SOLUTION

(a) Alison's accounts (which coincide with tax year 1997/98) show a net profit which is less than the small earnings exemption limit. Therefore she is not required to pay Class 2 NIC's in 1997/98.

(b) Amanda's accounts do not coincide with the tax year so some apportionment is necessary. Her actual net profit in 1997/98 is £3,492 (£3,370 x 270/365 + £3,840 x 95/365). This is not less than the small earnings exemption limit so she will be required to pay Class 2 NIC's in 1997/98.

Class 4 National Insurance contributions

In addition to the flat rate Class 2 liability described above, self-employed people may also be liable to pay earnings related Class 4 NIC's. A self-employed person's Class 4 liability for a given tax year is based on the tax-adjusted profits assessed for the year under Schedule D Case I or II and is collected along with the income tax liability. The amount due is calculated as follows :

(a) The liability is based on the Schedule D Case I or II assessment for the year (net of capital allowances) after deducting trade charges and loss reliefs, but before deducting retirement annuity or personal pension premiums.

(b) If a self-employed person has more than one business, the earnings from all businesses for the year are aggregated.

(c) If earnings from self-employment are less than or equal to a lower limit (£7,010 for 1997/98), the Class 4 liability is nil.

(d) If earnings from self-employment exceed the lower limit, Class 4 NIC's are payable (for 1997/98) at 6% on earnings lying between the lower limit of £7,010 and an upper limit of £24,180.

EXAMPLE 7

Calculate the Class 4 NIC's payable in 1997/98 in each of the following cases :

(a) Shawn has a 1997/98 Schedule D Case I assessment of £12,650.

(b) Catherine has a 1997/98 Schedule D Case I assessment of £30,000.

(c) Paul has a 1997/98 Schedule D Case I assessment of £6,900.

SOLUTION

(a) 6% x (£12,650 - £7,010) = £338.40.

(b) 6% x (£24,180 - £7,010) = £1,030.20. This is the maximum contribution since profits over the upper limit are not subject to Class 4 NIC's.

(c) Paul's profits are less than the lower limit so his Class 4 liability for the year is nil.

Class 3 National Insurance contributions

Any individual (employed or self-employed) whose earnings are too low in a contribution period to require a National Insurance contribution may make a voluntary Class 3 contribution so as to maintain a full contributions record. For 1997/98, the amount of the Class 3 contribution is £6.05 per week.

Annual maximum contributions

An employee who has more than one employment will normally be required to make Class 1 contributions in respect of each employment. Similarly, an individual who is both employed and self-employed will normally be required to make Class 1 contributions (in respect of the employment) and Class 2 and Class 4 contributions (in respect of the self-employment).

In these circumstances, the total NIC's payable could become onerous but relief is available in the form of limits on the amount of NIC's payable by any one person in any one year. There are two limits to consider :

(a) **Maximum Class 1 and 2 contributions.** The total of the Class 1 and Class 2 contributions payable by an individual in one year is limited to 53 primary Class 1 NIC's at the maximum weekly rate. For 1997/98 this is equal to £2,201.62 (53 x (2% x £62 + 10% x £403)). If this limit is exceeded then the excess is refunded.

(b) **Maximum Class 1, 2 and 4 contributions.** The total of the Class 1, 2 and 4 contributions payable by an individual in one year is limited to 53 Class 2 contributions for the year plus the maximum Class 4 contribution for the year. For 1997/98 this is equal to £1,356.15 (53 @ £6.15 + 6% x (£24,180 - £7,010)). If this limit is exceeded, Class 4 contributions are refunded, up to the amount of the excess.

EXAMPLE 8

(a) Stephanie is employed at a monthly salary of £1,800. She is not contracted out of SERPS. She also has a small business and pays Class 2 NIC's each week. Calculate the refund of NIC's due for 1997/98.

(b) Stewart is self-employed and pays Class 2 NIC's each week. His business profits assessed in 1997/98 are £21,500. He also receives directors' fees of £5,000 in the year. He is not contracted out of SERPS. Calculate the refund of NIC's due for 1997/98.

SOLUTION

(a) Stephanie will have paid NIC's as follows :

	£
Class 1 (12 x (2% x £269 + 10% x £1,531))	1,901.76
Class 2 (52 @ £6.15)	319.80
	2,221.56

This exceeds the maximum of £2,201.62, so Stephanie is entitled to a refund of £19.94.

(b) Stewart will have paid NIC's as follows :

	£
Class 1 (2% x £3,224 + 10% x £1,776)	242.08
Class 2 (52 @ £6.15)	319.80
Class 4 (6% x (£21,500 - £7,010))	869.40
	1,431.28

His combined Class 1 and Class 2 contributions are within the allowed maximum of £2,201.62 but his combined Class 1, 2 and 4 contributions exceed the allowed maximum of £1,356.15. Therefore he is entitled to a refund of Class 4 contributions amounting to £75.13.

Summary

- Class 1 NIC's are payable by employees (the primary contributions) and by employers (the secondary contributions).
- Class 1 NIC's are calculated with respect to earnings in a contribution period and each contribution period is considered independently.
- Both primary and secondary NIC's are reduced if the employee is contracted out of SERPS.
- The Class 1 NIC's of company directors are assessed on an annual basis and are unaffected by the distribution of the director's earnings over the year.
- Class 1A NIC's are payable by employers in relation to cars provided to employees as a benefit in kind.
- Class 2 NIC's are payable at a flat rate by self-employed people whose profits exceed the small earnings exemption limit.
- Class 4 NIC's are paid by self-employed people and are earnings-related.
- Class 3 NIC's are paid voluntarily in order to maintain a full contributions record.
- There are annual maximum limits on the amount of NIC's payable by an individual.

Exercises

15.1 Compute the primary and secondary Class 1 NIC's payable in relation to the following employees (none of whom are contracted out of SERPS) :

(a) A earns £78 for the week ending 1 September 1997.

(b) B earns £178 for the week ending 1 September 1997.

(c) C earns £475 for the week ending 1 September 1997.

(d) D earns £200 for the month of September 1997.

(e) E earns £413 for the month of September 1997.

(f) F earns £2,500 for the month of September 1997.

15.2 Rework your answer to Exercise 15.1, assuming now that each of the employees is a member of a COSR scheme.

15.3 Mark is self-employed and makes up his accounts annually to 30 November. His accounts for the year ended 30 November 1997 show a net profit of £6,890 and his accounts for the year ended 30 November 1998 show a net profit of £3,120. His 1997/98 Schedule D Case I assessment is £7,200. Calculate the NIC's payable by Mark for 1997/98.

***15.4** Brenda is a company director and earns a regular monthly salary of £1,750. In December 1997 she received a £5,000 bonus. She is provided with a one-year old 1,800cc diesel-engined company car which had a list price when new of £16,000 and she travels 10,000 miles a year of which 20% comprises business mileage. The company pays all the running costs of the car, including fuel. Her BUPA subscription of £350 per year is paid by the company.

Calculate the NIC's payable in respect of Brenda in 1997/98 (she is a member of a COSR scheme).

***15.5** Leonard is employed and receives a salary during 1997/98 of £1,200 per month. He is not contracted out of SERPS. He also has a small business and pays Class 2 NIC's each week. His 1997/98 Schedule D Case I assessment is £7,150. Calculate the refund of NIC's due to Leonard for 1997/98.

Review questions (Set A)

A 1 Tom Tulliver has been appointed sales director of Pembridge plc, a large company in the building industry. In addition to a basic salary of £50,000, he has been offered a comprehensive benefits package. The proposed deal is :

(i) The company will provide him with a new 1,800cc motor car which, together with accessories, will cost £19,500. Whilst the use would be primarily personal, he has carefully estimated that business mileage would be 2,400 miles per annum. Petrol for private use will be provided but Mr Tulliver must make a contribution of £400 per year towards its cost.

(ii) An interest-free loan of £5,250 will be made to him on appointment and need only be repaid on his leaving the company. The loan will be used to purchase a stereo system and other household items.

(iii) He has a choice of meals in the company canteen, which is open to all staff free of charge, or luncheon vouchers worth £5 per day, an amount equivalent to the normal cost of the meals. He has decided to accept the luncheon vouchers. The normal working year is 200 working days.

(iv) His son, aged three, is presently attending a nursery group at a cost of £2,000 per year. Pembridge plc has offered to give his son a free place in their own day nursery but Mr Tulliver would like to continue the existing arrangement and for Pembridge to pay the fees to the existing nursery.

Mrs Tulliver's wife earns £14,000 per year. She pays pension contributions to her employer's pension scheme of 6% of her salary. Both Mr and Mrs Tulliver have building society accounts which will yield net interest of £6,400 and £2,240 respectively in 1997/98. Mr Tulliver receives net preference dividends of £4,160 annually.

Mr Tulliver's appointment will begin on 1 April 1997 and he wishes to examine his and his wife's tax position before the start of fiscal year 1997/98.

Required :

(a) Advise Mr Tulliver on the taxation implications of his employment package as it stands.

(b) Advise him of any changes you consider that he should make to maximise the tax efficiency of the proposed package.

(c) Using your answer in (a) as to the amount of Mr Tulliver's income, advise him of the likely income tax borne by him and his wife for 1997/98 and, again, suggest how the tax position might be improved. (*Note* : Assume that the official rate of interest is 6.75%). *(AAT)*

A 2 Abel and Zoe were married on 17 May 1997 when they were both 20. On 21 March 1998 Zoe gave birth to twins, Brendan and Yvonne. On 7 June 1998 Abel and Zoe separated in circumstances likely to be permanent. Brendan stayed with his father and Yvonne stayed with her mother. On 7 December 1998 Abel and Zoe were divorced.

From 6 July 1998 Abel was required by a court order to pay maintenance of £40 per week to Zoe. This amount was increased on 6 January 2000 to £60 per week by court order.

Neither Abel nor Zoe plan to re-marry nor live with a new partner.

You are required :

To state the amount of the personal allowances to which Abel and Zoe are entitled for tax years 1997/98, 1998/99 and 1999/00. (You may assume that the amounts of the personal allowances in all three years are the same as those for 1997/98). *(ACCA)*

A 3 Sarah, who was born on 2 April 1953, is a self-employed computer consultant. Her agreed taxable profits were as follows :

	£
1997/98	50,000
1996/97	30,000
1995/96	10,000
1994/95	9,000
1993/94	8,000
1992/93	7,000
1991/92	6,000
1990/91	5,000
1989/90	4,000

On 1 June 1997, she tells you (her accountant) that she has never paid any personal pension premiums and that, in view of her recent high profits, she now wishes to make premium payments sufficient to utilise as much of the previous years' unused relief as possible.

You are required :

To calculate the amount of the premiums which Sarah should pay and to explain how these premiums should be applied. *(ACCA)*

A 4 In each of the following situations, show the tax position assuming that the maximum potential reliefs are claimed as soon as possible. Then advise your client of any alternatives that might be available.

(i) Mr de Praet - a married man - begins trading on 1 January 1995, preparing accounts to 31 December annually. Recent results are :

	£	
Year to 31 December 1996	20,000	Profit
Year to 31 December 1997	(30,000)	Loss

He receives rents of £5,000 annually. His wife is employed part-time at a salary of £4,200 per year. It is estimated that the trading profits for the year to 31 December 1998 are likely to be £68,000. (Ignore Section 381 relief).

(ii) Henry Percy is a single man who began trading on 1 July 1994 and makes up accounts to 30 June annually. His adjusted trading results (before capital allowances) for the last two years have been :

	£	
Year to 30 June 1997	16,000	Profit
Year to 30 June 1998	(10,000)	Loss

Up to 31 December 1997 he always leased his plant and machinery but on 1 January 1998 he purchased a new machine for £18,400. He has no income other than his business profits. *(AAT)*

A 5 In May 1997 Bernard, a self-employed plumber, and his son Gerald, a self-employed electrician, purchased 1,000 empty barrels from a Scottish whisky distillery. The barrels were over 100 years old and of no further use to the distillery. Bernard and Gerald sawed the barrels into halves and sold them to several local garden centres for use as ornamental flower tubs. Bernard and Gerald paid £10 per barrel to the distillery and sold a half-barrel for £8. Three-quarters of the barrels were sold by Bernard and Gerald in the summer of 1997 and the remainder in the summer of 1998.

You are required :

To prepare a list of points for consideration prior to writing a report to Bernard and Gerald on the liability to income tax of the profit generated by the venture. *(ACCA)*

***A 6** Your directors are considering paying substantial cash bonuses to a number of senior employees, including some directors.

You are required :

To draft a report to the board setting out the regulations for taxing these bonuses, indicating when the tax and National Insurance contributions on them would be payable. *(CIMA)*

***A 7** Claud Chapperon is a self-employed wholesale clothing distributor who began trading on 1 July 1994. His summarised accounts for the year to 30 June 1997 are shown below (figures in brackets refer to notes).

	£	£
Sales (1)		400,000
Opening stock (2)	40,000	
Purchases	224,000	
	264,000	
Closing stock (2)	32,000	232,000
Gross profit		168,000
Wages and national insurance (3)	52,600	
Rent and rates	29,100	
Repairs and renewals (4)	3,490	
Miscellaneous expenses (5)	665	
Taxation (Claud's income tax)	17,555	
Bad debts (6)	820	
Legal expenses (7)	1,060	
Depreciation	570	
Lease rental on Claud's car (8)	8,400	
Loss on sale of office furniture	60	
Deeds of covenant (9)	80	
Transport costs	4,250	
Interest (10)	990	
Running expenses of Claud's car (11)	2,000	
Premium on lease (12)	6,000	
Lighting and heating	1,250	
Sundry expenses (all allowable)	710	
Relocation expenditure (13)	2,400	132,000
Net profit		36,000

Notes :

1. Sales include £500 reimbursed by Claud's family for clothing taken from stock. The reimbursement represented cost price.
2. The basis of both the opening and closing stock valuations was "lower of cost or market value", less a contingency reserve of 50%.
3. Included in wages are Claud's drawings of £50 per week, his NIC's of £320 for the year and his wife's wages and NIC's totalling £11,750. His wife works full-time in the business as a secretary.
4. The charge for repairs and renewals includes £2,955 for fitting protective covers over the factory windows and doors to prevent burglary.

5. Miscellaneous expenses comprise :

	£
Theft of money by employee	65
Political donation to Green Party	100
Gifts of 100 "Chapperon" calendars	500
	665

6. Bad debts comprise :

	£
Trade debt written off	720
Loan to former employee written off	250
Reduction in general provision	(150)
	820

7. Legal expenses comprise :

	£
Defending action re alleged faulty goods	330
Costs re lease of new larger premises	250
Successful appeal against previous year's income tax assessment	200
Defending Claud in connection with speeding offence	190
Debt collection	90
	1,060

8. Claud's leased car was a BMW costing £20,000.

9. Deeds of covenant consist of £50 per annum to the local children's hospital and £30 per annum to Oxfam. Both covenants are payable for the next 4 years and both figures are shown gross in the accounts.

10. Interest is as follows :

	£
Bank overdraft interest (business account)	1,020
Interest on overdue tax	130
Interest credited on NSB ordinary a/c (see note 14)	(160)
	990

11. The Inland Revenue have agreed that one-third of Claud's mileage is private. Included in the charge for motor running expenses is £65 for a speeding fine incurred by Claud whilst delivering goods to a customer.

12. The premium was for a lease of six years.

13. The relocation expenditure was incurred in transferring the business to new and larger premises.

14. The NSB ordinary account was opened on 1 March 1996 and interest was credited as follows :

	£
31 December 1996	160
31 December 1997	140

The following information is also provided :

(i) Capital allowances for the year to 30 June 1997 are £480.

(ii) Claud was born on 10 April 1941 and always pays the maximum permitted personal pension contribution.

(iii) Claud and his wife have a joint mortgage on their home of £75,000. The interest payable for 1997/98 is £5,250. The MIRAS arrangements apply.

You are required :

(a) To prepare a profit adjustment statement in respect of the accounting period to 30 June 1997, showing the 1997/98 Schedule D Case I assessment.

(b) To calculate the Class 4 NIC's payable by Claud for 1997/98.

(c) To prepare an estimate of Claud's income tax borne for 1997/98. *(ACCA)*

***A8** When submitting a business's annual accounts to the Inspector of Taxes, it is usual to send schedules under the following expenditure headings :

(i) Gifts and entertainment

(ii) Major repairs

(iii) Redundancy payments to employees.

You are required :

To state the information which should be included under each of the above headings, explaining why such information will be required. *(CIMA)*

***A9** Joseph Kent commenced in business on 1 October 1994 as a joiner making conservatories. His tax-adjusted profits (before deduction of capital allowances) were as follows :

	£
Period to 31 December 1995	35,000
Year ended 31 December 1996	24,000
Year ended 31 December 1997	42,000

Capital additions and disposals were as follows :

		£
Additions		
1 October 1994	Car (at valuation)	12,200
1 October 1994	Trailer	2,000
1 October 1994	Plant and machinery	8,000
1 December 1996	Car	13,000
1 December 1997	Plant and machinery	6,000

		£
Disposals		
1 December 1996	Car acquired 1/10/94	7,000
1 January 1997	Plant and machinery (at less than cost)	2,000

Private use of both cars has been agreed with the Inland Revenue at 20%. No claim is made to treat any of the assets as short-life assets.

Joseph manufactured the conservatories in rented premises until 1 January 1997, when he purchased a new factory unit on an industrial estate for £20,000 (not in an enterprise zone). All assets were brought into use immediately upon acquisition.

Joseph's wife Sephora is a solicitor employed by a practising firm at a salary of £30,000 per annum. The following additional information is provided for 1997/98 :

(i) A new 2,500cc petrol-engined car was provided for Sephora's use in August 1996. The list price at that time was £25,000. Of this amount, £4,000 was contributed by Sephora so that a better car could be provided. She was required to pay £25 per month towards the private use of the car but not towards the private fuel, all of which was provided by her employers. The business mileage in 1997/98 is 10,000 miles.

(ii) Sephora has received a loan of £60,000 on the matrimonial home from her employers on which she pays interest at 3%. The interest is paid gross.

(iii) Sephora made a qualifying donation to the Oxfam charity on 1 July 1997 of £385 under the gift aid scheme.

(iv) Sephora had made the appropriate election to have one-half of the married couple's allowance set-off against her income for 1997/98. Both Joseph and Sephora are under 65 years old.

You are required :

(a) To calculate Joseph's Schedule D Case I assessments for 1994/95 to 1997/98 inclusive.

(b) To calculate Sephora's income tax liability for 1997/98 (assuming an official rate of interest of 6.75% per annum). *(ACCA)*

***A10** Thomas Pilkington bought an existing business, Marcus Fashionwear, a gentlemen's outfitters, on 1 December 1996. The summarised trading profit and loss account for the year to 30 November 1997 is set out below :

		£	£
Sales			201,600
Cost of sales			53,900
			147,700
Investment income			9,100
			156,800
Rent and rates		25,400	
Lighting and heating		3,200	
Wages and salaries		22,500	
Insurances		1,100	
Motor vehicle expenses		5,200	
Postage, stationery and telephone		800	
Repairs to premises		4,900	
Advertising		3,200	
Bad debts		2,100	
Subscriptions and donations		500	
Depreciation :	Motor vehicles	3,900	
	Fixtures and fittings	2,000	
	Office machinery	3,000	
Legal and professional charges		3,300	81,100
Net profit			75,700

You are required :

To state what further information you would require to enable you to calculate the income assessable under the various schedules. *(ACCA)*

PART 2
CAPITAL GAINS TAX

Chapter 16

Introduction to capital gains tax

Introduction

The next seven chapters of this book deal with capital gains tax (CGT), which was introduced in 1965 with the aim of taxing gains arising on the disposal of capital assets. CGT has undergone many changes since its inception and the changes made between 1965 and 1992 were consolidated into the Taxation of Chargeable Gains Act 1992. This Act has since been amended by subsequent Finance Acts.

Chargeable persons

A liability to CGT may arise when a "chargeable person" makes a "chargeable disposal" of a "chargeable asset". The main categories of chargeable person are as follows :

(a) individuals who are resident or ordinarily resident in the UK (husbands and wives being assessed independently)

(b) partners, who are each responsible for their share of the CGT due on a partnership's capital gains

(c) trustees and personal representatives.

The following are *not* chargeable persons for CGT purposes and therefore cannot incur a CGT liability :

(a) companies, which pay corporation tax on their capital gains, not CGT

(b) registered charities and friendly societies, local authorities, approved superannuation funds, unit trusts, investment trusts and approved scientific research associations, all of which are exempt from CGT.

Chargeable assets

All assets are regarded as chargeable assets except for those which are specifically exempted from CGT. The main exemptions are as follows :

(a) land and buildings comprising a taxpayer's principal private residence (see Chapter 21)

(b) motor cars, including vintage and veteran motor cars

(c) chattels (i.e. tangible, movable property) disposed of for less than £6,000 (see Chapter 18)

(d) wasting chattels (i.e. chattels with a predictable useful life of 50 years or less), unless used in business and eligible for capital allowances (see Chapter 18)

(e) gilt-edged securities and qualifying corporate bonds (see Chapter 19)

(f) works of art and collections of scientific interest if donated for the benefit of the nation

(g) national savings certificates, premium bonds, development bonds, defence bonds and SAYE deposits

(h) foreign currency if acquired for private use

(i) winnings from pools, lotteries, betting etc.

(j) decorations for valour (unless acquired by purchase)

(k) compensation or damages received for personal or professional injury

(l) life assurance policies

(m) personal equity plans.

If an asset is not a chargeable asset, then neither a chargeable gain nor an allowable loss can arise on its disposal.

Chargeable disposals

The main, and most obvious, instance of a chargeable disposal occurs when a chargeable asset is sold. However, the sale of an asset in the course of trade does *not* constitute a chargeable disposal for CGT purposes since trading profits are assessed instead to income tax under Schedule D Case I.

Before CGT was introduced in 1965 there was a great incentive for taxpayers to show that the gain arising on the sale of an asset was a capital gain (and so not taxable at all) rather than a trading profit (and so subject to income tax). With the introduction of CGT this incentive was diminished but it is still important to distinguish between capital gains and trading profits since the rules of computation for CGT and income tax are different.

As well as the sale of a chargeable asset, the following also rank as chargeable disposals :

(a) the sale of part of a chargeable asset

(b) the gift of all or part of chargeable asset

(c) the loss or destruction of all or part of a chargeable asset.

The date on which a chargeable disposal is deemed to occur is the date on which ownership of the asset changes hands, regardless of the date on which payment (if any) takes place.

Non-chargeable disposals

The following types of disposal are *not* chargeable disposals and therefore any gains (or losses) arising on such disposals are exempt from CGT :

(a) gifts to charities, art galleries, museums etc.

(b) disposals caused by the death of the taxpayer

(c) disposals between husband and wife who are living together (strictly speaking, such disposals are not actually exempt from CGT but are deemed to have occurred at a disposal value such that neither a chargeable gain nor an allowable loss arises).

Basis of assessment

A person's CGT liability for a tax year is based upon the chargeable disposals made by that person during the tax year. For example, the 1997/98 CGT assessment is based upon chargeable disposals made between 6 April 1997 and 5 April 1998 inclusive. No liability to CGT arises until an asset is disposed of, so the mere fact that an asset has appreciated in value will not of itself trigger a CGT assessment. The amount of the CGT assessment for a tax year is calculated as follows :

(a) The chargeable gain or allowable loss arising on each disposal made during the year is calculated separately (the method of calculation is described in great detail in subsequent chapters of this book).

(b) The chargeable gains are then aggregated to give the total gains for the year and the allowable losses are aggregated to give the total losses for the year.

(c) If total gains exceed total losses, the losses are subtracted from the gains to give the "net gains" for the year.

(d) If total losses exceed total gains, the gains are subtracted from the losses to give the "net losses" for the year.

(e) If there are net gains for the year, these are reduced by an "annual exemption" and then the remainder is subjected to CGT. The annual exemption for an individual in tax year 1997/98 is £6,500. If net gains are less than the annual exemption in any year, the CGT assessment for that year is £nil and the balance of the annual exemption is lost.

(f) If there are net losses for the year, the CGT assessment for that year is £nil and the whole of the annual exemption is lost. The net losses may then be carried forward for relief in future years, as described later in this chapter.

Note that husbands and wives are each entitled to the £6,500 annual exemption. This exemption is also available to the trustees of a trust established for a mentally disabled person or for certain other infirm or disabled persons. For trustees of other settlements the annual exemption is £3,250. The personal representatives of a deceased person are entitled to the full annual exemption for the year of death and for the following two years.

EXAMPLE 1

Four taxpayers each make three chargeable disposals during 1997/98. Compute their CGT assessments for the year, given that these disposals give rise to the following gains and losses :

(a) Taxpayer A has chargeable gains of £1,400, £2,600 and £4,750.

(b) Taxpayer B has chargeable gains of £2,800, £5,840 and an allowable loss of £1,250.

(c) Taxpayer C has chargeable gains of £450, £7,630 and an allowable loss of £3,250.

(d) Taxpayer D has a chargeable gain of £8,950 and allowable losses of £9,500 and £800.

SOLUTION

(a) Taxpayer A has total gains of £8,750 and no allowable losses. Net gains are therefore £8,750. Subtracting the annual exemption of £6,500 gives a CGT assessment for the year of £2,250.

(b) Taxpayer B has total gains of £8,640 and total losses of £1,250. Net gains are therefore £7,390. Subtracting the annual exemption of £6,500 gives a CGT assessment for the year of £890.

(c) Taxpayer C has total gains of £8,080 and total losses of £3,250. Net gains are therefore £4,830. This is less than the annual exemption of £6,500, so the CGT assessment for the year is £nil. The unused part of the annual exemption (£1,670) is lost.

(d) Taxpayer D has total gains of £8,950 and total losses of £10,300. Net losses are therefore £1,350. The CGT assessment for the year is £nil and the whole of the annual exemption is lost.

Rate of CGT

The amount of CGT payable for a tax year is equal to the amount of extra income tax which the taxpayer would be liable to pay if the CGT assessment for that year were regarded as extra taxable income. Therefore there is no single CGT rate. Tax may be payable at 20%, 23%, 40% or at a combination of these rates, depending upon the taxpayer's income tax situation.

It is important to note that non-taxpayers are *not* allowed to offset any unrelieved charges or unused personal allowances against their capital gains, and that tax reducers may be used only to reduce a taxpayer's income tax liability, not his or her CGT liability.

If a taxpayer has savings income, non-savings income and capital gains, the allocation of the lower rate and basic rate tax bands is as follows :

(a) The lower rate tax band (£4,100 in 1997/98) is allocated first to non-savings income, then to capital gains and finally to savings income.

(b) The basic rate tax band (£22,000 in 1997/98) is allocated first to non-savings income, then to savings income and finally to capital gains. As usual, any savings income falling into the basic rate band is taxed at only 20%.

EXAMPLE 2

Alan has net capital gains in 1997/98 of £7,900. Calculate the amount of CGT payable for 1997/98 if his taxable income for the year (i.e. his total income after deduction of charges and the personal allowance) comprises :

(a) non-savings income of £25,700 and savings income of £nil

(b) non-savings income of £nil and savings income of £13,300

(c) non-savings income of £2,900 and savings income of £30,000.

SOLUTION

(a)

	Non-savings	*Savings*	*Capital gains*	*Total*
	£	£	£	£
Lower rate band	4,100	0	0	4,100
Basic rate band	21,600	0	400	22,000
Higher rate band	0	0	1,000	1,000
	25,700	0	1,400	

The CGT assessment is £1,400 (£7,900 - £6,500). CGT payable is £400 @ 23% + £1,000 @ 40% = £492.

(b)

	Non-savings	Savings	Capital gains	Total
	£	£	£	£
Lower rate band	0	2,700	1,400	4,100
Basic rate band	0	10,600	0	10,600
Higher rate band	0	0	0	0
	0	13,300	1,400	

CGT payable is £1,400 @ 20% = £280.

(c)

	Non-savings	Savings	Capital gains	Total
	£	£	£	£
Lower rate band	2,900	0	1,200	4,100
Basic rate band	0	22,000	0	22,000
Higher rate band	0	8,000	200	8,200
	2,900	30,000	1,400	

CGT payable is £1,200 @ 20% + £200 @ 40% = £320.

Relief for capital losses

If a taxpayer has net losses for a year, the CGT assessment for that year is £nil and the annual exemption is lost. The amount of the net losses may then be carried forward without time limit and set against the net gains of future years.

Losses carried forward must be offset against the first available net gains, but are offset only to the extent that those net gains exceed the annual exemption for the year in which they arise, so preventing the annual exemption from being wasted. Any losses remaining unrelieved are carried forward again to subsequent years. This method of preserving the annual exemption applies *only* to losses brought forward from a previous year. It is *not* possible to preserve the annual exemption by restricting the set-off of current year losses.

Since married couples are taxed independently, the losses of one spouse cannot be offset against the gains of the other spouse.

EXAMPLE 3

Four taxpayers each have £3,000 of losses brought forward from previous years. Calculate their 1997/98 CGT assessments if their total gains and losses in 1997/98 are as follows :

(a) Taxpayer A has gains of £5,800 and losses of £1,100.

(b) Taxpayer B has gains of £7,500 and losses of £1,000.

(c) Taxpayer C has gains of £9,900 and losses of £1,700.

(d) Taxpayer D has gains of £12,900 and losses of £1,200.

SOLUTION

(a) Taxpayer A's net gains for the year are £4,700. This is less than the annual exemption of £6,500 so the CGT assessment for the year is £nil and the balance of the annual exemption is lost. There is no scope for relieving losses brought forward, so the entire £3,000 is carried forward to 1998/99.

(b) Taxpayer B's net gains for the year are £6,500. This is exactly equal to the annual exemption so the CGT assessment for the year is £nil. There is no scope for relieving losses brought forward, so the entire £3,000 is carried forward to 1998/99.

(c) Taxpayer C's net gains for the year are £8,200. This exceeds the annual exemption by £1,700 so £1,700 of the losses brought forward are relieved in 1997/98, giving a CGT assessment for the year of £nil. The remaining £1,300 of the losses are unrelieved and are therefore carried forward to 1998/99.

(d) Taxpayer D's net gains for the year are £11,700. This exceeds the annual exemption by £5,200 so the entire £3,000 of losses brought forward are relieved in 1997/98, giving a CGT assessment for the year of £2,200. There are no unrelieved losses to carry forward.

Losses in the year of death

As stated above, disposals caused by the death of a taxpayer are exempt from CGT, though such disposals may give rise to an inheritance tax liability. But disposals made in the year of death (i.e. from 6 April up to the date of death) are *not* exempt from CGT and are taxed in the usual way, with a full annual exemption given for the year.

If a taxpayer suffers net losses in the year of death, such losses cannot (for obvious reasons) be carried forward for relief in future years. However, a measure of relief is available in that net losses incurred in the year of death may be carried back and set off against the net gains of the previous 3 years (most recent years first). As is the case with losses carried forward, losses carried back are set against a year's net gains only to the extent that those net gains exceed the annual exemption for the year in which they arise.

EXAMPLE 4

Sarah dies on 16 December 1997, having made net capital losses of £7,300 between 6 April 1997 and the date of her death. Her net gains in the previous 3 years are :

	£
1994/95	6,950
1995/96	1,200
1996/97	10,650

Calculate her CGT assessments for the years 1994/95 to 1997/98 inclusive, given that the annual exemption was £5,800 in 1994/95, £6,000 in 1995/96 and £6,300 in 1996/97.

SOLUTION

Since losses in the year of death are carried back to the most recent year first, it is easier to begin with the year of death and then work backwards.

(a) In 1997/98, Sarah has net losses. Her CGT assessment for the year is therefore £nil and the annual exemption (available in full) is lost. The net losses of £7,300 may be carried back to 1996/97, 1995/96 and 1994/95, in that order.

(b) In 1996/97, Sarah's net gains of £10,650 exceed the annual exemption by £4,350 so £4,350 of the losses carried back are relieved in 1996/97, giving a CGT assessment for the year of £nil. The remaining £2,950 of the losses are carried back to 1995/96.

(c) In 1995/96, Sarah's net gains of £1,200 are less than the annual exemption of £6,000. Therefore the CGT assessment for the year is £nil and the balance of the annual exemption is lost. There is no scope for relieving losses carried back, so the £2,950 is now carried back to 1994/95.

(d) In 1994/95, Sarah's net gains of £6,950 exceed the annual exemption by £1,150 so £1,150 of the losses carried back are relieved in 1994/95, giving a CGT assessment for the year of £nil. The remaining £1,800 of the losses incurred in the year of death cannot be carried back any further and therefore cannot be relieved in any way.

Assuming that CGT assessments have already been issued for 1994/95 and 1996/97, it will be necessary to issue revised assessments to take into account the relief for losses carried back and to refund any CGT already paid for those years.

Losses on disposals to connected persons

A taxpayer is deemed to be "connected" with a number of persons, mainly relatives and business associates (a full list of "connected persons" is given in Chapter 17). As an anti-avoidance measure, the Taxation of Chargeable Gains Act 1992 states that losses incurred on a disposal to a connected person can be offset only against gains made on disposals to the *same connected person*, in the same or future years.

Relief for trading losses

Under Section 72 of the Finance Act 1991, a taxpayer's trading losses may in certain circumstances be offset against that taxpayer's net capital gains (the required circumstances are described in Chapter 11). If a Section 72 claim is made for a tax year, the amount of the claim must be for the *lower* of :

(a) the amount of the trading loss which is available for relief in that year, and

(b) the "maximum amount", which is the amount of the CGT assessment (*before* deducting the annual exemption) that would have been raised in that year had a Section 72 claim not been made.

The maximum amount of a Section 72 claim for a tax year consists therefore of the net capital gains for that year, less any capital losses brought forward (remembering that the amount of capital losses brought forward might be restricted so as to preserve the annual exemption). When the amount of the Section 72 claim has been determined, it is relieved *before* giving relief for capital losses brought forward.

EXAMPLE 5

(a) Richard is a sole trader and is considering making a Section 72 claim for 1997/98. His net gains for the year are £10,700 and he has capital losses brought forward of £2,300. Calculate his CGT assessment for 1997/98 (ignoring any Section 72 claim).

(b) Richard's unrelieved trading losses (eligible for a Section 72 claim in 1997/98) amount to £12,500. Calculate his CGT assessment for 1997/98 if he decides to make a Section 72 claim for the year.

(c) Now calculate the CGT assessment for 1997/98 if Richard's net gains for the year are £20,700 instead of £10,700.

SOLUTION

(a) If Richard does not make a Section 72 claim for 1997/98, his CGT assessment for the year will be :

	£
Net gains	10,700
Less : Capital losses b/f	2,300
	8,400
Less : Annual exemption	6,500
CGT assessment	1,900

There will be no unrelieved capital losses to carry forward.

(b) A Section 72 claim would have to be for the lower of :

(i) the trading loss (£12,500), and

(ii) the CGT assessment (before deducting the annual exemption) that would be raised if a Section 72 claim were not made (i.e. £8,400, as shown above).

Therefore the Section 72 claim would be for £8,400. This would be relieved in priority to capital losses brought forward and the CGT assessment would be :

	£
Net gains	10,700
Less : Section 72 claim	8,400
	2,300
Less : Annual exemption (restricted)	2,300
CGT assessment	nil

The remainder of the annual exemption (£4,200) would be lost. There would be no scope for relieving any of the capital losses brought forward, so the entire £2,300 would be carried forward to 1998/99.

(c) In the absence of a Section 72 claim, the amount of Richard's CGT assessment (before deducting the annual exemption) would be £18,400 (£20,700 - £2,300). Since the trading loss of £12,500 is less than this, a Section 72 claim would be for £12,500. The CGT assessment would then be :

	£
Net gains	20,700
Less : Section 72 claim	12,500
	8,200
Less : Capital losses b/f (restricted)	1,700
	6,500
Less : Annual exemption	6,500
CGT assessment	nil

The remainder of the losses brought forward (£600) would be carried forward to 1998/99.

Administration of CGT

The administration system which was described in Chapter 1 applies to CGT as well as to income tax. Note that :

(a) Details of the chargeable disposals made by a taxpayer during 1997/98 need not be entered on the tax return for that year if:

  (i) the total disposal proceeds for the year do not exceed £13,000, and

  (ii) the total gains for the year do not exceed £6,500, and

  (iii) the taxpayer does not wish to notify the Inland Revenue that there are net losses for the year.

(b) Net losses cannot be carried forward and set against subsequent capital gains unless these losses have been notified to the Inland Revenue. If the taxpayer has received a tax return for the year in which the losses are incurred, then notification must be made in the tax return. Otherwise, notification may be made in a later year's tax return or by sending a separate notice to the Inland Revenue. Losses are not allowed unless notified to the Inland Revenue by 31 January in the sixth year of assessment following the year in which the losses are incurred. For example, the latest date by which capital losses incurred in 1997/98 must be notified to the Inland Revenue is 31 January 2004.

(c) Acquisitions of chargeable assets do not need to be entered on the tax return.

Payment of CGT

As from tax year 1996/97, CGT is normally payable on 31 January following the end of the tax year to which the tax relates. For instance, the normal due date for the 1997/98 CGT liability is 31 January 1999. An important difference between the payment of CGT and the payment of income tax is that payments on account of the CGT liability are *not* required.

If the proceeds of a disposal are received by the taxpayer in instalments over a period of more than 18 months, the taxpayer may make a claim for the CGT due in relation to the disposal to be payable over the period of the instalments or over an 8-year period, whichever is the shorter.

Interest, surcharges and penalties

The regime of interest, surcharges and penalties which was described in Chapter 14 applies to both CGT and income tax.

Summary

- A liability to CGT may arise when a chargeable person makes a chargeable disposal of a chargeable asset. Individuals resident or ordinarily resident in the UK are chargeable persons. Companies are not chargeable persons.
- All assets are chargeable assets unless specifically exempted.
- A chargeable disposal occurs when all or part of a chargeable asset is sold (except in the course of trade), given away, lost or destroyed.
- An individual's CGT liability for a tax year is based upon the chargeable disposals made by that individual during the tax year. For 1997/98, the first £6,500 of net gains is exempt from CGT.
- CGT is payable at the taxpayer's marginal rates of income tax.
- Net losses may be carried forward and set against the net gains of subsequent years. Net losses incurred in the year of death of a taxpayer may be carried back for up to 3 years. Losses incurred on a disposal to a connected person may be offset only against gains made on disposals to the same connected person.
- In certain circumstances, trading losses may be set against net gains.
- CGT is normally payable on 31 January following the end of the tax year.

Exercises

16.1 Which of the following disposals might give rise to a CGT liability ?

(a) the sale of freehold property by a UK company

(b) the gift of shares from husband to wife

(c) the gift of an oil painting to a charity

(d) the sale of an oil painting by a charity

(e) the sale of an oil painting by an art dealer

(f) the sale of leasehold property by a partnership.

16.2 Which of the following are chargeable assets for CGT purposes ?

(a) shares in British Telecom plc

(b) gilt-edged securities

(c) an antique table worth £20,000

(d) an antique chair worth £5,000

(e) a taxpayer's home

(f) a vintage Bentley.

16.3 A taxpayer has allowable losses of £2,500 in 1997/98. Compute the 1997/98 CGT assessment if chargeable gains for the year are :

(a) £nil (b) £1,500 (c) £4,650 (d) £10,950.

16.4 A single man's only income in 1997/98 consists of a salary of £27,320. He has net gains of £9,900 for the year. Calculate his CGT liability.

16.5 A taxpayer has capital losses brought forward from previous years amounting to £4,800. Compute the CGT assessment for 1997/98 if total gains and losses for the year are :

(a) gains £7,700, losses £2,000

(b) gains £8,500, losses £1,400

(c) gains £12,700, losses £nil.

16.6 John dies on 3 March 1998. Between 6 April 1997 and 3 March 1998, he has total gains of £1,200 and total losses of £15,400. His net gains in recent years have been as follows :

	£
1993/94	51,800
1994/95	12,300
1995/96	8,800
1996/97	250

Show how the losses incurred in the year of John's death may be relieved, given that the annual exemption was £5,800 in 1993/94 and 1994/95, £6,000 in 1995/96 and £6,300 in 1996/97.

16.7 On what date is CGT for 1997/98 normally due for payment ?

***16.8** Rosemary has the following chargeable gains and allowable losses :

	Chargeable gains	*Allowable losses*
	£	£
1994/95	5,600	12,700
1995/96	6,700	2,350
1996/97	9,400	nil
1997/98	15,900	7,500

There were no unrelieved losses to bring forward from 1993/94 or earlier. Compute her CGT assessments for the years 1994/95 to 1997/98, given that the annual exemption was £5,800 in 1994/95, £6,000 in 1995/96 and £6,300 in 1996/97.

***16.9** In 1996/97, Ahmed (a UK resident) incurred an allowable loss of £3,750 on the disposal of an asset to his father. He also had chargeable gains in that year of £10,300. In 1997/98, Ahmed has chargeable gains of £37,200 and no allowable losses. The chargeable gains in 1997/98 include gains of £2,000 on a disposal to his father and £3,500 on a disposal to his mother.

Compute Ahmed's CGT assessments for the years 1996/97 and 1997/98. (The annual exemption was £6,300 in 1996/97).

***16.10** Melissa is a sole trader. She has trading losses eligible for a Section 72 claim in 1997/98 of £9,500. Her chargeable gains and allowable losses for 1997/98 are £24,000 and £1,300 respectively. She has capital losses brought forward from 1996/97 of £13,700.

Show Melissa's CGT assessment for 1997/98, assuming that :

(a) the Section 72 claim is not made

(b) the Section 72 claim is made.

Chapter 17

Computation of gains and losses

Introduction

The computation of the chargeable gain or allowable loss arising on the disposal of an asset involves subtracting the acquisition cost of the asset from its disposal value and then adjusting the gain to take account of inflation. The computation becomes more complex if the asset was acquired on or before 31 March 1982 and becomes more complex still if the asset was acquired before 6 April 1965. The purpose of this chapter is to explain the basic method of computation and to show how this method is modified for disposals of older assets.

Layout of a CGT computation

The computation of the chargeable gain or the allowable loss arising on a chargeable disposal is laid out as follows :

	£	£
Disposal value		x
Less : Incidental costs of disposal		x
		x
Less : *Allowable expenditure* :		
Acquisition cost of asset	x	
Incidental costs of acquisition	x	
Enhancement expenditure	x	
Cost of defending the owner's title to the asset	x	
Valuation fees	x	x
Unindexed gain (unindexed loss)		x
Less : Indexation allowance		x
Chargeable gain (allowable loss)		x

Each of the terms used in this layout is explained below.

Disposal value

If a disposal consists of the sale of an asset, disposal value is generally taken to be the proceeds of the sale. But if the sale is to a "connected person", sale proceeds are ignored and disposal value is taken to be the market value of the asset on the date of the sale. For this purpose, the main persons with whom a taxpayer is "connected" are his or her :

(a) spouse

(b) relatives (i.e. brothers, sisters, ancestors and direct descendants) and their spouses

(c) spouse's relatives and their spouses

(d) business partners and their spouses and relatives.

Market value is also used as disposal value if a disposal takes the form of a gift. In general, the market value of an asset is the amount which the asset would fetch if sold on the open market. Listed shares and securities are valued for CGT purposes in the same way as they are valued for inheritance tax purposes (see Chapter 31).

Incidental costs of disposal

The incidental costs of disposal which may be deducted when calculating the chargeable gain or allowable loss include legal fees, estate agents' and auctioneers' fees, advertising costs etc.

Allowable expenditure

The following expenditure may be set against disposal value when calculating the chargeable gain or allowable loss arising on the disposal :

(a) the acquisition cost of the asset (or market value on the date of acquisition if the asset was acquired by gift or from a connected person)

(b) incidental costs of acquisition, e.g. legal fees

(c) "enhancement expenditure", consisting of capital expenditure which has served to increase the disposal value of the asset (the costs of mere repairs and maintenance are disallowed)

(d) costs incurred in defending the owner's title to the asset (generally legal costs)

(e) valuation fees necessarily incurred for CGT purposes.

Indexation allowance

Indexation allowance was introduced by the Finance Act 1982 with the object of ensuring that only genuine gains are taxed and that any part of a gain which has been caused solely by the effects of inflation is not charged to tax.

An indexation allowance is calculated separately for each item of allowable expenditure shown in the CGT computation, based on the change in Retail Prices Index (RPI) between the month in which the expenditure took place and the month in which the disposal took place. These individual indexation allowances are then aggregated to give the total indexation allowance due.

The indexation allowance available in relation to an item of expenditure is calculated by multiplying the amount of that expenditure by an *indexation factor*, computed according to the following formula (rounded to 3 decimal places) :

$$\frac{\text{RPI for the month of disposal - RPI for the month of expenditure}}{\text{RPI for the month of expenditure}}$$

A table of RPI's is given at the end of this chapter.

EXAMPLE 1

An asset was acquired in June 1989 (RPI 115.4) at a cost of £1,200 and was sold in May 1997 (RPI 155.9) for £2,350. Compute the chargeable gain.

SOLUTION

	£
Sale proceeds	2,350
Less : Acquisition cost	1,200
Unindexed gain	1,150
Less : Indexation allowance	
$\frac{155.9 - 115.4}{115.4}$ = 0.351 x £1,200	421
Chargeable gain	729

EXAMPLE 2

An asset was acquired in August 1990 (RPI 128.1) at a cost of £15,000. Enhancement expenditure of £2,000 was incurred in January 1991 (RPI 130.2). The asset was sold in June 1997 (RPI 156.2) for £28,000. Compute the chargeable gain.

SOLUTION

		£	£
Sale proceeds			28,000
Less : Acquisition cost		15,000	
Enhancement expenditure		2,000	17,000
Unindexed gain			11,000
Less : Indexation allowance :			
(i) on acquisition cost			
$\frac{156.2 - 128.1}{128.1}$	= 0.219 x £15,000	3,285	
(ii) on enhancement expenditure			
$\frac{156.2 - 130.2}{130.2}$	= 0.200 x £2,000	400	3,685
Chargeable gain			7,315

Restrictions on indexation allowance

Note the following points about the indexation allowance :

(a) If RPI goes *down* between the month in which expenditure is incurred and the month of disposal, the indexation allowance available in relation to that expenditure is nil.

(b) No indexation allowance is available in respect of the incidental costs of disposal, even if they were incurred in a month earlier than the month of disposal.

(c) Indexation allowance cannot be used to convert an unindexed gain into an indexed loss. Therefore, if the indexation allowance (calculated in the normal way) exceeds the unindexed gain, the indexation allowance is restricted so as to produce neither a chargeable gain nor an allowable loss.

(d) Indexation allowance cannot be used to increase an unindexed loss. If there is an unindexed loss on a disposal then the indexation allowance is nil.

EXAMPLE 3

An asset was acquired in February 1987 (RPI 100.4) at a cost of £5,000. The asset was sold in July 1997 (RPI 156.5). Compute the chargeable gain if the sale proceeds were :

(a) £9,000

(b) £6,500

(c) £4,800

SOLUTION

	(a)	(b)	(c)
	£	£	£
Sale proceeds	9,000	6,500	4,800
Less : Acquisition cost	5,000	5,000	5,000
Unindexed gain (loss)	4,000	1,500	(200)
Less : Indexation allowance			
$\frac{156.5 - 100.4}{100.4}$ = 0.559 x £5,000	2,795	1,500	nil
Chargeable gain (allowable loss)	1,205	nil	(200)

Notes :

(a) The indexation allowance can be given in full.

(b) Giving the full indexation allowance would convert an unindexed gain of £1,500 into an allowable loss of £1,295. The indexation allowance is restricted to £1,500 to prevent this.

(c) There is an unindexed loss. Therefore the indexation allowance is restricted to £nil.

Part disposals

It was stated in Chapter 16 that the disposal of part of a chargeable asset ranks as a chargeable disposal for CGT purposes. Since only part of the asset has been disposed of, only part of its acquisition cost is allowable in the computation of the gain or loss arising on the disposal. The allowable part cost is the full cost of the asset multiplied by the following fraction :

$$\frac{A}{A+B}$$

where : A is the value of the part disposed of (i.e. the disposal value), and

B is the value of the part remaining in the taxpayer's ownership, and

A + B is the value of the entire asset on the day of disposal.

This part disposal fraction applies not only to the acquisition cost of the asset but also to any other items of allowable expenditure which relate to the whole asset. But any item of expenditure which relates only to the part of the asset which has been disposed of should be allowed in full.

EXAMPLE 4

Peter buys a piece of land for £26,000 in October 1985 (RPI 95.59). He sells one quarter of the land for £12,000 in August 1997 (RPI 156.8), incurring incidental costs of disposal of £500. The value of the remaining three-quarters of the land in August 1997 is £40,000. Calculate the chargeable gain.

SOLUTION

	£
Sale proceeds	12,000
Less : Incidental costs of disposal	500
	11,500
Less : Part cost : $\frac{£12,000}{£12,000 + £40,000}$ x £26,000	6,000
Unindexed gain	5,500
Less : Indexation allowance $\frac{156.8 - 95.59}{95.59}$ = 0.640 x £6,000	3,840
Chargeable gain	1,660

Notes :

(i) The fact that Peter has sold one quarter of the area of the land is irrelevant. What is relevant is that he has sold £12,000 worth of land out of a holding currently worth £52,000, as indicated by the part disposal fraction. Since the allowable part cost (£6,000) is slightly less than a quarter of the acquisition cost (£26,000), it is probable that the land he has sold is of slightly lower quality than the land he has retained.

(ii) The incidental costs of disposal clearly relate only to the part of the land that has been disposed of, not to the whole holding. Therefore these costs are allowed in full.

(iii) If Peter disposes of the remainder of the land at some future time, then the remainder of the cost i.e. £20,000 (£26,000 - £6,000) will be allowable in the computation of the chargeable gain arising on that disposal.

Small part disposals of land

An exception to the usual part disposal rules occurs when a taxpayer makes a "small" part disposal of land. For this purpose a disposal of land is regarded as "small" so long as the following conditions are met :

(a) The land in question must be freehold or long leasehold (i.e. held on a lease with more than 50 years left to run).

(b) If the land is disposed of because of a compulsory purchase order by a public authority, the disposal proceeds must be no more than 5% of the value of the whole piece of land.

(c) If the disposal is not caused by a compulsory purchase order, the disposal proceeds must be no more than 20% of the value of the whole piece of land and the total proceeds of all disposals of land in the year of assessment (excluding small disposals caused by compulsory purchases) must be no more than £20,000.

In these circumstances, the taxpayer may claim that there should be no chargeable gain and that, instead, the disposal proceeds should be subtracted from the original cost of the land for CGT purposes. This has the effect of increasing the chargeable gain arising on a subsequent disposal of the remainder of the land and therefore, in effect, the gain arising on the small part disposal is deferred. Obviously, the taxpayer will not make such a claim if the gain arising on the small part disposal is covered by the taxpayer's annual exemption for the year.

On a subsequent disposal of the remainder of the land, it would be unfair to calculate indexation allowance on the reduced cost only. Instead, indexation allowance is first calculated on the full original cost of the land and is then reduced by the proceeds of the small part disposal, multiplied by the percentage increase in RPI since the date of the small part disposal.

EXAMPLE 5

In July 1989 (RPI 115.5), Malcolm bought a piece of land for £40,000. In June 1993 (RPI 141.0) he sold part of the land for £11,000 (this being his only disposal of land in 1993/94). The value of the remainder of the land at the time of the part disposal was £50,000. Malcolm had substantial capital gains in 1993/94, sufficient to absorb his annual exemption for the year, and therefore decided to make the small part disposal claim.

Calculate the chargeable gain arising in June 1997 (RPI 156.2) when Malcolm sold the remainder of the land for £60,000.

SOLUTION

The small part disposal claim in 1993/94 was valid since the total value of the land immediately prior to the disposal was £61,000 (£11,000 + £50,000) and the disposal raised £11,000 which is less than 20% of £61,000. Also, the disposal proceeds of all land disposals in the year did not exceed £20,000. The chargeable gain on the June 1997 disposal is as follows :

	£
Sale proceeds	60,000
<u>Less</u> : Reduced cost (£40,000 - £11,000)	29,000
Unindexed gain	31,000

		£	£
Unindexed gain			31,000
Less : Indexation allowance :			
(i) on full original cost			
$\frac{156.2 - 115.5}{115.5}$	= 0.352 x £40,000	14,080	
(ii) on proceeds of small part disposal			
$\frac{156.2 - 141.0}{141.0}$	= 0.108 x £11,000	(1,188)	12,892
Chargeable gain			18,108

Assets with negligible value

If the value of a chargeable asset has become negligible, the owner of the asset may make a "negligible value" claim. If this claim is accepted, the asset is treated as if it had been disposed of at its current, negligible value (so triggering a disposal giving rise to an allowable loss) and then immediately re-acquired at that value. This claim is most frequently made in connection with stocks and shares which have become valueless.

Assets held on 31 March 1982

Capital gains tax was originally introduced in 1965 and applied to disposals made on or after 6 April 1965, which was the "base date" for CGT. Gains accruing before 6 April 1965 were not taxable. Therefore, if an asset acquired before 6 April 1965 was disposed of after that date, only the part of the gain accruing since 6 April 1965 was taxable. (The current treatment of assets held on 6 April 1965 is described later in this chapter).

The Finance Act 1988 changed the CGT base date to 31 March 1982. Therefore, if an asset is now disposed of which was acquired before 31 March 1982, only the part of the gain accruing since 31 March 1982 is taxable. The calculation of the taxable part of the gain is achieved by means of a technique known as "rebasing" whereby the market value of the asset at 31 March 1982 is substituted for its original acquisition cost in the CGT calculation. However, rebasing does *not* apply if the rebasing calculation results in a greater gain than the calculation based on original cost.

EXAMPLE 6

A chargeable asset was acquired in April 1975 for £2,000 and sold in January 1998 for £8,500. Compute the unindexed gain if the asset's market value at 31 March 1982 was :

(a) £4,200

(b) £1,500

SOLUTION

(a) The unindexed gain over the entire period of ownership, based on the original cost of the asset, is £6,500 (£8,500 - £2,000). But the rebasing calculation gives an unindexed gain of only £4,300 (£8,500 - £4,200). This is less than the gain based on original cost so rebasing applies and the unindexed gain is £4,300.

(b) The rebasing calculation gives an unindexed gain of £7,000 (£8,500 - £1,500). This is more than the gain based on original cost so rebasing does not apply and the unindexed gain is £6,500.

Indexation allowance for pre-31 March 1982 assets

The rules for calculating the indexation allowance available on the disposal of an asset held on 31 March 1982 are as follows :

(a) Indexation allowance is based on the change in RPI between March 1982 and the month of disposal. No further indexation allowance is available to compensate for the effects of pre-March 1982 inflation (which is why the table of RPI's at the end of this chapter begins with the RPI for March 1982).

(b) In *both* the rebasing calculation and in the calculation based on original cost, indexation allowance is calculated with reference to the *greater* of original cost and market value at 31 March 1982 i.e. the same indexation allowance is given in both calculations.

EXAMPLE 7

Calculate the chargeable gain arising on the disposal described in the above example. (RPI for March 1982 was 79.44 and RPI for January 1998 is 158.3).

SOLUTION

(a)

	Original cost	*Rebasing*
	£	£
Sale proceeds	8,500	8,500
Less : Original cost	2,000	
Market value 31/3/82		4,200
Unindexed gain	6,500	4,300
Less : Indexation allowance		
$\frac{158.3 - 79.44}{79.44}$ = 0.993 x £4,200	4,171	4,171
Chargeable gain	2,329	129

The rebasing calculation gives the lower gain, so rebasing applies and the chargeable gain is £129.

(b)

		Original cost	*Rebasing*
		£	£
Sale proceeds		8,500	8,500
Less : Original cost		2,000	
Market value 31/3/82			1,500
Unindexed gain		6,500	7,000
Less : Indexation allowance			
$\frac{158.3 - 79.44}{79.44}$	= 0.993 x £2,000	1,986	1,986
Chargeable gain		4,514	5,014

The rebasing calculation gives the higher gain, so rebasing does not apply and the chargeable gain is £4,514.

EXAMPLE 8

In January 1979, Margaret acquired a chargeable asset for £10,000. Enhancement expenditure was incurred of £2,000 in June 1980 and £3,000 in June 1984 (RPI 89.20). The asset had a market value of £16,000 on 31 March 1982 (RPI 79.44) and was sold in July 1997 (RPI 156.5) for £40,000. Compute the chargeable gain.

SOLUTION

			Original cost	*Rebasing*
		£	£	£
Sale proceeds			40,000	40,000
Less : Acquisition cost		10,000		
Enhancement expenditure June 1980		2,000	(12,000)	
Market value 31 March 1982				(16,000)
Enhancement expenditure June 1984			(3,000)	(3,000)
Unindexed gain			25,000	21,000
Less : Indexation allowance :				
(i) on cost to 31 March 1982				
$\frac{156.5 - 79.44}{79.44}$	= 0.970 x £16,000	15,520		
(ii) on enhancement June 1984				
$\frac{156.5 - 89.20}{89.20}$	= 0.754 x £3,000	2,262	17,782	17,782
Chargeable gain			7,218	3,218

The rebasing calculation gives the lower gain, so rebasing applies and the chargeable gain is £3,218.

Notes :

(i) Margaret has spent a total of £15,000 (£10,000 + £2,000 + £3,000) on buying and enhancing the asset. Therefore the calculation based on original cost takes into account total allowable expenditure of £15,000.

(ii) The market value at 31 March 1982 is the value of the asset as it stood on that date (i.e. the value of the asset including the June 1980 enhancement). But this valuation did not take into account the second enhancement, which did not occur until June 1984. Therefore the rebasing calculation takes into account both the market value at 31 March 1982 and the cost of the second enhancement.

(iii) Indexation allowance based on the change in RPI from March 1982 to July 1997 is given on the greater of total cost up to 31 March 1982 and market value at 31 March 1982. Indexation allowance is also given on the second enhancement, based on the change in RPI from June 1984 to July 1997.

Losses on disposal of pre-31 March 1982 assets

As shown above, if the rebasing calculation gives a gain and the original cost calculation also gives a gain, the chargeable gain is the *smaller* of these two gains. Similarly, if the rebasing calculation gives a loss and the original cost calculation also gives a loss, the allowable loss is the *smaller* of these two losses. Finally, if the rebasing calculation gives a loss and the original cost calculation gives a gain (or vice-versa), or if either of the calculations gives a nil result, the situation is "no gain, no loss" i.e. there is no chargeable gain and no allowable loss.

EXAMPLE 9

Neil acquired a chargeable asset in 1978. The asset was sold in April 1997 (RPI 155.6) for £2,000. Compute the chargeable gain or allowable loss if the original cost of the asset and its market value on 31 March 1982 (RPI 79.44) were :

	Original cost	*MV 31 March 1982*
(a)	750	850
(b)	3,500	4,000
(c)	10	2,050

SOLUTION

(a)

	Original cost	Rebasing
	£	£
Sale proceeds	2,000	2,000
Less : Original cost	750	
Market value 31/3/82		850
Unindexed gain	1,250	1,150
Less : Indexation allowance		
$\frac{155.6 - 79.44}{79.44}$ = 0.959 x £850	815	815
Chargeable gain	435	335

The rebasing calculation gives the lower gain, so rebasing applies and the chargeable gain is £335.

(b)

	Original cost	Rebasing
	£	£
Sale proceeds	2,000	2,000
Less : Original cost	3,500	
Market value 31/3/82		4,000
Unindexed loss	(1,500)	(2,000)
Less : Indexation allowance		
$\frac{155.6 - 79.44}{79.44}$ = 0.959 x £4,000	nil	nil
Allowable loss	(1,500)	(2,000)

The rebasing calculation gives the higher loss, so rebasing does not apply and the allowable loss is £1,500. Indexation allowance was restricted to £nil in both calculations, since indexation allowance cannot be used to increase an unindexed loss.

(c)

	Original cost	Rebasing
	£	£
Sale proceeds	2,000	2,000
Less : Original cost	10	
Market value 31/3/82		2,050
Unindexed gain (loss)	1,990	(50)
Less : Indexation allowance		
$\frac{155.6 - 79.44}{79.44}$ = 0.959 x £2,050	1,966	nil
Chargeable gain (allowable loss)	24	(50)

The rebasing calculation gives a loss, whilst the calculation based on original cost gives a gain. Therefore the situation is "no gain, no loss". Indexation allowance was restricted to £nil in the rebasing calculation, since indexation allowance cannot be used to increase an unindexed loss.

Part disposals of pre-31 March 1982 assets

When a part disposal is made of an asset which was owned on 31 March 1982, the part disposal fraction which is applied to the original cost of the asset (see earlier in this chapter) is also applied to the market value at 31 March 1982 for the purposes of the rebasing calculation.

EXAMPLE 10

A chargeable asset was purchased in November 1975 for £2,000. The asset had a market value on 31 March 1982 (RPI 79.44) of £5,000. Part of the asset was disposed of for £8,000 in November 1997 (RPI 157.7), at which time the remainder of the asset was valued at £12,000. Compute the chargeable gain.

SOLUTION

The part disposal fraction to be used in this case is :

$$\frac{£8,000}{£8,000 + £12,000}$$

The computation of the chargeable gain is therefore as follows :

	Original cost	*Rebasing*
	£	£
Sale proceeds	8,000	8,000
Less : Part cost :		
$\frac{£8,000}{£8,000 + £12,000} \times £2,000$	800	
Part market value 31/3/82 :		
$\frac{£8,000}{£8,000 + £12,000} \times £5,000$		2,000
Unindexed gain	7,200	6,000
Less : Indexation allowance		
$\frac{157.7 - 79.44}{79.44} = 0.985 \times £2,000$	1,970	1,970
Chargeable gain	5,230	4,030

The rebasing calculation gives the lower gain, so rebasing applies and the chargeable gain is £4,030.

The rebasing election

A taxpayer may make an *irrevocable* election to the effect that gains and losses arising on all future disposals of assets held on 31 March 1982 should be calculated by the rebasing method, with no reference whatsoever to the costs incurred before 31 March 1982. Such an election must be made on or before 31 January in the second tax year following the year in which the first disposal of a pre-31 March 1982 asset occurs after 5 April 1988. For example, if the first such disposal occurs during 1997/98, the election must be made by 31 January 2000.

If this election is made, costs incurred before 31 March 1982 are completely ignored for all purposes, including calculation of the indexation allowance. Therefore indexation allowance will always be based upon market value at 31 March 1982, even if this is lower than the costs incurred before 31 March 1982.

Assets acquired before 6 April 1965

When CGT was first introduced, special rules were devised for the calculation of the chargeable gain arising on the disposal of an asset acquired before 6 April 1965 (since only the part of the gain accruing since 6 April 1965 was taxable).

However, from the perspective of disposals made in the late 1990's, the disposal of an asset acquired before 6 April 1965 must also be the disposal of an asset held on 31 March 1982. Therefore rebasing is available in relation to such disposals. Rebasing will generally give a lower gain than the gain calculated according to the special rules referred to above but these rules will still be used if they give the lower gain.

In summary, the calculation of the chargeable gain arising on the disposal of an asset acquired before 6 April 1965 is as follows :

(a) The gain is first calculated by the "time apportionment" method. This method calculates the total gain arising since the asset was acquired and then apportions the gain between the period before 6 April 1965 (which is not taxable) and the period after 6 April 1965 (which is taxable). For the purposes of this method, indexation allowance is based on the higher of original cost and market value at 31 March 1982. If the asset was acquired before 6 April 1945 it is assumed to have been acquired on that date for time apportionment purposes.

(b) Alternatively, the taxpayer may elect for the "6 April 1965 market value" method (and will presumably do so if this produces a lower gain). This method calculates the gain by comparing disposal proceeds with the market value of the asset on 6 April 1965. For the purposes of this method, indexation allowance is based on the higher of market value at 6 April 1965 and market value at 31 March 1982.

(c) Finally, the gain produced by the above rules is compared with the gain produced by the rebasing rules and the lower gain is taken as the chargeable gain. The indexation allowance used in the rebasing calculation is based on either :

(i) the greater of original cost and market value at 31 March 1982 (if the time apportionment method is being used), or

(ii) the greater of market value at 6 April 1965 and market value at 31 March 1982 (if the taxpayer has elected for the 6 April 1965 market value method).

EXAMPLE 11

A chargeable asset was purchased on 6 October 1951 for £50,000 and sold on 6 October 1997 (RPI 157.4) for £250,000. The market value of the asset was £25,000 on 6 April 1965 and £75,000 on 31 March 1982 (RPI 79.44). Compute the chargeable gain, performing apportionment calculations to the nearest month.

SOLUTION

	Time apportionment	*MV 6/4/65*
	£	£
Sale proceeds	250,000	250,000
Less : Original cost	50,000	
Market value 6/4/65		25,000
Unindexed gain	200,000	225,000
Less : Indexation allowance		
$\frac{157.4 - 79.44}{79.44} = 0.981 \times £75,000$	73,575	73,575
Chargeable gain	126,425	151,425
Time apportioned $\frac{32.5}{46.0} \times £126,425$	89,322	

The gain produced by the time apportionment method is lower than the gain produced by the 6 April 1965 market value method. Therefore the taxpayer will not elect for the 6 April 1965 market value method and the gain (before considering rebasing) is £89,322. The gain produced by the rebasing calculation is £101,425 (£250,000 - £75,000 - £73,575). This is higher than the gain based on cost, so rebasing will not apply and the chargeable gain is £89,322.

Notes :

(i) Indexation allowance was based on 31 March 1982 market value in each case, since this was greater than original cost or 6 April 1965 market value.

(ii) The asset was owned for 46 years and disposal took place 32 years and 6 months after 6 April 1965, hence the time apportionment fraction used above.

Losses on disposal of pre-6 April 1965 assets

If all three of the computations required on the disposal of an asset held on 6 April 1965 result in a gain (as in the above example), the chargeable gain is the lowest of these three gains. But the situation is more complex if any of the computations result in a loss. If this happens then the following rules apply :

(a) If time apportionment gives a loss and market value at 6 April 1965 gives a gain (or a smaller loss), then the taxpayer will not elect (and cannot be forced to elect) for the 6 April 1965 market value method of calculation. The time apportioned loss is then compared with the outcome of the rebasing calculation in the usual way.

(b) If time apportionment gives a gain and market value at 6 April 1965 gives a loss then the situation is no gain, no loss and there is no point in performing a rebasing calculation.

(c) If time apportionment gives a loss and market value at 6 April 1965 gives a greater loss, the allowable loss is restricted to the amount of the loss based on original cost, *ignoring time apportionment.* This loss is then compared with the outcome of the rebasing calculation in the usual way.

EXAMPLE 12

A chargeable asset was purchased on 6 April 1962 for £24,000 and sold on 6 April 1997 (RPI 155.6) for £18,000. The market value of the asset was £26,000 on 6 April 1965 and £30,000 on 31 March 1982 (RPI 79.44). Compute the chargeable gain.

SOLUTION

	Time apportionment	*MV 6/4/65*
	£	£
Sale proceeds	18,000	18,000
Less : Original cost	24,000	
Market value 6/4/65		26,000
Unindexed loss	(6,000)	(8,000)
Less : Indexation allowance		
$\frac{155.6 - 79.44}{79.44} = 0.959 \times £30,000$	nil	nil
Allowable loss	(6,000)	(8,000)
Time apportioned $\frac{32}{35} \times £6,000$	(5,486)	

Time apportionment gives a loss and market value at 6 April 1965 gives a greater loss, therefore the allowable loss is restricted to the amount of the loss based on original cost, ignoring time apportionment i.e. £6,000. This loss is then compared with the loss produced by the rebasing calculation, which is £12,000 (£18,000 - £30,000). The allowable loss is the lower of these figures i.e. £6,000.

Summary

- The disposal value of an asset is normally equal to the sale proceeds, but if an asset is given away or is sold to a connected person, the disposal value is deemed to be the market value of the asset on the date of the sale.
- Allowable costs include acquisition cost of the asset, costs of acquisition and disposal, enhancement expenditure, costs of defending the owner's title and valuation fees.
- Indexation allowance is calculated for each allowable cost (apart from the costs of disposal) and is based on the change in RPI between the month in which the cost was incurred and the month of the disposal.
- Indexation allowance cannot be used to create or increase a loss.
- On a part disposal, the allowable part cost is calculated by multiplying the full cost by the part disposal fraction.
- A taxpayer may claim that an asset has negligible value, so triggering a disposal which gives rise to an allowable loss.
- If an asset is disposed of which was owned on 31 March 1982, it is necessary to perform a calculation based on original cost and a "rebasing" calculation based on market value at 31 March 1982. The chargeable gain (or allowable loss) is the lower of the gains (or losses) produced by these two calculations. If one calculation produces a gain and the other produces a loss then the situation is no gain, no loss.
- A taxpayer may make a once-and-for-all election for the rebasing method to be used on all disposals of pre-31 March 1982 assets.
- Special rules apply to the disposal of assets owned on 6 April 1965.

Retail price index (RPI)

(*Source* : Central Statistical Office)

	Jan	Feb	Mar	Apr	May	Jun	Jul	Aug	Sep	Oct	Nov	Dec
1982			79.44	81.04	81.62	81.85	81.88	81.90	81.85	82.26	82.66	82.51
1983	82.61	82.97	83.12	84.28	84.64	84.84	85.30	85.68	86.06	86.36	86.67	86.89
1984	86.84	87.20	87.48	88.64	88.97	89.20	89.10	89.94	90.11	90.67	90.95	90.87
1985	91.20	91.94	92.80	94.78	95.21	95.41	95.23	95.49	95.44	95.59	95.92	96.05
1986	96.25	96.60	96.73	97.67	97.85	97.79	97.52	97.82	98.30	98.45	99.29	99.62
1987	100.0	100.4	100.6	101.8	101.9	101.9	101.8	102.1	102.4	102.9	103.4	103.3
1988	103.3	103.7	104.1	105.8	106.2	106.6	106.7	107.9	108.4	109.5	110.0	110.3
1989	111.0	111.8	112.3	114.3	115.0	115.4	115.5	115.8	116.6	117.5	118.5	118.8
1990	119.5	120.2	121.4	125.1	126.2	126.7	126.8	128.1	129.3	130.3	130.0	129.9
1991	130.2	130.9	131.4	133.1	133.5	134.1	133.8	134.1	134.6	135.1	135.6	135.7
1992	135.6	136.3	136.7	138.8	139.3	139.3	138.8	138.9	139.4	139.9	139.7	139.2
1993	137.9	138.8	139.3	140.6	141.1	141.0	140.7	141.3	141.9	141.8	141.6	141.9
1994	141.3	142.1	142.5	144.2	144.7	144.7	144.0	144.7	144.7	145.2	145.3	146.0
1995	146.0	146.9	147.5	149.0	149.6	149.8	149.1	149.9	150.6	149.8	149.8	150.7
1996	150.2	150.9	151.5	152.6	152.9	153.0	152.4	153.1	153.8	153.8	153.9	154.4
1997	*154.7*	*155.0*	*155.3*	*155.6*	*155.9*	*156.2*	*156.5*	*156.8*	*157.1*	*157.4*	*157.7*	*158.0*
1998	*158.3*	*158.6*	*158.9*	*159.2*	*159.5*	*159.8*	*160.1*	*160.4*				

(RPI's for January 1997 onwards have been estimated by the author).

Exercises

17.1 Carol purchased a holiday flat in December 1987 (RPI 103.3) for £35,000. She spent £3,000 on installing central heating in February 1988 (RPI 103.7) and a further £650 on repainting the interior of the flat in March 1992 (RPI 136.7). She sold the flat at auction in August 1997 (RPI 156.8) for £62,000, paying a 5% fee to the auctioneer. The flat was never Carol's residence. Compute the chargeable gain.

17.2 David was given a chargeable asset in November 1991 (RPI 135.6) at which time the asset had a market value of £4,500. He sold the asset in January 1998 (RPI 158.3). Compute the chargeable gain if the sale proceeds were :

(a) £4,950

(b) £4,350

(c) £5,380.

17.3 Edwina bought a chargeable asset in August 1991 (RPI 134.1) for £240,000, paying acquisition costs of £12,000. In June 1997 (RPI 156.2) she sold a one-quarter interest in the asset for £100,000, incurring disposal costs of £5,000. The remaining three-quarter interest in the asset was valued at £500,000 in June 1997. Compute the chargeable gain.

In January 1998 (RPI 158.3), Edwina sold her remaining three-quarter interest in the asset for £520,000. Compute the chargeable gain.

17.4 Francis acquired an oil painting for £12,500 in March 1975. He sold the painting for £37,500 in March 1998 (RPI 158.9). Compute the chargeable gain if the market value of the painting on 31 March 1982 (RPI 79.44) was :

(a) £10,000
(b) £15,000.

17.5 In April 1990 (RPI 125.1) Gillian was given some shares with a market value at that time of £6,000. Unfortunately the company was forced to appoint a receiver in 1997 and Gillian's shares became virtually valueless. In October 1997 (RPI 157.4) Gillian made a successful claim to the effect that her shares had a negligible value of only £80.

(a) Compute the allowable loss.
(b) If Gillian sold the shares for £120 in March 1998 (RPI 158.9), compute the chargeable gain.

17.6 Henry acquired a chargeable asset in August 1970 at a cost of £100. The asset was sold in August 1997 (RPI 156.8) for £8,450. Compute the chargeable gain or allowable loss if the asset had a market value on 31 March 1982 of :

(a) £8,500
(b) £12,500.

***17.7** Iris bought a chargeable asset on 6 April 1958 for £400. The asset had a market value of £600 on 6 April 1965 and £850 on 31 March 1982 (RPI 79.44). She sold the asset on 6 April 1997 (RPI 155.6) for £4,200. Compute the chargeable gain.

***17.8** Jon bought a holiday cottage in 1975 for £23,000. He spent £10,000 on building an extension in 1979 and a further £4,000 on building a garage in June 1985 (RPI 95.41). The cottage was valued at £33,500 on 31 March 1982 (RPI 79.44) and was sold for £85,000 in May 1997 (RPI 155.9). Compute the chargeable gain. (The cottage was never Jon's residence).

***17.9** Karen bought a house in 1979 for £30,000. The house was valued at £32,000 on 31 March 1982 (RPI 79.44). In November 1986 (RPI 99.29) she spent £18,000 on dividing the house into two self-contained flats and in May 1997 (RPI 155.9) she sold one of the flats for £95,000, at which time the other flat was valued at £105,000. In January 1998 (RPI 158.3) she sold the second flat for £110,000. Karen never lived in either of the flats. Compute the chargeable gains arising on the two disposals.

Chapter 18

Chattels and wasting assets

Introduction

A "chattel" is an item of tangible, movable property. A "wasting asset" is one with an expected useful life of 50 years or less at the time of disposal. If an asset is both a chattel and a wasting asset (e.g. a domestic television set) it is a "wasting chattel". Special CGT rules apply to the disposal of chattels, wasting assets and wasting chattels, and the purpose of this chapter is to explain these special rules.

The chattels exemption

If a chattel is disposed of for £6,000 or less, the disposal is exempt from CGT. This provision removes from charge a great many trivial disposals and ensures that CGT is levied only if the disposal is material. The following points relate to the chattels exemption :

(a) This exemption applies only to chattels, not to assets in general.

(b) The exemption means that gains arising on the disposal of a chattel for £6,000 or less are not chargeable to CGT but it also means that losses arising on such disposals are not allowable (but see below for more information on chattels disposed of at a loss).

(c) The £6,000 figure relates to the *gross* disposal proceeds i.e. the proceeds before deducting incidental costs of disposal.

(d) If the gross disposal proceeds of a chattel exceed £6,000, the chargeable gain cannot exceed five-thirds of the amount by which the proceeds exceed £6,000. This "marginal relief" ensures that taxpayers who dispose of chattels for slightly more than £6,000 are not unduly penalised by the tax system.

EXAMPLE 1

In 1997/98, a taxpayer makes a number of disposals, as listed below. Which of these disposals would be exempt from CGT ?

(a) An antique table sold for £5,000.

(b) A watercolour painting sold at auction, The auctioneer deducted his 10% commission from the selling price and sent the taxpayer a cheque for the remaining £5,670.

(c) A holding of shares sold for £4,500.

SOLUTION

(a) The antique table is a chattel disposed of for £6,000 or less. Therefore the disposal is exempt from CGT.

(b) A watercolour painting is a chattel, but the gross disposal proceeds must have been £6,300 (since £6,300 less 10% = £5,670). The chattels exemption will not apply but the chargeable gain cannot exceed five-thirds of £300 i.e. £500.

(c) A shareholding is not a chattel. Therefore the £6,000 exemption does not apply and the disposal will be chargeable to CGT.

EXAMPLE 2

In December 1997 (RPI 158.0), Michael sells a piece of antique furniture for £6,360. He pays incidental disposal costs of £420. He had acquired the furniture as a gift from his mother in January 1991 (RPI 130.2). Compute the chargeable gain if the market value of the furniture in January 1991 was :

(a) £4,800 (b) £4,300

SOLUTION

	(a)	(b)
	£	£
Sale proceeds	6,360	6,360
<u>Less</u> : Incidental costs of disposal	420	420
	5,940	5,940
<u>Less</u> : Deemed acquisition cost	4,800	4,300
Unindexed gain	1,140	1,640
<u>Less</u> : Indexation allowance		
$\frac{158.0 - 130.2}{130.2}$ = 0.214 x £4,800	1,027	
$\frac{158.0 - 130.2}{130.2}$ = 0.214 x £4,300		920
Chargeable gain	113	720

Notes :

(a) £113 is less than the maximum chargeable gain of £360 x 5/3 = £600, so the chargeable gain is £113.

(b) £720 exceeds £600, so the chargeable gain is restricted to £600.

Chattels disposed of at a loss

If a chattel is disposed of at a loss, there are two possibilities. Either :

(a) the disposal proceeds are more than £6,000, in which case the allowable loss is calculated in the usual way, or

(b) the disposal proceeds are £6,000 or less, in which case the chattels exemption applies and it appears that no allowable loss could arise.

However, if a chattel is acquired for more than £6,000 and then disposed of for less than £6,000, the chattels exemption is overruled and an allowable loss is given. But the amount of the loss is restricted to the amount that would arise if the disposal proceeds were exactly £6,000.

EXAMPLE 3

In March 1998, Naomi sells an oil painting which she had acquired some years previously for £10,000. Compute the allowable loss is she sells the painting for :

(a) £7,200 (b) £5,700

SOLUTION

(a) Naomi has disposed of a chattel for more than £6,000, so the disposal is not exempt from CGT. The allowable loss is calculated in the usual way as £10,000 - £7,200 = £2,800. There is of course no indexation allowance to consider, since indexation allowance cannot be used to increase a loss.

(b) Naomi has disposed of a chattel for less than £6,000 and normally this disposal would be exempt from CGT. However, since the asset was acquired for more than £6,000 a loss is allowed, calculated by substituting £6,000 for the disposal proceeds. The allowable loss is £10,000 - £6,000 = £4,000. Again, there is no point in calculating indexation allowance.

Part disposals of chattels

A part disposal of a chattel may be made in one of two ways. Either :

(a) a part interest in a chattel may be disposed of, or

(b) for chattels forming a set, one or more of the items in the set may be disposed of.

Each of these forms of part disposal is considered below.

Disposal of a part interest in a chattel

If a disposal is made of a part interest in a chattel, this part disposal will be exempt from CGT only if the value of the *whole* chattel immediately prior to the part disposal is £6,000 or less.

If the value of the whole chattel exceeds £6,000 the disposal is not exempt from CGT and the usual part disposal calculation is performed. However, the chargeable gain on the part disposal is limited to five-thirds of the amount by which the value of the whole chattel exceeds £6,000, multiplied by the usual part disposal fraction.

EXAMPLE 4

In October 1989 (RPI 117.5) Jackie bought a statuette for £3,500. In October 1997 (RPI 157.4), she sells a one-third interest in the statuette for £2,000. Compute the chargeable gain if the value of the remaining two-thirds interest in October 1997 is :

(a) £4,000 (b) £5,000

SOLUTION

(a) The value of the whole chattel on the date of the part disposal is £6,000. Since this value does not exceed £6,000 the part disposal is exempt from CGT.

(b) The value of the whole chattel on the date of the part disposal is £7,000. Since this value exceeds £6,000 the part disposal is not exempt from CGT. The computation of the chargeable gain is as follows :

	£
Sale proceeds	2,000
<u>Less</u> : Part cost :	
$\frac{£2,000}{£2,000 + £5,000} \times £3,500$	1,000
Unindexed gain	1,000
<u>Less</u> : Indexation allowance	
$\frac{157.4 - 117.5}{117.5} = 0.340 \times £1,000$	340
Chargeable gain	660

The part disposal fraction cancels down to 2/7th, so the chargeable gain is restricted to £1,000 x 5/3 x 2/7 = £476.

Disposal of part of a set

If a taxpayer acquires a set of chattels (e.g. a set of dining chairs) and then disposes of them individually, each disposal is regarded as a part disposal and will in general only be chargeable to CGT if the disposal proceeds exceed £6,000.

However, a taxpayer who wished to dispose of a set of chattels with a total value exceeding £6,000 could use this rule to avoid CGT by disposing of the items one by one (with each disposal raising less than £6,000). In order to prevent such avoidance, a series of disposals of chattels which form part of a set will be treated as a single transaction for the purposes of calculating the chattels exemption if all the disposals are *to the same person* or to persons connected with each other or acting together.

EXAMPLE 5

Andrew acquired a set of six dining chairs in January 1987 (RPI 100.0) for £4,300. In June 1997 (RPI 156.2) he sold three of the chairs to a friend for £3,500 (the other 3 chairs also being valued at £3,500). In August 1997 (RPI 156.8) he sold the remaining chairs to the friend's brother for £3,700. Compute the chargeable gain on each disposal.

SOLUTION

If it were not for the rule introduced above, neither of these disposals would be chargeable to CGT since neither of them raises more than £6,000. However, the two disposals are made to connected persons and are therefore to be regarded as a single transaction for the purposes of calculating the chattels exemption. The total disposal proceeds are £7,200 (£3,500 + £3,700). This exceeds £6,000 so the disposals are chargeable. The computations are as follows :

	June 1997	*August 1997*
	£	£
Sale proceeds	3,500	3,700
Less : Part cost :		
$\frac{£3,500}{£3,500 + £3,500} \times £4,300$	2,150	
Remainder of cost (£4,300 - £2,150)		2,150
Unindexed gain	1,350	1,550
Less : Indexation allowance		
$\frac{156.2 - 100.0}{100.0} = 0.562 \times £2,150$	1,208	
$\frac{156.8 - 100.0}{100.0} = 0.568 \times £2,150$		1,221
Chargeable gain	142	329

This gives a total chargeable gain of £471 (£142 + £329). The two transactions are also treated as one for the purpose of calculating the chattels marginal relief, so that the total chargeable gain cannot exceed (£7,200 - £6,000) x 5/3 = £2,000. Since this exceeds £471, the chargeable gain remains £471.

Wasting chattels

Wasting chattels (i.e. chattels with an expected useful life of 50 years or less at the time of disposal) are generally exempt from CGT. Therefore no chargeable gain or allowable loss can in general arise on the disposal of a wasting chattel.

The only exception to this rule relates to movable plant and machinery used in business and eligible for capital allowances. Plant and machinery is always regarded as a wasting asset for CGT purposes and therefore movable plant and machinery is a wasting chattel. Disposals of such plant and machinery are *not* exempt from CGT (unless disposal proceeds do not exceed £6,000 in which case the chattels exemption applies). One of two situations may arise on disposal :

(a) Disposal proceeds may be less than original cost. In this (the most likely) case, the unindexed loss is reduced by the total capital allowances which have been available on the asset. This will reduce the loss to £nil and since no indexation allowance is available on assets sold at a loss, the allowable loss will also be £nil.

(b) Disposal proceeds may be greater than original cost. In this case, the total of available capital allowances on the asset is £nil and therefore capital allowances have no effect on the computation which will proceed in the usual way.

In fact, these rules (other than the £6,000 exemption) also apply to immovable plant and machinery used in business and eligible for capital allowances.

EXAMPLE 6

An item of movable plant and machinery is bought in February 1992 (RPI 136.3) for £8,000 and used solely for trade purposes. Capital allowances are available in relation to this item. Compute the chargeable gain arising if the item is sold in July 1997 (RPI 156.5) and the sale proceeds are :

(a) £4,500 (b) £6,500 (c) £8,500 (d) £10,500.

SOLUTION

In case (a), sale proceeds do not exceed £6,000 so the disposal is exempt from CGT. In cases (b), (c) and (d), the sale proceeds exceed £6,000 so there is no exemption. The computations are as follows :

	(b)	(c)	(d)
	£	£	£
Sale proceeds	6,500	8,500	10,500
Less : Acquisition cost	8,000	8,000	8,000
	(1,500)	500	2,500
Less : Available capital allowances	1,500	0	0
Unindexed gain/(loss)	nil	500	2,500
Less : Indexation allowance			
$\frac{156.5 - 136.3}{136.3}$ = 0.148 x £8,000 = £1,184	nil	500	1,184
Chargeable gain	nil	nil	1,316

In case (d), the gain of £1,316 is less than the maximum chargeable gain of £4,500 x 5/3 = £7,500, so the chargeable gain is £1,316.

Wasting assets

A wasting asset which is not a chattel is *not* exempt from CGT. Typical examples of such wasting assets include :

(a) immovable plant and machinery (but see earlier in this chapter for a description of the CGT treatment if the plant is eligible for capital allowances)

(b) leases with less than 50 years' life remaining (to which special rules apply, as described later in this chapter)

(c) intangible assets such as copyrights, options etc. with less than 50 years' life remaining.

In general, the original cost of a wasting asset (less its scrap value, if any) is deemed to "waste away" on a straight line basis over the asset's predictable life. The computation of the gain or loss arising on the disposal of the asset is then achieved by comparing disposal proceeds with the unexpired portion of the asset's cost at the time of disposal.

EXAMPLE 7

In January 1990 (RPI 119.5), Fiona acquired a 20-year copyright at a cost of £30,000. In January 1998 (RPI 158.3) she sold the copyright for £35,500. Compute the chargeable gain.

SOLUTION

When the copyright was bought it had a 20-year life. When it was sold there were 12 years remaining. Therefore the computation is as follows :

	£
Sale proceeds	35,500
Less : Unexpired portion of cost	
$\frac{12}{20}$ x £30,000	18,000
Unindexed gain	17,500
Less : Indexation allowance	
$\frac{158.3 - 119.5}{119.5}$ = 0.325 x £18,000	5,850
Chargeable gain	11,650

EXAMPLE 8

In March 1979, Philip acquired a 25-year copyright at a cost of £50,000. The copyright was valued at £63,000 on 31 March 1982 (RPI 79.44). In March 1998 (RPI 158.9) Philip sold the copyright for £42,000. Compute the chargeable gain.

SOLUTION

When the copyright was bought it had a 25-year life and when it was valued on 31 March 1982 it had a 22-year life. When it was sold there were 6 years remaining. Therefore the computation is as follows :

	Original cost £	*Rebasing* £
Sale proceeds	42,000	42,000
Less : Unexpired portion of cost		
$\frac{6}{25}$ x £50,000	12,000	
Unexpired portion of MV 31/3/82		
$\frac{6}{22}$ x £63,000		17,182
Unindexed gain	30,000	24,818
Less : Indexation allowance		
$\frac{158.9 - 79.44}{79.44}$ = 1.000 x £17,182	17,182	17,182
Chargeable gain	12,818	7,636

The rebasing calculation gives the lower gain, so rebasing applies and the chargeable gain is £7,636.

Leases

For CGT purposes, leases are classified into "long leases" (i.e. those with more than 50 years to run) and "short leases" (i.e. those with 50 years or less to run). A chargeable disposal may occur in connection with a lease in any of the following ways :

(a) A taxpayer who has a long lease on a piece of property assigns that long lease to someone else.

(b) A taxpayer who has a short lease on a piece of property assigns that short lease to someone else.

(c) A taxpayer who has the freehold (or a long head-lease) grants a long lease (or sub-lease) on the property to someone else, the property eventually reverting to the taxpayer.

(d) A taxpayer who has the freehold (or a long head-lease) grants a short lease (or sub-lease) on the property to someone else, the property eventually reverting to the taxpayer.

(e) A taxpayer who has a short head-lease grants a shorter sub-lease on the property to someone else, the property eventually reverting to the taxpayer.

Each of these cases is considered below. Note that if a property is or has been the taxpayer's main residence, the gain arising on the disposal of a lease on the property may be subject to the principal private residence exemption described in Chapter 21.

Assignment of a long lease

The assignment of a long lease is treated as a disposal of the whole asset and therefore causes no CGT difficulties at all. The computation proceeds in precisely the same way as the computation on the disposal of any other whole asset.

EXAMPLE 9

In 1988, Jim acquired a 99 year lease on a flat for £60,000. In 1997, he assigned the lease to a third party for £92,000. The flat was never Jim's residence. Compute the chargeable gain, assuming an indexation factor of 49%.

SOLUTION

The unindexed gain is £32,000. Indexation allowance of £29,400 (49% x £60,000) reduces this to a chargeable gain of £2,600.

Assignment of a short lease

A short lease is, by definition, a wasting asset. Therefore the computation of the chargeable gain arising on the disposal of a short lease should be achieved by comparing disposal proceeds with the unexpired portion of the lease's cost at the time of disposal.

However, unlike other wasting assets, the cost of a short lease is not deemed to waste away on a straight line basis. Instead, the cost of a short lease is deemed to waste away according to a table of percentages given in Schedule 8 of the Taxation of Chargeable Gains Act 1992. The effect of this table is to write off the cost of a short lease slowly in the early years and more quickly in the closing years. The table is reproduced at the end of this chapter.

The proportion of the cost of a short lease which is allowed in the CGT computation on its disposal is :

$$\frac{\text{\% relating to number of years lease has left to run on disposal}}{\text{\% relating to original length of lease}}$$

If the lease was originally a long lease but the taxpayer has occupied the property for some years so that the lease now being assigned is a short lease, the denominator in the above fraction is taken as 100%, corresponding to "50 or more" in the Schedule 8 table.

EXAMPLE 10

Jean acquired a 30-year lease on a property in July 1987 (RPI 101.8) for £32,000. In July 1997 (RPI 156.5), she assigned the lease to a third party for £45,000. The property was never Jean's residence. Compute the chargeable gain.

SOLUTION

When the lease was acquired it had a 30-year life (Sch 8 percentage 87.330%). When it was assigned there were 20 years remaining (Sch 8 percentage 72.770%). Therefore the computation is as follows :

	£
Sale proceeds	45,000
Less : Unexpired portion of cost	
$\frac{72.770}{87.330}$ x £32,000	26,665
Unindexed gain	18,335
Less : Indexation allowance	
$\frac{156.5 - 101.8}{101.8}$ = 0.537 x £26,665	14,319
Chargeable gain	4,016

Schedule 8 gives percentages only for whole numbers of years. If the duration of a lease is not a whole number of years, then the appropriate percentage is calculated from the table on a pro rata basis.

EXAMPLE 11

A taxpayer assigns a lease of duration 12 years and 5 months. Calculate the appropriate percentage for use in the CGT computation on the disposal.

SOLUTION

The percentage for 12 years is 53.191%. The percentage for 13 years is 56.167%. The difference between these percentages is 2.976%. Therefore the appropriate percentage for a lease of duration 12 years and 5 months is 53.191 + 2.976 x 5/12 = 54.431%.

EXAMPLE 12

Joan acquired a 40-year lease on a property on 31 May 1981 for £38,000. The market value of the lease on 31 March 1982 (RPI 79.44) was £35,000. On 30 November 1997 (RPI 157.7), she assigned the lease to a third party for £65,000. The property was never Joan's residence. Compute the chargeable gain.

SOLUTION

When the lease was acquired it had a 40-year life (Sch 8 percentage 95.457%). On 31 March 1982 there were 39 years and 2 months remaining (Sch 8 percentage 94.842 + 0.615 x 2/12 = 94.945%). When it was assigned there were 23 years and 6 months remaining (Sch 8 percentage = 78.055 + 1.567 x 6/12 = 78.839%). The computation is as follows :

	Original cost	*Rebasing*
	£	£
Sale proceeds	65,000	65,000
Less : Unexpired portion of cost		
$\frac{78.839}{95.457}$ x £38,000	31,385	
Unexpired portion of MV 31/3/82		
$\frac{78.839}{94.945}$ x £35,000		29,063
Unindexed gain	33,615	35,937
Less : Indexation allowance		
$\frac{157.7 - 79.44}{79.44}$ = 0.985 x £31,385	30,914	30,914
Chargeable gain	2,701	5,023

The rebasing calculation gives the higher gain, so rebasing does not apply and the chargeable gain is £2,701.

Grant of a long lease

The grant of a long lease (or sub-lease) out of a freehold (or a long head-lease) is treated as a part disposal for CGT purposes and the normal part disposal rules apply. The value of the part disposed of is clearly the proceeds of the disposal. The value of the part remaining takes into account both :

(a) the right of the taxpayer making the disposal to receive rents from the tenant, and

(b) the taxpayer's "reversionary interest" i.e. the right to take back the property when the lease (or sub-lease) finishes.

Grant of a short lease

The grant of a short lease (or sub-lease) out of a freehold (or a long head-lease) is also treated as a part disposal for CGT purposes and once again the part disposal rules apply. However, the premium received on the grant of a short lease (or sub-lease) will be assessable to Schedule A income tax (see Chapter 5) and therefore, in order to avoid double taxation, the disposal proceeds are reduced by the amount of the Schedule A assessment.

EXAMPLE 13

Jeffrey acquired a freehold property in 1991 for £117,000. In 1997 he granted Jill a lease on the property for £80,000. The market value of the freehold after the lease had been granted was £100,000. The property was never Jeffrey's residence. Compute the chargeable gain, given that the lease granted to Jill was of duration :

(a) 99 years (b) 40 years.

Assume an indexation factor of 18%.

SOLUTION

(a) This is a part disposal with A = £80,000 and B = £100,000. The computation is as follows :

	£
Sale proceeds	80,000
Less : Part cost :	
$\frac{£80,000}{£80,000 + £100,000} \times £117,000$	52,000
Unindexed gain	28,000

	£
Unindexed gain	28,000
Less : Indexation allowance	
18% of £52,000	9,360
Chargeable gain	18,640

(b) This is also a part disposal but the disposal proceeds will be subject to a Schedule A assessment of £17,600 (£80,000 - 2% x £80,000 x 39) and this must be taken into account in the CGT computation. The computation is as follows :

	£
Sale proceeds (£80,000 - £17,600)	62,400
Less : Part cost :	
$\frac{£62,400}{£80,000 + £100,000} \times £117,000$	40,560
Unindexed gain	21,840
Less : Indexation allowance	
18% of £40,560	7,301
Chargeable gain	14,539

Note that the numerator of the part disposal fraction is taken as the disposal proceeds *after* deducting the Schedule A assessment, whilst the denominator takes into account the disposal proceeds *before* deducting the Schedule A assessment.

Grant of a short sub-lease out of a short head-lease

In essence, the grant of a short sub-lease out of a short head-lease is treated in a similar fashion to the assignment of a short lease, as discussed earlier in this chapter. Once again, the Schedule 8 table of percentages is called into use to determine the part cost that should be deducted in the CGT computation. But since the property will be returning to the original tenant when the sub-lease finishes, the proportion of the cost of the short head-lease which is allowed in the CGT computation on the granting of the sub-lease is equal to:

$$\frac{P1 - P2}{P3}$$

where :

P1 = % relating to the number of years left of the short head-lease when the sub-lease begins

P2 = % relating to the number of years left of the short head-lease when the sub-lease ends

P3 = % relating to original length of the short head-lease.

Since the premium received by the taxpayer on the grant of a short sub-lease will be assessable to Schedule A income tax, the chargeable gain is reduced by the amount of the Schedule A assessment. However, this reduction cannot be used to convert a gain into a loss or to increase a loss.

EXAMPLE 14

Joanna acquired a 15-year lease on a property in September 1991 (RPI 134.6) for £45,000. In September 1997 (RPI 157.1), she granted a 4-year sub-lease to a third party for £20,000. The property was never Joanna's residence. Compute the chargeable gain.

SOLUTION

The computation of the chargeable gain is as follows :

	£
Sale proceeds	20,000
Less : Proportion of cost	
$\frac{43.154 - 26.722}{61.617}$ x £45,000	12,001
Unindexed gain	7,999
Less : Indexation allowance	
$\frac{157.1 - 134.6}{134.6}$ = 0.167 x £12,001	2,004
	5,995
Less : Schedule A assessment (£10,160)	5,995
Chargeable gain (allowable loss)	nil

Notes :

(i) P1 = 43.154 (9 years), P2 = 26.722 (5 years) and P3 = 61.617 (15 years)

(ii) The Schedule A assessment (see Chapter 5) is :

	£
Premium received	20,000
Less : £20,000 x (4 - 1) x 2%	1,200
	18,800
Less : Relief for premium paid :	
$\frac{4}{15}$ x (£45,000 - £45,000 x (15 - 1) x 2%)	8,640
	10,160

(iii) The relief given for the Schedule A assessment is restricted to £5,995 so as not to turn a gain into a loss.

Summary

- A chattel is an item of tangible, movable property. A wasting asset is one with an expected useful life of 50 years or less at the time of disposal. A wasting asset that is also a chattel is a wasting chattel.
- Chattels disposed of for £6,000 or less are exempt from CGT.
- The allowable loss on chattels acquired for more than £6,000 and disposed of for less than £6,000 is restricted by substituting £6,000 for the disposal proceeds.
- Disposals of a part interest in a chattel are exempt from CGT if the value of the whole chattel is £6,000 or less,
- A series of disposals of chattels forming a set will be treated as a single transaction for CGT purposes if the disposals are to connected persons.
- Wasting chattels are exempt from CGT apart from movable plant and machinery used in business on which capital allowances are available.
- Wasting assets are not exempt from CGT. In general, the original cost of a wasting asset is written off over its predictable life using the straight line method. However, special rules apply to plant and machinery used for trade purposes and to leases.
- An assignment of a long lease is regarded as the disposal of a whole asset.
- An assignment of a short lease is a disposal of a wasting asset. The original cost of a short lease is written off over its predictable life, using a table of percentages contained in Schedule 8, TCGA 1992.
- The grant of a long lease is treated as a part disposal.
- The grant of a short lease (or sub-lease) out of a freehold (or long head-lease) is treated as a part disposal. The Schedule A assessment raised on the premium received is deducted from disposal proceeds in the CGT computation.
- The grant of a short sub-lease out of a short head-lease is a part disposal of a wasting asset. The Schedule 8 table is used to determine the allowable cost used in the CGT computation. The Schedule A assessment raised on the premium received is deducted from the chargeable gain but cannot be used to convert a gain into a loss or to increase a loss.

Short lease amortisation table

(Schedule 8 of TCGA 1992)

Years	*Percentage*	*Years*	*Percentage*	*Years*	*Percentage*
50 or more	100	33	90.280	16	64.116
49	99.657	32	89.354	15	61.617
48	99.289	31	88.371	14	58.971
47	98.902	30	87.330	13	56.167
46	98.490	29	86.226	12	53.191
45	98.059	28	85.053	11	50.038
44	97.595	27	83.816	10	46.695
43	97.107	26	82.496	9	43.154
42	96.593	25	81.100	8	39.399
41	96.041	24	79.622	7	35.414
40	95.457	23	78.055	6	31.195
39	94.842	22	76.399	5	26.722
38	94.189	21	74.635	4	21.983
37	93.497	20	72.770	3	16.959
36	92.761	19	70.791	2	11.629
35	91.981	18	68.697	1	5.983
34	91.156	17	66.470	0	0

Exercises

18.1 Classify each of the following assets as either chattels, wasting assets or wasting chattels :

(a) A domestic washing machine.

(b) A gold ring.

(c) A personal computer.

(d) A central heating system.

(e) A 20-year lease on a building.

(f) A suit of clothes.

(g) An antique vase.

18.2 In October 1997 (RPI 157.4), Keith sells an antique cabinet for £7,200. He incurs incidental costs of disposal amounting to £200. The cabinet cost £2,000 in July 1989 (RPI 115.5). Compute the chargeable gain.

18.3 In September 1997 (RPI 157.1), Kevin sells a drawing for £2,000. He was given the drawing in February 1990 (RPI 120.2) when it was thought (incorrectly) to be by a famous artist and had a market value of £50,000. Compute the allowable loss.

18.4 In January 1998 (RPI 158.3), Karl sells a one-quarter interest in a painting for £25,000. The remaining three-quarter interest is valued at £85,000. The painting had cost Karl £38,500 in January 1984 (RPI 86.84). Compute the chargeable gain.

18.5 In February 1991 (RPI 130.9), Katrina buys an item of movable plant and machinery for use in her business. The plant costs her £50,000 and capital allowances are claimed. Compute the chargeable gain in March 1998 (RPI 158.9) when she sells the plant, assuming that sale proceeds are :

(a) £60,000

(b) £35,000.

18.6 In June 1995 (RPI 149.8), Katie acquired a 5-year option to buy a piece of land. The option cost her £10,000. In June 1997 (RPI 156.2), she sold the option for £8,000. Compute the chargeable gain.

18.7 Katherine acquired a 25-year lease on a property on 31 August 1980 for £12,500. The lease was valued at £15,000 on 31 March 1982 (RPI 79.44). On 31 August 1997 (RPI 156.8), she assigned the lease to a third party for £20,000. The property was never Katherine's residence. Compute the chargeable gain.

***18.8** In March 1987 (RPI 100.6), Sean acquired a pair of matching antique silver candlesticks at a cost of £4,000. In August 1997 (RPI 156.8) he sold one of the candlesticks to James for £6,750. At that time the other candlestick was valued at £5,750. In September 1997 (RPI 157.1) he sold the other candlestick to Julia for £5,800. Calculate the chargeable gain on these two disposals if :

(a) James and Julia are unconnected.

(b) James and Julia are a married couple.

***18.9** On 31 March 1976, Estelle acquired a patent with a 30 year life at a cost of £21,000. The patent was valued at £18,000 on 31 March 1982 (RPI 79.44) and Estelle sold the patent on 31 March 1998 (RPI 158.9) for £13,000. Compute the chargeable gain.

***18.10** Edward bought a 20-year lease on a flat in May 1989 (RPI 115.0) at a cost of £35,000. In November 1997 (RPI 157.7) he granted a 5-year sub-lease to a third party for £15,000. The flat was never Edward's principal private residence. Compute the chargeable gain.

Chapter 19
Shares and securities (1)

Introduction

A disposal of shares or securities causes no CGT problems unless a taxpayer disposes of part of a shareholding which was originally acquired over a period of time in several separate transactions. If this happens, it is not possible to identify the shares which have been disposed of. But the calculation of the gain or loss arising on the disposal cannot proceed until the cost and acquisition date of the shares concerned have been established. It is necessary, therefore, to devise a set of *matching rules* which may be used to match disposals against acquisitions in these circumstances. The purpose of this chapter is to explain these matching rules and to show how they are used to calculate the gain or loss arising on a disposal of shares.

The matching rules

A disposal of shares is matched against acquisitions of those shares in the following order :

(a) First, against any acquisitions made on the same day as the day of the disposal.

(b) Next, against any acquisitions made during the previous 9 days, on a first-in, first-out basis (no indexation allowance is available on a disposal of shares acquired during the previous 9 days, even if the acquisition and disposal occur in different months).

(c) Next, against shares forming the "Finance Act 1985 pool", which is a pool of shares acquired on or after 6 April 1982 (excluding those already considered in (a) and (b) above).

(d) Next, against shares forming the "1982 holding", which is a pool of shares acquired between 6 April 1965 and 5 April 1982 inclusive.

(e) Finally, against shares acquired before 6 April 1965, on a last-in, first-out basis.

The operation of the Finance Act 1985 pool and the 1982 holding are considered later in this chapter, as is the treatment of shares acquired before 6 April 1965.

EXAMPLE 1

Paul makes the following purchases of ordinary shares in Crimson plc :

Date	*No of shares purchased*
11 May 1962	2,000
15 January 1965	400
12 May 1979	800
27 November 1997	300
29 November 1997	200
1 December 1997	100

Against which of these purchases are the following sales matched ?

(a) 450 shares sold on 1 December 1997

(b) 750 shares sold on 11 January 1998

(c) 300 shares sold on 18 February 1998.

SOLUTION

(a) The 450 shares sold on 1 December 1997 are matched first against the 100 shares bought on the same day, leaving 350 shares still to be matched. 300 of these are matched against the 300 shares bought on 27 November 1997 (the earliest acquisition within the previous 9 days) and the remaining 50 are matched against 50 of the shares bought on 29 November 1997 (also within the previous 9 days).

(b) The sale of 750 shares on 11 January 1998 cannot be matched against any acquisitions on the same day or during the previous 9 days. Therefore the next step is to match against the pool of shares acquired on or after 6 April 1982. This pool currently comprises only 150 shares bought on 29 November 1997 (200, less 50 already matched). Therefore 150 of the sold shares are matched against this purchase, leaving 600 shares still to be matched.

The next step is to match against the pool of shares acquired between 6 April 1965 and 5 April 1982 inclusive. This pool contains only the 800 shares bought on 12 May 1979 so the remaining 600 sold shares are matched against 600 of these shares.

(c) The sale of 300 shares on 18 February 1998 cannot be matched against any acquisitions on the same day, during the previous 9 days or on or after 6 April 1982. The next step is to match against the pool of shares acquired between 6 April 1965 and 5 April 1982 inclusive. This pool now contains only 200 shares (800, less 600 already matched) so 200 of the sold shares are matched against this purchase, leaving 100 shares still to be matched. These are matched against 100 of the shares bought on 15 January 1965 (i.e. the most recent acquisition made before 6 April 1965).

The Finance Act 1985 pool

The "Finance Act 1985 pool" consists of a pool of shares acquired on or after 6 April 1982, excluding any shares disposed of within 10 days of their acquisition. The name of this pool is derived from the Finance Act 1985, which introduced the matching rules described above. The pool is also known as the "new pool" or the "new holding" to distinguish it from the 1982 holding.

The pooling of shares acquired on or after 6 April 1982 removes the need to keep detailed records of individual acquisitions. Instead, all that is required is to keep a record of :

(a) the total number of shares in the pool, and

(b) their total cost, and

(c) their total *indexed cost,* which consists of total cost plus all indexation allowance due up to the date of the most recent "operative event". An operative event occurs whenever shares enter or leave the pool and an indexation calculation is required on each such occasion, as demonstrated by the following example.

EXAMPLE 2

Pauline makes the following purchases of preference shares in Violet plc :

Date	*No of shares*	*Cost*
		£
23 June 1990	1,000	1,100
14 May 1992	2,000	2,300
8 December 1997	3,000	3,150

Assuming an indexation factor of 10% between June 1990 and May 1992, and a further 13% between May 1992 and December 1997, calculate the value of the FA1985 pool at :

(a) 14 May 1992

(b) 8 December 1997.

SOLUTION

(a) The FA 1985 pool commences on 23 June 1990 with the purchase of 1,000 shares at a cost of £1,100. On 14 May 1992, an operative event occurs i.e. the purchase of a further 2,000 shares. Before adding these shares to the pool it is necessary to index the pool up to May 1992. The calculation is as follows :

	No. of shares	Cost	Indexed cost
		£	£
Bought 23 June 1990	1,000	1,100	1,100
Add : Indexation to May 1992			
10% x £1,100			110
			1,210
Bought 14 May 1992	2,000	2,300	2,300
FA 1985 pool at 14 May 1992	3,000	3,400	3,510

The total of the indexed cost column represents the cost *in May 1992 terms* of the FA1985 pool and includes all indexation allowance due up to that date.

(b) The next operative event is the purchase of 3,000 shares in December 1997. Before adding these shares to the pool it is necessary to index the pool from May 1992 (when the previous indexation calculation took place) to December 1997. The calculation is :

	No. of shares	Cost	Indexed cost
		£	£
FA 1985 pool b/f at 14 May 1992	3,000	3,400	3,510
Add : Indexation to Dec 1997			
13% x £3,510			456
			3,966
Bought 8 December 1997	3,000	3,150	3,150
FA 1985 pool at 8 December 1997	6,000	6,550	7,116

The three acquisitions forming the FA1985 pool have now been combined into a single pool of 6,000 shares, costing £6,550 but with an indexed cost (including all indexation allowance due to December 1997) of £7,116. It is now necessary to carry forward only these three "bottom line" figures, rather than the details of each individual acquisition.

Calculation of the indexed cost of the FA1985 pool

The example given above was a slight simplification of the way in which the indexed cost of the FA1985 pool is actually calculated. The full method of calculation is as follows :

(a) The number of shares in the pool at 5 April 1985 is totalled and the cost of these shares is also totalled. The indexed cost of the pool at 5 April 1985 is calculated as total cost, plus an indexation allowance for each acquisition forming part of the pool, based on the change in RPI between the date of the acquisition and April 1985.

(b) On the occurrence of a subsequent operative event, the indexed cost of the pool is increased by reference to the change in RPI since the previous operative event (or since April 1985 if this is the first operative event). The indexation factor used in this calculation is *not* rounded to 3 decimal places. The pool value is then adjusted to take account of the operative event as follows :

(i) for an acquisition, the number of shares acquired is added to the number of shares in the pool and their cost is added to the cost and to the indexed cost of the pool.

(ii) for a disposal, the number of shares disposed of is subtracted from the number of shares in the pool and amounts are subtracted from the cost and from the indexed cost of the pool, in proportion to the number of shares disposed of.

The unindexed gain (or loss) arising on a disposal from the pool is calculated as the difference between the disposal proceeds and the amount which has been subtracted from the cost of the pool as a consequence of the disposal. The indexation allowance due on the disposal is the difference between the amount subtracted from the cost of the pool and the amount subtracted from the indexed cost of the pool. As usual, indexation allowance cannot be used to create a loss or to increase a loss.

EXAMPLE 3

Paula makes the following acquisitions of ordinary shares in Indigo plc :

Date	*No of shares*	*Cost*	*RPI*
		£	
1 July 1983	5,000	6,300	85.30
2 August 1984	2,000	2,500	89.94
3 February 1987	1,200	2,300	100.4
4 June 1993	1,800	3,400	141.0

She sells 500 shares on 8 May 1997 (RPI 155.9).

(a) Calculate the value of the FA1985 pool on 8 May 1997, just prior to and just after the above disposal (RPI for April 1985 is 94.78).

(b) Compute the chargeable gain or allowable loss on the disposal if the sale proceeds are :

(i) £1,200 (ii) £1,000 (iii) £700

SOLUTION

(a) The calculation of the value of the FA1985 pool on 8 May 1997 is as follows :

	No. of shares	*Cost*	*Indexed cost*
		£	£
Bought 1 July 1983	5,000	6,300	6,300
Bought 2 August 1984	2,000	2,500	2,500
Add : Indexation to April 1985			
(a) $\frac{94.78 - 85.30}{85.30} = 0.111$			
0.111 x £6,300			699
(b) $\frac{94.78 - 89.94}{89.94} = 0.054$			
0.054 x £2,500			135
FA 1985 pool at 5 April 1985	7,000	8,800	9,634
Add : Indexation to February 1987			
$\frac{100.4 - 94.78}{94.78}$ x £9,634			571
			10,205
Bought 3 February 1987	1,200	2,300	2,300
FA 1985 pool at 3 February 1987	8,200	11,100	12,505
Add : Indexation to June 1993			
$\frac{141.0 - 100.4}{100.4}$ x £12,505			5,057
			17,562
Bought 4 June 1993	1,800	3,400	3,400
FA 1985 pool at 4 June 1993	10,000	14,500	20,962
Add : Indexation to May 1997			
$\frac{155.9 - 141.0}{141.0}$ x £20,962			2,215
			23,177
Sold 8 May 1997 (500/10,000th)	(500)	(725)	(1,159)
FA 1985 pool at 8 May 1997	9,500	13,775	22,018

Notes :

(i) The indexation allowance calculated on operative events occurring after 5 April 1985 has not been rounded off to 3 decimal places.

(ii) The disposal is of 500 shares out of a holding of 10,000. Therefore 500/10,000th or 1/20th of the pool has been sold and so 1/20th of the cost and indexed cost are subtracted from the pool.

(iii) The cost of the shares disposed of is £725. Since the equivalent indexed cost is £1,159, the maximum indexation allowance due on the disposal is £434 (£1,159 - £725).

(b)

	(i)	(ii)	(iii)
	£	£	£
Sale proceeds	1,200	1,000	700
Less : Cost	725	725	725
Unindexed gain (loss)	475	275	(25)
Less : Indexation allowance	434	275	nil
Chargeable gain (allowable loss)	41	nil	(25)

The 1982 holding

The 1982 holding consists of a pool of shares acquired between 6 April 1965 and 5 April 1982 inclusive. All the shares in this pool (including those acquired during the first 5 days of April 1982) are deemed to attract the same rate of indexation allowance, based on the change in RPI between March 1982 (79.44) and the date of a subsequent disposal. This means that the calculation of the pool value is much simpler than the calculation of the FA1985 pool value. All that is needed is a record of :

(a) the number of shares acquired between 6 April 1965 and 5 April 1982 inclusive, and

(b) the total cost of these shares.

When a disposal occurs which is deemed to have come from the 1982 holding, the number of shares disposed of is subtracted from the number of shares in the holding. An amount is also subtracted from the cost of the holding (in proportion to the number of shares disposed of) and this amount is taken to be the cost of the disposal. The chargeable gain or allowable loss arising on the disposal is then calculated in the usual way, as for any disposal of a pre-31 March 1982 asset.

EXAMPLE 4

Patrick made the following acquisitions of ordinary shares in Cornflower plc :

Date	*No of shares*	*Cost*
		£
1 June 1970	1,000	3,000
30 October 1975	800	2,500
15 August 1981	900	3,100

The shares had a market value of £3.10 per share on 31 March 1982 (RPI 79.44). Patrick made no other acquisitions of shares in the company. He sold 750 shares on 18 July 1997 (RPI 156.5) for £6,500. Compute the chargeable gain.

SOLUTION

The sale of 750 shares on 18 July 1997 cannot be matched against any acquisitions on the same day, during the previous 9 days or on or after 6 April 1982. The next step is to match against the 1982 holding. The value of the 1982 holding is as follows :

	No. of shares	*Cost*
		£
Acquired 1 June 1970	1,000	3,000
Acquired 30 October 1975	800	2,500
Acquired 15 August 1981	900	3,100
	2,700	8,600
Sold 18 July 1997 (750/2,700th)	(750)	(2,389)
1982 holding c/f	1,950	6,211

The sold shares are deemed to have cost £2,389 and their market value at 31 March 1982 was £2,325 (750 @ £3.10). The calculation of the chargeable gain arising on the disposal is :

	Original cost	*Rebasing*
	£	£
Sale proceeds	6,500	6,500
Less : Original cost	2,389	
Market value 31/3/82		2,325
Unindexed gain	4,111	4,175
Less : Indexation allowance		
$\frac{156.5 - 79.44}{79.44}$ = 0.970 x £2,389	2,317	2,317
Chargeable gain	1,794	1,858

The rebasing calculation gives the higher gain, so rebasing does not apply and the chargeable gain is £1,794.

Shares acquired before 6 April 1965

The CGT treatment of shares acquired before 6 April 1965 depends upon whether the shares are listed or unlisted. Each of these classifications is considered separately below.

Listed shares - the pooling election

A taxpayer who owns listed shares acquired before 6 April 1965 may elect *irrevocably* for these shares to be incorporated into the 1982 holding at their market value on 6 April 1965. This is known as the "pooling election" and a taxpayer who makes the election is left with only a 1982 holding and (possibly) a Finance Act 1985 pool. The chargeable gain or allowable loss arising on subsequent disposals can then be calculated as described earlier in this chapter.

The pooling election was first made available in 1968 and could be made either for equities or for fixed interest shares and securities (or for both). The election had to be made within two years of the end of the tax year in which the first disposal of such shares took place after 19 March 1968. Another opportunity to make the election is provided by the Taxation of Chargeable Gains Act 1992. The Act allows taxpayers to make the election (this time, for *all* types of listed shares and securities) by 31 January in the second year of assessment following the year in which the first disposal of such shares takes place after 5 April 1985.

EXAMPLE 5

Roseanne made the following acquisitions of ordinary shares in Magenta plc (a listed company) :

Date	*No of shares*	*Cost*	*RPI*
		£	
12 October 1960	100	1,100	
17 March 1963	120	1,400	
18 March 1979	80	800	
23 July 1988	150	1,800	106.7

The shares had a market value of £9 per share on 6 April 1965 and £11 per share on 31 March 1982 (RPI 79.44). Roseanne sold 200 shares on 9 October 1997 (RPI 157.4) for £21 each. Compute the chargeable gain, assuming that an election has been made to incorporate pre-6 April 1965 shares into the 1982 holding.

SOLUTION

The sale of 200 shares on 9 October 1997 cannot be matched against any acquisitions on the same day or during the previous 9 days. The next step is to match against the FA1985 pool. This pool consists only of the shares acquired in July 1988, so only 150 shares can be matched. The computation of the FA1985 pool value is as follows :

	No. of shares	Cost	Indexed cost
		£	£
Bought 23 July 1988	150	1,800	1,800
Add : Indexation to October 1997			
$\frac{157.4 - 106.7}{106.7}$ x £1,800			855
			2,655
Sold 9 October 1997	(150)	(1,800)	(2,655)
FA1985 pool c/f	nil	nil	nil

The chargeable gain on the disposal of these 150 shares is :

	£
Sale proceeds (150 @ £21)	3,150
Less : Cost	1,800
Unindexed gain	1,350
Less : Indexation allowance (£2,655 - £1,800)	855
Chargeable gain	495

The 50 remaining shares must be matched against the 1982 holding, which incorporates the pre-6 April 1965 shares (included at 6 April 1965 market value, *not* at original cost). The 1982 holding is :

	No. of shares	Cost
		£
Acquired 12 October 1960 (@ £9)	100	900
Acquired 17 March 1963 (@ £9)	120	1,080
Acquired 18 March 1979	80	800
	300	2,780
Sold 9 October 1997 (50/300th)	(50)	(463)
1982 holding c/f	250	2,317

The chargeable gain on the disposal of these 50 shares is :

	Original cost	Rebasing
	£	£
Sale proceeds (50 @ £21)	1,050	1,050
Less : Original cost	463	
Market value 31/3/82		550
Unindexed gain	587	500
Less : Indexation allowance		
$\frac{157.4 - 79.44}{79.44}$ = 0.981 x £550	540	500
Chargeable gain	47	nil

The rebasing calculation gives the lower gain, so rebasing applies and the chargeable gain is £nil. The total chargeable gain on the disposal of the entire 200 shares is therefore £495.

Listed shares - no pooling election made

Without a pooling election, the disposal of listed shares acquired before 6 April 1965 is treated in a broadly similar way to the disposal of any other pre-6 April 1965 asset (see Chapter 17). Basically, the gain produced by a calculation based on original cost is compared with the gain produced by a calculation based on market value at 6 April 1965 and the lower of these two gains is then compared with the gain produced by a rebasing calculation. But there are some significant differences between a disposal of listed shares and a disposal of other types of asset. These differences are :

(a) The calculation based on original cost is performed *without* time apportionment.

(b) The comparison of the calculation based on original cost and the calculation based on market value at 6 April 1965 is mandatory, rather than depending on an election by the taxpayer.

(c) The treatment of losses is as follows :

   (i) If the calculation based on original cost gives a loss and the calculation based on market value at 6 April 1965 also gives a loss, then the lower of these two losses is compared with the outcome of the rebasing calculation in order to arrive at the allowable loss.

   (ii) If the calculation based on original cost gives a gain and the calculation based on market value at 6 April 1965 gives a loss (or vice-versa), then the situation is no gain, no loss. In these circumstances there is no need to perform a rebasing calculation.

EXAMPLE 6

In June 1964, Samuel acquired 1,000 shares in Orange plc (a listed company) at a cost of £500. The shares had a market value of £2 each on 6 April 1965 and £1 each on 31 March 1982. Samuel made no further acquisitions of shares in the company and no election was made to incorporate pre-6 April 1965 shares into the 1982 holding. He sold his entire shareholding in January 1998 (RPI 158.3). Compute the chargeable gain if sale proceeds were :

(a) £10 per share (b) £1.80 per share.

SOLUTION

(a)

	Cost	*MV 6/4/65*	*MV 31/3/82*
	£	£	£
Sale proceeds	10,000	10,000	10,000
Less : Original cost	500		
Market value 6/4/65		2,000	
Market value 31/3/82			1,000
Unindexed gain	9,500	8,000	9,000
Less : Indexation allowance			
$\frac{158.3 - 79.44}{79.44}$ = 0.993 x £1,000	993		
$\frac{158.3 - 79.44}{79.44}$ = 0.993 x £2,000		1,986	1,986
Chargeable gain	8,507	6,014	7,014

Comparing the gains based on cost and on market value at 6 April 1965 gives a gain of £6,014. This gain is lower than the gain produced by the rebasing calculation, so rebasing will not apply and the chargeable gain is £6,014.

Notes :

(i) The indexation allowance in the original cost calculation is based on the greater of original cost (£500) and market value at 31 March 1982 (£1,000).

(ii) The indexation allowance in the 6 April 1965 market value calculation is based on the greater of market value at 6 April 1965 (£2,000) and market value at 31 March 1982 (£1,000).

(iii) The indexation allowance in the rebasing calculation is also based on the greater of market value at 6 April 1965 (£2,000) and market value at 31 March 1982 (£1,000), since the rebasing calculation is being compared with the 6 April 1965 market value calculation (see Chapter 17).

(b)

	Cost	*MV 6/4/65*
	£	£
Sale proceeds	1,800	1,800
Less : Original cost	500	
Market value 6/4/65		2,000
Unindexed gain	1,300	(200)
Less : Indexation allowance	993	nil
Chargeable gain	307	(200)

The situation is no gain, no loss. There is no need to perform a rebasing calculation.

Unlisted shares acquired before 6 April 1965

None of the rules described above for listed shares apply to unlisted shares. There is no pooling election available in respect of unlisted shares and the computation of the gain or loss arising on a disposal of unlisted shares acquired before 6 April 1965 is performed in the same way as for any other pre-6 April 1965 asset.

Gilts and qualifying corporate bonds

Gilt-edged securities and "qualifying corporate bonds" are not chargeable assets. Therefore neither a chargeable gain nor an allowable loss can arise on their disposal. For CGT purposes :

(a) Gilt-edged securities are British Government securities such as Treasury Stock, Exchequer Stock, War Loan etc.

(b) "Qualifying corporate bonds" consist of company debentures and other fixed-interest securities which are expressed in sterling and which comprise a normal commercial loan.

Summary

- Special matching rules are used to match disposals of shares and securities against acquisitions.
- Disposals are matched first against shares acquired on the same day as the disposal, then against shares acquired in the previous nine days, then against the FA1985 pool, then against the 1982 holding, then against shares acquired before 6 April 1965.
- The FA1985 pool consists of a pool of shares acquired after 6 April 1982. It is necessary to keep a record of the number of shares in this pool, their total cost and their total indexed cost.
- The 1982 holding consists of a pool of shares acquired between 6 April 1965 and 5 April 1982 inclusive. It is necessary to keep a record only of the number of shares in this pool and their total cost.
- Listed shares acquired before 6 April 1965 may join the 1982 holding at their 6 April 1965 market value if the taxpayer makes a pooling election to this effect.
- In the absence of a pooling election, disposals of listed shares acquired before 6 April 1965 are dealt with according to a special set of rules which differ in some respects from the usual rules for dealing with pre-6 April 1965 assets.

- Disposals of unlisted shares acquired before 6 April 1965 are dealt with according to the usual rules for dealing with pre-6 April 1965 assets.
- Gilt-edged securities and qualifying corporate bonds are not chargeable assets for CGT purposes.

Exercises

19.1 A taxpayer makes the following purchases of preference shares in Mauve Ltd (an unlisted company) :

Date	*No of shares purchased*
1 August 1959	200
10 September 1962	500
4 August 1981	1,000
17 October 1997	100
20 October 1997	200

How will the following disposals be matched against these purchases ?

(a) 250 shares sold on 20 October 1997

(b) 100 shares sold on 25 January 1998

(c) 1,200 shares sold on 1 February 1998.

19.2 Sandra acquired the following ordinary shares in Pink plc :

Date	*No of shares*	*Cost*	*RPI*
		£	
29 June 1982	1,000	3,000	81.85
5 May 1984	1,000	3,500	88.97
13 August 1987	1,350	6,500	102.1
7 September 1990	2,650	14,150	129.3
4 October 1995	2,000	22,500	149.8

Calculate the value of the FA1985 pool at 4 October 1995 (RPI for April 1985 was 94.78).

19.3 In April 1997 (RPI 155.6) Sandra (in question 19.2 above) sells 2,000 of her shares in Pink plc. Calculate the chargeable gain (or allowable loss) if the sale proceeds are :

(a) £14,000

(b) £12,000

(c) £16,000.

19.4 Dennis acquired the following ordinary shares in Bronze plc :

Date	*No of shares*	*Cost*
		£
5 August 1978	300	2,400
12 May 1980	200	1,700
11 July 1981	250	2,000

Dennis made no other acquisitions and the shares had a market value of £10 per share on 31 March 1982 (RPI 79.44). Calculate the chargeable gain arising in August 1997 (RPI 156.8) when Dennis sold 150 shares for £3,000.

19.5 Denise acquired the following ordinary shares in Turquoise plc :

Date	*No of shares*	*Cost*	*RPI*
		£	
28 December 1980	10,000	5,000	
21 June 1990	10,000	9,000	126.7
3 March 1993	10,000	11,000	139.3

The shares were valued at 60p each on 31 March 1982 (RPI 79.44). In December 1997 (RPI 158.0), Denise sold 25,000 shares for £1.25 per share. Compute the chargeable gain.

19.6 Raymond acquired the following ordinary shares in Buff plc (which are listed on the Stock Exchange) :

Date	*No of shares*	*Cost*
		£
17 February 1963	500	4,000
8 January 1980	700	8,500

The shares were valued at £9 each on 6 April 1965 and £15 each on 31 March 1982. Raymond elected to incorporate pre 6-April 1965 shares into the 1982 holding. In September 1997 (RPI 157.1), Raymond sold 1,000 shares for £40 each. Compute the chargeable gain.

19.7 Rework exercise 19.6, assuming now that Raymond had *not* elected to incorporate pre 6-April 1965 shares into the 1982 holding.

***19.8** Suzanne acquired the following ordinary shares in Aquamarine plc :

Date	*No of shares*	*Cost*	*RPI*
		£	
2 October 1979	100	300	
10 January 1981	150	500	
5 December 1983	200	700	86.89
8 November 1984	250	1,000	90.95
4 July 1991	300	1,400	133.8
30 September 1997	400	2,500	157.1

The shares were valued at £3.25 each on 31 March 1982 (RPI 79.44). RPI for April 1985 was 94.78. On 5 October 1997 (RPI 157.4), Suzanne sold 1,200 shares for £7 per share. Compute the chargeable gain.

***19.9** Stephen acquired the following ordinary shares in Olive plc (a listed company) :

Date	*No of shares*	*Cost*
		£
1 June 1943	10	100
1 January 1960	90	9,000

The shares had a market value of £85 each on 6 April 1965 and £120 each on 31 March 1982 (RPI 79.44). Stephen sold all his shares in January 1998 (RPI 158.3) at £80 each. Compute the chargeable gain (or allowable loss), given that no pooling election had been made (or will be made) in relation to shares acquired before 6 April 1965.

Chapter 20

Shares and securities (2)

Introduction

Subject to what is permitted by company law, a company may reorganise its share capital by making bonus issues or rights issues or by repaying shareholders part of their share capital. This chapter considers the CGT impact of a reorganisation of share capital and also describes the treatment of disposals occurring on the takeover of one company by another.

Bonus issues

A bonus issue consists of an issue of free extra shares by a company to its shareholders, generally in proportion to their existing shareholdings. For instance, a "1 for 5" bonus issue would give shareholders one free extra share for each five shares previously held. The CGT effect of a bonus issue is to increase the number of shares in each of the taxpayer's holdings prior to the bonus issue. The cost of those holdings is not affected, since bonus shares are issued free of charge.

EXAMPLE 1

Sherjeel made the following acquisitions of ordinary shares in Triangle plc :

Date	*No of shares*	*Cost*	*RPI*
		£	
22 January 1978	1,000	2,000	
27 September 1981	200	500	
28 July 1986	800	2,800	97.52
3 February 1993	500	2,200	138.8

In May 1997 (RPI 155.9), the company made a 1 for 10 bonus issue. Calculate the value of the FA1985 pool and the 1982 holding immediately after this bonus issue.

SOLUTION

Prior to the bonus issue, Sherjeel owned 2,500 shares in Triangle plc, of which 1,200 comprised the 1982 holding and 1,300 comprised the FA1985 pool. He received a further 250 shares as a consequence of the bonus issue but these 250 shares do *not* all join the FA1985 pool, even though they were all received in May 1997. Instead, the bonus shares are regarded as increasing the size of Sherjeel's holdings prior to the bonus issue. Therefore 120 shares (1/10th of 1,200) join the 1982 holding and 130 shares (1/10th of 1,300) join the FA1985 pool.

The 1982 holding is :

	No. of shares	*Cost*
		£
Acquired 22 January 1978	1,000	2,000
Acquired 27 September 1981	200	500
	1,200	2,500
Bonus issue May 1997 (1 for 10)	120	nil
1982 holding c/f	1,320	2,500

The FA1985 pool is :

	No. of shares	*Cost*	*Indexed cost*
		£	£
Bought 28 July 1986	800	2,800	2,800
Add : Indexation to February 1993			
$\frac{138.8 - 97.52}{97.52} \times £2,800$			1,185
			3,985
Bought 3 February 1993	500	2,200	2,200
FA 1985 pool at 3 February 1993	1,300	5,000	6,185
Bonus issue May 1997 (1 for 10)	130	nil	nil
FA 1985 pool (indexed to Feb 1993)	1,430	5,000	6,185

There is no need to perform an indexation calculation when the bonus issue is added to the pool since the bonus shares are issued at zero cost. However, it is important to remember that the pool has been indexed only up to February 1993 (not May 1997). When the next operative event occurs, it will be necessary to index from February 1993 up to the date of that event.

Bonus issues and market value at 31 March 1982

The only other effect of a bonus issue is concerned with market value at 31 March 1982. If a bonus issue is made after 31 March 1982, the market value of the relevant shares at 31 March 1982 does not reflect the bonus issue and should be adjusted to a post-bonus equivalent. For instance, if a 1 for 4 bonus issue is made after 31 March 1982, 5 shares now exist for each 4 which existed on 31 March 1982. The market value at 31 March 1982 should therefore be multiplied by 4/5th so as to obtain a post-bonus equivalent.

EXAMPLE 2

The shares of Triangle plc (see above example) had a market value of £3.19 per share on 31 March 1982 (RPI 79.44).

(a) Compute the post-bonus equivalent of this figure that will be used in CGT computations made after May 1997.

(b) Compute the chargeable gain arising in December 1997 (RPI 158.0) when Sherjeel sells 1,500 shares for £6 each.

SOLUTION

(a) After the bonus issue, 11 shares exist for each 10 shares which previously existed. Therefore the market value at 31 March 1982 which will be used in future CGT computations is 10/11th of £3.19 = £2.90 per share.

(b) *FA1985 pool (1,430 shares sold)* :

	No. of shares	*Cost*	*Indexed cost*
		£	£
b/f (indexed to Feb 1993)	1,430	5,000	6,185
Add : Indexation to Dec. 1997			
$\frac{158.0 - 138.8}{138.8}$ x £6,185			856
			7,041
Sold December 1997	(1,430)	(5,000)	(7,041)
FA 1985 pool c/f	nil	nil	nil

The chargeable gain on the disposal of the FA1985 pool is :

	£
Sale proceeds (1,430 @ £6)	8,580
Less : Cost	5,000
Unindexed gain	3,580
Less : Indexation allowance (£7,041 - £5,000)	2,041
Chargeable gain	1,539

1982 holding (70 shares sold) :

	No. of shares	*Cost*
		£
b/f	1,320	2,500
Sold December 1997 (70/1,320th)	(70)	(133)
1982 holding c/f	1,250	2,367

The chargeable gain on the disposal from the 1982 holding is :

	Original cost	*Rebasing*
	£	£
Sale proceeds (70 @ £6)	420	420
Less : Original cost	133	
Market value 31/3/82 (70 @ £2.90)		203
Unindexed gain	287	217
Less : Indexation allowance		
$\frac{158.0 - 79.44}{79.44}$ = 0.989 x £203	201	201
Chargeable gain	86	16

The rebasing calculation gives the lower gain, so rebasing applies and the chargeable gain is £16. The total gain on the entire disposal of 1,500 shares is therefore £1,555 (£1,539 + £16).

Rights issues

A rights issue consists of an offer of extra shares to existing shareholders, generally at an attractive price. Shareholders who are offered a rights issue may either :

(a) ignore the rights issue completely, in which case there is no CGT impact at all, or

(b) sell their "rights" to someone else (see later in this chapter), or

(c) buy the shares which they are offered.

If shareholders buy the shares which they are offered, then (as for a bonus issue) the extra shares acquired are deemed to increase the number of shares in each of the taxpayer's holdings prior to the rights issue. But the value of each holding is also affected, since rights issues are not made free of charge.

EXAMPLE 3

Tina made the following acquisitions of ordinary shares in Rhombus plc :

Date	*No of shares*	*Cost*	*RPI*
		£	
15 August 1980	500	1,000	
23 January 1987	600	2,500	100.0

In June 1997 (RPI 156.2), the company made a 1 for 20 rights issue at £8 per share and Tina decided to buy the shares which she was offered. Calculate the value of the FA1985 pool and the 1982 holding immediately after the rights issue.

SOLUTION

The 1982 holding is :

	No. of shares	*Cost*
		£
Acquired 15 August 1980	500	1,000
Rights issue June 1997 (1 for 20)	25	200
1982 holding c/f	525	1,200

The FA1985 pool is :

	No. of shares	*Cost*	*Indexed cost*
		£	£
Bought 23 January 1987	600	2,500	2,500
Add : Indexation to June 1997			
$\frac{156.2 - 100.0}{100.0} \times £2,500$			1,405
			3,905
Rights issue June 1997 (1 for 20)	30	240	240
FA 1985 pool c/f	630	2,740	4,145

Disposals from the 1982 holding after a rights issue

A disposal made subsequent to a rights issue is treated in much the same way as any other disposal. However, if a disposal is made from the 1982 holding, it is necessary to make a pro-rata apportionment of the disposal between :

(a) shares originally forming the 1982 holding (which attract indexation allowance based on the RPI in March 1982), and

(b) shares acquired as a result of the rights issue (which attract indexation allowance based on the RPI on the date of the rights issue).

In effect, the cost of shares acquired as a result of a rights issue and attached to the 1982 holding is treated as enhancement expenditure in the CGT computation.

EXAMPLE 4

The shares of Rhombus plc (see above example) had a market value of £2.50 per share on 31 March 1982 (RPI 79.44). Compute the chargeable gain arising in November 1997 (RPI 157.7) when Tina sells 840 shares for £7 each.

SOLUTION

FA1985 pool (630 shares sold) :

	No. of shares	*Cost*	*Indexed cost*
		£	£
b/f at June 1997	630	2,740	4,145
Add : Indexation to Nov. 1997			
$\frac{157.7 - 156.2}{156.2}$ x £4,145			40
			4,185
Sold November 1997	(630)	(2,740)	(4,185)
FA 1985 pool c/f	nil	nil	nil

The chargeable gain on the disposal of the FA1985 pool is :

	£
Sale proceeds (630 @ £7)	4,410
Less : Cost	2,740
Unindexed gain	1,670
Less : Indexation allowance	
(£4,185 - £2,740)	1,445
Chargeable gain	225

1982 holding (210 shares sold) :

	No. of shares	*Cost*
		£
b/f	525	1,200
Sold November 1997 (210/525th)	(210)	(480)
1982 holding c/f	315	720

Since the 1982 holding contains 1 rights share for each 20 original shares, the 210 shares taken from this holding are deemed to be 210 x 1/21 = 10 rights shares and 210 x 20/21 = 200 original shares. The cost of the 10 rights shares is treated as enhancement expenditure in the computation of the chargeable gain arising on the disposal :

	Original cost	Rebasing
	£	£
Sale proceeds (210 @ £7)	1,470	1,470
Less : (i) *200 original shares* :		
Cost (£1,000 x 200/500)	(400)	
Market value 31/3/82 (200 @ £2.50)		(500)
(ii) *10 rights shares* :		
Cost (£200 x 10/25)	(80)	(80)
Unindexed gain	990	890
Less : Indexation allowance :		
(i) *200 original shares* :		
$\frac{157.7 - 79.44}{79.44} = 0.985 \times £500$	(493)	(493)
(ii) *10 rights shares* :		
$\frac{157.7 - 156.2}{156.2} = 0.010 \times £80$	(1)	(1)
Chargeable gain	496	396

The rebasing calculation gives the lower gain, so rebasing applies and the chargeable gain is £396. The total gain on the entire disposal of 840 shares is therefore £621 (£225 + £396).

Capital distributions

A capital distribution occurs when shareholders are repaid part of their share capital, usually when a company goes into liquidation. Unless the capital distribution is regarded as "small" (see later in this chapter) a capital distribution is treated for CGT purposes as a part disposal.

EXAMPLE 5

In March 1990 (RPI 121.4), Vincent bought 1,000 ordinary shares in Trapezium plc for £4,400. In June 1997 (RPI 156.2), the company went into liquidation and Vincent received a first distribution of £0.50 per share. The market value of an ordinary share in Trapezium plc just after this distribution was £0.75. Compute the allowable loss arising in June 1997.

SOLUTION

The value of the part disposed of is £500 (1,000 @ £0.50) and the value of the part remaining is £750 (1,000 @ £0.75). Therefore there has been a 500/1,250th part disposal.

The FA1985 pool is :

	No. of shares	Cost	Indexed cost
		£	£
Bought March 1990	1,000	4,400	4,400
Add : Indexation to June 1997			
$\frac{156.2 - 121.4}{121.4} \times £4,400$			1,261
			5,661
Distribution June 1997 (500/1,250th)	-	(1,760)	(2,264)
FA 1985 pool c/f	1,000	2,640	3,397

The computation of the allowable loss is as follows :

	£
Disposal proceeds	500
Less : Part cost	(1,760)
Unindexed loss	(1,260)
Less : Indexation allowance (£2,264 - £1,760)	nil
Allowable loss	(1,260)

Sale of rights

Another example of a capital distribution occurs when a company makes a rights issue and a shareholder decides to sell his or her rights to someone else. When shareholders sell their rights they are *not* selling shares. What they are selling is the right to buy shares, often at an attractive price. The proceeds of such a sale are treated as a capital distribution and if the amount of money involved is "small" (see below) the amount received will be treated as a small capital distribution.

Small capital distributions

A "small" capital distribution is one which consists of less than 5% of the value of the company's shares immediately prior to the distribution. At the discretion of the Inland Revenue, the gain arising on a small capital distribution may be deferred or "rolled over". This is achieved by subtracting the proceeds of the distribution from the original cost of the shares, so reducing their allowable cost on a later disposal. (This is similar to the treatment of small part disposals of land, described in Chapter 17).

The Inland Revenue will not insist upon the gain arising on a small capital distribution being rolled over if this is not to the taxpayer's advantage (e.g. if the gain would be covered by the annual exemption).

EXAMPLE 6

In April 1989 (RPI 114.3), Vanessa bought 100 shares in Pentagon plc at a cost of £5 per share. The company went into liquidation and Vanessa received a first distribution of 40p per share in July 1997 (RPI 156.5). The shares had a market value of £9.75 immediately after the distribution.

(a) Show how the distribution will be dealt with for CGT purposes.

(b) Calculate the chargeable gain arising in March 1998 (RPI 158.9), when Vanessa received a second and final distribution of £9.82 per share.

SOLUTION

(a) The value of the shares immediately prior to the distribution must have been £10.15 (£9.75 + £0.40). 40p is 3.9% of £10.15 so the distribution ranks as a small capital distribution. The £40 received by Vanessa may be deducted from the £500 that she paid for her shares, reducing the allowable cost on a future disposal to £460.

(b) Assuming that the gain arising on the small capital distribution is rolled over, the FA1985 pool is :

	No. of shares	*Cost*	*Indexed cost*
		£	£
Bought April 1989	100	500	500
Add : Indexation to July 1997 $\frac{156.5 - 114.3}{114.3} \times £500$			185
			685
Distribution July 1997	-	(40)	(40)
	100	460	645
Add : Indexation to March 1998 $\frac{158.9 - 156.5}{156.5} \times £645$			10
			655
Distribution March 1998	(100)	(460)	(655)
FA1985 pool c/f	nil	nil	nil

The chargeable gain on the disposal is :

	£
Sale proceeds (100 @ £9.82)	982
Less : Cost	460
Unindexed gain	522
Less : Indexation allowance (£655 - £460)	195
Chargeable gain	327

Small capital distributions and the 1982 holding

If a small capital distribution is made and the shareholder has a 1982 holding, the value of the 1982 holding will be reduced as a consequence of the small capital distribution. The proceeds of the distribution are also subtracted from the market value of the shares at 31 March 1982.

On a subsequent disposal from the 1982 holding, it would be unfair to calculate indexation allowance on the reduced cost or on the reduced 31 March 1982 market value. Instead, indexation allowance is first calculated on the value of the 1982 holding as it stood before the small capital distribution and is then reduced by the proceeds of the distribution, multiplied by the % increase in RPI since the date of the distribution.

EXAMPLE 7

In January 1980, Wendy bought 2,000 shares in Square plc at a cost of £2.50 per share. On 31 March 1982 (RPI 79.44), the company's shares had a market value of £3.00 each. In July 1997 (RPI 156.5), when shares in Square plc had a market value of £12 each, the company made a rights issue but Wendy decided to sell her rights, realising £100. Compute the chargeable gain arising in December 1997 (RPI 158.0), when Wendy sold all her shares for £25,000.

SOLUTION

The value of Wendy's shares immediately prior to the sale of rights was £24,000 (2,000 @ £12). Wendy realised £100, which is 0.4% of £24,000. Therefore the sale of rights may be treated as a small capital distribution. Assuming that the gain arising is rolled over :

The 1982 holding is :

	No. of shares	*Cost*
		£
Bought January 1980	2,000	5,000
Distribution July 1997	-	(100)
1982 holding c/f	2,000	4,900
Sold December 1997	(2,000)	(4,900)
1982 holding c/f	nil	nil

The market value of the shares at 31 March 1982 is £5,900 (£6,000 - £100). The computation of the chargeable gain in December 1997 is as follows :

	Original cost	*Rebasing*
	£	£
Sale proceeds	25,000	25,000
Less : Cost	4,900	
Market value 31/3/82		5,900
Unindexed gain	20,100	19,100

	Original cost £	Rebasing £
Unindexed gain	20,100	19,100
Less : Indexation allowance :		
(i) *on original 1982 holding* : $\frac{158.0 - 79.44}{79.44}$ = 0.989 x £6,000	(5,934)	(5,934)
(ii) *on distribution* : $\frac{158.0 - 156.5}{156.5}$ = 0.010 x £100	1	1
Chargeable gain	14,167	13,167

The rebasing calculation gives the lower gain, so rebasing applies and the chargeable gain is £13,167.

Takeovers

A takeover occurs if one company acquires the shares of another company. Shareholders of the "target" company exchange their shares in return for cash, or shares of the acquiring company, or a combination of both cash and shares. The CGT treatment of such disposals is as follows :

(a) If a takeover is entirely for cash, the shareholders of the target company have sold their shares and have made chargeable disposals. The fact that shares have been sold as a consequence of a takeover is irrelevant and the chargeable gain is computed in the usual way.

(b) If a takeover is entirely for shares (a "paper for paper" takeover), no chargeable disposals have taken place. A shareholder's newly-acquired shares in the acquiring company replace the shares originally held in the target company and are deemed for CGT purposes to have been acquired on the same date and at the same cost as the original holding.

(c) If a takeover is partly for cash and partly for shares, a part disposal has taken place and a part disposal calculation is usually required. The value of the part disposed of is the amount of cash received and the value of the part remaining is the value of the shares received. However, if the amount of cash received is less than 5% of the total consideration, the cash received may be treated as a small capital distribution.

EXAMPLE 8

In October 1992 (RPI 139.9), Winston bought 400 shares in Hexagon plc at a cost of £3 per share. In October 1997 (RPI 157.4), Circle plc made a takeover bid for Hexagon plc, offering the Hexagon shareholders 3 Circle shares plus £1 in cash for every 2 Hexagon shares. The offer was accepted on 29 October 1997 when the market value of shares in Circle plc was £5.50 per share. Compute Winston's chargeable gain.

SOLUTION

Winston received 600 shares in Circle plc, worth £3,300, plus £200 in cash i.e. a total of £3,500. The amount received in cash is approximately 5.7% of the total, so this cannot be treated as a small capital distribution. The FA1985 pool is :

	No. of shares	*Cost*	*Indexed cost*
		£	£
Bought (Hexagon plc) Oct. 1992	400	1,200	1,200
Add : Indexation to Oct. 1997			
$\frac{157.4 - 139.9}{139.9} \times £1,200$			150
			1,350
Distribution Oct. 1997 (200/3,500th)	-	(69)	(77)
FA1985 pool after distribution	400	1,131	1,273
FA 1985 pool (Circle plc) c/f	600	1,131	1,273

The chargeable gain on the disposal is :

	£
Disposal proceeds	200
Less : Cost	69
Unindexed gain	131
Less : Indexation allowance (£77 - £69)	8
Chargeable gain	123

Summary

- The CGT effect of a bonus issue is to increase the number of shares in each of the taxpayer's holdings prior to the bonus issue. The cost of the holdings is not affected.
- If a bonus issue is made after 31 March 1982, the market value at 31 March 1982 should be adjusted to a post-bonus equivalent.
- The CGT effect of a rights issue which is taken up is to increase both the number and the value of the shares in each of the taxpayer's holdings prior to the rights issue.

- A capital distribution is treated for CGT purposes as a part disposal, unless it ranks as a small capital distribution.
- A small capital distribution is one which consists of less than 5% of the value of the company's shares immediately prior to the distribution. Gains arising on small capital distributions may be rolled over.
- If a takeover is entirely for cash, the shareholders of the target company have made chargeable disposals.
- If a takeover is entirely for shares, no chargeable disposals have taken place.
- If a takeover is partly for cash and partly for shares, a part disposal has taken place.

Exercises

20.1 William made the following acquisitions of preference shares in Heptagon plc :

Date	*No of shares*	*Cost*	*RPI*
		£	
17 February 1980	600	900	
13 November 1988	200	400	110.0

The market value of the shares at 31 March 1982 (RPI 79.44) was £1.70 per share. In July 1997 (RPI 156.5), the company made a 1 for 4 bonus issue.

Calculate the value of the FA1985 pool and the 1982 holding immediately after this bonus issue. Also calculate the market value at 31 March 1982 to be used when calculating the gain on subsequent disposals.

20.2 In March 1998 (RPI 158.9), William (in exercise 20.1) sells 300 shares for £4 per share. Calculate the chargeable gain.

20.3 Yvonne made the following acquisitions of ordinary shares in Rectangle plc :

Date	*No of shares*	*Cost*	*RPI*
		£	
30 September 1979	2,000	1,200	
1 December 1992	3,000	3,600	139.2

In January 1998 (RPI 158.3), the company made a 1 for 8 rights issue at £1 per share and Yvonne decided to buy the shares which she was offered. Calculate the value of the FA1985 pool and the 1982 holding immediately after the rights issue.

20.4 In March 1998 (RPI 158.9), Yvonne (in exercise 20.3) sells all her shares for £1.80 per share. The market value of ordinary shares in Rectangle plc on 31 March 1982 (RPI 79.44) was 75p per share. Calculate the chargeable gain arising in March 1998.

20.5 In November 1989 (RPI 118.5), Yorick bought 100 ordinary shares in Octagon plc for £500. In May 1997 (RPI 155.9), the company went into liquidation and Yorick received a first distribution of £1 per share. The market value of an ordinary share in Octagon plc just after this distribution was £1.50. Compute the allowable loss arising in May 1997.

20.6 In January 1990 (RPI 119.5), Yolande bought 300 ordinary shares in Ellipse plc at a cost of £1.20 per share. In March 1993 (RPI 139.3), when shares in Ellipse plc had a market value of £2 each, the company made a rights issue. Yolande sold her rights, realising £25. Compute the chargeable gain arising in November 1997 (RPI 157.7), when Yolande sold all her shares for £780.

20.7 In April 1993 (RPI 140.6), Walter bought 4,000 shares in Oval plc at a cost of £5.85 per share. In September 1997 (RPI 157.1), Round plc made a takeover bid for Oval plc, offering the Oval shareholders 8 Round shares plus £2.50 in cash for every 5 Oval shares. The offer was accepted on 2 September 1997 when the market value of shares in Round plc was £4.30 per share. Compute Walter's chargeable gain.

***20.8** Saeed made the following purchases of ordinary shares in Hyperbola plc :

Date	*No of shares*	*Cost*	*RPI*
		£	
24 August 1975	800	800	
25 November 1980	1,200	1,350	
26 February 1985	1,600	2,400	91.94
11 October 1993	400	800	141.8

The company's shares had a market value of £1.20 each on 31 March 1982 (RPI 79.44). In March 1994 (RPI 142.5), the company made a 1 for 40 rights issue at £1.50 per share and Saeed took up the shares which he was offered.

Calculate the chargeable gain in November 1997 (RPI 157.7) when Saeed sold 3,000 shares at £3 each. (RPI for April 1985 was 94.78).

***20.9** Susan made the following purchases of ordinary shares in Semicircle plc :

Date	*No of shares*	*Cost*
		£
11 January 1981	750	2,400
20 January 1982	570	2,850

The market value of the company's shares on 31 March 1982 (RPI 79.44) was £4. In January 1998 (RPI 158.3), the company went into liquidation and Susan received a first distribution of £2 per share. The market value of an ordinary share in Semicircle plc just after this distribution was £1. Compute the allowable loss arising in January 1998.

***20.10** Steven made the following purchases of ordinary shares in Convex plc :

Date	*No of shares*	*Cost*
		£
9 May 1977	2,000	8,000
28 November 1981	500	2,500

The market value of the company's shares on 31 March 1982 (RPI 79.44) was £5 per share. In June 1997 (RPI 156.2), Concave plc made a takeover bid for Convex plc, offering the Convex shareholders 2 Concave shares plus £2 in cash for every Convex share. The offer was accepted on 21 June 1997 when the market value of shares in Concave plc was £4 per share. Compute Steven's chargeable gain.

Chapter 21

Principal private residences

Introduction

This chapter examines the CGT consequences of the disposal of a taxpayer's private residence. It was stated in Chapter 16 that a principal private residence is not a chargeable asset for CGT purposes. However, a CGT liability may arise when a property is disposed of which has been used as a residence for only part of the period of ownership or which has been used partly as a residence and partly for other purposes.

Principal private residence

A dwelling which is a taxpayer's only or main residence is known as that taxpayer's "principal private residence" (PPR). A PPR is not a chargeable asset for CGT purposes. Therefore any gain arising on the disposal of a PPR is not chargeable and any loss arising on the disposal of a PPR is not allowable.

In order for a property to be regarded as a PPR the taxpayer must actually reside in the property for at least part of the time. Mere ownership (without residence) is not sufficient.

The large majority of taxpayers own (at most) a single property and reside in that property, so that it is perfectly obvious that the property is the taxpayer's PPR. However, the following points are relevant in more complex cases :

(a) A taxpayer may have only one PPR at any given time.

(b) If a taxpayer owns and lives in two (or more) properties, the taxpayer may elect which property is to be regarded as the PPR. Such an election must be made within two years of the date from which it is to take effect.

(c) A married couple may have only one PPR between them (even though they are taxed independently).

(d) The PPR exemption covers the residence itself together with grounds or gardens of up to half a hectare (500 square metres) in area. Larger areas of grounds or gardens may be included in the exemption if they are warranted by the size of the residence.

(e) The requirement that there must be actual residence in the property is relaxed if the taxpayer is required to live in job-related accommodation (see Chapter 7). In these circumstances, the PPR exemption is extended to any property which the taxpayer owns so long as he or she intends to occupy the property at some future time.

Partial exemption

If a property has been occupied as a PPR for only a part of the period of ownership, only a part of the gain realised on disposal will be exempt from CGT. The exempt part of the gain is equal to :

$$\frac{\text{length of period of residence}}{\text{length of period of ownership}} \times \text{whole gain}$$

The lengths of the periods of residence and ownership are usually calculated to the nearest month. Note the following important points :

(a) If the property was acquired before 31 March 1982, the period of ownership and any period of residence prior to that date are ignored in the calculation of the exempt part of the gain.

(b) The last 36 months of ownership always count as a period of residence, whether or not the taxpayer was actually resident (so helping taxpayers who move house and then experience difficulty in selling their previous residence).

EXAMPLE 1

Allan bought a house in January 1979 for £20,000. The market value of the house on 31 March 1982 (RPI 79.44) was £29,000. Allan lived in the house until 1 May 1994 on which date he bought another house and made this his principal private residence. The house bought in January 1979 was sold on 31 January 1998 (RPI 158.3) for £65,000. Compute the chargeable gain.

SOLUTION

In examples of this type it is necessary first to calculate the gain arising (ignoring any PPR exemption) and then to consider the PPR exemption as a second stage. The gain arising is as follows :

	Original cost	Rebasing
	£	£
Sale proceeds	65,000	65,000
Less : Original cost	20,000	
Market value 31/3/82		29,000
Unindexed gain	45,000	36,000
Less : Indexation allowance		
$\frac{158.3 - 79.44}{79.44} = 0.993 \times £29,000$	28,797	28,797
Gain before PPR exemption	16,203	7,203

The rebasing calculation gives the lower gain, so rebasing applies and the gain arising (before considering the PPR exemption) is £7,203.

After 31 March 1982, Allan owned the house for 15 years and 10 months (190 months). He was actually resident for 12 years and 1 month (145 months) and the last 36 months of ownership also count as a period of residence, making a total of 181 months during which the PPR exemption applies. The chargeable gain is therefore as follows :

	£
Total gain (as above)	7,203
Less : $\frac{181}{190} \times £7,203$	6,862
Chargeable gain	341

Deemed residence

The period of residence in a property is deemed to include certain periods when the taxpayer was not actually resident, so long as :

(a) there is a period of actual residence both at some time before the period of absence and at some time after the period of absence, and

(b) the taxpayer claims no other property to be a PPR during the period of absence.

These periods of "deemed residence" are as follows :

(a) any period or periods of absence during which the taxpayer is working abroad

(b) a total of up to 4 years of absence during which the taxpayer is working elsewhere in the UK

(c) a total of up to 3 years of absence for any reason.

By concession, the requirement that the taxpayer must reside in the property at some time after the period of absence is waived if the absence is work-related and the terms of the taxpayer's employment prevent him or her from returning to the residence.

EXAMPLE 2

On 1 June 1983 (RPI 84.84), Alice bought a house in Derby for £35,000. She occupied the house as her PPR until 1 May 1985 when she left to work in Exeter, living in rented accommodation. She returned to the house in Derby on 1 November 1986 and stayed until 1 July 1989 when she left to take up a post in the USA, again living in rented accommodation. She returned to Derby on 1 February 1992 and stayed until 1 December 1994 when she bought another house in Nottingham and made this her principal private residence. She had trouble in selling the Derby house but eventually managed to sell it for £74,000 on 1 February 1998 (RPI 158.6). Compute the chargeable gain.

SOLUTION

	£
Sale proceeds	74,000
Less : Acquisition cost	35,000
Unindexed gain	39,000
Less : Indexation allowance	
$\frac{158.6 - 84.84}{84.84}$ = 0.869 x £35,000	30,415
Gain before PPR exemption	8,585

Alice's period of ownership of the house in Derby (a total of 176 months) can be broken down into the following periods :

(i)	1 June 1983 to 30 April 1985	23 months	Actual residence
(ii)	1 May 1985 to 31 October 1986	18 months	Working in UK
(iii)	1 November 1986 to 30 June 1989	32 months	Actual residence
(iv)	1 July 1989 to 31 January 1992	31 months	Working abroad
(v)	1 February 1992 to 30 November 1994	34 months	Actual residence
(vi)	1 December 1994 to 31 January 1998	38 months	Living in new PPR

Periods (i), (iii) and (v) are exempt since Alice was actually resident in the property during those periods. Period (ii) is exempt since Alice was working elsewhere in the UK, the 4-year time limit has not been exceeded and she was resident in the property both before and after the absence. Similarly, period (iv) is exempt. The last 36 months of ownership are always exempt, which leaves the first 2 months of period (vi) to consider. During these 2 months Alice was claiming another property to be her PPR, so the period cannot count as a period of deemed residence and the gain arising during these 2 months is chargeable. The remaining 174 months benefit from the PPR exemption. The chargeable gain is therefore as follows :

	£
Total gain (as above)	8,585
Less : $\frac{174}{176}$ x £8,585	8,487
Chargeable gain	98

Letting relief

An extension to the PPR exemption, known as "letting relief", applies if a PPR has been let to tenants as residential accommodation. There are two situations to consider :

(a) A property might have been used entirely as a residence for part of the period of ownership but let to tenants during periods of absence by the owner. A chargeable gain will arise if the periods of absence are not entirely covered by the exemptions already described in this chapter, but letting relief will then be available in relation to this gain.

(b) Part of a property might have been used as a residence whilst the other part has been let. In this case, the PPR exemption will cover :

    (i) the gain arising on the whole property during the last 36 months of ownership, and

    (ii) the remainder of the gain, to the extent that this is attributable to the part of the property which was occupied by the owner.

    The balance of the gain will be chargeable to CGT, but letting relief may then be available. In general, letting relief will *not* be granted if the part that has been let forms a dwelling which is entirely separate from the accommodation which forms the owner's residence (e.g. a self-contained flat with its own access from the road). Relief *will* normally be granted if the let accommodation forms part of the owner's dwelling and the owner previously resided in the entire premises.

Letting relief is calculated as the *lowest* of :

(a) the part of the gain which relates to the let part of the property or to the letting period

(b) the part of the gain which is exempt because of the PPR exemptions

(c) £40,000.

EXAMPLE 3

In relation to the previous example in this chapter, assume now that Alice always let her Derby house when she was not resident there. Compute the chargeable gain.

SOLUTION

The only chargeable period was a period of 2 months during which a gain of £98 arose and during which the property was let. Letting relief is available as the lowest of :

(a) The part of the gain which relates to the letting period (£98)

(b) The part of the gain which is exempt because of the PPR exemptions (£8,487)

(c) £40,000.

The lowest of these is £98. Therefore letting relief of £98 is available and the chargeable gain is reduced to £nil.

EXAMPLE 4

Alistair bought a house in 1978 for £19,500 and occupied the entire house until 1 May 1989 when he rented the top floor (comprising one-half of the house) to tenants, retaining the ground floor as his own residence. This arrangement continued until 1 October 1997 (RPI 157.4) when he sold the house for £103,000. The house had a market value of £25,000 on 31 March 1982 (RPI 79.44). Compute the chargeable gain.

SOLUTION

	Original cost	*Rebasing*
	£	£
Sale proceeds	103,000	103,000
Less : Original cost	19,500	
Market value 31/3/82		25,000
Unindexed gain	83,500	78,000
Less : Indexation allowance		
$\frac{157.4 - 79.44}{79.44}$ = 0.981 x £25,000	24,525	24,525
Gain before PPR exemption	58,975	53,475

The rebasing calculation gives the lower gain, so rebasing applies and the gain arising (before considering exemptions) is £53,475.

After 31 March 1982, Alistair owned the house for 15 years and 6 months (186 months). Full exemption is available for the 85 months during which he occupied the whole property and for the last 36 months (a total of 121 months). He was resident in half of the property for the remaining 65 months, so 50% of the gain arising during these 65 months is also exempt. The other 50% is chargeable but letting relief is available. The chargeable gain is calculated as follows :

	£	£
Total gain (as above)		53,475
Less : PPR exemption :		
£53,475 x 121/186	34,787	
£53,475 x 65/186 x 1/2	9,344	44,131
		9,344
Less : Letting relief, lowest of :		
(a) £9,344		
(b) £44,131		
(c) £40,000		9,344
Chargeable gain		nil

Business use

If a property is used partly as a residence and partly for business purposes, the gain which is attributable to the part used for business purposes is chargeable to CGT. No reliefs are available in relation to this gain. The usual exemption for the last 36 months of ownership does not apply to the part of the property which has been used for business purposes.

EXAMPLE 5

Ava bought a house on 1 July 1985 (RPI 95.23) for £32,000. She occupied the entire property as her PPR until 1 August 1989 when she began using one-quarter of the house for business purposes. This continued until 1 November 1997 (RPI 157.7) when she sold the house for £87,000. Compute the chargeable gain.

SOLUTION

	£
Sale proceeds	87,000
Less : Acquisition cost	32,000
Unindexed gain	55,000
Less : Indexation allowance	
$\frac{157.7 - 95.23}{95.23}$ = 0.656 x £32,000	20,992
Gain before PPR exemption	34,008

Ava owned the house for 12 years and 4 months (148 months). For the first 4 years and 1 month (49 months) she occupied the entire house as her PPR but for the remaining 99 months she occupied only three-quarters of the house. The chargeable gain is as follows :

	£	£
Total gain (as above)		34,008
Less : PPR exemption :		
£34,008 x 49/148	11,259	
£34,008 x 99/148 x 3/4	17,061	28,320
Chargeable gain		5,688

Summary

- ► A taxpayer's principal private residence (PPR) is exempt from CGT.
- ► Taxpayers with two or more residences may elect which property is to be regarded as the PPR.
- ► A married couple may have only one PPR between them.
- ► If a property has been occupied as a PPR for only a part of the period of ownership, only a part of the gain realised on disposal will be exempt from CGT.
- ► The last 36 months of ownership always count as a period of residence.
- ► Certain periods of absence are deemed to be periods of residence.
- ► Letting relief may be available if a residence has been let to tenants as residential accommodation.
- ► If a residence is used partly for business purposes, the gain relating to the part used for business purposes is chargeable to CGT.

Exercises

21.1 Mohammed owns two properties - a flat in Central London and a country cottage in Sussex. In general he lives in his London flat during the week and spends the weekends in his Sussex cottage. Which of his two properties will be regarded as his principal private residence ?

21.2 Melanie bought a house in November 1979 for £18,000. The house had a market value of £21,000 on 31 March 1982 (RPI 79.44) and was sold on 31 October 1997 (RPI 157.7) for £58,000. Compute the chargeable gain in each of the following cases :

(a) Melanie occupied the house as her principal private residence throughout the period of ownership.

(b) Melanie occupied the house throughout her period of ownership with the exception of the period between 1 June 1985 and 31 May 1989 when she lived with a friend. During this time the house stood empty.

(c) As (b) except that the house was let as residential accommodation during Melanie's absence.

21.3 Rupert bought a house in Manchester on 1 November 1983 (RPI 86.67) for £55,000. He occupied the house until 1 November 1987 when he left to work abroad for a year, moving back into the house on 1 November 1988. He stayed until 1 February 1989 when he left again, this time to work in Aberdeen, where he stayed until his return on 1 May 1993. This time he stayed for only a month, leaving on 1 June 1993 to go to live with a friend. He never returned to the house and it was sold on 1 March 1998 (RPI 158.9) for £172,000. During his absences, Rupert always let his house and he claimed no other property to be his principal private residence. Compute the chargeable gain arising on the disposal.

21.4 Samantha bought a house for £37,500 on 1 August 1984 (RPI 89.94) and occupied the house as her principal private residence. On 1 June 1986 she began to use one-fifth of the house for business purposes. Unfortunately her business eventually failed and on 1 June 1992 she ceased trading. From that date onwards she resided in the entire house until it was sold on 1 August 1997 (RPI 156.8) for £75,000. Compute the chargeable gain.

***21.5** Terry bought a house for £65,000 on 1 June 1984 (RPI 89.20) and occupied the house as his principal private residence. He lived in the house until 1 June 1987 when he went to stay with relatives in Australia, letting the house in his absence. He did not return until 1 June 1991, when he began using one-quarter of the house for business purposes and the other three-quarters as his residence. This arrangement continued until 1 June 1997 (RPI 156.2) when he sold the house for £190,000. Compute the chargeable gain.

Chapter 22

CGT reliefs

Introduction

In certain circumstances, a taxpayer's CGT liability may be reduced (or at least deferred) by taking advantage of a variety of CGT reliefs. The purpose of this chapter is to explain, for each of these reliefs, the circumstances in which the relief is available and the way in which the amount of relief is calculated.

Damaged assets

If an asset has been damaged and insurance money or other compensation is received in consequence, the amount received is generally subject to CGT. The situation is treated as a part disposal (see Chapter 17). The value of the part disposed of (A) is the amount of money received and the value of the part remaining (B) is the value of the asset on the date that the money is received. Any money spent on restoration is treated as enhancement expenditure.

In certain circumstances, however, the taxpayer may elect that the situation should *not* be treated as a part disposal and that the amount received should instead be deducted from the allowable expenditure relating to the asset. This has the effect of increasing the chargeable gain arising on a subsequent disposal of the asset and is very similar to the CGT treatment of small part disposals of land (see Chapter 17). The circumstances in which a part disposal can be avoided are as follows :

(a) The money received is wholly applied in restoring the asset, or

(b) The asset is not a wasting asset and at least 95% of the money received is applied in restoring the asset (providing that the remainder is not reasonably required for restoration purposes), or

(c) The asset is not a wasting asset and the amount of money received is no more than 5% of the value of the asset.

If less than 95% of the money received is spent on restoring the asset (and (c) above does not apply) then a part disposal calculation is unavoidable, but the taxpayer may elect that this calculation should relate only to that part of the amount received which is not spent on restoration work. If this election is made, the amount spent on restoration is deducted from the allowable expenditure relating to the asset (so increasing the gain arising on a subsequent disposal).

EXAMPLE 1

Laura bought an item of antique furniture in July 1987 (RPI 101.8) for £8,000. The furniture was damaged by fire and, as a result, Laura received compensation from her insurance company of £3,000 in February 1998 (RPI 158.6). Compute the chargeable gain or allowable loss arising in each of the following circumstances :

(a) Laura spent none of the insurance money on restoration and the damaged asset was valued at £17,000 in February 1998.

(b) Laura spent £3,000 on restoring the asset in November 1997 (RPI 157.7) and elected that the situation should not be treated as a part disposal.

(c) Laura spent £2,900 on restoring the asset in November 1997 and elected that the situation should not be treated as a part disposal.

(d) Laura spent £2,000 on restoring the asset in November 1997 and elected that the part disposal should relate only to the retained £1,000. The restored asset was valued at £20,000 in February 1998.

SOLUTION

(a) This is a part disposal, with A = £3,000 and B = £17,000. The computation is :

	£
Disposal proceeds	3,000
Less : Part cost :	
$\frac{£3,000}{£3,000 + £17,000} \times £8,000$	1,200
Unindexed gain	1,800
Less : Indexation allowance	
$\frac{158.6 - 101.8}{101.8} = 0.558 \times £1,200$	670
Chargeable gain	1,130

The balance of allowable expenditure carried forward and used in the calculation of the chargeable gain arising on a subsequent disposal of the furniture is £6,800 (£8,000 - £1,200).

(b) The entire amount received is spent on restoration so the election to avoid a part disposal is valid. The balance of allowable expenditure carried forward is :

	£
Incurred July 1987	8,000
Incurred November 1997	3,000
	11,000
Less : Received February 1998	3,000
	8,000

On a subsequent disposal, indexation allowance will run from July 1987 on the original expenditure and from November 1997 on the restoration expenditure. There will be a negative indexation allowance relating to the compensation money received, running from February 1998.

(c) The £2,900 spent on restoration is over 96% of the amount received and so the election to avoid a part disposal is valid (so long as the remaining £100 is not reasonably required for restoration purposes). The balance of allowable expenditure carried forward is :

	£
Incurred July 1987	8,000
Incurred November 1997	2,900
	10,900
Less : Received February 1998	3,000
	7,900

On a subsequent disposal, indexation allowance will be calculated as in (b) above.

(d) More than 5% of the compensation money has been retained so a part disposal is unavoidable. However, by virtue of Laura's election, this will relate only to the retained £1,000, not to the entire £3,000 received. The computation is :

	£	£
Disposal proceeds		1,000
Less : Part original expenditure :		
$\frac{£1,000}{£1,000 + £20,000} \times £8,000$	381	
Part restoration expenditure :		
$\frac{£1,000}{£1,000 + £20,000} \times £2,000$	95	476
Unindexed gain		524
Less : Indexation allowance		
$\frac{158.6 - 101.8}{101.8} = 0.558 \times £381$	213	
$\frac{158.6 - 157.7}{157.7} = 0.006 \times £95$	1	214
Chargeable gain		310

The balance of allowable expenditure carried forward in this case is :

	£
Incurred July 1987 (£8,000 - £381)	7,619
Incurred November 1997 (£2,000 - £95)	1,905
	9,524
Less : Received February 1998 and spent on restoration	2,000
	7,524

Destroyed assets

If an asset has been lost or totally destroyed and insurance or compensation money is received in consequence, this constitutes a chargeable disposal and the normal computation is performed. However, if all of the money received is spent (within 12 months) on the purchase of a replacement asset, the taxpayer may elect for the gain arising on the disposal to be deferred or "rolled-over" until the replacement asset is disposed of. This is achieved by subtracting the gain arising on the lost or destroyed asset from the allowable cost of the replacement asset.

If only *part* of the money received is spent on the purchase of a replacement asset, the taxpayer may elect for the chargeable gain arising on the disposal of the original asset to be restricted to the amount of money retained. The balance of the gain is then rolled-over against the cost of the replacement asset.

EXAMPLE 2

Maurice bought an item of jewellery in November 1990 (RPI 130.0) for £125,000. In 1993 the jewellery was stolen and, as a result, an insurance payment of £141,500 was received in October 1993 (RPI 141.8). In December 1993 (RPI 141.9), Maurice spent £150,000 on the purchase of replacement jewellery and elected that the gain arising on the disposal of the original jewellery should be rolled-over.

(a) Compute the chargeable gain arising in March 1998 (RPI 158.9) when the replacement jewellery was sold for £180,000.

(b) How would this computation alter if the jewellery bought in December 1993 had cost only £140,000 ?

SOLUTION

(a) The gain arising on the loss of the original jewellery is :

	£
Disposal proceeds	141,500
Less : Acquisition cost	125,000
Unindexed gain	16,500

	£
Unindexed gain	16,500
Less : Indexation allowance	
$\frac{141.8 - 130.0}{130.0}$ = 0.091 x £125,000	11,375
Chargeable gain	5,125

The entire proceeds were spent on a replacement asset within 12 months so Maurice is entitled to roll-over the above gain. This reduces the allowable cost of the new jewellery to £144,875 (£150,000 - £5,125). The gain arising on the subsequent sale of this jewellery is as follows :

	£
Disposal proceeds	180,000
Less : Deemed acquisition cost	144,875
Unindexed gain	35,125
Less : Indexation allowance	
$\frac{158.9 - 141.9}{141.9}$ = 0.120 x £144,875	17,385
Chargeable gain	17,740

(b) £1,500 of the insurance money was retained and so £1,500 of the gain arising on the stolen jewellery is immediately chargeable. The remaining £3,625 of the gain may be rolled-over, reducing the deemed acquisition cost of the new jewellery to £136,375 (£140,000 - £3,625). The gain arising on the March 1998 disposal (assuming that the disposal proceeds remain at £180,000) becomes £27,260 (£180,000 - £136,375 - 0.120 x £136,375).

Replacement of business assets

Subject to certain conditions, the gain arising on the disposal of a business asset may be rolled-over against the cost of acquiring a replacement business asset. If this relief did not exist, the owners of businesses might be discouraged from selling business assets in order to acquire better ones. The conditions which must be satisfied are :

(a) Both the asset which is disposed of and the replacement asset must be drawn from the following list (though they need not both be the same type of asset) :

(i) land and buildings used solely for the purposes of a trade

(ii) fixed (i.e. immovable) plant and machinery

(iii) ships, aircraft and hovercraft

(iv) goodwill

(v) satellites, space stations and spacecraft

(vi) milk and potato quotas and certain EU agricultural quotas.

(b) Both the asset which is disposed of and the replacement asset must be used for trade purposes throughout the period of ownership.

(c) The replacement asset must be acquired during a period beginning one year before and ending three years after the date of disposal of the original asset.

(d) The taxpayer concerned must claim the relief by 31 January in the sixth year of assessment following the year in which the disposal occurred.

If only part of the disposal proceeds of the original asset are used to acquire a replacement asset, then only part of the gain may be rolled-over. The part which cannot be rolled-over and is therefore immediately chargeable is the *lower* of :

(a) the amount of money retained and not used in the purchase of the replacement asset

(b) the whole of the gain arising on the disposal of the original asset.

EXAMPLE 3

Janine bought a building for use in her business in May 1982 (RPI 81.62) for £75,000. In July 1997 (RPI 156.5) she sold the building for £160,000 and, in the same month, bought another building for use in her business. Assuming that Janine claims roll-over relief, calculate the chargeable gain arising on the July 1997 disposal if the replacement building has a cost of :

(a) £170,000

(b) £150,000

(c) £130,000.

SOLUTION

The gain on the disposal of the original building is computed as follows :

	£
Sale proceeds	160,000
Less : Acquisition cost	75,000
Unindexed gain	85,000
Less : Indexation allowance	
$\frac{156.5 - 81.62}{81.62}$ = 0.917 x £75,000	68,775
Chargeable gain	16,225

(a) The entire sale proceeds have been spent on a replacement building. Therefore none of the gain is immediately chargeable and the entire gain may be rolled-over against the cost of the new building, reducing its allowable cost to £153,775 (£170,000 - £16,225).

(b) £10,000 of the sale proceeds have been retained. Therefore £10,000 of the gain is immediately chargeable. The remaining £6,225 may be rolled-over against the cost of the new building, reducing its allowable cost to £143,775 (£150,000 - £6,225).

(c) £30,000 of the sale proceeds have been retained. This exceeds the chargeable gain. Therefore the whole gain is immediately chargeable and no part of the gain may be rolled-over. The allowable cost of the new building is the full £130,000.

Replacement with a depreciating asset

If the replacement business asset is a "depreciating asset" (defined as one which has an expected life of 60 years or less) the gain arising on disposal of the original asset cannot be permanently rolled-over. Instead, the gain is temporarily "held-over" until the earliest of the following three dates :

(a) The date on which the replacement asset is disposed of. If this is the earliest of the three dates, the usual roll-over provisions apply (as described above).

(b) A date 10 years after the acquisition of the depreciating asset. The held-over gain "crystallises" on this date i.e. becomes chargeable.

(c) The date on which the depreciating asset ceases to be used in the owner's business.

EXAMPLE 4

In June 1997, Ian sells a freehold building (which he used exclusively for business purposes) for £100,000, realising a chargeable gain of £25,000. In the same month he acquires fixed plant and machinery costing £120,000 and elects to hold-over the gain on the freehold property against the plant and machinery. Explain the way in which the held-over gain will be treated in each of the following situations :

(a) Ian sells the plant and machinery in July 2001.

(b) Ian sells the plant and machinery in March 2010.

SOLUTION

(a) In this case the replacement asset is sold before the 10th anniversary of its acquisition, so the usual roll-over provisions apply. The allowable cost of the plant and machinery is reduced to £95,000 (£120,000 - £25,000) and this figure is used in the computation of the chargeable gain (if any) arising on its disposal.

(b) In this case, the replacement asset is still in Ian's possession on the 10th anniversary of its acquisition, so the held-over gain of £25,000 crystallises in June 2007 and will form part of Ian's chargeable gains in 2007/08.

A gain which is held-over against a depreciating asset will normally become chargeable no more than 10 years after the date of acquisition of the depreciating asset. However, if a suitable non-depreciating asset is acquired at any time before the end of this 10-year period, the held-over gain can be transferred to this new asset, so converting a temporarily held-over gain into a permanently rolled-over gain.

EXAMPLE 5

Imagine now that Ian (in the above example) bought another freehold building (for business use) in November 2000 and elected to transfer the held-over gain on the plant and machinery to the new freehold building. Explain the treatment of the held-over gain if the new building cost :

(a) £150,000 (b) £90,000.

SOLUTION

(a) The entire proceeds of the sale of the original building have been invested in a new building so the whole held-over gain of £25,000 can be converted into a rolled-over gain, reducing the allowable cost of the new building to £125,000.

(b) £10,000 out of the sale proceeds of the original building have not been invested in the new building and therefore cannot be rolled-over against its cost. This £10,000 will continue to be held-over against the plant and machinery and will become chargeable no later than June 2007. However, the remaining £15,000 is converted into a rolled-over gain, reducing the allowable cost of the new building to £75,000.

Gains rolled over between 31 March 1982 and 6 April 1988

Special provisions apply to a claim for roll-over relief on the replacement of a business asset which was originally acquired before 31 March 1982 and replaced between 31 March 1982 and 6 April 1988. In these circumstances, some part of the rolled-over gain relates to the period before 31 March 1982 and it would now be unfair to bring such gains to charge when the replacement asset is sold (since gains arising before 31 March 1982 have been exempt from CGT since 6 April 1988).

So as to avoid detailed calculations of the amount of the rolled-over gain which relates to the period before 31 March 1982, the Finance Act 1988 provided that such rolled-over gains are to be reduced by a flat-rate 50%.

Gift of business assets

The gift of an asset is a chargeable disposal for CGT purposes and this is the case whether or not the asset concerned is used in business. However, subject to certain conditions, the gain arising on a gift of business assets may be held-over until the transferee in turn disposes of the assets concerned. The conditions which must be satisfied are as follows :

(a) Both the transferor and the transferee must elect for the gain arising on the gift to be held-over. This election must be made by 31 January in the sixth year of assessment following the year in which the gift is made.

(b) The gifted assets must consist of either :

  (i) assets used in a business carried on by the transferor or by the transferor's personal company (i.e. a company in which the transferor has at least 5% of the voting rights), or

  (ii) shares in an unlisted trading company, or

  (iii) shares in the transferor's personal company.

If the gift is of shares, rather than of individual business assets, the gain arising on the disposal will be apportioned between the amount relating to chargeable business assets (i.e. chargeable assets used for business purposes) and the amount relating to other chargeable assets owned by the company (e.g. investments). Only the part of the gain relating to chargeable business assets is eligible for hold-over relief.

EXAMPLE 6

Kathy is the managing director of Kathy Ltd. She bought 90% of the voting share capital of the company for £70,000 in July 1985 (RPI 95.23). In August 1993 (RPI 141.3) she gave all her shares to her son and both Kathy and her son elected that the gain arising on this gift should (as far as possible) be held-over. The net assets of the company on the date of the gift (at market value) were as follows :

	£
Goodwill	100,000
Freehold building (used only for business purposes)	150,000
Listed investments	50,000
Net current assets (none of which are chargeable)	40,000
Total net assets	340,000

(a) Compute the gain arising on the gift and the amount which may be held-over.

(b) Compute the gain arising in December 1997 (RPI 158.0) when Kathy's son sold the shares for £350,000.

SOLUTION

(a) The value of the shares on the date of the gift was 90% of £340,000 = £306,000. The gain arising on the gift is therefore as follows :

	£
Deemed disposal proceeds	306,000
Less : Acquisition cost	70,000
Unindexed gain	236,000

	£
Unindexed gain	236,000
Less : Indexation allowance	
$\frac{141.3 - 95.23}{95.23}$ = 0.484 x £70,000	33,880
Chargeable gain	202,120

The total chargeable assets on the company on the date of the gift are £300,000 (£100,000 + £150,000 + £50,000) of which £250,000 are chargeable business assets. Therefore £202,120 x 250,000/300,000 = £168,433 of the gain may be held-over whilst the remaining £33,687 is immediately chargeable.

(b) The gain arising in December 1997 is as follows :

	£
Sale proceeds	350,000
Less : Deemed acquisition cost	
(£306,000 - £168,433)	137,567
Unindexed gain	212,433
Less : Indexation allowance	
$\frac{158.0 - 141.3}{141.3}$ = 0.118 x £137,567	16,233
Chargeable gain	196,200

Gifts between 31 March 1982 and 6 April 1988

Special provisions apply to a claim for hold-over relief on the gift of a business asset which was originally acquired before 31 March 1982 and gifted between 31 March 1982 and 6 April 1988. These special provisions are identical to those described above for roll-over relief on replacement of business assets i.e. the held-over gain is reduced by a flat-rate 50%.

Transfer of a business to a limited company

Subject to certain conditions, all or part of the gain arising on the transfer of a business to a limited company may be held-over until the vendor of the business disposes of the shares that he or she has received in exchange for the business. The conditions which must be satisfied are as follows :

(a) The business must be transferred as a going concern.

(b) All the assets of the business (apart from cash balances) must be transferred to the company.

(c) The consideration received by the vendor of the business must consist wholly or partly of shares in the company.

The relief is applied automatically so there is no need for the taxpayer to elect for the gain to be held-over. The part of the gain that is held-over is calculated as follows :

$$\frac{\text{value of the shares received}}{\text{total consideration received}} \text{ x whole gain.}$$

If a transfer of this type was made between 31 March 1982 and 6 April 1988 and at least some of the assets transferred were acquired before 31 March 1982, the held-over gain is reduced by a flat-rate 50%.

EXAMPLE 7

In April 1997, Leroy transferred his business to a limited company in exchange for £5,000 in cash and shares valued at £60,000. The gain arising on the transfer was £26,000. Calculate the amount of the gain which is immediately chargeable and the amount which is held-over.

SOLUTION

The held-over gain is £26,000 x 60,000/65,000 = £24,000. The remaining £2,000 of the gain is immediately chargeable. The allowable cost of the shares which will be used in the computation on their eventual disposal is £36,000 (£60,000 - £24,000).

Retirement relief

Subject to certain conditions, a relief known as "retirement relief" is available when a taxpayer makes a material disposal of business assets. The disposal may consist of the disposal of business assets by a sole trader, the disposal of a partnership share or the disposal of shares in a personal company. It is not necessary for the taxpayer actually to retire in order to benefit from retirement relief but the following conditions must be satisfied :

(a) There must be a *material* disposal of business assets. It is not sufficient merely for business assets to have been disposed of. Rather, the assets disposed of must constitute a whole business or a part of a business.

(b) The taxpayer must be at least 50 years old or must be disposing of the assets because ill-health renders him or her permanently unable to continue in business.

(c) For sole traders and partnerships, the business must have been owned by the taxpayer for at least 10 years. A proportionate relief is available if the business has been owned for at least one year but less than 10 years.

(d) For disposals of shares in a personal company the shares must have been owned for at least 10 years and the taxpayer must have been a full-time working director or full-time employee of the company for at least 10 years. Again, a proportionate relief is available if either of the 10 year requirements is not satisfied.

Retirement relief is granted automatically so there is no need for the taxpayer to make a claim (except when retiring on grounds of ill-health). The relief is calculated in two stages, as follows :

(a) The first £250,000 of gains is exempt from CGT.

(b) 50% of any remaining gains between £250,000 and £1,000,000 (i.e. 50% of the next £750,000) are also exempt from CGT.

The limits of £250,000 and £1,000,000 are scaled down proportionately if the taxpayer has a qualifying period of at least one year but less than 10 years.

EXAMPLE 8

Compute the amount of retirement relief available to the following taxpayers, each of whom is a sole trader (in good health) making a material disposal of business assets :

	Age	*No of years trading*	*Amount of chargeable gains*
(a)	65	12	£130,000
(b)	68	27	£540,000
(c)	67	20	£2,240,000
(d)	48	12	£26,000
(e)	58	8	£210,000
(f)	62	7	£750,000

SOLUTION

(a) The taxpayer is fully eligible for retirement relief. The total gains of £130,000 are less than £250,000, so retirement relief of £130,000 will be given, reducing the chargeable gain to £nil.

(b) The taxpayer is fully eligible for retirement relief. The first £250,000 is fully exempt and half of the remaining £290,000 is also exempt. Total retirement relief is £395,000 (£250,000 + £145,000), leaving a chargeable gain of £145,000.

(c) The taxpayer is fully eligible for retirement relief. The first £250,000 is fully exempt and 50% relief will be granted on the gains lying between £250,000 and £1,000,000 (i.e. the next £750,000). Total retirement relief is £625,000 (£250,000 + £375,000), leaving a chargeable gain of £1,615,000.

(d) The taxpayer (who is in good health) is too young for retirement relief and so none is available.

(e) The taxpayer is entitled to a proportionate relief based on 8 years of trading. The lower and upper limits are scaled down to £200,000 and £800,000 respectively, so the first £200,000 is fully exempt and half of the remaining £10,000 is also exempt. Total retirement relief is £205,000 (£200,000 + £5,000), leaving a chargeable gain of £5,000.

(f) The taxpayer is entitled to a proportionate relief based on 7 years of trading. The lower and upper limits are scaled down to £175,000 and £700,000 respectively, so the first £175,000 is fully exempt and 50% relief will be granted on the gains lying between £175,000 and £700,000 (i.e. the next £525,000). Total retirement relief is £437,500 (£175,000 + £262,500), leaving a chargeable gain of £312,500.

Disposals of shares in a personal company

As stated above, retirement relief may be available when a taxpayer disposes of shares in a personal company. In these circumstances, the gain arising on the disposal is apportioned between the amount relating to chargeable business assets owned by the company and the amount relating to other chargeable assets owned by the company. Only the part of the gain relating to chargeable business assets is eligible for retirement relief. This is identical to the way in which hold-over relief is given on a gift of shares in a personal company (see earlier in this chapter).

EXAMPLE 9

Gita (who was born in 1940) acquired a 50% shareholding in G Ltd in 1973. She has been a full-time working director of the company ever since. In January 1998 she sold her entire shareholding. The gain arising on this disposal (before deduction of retirement relief) was £650,000. On the day that Gita sold her shares the company had chargeable assets of £3.2 million, of which £2.8 million comprised chargeable business assets. Compute Gita's chargeable gain.

SOLUTION

Gita is fully eligible for retirement relief but relief is available only in relation to the part of her gain which relates to chargeable business assets. This part of the gain is £650,000 x 2.8/3.2 = £568,750. The remaining £81,250 (which relates to non-business chargeable assets) does not attract retirement relief. The computation is :

	£
Gain eligible for retirement relief	568,750
Less : Retirement relief :	
(£250,000 + 50% x £318,750)	409,375
	159,375
Add : Gain not eligible for retirement relief	81,250
Chargeable gain	240,625

Relationship between retirement relief and gift relief

If a taxpayer makes a gift of business assets on retirement it is quite possible that both retirement relief and hold-over relief might be available in relation to the gift. In this situation, retirement relief (which is mandatory) is first subtracted from the gain arising on the disposal. Hold-over relief may then be claimed in relation to the balance of the gain (if both the transferor and the transferee agree to do so).

Reinvestment relief

Subject to certain conditions, the chargeable gain arising on the disposal of *any* asset may be held-over if the gain is reinvested in the ordinary shares of an unlisted trading company. The conditions which must be satisfied are :

(a) The company must carry on a "qualifying trade" on a commercial basis with a view to the realisation of profits. The definition of a "qualifying trade" is fairly broad but excludes activities such as commodity dealing, banking, insurance and the provision of financial or leasing services. The trade must be carried on wholly or mainly in the UK.

(b) The reinvestment must be made within the period starting one year before and finishing three years after the relevant disposal.

The maximum amount which may be held-over is equal to the lower of the amount reinvested and the amount of the chargeable gain. Therefore the entire gain may be held-over if an amount equal to the gain is reinvested - it is not necessary to reinvest the entire sale proceeds of the original disposal. Furthermore, a taxpayer claiming reinvestment relief may restrict the amount of relief claimed so as to avoid wasting the annual exemption.

Loans to traders

If a taxpayer lends money to a trader and then finds that all or part of the loan is irrecoverable, the loss incurred may be treated as a capital loss and set against the taxpayer's capital gains. This relief is subject to the following conditions :

(a) the trader who has borrowed the money must be resident in the UK

(b) the money must have been borrowed for trading purposes (but not for the trade of money-lending)

(c) the debt must be unsecured.

Subject to these conditions, the amount lost is treated as a capital loss of the year in which the taxpayer makes the claim for relief, though a claim may be backdated for up to two years if it can be shown that the debt was irrecoverable then. If relief is given and then all or part of the loan is recovered, the amount recovered is treated as a capital gain of the year in which recovery takes place.

Summary

- ► If the compensation received on the destruction of an asset is spent on a replacement asset, the gain arising on the original asset's disposal may be rolled-over against the cost of the replacement asset.
- ► The gain arising on the disposal of a business asset may be rolled-over against the cost of a replacement.
- ► If a business asset is replaced by a depreciating asset the held-over gain will become chargeable in 10 years at most, unless the gain can be transferred to a non-depreciating asset in the meantime.
- ► The gain arising on the gift of a business asset may be held-over until the transferee disposes of the asset.
- ► The gain arising on the transfer of a business to a limited company is held-over until the transferor disposes of the shares received in exchange for the assets of the business.
- ► Retirement relief may be available when a taxpayer makes a material disposal of business assets.
- ► The chargeable gain arising on the disposal of any asset may be held-over if the disposal proceeds are reinvested in the ordinary shares of a qualifying company.
- ► A loss incurred in connection with a loan to a trader may be treated as a capital loss.

Exercises

22.1 Matthew bought a piece of antique porcelain in March 1986 (RPI 96.73) for £10,000. The porcelain was damaged in early 1992 and Matthew spent £3,850 on restoration work in March of that year (RPI 136.7). In July 1992 (RPI 138.8) Matthew's insurance company paid him £4,000 and Matthew successfully elected that this should not be treated as a part disposal. In March 1998 (RPI 158.6) he sold the porcelain for £23,500. Compute the chargeable gain.

22.2 Maria bought a diamond necklace in February 1988 (RPI 103.7) for £13,500. In 1993 the necklace was stolen and, as a result, an insurance payment of £19,000 was received in February 1994 (RPI 142.1). In the same month, Maria spent £19,500 on the purchase of a replacement necklace and elected that the gain arising on the disposal of the original necklace should be rolled-over. Compute the chargeable gain arising in January 1998 (RPI 158.3) when the replacement necklace was sold for £22,000.

22.3 Pamela bought a building for business use in September 1990 (RPI 129.3) at a cost of £50,000. In September 1997 (RPI 157.1) she sold the building for £64,300 and immediately bought another building, again for business use. Assuming that Pamela claims roll-over relief, calculate the chargeable gain arising in September 1997 if the cost of the new building is :

(a) £61,800

(b) £59,300

(c) £66,800.

22.4 Phillip is a sole trader. In July 1997 he gives his entire business to his grandson. Both Phillip and his grandson elect that the gains arising on this gift should be held-over. The gains arising are as follows :

	£
Freehold buildings	23,500
Goodwill	40,000
Listed investments	10,600

Calculate the amount which may be held-over and the amount which is immediately chargeable.

22.5 Compute the amount of retirement relief available to each of the following taxpayers, each of whom is a sole trader (in good health) making a material disposal of business assets :

	Age	*No of years trading*	*Amount of chargeable gains*
(a)	57	35	£550,000
(b)	69	9	£1,200,000
(c)	56	2	£200,000

***22.6** In January 1981, Norman bought a freehold building for use in his business at a cost of £120,000. The building had a market value on 31 March 1982 (RPI 79.44) of £125,000. In June 1990 (RPI 126.7) he sold the building for £275,000 and in August 1990 (RPI 128.1) he spent £270,000 on buying another building for use in his business. This building was sold in December 1997 (RPI 158.0) for £330,000. Compute the chargeable gains arising on the disposal of each building (assuming that Norman claims roll-over relief).

***22.7** In May 1997, Ruth sold a freehold building which she had used exclusively for business purposes. The building was sold for £120,000, realising a chargeable gain of £42,500. In the following month, Ruth acquired fixed plant for £120,000 and elected to hold-over the gain on the freehold property against this plant and machinery. In August 2001, she acquired another freehold building for £105,000 and elected to transfer the held-over gain to this new building. Explain the treatment of the £42,500 gain.

***22.8** In October 1997 (RPI 157.4), Roger sold the goodwill of his business for £100,000. He had acquired the goodwill in the form of a gift from his brother in January 1986 (RPI 96.25) when it was valued at £50,000. Roger's brother had purchased the goodwill in 1980 and the gain arising on the gift to Roger was £37,350. Both Roger and his brother elected that this gain should be held-over. Compute the chargeable gain in October 1997.

***22.9** Susannah has reached her 60th birthday and has decided to retire after over 20 years of owning her own business. In June 1997 (RPI 156.2) she gives her entire business to her daughter, realising chargeable gains (all relating to chargeable business assets) of £320,000. Calculate the amount of retirement relief which is available and the amount of the gain which may be held-over (if Susannah and her daughter so elect).

***22.10** For the last 15 years, Shaun has been a full-time working director of a company in which he has a 10% stake. He has now reached the age of 59 and has decided to retire, so in January 1998 (RPI 158.3) he sells his entire shareholding for £250,000. He bought the shares in 1981 for £80,000 and they had a market value of £75,000 in March 1982 (RPI 79.44). In January 1998, the company's assets are valued as follows :

	£
Freehold land and buildings	1,700,000
Goodwill	500,000
Investments	100,000
Motor cars	40,000
Plant and machinery	60,000
Net current assets	100,000

The plant and machinery consist entirely of small movable items costing less than £6,000 each and with a current value of less than £6,000 each. Calculate the chargeable gain.

Review questions (Set B)

B1 On 31 March 1998, her 58th birthday, Angela sold all her shares in Scott Stockings Ltd, a manufacturing company. Angela had been a full-time working director of the company for six years and had owned 15% of the company's ordinary shares for the last eight years. The capital gain, after indexation, was £290,000. The market values of the company's assets on 31 March 1998 were :

	£'000
Land and buildings	2,000
Plant and machinery	1,000
Goodwill	500
Investments in gilt-edged securities	250
Net current assets	1,500
	5,250

All items of plant and machinery had a market value of more than £6,000.

You are required to :

Calculate Angela's assessable capital gain for 1997/98, assuming no other disposals of chargeable assets in the year. *(ACCA)*

B2 Victor had the following transactions in the ordinary shares of Victorious Vulcanising plc, a listed company :

		No of shares	*Total amount*	*RPI*
			£	
1/8/78	Bought	600	7,200	
1/4/87	Bought	1,000	11,000	101.8
1/9/89	(1 for 2 rights) Bought	800	4,800	116.6
1/8/97	Sold	2,100	42,000	156.8

The value per share on 31 March 1982 (RPI 79.44) was £8.

You are required to :

Calculate Victor's capital gain for 1997/98, before the annual exemption. *(ACCA)*

B3 Ranek Innovators Ltd sold a factory in November 1997 (RPI 157.7) for £200,000 and moved into rented premises. The factory had been purchased in April 1984 (RPI 88.64) for £100,000. The company purchased fixed plant in December 1996 costing £190,000 and elected to "hold-over" any gain on the sale of the building against the cost of the plant.

You are required to :

(i) Calculate the chargeable gain on the sale of the factory and the effect of the "hold-over" claim on the chargeable gain.

(ii) State the earliest time that the "hold-over" would cease to be effective. *(ACCA)*

B4 ST Ltd, a UK resident company, made the following disposals during the twelve months to 31 March 1998 :

(a) On 30 June 1997, ST Ltd sold 25,000 shares in AD Ltd for £65,000 (net of costs). The holding in AD Ltd had been acquired as follows :

Date	*Shares*	*Cost*
		£
10 July 1979	12,000	12,000
15 February 1981	Bonus issue 1 for 4	
25 March 1984	6,000	9,000
3 June 1987	Bonus issue 1 for 3 (on all shares held)	
10 April 1989	7,000	14,000

The market value of each share on 31 March 1982 was £1.80 (adjusted for the bonus issues).

(b) In August 1988, ST Ltd sold a factory for £180,000 on which a chargeable gain of £50,000 arose. Of the proceeds, £150,000 was immediately invested in a major item of fixed plant and the maximum roll-over relief was claimed. In August 1997 the item of plant was scrapped. (Ignore capital allowances).

(c) In December 1997, the company cleared out the contents of the board room and made the following disposals :

- A painting purchased in May 1982 for £3,000 was sold for £7,500.
- A chandelier purchased in August 1983 for £2,000 was sold for £4,000.
- Two matching sculptures were purchased in January 1984 for £2,000 each. One was sold to a senior employee for £4,000 and the other was sold to his wife for £4,000, the market values at the date of the sales.

The indexation factors to be used in this question are :

March 1982 - June 1997	0.966
March 1984 - April 1985	0.083
April 1985 - April 1989	0.206
April 1989 - June 1997	0.367
May 1982 - December 1997	0.936
August 1983 - December 1997	0.844
January 1984 - December 1997	0.819

You are required :

To compute the amount of gains chargeable to corporation tax on ST Ltd for each of the above transactions. *(CIMA)*

B5 In the year to 5 April 1998, Thomas More, who was born on 1 October 1948, made the following disposals :

(i) A flat in a house that he had purchased on 1 December 1981 for £29,000. It had never been occupied as the main residence and had been consistently let during his period of ownership. The property had been converted into two flats in September 1984 at a cost of £18,000. The flat was sold for £71,000 on 1 December 1997 and out of this legal fees of £2,000 were paid. It was agreed that the value of the other flat was £65,000 in December 1997 and that the entire house was valued at £40,000 in March 1982.

(ii) 20,000 shares in ICI plc which cost £60,000 in December 1983 and which were sold for £150,000 in December 1997.

Thomas also received an offer to sell his 10,000 shares in Hampton Ltd on 30 June 1998. An estimated balance sheet at that date is as follows :

	£	£
Freehold land and buildings - cost		200,000
Plant and machinery (all small items)		
cost less depreciation		60,000
Investment in shares of a major supplier - cost		100,000
		360,000
Current Assets :		
Stock	360,000	
Debtors	140,000	
	500,000	
Less : Bank overdraft	130,000	370,000
		730,000
Share Capital - 30,000 shares of £1		30,000
Reserves		700,000
		730,000

On 30 June 1998, it was agreed that the freehold land and buildings, which were all used in the trade, would have a market value of £800,000 and that the investments would be worth £300,000. The offer made to Thomas is that his shares would be bought at asset value less 10%. The purchaser is also willing to buy them in December 1998 at the same asset values as indicated above but less a discount of 15%. The shares cost Thomas £40,000 on 31 March 1982 when he joined the Board as the production director of the company. Goodwill has been valued at £280,000 in June 1998.

Assume that the Retail Prices Index has the following values :

March 1982	79.44	December 1983	86.89
September 1984	90.11	April 1985	94.78
December 1997	158.0	June 1998	159.8
December 1998	161.6		

Required :

(a) Calculate the capital gains tax payable on the sale of the flat and the shares in ICI plc, assuming that Thomas is married and has taxable income of £20,000 after the personal allowance for 1997/98. None of his income is derived from savings.

(b) If you were told that Mrs More had capital losses of £35,000 brought forward and had made no capital disposals in 1997/98, would there be any advice that you should consider giving to Thomas ?

(c) What will be the capital gain arising to Thomas if he sells his shares in Hampton Ltd on 30 June 1998 ? Again, is there any advice that you should consider giving to him ? Illustrate your answer with appropriate computations. *(AAT)*

***B6** Mrs Laura Stapleton, a widow, has decided to dispose of her residence and retire to Canada, where she will live with her son, Danny.

She acquired her house on 1 June 1984 and lived there until 31 March 1985 when she left the UK in order to care for Danny and his wife who had been injured in a serious car accident in Canada. Liking it there, she extended her stay and on 1 November 1985 she took a job at a local hospital until 31 December 1986 when she returned to the UK and resumed residence in her property.

Having incorporated a company, which commenced to operate a nursing agency on 1 February 1987, she remained living in her house until 31 December 1992, when she left it permanently in order to live in a flat over the company's offices. Contracts were exchanged for the sale of the house on 31 May 1997 with completion scheduled for 30 June 1997.

The house originally cost £50,000 and an extension was completed in December 1989 at a cost of £20,000. The agreed sale proceeds are £300,000 and the expenses of sale are £5,200. Throughout the periods of Mrs Stapleton's absence, the property was let at a market rent.

Assume that the Retail Prices Index has the following values :

June 1984	89.20	December 1989	118.8
May 1997	155.9	June 1997	156.2

Required :

Calculate the capital gain arising on the disposal of Mrs Stapleton's residence. *(AAT)*

***B7** You have been consulted by Mr Christopher Rodrigues on two matters relating to capital gains tax. Extracts from his letter to you are :

"On 31 January 1998, I sold my shares in Fledgeby plc, a listed company. I had acquired them as follows :

1 January 1983	1,000	shares cost £4,200
19 June 1984	700	shares cost £2,950
31 December 1986	1,200	shares cost £5,620
11 August 1988	400	shares cost £2,100

I also took up a 1 for 4 rights issue at £3.50 per share on 31 May 1987. The shares were sold for £38,000.

Also on 31 January 1998, I sold for £100,000 a plot of land that I acquired in January 1970 for £10,000. A friend has told me that the gain might be either a capital gain or a trading gain but, as capital gains are broadly charged at income tax rates, it doesn't really matter which way it is dealt with".

Assume that the Retail Prices Index has the following values :

January 1983	82.61	June 1984	89.20
April 1985	94.78	December 1986	99.62
May 1987	101.9	August 1988	107.9
January 1998	158.3		

Required :

(a) Calculate the capital gain or allowable loss arising on the sale of the shares in Fledgeby plc.

(b) Do you agree with the statement of the other taxation practitioner ? Draft brief notes that will form the basis of the letter that you will write to Mr Rodrigues.

(AAT)

***B8** On 8 August 1978, Alison purchased 500 ordinary shares in Langdale Holdings plc, a listed company, for £3,000. In August 1988 (RPI 107.9), the company made a 1 for 2 rights issue at £10 per ordinary share which Alison took up in respect of her holding. On 15 April 1997 (RPI 155.6), Alison sold 500 shares for £7,500. The market value of the shares on 31 March 1982 (RPI 79.44) was £7 each.

You are required to :

Calculate , before annual exemption, the capital gain assessable on Alison in 1997/98.

(ACCA)

***B9** In October 1997 (RPI 157.4), Kathleen had her 57th birthday and decided to retire immediately from her personal company. She had two children, Corinne and Stephen, to whom she gave all her shares in the company in equal shares. In October 1997 the total value of the shares was £750,000. The shares had cost £250,000 in September 1981 and were valued at £200,000 in March 1982 (RPI 79.44). Kathleen had been a full-time working director in the company since October 1992. The company did not own any "non-business" chargeable assets.

No election has been made, or will be made, to have all pre-31 March 1982 acquisitions re-based to 31 March 1982 (S35(5) TCGA 1992).

You are required to :

(i) Calculate the capital gain (before annual exemption) assessable on Kathleen for 1997/98.

(ii) Explain the present and future consequences of a joint election made by Kathleen, Corinne and Stephen to "hold-over" any capital gain. *(ACCA)*

***B10** The directors of P Ltd have taken the view that the economy will soon start to recover and have decided to make an investment in manufacturing machinery of approximately £1 million. In order to raise most of the required funds they decided to make a number of asset disposals during the accounting period to 31 March 1998. The assets sold were as follows :

(A) On 31 October 1997 an office block was sold for £500,000. Its cost was made up of :

		£
November 1979	Original cost	120,000
December 1980	Extension built	25,000
October 1986	Lift installed	80,000
August 1990	New roof fitted	30,000

This building had been acquired as an investment property for renting. It has never been used for the purpose of P Ltd's trade. Its market value at 31 March 1982 was £160,000.

(B) On 30 November 1997 a plot of land was sold for £140,000. This had been acquired in February 1982 at a cost of £40,000. This purchase had been partly funded from the sale of a plot of land sold in February 1982 for £38,000. This latter plot cost £30,000 in July 1980 and the gain arising on it had been rolled over against the replacement land. The plot now being sold had a market value at 31 March 1982 of £41,000.

(C) On 30 December 1997 an office building, which had been used for business purposes but was now surplus to requirements, was sold for £210,000 (net of costs). This had been bought in April 1983 for £120,000, using all of the proceeds of the sale, during April 1983, of a previously-owned building. This latter building had been purchased in August 1978 for £50,000 and, on its sale, full roll-over relief had been claimed against the new building for the gain arising in April 1983.

The indexation factors to be used in this question are :

March 1982 - April 1983	0.061
April 1983 - December 1997	0.875
March 1982 - November 1997	0.985
March 1982 - October 1997	0.981
October 1986 - October 1997	0.599
August 1990 - October 1997	0.229

You are required :

(a) to compute the capital gains arising from each of the above disposals

(b) to advise the directors on the extent to which they may claim to have the above gains rolled over against their proposed investment in the new machinery. *(CIMA)*

PART 3
CORPORATION TAX

Chapter 23

Introduction to corporation tax

Introduction

The next seven chapters of this book deal with corporation tax, which was introduced in 1965 as the tax payable on the profits of companies. Prior to 1965, companies paid income tax on their profits. The purpose of this first chapter is to provide an introduction to the basic principles of corporation tax.

As stated in Chapter 1, current corporation tax legislation is to be found in the Income and Corporation Taxes Act 1988, as amended by subsequent Finance Acts.

Scope of corporation tax

Companies which are resident in the UK are liable to corporation tax on their "chargeable profits", no matter where in the world those profits arise. Companies which are not UK resident but which operate in the UK through a branch or agency are liable to corporation tax on the chargeable profits of that branch or agency (see Chapter 32).

A company's "chargeable profits" consist of its income plus capital gains, less charges on income. The system of Schedules and Cases used for income tax purposes also applies to corporation tax, but there are some important distinctions between the assessment of an individual's income and the assessment of a company's income. These distinctions are explained later in this chapter.

For corporation tax purposes, the word "company" is taken to mean any corporate body or unincorporated association, excluding partnerships, local authorities and local authority associations. Some of the main types of organisation, other than limited companies, which are liable to corporation tax are :

(a) clubs and societies (e.g. sports clubs)

(b) political associations

(c) building societies

(d) nationalised corporations.

Charities are generally exempt from corporation tax, as are agricultural societies, scientific research associations, friendly societies, trade unions (subject to certain conditions) and approved pension schemes.

Chargeable accounting periods (CAP's)

A company receives one corporation tax assessment per "chargeable accounting period" (CAP). A CAP *begins* when :

(a) the company starts to trade, or otherwise comes within the charge to corporation tax, or

(b) when the previous CAP ends, so long as the company remains within the charge to corporation tax.

A CAP *ends* on the *earliest* occurrence of any of the following events:

(a) the expiration of 12 months from the beginning of the CAP

(b) the end of a period for which the company prepares a set of accounts

(c) the commencement of winding-up proceedings

(d) the company ceasing to be UK resident

(e) the company ceasing to be within the charge to corporation tax.

These rules have the following consequences :

(a) The length of a CAP can never exceed 12 months.

(b) If a set of accounts covers a period of 12 months or less, the period covered by the accounts is regarded as a CAP in its own right and a corporation tax assessment is raised for this period of account.

(c) If a set of accounts covers a period exceeding 12 months, the period covered by the accounts is broken down into two or more CAP's, each giving rise to a separate corporation tax assessment. The first CAP consists of the first 12 months of the period covered by the accounts. The second CAP consists of the next 12 months and so forth. If the period covered by the accounts is not an exact multiple of 12 months, the final CAP will be of less than 12 months' duration.

EXAMPLE 1

Identify the CAP's which relate to the following sets of company accounts :

(a) A Ltd makes up accounts for the year to 31 December 1997.

(b) B Ltd makes up accounts for the six months to 31 October 1997.

(c) C Ltd makes up accounts for the sixteen months to 31 December 1997.

(d) D Ltd makes up accounts for the thirty months to 31 March 1998.

SOLUTION

(a) The year to 31 December 1997 is a CAP in its own right.

(b) The six months to 31 October 1997 is a CAP in its own right.

(c) The sixteen months to 31 December 1997 is divided into two CAP's. These are the 12 months to 31 August 1997 and the 4 months to 31 December 1997.

(d) The thirty months to 31 March 1998 is divided into three CAP's. These are the 12 months to 30 September 1996, the 12 months to 30 September 1997 and the 6 months to 31 March 1998.

Allocation of profits between CAP's

As stated above, a period of account exceeding 12 months must be divided into two or more CAP's, each of which will give rise to a separate corporation tax assessment. The company's profit for a long period of account is allocated between CAP's as follows :

(a) Trading profits assessable under Schedule D Case I (before deduction of capital allowances) are time-apportioned between CAP's. A separate capital allowances computation is then performed for each CAP.

(b) Schedule D Case VI income is usually also time-apportioned between CAP's.

(c) Other income is allocated between CAP's according to the relevant basis of assessment. For example :

  (i) Bank or building society interest (received gross by a company and assessed under Schedule D Case III on the receipts basis) is allocated to the CAP in which the interest is received.

  (ii) Rental income assessed under Schedule A on the due basis (see later in this chapter) is allocated to the CAP in which the rents fall due.

  (iii) A net credit on "non-trading loan relationships" (see later in this chapter) is allocated between CAP's on the accruals basis.

(d) Capital gains are allocated to the CAP in which the disposals take place.

(e) Charges on income are allocated to the CAP in which they are paid.

As for income tax, all time-apportionments should be made exactly, according to the number of days in the period concerned. This is the approach adopted in this book (although, for the sake of simplicity, the existence of February 29th has been ignored and all years have been assumed to contain 365 days).

In practice, the time-apportionment method normally used for income arising under Schedule D Cases I and VI may be replaced by a more accurate method of allocation if one is available. For instance, if a company's trading profits are earned as a result of a small number of transactions and the profit arising on each transaction can be calculated individually, the company's Schedule D Case I income may be allocated between CAP's according to the transactions occurring in each CAP.

EXAMPLE 2

A company makes up accounts for the 21 months to 30 September 1997. The company's income, gains and charges for this period are as follows :

	£
Trading income (before capital allowances)	630,000
Gross bank interest received on :	
30 June 1996	500
31 December 1996	550
30 June 1997	600
Chargeable gains :	
Disposal on 25 May 1996	2,300
Disposal on 12 December 1996	700
Disposal on 15 February 1997	10,500
Charges on income :	
Paid 31 March 1996	4,000
Paid 31 March 1997	4,000

Show how the company's period of account will be divided into CAP's and compute the chargeable profits for each CAP (ignoring capital allowances).

SOLUTION

The period of account (638 days) is divided into two CAP's i.e. the 12 months to 31 December 1996 (365 days) and the 9 months to 30 September 1997 (273 days). The chargeable profits for each CAP are as follows :

	12 months to 31/12/96	*9 months to 30/9/97*
	£	£
Trading income (365/638th, 273/638th)	360,423	269,577
Bank interest received	1,050	600
Chargeable gains	3,000	10,500
	364,473	280,677
Less : Charges on income	4,000	4,000
	360,473	276,677

Note :

The bank interest received is allocated according to the date received, the chargeable gains are allocated according to the date of disposal and the charges on income are allocated according to the date of payment.

Chargeable profits

A company's chargeable profits for a CAP are calculated as follows :

	£
Schedule D Case I (trading income, less capital allowances)	x
Schedule D Case III (interest received gross and non-trading loan relationships)	x
Schedule D Case V (income from foreign possessions)	x
Schedule D Case VI (furnished lettings and miscellaneous income)	x
Schedule A (unfurnished lettings and other income from property)	x
Unfranked investment income	x
Chargeable gains	x
	x
Less : Charges on income	x
Chargeable profits	x

Notes :

(i) A company cannot be assessed under Schedule E, since Schedule E relates to income from employment and a company cannot be an employee. Similarly, a company cannot exercise a profession or a vocation and therefore cannot be assessed under Schedule D Case II.

(ii) Schedule D Case IV (income from foreign securities) no longer applies to companies. The tax treatment of a company's foreign income is described in Chapter 32 of this book.

(iii) In general, a company's income under each Schedule and Case is computed in accordance with income tax principles and its chargeable gains are computed in accordance with CGT principles. However, this general rule is over-ridden by special corporation tax provisions in some instances (see below).

(iv) A company is not a "person" and is not entitled to claim personal allowances.

Schedule D Case I

A company's Schedule D Case I assessment for a CAP is always based on its actual trading income for that CAP, adjusted for tax purposes in the usual way. There are no special rules relating to the commencement or cessation of trade. Companies are entitled to claim capital allowances, but note that :

(a) There is no restriction relating to the private use of assets, because private use of company assets by a company's employees is charged to income tax under Schedule E as a benefit in kind.

(b) WDA is scaled down if a CAP is of less than 12 months' duration.

(c) The capital allowances of companies are treated as a trading expense and are taken into account when computing adjusted trading profits. This is in line with the treatment of capital allowances accorded to "new" unincorporated businesses (and to old unincorporated businesses as from 1997/98).

The provisions whereby farmers may average their profits (see Chapter 9) do *not* apply to companies.

Schedule D Case III

The main classes of income assessed under Schedule D Case III for a company are as follows :

(a) bank deposit interest received gross

(b) building society interest received gross

(c) net credits arising from non-trading loan relationships (see later in this chapter).

Unlike individuals, companies receive all bank deposit and building society interest gross and this is assessed under Schedule D Case III *on the receipts basis.* Any bank or building society interest accrued at the end of a CAP is disregarded. (Note that the first £70 p.a. of National Savings Bank interest received by a company is *not* exempt from corporation tax).

Property income

As explained in Chapter 5, a company's income from property is assessed according to pre-FA1995 rules which no longer apply to individuals. One consequence of these rules is that a company's income from the letting of furnished property is assessed under Schedule D Case VI rather than under Schedule A. Income from the letting of unfurnished property and other property income is assessed under Schedule A but on a different basis from that which is used for income tax purposes. The rules which are used to assess a company's property income are explained in detail at the end of this chapter.

Unfranked investment income

The term "unfranked investment income" (UFII) refers to income received by a company net of *basic rate* income tax (e.g. patent royalties). A company receiving such income is able to reclaim the income tax deducted at source (see Chapter 26) but the grossed-up amount of the income is then assessed to corporation tax *on the receipts basis.*

Before the introduction of the provisions relating to loan relationships (see below) interest received net of lower rate income tax was also classed as UFII but this is now assessed instead under Schedule D Case I or Case III.

Franked investment income

Dividends received from other UK companies are known as "franked investment income" (FII). Such dividends are paid out of profits which have already been subject to corporation tax once in the hands of the paying company and are therefore not subjected to corporation tax a second time in the hands of the receiving company. A company's FII does not form part of its chargeable profits.

Chargeable gains

A company's chargeable profits for a CAP include any chargeable gains arising in respect of disposals made during that CAP. Note that :

(a) Companies are not entitled to the £6,500 annual exemption.

(b) If a company owns shares or securities, the FA1985 pool consists of shares acquired on or after 1 April 1982 (not 6 April 1982) and the 1982 holding consists of shares acquired between 6 April 1965 and 31 March 1982 (not 5 April 1982).

Charges on income

A company's charges on income consist largely of payments made net of *basic rate* income tax. The main types of payment classified as charges on income are patent royalties and certain charitable donations (see below). A company making such a payment must account to the Inland Revenue for the income tax deducted at source (see Chapter 26) but the grossed-up amount of the payment is then deducted as a charge on income when calculating the company's chargeable profits. Note the following important points :

(a) The amount of charges deducted when computing the chargeable profits for a CAP is the grossed-up amount of the charges actually *paid* during the CAP.

(b) Companies may obtain tax relief on their charitable donations as follows :

 (i) A payment made to a charity under a qualifying deed of covenant is a charge on income.

 (ii) A payment made under the Gift Aid scheme is a charge on income. The £250 minimum which applies to individuals applies also to close companies (see Chapter 28) but does not apply to non-close companies.

 (iii) A charitable donation incurred for trade purposes is an allowable expense under Schedule D Case I and is not treated as a charge on income.

Before the introduction of the provisions relating to loan relationships (see below) interest paid net of lower rate income tax was regarded as a charge on income but this is no longer the case. Such interest is now deductible when computing the company's assessment under Schedule D Case I or Case III.

Loan relationships

The Finance Act 1996 introduced a new tax regime for the treatment of company "loan relationships". A company has a loan relationship if it is a debtor or creditor with regard to any debt which is a loan under general law. The main classes of debt to which the term "loan relationship" refers are Government securities (also known as gilt-edged securities), corporate bonds (e.g. debentures) and bank overdrafts. The tax treatment of income and expenditure relating to a loan relationship depends upon whether the relationship has been entered into for trade purposes :

(a) **Trading loan relationships.** If a company has entered into a loan relationship for trade purposes, then :

    (i) Any interest payable (and any other cost relating to the debt) is allowable as a trading expense and is deducted when computing the company's Schedule D Case I income.

    (ii) Any interest receivable (and other income relating to the debt) is regarded as a trading receipt and is treated as Schedule D Case I income. This will usually apply only if the company's trade is that of lending money.

(b) **Non-trading loan relationships.** If a company has entered into one or more loan relationships for non-trading purposes, then all of the "debits" and "credits" (costs and income) relating to such relationships for a CAP are aggregated. Then :

    (i) If total credits exceed total debits, the net credits are assessable under Schedule D Case III.

    (ii) If total debits exceed total credits, the net debits may be relieved in a variety of ways (see Chapter 27).

It is important to appreciate that the above treatment of costs and income relating to loan relationships applies to all such costs and income, *whether of a revenue or capital nature*. This means that the profit (or loss) arising on a disposal of Government securities or corporate bonds by a company is taxable (or allowable) even though such assets would not be chargeable assets for CGT purposes if held by individuals.

In most cases, the amount of income and expenditure brought into account for a loan relationship in a given CAP will be calculated on the *accruals basis*. If receipts or payments are made net of income tax (at the lower rate) they must be grossed-up. Any income tax deducted from the income received in a CAP may be reclaimed from the Inland Revenue and any income tax deducted from the payments made in a CAP must be accounted for to the Inland Revenue (see Chapter 26).

EXAMPLE 3

A company has the following results for the year to 31 March 1998 :

	£
Trading income	875,000
Income from property let unfurnished	14,200
Bank interest received gross	8,300
Patent royalties (net amount received)	6,160
Interest on Government securities (net amount received)	22,400
Dividends from UK companies (net amount received)	16,400
Chargeable gains	123,000
Charitable covenant (net amount paid)	18,480

The following information is also relevant :

(a) Patent royalties of £3,080 (net) were owing to the company on 31 March 1998 but were not received until May 1998.

(b) The Government securities were acquired on 1 July 1997. Interest of £22,400 (net) is payable to the company on 30 June and 31 December each year.

(c) The charitable covenant began on 1 January 1998 and, on that date, the company made the first annual payment of £18,480 (net).

Compute the company's chargeable profits for the year to 31 March 1998.

SOLUTION

	£
Schedule D Case I	875,000
Schedule A	14,200
Schedule D Case III (£8,300 + £42,000)	50,300
Unfranked Investment Income	8,000
Chargeable gains	123,000
	1,070,500
Less : Charges on income	24,000
Chargeable profits	1,046,500

Notes :

(i) The patent royalties are unfranked investment income. The company may reclaim the £1,840 (£6,160 x 23/77) income tax suffered by deduction at source but the gross income of £8,000 (£6,160 x 100/77) forms part of the company's chargeable profits for corporation tax purposes. Since UFII is assessed on the receipts basis, the amount owing to the company at the end of the year is irrelevant.

(ii) The interest on Government securities is income from a non-trading loan relationship and is assessed under Schedule D Case III on the accruals basis. The company may reclaim the income tax of £5,600 (£22,400 x 20/80) suffered during the CAP but the gross income accrued in the CAP of £42,000 (£33,600 x 100/80) forms part of the company's chargeable profits for corporation tax purposes.

(iii) The dividends received from UK companies are franked investment income and do not form part of the company's chargeable profits for corporation tax purposes.

(iv) The company must account to the Inland Revenue for the income tax deducted at source from the charges on income but the gross payment of £24,000 (£18,480 x 100/77) is then deducted from the company's chargeable profits for corporation tax purposes. Since charges are dealt with on a payments basis, the whole of the £24,000 is deductible in the year to 31 March 1998.

(v) In this example, interest on Government securities, UFII, FII and charges on income were stated net. However, it is standard accounting practice for a company's profit and loss account to show all such items gross.

Schedule A

A company's property income is assessed under Schedule A, unless the income arises from furnished lettings, in which case it is assessed under Schedule D Case VI. The rules used to compute a company's Schedule A assessment for a CAP are as follows :

(a) The income assessable under Schedule A for the CAP is the income *due to be received* in that CAP, regardless of the period to which the income relates and regardless of whether or not the income is actually received (though relief is given for bad debts if the company has taken all reasonable steps to enforce payment).

(b) Short lease premiums are assessed as for individuals (see Chapter 5).

(c) The expenditure which is allowable against property income is restricted to the following items :

    (i) maintenance and repairs (excluding improvements and excluding the cost of rectifying dilapidations which had occurred before the property was acquired by the company)

    (ii) insurance and management expenses

    (iii) council tax, business rates and water rates

    (iv) rent payable to a superior landlord (in the case of a sublet)

    (v) cost of services provided by the landlord.

    Expenditure incurred during a period of owner-occupation is not allowable under Schedule A but may instead be allowed under Schedule D Case I (if the company is occupying the property for trade purposes).

(d) Interest payable on a loan to buy or improve rented property is subject to the rules relating to non-trading loan relationships (see above).

(e) Special rules relate to expenditure incurred during "void periods" i.e. periods during which a property is neither occupied by the owner nor let to a tenant. Any expenditure which would normally be allowable under the Schedule A rules but which is incurred during a void period will be allowed only if :

(i) the void period is immediately preceded by and immediately followed by a lease at full rent, or

(ii) the void period is between initial acquisition of the property and a lease at full rent and the expenses do not relate to the pre-acquisition period.

A "full rent" is a rent which is sufficient, taking one CAP with another, to cover expenditure. Allowable expenditure on a property during a void period is set against income from the full rent lease which follows that period.

(f) Expenditure on plant and machinery used in the management of let property attracts capital allowances, as does expenditure on industrial buildings let for industrial use.

EXAMPLE 4

On 1 August 1997, a company receives a £7,000 premium in return for granting a 15-year lease on an unfurnished property. The rent of £6,000 per annum is payable quarterly in advance on 1 February, 1 May, 1 August and 1 November. The company's annual accounting date is 31 December and allowable expenses up to 31 December 1997 are £1,920. Compute the Schedule A assessment for the year to 31 December 1997.

SOLUTION

The rent due to be received in the year to 31 December 1997 is £3,000 (i.e. £1,500 on 1 August and £1,500 on 1 November). The assessable part of the premium is £5,040 (£7,000 - 14 x 2% x £7,000), so the Schedule A assessment is £6,120 (£3,000 + £5,040 - £1,920).

Schedule A losses

When computing a company's Schedule A assessment for a CAP, the profit or loss arising on each lease must be calculated separately. If any lease shows a loss, the treatment of that loss depends whether the lease in question is a "landlord's repairing lease" (a lease at full rent where the landlord is responsible for the cost of repairs) or a "tenant's repairing lease" (a lease at full rent where the tenant is responsible for the cost of repairs) or a "nominal rent lease" (a lease at less than full rent). Losses are dealt with as follows :

(a) A loss arising on a landlord's repairing lease may be set against surpluses arising on landlord's repairing leases in the same or future CAP's.

(b) A loss arising on a tenant's repairing lease may be set against surpluses arising on landlord's repairing leases in the same CAP or, failing this, may be carried forward and set against future surpluses arising from the same property.

(c) A loss arising on a nominal rent lease may only be carried forward and set against future surpluses (if any) arising from the same lease.

EXAMPLE 5

A company which makes up accounts to 31 March each year owns four properties, all of which are let unfurnished. Income and expenditure in relation to these properties for the years to 31 March 1997 and 31 March 1998 are as follows :

	Property A	*Property B*	*Property C*	*Property D*
	£	£	£	£
y/e 31 March 1997 :				
Income	2,000	1,850	100	2,500
Expenditure	700	2,360	1,300	2,200
y/e 31 March 1998 :				
Income	2,100	1,950	100	2,500
Expenditure	750	1,700	1,400	1,900

Properties A and B are let under tenant's repairing leases. Property C is let at nominal rent. Property D is let under a landlord's repairing lease. Compute the Schedule A assessment for the two years.

SOLUTION

	Property A	*Property B*	*Property C*	*Property D*
	£	£	£	£
y/e 31 March 1997 :				
Income	2,000	1,850	100	2,500
Expenditure	700	2,360	1,300	2,200
Surplus/(loss)	1,300	(510)	(1,200)	300
Loss on Property B		300		(300)
	1,300	(210)	(1,200)	0
		c/f	c/f	

Schedule A assessment for y/e 31 March 1997 = £1,300.

	Property A	*Property B*	*Property C*	*Property D*
	£	£	£	£
y/e 31 March 1998 :				
Income	2,100	1,950	100	2,500
Expenditure	750	1,700	1,400	1,900
Surplus/(loss)	1,350	250	(1,300)	600
Loss b/f		(210)	(1,200)	
	1,350	40	(2,500)	600
			c/f	

Schedule A assessment for y/e 31 March 1998 = £1,990 (£1,350 + £40 + £600).

Notes :

(i) £300 of the loss on property B (tenant's repairing) in the year to 31 March 1997 is set against the surplus arising in the same year on Property D (landlord's repairing). The remaining £210 of the loss can only be carried forward and set against future surpluses from the same property.

(ii) The losses on Property C (nominal rent) can only be carried forward and set against future surpluses (if any) from the same lease.

Schedule D Case VI

A company's income from the letting of furnished property is assessed under Schedule D Case VI (usually on the accruals basis). Allowable expenditure includes all of the expenditure allowable under Schedule A, together with repairs and insurance of the contents of the property and the "wear and tear" allowance (see Chapter 5). The renewals basis may be used as an alternative to the wear and tear allowance. If the property is not made available for letting throughout the whole of a CAP, the allowable expenditure is restricted to a proportion, based upon the length of the period during which the property was available for letting.

A company may elect that an assessment on income from furnished property should be subdivided into a Schedule A assessment on the portion of the income relating to the premises and a Schedule D Case VI assessment on the portion of the income relating to the furniture. The Schedule A part of the assessment may then be used to relieve other Schedule A losses incurred by the company (subject to the Schedule A loss relief rules described above). A company's Schedule D Case VI losses may be set against any other Schedule D Case VI income for the same CAP. Unrelieved losses are carried forward and set against Schedule D Case VI income in future CAP's.

EXAMPLE 6

A company produces the following profit and loss account for the year to 31 March 1998 :

	£	£
Gross profit brought down from trading account		758,950
Add : Rents from unfurnished property (Notes 1,3)	2,500	
Rents from furnished property (Notes 2,3)	2,500	
Loan interest receivable (Note 4)	2,600	
Dividends received (Note 5)	18,750	
Bank interest received gross	4,789	
Profit on sale of building (Note 6)	12,500	43,639
		802,589
Less : Operating expenses (Note 7)		568,912
Net profit for the year		233,677

Notes :

1. The unfurnished property was let on 1 January 1998 at a rent of £10,000 per annum, payable annually in advance. The figure shown in the profit and loss account represents the rent for the period 1 January 1998 to 31 March 1998.
2. Coincidentally, the furnished property was let on precisely the same terms (and on the same date) as the unfurnished property.
3. No allowable expenditure has been incurred in relation to either of the let properties.
4. Net loan interest of £1,560 was received during the year and a further £520 (net) was owing to the company at the end of the year. The profit and loss account shows the gross equivalent figure (i.e. £2,080 x 100/80 = £2,600).
5. Dividends of £15,000 were received from other UK companies during the year. The profit and loss account shows the gross equivalent figure (i.e. £15,000 x 100/80 = £18,750).
6. The chargeable gain on the sale of the building (after deduction of indexation allowance) is £2,350.
7. Operating expenses include :

	£
Directors' fees	100,000
Debenture interest (grossed-up amounts) :	
Paid 1 July 1997	2,000
Paid 1 January 1998	2,000
Accrued at 31 March 1998	1,000
Depreciation	102,500
Entertaining expenses	2,400
Charitable covenant (grossed-up amounts) :	
Paid during the year	500
Accrued at 31 March 1998	250

All of the remaining operating expenses are allowable under the rules of Schedule D Case I. The debentures were issued for trade purposes. The company claims capital allowances for the year of £87,450.

Required :

(a) Compute the company's trading profit assessable under Schedule D Case I for the year to 31 March 1998.

(b) Compute the company's chargeable profits for the year to 31 March 1998.

SOLUTION

(a) The Schedule D Case I assessment is as follows :

		£	£
Net profit per accounts			233,677
Less : *Non-trading income* :			
	Rents from unfurnished property	2,500	
	Rents from furnished property	2,500	
	Loan interest receivable	2,600	
	Dividends received	18,750	
	Bank interest received	4,789	
	Profit on sale of building	12,500	43,639
			190,038
Add : *Disallowed expenses* :			
	Depreciation	102,500	
	Entertaining	2,400	
	Charitable covenant	750	105,650
			295,688
Less : Capital allowances			87,450
Schedule D Case I assessment			208,238

(b) The chargeable profits for the year are :

	£
Schedule D Case I	208,238
Schedule A	10,000
Schedule D Case VI	2,500
Schedule D Case III (£2,600 + £4,789)	7,389
Chargeable gain	2,350
	230,477
Less : Charges on income (charitable covenant)	500
Chargeable profits	229,977

Notes :

(i) The computation of the Schedule D Case I assessment is performed in the same way as that of an individual. The starting point is the net profit shown by the accounts. Non-trading income included in this net profit is subtracted and disallowed expenses are added back. The aim is to separate out the company's trading profit from the total net profit shown in the accounts. (Note that debenture interest payable for the CAP is an allowable expense).

It is extremely important to classify the company's profits correctly and to arrive at a separate figure for each category of profit (e.g. trading income, rents, interest, chargeable gains etc). This analysis is necessary because different rules of assessment apply to each category of profit and is especially vital if the company has incurred any losses (see Chapter 27).

(ii) The Schedule A assessment is based on the rents due to be received during the CAP but the Schedule D Case VI assessment is made on the accruals basis.

(iii) The gross amount of the loan interest accrued for the CAP forms part of the Schedule D Case III assessment (assuming that the loan was not made for trade purposes).

(iv) FII is not chargeable to corporation tax and does not form part of the chargeable profit.

(v) The chargeable gain on the sale of the building is fully chargeable to corporation tax since the company is not entitled to the annual exemption.

(vi) The grossed-up charitable covenant actually paid in the CAP (£500) is treated as a charge on income when computing chargeable profits.

Summary

- Corporation tax is charged on the profits of UK resident companies. The term "company" includes clubs, societies and other unincorporated associations.
- A company receives one corporation tax assessment per chargeable accounting period (CAP). A CAP can never be more than 12 months in length. Accounts covering a period exceeding 12 months are divided into two or more CAP's.
- A company's chargeable profits consist of its income and capital gains, less charges on income.
- A company's Schedule D Case III income consists of interest received gross and net credits on non-trading loan relationships. Income and expenditure relating to loan relationships entered into for trade purposes is taken into account when computing Schedule D Case I income.
- A company's income from property is assessed according to pre-FA1995 rules which no longer apply to individuals.
- Income received net of basic rate income tax is known as "unfranked investment income" (UFII). The gross equivalent of the UFII received in a CAP forms part of the chargeable profits for that CAP.
- Dividends received from other UK companies are known as "franked investment income" (FII) and do not form part of the chargeable profits of the receiving company.
- A company's charges on income consist mainly of payments made net of basic rate income tax. The gross equivalent of the payments made in a CAP are deducted when computing the chargeable profits for that CAP.

Exercises

23.1 Identify the chargeable accounting periods relating to the following sets of company accounts :

(a) year to 30 November 1997
(b) 1 October 1996 to 31 July 1997
(c) 1 January 1998 to 31 January 1998
(d) 33 months to 31 August 1997
(e) 1 April 1996 to 30 September 1997.

23.2 On 1 January 1998, a company receives a dividend from another UK company of £5,600. On the same date, the company also receives debenture interest of £1,280 (net of income tax) and pays debenture interest of £8,640 (net of income tax).

(a) Outline the corporation tax treatment of each of these three items.
(b) Explain how each of these items would appear in the company's accounts.

23.3 On 1 February 1998, a company receives bank interest of £1,500. On the same date, the company also receives interest of £1,500 on its holding of Government securities. Describe the corporation tax treatment of each of these items.

23.4 A company's accounts for the 17 months to 30 June 1997 include :

	£
Trading income	425,000
Building society interest received on :	
30 April 1996	2,450
30 April 1997	2,675
Rents from furnished property	9,010
Rents from unfurnished property :	17,000
(let in 1992 at a rent of £12,000 p.a. payable quarterly in advance on 1 May, 1 August, 1 November and 1 February)	
Chargeable gains :	
Disposal on 31 January 1997	28,700
Disposal on 1 February 1997	49,760
Dividend received from UK company (gross amount)	10,000
Patent royalties paid net (gross amounts) :	
Paid 31 July 1996	6,000
Paid 31 January 1997	6,000
Accrued to 30 June 1997	5,000

Show how the company's period of account will be divided into chargeable accounting periods and compute the chargeable profits for each CAP.

23.5 A company has the following results for the year to 31 March 1998 :

		£
Trading profits, after capital allowances		1,549,400
Bank deposit interest (gross) :		
Received 30 June 1997		43,800
Received 31 December 1997		44,670
Accrued to 31 March 1998		23,980
Chargeable gain on sale of factory		531,000
Dividends received from UK companies (net amount)		132,000
Debenture interest receivable (net amounts) :		
Received 28 February 1998		9,000
Accrued to 31 March 1998		1,500
Deed of covenant payable to charity (net amounts)		
Paid 1 October 1997, for year to 30 September 1998	6,930	
Less : Prepayment	3,465	3,465

Compute the company's chargeable profits for the year. (Assume that the debentures were not acquired for trade purposes).

23.6 A company with an accounting date of 31 March owns 4 houses in North Street (numbers 21, 23, 25 and 27). During the year to 31 March 1998, the houses are let unfurnished as described below, all rents being payable quarterly in advance on the English quarter days (25 March, 24 June, 29 September and 25 December) :

21 Let all year at a full rent of £2,000 per annum, the company being responsible for all repairs.

23 Let all year at a nominal rent of £100 per annum.

25 Let at a nominal rent of £40 per annum until 23 June 1997, then empty until 29 September 1997 when let at a full rent of £3,000 per annum. The new tenant is responsible for all repairs.

27 Let at a full rent of £2,500 per annum until the tenant moved out on 25 December 1997, then empty until 25 March 1998 when let at a full rent of £2,600 per annum. The company is responsible for repairs under both leases.

The company incurred the following expenses during the year :

		Insurance	*Rent collector's fees*	*Repairs*
		£	£	£
21		200	120	3,450
23		120		180
25	- during first lease			28
	- whilst vacant			187
	- during second lease	150	135	
27	- during first lease		75	
	- whilst vacant			154
	- during second lease	125	39	77

Calculate the Schedule A assessment for the year to 31 March 1998.

***23.7** A company's profit and loss account (drawn up in accordance with standard accounting practice) for the year to 31 March 1998 is as follows :

		£
Gross trading profit		373,870
Receivable from other UK companies :		
Dividends		4,000
Debenture interest (Note 1)		6,000
Bank interest received		12,600
Rents from unfurnished property (Note 2)		4,000
Profit on sale of investments (Note 3)		22,490
		422,960
Less :		
Distribution costs (all allowable)	97,500	
Administrative expenses (all allowable)	101,150	
Directors' fees	50,000	
Interest on bank overdraft	23,780	
Debenture interest payable (Note 4)	50,000	
Patent royalties payable (Note 5)	7,500	
Depreciation	108,300	438,230
Net loss for the year		15,270

Notes :

1. The company acquired £240,000 of 10% debentures (for non-trade purposes) on 1 January 1998. Interest is receivable half-yearly on 30 June and 31 December.
2. The unfurnished property was let on 1 December 1997 at a rent of £1,000 per month payable quarterly in advance on 1 December, 1 March, 1 June and 1 September.
3. The agreed chargeable gain on the sale of the investments was £8,450.
4. £500,000 of 10% debentures were issued (for trade purposes) on 1 April 1997. The interest is payable annually on 1 January.
5. As from 1 July 1997, the company is required to pay patent royalties of £10,000 per annum, less basic rate income tax deducted at source. The net amount actually paid in the year to 31 March 1998 is £3,850.
6. Capital allowances of £32,700 are claimed for the year.

Compute the company's chargeable profits for the year.

Chapter 24

Computation and payment of the corporation tax liability

Introduction

Having ascertained a company's chargeable profits for a chargeable accounting period (CAP), the next step is to compute the corporation tax liability arising in that CAP. The purpose of this chapter is to describe the way in which the corporation tax liability is computed and to explain the system by means of which the tax is collected.

Corporation tax financial years

A corporation tax financial year (FY) runs from 1 April to the following 31 March and is identified by the year in which it *begins*. For example, FY96 ran from 1 April 1996 to 31 March 1997 and FY97 runs from 1 April 1997 to 31 March 1998. The income tax year (6 April to the following 5 April) is largely irrelevant when dealing with corporation tax matters.

The rates of corporation tax are fixed for each financial year, so if a CAP coincides with a financial year (i.e. the year ended 31 March), or is entirely contained within a CAP (e.g. the six months from 1 July to 31 December), the computation of the corporation tax liability for the CAP is very straightforward. The appropriate rate of corporation tax for the FY is applied to the chargeable profits for the CAP, giving the corporation tax liability.

However, if a CAP straddles 31 March, the chargeable profits for the CAP are time-apportioned between the two FY's involved and are charged to corporation tax at the rates applicable to each FY. Clearly, this apportionment will be required only if corporation tax rates have changed from one FY to the next. It is important to note that a simple time-apportionment is always made in these circumstances. This differs from the method described in Chapter 23 for the apportionment between CAP's of the income, gains and charges of long periods of account.

EXAMPLE 1

A company has chargeable profits of £5,000,000 for a CAP. Explain how the corporation tax liability for this CAP will be calculated if :

(a) the CAP is the 12 months to 31 March 1998

(b) the CAP is the 9 months to 31 January 1998

(c) the CAP is the 10 months to 31 October 1997.

SOLUTION

(a) The 12 months to 31 March 1998 coincide with FY97, so the chargeable profits of £5,000,000 will be charged to corporation tax at the rates applicable to FY97.

(b) The 9 months to 31 January 1998 are entirely contained within FY97, so the chargeable profits of £5,000,000 will be charged to corporation tax at the rates applicable to FY97.

(c) The 10 months to 31 October 1997 (304 days) are contained partly within FY96 (90 days) and partly within FY97 (214 days). The chargeable profits of £5,000,000 will be apportioned between FY's as follows :

FY96	1 January 1997 to 31 March 1997	£5,000,000 x 90/304	= £1,480,263
FY97	1 April 1997 to 31 October 1997	£5,000,000 x 214/304	= £3,519,737

The profits of £1,480,263 falling into FY96 will be taxed at FY96 rates whilst the profits of £3,519,737 falling into FY97 will be taxed at FY97 rates.

Rates of corporation tax

For each corporation tax financial year, there are two rates of corporation tax. The "full rate" applies to companies with profits exceeding a specified upper limit whilst the "small companies rate" applies to companies with profits not exceeding a specified lower limit. Companies with profits which lie between the lower and upper limits are charged to corporation tax at the full rate but are then entitled to a deduction known as the "marginal relief" (see below). Recent corporation tax rates and limits have been as follows :

	Full rate	*Small companies rate*	*Upper limit*	*Lower limit*
			£	£
FY91	33%	25%	1,250,000	250,000
FY92	33%	25%	1,250,000	250,000
FY93	33%	25%	1,250,000	250,000
FY94	33%	25%	1,500,000	300,000
FY95	33%	25%	1,500,000	300,000
FY96	33%	24%	1,500,000	300,000
FY97	33%	23%	1,500,000	300,000

The upper and lower limits are reduced pro rata if the CAP (or the part of the CAP that falls into the corporation tax FY) is of less than 12 months' duration.

Profits and chargeable profits

The "profits" which are compared with the upper and lower limits in order to determine the applicable rate of corporation tax are *not* the company's chargeable profits as defined in Chapter 23. For this purpose alone, the term "profits" is defined as the company's chargeable profits plus its grossed-up franked investment income. Even though, as stated in Chapter 23, FII is not charged to corporation tax in the hands of the receiving company, the amount of FII received by a company *is* taken into account when determining the applicable rate of corporation tax. The process of calculating a company's corporation tax liability for a CAP involves the following steps :

(a) The chargeable profits for the CAP are calculated (the term "basic profits" is sometimes used instead of "chargeable profits").

(b) The "profits" for the CAP are calculated by adding the grossed-up FII for that CAP (if any) to the chargeable profits.

(c) The profits figure calculated at (b) is used to determine the applicable rate of corporation tax but that rate is then applied to the chargeable profits.

(d) If the CAP straddles 31 March, profits and chargeable profits are both time-apportioned between the two FY's involved and a separate tax computation is performed for each FY. The results of these two computations are aggregated to give the corporation tax liability for the CAP.

EXAMPLE 2

Calculate the corporation tax liability arising in each of the following cases :

(a) A Ltd has chargeable profits of £2,000,000 for the year to 31 March 1998 and no FII.

(b) B Ltd has chargeable profits of £143,000 for the year to 31 March 1998 and FII (net) of £8,000.

(c) C Ltd has chargeable profits of £282,500 for the year to 31 March 1998 and FII (net) of £1,000,000.

SOLUTION

	(a)	(b)	(c)
	£	£	£
Chargeable profits	2,000,000	143,000	282,500
FII (gross)	0	10,000	1,250,000
Profits	2,000,000	153,000	1,532,500

	(a)	(b)	(c)
Applicable rate of corporation tax	33%	23%	33%
Corporation tax due :			
£2,000,000 @ 33%	£660,000		
£143,000 @ 23%		£32,890	
£282,500 @ 33%			£93,225

Notes :

(i) Each company's CAP coincides with FY97. Therefore the lower limit, upper limit and rates of tax used are those for FY97.

(ii) FII is grossed up at 100/80.

(iii) In each case, the profits figure is used to determine the applicable rate of tax but this rate is then applied to chargeable profits.

EXAMPLE 3

D Ltd has chargeable profits of £211,200 for the 11 months to 30 November 1997 and received net FII of £2,640 on 30 June 1997. Calculate the corporation tax liability for this period.

SOLUTION

The company has chargeable profits of £211,200 and profits of £214,500 (£211,200 + £2,640 x 100/80) for its 334-day CAP. 90 days of the CAP fall into FY96 and the remaining 244 days fall into FY97. Chargeable profits, profits, the lower limit and the upper limit are apportioned between the two FY's as follows :

	FY96 (1/1/97 to 31/3/97)	*FY97 (1/4/97 to 30/11/97)*
Chargeable	£211,200 x 90/334 = £56,910	£211,200 x 244/334 = £154,290
Profits	£214,500 x 90/334 = £57,799	£214,500 x 244/334= £156,701
Lower limit	£300,000 x 90/365 = £73,973	£300,000 x 244/365 = £200,548
Upper limit	£1,500,000 x 90/365 = £369,863	£1,500,000 x 244/365 = £1,002,740

Notes :

(i) The date on which the FII was received is irrelevant in this apportionment process.

(ii) The lower and upper limits used are those of the relevant FY.

(iii) In both FY96 and FY97, profits are less than the lower limit so the small companies rate applies.

(iv) The corporation tax liability for the CAP is 24% x £56,910 + 23% x £154,290 = £49,145.10.

(v) Since the lower and upper limits are the same in FY96 and FY97, it would have been possible in this case to compare profits of £214,500 with the scaled-down lower limit of £274,521 (£300,000 x 334/365) and so detect that the small companiès rate applies in both FY's. This would have saved the effort of apportioning the lower and upper limits between the two FY's.

Marginal relief

If a company's profits exceed the lower limit but do not exceed the upper limit, the corporation tax liability is calculated at the full rate but the company is entitled to a deduction known as the "marginal relief". This marginal relief (or "taper relief") is calculated according to the following formula :

$$\text{fraction} \times (M - P) \times \frac{I}{P}$$

where : M = the upper limit
P = profits
I = chargeable profits.

The fraction is fixed for each financial year. For FY91 through to FY95 the fraction was 1/50, for FY96 it was 9/400 and for FY97 it is 1/40.

EXAMPLE 4

(a) A company makes up accounts annually to 31 March. In the year to 31 March 1998, the company has chargeable profits of £600,000 and no FII. Compute the corporation tax liability for the year.

(b) Another company, which also makes up accounts annually to 31 March, has chargeable profits of £975,000 in the year to 31 March 1998 and FII (net) of £40,000. Compute the corporation tax liability for the year.

SOLUTION

(a) The company's profits are £600,000, a figure which lies between the lower limit and the upper limit for FY97. Therefore the chargeable profits (also £600,000) are taxed at the full rate and marginal relief is available. The computation is as follows :

	£
Corporation tax on £600,000 @ 33%	198,000.00
Less : Marginal relief :	
$\frac{1}{40} \times (£1,500,000 - £600,000) \times \frac{£600,000}{£600,000}$	22,500.00
Corporation tax due	175,500.00

(b) The company's profits are £1,025,000 (£975,000 + £40,000 x 100/80), which lie between the lower limit and the upper limit for FY97. The chargeable profits (£975,000) are taxed at the full rate and marginal relief is available. The computation is as follows :

	£
Corporation tax on £975,000 @ 33%	321,750.00
Less : Marginal relief :	
$\frac{1}{40} \times (£1,500,000 - £1,025,000) \times \frac{£975,000}{£1,025,000}$	11,295.73
Corporation tax due	310,454.27

Marginal rate

The above example shows that the marginal relief formula seems to be achieving its object, which is to set a corporation tax rate (in FY97) of somewhere between 23% and 33% for companies whose profits lie between the lower and upper limits. In part (a) of the example, tax of £175,500 on chargeable profits of £600,000 gives a tax rate of 29.25%. In part (b), tax of £310,454.27 on chargeable profits of £975,000 gives a tax rate of approximately 31.8%.

However, if a company is entitled to the marginal relief, each extra £1 of chargeable profits gives rise to 35.5p of extra corporation tax. For instance, in part (a) of the above example, profits of £600,002 would have given rise to a corporation tax liability of £175,500.71 (the calculation is left to the reader). Therefore a marginal rate of 35.5% applies in these circumstances, higher than the full rate of 33%.

Marginal relief when CAP straddles 31 March

If a CAP straddles 31 March it is necessary to apportion profits and chargeable profits between the two FY's involved and calculate the corporation tax liability separately for each FY. Marginal relief creates no new problems in these circumstances, as illustrated by the following example.

EXAMPLE 5

In the year ended 31 December 1997, a company has chargeable profits of £475,000 and FII (gross) of £25,000. Compute the corporation tax liability for the year.

SOLUTION

The company has chargeable profits of £475,000 and profits of £500,000 (£475,000 + £25,000) for the CAP. Apportionment between the two FY's is as follows :

	FY96 (1/1/97 to 31/3/97)	*FY97 (1/4/97 to 31/12/97)*
Chargeable	£475,000 x 90/365 = £117,123	£475,000 x 275/365 = £357,877
Profits	£500,000 x 90/365 = £123,288	£500,000 x 275/365 = £376,712
Lower limit	£300,000 x 90/365 = £73,973	£300,000 x 275/365 = £226,027
Upper limit	£1,500,000 x 90/365 = £369,863	£1,500,000 x 275/365 = £1,130,137

In both FY's, profits are between the lower and upper limits so marginal relief is available. The computation is :

	£	£
FY96		
Corporation tax on £117,123 @ 33%	38,650.59	
Less : Marginal relief :		
$\frac{9}{400} \times (£369,863 - £123,288) \times \frac{£117,123}{£123,288}$	5,270.51	33,380.08
FY97		
Corporation tax on £357,877 @ 33%	118,099.41	
Less : Marginal relief :		
$\frac{1}{40} \times (£1,130,137 - £376,712) \times \frac{£357,877}{£376,712}$	17,893.87	100,205.54
Corporation tax liability for the CAP		133,585.62

Pay and file

The corporation tax due in relation to a CAP is payable nine months and one day after the end of that CAP, though the amount payable may be reduced by any Advance Corporation Tax (ACT) paid earlier. The circumstances in which ACT is paid and the calculation of the amount payable are described in Chapter 25.

EXAMPLE 6

A company makes up its accounts to 31 December each year. What is the due date of payment of the corporation tax liability for the year to 31 December 1997 ?

SOLUTION

The due date of payment is 1 October 1998, i.e. nine months and one day after the end of the chargeable accounting period.

Prior to the introduction of the "Pay and File" system in 1993, companies could defer the payment of corporation tax by delaying the submission of their accounts to the Inspector of Taxes and then appealing against the estimated assessment which the Inspector was obliged to raise. But Pay and File prevents companies from adopting this tactic and makes it far more likely that corporation tax is paid on the due date. The main features of the Pay and File system are as follows :

(a) Companies are required to estimate their own corporation tax liability and make the necessary payment on the due date, without waiting for the Inspector of Taxes to raise an assessment.

(b) A company making a late payment or an inadequate payment will be subject to an interest charge (see below).

(c) On the issue of a notice by the Inspector of Taxes, companies are also required to file a corporation tax return (form CT200) together with their accounts and computations. This information must normally be filed by the *latest* of the following dates :

   (i) 12 months after the end of the CAP

   (ii) 12 months after the end of the period of account in which the end of the CAP falls (though never more than 30 months after the beginning of a period of account)

   (iii) 3 months after issue of the notice.

   Most companies make up their accounts to the same date each year and notices are usually issued within a few months of the end of each period of account, so the required filing date is normally 12 months after the end of a period of account. There is nothing to prevent a company from submitting an early return so that the tax liability can be agreed before the due date of payment.

(d) On the basis of the filed information, the Inspector calculates the correct amount of tax due and raises an assessment. If the assessed amount exceeds the amount previously paid by the company, interest is charged on the underpaid tax, running from the due date to the eventual date of payment. Any tax overpaid is refunded, also with interest.

(e) The Inspector may issue an estimated assessment if form CT200 is not submitted on time or if he or she believes that the CT200 is not correct. A company has 30 days in which to appeal against any assessment raised by the Inspector and may apply to postpone payment of all or part of the tax charged pending determination of the appeal.

(f) A company which is chargeable to corporation tax for a CAP but has neither filed a return nor been issued with a notice must notify the Inspector of Taxes of its chargeability within 12 months of the end of the CAP.

Interest and penalties

Under the Pay and File system, interest is charged on any corporation tax not paid by the due date. Interest runs from the due date until the date on which payment is made. The rate at which the interest is calculated rises and falls in line with base rates.

Repayments of overpaid tax are also made with interest, though this is calculated at a lower rate than the interest charged on unpaid tax. Interest on overpaid tax usually runs from the due date (or the date on which the tax was paid, if later) until the date on which the repayment is made.

EXAMPLE 7

(a) Hay Ltd estimates its corporation tax liability for the year to 30 September 1997 at £550,000 and pays this amount on the due date. The company's return and accounts are submitted in August 1998 and the Inspector calculates that a further £24,000 is due. The company pays the £24,000 on 12 September 1998. Calculate the interest payable by Hay Ltd (assuming an interest rate of 6.25% per annum).

(b) Bee Ltd also estimates its corporation tax liability for the year to 30 September 1997 at £550,000 and also pays this amount on the due date. The Inspector calculates that the correct liability for the year is only £493,000. The necessary repayment is made on 18 December 1998. Calculate the interest payable to Bee Ltd (assuming an interest rate of 3.25% per annum).

SOLUTION

(a) The due date is 1 July 1998 (9 months and one day after 30 September 1997). Most of the corporation tax was paid on this date but the final £24,000 was paid on 12 September 1998, 73 days late. The interest payable by the company is :

$$\pounds 24{,}000 \times 6.25\% \times \frac{73}{365} = \pounds 300.00.$$

(b) The overpaid tax of £57,000 was paid on the due date of 1 July 1998 and repaid on 18 December 1998, 170 days later. The interest payable to the company is :

$$\pounds 57{,}000 \times 3.25\% \times \frac{170}{365} = \pounds 862.81.$$

Penalties

Penalties are charged if a company does not file its CT200 return (together with accompanying accounts and other necessary information) by the required date, normally 12 months after the end of the CAP. The penalties are as follows :

(a) If the return is up to 3 months late, a fixed penalty of £100 is charged, increased to £500 for a third consecutive late return.

(b) If the return is over 3 months late, a fixed penalty of £200 is charged, increased to £1,000 for a third consecutive late return.

(c) In addition to the above penalties, a further tax-related penalty is charged if the return is submitted more than 6 months late. In these circumstances the penalty is expressed as a percentage of the amount of tax outstanding at the end of the 6 months, as follows :

(i) If the return is made between 6 and 12 months late, the penalty is 10% of the tax outstanding 6 months after the return was due.

(ii) If the return is made more than 12 months late, the penalty rises to 20% of the tax outstanding 6 months after the return was due.

(d) If a company which has neither filed a return nor been issued with a notice fails to notify the Inspector of Taxes of its chargeability to corporation tax within 12 months of the end of the CAP, a penalty may be charged of up to 100% of the tax unpaid.

EXAMPLE 8

A company makes up accounts to 31 July annually. It estimates its corporation tax liability for the year to 31 July 1996 at £4,500,000 and pays this sum on 1 May 1997. Despite being issued with a notice by the Inspector of Taxes in October 1996, the company fails to submit its return for the year to 31 July 1996 until 31 March 1998. The corporation tax liability for the year was finally agreed at £5,150,000. Calculate the penalties that would be charged.

SOLUTION

The return was made 8 months late and tax of £650,000 was still outstanding 6 months after the return was due. Assuming that the company is not a persistent offender, a fixed penalty of £200 would be charged, together with a tax-related penalty of £65,000 (10% of £650,000). Interest would also be charged on the unpaid tax.

Summary

- A corporation tax financial year runs from 1 April to the following 31 March.
- The full rate of corporation tax applies to companies with profits (including grossed-up FII) exceeding a specified upper limit.
- The small company rate of corporation tax applies to companies with profits (including grossed-up FII) not exceeding a specified lower limit.
- If a company's profits exceed the lower limit but do not exceed the upper limit, the corporation tax liability is calculated at the full rate, less marginal relief.
- The due date of payment for corporation tax is nine months and one day after the end of the chargeable accounting period.
- The Pay and File system requires companies to estimate and pay their corporation tax liability on the due date, without waiting for a formal assessment to be raised.
- Interest is charged on unpaid tax and is paid on refunds of overpaid tax.

- The Pay and File system requires companies to file a CT200 return, together with accounts and computations, usually within 12 months of the end of the company's period of account.
- Penalties are charged if a return is submitted late.

Exercises

24.1 A company has chargeable profits of £2,500,000 for the year to 30 June 1997. Show how these profits will be apportioned between corporation tax financial years.

24.2 Three companies each have an accounting year ending on 31 March 1998. Compute the corporation tax liability of each company, given the following information :

(a) Company A has chargeable profits of £267,000 and net FII of £16,400.

(b) Company B has chargeable profits of £1,450,000 and net FII of £44,000.

(c) Company C has chargeable profits of £10,000,000 and no FII.

24.3 A company has chargeable profits of £536,000 for the year to 31 March 1998 and net FII of £32,800. Compute the corporation tax liability for the year.

24.4 A company has chargeable profits of £875,983 for the year to 28 February 1998 and gross FII of £32,800. Compute the corporation tax liability for the year.

24.5 A company estimates its corporation tax liability for the year to 31 August 1996 at £1,200,000 and pays this amount on 1 June 1997. The company's CT200 return is submitted during August 1997 and the Inspector of Taxes calculates that a further £46,500 is due to be paid. This amount is paid on 3 October 1997. Calculate the interest payable (assuming an interest rate of 6.25% per annum).

***24.6** A company has the following results for the year to 31 March 1998 :

	£
Trading profits, less capital allowances	349,782
Bank deposit interest :	
Received 31 December 1997	12,957
Accrued to 31 March 1998	3,000
Patent royalties received net of income tax (net amount)	8,085
Dividends received from UK companies (net amount)	21,600
Chargeable gains	295,327
Charges on income (net amounts) :	
Paid 30 November 1997	18,942
Accrued to 31 March 1998	6,314

Compute the company's corporation tax liability for the year.

***24.7** A company has the following results for the 14 months to 31 December 1997 :

	£
Trading profits, before deduction of capital allowances	1,413,508
Capital allowances claimed :	
Year to 31 October 1997	222,650
2 months to 31 December 1997	37,210
Building society interest received on :	
31 December 1996	16,575
31 December 1997	17,492
Rents from unfurnished property :	7,500
(the property was let on 1 August 1997 at a rent of £18,000 p.a., payable quarterly in advance)	
UK dividend received on 25 September 1997 (net amount)	2,800

Compute the corporation tax liability.

Chapter 25

Advance corporation tax

Introduction

Although the due date for the payment of corporation tax falls nine months and one day after the end of the chargeable accounting period, companies may be required to make payments of "Advance Corporation Tax" (ACT) prior to this date. The main purpose of this chapter is to explain the circumstances in which ACT is payable and to describe the way in which the amount of ACT due is calculated.

Qualifying distributions

A company's corporation tax liability for a chargeable accounting period is entirely dependent upon its chargeable profits in that period and is unaffected by the use to which the company puts those profits. In general, therefore, two companies with identical chargeable profits will each pay the same amount of corporation tax, even though one of the companies may retain all of its profits whilst the other company may distribute all or part of its profits to the shareholders.

However, the making of a distribution does affect the *timing* of the corporation tax payment, since a company which makes a "qualifying distribution" during a CAP must also make a payment of Advance Corporation Tax, calculated as a fraction of the amount of the distribution (see below). The ACT paid for a CAP is not additional corporation tax but is regarded instead as a payment on account of the corporation tax liability for that CAP. The term "Mainstream Corporation Tax" (MCT) is used to refer to the balance of the corporation tax liability, payable nine months after the end of the CAP.

By far the most common example of a qualifying distribution is the payment of a dividend and so, for the sake of simplicity, the remainder of this chapter refers throughout to "dividends" rather than "qualifying distributions". Some examples of other qualifying distributions are :

(a) any distribution in respect of shares in the company (except for distributions representing a repayment of share capital), if the cost of the distribution is borne by the company
(b) any issue of redeemable share capital, unless the new issue is paid for otherwise than out of the assets of the company
(c) any payments of interest over and above interest calculated at a reasonable commercial rate
(d) certain bonus issues of shares
(e) the transfer of assets or liabilities between a company and its members at less than full market value.

The ACT fraction

The amount of ACT payable in relation to a dividend (or other qualifying distribution) is calculated as a fraction of the amount of the dividend paid to the shareholders. Recent ACT fractions have been as follows :

FY91, FY92	25/75	(i.e. one-third of the dividend paid)
FY93	22.5/77.5	(i.e. 9/31th of the dividend paid)
FY94, FY95, FY96, FY97	20/80	(i.e. one-quarter of the dividend paid)

In general, the ACT fraction is equal to $\frac{I}{100 - I}$, where I is determined as follows :

(a) For corporation tax financial years up to and including FY92, I was equal to the basic rate of income tax for the fiscal year beginning in the financial year.
(b) For FY94 onwards, I is equal to the *lower* rate of income tax for the fiscal year beginning in the financial year.
(c) For FY93 alone, I was fixed at the transitional figure of 22.5 (halfway between the basic and lower rates of income tax for fiscal year 1993/94).

The amount of the dividend paid, plus the ACT attributable to that dividend, is known as the "franked payment". For dividends paid in FY97 :

(a) the franked payment is equal to the dividend paid multiplied by 100/80
(b) the ACT attributable to a dividend may be expressed at 20% of the franked payment (i.e. the "rate of ACT" is 20%).

EXAMPLE 1

A company has an issued share capital consisting of ten million £1 ordinary shares. On 17 February 1998, the company pays a dividend of 40p per share.

(a) Compute the amount of ACT payable.

(b) Compute the amount of the franked payment.

SOLUTION

(a) The amount of the dividend paid to the shareholders is £4,000,000. The ACT fraction for FY97 (in which 17 February 1998 falls) is 20/80, so the amount of ACT payable is £4,000,000 x 20/80 = £1,000,000.

(b) The franked payment is equal to £5,000,000 (i.e. the dividend plus the attributable ACT). Alternatively, the franked payment may be calculated as £4,000,000 x 100/80 = £5,000,000 and the ACT payable may be expressed as 20% of £5,000,000 = £1,000,000.

The imputation system

The system which links the corporation tax treatment of dividends paid by UK companies with the income tax treatment of dividends received by individuals from such companies is known as the "imputation system". The main features of this system are as follows :

(a) Dividends received by individuals from UK companies are "imputed" with a tax credit equal, in 1997/98, to 20/80th of the amount of the dividend received (see Chapter 2).

(b) Dividends paid by UK companies trigger a payment of ACT equal, in FY97, to 20/80th of the amount of the dividend paid.

(c) In effect, the ACT payment made by the company satisfies the company's Schedule F liability and supplies the funds for the tax credit enjoyed by the shareholder.

Franked investment income

In Chapter 23, the term "franked investment income" (FII) was used to refer to a dividend received by one UK company from another UK company. Strictly speaking, this term refers to the *gross* amount of the dividend i.e. the amount of the dividend received plus the associated tax credit. As explained in Chapter 23, dividends paid by UK companies are paid out of profits which have already borne corporation tax once and are therefore not chargeable to corporation tax a second time in the hands of the receiving company.

Since FII does not give rise to a corporation tax liability, it would seem that a company receiving dividends would be unable to make use of the tax credits attached to those dividends. However, such tax credits *can* be used to reduce the receiving company's ACT liability in relation to its own dividends paid.

EXAMPLE 2

On 1 January 1998, a company both pays a dividend of £400,000 and receives a dividend of £20,000. Calculate the required ACT payment.

SOLUTION

If it were not for the dividend received, the company would have to pay ACT of £100,000 (£400,000 x 20/80). However, the dividend received is accompanied by a tax credit of £5,000 (£20,000 x 20/80). This reduces the required ACT payment to £95,000.

The following points should be noted :

(a) This use of the tax credits accompanying dividends received does not actually reduce the receiving company's corporation tax liability. A reduction in ACT payable may provide a welcome cash flow benefit in the short term but this is at the expense of a correspondingly greater MCT payment 9 months and one day after the end of the CAP.

(b) Dividends received from foreign companies are not FII and cannot be used to reduce the receiving company's ACT liability. Such dividends are taxed under Schedule D Case V (see Chapter 32).

EXAMPLE 3

A company which makes up accounts annually to 31 March has a corporation tax liability of £150,000 for the year to 31 March 1998. On 1 July 1997, the company pays a £48,000 dividend to its shareholders.

(a) Compute the ACT due on the dividend paid on 1 July 1997.

(b) Compute the MCT payable by the company on 1 January 1999.

(c) If, on 1 July 1997, the company also receives a dividend of £16,000, re-compute the ACT and MCT due for the year.

(d) What is the net effect of the dividend received ?

SOLUTION

(a) The ACT due on the dividend paid is £12,000 (£48,000 x 20/80).

(b) The MCT due on 1 January 1999 is the remaining £138,000 of the company's corporation tax liability (£150,000 - £12,000).

(c) The dividend received is accompanied by a tax credit of £4,000 (£16,000 x 20/80), which reduces the ACT due on the dividend paid to £8,000. The MCT due on 1 January 1999 is now £142,000 (£150,000 - £8,000).

(d) The effect of the dividend received is to reduce the ACT payment by £4,000 but to increase the eventual MCT payment, also by £4,000. The total amount of corporation tax payable by the company is the same with or without the dividend received.

The quarterly accounting system

Companies must account to the Inland Revenue for ACT at quarterly intervals. An ACT return, on form CT61(Z), is required for :

(a) each of the four quarters ending on 31 March, 30 June, 30 September and 31 December which fall completely into a CAP, and

(b) each part of a CAP which does not comprise a complete quarter.

A company with an annual accounting date which coincides with one of the above four dates will make four returns each year but companies with any other annual accounting date will need to submit a fifth return each year. The period in respect of which an ACT return is made is known as a "return period".

EXAMPLE 4

(a) A company makes up accounts annually to 30 June. Identify the ACT return periods for the year to 30 June 1997.

(b) A company makes up accounts annually to 31 January. Identify the ACT return periods for the year to 31 January 1998.

SOLUTION

(a) The company's accounting date coincides with one of the four standard dates, so there will be four return periods each year. The four return periods for the year to 30 June 1997 are :

  (i) 1 July 1996 to 30 September 1996
  (ii) 1 October 1996 to 31 December 1996
  (iii) 1 January 1997 to 31 March 1997
  (iv) 1 April 1997 to 30 June 1997.

(b) The company's accounting date does not coincide with one of the four standard dates, so there will be five return periods each year. The five return periods for the year to 31 January 1998 are :

  (i) 1 February 1997 to 31 March 1997
  (ii) 1 April 1997 to 30 June 1997

(iii) 1 July 1997 to 30 September 1997
(iv) 1 October 1997 to 31 December 1997
(v) 1 January 1998 to 31 January 1998.

An ACT return gives the following information for the return period to which it relates :

(a) franked payments made during the return period
(b) FII received during the return period
(c) the amount of ACT payable or repayable for the return period (see below).

An ACT return shows dividends actually paid and received during the return period, *regardless of the accounting year to which those dividends relate.* The return must be submitted, and any ACT due must be paid, within 14 days of the end of the return period. Nil returns are not required.

EXAMPLE 5

A company makes up accounts annually to 31 December. On 17 May 1997, the company pays an interim dividend for the year ended 31 December 1997 of £100,000. No other dividends are paid or received in the year.

(a) Compute the amount of ACT payable for the year and state the date on which this ACT falls due.
(b) What difference would it make if the dividend paid on 17 May 1997 had been the final dividend for the year ended 31 December 1996 ?

SOLUTION

(a) The company's year-end coincides with one of the four standard dates, so there are four return periods each year. The only period for which a return is required is the quarter to 30 June 1997. This will show a franked payment of £125,000 (£100,000 x 100/80) and ACT payable of £25,000 (£100,000 x 20/80). The return must be submitted by 14 July 1997 and this is also the date upon which the ACT is due to be paid.
(b) It would make no difference at all if the dividend paid on 17 May 1997 had been the final dividend for 1996, rather than the interim for 1997. All that matters is the date on which the dividend was paid. The accounting year to which the dividend relates is irrelevant.

The quarterly accounting procedure

For each return period, the calculation of the ACT payable or repayable for that return period is accomplished by means of a procedure which is cumulative in nature, automatically taking into account events in previous return periods during the same CAP. The procedure is as follows :

(a) FII for the return period is subtracted from franked payments for the return period, giving the excess of franked payments over FII (or vice-versa).

(b) The cumulative excess of franked payments over FII (or vice-versa) for the CAP to date is then calculated.

(c) If the figure calculated at (b) represents an excess of franked payments over FII, the company's ACT liability for the CAP to date is equal to the excess multiplied by the rate of ACT (20% for FY97). This liability is then compared with the total amount of ACT paid in previous return periods during the same CAP (if any) and the difference is either payable by the company or repayable to the company.

(d) If the figure calculated at (b) represents an excess of FII over franked payments, the company's ACT liability for the CAP to date is £nil. Any ACT paid in previous return periods during the same CAP is repayable to the company. (But note that the tax credit on excess FII is *not* repayable to the company).

It is important to use the *gross* figures for FII and franked payments when performing these computations and to avoid shortcuts in which net figures are used instead. Although these shortcuts will often produce the right answers they may fail to do so when a change is made to the rate of ACT (see later in this chapter).

EXAMPLE 6

A company pays and receives the following dividends (net amounts) in the year to 31 March 1998 :

	Paid	*Received*
	£	£
12 April 1997	2,600	
30 June 1997		1,000
15 July 1997		2,400
1 October 1997		1,000
5 November 1997	3,000	
2 January 1998	400	
6 February 1998		900

Compute the amounts of ACT payable or repayable in each return period.

SOLUTION

Return period	*FP*	*FII*	*FP - FII*	*Cumulative FP - FII*	*ACT payable (repayable)*
	£	£	£	£	£
1/4/97 - 30/6/97	3,250	1,250	2,000	2,000	400.00
1/7/97 - 30/9/97		3,000	(3,000)	(1,000)	(400.00)
1/10/97 - 31/12/97	3,750	1,250	2,500	1,500	300.00
1/1/98 - 31/3/98	500	1,125	(625)	875	(125.00)
	7,500	6,625	875		175.00

Notes :

(i) The dividends paid and received are first multiplied by 100/80, giving the corresponding franked payments and FII. The franked payments and FII for each return period are shown in the first two columns of the table.

(ii) For each return period, the excess of franked payments over FII is shown in the third column. If FII exceeds franked payments, the figure is shown in parentheses. The cumulative total of FP - FII for the CAP is shown in the fourth column.

(iii) At the end of the first return period, the excess of franked payments over FII is £2,000. ACT of £400 (20% of £2,000) is due for payment on 14 July 1997.

(iv) At the end of the second return period, there is a cumulative excess of FII over franked payments. The company now has no ACT liability for the CAP to date and may reclaim the £400 paid in the previous return period. The tax credit attached to the £1,000 of excess FII (£200) is *not* repayable to the company but this excess will automatically be taken into account in future return periods.

(v) At the end of the third return period, the cumulative excess of franked payments over FII is £1,500. ACT of £300 (20% of £1,500) is due for the CAP to date. Since the ACT paid in previous return periods is £nil (£400 paid less £400 reclaimed) ACT of £300 is due for payment on 14 January 1998.

(vi) At the end of the fourth return period, the cumulative excess of franked payments over FII is £875. ACT of £175 (20% of £875) is due for the CAP to date. Since the ACT paid in previous return periods amounts to £300, a repayment of £125 (£300 - £175) will be made.

It is not strictly necessary to calculate the total of each column in the above table but this does provide a check on the arithmetic accuracy of the calculations, as follows :

(a) The total of the FP-FII column should be equal to the difference between the total of the FP column and the total of the FII column.

(b) The total of the FP-FII column should also be equal to the last figure in the cumulative column.

(c) If franked payments for the CAP exceed FII, the total of the ACT payable/repayable column should be equal to the total of the FP-FII column multiplied by the rate of ACT.

(d) If FII for the CAP exceeds franked payments, the total of the ACT payable/repayable column should be £nil.

Surplus FII

If there is a cumulative excess of FII over franked payments at the end of a return period, the quarterly accounting system described above will automatically carry this excess forward to subsequent return periods in the same CAP, where it can be used to reduce the ACT liability on dividends paid in those subsequent return periods.

If, however, there is an excess of FII over franked payments for an entire CAP then the company has "surplus FII". Surplus FII cannot be used in the CAP in which it arises but is carried forward to the next CAP and is treated as if it were received on the first day of that CAP. In this way, surplus FII arising in one CAP may be used to reduce a company's ACT liability in a subsequent CAP.

EXAMPLE 7

A company pays and receives the following dividends (net amounts) in the years to 31 March 1997 and 1998 :

	Paid	*Received*
	£	£
21 August 1996	6,000	
1 February 1997		10,000
18 September 1997	4,800	

Compute the amounts of ACT payable or repayable in each year.

SOLUTION

Year to 31 March 1997 :

Return period	*FP*	*FII*	*FP - FII*	*Cumulative FP - FII*	*ACT payable (repayable)*
	£	£	£	£	£
1/7/96 - 30/9/96	7,500		7,500	7,500	1,500.00
1/1/97 - 31/3/97		12,500	(12,500)	(5,000)	(1,500.00)
	7,500	12,500	(5,000)		0.00

Year to 31 March 1998 :

Return period	*FP*	*FII*	*FP - FII*	*Cumulative FP - FII*	*ACT payable (repayable)*
	£	£	£	£	£
Surplus FII b/f		5,000	(5,000)	(5,000)	
1/7/97 - 30/9/97	6,000		6,000	1,000	200.00
	6,000	5,000	1,000		200.00

Notes :

(i) Surplus FII of £5,000 arises in the year to 31 March 1997. The company may *not* reclaim the tax credit relating to this surplus FII but the surplus may be carried forward to the following year.

(ii) The surplus FII brought forward from the year to 31 March 1997 is used to reduce the ACT payable on the September 1997 dividend (from £1,200 to only £200).

Surplus FII when there is a change in the rate of ACT

It is important to appreciate that, if surplus FII arises, the figure carried forward to the next CAP is the gross amount of the surplus FII *not* the tax credit attached to this surplus FII. This distinction is important if the rate of ACT changes between the CAP in which surplus FII arises and the CAP in which it is used.

EXAMPLE 8

A company pays and receives the following dividends (net amounts) in the years to 31 March 1998 and 1999 :

	Paid	*Received*
	£	£
1 January 1998	4,800	
19 March 1998		7,200
5 February 1999	6,800	

Compute the amounts of ACT payable or repayable in each year, assuming that the ACT rate for FY98 is set at 15%.

SOLUTION

The ACT fraction for FY97 is 20/80, so the dividend of £4,800 paid on 1 January 1998 is equivalent to a franked payment of £6,000 (£4,800 x 100/80) and the dividend received on 19 March 1998 has a gross equivalent of £9,000 (£7,200 x 100/80).

Assuming an ACT fraction for FY98 of 15/85, the dividend paid on 5 February 1999 is equivalent to a franked payment of £8,000 (£6,800 x 100/85). The computation is as follows :

Year to 31 March 1998:

Return period	*FP*	*FII*	*FP - FII*	*Cumulative FP - FII*	*ACT payable (repayable)*
	£	£	£	£	£
1/1/98 - 31/3/98	6,000	9,000	(3,000)	(3,000)	0.00

Year to 31 March 1999:

Return period	*FP*	*FII*	*FP - FII*	*Cumulative FP - FII*	*ACT payable (repayable)*
	£	£	£	£	£
Surplus FII b/f		3,000	(3,000)	(3,000)	
1/1/99 - 31/3/99	8,000		8,000	5,000	750.00
	8,000	3,000	5,000		750.00

Note:

The tax credit attached to the surplus FII of £3,000 arising in the year to 31 March 1998 is £600 (20% of £3,000). However, when this surplus FII is carried forward to the following year, it reduces the ACT due on the dividends paid in that year by only £450 (15% of £3,000) since the rate of ACT has changed between FY97 and FY98. In effect a reduction (or increase) in the rate of ACT serves to reduce (or increase) the value of any surplus FII brought forward from a previous CAP.

Changes in the rate of ACT

As noted above, the rate of ACT has changed a number of times in recent years and will presumably change again in the future if alterations are made to the lower rate of income tax. Since income tax rates are changed with effect from 6 April and the ACT fraction is set for financial years beginning on 1 April, a special rule is needed to deal with the 5-day period at the start of the financial year. This rule states that the rate of ACT used during this 5-day period is the rate of ACT for the *previous* financial year.

One effect of a change in the rate of ACT has already been mentioned (i.e. the consequent change in the value of any surplus FII carried forward). Another effect of a change in the rate of ACT is described below :

(a) If the rate of ACT changes part-way through a company's CAP, that CAP is subdivided (*for ACT accounting purposes only*) into two separate "notional CAP's", one covering the period before the change in rate and the other covering the period after the change in rate.

(b) As a consequence of this subdivision, any FII received after the change in rate cannot be offset against franked payments made before the change in rate (since surplus FII cannot be carried back to a previous CAP, even if that previous CAP is only a notional CAP).

EXAMPLE 9

A company pays and receives the following dividends (net amounts) in the year to 31 October 1998 :

	Paid	*Received*
	£	£
3 April 1998	6,080	
24 June 1998	3,400	
17 September 1998		10,200

Given that the rate of ACT is 20% in FY97 and assuming that the rate reduces to 15% in FY98, compute the amounts of ACT payable or repayable by the company.

SOLUTION

The ACT rate of 20% is applicable to dividends paid on or before 5 April 1998 and the assumed rate of 15% applies thereafter. Therefore the company's CAP must be divided (for ACT accounting purposes only) into two notional CAP's, namely 1 November 1997 to 5 April 1998 and 6 April 1998 to 31 October 1998. The computation is as follows :

Notional CAP 1/11/97 to 5/4/98 :

Return period	*FP*	*FII*	*FP - FII*	*Cumulative FP - FII*	*ACT payable (repayable)*
	£	£	£	£	£
1/4/98 - 30/6/98 (up to 5/4/98)	7,600		7,600	7,600	1,520.00

Notional CAP 6/4/98 to 31/10/98 :

Return period	*FP*	*FII*	*FP - FII*	*Cumulative FP - FII*	*ACT payable (repayable)*
	£	£	£	£	£
1/4/98 - 30/6/98 (from 6/4/98)	4,000		4,000	4,000	600.00
1/7/98 - 30/9/98		12,000	(12,000)	(8,000)	(600.00)
	4,000	12,000	(8,000)		0.00

Notes :

(i) ACT due on the dividend paid on 3 April 1998 is calculated at the rate in force for the previous financial year.

(ii) The tax credit attached to the dividend received on 17 September 1998 is more than sufficient to generate a repayment of the ACT of £600 paid in relation to the June dividend but the excess cannot be used to obtain repayment of the ACT paid in relation to the April dividend. If the rate of ACT had not changed, and the CAP had not been subdivided into two notional CAP's, the usual accumulative accounting system would have ensured repayment of all the ACT paid earlier in the CAP.

(iii) The surplus FII of £8,000 can only be carried forward to subsequent CAP's.

(iv) The return period from 1 April 1998 to 30 June 1998 is still regarded as a single return period (despite the split between two notional CAP's) and the ACT of £2,120 due for that period (£1,520 + £600) is payable on the 14 July 1998.

Set-off of ACT

When a dividend (or other qualifying distribution) is paid during a CAP, the ACT relating to that dividend is treated as a payment on account of the company's corporation tax liability for the CAP.

However, there is an upper limit on the amount of ACT which may be offset against a company's corporation tax liability. This "maximum ACT set-off" is equal to the ACT which would be attributable to a franked payment equal in size to the company's entire chargeable profits for the CAP. If the rate of ACT changes during a CAP then the calculation of the maximum ACT set-off will involve time-apportionment of the company's chargeable profits.

EXAMPLE 10

(a) A company which makes up accounts annually to 31 March has chargeable profits of £2,300,000 for the year to 31 March 1998. Calculate the maximum ACT set-off for the year.

(b) A company which makes up accounts annually to 31 December has chargeable profits of £800,000 for the year to 31 December 1998. Calculate the maximum ACT set-off for the year, assuming that the ACT rate for FY98 is set at 15%.

SOLUTION

(a) The maximum ACT set-off is the amount of ACT attributable to a franked payment of £2,300,000 i.e. 20% of £2,300,000 = £460,000. The company could pay dividends during the year totalling £1,840,000, giving rise to an ACT liability of £460,000 (£1,840,000 x 20/80) and offset all of this ACT against the corporation tax liability for the year.

(b) The rate of ACT for 1/1/98 - 5/4/98 (95 days) is 20% and the assumed rate for 6/4/98 - 31/12/98 (270 days) is 15%. The maximum ACT set-off is :

		£
£800,000 x 95/365 @ 20%	=	41,643.83
£800,000 x 270/365 @ 15%	=	88,767.12
		130,410.95

Surplus ACT

If the amount of ACT paid by a company in relation to a CAP exceeds the maximum set-off allowed, the company has "surplus ACT".

EXAMPLE 11

A company has chargeable profits of £100,000 for the year to 31 March 1998 and pays a dividend of £88,000 on 1 January 1998. No other dividends are paid or received during the year. Calculate the ACT and MCT due for the year.

SOLUTION

ACT of £22,000 (£88,000 x 20/80) is payable on 14 April 1998. But the maximum ACT set-off for the CAP is £20,000 (20% of £100,000), so there is surplus ACT of £2,000. The MCT payable on 1 January 1999 is calculated as follows :

	£	£
Corporation tax liability (£100,000 @ 23%)		23,000
Less : Lower of :		
(a) ACT payable for the year	22,000	
(b) Maximum ACT set-off	20,000	20,000
MCT payable		3,000

Relief of surplus ACT

Surplus ACT may be relieved in two main ways :

(a) It may be *carried back* and relieved against the corporation tax liability of CAP's beginning in the six years prior to the CAP in which the surplus ACT has arisen. Relief is given in more recent years first and a carry-back election must be made within two years of the end of the CAP in which the surplus ACT arises.

(b) If no carry-back election is made (or if surplus ACT still remains after a carry-back election has been made) surplus ACT is *carried forward* and relieved against the corporation tax liability of the next CAP. To the extent that it cannot be relieved in that CAP it may be carried forward again, without time limit, until it can eventually be relieved.

It is important to note that the total amount of ACT relieved in any CAP (including any surplus ACT carried back from subsequent years or carried forward from previous years) cannot exceed the maximum ACT set-off for that CAP, calculated as described above.

EXAMPLE 12

A company began trading on 1 April 1994. The first 4 years' results are :

	year to 31/3/95	*year to 31/3/96*	*year to 31/3/97*	*year to 31/3/98*
	£	£	£	£
Chargeable profits	6,600	6,800	4,000	10,000
Dividends paid in the year	4,920	4,500	4,800	3,200
Dividends received in the year	0	0	0	0

None of the dividends were paid or received in the period between 1 April and 5 April. Calculate the maximum ACT set-off in each year (assuming, for this purpose, that changes in the rate of ACT occur on 1 April rather than on 6 April) and calculate the surplus ACT (if any) arising in each year. Show how any surplus ACT may be relieved at the earliest opportunity and show the MCT payable for each year. (The small companies rate of corporation tax was 25% in FY94 and FY95 and 24% in FY96).

SOLUTION

	year to 31/3/95	*year to 31/3/96*	*year to 31/3/97*	*year to 31/3/98*
	£	£	£	£
Maximum ACT set-off :				
20% x £6,600	1,320			
20% x £6,800		1,360		
20% x £4,000			800	
20% x £10,000				2,000
ACT paid for the year :				
£4,920 x 20/80	1,230			
£4,500 x 20/80		1,125		
£4,800 x 20/80			1,200	
£3,200 x 20/80				800
Spare capacity/(Surplus ACT)	90	235	(400)	1,200

A total of £325 (£90 + £235) of the surplus ACT arising in the year to 31 March 1997 may be carried back (provided that a carry-back election is made by 31 March 1999). The remaining £75 can only be carried forward. The MCT payable for each year becomes :

	year to 31/3/95	*year to 31/3/96*	*year to 31/3/97*	*year to 31/3/98*
	£	£	£	£
Chargeable profits x 25%, 24% or 23%	1,650	1,700	960	2,300
Less : Lower of ACT paid for the year and maximum ACT set-off	(1,230)	(1,125)	(800)	(800)
Less : Surplus ACT carried back	(90)	(235)		
Less : Surplus ACT carried forward				(75)
MCT payable	330	340	160	1,425

The effect of carrying back surplus ACT is to reduce the MCT payable in respect of earlier CAP's and therefore to generate repayments of MCT. In general, repayments of corporation tax are made with interest (see Chapter 24) and therefore a repayment of MCT originally paid up to 6 years previously might seem likely to attract substantial amounts of interest. However, if a repayment is triggered by a carry-back of surplus ACT, interest does not begin to run until 9 months after the end of the CAP in which the surplus ACT arose.

Surplus ACT on a change of ownership

A company which incurs losses over a period of several years and yet manages to maintain dividend payments during those years may accumulate substantial amounts of surplus ACT. The existence of this surplus ACT might make the company a desirable acquisition, since a new owner could :

(a) use the company to operate a profitable business (perhaps very different in nature from the company's business before the acquisition), and then

(b) set the pre-acquisition surplus ACT against the tax payable on the post-acquisition profits, so avoiding liability to corporation tax.

This manoeuvre is prevented from succeeding by anti-avoidance legislation which provides that, under certain conditions, surplus ACT arising before a change in the ownership of a company cannot be set against a corporation tax liability arising after that change. Nor can surplus ACT arising after the change be set against a corporation tax liability arising before it. The required conditions are that :

(a) a change in ownership and a major change in the nature or conduct of the company's business both occur within the same three-year period, or

(b) a change in ownership occurs at a time when the company's business has become negligible and then, at any time after the change, there is a revival of the company's business.

For this purpose, a change in ownership is deemed to occur if over half of the company's ordinary share capital is acquired either by one person or by a group of people, each acquiring at least a 5% shareholding.

Summary

- ACT is payable when a company makes a qualifying distribution. The most common example of a qualifying distribution is the payment of a dividend.
- ACT is calculated as a fraction of the amount of the dividend paid. The ACT fraction is determined for each corporation tax financial year.
- The amount of the dividend paid, plus its associated ACT, is known as the franked payment.
- The imputation system provides the link between the corporation tax treatment of dividends paid by companies and the income tax treatment of dividends received by shareholders.
- ACT is accounted for by means of a quarterly accounting system and is payable on the excess of franked payments over franked investment income.
- Surplus FII may be carried forward to subsequent CAP's and used to reduce the company's ACT liability in those CAP's.
- If a change occurs in the rate of ACT part-way through a company's CAP, that CAP is divided into 2 notional CAP's for ACT accounting purposes.
- The maximum ACT set-off for a CAP is equal to the ACT attributable to a franked payment equal to the entire chargeable profits for that CAP.
- Surplus ACT may be carried back for up to 6 years or carried forward without time limit.

Exercises

25.1 On 29 December 1997, a company with an issued share capital of 2 million £1 ordinary shares pays a dividend of 7 pence per share. The company makes up accounts annually to 31 December.

(a) Compute the amount of ACT payable and the amount of the franked payment (assuming that the company receives no dividends from other UK companies).

(b) State the date on which this ACT must be paid.

(c) Identify the corporation tax payment which will be reduced as a consequence of paying this ACT.

(d) How would the answers to (a), (b) and (c) differ if the dividend had been paid a week later ?

25.2 A company makes up accounts annually to 30 November. Identify the company's ACT return periods for the year to 30 November 1997.

25.3 A company makes up accounts annually to 30 April. On 1 June 1996, the company paid a final dividend for the year to 30 April 1996 amounting to £160,000. On 1 April 1997, the company paid an interim dividend for the year to 30 April 1997 amounting to £72,000. For each of these two dividends :

(a) Compute the amount of ACT payable and the amount of the franked payment (assuming that the company has no dividend income).

(b) State the date on which the ACT must be paid.

(c) Identify the corporation tax liability against which the ACT is offset.

25.4 A company pays and receives the following dividends (net amounts) in the year to 31 March 1998 :

	Paid	*Received*
	£	£
17 June 1997		4,400
2 August 1997	6,400	
11 October 1997	7,000	
15 December 1997		3,200
16 March 1998		1,200

Compute the amounts of ACT payable or repayable in each return period.

25.5 A company has chargeable profits of £24,000,000 for the year to 31 March 1998. Calculate the maximum ACT set-off for the year.

25.6 A company with chargeable profits of £78,000 for the year to 31 March 1998 pays a dividend of £64,000 on 1 February 1998. No other dividends are paid or received during the year. Calculate the MCT payable on 1 January 1999.

***25.7** A company has surplus FII brought forward on 1 April 1997 of £2,400. The company pays and receives the following dividends (net amounts) in the year to 31 March 1998 :

Return period	*Paid*	*Received*
	£	£
30 June 1997	2,800	1,000
30 September 1997	1,400	300
31 December 1997	1,400	
31 March 1998		1,200

Compute the amounts of ACT payable or repayable in each return period.

***25.8** A company pays and receives the following dividends (net amounts) in the year to 30 September 1998 :

	Paid	*Received*
	£	£
21 January 1998	8,000	3,200
1 April 1998	2,560	
31 May 1998		1,700
31 August 1998	1,275	

Compute the amounts of ACT payable or repayable in each return period, assuming that the rate of ACT is set to 15% in FY98.

***25.9** A company began trading on 1 October 1994. Accounts were made up for the 6 months to 31 March 1995 and annually to 31 March thereafter. The first four sets of accounts showed the following results :

	period to 31/3/95	*year to 31/3/96*	*year to 31/3/97*	*year to 31/3/98*
	£	£	£	£
Trading profits	10,200	8,800	3,000	11,000
Chargeable gains	2,100	3,000	0	0
Charges on income (gross)	500	500	500	500
Dividends paid	7,460	7,440	7,440	7,440

None of the dividends were paid in the period 1 April to 5 April and the company received no dividends at all. Calculate the ACT and MCT payable for each CAP, assuming that :

(i) changes in the rate of ACT occur on 1 April rather than on 6 April (for the purpose of calculating the maximum ACT set-off in each year), and

(ii) surplus ACT (if any) is to be relieved as soon as possible.

Note : The small companies rate of corporation tax was 25% in FY94 and FY95 and 24% in FY96.

Chapter 26

Companies and income tax

Introduction

Companies are liable to corporation tax, not income tax. Therefore, companies which suffer income tax by deduction at source from any of their income are entitled to repayment of the income tax suffered. Similarly, companies which deduct income tax at source from any of their payments must account for this income tax to the Inland Revenue. The purpose of this chapter is to explain how the necessary repayments and payments of income tax are made.

Income received net of income tax

As was explained in Chapter 23, certain types of income received by a company are received net of income tax. A company receiving such income is able to reclaim the income tax deducted at source but the grossed-up amount of the income is then liable to corporation tax. The main sources of taxed income are as follows :

Type of income	*Rate of income tax deducted at source*
Patent royalties	23%
Debenture and other loan interest	20%
Interest from gilt-edged securities	20%

Patent royalties are assessed as UFII on the receipts basis. Debenture interest, loan interest and interest on gilt-edged securities are all assessed under the loan relationships system, usually on the accruals basis. But in all cases, the income tax which may be reclaimed for a CAP is the amount of income tax suffered on the taxed income actually *received* during the CAP. The procedure for reclaiming this income tax is explained below.

Remember that companies (unlike individuals) receive bank deposit interest and building society interest gross. Therefore such income does not rank as income received net of income tax.

Payments made net of income tax

Certain types of payment made by a company are made net of income tax. A company making such a payment must account to the Inland Revenue for the income tax deducted at source but the grossed-up amount of the payment is then granted relief in the company's corporation tax computation. The main types of payment made net of income tax are :

Type of payment	*Rate of income tax deducted at source*
Patent royalties	23%
Deeds of covenant to charities	23%
Donations under the "gift aid" scheme	23%
Debenture and other loan interest	20%

Patent royalties, payments made under the terms of a charitable covenant and gift aid donations are all relieved as charges on income on the payments basis. Debenture and other loan interest is relieved under the loan relationships system, usually on the accruals basis. But in all cases, the income tax which must be accounted for to the Inland Revenue for a CAP is the income tax deducted from the amounts actually *paid* during the CAP. The accounting procedure is explained below.

Note that interest paid by a company to a UK bank is paid without deduction of income tax. Therefore interest payments of this type do not rank as payments made net of income tax.

The quarterly accounting system

Companies must make quarterly returns to the Inland Revenue of the income tax suffered on taxed income and the income tax deducted from relevant payments. Returns are required for the same return periods as those for ACT (see Chapter 25) so a company may be required to make five "quarterly" returns each year. Returns must be submitted, and any required income tax payment must be made, within 14 days of the end of the return period. Nil returns are not required.

Returns are made on form CT61(Z) along with the ACT return but the calculations of income tax payable/repayable are kept *completely separate* from the calculations of ACT payable/repayable. In each return period, the procedure is as follows :

(a) The income tax suffered on taxed income received during the return period is subtracted from the income tax deducted from relevant payments made during the return period. The result of this calculation is the excess of income tax deducted over income tax suffered (or vice-versa).

(b) The cumulative excess of income tax deducted over income tax suffered (or vice-versa) for the CAP to date is then calculated.

(c) If there is a cumulative excess of income tax deducted over income tax suffered, this excess is compared with the total of the income tax payments made to the Inland Revenue in previous return periods during the same CAP (if any) and the difference is either payable by the company or repayable to the company.

(d) If there is a cumulative excess of income tax suffered over income tax deducted, then no income tax payment is required for the current return period and any payments made to the Inland Revenue in previous return periods during the same CAP may be reclaimed. However, the excess itself is *not* repayable to the company but is carried forward to the next return period.

There an important difference between this procedure and the very similar procedure relating to ACT. As explained in Chapter 25, ACT returns are prepared at the *gross* level, showing gross amounts of FII and franked payments for each return period and keeping track of cumulative gross figures for the CAP to date. Income tax returns, on the other hand, are prepared at the *tax* level, showing only the amounts of income tax deducted and suffered for each return period and keeping track of the cumulative tax figures for the CAP to date. As a consequence, income tax returns are simpler to complete than ACT returns and no complications arise when income tax rates change.

EXAMPLE 1

A company has the following payments made net of income tax and income received net of income tax for the year to 31 March 1998 (amounts are stated net) :

		Payments	*Income*
		£	£
1 May 1997	Debenture interest paid	4,000	
5 July 1997	Gift aid payment	770	
1 September 1997	Debenture interest received		6,000
1 November 1997	Debenture interest paid	4,000	
12 January 1998	Patent royalties paid	9,240	
31 March 1998	Gilt interest received		1,600

Compute the amounts of income tax payable or repayable in each return period.

SOLUTION

Return period	*Tax deducted*	*Tax suffered*	*Tax deducted less tax suffered*	*Cumulative*	*Income tax payable (repayable)*
	£	£	£	£	£
1/4/97 - 30/6/97	1,000		1,000	1,000	1,000
1/7/97 - 30/9/97	230	1,500	(1,270)	(270)	(1,000)
1/10/97 - 31/12/97	1,000		1,000	730	730
1/1/98 - 31/3/98	2,760	400	2,360	3,090	2,360
	4,990	1,900	3,090		3,090

Notes :

(i) The net payments and the net income in each return period are multiplied by either 20/80 or 23/77 (depending upon the type of payment or income) to give the amounts of income tax deducted and suffered, as shown in the first two columns of the table. For each return period, the excess of tax deducted over tax suffered is shown in the third column. If tax suffered exceeds tax deducted, the figure is shown in parentheses. The cumulative total of tax deducted less tax suffered is shown in the fourth column.

(ii) At the end of the first return period, tax deducted exceeds tax suffered by £1,000, so £1,000 is due for payment on 14 July 1997.

(iii) At the end of the second return period, there is a cumulative excess of tax suffered over tax deducted of £270. The company now has no income tax liability for the CAP to date and may reclaim the £1,000 paid in the previous return period. The excess tax suffered of £270 is *not* repayable to the company but the cumulative nature of the system ensures that this excess will automatically be taken into account in future return periods.

(iv) At the end of the third return period, there is a cumulative excess of tax deducted over tax suffered of £730. Since the tax paid in previous return periods is £nil (£1,000 paid less £1,000 reclaimed), income tax of £730 is due for payment on 14 January 1998.

(v) At the end of the fourth return period, there is a cumulative excess of tax deducted over tax suffered of £3,090. Since the tax paid in previous return periods is £730, income tax of £2,360 is due for payment on 14 April 1998.

(vi) Strictly speaking, calculations of income tax due and suffered should be made to the nearest penny. However, in the interests of clarity, pence have been omitted from the above table.

Tax suffered in excess of tax deducted

At the end of a CAP, one of two possible situations will apply :

(a) The income tax deducted from payments made in the CAP exceeds the income tax suffered on income received during the CAP. In this case, the excess will have been paid over to the Inland Revenue by virtue of the system described above and no further action is required.

(b) The income tax suffered on income received during the CAP exceeds the income tax deducted from payments made in the CAP. In this case the system described above will not have provided the necessary income tax repayment.

EXAMPLE 2

A company has the following net payments and net income for the year to 31 March 1998 (amounts are stated net) :

		Payments	*Income*
		£	£
1 April 1997	Debenture interest paid	8,000	
1 July 1997	Gilt interest received		9,600
1 October 1997	Debenture interest paid	8,000	
1 January 1998	Gilt interest received		9,600

Compute the amounts of income tax payable or repayable in each return period.

SOLUTION

Return period	*Tax deducted*	*Tax suffered*	*Tax deducted less tax suffered*	*Cumulative*	*Income tax payable (repayable)*
	£	£	£	£	£
1/4/97 - 30/6/97	2,000		2,000	2,000	2,000
1/7/97 - 30/9/97		2,400	(2,400)	(400)	(2,000)
1/10/97 - 31/12/97	2,000		2,000	1,600	1,600
1/1/98 - 31/3/98		2,400	(2,400)	(800)	(1,600)
	4,000	4,800	(800)		0

Note :
The income tax suffered exceeds the income tax deducted by £800 but the operation of the quarterly accounting system has not resulted in repayment of this income tax.

In these circumstances, the required repayment of income tax is made by means of a reduction in the company's mainstream corporation tax liability for the CAP in which the surplus arises (after deduction of any ACT). If the MCT liability is less than the required repayment, the balance is repaid in cash.

EXAMPLE 3

In the year to 31 March 1998, a company receives net debenture interest of £40,000 and makes no payments net of income tax. Calculate the required income tax repayment and show how this repayment will be made if the company's MCT liability for the year is :

(a) £100,000

(b) £7,000.

SOLUTION

(a) The required repayment is £40,000 x 20/80 = £10,000. This will be offset against the company's MCT liability for the year, reducing this liability from £100,000 to £90,000.

(b) If the company's MCT liability for the year is only £7,000, this liability will be reduced to £nil and the remaining £3,000 will be repaid to the company in cash.

Summary

- ► Companies receive certain types of income net of income tax at either the basic rate or the lower rate, depending upon the type of income.
- ► Companies make certain types of payment net of income tax at either the basic rate or the lower rate, depending upon the type of payment.
- ► Companies must submit quarterly returns of the income tax suffered on taxed income and deducted from relevant payments. From the information given in these returns, the amount of income tax payable/repayable for each return period can be calculated.
- ► If the income tax suffered in a CAP exceeds the income tax deducted from payments made in that CAP, the income tax suffered on the excess is repaid by means of a reduction in the company's MCT liability.

Exercises

26.1 Classify each of the following as either a payment made net of income tax, income received net of income tax or neither :

(a) debenture interest paid

(b) debenture interest received

(c) dividends paid

(d) dividends received

(e) interest paid to a UK bank

(f) interest received from a UK bank.

Also specify the rate at which income tax (if any) is deducted or suffered in each case.

26.2 A company has the following payments made net of income tax and income received net of income tax for the year to 31 March 1998 (amounts are stated net) :

		Payments	*Income*
		£	£
1 May 1997	Debenture interest paid	16,000	
30 June 1997	Patent royalties received		7,700
1 November 1997	Debenture interest paid	16,000	
1 January 1998	Loan interest received		5,200

Compute the amounts of income tax payable or repayable in each return period.

26.3 A company with chargeable profits of £2,400,000 for the year to 31 March 1998 paid a dividend of £420,000 on 2 January 1998. No other dividends were paid or received during the year. Payments made net of income tax and income received net of income tax during the year (net amounts) were as follows :

		Payments	*Income*
		£	£
30 June 1997	Loan interest received		280,000
17 August 1997	Debenture interest paid	360,000	
1 January 1998	Loan interest received		280,000

Compute the mainstream corporation tax payable on 1 January 1999.

***26.4** A company's profit and loss account for the year to 31 March 1998 is as follows :

		£	£
Sales			254,628
Less :	Cost of sales		112,876
Gross profit			141,752
Add :	Profit on sale of fixed asset	542	
	Income from investments	16,000	16,542
			158,294
Less :	Distribution costs	32,189	
	Administrative expenses	42,974	
	Interest payable	22,876	98,039
Net profit			60,255

Notes :

(i) The sale of the fixed asset gave rise to a chargeable gain of £212.

(ii) Income from investments consists of :

	£
Dividends from UK companies (gross amount)	10,000
Debenture interest received (gross amount)	4,000
Debenture interest accrued (gross amount)	2,000
	16,000

(iii) Administrative expenses include :

	£
Directors' fees	20,000
Depreciation	5,764
Audit fee	1,000

(iv) Interest payable consists of :

	£
Debenture interest paid (gross amount)	2,000
Debenture interest accrued (gross amount)	1,000
Bank overdraft interest	19,876
	22,876

(v) Capital allowances of £5,318 are claimed for the year.

(vi) During the year, the company paid a dividend of 10 pence per share on its issued share capital of 200,000 ordinary shares.

Calculate the mainstream corporation tax payable on 1 January 1999.

Chapter 27

Corporation tax losses

Introduction

A variety of loss reliefs is available to a company which incurs a trading loss. The main reliefs are similar to those available to individuals (see Chapter 11) and involve either carrying the loss forward against future trading profits or setting the loss against total profits for a specified period. The main purpose of this chapter is to describe the reliefs available in relation to a trading loss and to explain the factors which might influence the company when choosing between these reliefs. The chapter also considers the tax treatment of a company's non-trading losses.

Relief for trading losses

A company's trading losses may be relieved in any of the following ways :

(a) Under Section 393(1) of ICTA 1988, trading losses may be carried forward and relieved against future trading profits.

(b) Under Section 393A(1)(a) of ICTA 1988, trading losses may be relieved against the total profits of the CAP in which the loss arises.

(c) Under Section 393A(1)(b) of ICTA 1988, trading losses may be relieved against the total profits of the three years prior to the CAP in which the loss arises.

(d) Under Section 242 of ICTA 1988, trading losses may be relieved against surplus FII.

Each of these forms of loss relief is described below. The loss reliefs are usually referred to by their section numbers in the Income and Corporation Taxes Act 1988 and this practice is followed for the remainder of this chapter.

As stated in Chapter 23, the capital allowances of companies are treated as a trading expense and are therefore included automatically in any trading loss.

Section 393(1) relief

Unless a company claims any other form of loss relief, trading losses are carried forward under S393(1) and relieved against the company's future trading profits. It is important to note the following points :

(a) Relief under S393(1) is given only against future *trading* profits, not against any other form of profits.

(b) Furthermore, relief is given only against future trading profits arising from *the same trade* as that in which the loss was incurred. If a company ceases one trade and commences another, the losses of the old trade cannot be carried forward and relieved against the future profits of the new trade. Similarly, if a company carries on two trades simultaneously, a loss incurred in one of the trades cannot be carried forward and relieved against the future profits of the other trade.

(c) Relief must be given against the *first available* trading profits of future CAP's.

(d) There are restrictions on the carry-forward of trading losses when there is a change in the ownership of a company. These restrictions are similar to those relating to the carry-forward of surplus ACT (see Chapter 25) and apply also to the carry-forward of unrelieved trade charges (see below).

EXAMPLE 1

In the year to 31 March 1996, a company incurred a trading loss of £240,000 which was carried forward under S393(1). The company's results for the next two accounting years were as follows :

	y/e 31 March 1997	*y/e 31 March 1998*
	£	£
Trading profits	210,000	1,850,000
Bank interest received	50,000	60,000
Chargeable gains	125,000	572,000

Compute the company's chargeable profits for the years to 31 March 1997 and 1998.

SOLUTION

	y/e 31 March 1997	*y/e 31 March 1998*
	£	£
Schedule D Case I	210,000	1,850,000
Less : S393(1) relief	210,000	30,000
	0	1,820,000
Schedule D Case III	50,000	60,000
Chargeable gains	125,000	572,000
Chargeable profits	175,000	2,452,000

Notes :

(i) In the year to 31 March 1997, the trading losses brought forward are relieved to the fullest possible extent against the trading profits of the year. The trading losses of £30,000 which remain unrelieved cannot be offset against the bank interest or chargeable gains but must instead be carried forward and relieved against the trading profits of the following year.

(ii) In the year to 31 March 1997 the company pays corporation tax at only 24% (the small companies rate for FY96), but in the following year it pays corporation tax at 33%. If the company were able to defer the whole £240,000 of S393(1) relief until the year to 31 March 1998 it would make a tax saving. However, relief under S393(1) must be given at the first available opportunity and therefore the company cannot prevent relief being given to the fullest possible extent in the year to 31 March 1997.

Unrelieved charges on income

Charges on income fall into two categories :

(a) trade charges, which are those incurred wholly and exclusively for trade purposes (e.g. patent royalties), and

(b) non-trade charges (e.g. payments made under charitable covenants).

As explained in Chapter 23, charges are deducted when calculating a company's chargeable profits and so long as charges can be fully relieved in this way the distinction between trade and non-trade charges is not important. However, if a company's total profits are insufficient to cover its charges (perhaps because the company has incurred a trading loss) some or all of the charges will be unrelieved.

Under Section 393(9) of ICTA 1988 unrelieved *trade* charges may be carried forward in the same way as trading losses and set against future trading profits. But non-trade charges cannot be carried forward in this way and will remain permanently unrelieved to the extent that they cannot be relieved in the CAP in which they are incurred. (In practice, unrelieved trade charges are often added onto trading losses carried forward rather than being treated as a separate item).

In a CAP in which charges exceed total profits, non-trade charges are relieved in priority to trade charges, so giving non-trade charges the greatest possible chance of relief.

EXAMPLE 2

A company has the following results for the three years to 30 June 1997 :

	y/e 30/6/95	*y/e 30/6/96*	*y/e 30/6/97*
	£	£	£
Trading profits/(losses)	(17,600)	8,700	14,900
Bank interest received	1,000	-	-
Patent royalties paid (gross)	2,000	2,400	2,800
Deed of covenant to charity (gross)	300	300	300

Assuming that the trading loss of £17,600 is to be carried forward under S393(1), calculate the company's chargeable profits for each of the three years.

SOLUTION

	y/e 30/6/95	*y/e 30/6/96*	*y/e 30/6/97*
	£	£	£
Schedule D Case I	-	8,700	14,900
Less : S393(1)/(9) relief	-	8,700	12,600
	-	0	2,300
Bank interest received	1,000	-	-
Less : Non-trade charges	300	-	300
	700	0	2,000
Less : Trade charges	700	-	2,000
Chargeable profits	0	0	0
Trading losses and trade charges c/f	18,900	12,600	800
Non-trade charges unrelieved	-	300	-

Notes :

(i) In the year to 30 June 1995, the £300 of non-trade charges and £700 of the trade charges can be relieved against the bank interest received. This leaves £1,300 of unrelieved trade charges to be carried forward together with the £17,600 of trading losses, giving a total of £18,900.

(ii) In the year to 30 June 1996, the trading profit of £8,700 is used to relieve part of the losses brought forward, leaving £10,200 unrelieved. This is increased by the trade charges for the year of £2,400, giving a total of £12,600 to carry forward. The non-trade charges for the year are completely unrelieved.

(iii) In the year to 30 June 1997, the losses brought forward are fully relieved. The remaining profits of £2,300 are used to relieve the non-trade charges and £2,000 of the trade charges, leaving £800 of unrelieved trade charges to carry forward to the following year.

Section 393A(1) relief

As indicated earlier in this chapter, Section 393A(1) relief is available in two parts :

(a) Under S393A(1)(a), a company may claim that a trading loss incurred during a CAP should be relieved against the total profits of that CAP. For this purpose, the term "total profits" means the income and gains of the company, *before* deducting any charges on income.

(b) Under S393A(1)(b), the company may further claim that any part of the trading loss which remains unrelieved after a claim has been made under S393A(1)(a) should be relieved against the total profits of the previous 3 years (most recent years first). For this purpose, the term "total profits" means the income and gains of the company, *after* deducting trade charges but *before* deducting non-trade charges.

S393A(1) relief is voluntary in its operation and a company wishing to relieve a trading loss in this way must make the appropriate claim within two years of the end of the CAP in which the trading loss arises. A claim may be made under S393A(1)(a) without a corresponding S393A(1)(b) claim but a claim under S393A(1)(b) cannot be made without a prior S393A(1)(a) claim.

The company may not specify how much of its trading loss should be relieved under S393A(1). The effect of a claim is to relieve trading losses to the fullest possible extent in each affected CAP. Any part of the trading loss which remains unrelieved after a S393A(1) claim has been made is automatically carried forward under S393(1). If no claim at all is made under S393A(1) then the entire trading loss is carried forward under S393(1).

EXAMPLE 3

A company has the following results for the year to 31 December 1997 :

	£
Trading loss (adjusted for tax purposes)	(22,500)
Building society interest received	4,000
Unfranked investment income (gross)	23,000
Patent royalties paid (gross)	7,500
Deed of covenant to charity (gross)	1,200

Assuming that a claim is made for the trading loss to be relieved under S393A(1)(a), compute the company's chargeable profits for the year.

SOLUTION

	£
Schedule D Case I	-
Building society interest	4,000
Unfranked investment income	23,000
	27,000
Less : S393A(1)(a) relief	22,500
	4,500
Less : Non-trade charges	1,200
	3,300
Less : Trade charges	3,300
Chargeable profits	0

Note :

Under S393A(1)(a), relief for the trading loss is given against the total profits of the company, before deducting charges. As a consequence, only £3,300 of the trade charges can be relieved and the balance of £4,200 must be carried forward under S393(9).

EXAMPLE 4

A company has the following results for the four years to 31 July 1997 :

	y/e 31/7/94	*y/e 31/7/95*	*y/e 31/7/96*	*y/e 31/7/97*
	£	£	£	£
Trading profits/(losses)	14,000	12,500	10,700	(36,700)
Income from property	3,000	3,300	3,800	4,200
Trade charges	1,500	1,500	1,500	1,500
Non-trade charges	500	500	500	500

Assuming that a claim is made under both S393A(1)(a) and S393A(1)(b) in relation to the trading loss incurred in the year to 31 July 1997, calculate the company's chargeable profits for each of the four years.

SOLUTION

	y/e 31/7/94	*y/e 31/7/95*	*y/e 31/7/96*	*y/e 31/7/97*
	£	£	£	£
Schedule D Case I	14,000	12,500	10,700	-
Schedule A	3,000	3,300	3,800	4,200
	17,000	15,800	14,500	4,200
Less : S393A(1)(a) relief	-	-	-	4,200
c/f	17,000	15,800	14,500	0

		y/e 31/7/94	y/e 31/7/95	y/e 31/7/96	y/e 31/7/97
		£	£	£	£
b/f		17,000	15,800	14,500	0
Less : Trade charges		1,500	1,500	1,500	-
		15,500	14,300	13,000	0
Less : S393A(1)(b) relief	(1)			13,000	
	(2)		14,300		
	(3)	5,200			
		10,300	0	0	0
Less : Non-trade charges		500	-	-	-
Chargeable profits		9,800	0	0	0
Trade charges c/f		-	-	-	1,500
Non-trade charges unrelieved		-	500	500	500

Notes :

(i) In the year to 31 July 1997, the claim under S393A(1)(a) must be for the maximum possible amount of £4,200, leaving nothing against which to relieve charges. The trade charges may be carried forward under S393(9) but the non-trade charges are permanently unrelieved.

(ii) S393A(1)(b) relief is given first in the year to 31 July 1996, then in 1995 and finally in 1994. The relief is given after trade charges have been relieved and must be for the maximum possible amount. This leaves nothing against which to relieve the non-trade charges in 1996 and 1995.

(iii) In the year to 31 July 1994, the S393A(1)(b) relief of £5,200 consists of the balance of the trading loss after taking into account the loss reliefs given in 1997, 1996 and 1995 (i.e. £36,700 - £4,200 - £13,000 - £14,300).

(iv) Since the trading loss has been entirely relieved under S393A(1)(a) and S393A(1)(b), there are no unrelieved trading losses to carry forward under S393(1).

Restrictions on S393A(1) relief

Note the following further points in relation to S393A(1) relief :

(a) Relief under S393A(1) is available only if the loss-making trade is being carried on on a commercial basis with a view to profit. In the case of companies which carry on the trade of farming or market gardening, a loss is not normally eligible for relief under S393A(1) if losses have also been incurred in each of the previous 5 years.

(b) A trading loss can be carried back under S393A(1)(b) only to CAP's in which the loss-making trade was being carried on.

(c) If the beginning of the 3-year period to which losses may be carried back under S393A(1)(b) falls part-way through a CAP, the profits of that CAP are apportioned on a time basis. The profits eligible for loss relief are those which fall into the 3-year period.

(d) When a company ceases to trade, any unrelieved trade charges incurred in the company's final CAP may be used to increase or create a loss eligible for carry-back under S393A(1)(b).

(e) If more than one loss is eligible for relief against the profits of a given CAP, earlier losses are relieved before later losses.

(f) There are restrictions on the carry-back of trading losses under S393A(1)(b) when there is a change in the ownership of a company. These restrictions are similar to those relating to the carry-back of surplus ACT (see Chapter 25).

Losses and ACT

If a trading loss is carried back to an earlier CAP under S393A(1)(b), then the chargeable profits of that earlier CAP are reduced. This in turn reduces the maximum ACT set-off allowed in that CAP (see Chapter 25) and surplus ACT may arise as a consequence.

Surplus ACT created in this way might be difficult to relieve and it is clearly of no benefit to use S393A(1)(b) to relieve a trading loss if the result is a substantial amount of unrelieved surplus ACT. Therefore, the possibility that surplus ACT might be created as a consequence of a claim under S393A(1)(b) should be taken into account when choosing the most effective form of relief for a trading loss (see below).

EXAMPLE 5

A company has the following results for the four years to 31 March 1998 :

	y/e 31/3/95	*y/e 31/3/96*	*y/e 31/3/97*	*y/e 31/3/98*
	£	£	£	£
Chargeable profits	30,000	35,000	32,000	nil
ACT paid for the year	5,450	7,000	6,000	-

A claim is made under S393A(1)(b) in relation to trading losses of £75,000 incurred in the year to 31 March 1998. Calculate the surplus ACT arising in each of the three years to 31 March 1997 (assuming, for this purpose, that changes in the rate of ACT occur on 1 April rather than on 6 April).

SOLUTION

	y/e 31/3/95	*y/e 31/3/96*	*y/e 31/3/97*
	£	£	£
Chargeable profits (before loss relief)	30,000	35,000	32,000
Less : S393A(1)(b) relief (1)			32,000
(2)		35,000	
(3)	8,000		
Chargeable profits (after loss relief)	22,000	0	0
ACT rate	20%	20%	20%
Maximum ACT set-off	4,400	0	0
Less : ACT paid for the year	5,450	7,000	6,000
Surplus ACT	1,050	7,000	6,000

The total amount of surplus ACT created (where previously there was none) is £14,050.

Repayments of corporation tax

If a claim under S393A(1)(b) results in a repayment of corporation tax for an earlier CAP, this repayment will attract interest. The interest is calculated in the usual way (see Chapter 24) unless the CAP for which repayment is being made began more than 12 months before the loss-making CAP. In these circumstances, the interest is calculated as if the repayment were a repayment of tax for the loss-making CAP itself.

EXAMPLE 6

A company has the following results for the three years to 31 March 1998 :

	y/e 31/3/96	*y/e 31/3/97*	*y/e 31/3/98*
	£	£	£
Chargeable profits	180,000	120,000	nil
Franked investment income	nil	nil	nil

A claim is made under S393A(1)(b) in relation to trading losses of £250,000 incurred in the year to 31 March 1998. All corporation tax was originally paid on the due date and the necessary repayment of corporation tax is made on 1 February 1999. Calculate the amount of the repayment and the amount of interest which will accompany this repayment, assuming an interest rate of 3.25% per annum.

SOLUTION

In the year to 31 March 1996 and the year to 31 March 1997, the company's corporation tax liability was calculated at the small companies rate (25% in FY95 and 24% in FY96). The S393A(1)(b) claim will generate the following repayment :

		£
y/e 31 March 1997	120,000 @ 24%	28,800
y/e 31 March 1996	130,000 @ 25%	32,500
Total repayment		61,300

The year to 31 March 1997 began no more than 12 months before the loss-making year so interest on the £28,800 will run from 1 January 1998 (i.e. the due date of payment for the year to 31 March 1997).

But the year to 31 March 1996 began more than 12 months before the loss-making year so interest on the £32,500 will run only from 1 January 1999 (i.e. the due date of payment for the loss-making year itself, which ended on 31 March 1998).

The repayment took place on 1 February 1999, which is 396 days after 1 January 1998 and 31 days after 1 January 1999. Therefore the interest due is :

$$\text{£}28{,}800 \times 3.25\% \times \frac{396}{365} + \text{£}32{,}500 \times 3.25\% \times \frac{31}{365} = \text{£}1{,}105.20.$$

Choice of loss relief

A company which incurs a trading loss may choose between the following main courses of action :

(a) to carry the loss forward against future trading profits

(b) to relieve as much of the loss as possible against the total profits of the CAP in which the loss was incurred and then carry forward any unrelieved balance of the loss against future trading profits

(c) to relieve the loss against the total profits of the CAP in which the loss was incurred and the total profits of the previous three years and then carry forward any unrelieved balance of the loss against future trading profits.

Some of the main criteria which will influence this choice are as follows :

(a) the likelihood and expected amount of future profits arising from the same trade as that in which the loss was incurred

(b) the company's cash flow situation (a cash shortage may dictate that loss relief should be obtained as soon as possible)

(c) the possibility of creating surplus ACT

(d) the possibility that non-trade charges might become unrelieved

(e) the rates of corporation tax in earlier CAP's and the expected rates in future CAP's

(f) the possibility that trading losses carried back may so reduce the chargeable profits of an earlier CAP that the rate of corporation tax payable for that CAP becomes only the small companies rate (or the company becomes entitled to the marginal relief)

(g) the desire to maximise the amount of tax saved as a result of loss relief claims.

Relief of trading losses against surplus FII

Another choice which may be available to a company seeking to relieve a trading loss is to use its surplus FII for this purpose. Under Section 242 of ICTA 1988, a company which has surplus FII in a CAP may claim that this surplus FII should be treated as trading profits for the purpose of relieving trading losses under S393A(1)(a) or S393A(1)(b). Note the following points :

(a) The surplus FII available for S242 relief is the surplus FII of the CAP itself, excluding any surplus FII brought forward from previous CAP's.

(b) A claim cannot be made under S242 for a CAP unless relief has first been given in that CAP under S393A(1)(a) or S393A(1)(b).

(c) The effect of the claim is to generate a repayment of the tax credit attached to the amount of surplus FII which is used to relieve trading losses. This surplus FII is no longer available to be carried forward and set against future franked payments.

(d) If a claim is made under S242 and then, in a later CAP, there is an excess of franked payments over FII, the following consequences ensue :

    (i) the company pays ACT on this excess in the usual way, but

    (ii) the amount of this ACT which is available for set-off against the year's corporation tax liability is reduced by the amount of the tax credit which was repaid as a result of the previous S242 claim, and

    (iii) the loss which was relieved under S242 is reinstated and treated as a trading loss brought forward from a previous year.

    If the excess of franked payments over FII is less than the amount of surplus FII which was used in the S242 claim, the reduction at (ii) and the reinstatement at (iii) will occur only in part and the balance of the tax credit and loss will be carried forward to subsequent CAP's. This will continue until the entire S242 claim has been reversed.

The main benefit of a claim under S242 is that the company obtains a cash flow advantage, as illustrated by the following example.

EXAMPLE 7

A company has the following results for the years to 31 March 1997 and 1998 :

	y/e 31 March 1997	*y/e 31 March 1998*
	£	£
Trading profit/(loss)	(20,000)	50,000
Bank interest received	1,000	1,000
Dividends received	8,000	8,000
Dividends paid	nil	24,000

A claim is made under S393A(1)(a) in respect of the trading loss incurred in the year to 31 March 1997 but no claim is made under S393A(1)(b) in respect of this loss. A claim is made under Section 242. Show the corporation tax computation for each of the two years.

SOLUTION

	y/e 31 March 1997	*y/e 31 March 1998*
	£	£
Schedule D Case I	-	50,000
Less : S393(1) relief	-	19,000
	-	31,000
Schedule D Case III	1,000	1,000
Less : S393A(1)(a) relief	1,000	-
Chargeable profits	0	32,000
Corporation tax due @ 24%	0	
Corporation tax due @ 23%		7,360
Less : ACT set-off	0	2,000
MCT payable	0	5,360
Tax credit on FII refunded	2,000	-

Notes :

(i) The trading loss remaining in the year to 31 March 1997, after deduction of S393A(1)(a) relief, is £19,000 (£20,000 - £1,000).

(ii) Surplus FII in the year to 31 March 1997 is £10,000 (£8,000 x 100/80). A claim under S242 results in a repayment of the £2,000 tax credit attached to this FII and relieves £10,000 of the loss. The remaining £9,000 of the loss is carried forward.

(iii) In the year to 31 March 1998, franked payments (£24,000 x 100/80) exceed FII (£8,000 x 100/80) by £20,000 and the company pays ACT of 20% x £20,000 = £4,000.

(iv) The amount of ACT available for set-off in the year to 31 March 1998 is only £2,000 (£4,000 paid, less £2,000 tax credit previously refunded) but the loss previously relieved under S242 is reinstated, bringing trading losses brought forward to £19,000 (£9,000 + £10,000).

(v) The total corporation tax payable is the same with or without the S242 claim. If the company had not made the S242 claim, the £2,000 tax refund would not have been received but the surplus FII of £10,000 would have reduced the ACT payable for the year to 31 March 1998 by £2,000. However, the company's cash flow situation has been improved by making the S242 claim.

Non-trading losses

A company may incur non-trading losses in any of the following ways :

(a) **Schedule A losses**. A Schedule A loss arises if allowable expenditure exceeds assessable property income. Depending upon the type of lease involved, such a loss may be relieved against other Schedule A income in the same CAP. Unrelieved losses are carried forward and relieved against Schedule A income in future CAP's. The precise rules involved are explained in Chapter 23. Schedule A losses can never be relieved against any other form of income.

(b) **Schedule D Case VI losses**. A Schedule D Case VI loss is relieved first against any other Schedule D Case VI income of the same CAP and then against the Schedule D Case VI income of subsequent CAP's.

In general, Schedule D Case VI losses cannot be relieved against any other form of income. However, losses arising from the letting of "furnished holiday accommodation" (see Chapter 5) are regarded as trading losses and are relieved as such. In these circumstances it is possible that a Schedule D Case VI loss might be relieved against a company's other income.

(c) **Net debits on non-trading loan relationships**. If a company incurs a deficit on its non-trading loan relationships (see Chapter 23), a claim may be made within two years of the end of the relevant CAP for the deficit to be relieved in any of the following ways :

   (i) by set-off against the company's chargeable profits for the CAP in which the deficit occurs (after any S393(1) relief has been given but before S393A(1) relief)

   (ii) by group relief (see Chapter 29)

   (iii) by set-off against the company's income from non-trading loan relationships in the previous three years (most recent periods first).

Part of the deficit may be relieved in one way and part in another, if the company so wishes. Any part of the deficit which is not subject to such a claim is carried forward automatically and set against the first available non-trading profits in subsequent CAP's.

(d) **Capital losses**. A company's capital losses are treated in much the same way as an individual's capital losses (see Chapter 16). Capital losses are relieved first against capital gains of the same CAP and then against the capital gains of subsequent CAP's. Since companies are not entitled to the annual exemption, there is no need to restrict capital losses brought forward so as to conserve the exemption. Capital losses can never be relieved against any other form of income.

Summary

- A company's trading losses are carried forward under S393(1) and relieved against the first available profits of the same trade, unless the company makes a claim under S393A(1).
- Unrelieved trade charges may be carried forward under S393(9) but unrelieved non-trade charges are lost.
- Under S393A(1)(a), a trading loss may be relieved against the total profits of the loss making CAP.
- Under S393A(1)(b), a trading loss may be relieved against the total profits of the three years prior to the loss making CAP.
- Trading losses carried back under S393A(1)(b) may create surplus ACT in the CAP's to which they are carried back.
- If a claim under S393A(1)(b) results in a repayment of corporation tax for an earlier CAP, this repayment will attract interest.
- Under S242, a trading loss may be relieved against surplus FII.
- In general, a company's non-trading losses are relieved against income or gains of the same type arising in the same year or in future years. However, the loss reliefs available in relation to a deficit on non-trading loan relationships are more extensive.

Exercises

27.1 A Ltd has the following results for the three years to 31 May 1997 :

	y/e 31/5/95	*y/e 31/5/96*	*y/e 31/5/97*
	£	£	£
Trading profits/(losses)	(31,200)	23,800	11,500
Trade charges	1,000	1,200	1,400
Non-trade charges	400	500	600

Assuming that the trading loss is to be carried forward under S393(1), calculate the company's chargeable profits for each of the three years, showing the amount of the losses carried forward at the end of each year.

27.2 B Ltd has the following results for the year to 31 October 1997 :

	£
Trading loss	(7,300)
Income from property	10,200
Capital gains	540
Patent royalties paid (gross)	9,000
Deed of covenant to charity (gross)	4,000

Assuming that a loss relief claim is made under S393A(1)(a), calculate the chargeable profits for the year.

27.3 Which of the following statements is true ?

(a) Capital losses may be carried forward and relieved against future trading profits.

(b) Trading losses may be carried forward and relieved against future capital gains.

(c) Trading losses may be relieved against capital gains of the same CAP.

(d) Capital losses may be relieved against trading profits of the same CAP.

27.4 C Ltd has the following results for the four years to 30 June 1997 :

	y/e 30/6/94	*y/e 30/6/95*	*y/e 30/6/96*	*y/e 30/6/97*
	£	£	£	£
Trading profits/(losses)	54,800	22,700	8,600	(41,900)
Capital gains	-	-	-	8,700
Trade charges	5,000	5,000	5,000	5,000
Non-trade charges	1,000	1,000	1,000	1,000

Assuming that a claim is made under both S393A(1)(a) and S393A(1)(b) in relation to the trading loss incurred in the year to 30 June 1997, calculate the company's chargeable profits for each of the four years.

27.5 In the year to 31 March 1997, D Ltd had chargeable profits of £1,800,000 and paid a dividend of £500,000. In the year to 31 March 1998, the company incurred a trading loss of £1,200,000 and had no other income or gains. The company has no franked investment income and there were no charges on income in either year.

Describe the corporation tax effects of a claim under S393A(1)(b) in relation to the trading loss (detailed computations are not required).

***27.6** E Ltd has the following results for the four years to 31 March 1998 :

	y/e 31/3/95	*y/e 31/3/96*	*y/e 31/3/97*	*y/e 31/3/98*
	£	£	£	£
Trading profits/(losses)	61,900	27,400	4,200	(72,500)
Capital gains/(losses)	(7,500)	4,300	2,700	5,700
Trade charges	2,500	2,500	2,500	2,500
Non-trade charges	900	900	900	900

Calculate the total repayment of corporation tax (together with interest) to which the company is entitled, assuming that :

(a) claims under S393A(1)(a) and S393A(1)(b) are made in relation to the trading loss for the year to 31 March 1998

(b) any repayment of corporation tax which is generated by these claims is made on 15 January 1999

(c) corporation tax for each of the three years to 31 March 1997 was paid on the due date

(d) the company has neither paid not received any dividends in any of the four years

(e) the rate of interest paid on repayments of corporation tax is 3.25%.

The small companies rate of corporation tax was 25% in FY94 and FY95 and 24% in FY96.

Chapter 28

Close companies and investment companies

Introduction

In general terms, a "close company" is one which is controlled by a small number of people and an "investment company" is one whose principal activity is the making of investments. Special corporation tax rules apply to each of these types of company and the main purpose of this chapter is to explain the nature of these special rules. The tax implications of incorporation are also considered in this chapter.

Close companies

The essence of a close company is that its affairs can be controlled and manipulated by a small group of people, possibly for tax-avoidance purposes. (In fact, most UK companies are close companies). A body of anti-avoidance legislation has grown up over the years in relation to close companies and the main points of this legislation are explained later in this chapter. The first step, however, is to provide a precise definition of the term "close company".

Definition of a close company

A close company is defined as a UK resident company which is under the *control* of either :

(a) five or fewer *participators*, or

(b) any number of participators who are also *directors* of the company.

The rights of a participator's *associates* are aggregated with that participator's own rights for the purpose of determining whether or not a company is a close company.

Some important terms used in this definition are explained below.

Control

Persons are deemed to have "control" over a company if, taken together, they :

(a) own over 50% of the company's issued share capital, or
(b) have over 50% of the company's voting power, or
(c) would receive over 50% of the company's income, if all that income were distributed, or
(d) would receive over 50% of the company's assets, if the company were wound up.

Participators

A "participator" is defined as someone who has a share or interest in the capital or income of the company. In most cases, a company's only participators are its shareholders, but other persons (e.g. option holders) might also rank as participators.

Directors

A "director", for this purpose, is any person :

(a) who occupies the position of director (whether called a director or not), or
(b) whose directions or instructions are normally obeyed by the directors, or
(c) who is a manager of the company and (possibly together with associates) controls at least 20% of the company's ordinary share capital.

Associates

The "associates" of a participator are defined as :

(a) the participator's business partners
(b) the participator's relatives (which, for this purpose, consist of spouses, parents or remoter ancestors, children or remoter issue, brothers and sisters)
(c) the trustee(s) of any settlement established by the participator or by the participator's relatives.

EXAMPLE 1

A company's issued share capital consists of 1,000 £1 ordinary shares, held as follows :

	Number of shares
David	200
Emma	50
Frederick	100
George	50
c/f	400

	Number of shares
b/f	400
Helen	50
Ian	30
Jacqueline	40
Others (none owning more than 10 shares)	480
Total	1,000

None of the shareholders are associated in any way and no shareholder is also a director.

(a) Is the company a close company ?

(b) Would the company be a close company :

 (i) if David were Jacqueline's brother, or

 (ii) if Emma married Ian, or

 (iii) if David were Jacqueline's brother and Emma married Ian ?

SOLUTION

(a) The five largest shareholders own 45% of the share capital, so the company is not under the control of five or fewer participators. The company is also not under the control of its directors. Therefore the company is not a close company.

(b) (i) If David were Jacqueline's brother, her 4% holding would be aggregated with his and the five largest shareholders would control 49% (45% + 4%) of the share capital. The company would not be a close company.

 (ii) If Emma married Ian, his 3% would be aggregated with hers and the five largest shareholders would control 48% (45% + 3%) of the share capital. The company would still not be a close company.

 (iii) If David were Jacqueline's brother and Emma married Ian, the five largest shareholders would control 52% (45% + 4% + 3%) of the share capital. The company would then be a close company.

EXAMPLE 2

A company's issued share capital consists entirely of ordinary shares, held as follows :

	% holding	Director
Keith	7	Yes
Leonora	7	Yes
Martin	7	Yes
Norma	7	Yes
Oliver	7	Yes
Penny	16	No
Richard	4	No
Others (all non-directors owning under 1%)	45	
Total	100	

None of the shareholders are associated in any way

(a) Is the company a close company ?

(b) Would the company be a close company :

    (i) if Penny were a manager, or

    (ii) if Penny were Richard's daughter, or

    (iii) if Penny were both a manager and Richard's daughter ?

SOLUTION

(a) The five largest shareholders own 44% of the share capital, so the company is not under the control of five or fewer participators. The company is also not under the control of its directors, who own 35% of the share capital. Therefore the company is not a close company.

(b) (i) If Penny were a manager, she would not rank as a director since her shareholding is less than 20%. The situation would be unaltered and the company would not be a close company.

    (ii) If Penny were Richard's daughter, then his 4% holding would be aggregated with hers and the five largest shareholders would control 48% (44% + 4%) of the share capital. The company would still not be a close company.

    (iii) If Penny were both a manager and Richard's daughter, then her deemed 20% holding (16% + 4%) would make her a director. The six directors would control 55% of the share capital and the company would then be a close company.

Exceptions

Certain types of company are statutorily excepted from close company status, even if controlled by five or fewer participators (or by the participator directors). The main exception consists of listed companies with "a substantial public interest". In order for this exception to apply, a company must satisfy all of the following conditions :

(a) The company's voting shares must have been both dealt in and listed on a recognised stock exchange within the 12 months prior to the date on which the company's status is being determined.

(b) The total voting power possessed by the "principal members" of the company must not exceed 85% of the total voting power.

(c) At least 35% of the company's voting power must be in the hands of the "public".

For this purpose, a "principal member" is a shareholder who (possibly with associates) has more than 5% of the voting power of the company and is also one of the top five shareholders. If two or more shareholders, each holding more than 5%, tie for fifth place, there will be more than five principal members.

The "public" excludes directors, their associates and most principal members. However, principal members which are themselves either :

(a) non-close companies, or

(b) occupational pension schemes (other than schemes established for the benefit of the company's own employees or directors)

are included within the definition of the "public".

EXAMPLE 3

The issued share capital of XYZ plc consists entirely of ordinary shares. For many years, these shares have been listed on the London Stock Exchange and there have been frequent dealings in these shares within the last 12 months. The company's shares are owned as follows :

	% holding	*Director*
ABC Ltd (a non-close company)	13	-
DEF Ltd (a close company)	7	-
Terry	8	Yes
Ursula	10	Yes
Vincent (a manager)	33	No
Wendy	4	No
Others (all non-directors owning under 1%)	25	
Total	100	

None of the shareholders are associated in any way. Is the company a close company ?

SOLUTION

At first sight, XYZ plc seems to be a close company. It is under the control of its directors (since Vincent ranks as a director) and it is also under the control of five or fewer participators. However, the company is listed on a recognised stock exchange and its shares have been dealt in within the past 12 months. Furthermore, its principal members (the top five shareholders, each owning more than 5% of the voting shares) hold only 71% of the company's voting power and the public (ABC Ltd, Wendy and the others) hold 42%. Therefore the company is excepted from being a close company.

Consequences of close company status

There are two main tax consequences of being a close company. These are :

(a) Benefits in kind provided to participators and their associates are treated as distributions and therefore attract ACT.

(b) Loans made to participators are assessed to tax.

Benefits in kind provided to participators

Benefits in kind provided by a close company to its participators (or to their associates) are generally regarded as distributions. The taxation effects of this are as follows :

(a) The cost to the company of the benefit in kind is disallowed when computing its corporation tax liability.

(b) The company is deemed to have made a net distribution equal to the amount which would be assessed on a P11D employee if the benefit in kind had been received by such a employee (see Chapter 7). ACT is due on this amount exactly as if a dividend of the same amount had been paid. This ACT may then be set against the company's corporation tax liability for the CAP in the usual way.

(c) The person receiving the benefit is taxed as if he or she had received a dividend of the same amount.

Note that a benefit in kind provided to a participator is *not* treated as a distribution if the participator is an employee of the company (in which case the benefit is taxed under Schedule E in the usual way) or if the benefit consists of job-related living accommodation.

EXAMPLE 4

During the year to 31 March 1998, a close company provides the brother of one of its major shareholders with a free holiday abroad. The cost of the holiday is £3,200 and this amount is charged to the profit and loss account for the year. Explain the tax treatment of this item.

SOLUTION

The £3,200 will be disallowed in the computation of the company's corporation tax liability for the year and the company will be deemed to have made a distribution of £3,200. ACT of £800 (£3,200 x 20/80) will be payable but this may be set against the corporation tax liability for the year to 31 March 1998. The shareholder's brother will be taxed on a gross distribution of £4,000 (tax credit £800).

Loans made to participators

If a close company makes a loan to a participator (or associate), the tax consequences are as follows :

(a) The company must pay an amount of tax equal to the ACT which would be payable if the loan were a dividend. This tax is payable 9 months and one day after the end of CAP in which the loan is made. However, no tax is payable in relation to any part of a loan which is repaid to the company before the date on which the tax would have fallen due.

(b) Though often referred to as "notional ACT", the tax payable is actually not ACT at all and cannot be set against the company's corporation tax liability for the CAP. The tax will be repaid to the company only if the loan is repaid. This tax repayment is made 9 months after the end of the CAP in which the loan is repaid.

(c) If the company writes off the loan, the notional ACT will never be refunded and the participator is treated as having received a distribution equal to the amount of the loan written off. This distribution is accompanied by a tax credit in the usual way, but the tax credit cannot be repaid to the participator in full or in part, even if the participator is a non-taxpayer.

(d) Certain loans are excluded from the treatment described above. These include :

  (i) loans made to a participator in the normal course of business (e.g. by a close company whose business is that of lending money)

  (ii) loans not exceeding £15,000 made to a participator who is a full-time employee or director of the company, so long as that participator (with associates) has no more than a 5% interest in the company

  (iii) loans made to companies which are not UK resident.

EXAMPLE 5

On 1 July 1996, a close company (which makes up accounts to 31 March annually) lends £30,000 to Ravi, who is one of its directors. No interest is charged on this loan. Ravi owns 25% of the company's ordinary share capital. Explain the tax treatment of the loan if :

(a) it is repaid in full on 30 June 1998.

(b) £10,000 is repaid on 30 June 1998 and the remainder of the loan is written off on the same day.

SOLUTION

Ravi has more than a 5% interest in the company, so notional ACT of £7,500 (£30,000 x 20/80) will be payable by 1 January 1998. Since the loan is made interest-free, it will be treated as a beneficial loan and Ravi will be subject to Schedule E income tax on the related benefit in kind (see Chapter 7).

(a) If the loan is repaid in full on 30 June 1998, the company will be entitled to a tax repayment of £7,500. This will be made on 1 January 2000.

(b) If £10,000 is repaid on 30 June 1998 (and the rest of the loan is written off), the company will be entitled to a tax repayment of only £2,500. The remaining £5,000 is irrecoverable. Ravi will be taxed as if he had received a dividend of £20,000 (tax credit

£5,000) but will not be able to reclaim any part of the tax credit even if this exceeds his income tax liability for the year.

Investment companies

An investment company is defined in ICTA 1988 as "any company whose business consists wholly or mainly in the making of investments and the principal part of whose income is derived therefrom". The chargeable income of such a company will normally consist of :

(a) income from property

(b) bank and building society interest (received gross)

(c) net credits on non-trading loan relationships.

The company may also receive franked investment income, but (as explained in Chapter 23) this is not chargeable to corporation tax. The expenses incurred by an investment company fall into two categories :

(a) expenses which are directly related to one of the company's sources of income and which may be set against that income (e.g. property expenses offset against property income, debits on non-trading loan relationships set against credits), and

(b) general management expenses, which are not related to any particular source of income but which may be set against the company's total income.

Note that only genuine management expenses are allowed. For example, in *L G Berry Investments Ltd* v *Attwooll* (1964), excessive directors' remuneration included in general management expenses was disallowed.

To the extent that general management expenses cannot be relieved in the CAP in which they are incurred they may be carried forward (without time limit) to future CAP's. Unrelieved trade charges may be carried forward in the same way. There are restrictions on the carry-forward of management expenses and trade charges when there is a change in the ownership of a company. These restrictions are similar to those relating to the carry-forward of trading losses (see Chapter 27).

Close investment-holding companies

A close company is also a close investment-holding company unless it exists wholly or mainly for one or more of a number of purposes defined by statute. The main purposes which except a company from close investment-holding company status are :

(a) the carrying on of a trade on a commercial basis, or

(b) the letting of property (other than to connected persons).

Therefore a close company which is also an investment company will probably be a close investment-holding company, unless its main purpose is the letting of property.

A close investment-holding company is subject to all the close company rules described above, but is also subject to further provisions. The main provisions affecting close investment-holding companies (CIC's) are as follows :

(a) A CIC is not entitled to the small companies rate of corporation tax, no matter how small its chargeable profits. A CIC always pays corporation tax at the full rate (33% for FY97).

(b) In certain circumstances, the Inspector of Taxes has the right to restrict the repayment of tax credits to a person who receives a distribution from a CIC. This power is exercised only if the Inspector believes that the purpose of making the distribution is gain a tax advantage.

Unincorporated business or close company ?

An individual who starts trading is faced with a choice between two alternatives :

(a) To trade as an unincorporated business, either as a sole trader or in partnership with others. In this case the individual is self-employed and the business profits are assessed under Schedule D Case I.

(b) To trade as a limited company (almost certainly a close company), with the individual concerned being a director and/or shareholder of the company. In this case, the company's profits are assessed to corporation tax and the individual's emoluments and dividends from the company are assessed to income tax.

The choice between these two alternatives will be determined partly (though not solely) by taxation considerations.

A full analysis of these considerations is beyond the scope of this book but some of the main factors which should be taken into account when deciding whether to trade as an unincorporated business or as a limited company are outlined below.

Rates of tax

The entire profits of an unincorporated business are charged to income tax, regardless of whether the profits are drawn out of the business or not. The rate of tax in 1997/98 is 20%, 23% or 40%, depending upon the owner's taxable income. A marginal rate of 40% applies if the owner's taxable income exceeds £26,100 (a relatively small sum).

By contrast, the profits of a company for FY97 are charged to corporation tax at 23% (profits up to £300,000), 33% (profits exceeding £1,500,000) or 35.5% (marginal rate if profits lie between £300,000 and £1,500,000). The "owner" of the company can decide the amount of profits (if any) which should be paid out in the form of directors' remuneration and can therefore control the extent to which the profits are assessed to personal income tax rather than corporation tax.

Note, however, that retaining profits in a company so as to minimise the tax liability in the short term will serve to increase the value of the company's shares. This will result in an increased CGT liability in the long term when shareholders dispose of their shares, though a variety of CGT reliefs (e.g. retirement relief) may be available.

National Insurance

A self-employed person pays Class 2 NIC's in 1997/98 of £6.15 per week. Profits-related Class 4 NIC's are also payable, with a maximum contribution for 1997/98 of £1,030.20.

The NIC's payable in respect of a company director's emoluments are potentially much higher than this. The director pays primary Class 1 contributions (maximum £2,160.08 in 1997/98) and the company pays unlimited secondary contributions (10% of emoluments if these exceed £10,919.99). The secondary contributions are, however, an allowable deduction in the company's corporation tax computation.

Distribution of profits

As mentioned above, the amount of income tax payable on the profits of an unincorporated business is entirely unaffected by the level of the owner's drawings from the business. But in the case of a company, the distribution of profits (either as directors' emoluments or as dividends) has tax implications :

(a) The payment of directors' emoluments reduces the company's corporation tax liability at the expense of increasing the income tax liability of the directors concerned and creating a liability to both primary and secondary NIC's.

(b) The payment of a dividend avoids the national insurance liability and the dividend is accompanied by a tax credit. But dividends are an appropriation of profit and are not allowed in the company's corporation tax computation, so the company's corporation tax liability will be higher than if the payment took the form of directors' emoluments. The payment of a dividend also results in a payment of ACT, which might or might not be recoverable.

The decision as to whether to pay out a company's profits as directors' emoluments or dividends (or a mixture of both) is a complex one and should take into account the personal circumstances of the shareholders and directors as well as all the factors mentioned above.

A further possibility is to provide a director with benefits in kind (many of which do not attract NIC's) instead of or as well as other emoluments.

EXAMPLE 6

A close company is effectively owned and managed by a single director who has no income other than that derived from the company, claims only the personal allowance and is not contracted out of SERPS. In the year to 31 March 1998, the company has chargeable profits of £50,000. Compute the tax and national insurance implications of :

(a) paying a dividend during the year such that the total of the dividend and the company's tax liability exactly absorbs the £50,000 profit

(b) paying a director's salary during the year which is sufficient, together with the company's secondary NIC's, to absorb the £50,000 profit.

Perform all calculations to the nearest £.

SOLUTION

				(a)		(b)
				£	£	£
Company's corporation tax & NIC's :						
Profits before salary & NIC's				50,000		50,000
Less : Salary				-	45,455	
Secondary NIC's @ 10%				-	4,545	50,000
Chargeable profits				50,000		0
Less : Corporation tax @ 23%				11,500		0
				38,500		0
Less : Dividend				38,500		0
Profits left in company				0		0
Director's income tax & NIC's :						
Salary				-		45,455
Dividends £38,500 x 100/80				48,125		-
				48,125		45,455
Less : Personal allowance				4,045		4,045
Taxable income				44,080		41,410
	(a)	(b)				
	26,100	4,100	@ 20%	5,220		820
	0	22,000	@ 23%	0		5,060
	17,980	15,310	@ 40%	7,192		6,124
	44,080	41,410		12,412		12,004
Less : Tax credit				9,625		-
Tax payable				2,787		12,004
Add : Primary Class 1 NIC's				-		2,160
Income tax and NIC's payable				2,787		14,164

Notes :

(i) If the company's profits are paid out during the year in the form of a dividend, ACT of £9,625 (£38,500 x 20/80) will be payable. But this will be deducted from the MCT liability, leaving the total corporation tax liability unchanged at £11,500.

(ii) If the profits are distributed as a dividend, the director receives a net dividend of £38,500, out of which income tax of £2,787 is payable, leaving a net figure of £35,713.

(iii) If the profits are paid out as a salary, the director receives a gross salary of £45,455, out of which income tax of £12,004 and primary Class 1 NIC's of £2,160 are payable, leaving a net figure of £31,291.

(iv) In this case, the payment of a dividend seems to be more tax-effective, but this cannot be taken as a general rule and each case must be considered individually.

(v) It is also worth noting that adoption of the dividend solution means that no NIC's are paid, which may have an impact on the director's entitlement to social security benefits.

Pension contributions

A self-employed person may contribute up to 17.5% per annum of net relevant earnings (more for older taxpayers) into a pension scheme and obtain tax relief on the contributions.

A company director (being employed rather than self-employed) may obtain tax relief on payments of up to 15% of emoluments into a company pension scheme and the company may make further substantial contributions on the director's behalf, these payments being allowed in the company's corporation tax computation.

In general, the total of the tax-deductible contributions which may be made is greater for a company director than for a self-employed person but this depends to some extent upon profits being paid out in the form of emoluments (which are earned income and so relevant for pension contributions relief purposes) rather than as dividends (which are unearned income).

Dates of payment of tax and NIC's

A self-employed person must make payments on account of his or her liability to income tax and Class 4 NIC's. Note that :

(a) As from tax year 1996/97, these payments are due on 31 January in the tax year and on the following 31 July. The balance of the liability (if any) is payable on the following 31 January.

(b) Choosing an accounting date early in the tax year (e.g. 30 April) maximises the delay between earning profits and paying tax on them. For example, the tax on profits for the year to 30 April 1998 (basis period for 1998/99) will be payable on 31 January 1999 and 31 July 1999 with a balancing payment due on 31 January 2000.

(c) However, choosing an accounting date early in the tax year has the adverse effect of maximising the amount of overlap profits which are taxed twice on the commencement of trade.

(d) Class 2 NIC's of £6.15 per week are payable throughout the tax year.

A company must pay corporation tax 9 months and one day after the end of the chargeable accounting period and will have to account for ACT earlier than this if dividends are paid. Income tax and Class 1 NIC's in relation to directors' emoluments must be accounted for monthly via the PAYE system.

Relief for trading losses

For both individuals (Section 385) and companies (Section 393(1)) trading losses may be carried forward and set against future trading profits. The main distinctions between trading loss reliefs for individuals and companies are concerned with the opportunities to set such losses against total income :

(a) Section 380 of ICTA 1988 allows the trading losses of a self-employed person to be relieved against that person's total income for the year of the loss and/or the previous year. A company's equivalent of Section 380 (Section 393A(1)) is rather more generous, allowing a trading loss to be relieved against total income of the CAP in which the loss is incurred and total income of the previous 3 years.

(b) Section 72 of FA1991 allows the trading losses of an individual to be set against capital gains. Companies receive a similar relief by virtue of the fact that a company's capital gains are automatically included in its total income.

(c) Trading losses of an individual incurred in the opening years of a business may be relieved against total income of the previous three years. There is no equivalent relief for companies.

Note that a company's losses can be relieved only against the company's own income and gains, never against the income and gains of individual shareholders.

Chargeable gains

If an unincorporated business disposes of a chargeable asset, the resulting gain is assessed to CGT on the owner of the business. The rate of CGT is equal to the owner's marginal rate of income tax and so may be 20%, 23% or 40% but the annual exemption (£6,500 for 1997/98) is available.

If a company makes a chargeable disposal, the gain arising is subject to corporation tax (at 23%, 33% or 35.5%) but no annual exemption is available. If the gain is retained in the company, this will increase the value of the company's shares, so resulting in an increased CGT liability when shareholders eventually dispose of their shares. In effect, the gain may be taxed twice, first to corporation tax and then to capital gains tax.

Close company loans to participators

As explained earlier in this chapter, close companies must account for "notional ACT" when making loans to participators and this tax is irretrievably lost if the loan is written off. A tax charge of this type can sometimes be triggered accidentally if a director overdraws his or her current account with the company. These provisions have no relevance to unincorporated businesses.

Incorporation

If the initial choice is to trade as an unincorporated business, the trader may still consider incorporation at some future time. Some of the main consequences of incorporation are as follows :

(a) The transfer of the assets of a business to a company might give rise to a CGT liability. However, subject to certain conditions, the gains arising may be held-over until the shares which were acquired in exchange for the business assets are disposed of (see Chapter 22).

(b) Presuming that the company is under the control of the person who was previously the owner of the unincorporated business, assets which are eligible for capital allowances can be transferred at their written down values for capital allowances purposes, so avoiding the need for balancing adjustments (see Chapter 10).

(c) The transfer of assets to the company will not be treated as a supply for VAT purposes so long as the business is transferred as a going concern and the company is a taxable person at the time of the transfer (see Chapter 30).

(d) If the proprietor of the unincorporated business has unrelieved trade losses, these cannot be carried forward and used by the company but may, subject to certain conditions, be relieved against the proprietor's income from the company (see Chapter 11).

Summary

- A close company is one which is under the control either of five or fewer participators or of any number of participator-directors. The rights of the associates of a participator are aggregated with that participator's own rights when determining whether or not a company is a close company.
- Certain types of company (mainly listed companies with a substantial public interest) are excepted from close company status.
- Benefits in kind provided to the participators of a close company are treated as distributions and attract an ACT liability. Loans made to the participators of a close company are charged to tax.
- An investment company is one whose main purpose is the making of investments.
- A close company is also a close investment-holding company unless it exists wholly or mainly for the purposes of trading or the letting of property. A close investment-holding company is not entitled to the small companies rate of corporation tax.

Exercises

28.1 Andrew Pearson is a shareholder of A Pearson (Nottingham) Ltd. Which of the following (if any) are his associates for the purposes of deciding whether the company is a close company ?

(a) his married sister, Angela Birt
(b) his brother-in-law, Eric Birt
(c) his nephew, Michael Birt
(d) his father, Bill Pearson
(e) his partner in a firm of practising accountants, Alan Johnson.

28.2 The share capital of Romans Ltd consists of 5,000 ordinary shares, held as follows :

	Number of shares
Sejanus (a manager)	900
Claudius (a director)	400
Agrippa (a director)	300
Cleopatra (a director)	300
Tiberius (a director)	200
Gaius (a director)	200
Ptolemy	190
Livia (the grandmother of Claudius)	190
Apicata (the wife of Sejanus)	120
Others (all non-directors owning 10 shares or less)	2,200
Total	5,000

Is the company a close company ?

28.3 During the year to 31 March 1998, a close company provides one of its full-time working directors with :

(a) an interest-free loan of £12,000 (the company does not provide loans in the ordinary course of its business), and

(b) a season ticket for the opera, costing the company £1,500.

Explain the tax treatment of these two items, assuming that the director in question owns 10% of the company's ordinary share capital.

***28.4** On 19 April 1996, a close company (which makes up accounts to 31 March annually) lends £100,000 to Siobhan, who is a director of the company and who owns 30% of its ordinary share capital. The company does not provide loans in the ordinary course of its business. Siobhan pays a commercial rate of interest on this loan until 1 October 1997, when she repays £40,000. On that date the company writes off the remaining £60,000 of the loan. Explain the tax implications of these transactions.

***28.5** A close company has the following results for the year to 31 March 1998 :

	£
Income from letting unfurnished property	89,000
Bank interest received	600
Dividends from UK companies (net amount)	1,200

(a) Compute the corporation tax payable for the year.

(b) Would it make any difference if the property income were trading income instead ?

(c) Would it make any difference if the property income were a net credit on non-trading loan relationships instead ?

Chapter 29

Groups of companies and reorganisations

Introduction

For corporation tax purposes, group of companies are divided into a number of categories and each category enjoys certain tax advantages. These advantages may include :

(a) the payment of dividends, charges and annual interest from one group member to another without accounting for ACT or income tax

(b) the "surrender" of ACT from one group member to another

(c) the transfer of trading losses from one group member to another

(d) the transfer of chargeable assets from one group member to another in such a way that no chargeable gain arises on the transfer.

However, groups of companies also incur certain tax disadvantages, principally a restriction of small companies relief. The main purpose of this chapter is to describe the categories of group which exist and the extent to which these advantages and disadvantages apply to each category. The tax implications of company reorganisations are also considered in this chapter.

Associated companies

For taxation purposes, two companies are "associated" if one of the companies is under the control of the other, or if they are both under the control of a third party (which may be an individual, a partnership or a company).

In this context, the word "control" means the same as it does in connection with close companies (see Chapter 28). Control over a company is deemed to accompany :

(a) ownership of over 50% of the company's issued share capital, or

(b) ownership of over 50% of the company's voting power, or

(c) entitlement to over 50% of the company's income, if all that income were distributed, or

(d) entitlement to over 50% of the company's assets, if the company were wound up.

The main consequence of two or more companies being associated with one another is that the upper and lower limits for small company relief purposes are divided equally between the companies concerned. This is an anti-avoidance measure, designed to block the practice of breaking large companies into several smaller ones in order to take advantage of the small companies rate of corporation tax. The following points should be noted :

(a) Companies which are associated for only part of a CAP are deemed for this purpose to be associated for the entire CAP.

(b) But if a company's CAP straddles two FY's and the SCR limits have changed between the two FY's, the CAP is treated as two separate "notional CAP's" for this purpose.

(c) Associated companies which are dormant are ignored.

EXAMPLE 1

S Ltd had chargeable profits of £240,000 for the year to 30 September 1994 and no franked investment income. Until 1 July 1994 the company had no associated companies but, on that date, its entire share capital was acquired by H Ltd. H Ltd has five other wholly-owned subsidiaries, two of which are dormant. Compute S Ltd's corporation tax liability for the year.

SOLUTION

The SCR limits changed on 1 April 1994 (see Chapter 24), so the CAP is divided into two notional CAP's for SCR purposes, as follows :

(i) 1 October 1993 to 31 March 1994 (182 days), during which S Ltd had no associated companies, and

(ii) 1 April 1994 to 30 September 1994 (183 days), during which S Ltd is deemed to have had four associated companies (i.e. H Ltd and its three active subsidiaries). During this period, S Ltd is entitled to only one-fifth of the SCR limits.

The computation is :

	FY93 (1/10/93 to 31/3/94)	*FY94 (1/4/94 to 30/9/94)*
Chargeable	£240,000 x 182/365 = £119,671	£240,000 x 183/365 = £120,329
Profits	£240,000 x 182/365 = £119,671	£240,000 x 183/365 = £120,329
Lower limit	£250,000 x 182/365 = £124,658	£300,000 x 183/365 x 1/5 = £30,082
Upper limit	£1.25m x 182/365 = £623,288	£1.5m x 183/365 x 1/5 = £150,411

Corporation tax due is as follows :

	£
FY93	
£119,671 @ 25%	29,917.75
FY94	
£120,329 @ 33%	39,708.57
Less : Marginal relief :	
$\frac{1}{50}$ x (£150,411 - £120,329) x $\frac{£120,329}{£120,329}$	601.64
	39,106.93
Total corporation tax liability	69,024.68

51% groups

Company A is a "51% subsidiary" of Company B (and Company B is the "parent" of Company A) if all of the following conditions are satisfied :

(a) Both companies are resident in the UK, and

(b) Company B owns, either directly or indirectly, more than 50% of Company A's ordinary share capital (ignoring any shares held indirectly through a non-UK resident company), and

(c) Company B is entitled to more than 50% of the profits available to Company A's ordinary shareholders, and

(d) Company B would be entitled to more than 50% of the assets available to Company A's ordinary shareholders if Company A were wound-up.

Two companies are said to be "members of a 51% group" if one is a 51% subsidiary of the other, or if they are both 51% subsidiaries of a third company.

EXAMPLE 2

P Ltd owns 80% of the ordinary share capital of Q Ltd, which owns 70% of the ordinary share capital of R Ltd and 60% of the ordinary share capital of S Ltd. All the companies are UK resident. Describe the relationship which exists between the following pairs of companies.

(a) P Ltd and Q Ltd
(b) Q Ltd and R Ltd
(c) Q Ltd and S Ltd
(d) P Ltd and R Ltd
(e) P Ltd and S Ltd.
(f) R Ltd and S Ltd

SOLUTION

(a) P Ltd owns more than 50% of the ordinary share capital of Q Ltd, so Q Ltd is a 51% subsidiary of P Ltd.

(b) Q Ltd owns more than 50% of the ordinary share capital of R Ltd, so R Ltd is a 51% subsidiary of Q Ltd.

(c) Q Ltd owns more than 50% of the ordinary share capital of S Ltd, so S Ltd is a 51% subsidiary of Q Ltd.

(d) P Ltd owns (indirectly) 80% x 70% = 56% of the ordinary share capital of R Ltd, so R Ltd is a 51% subsidiary of P Ltd.

(e) P Ltd owns (indirectly) 80% x 60% = 48% of the ordinary share capital of S Ltd, so S Ltd is not a 51% subsidiary of P Ltd.

(f) R Ltd and S Ltd are both 51% subsidiaries of the same parent company (Q Ltd).

By definition, members of a 51% group are also associated companies and therefore suffer from the restriction on small companies relief which is described above. On the other hand, 51% groups enjoy a number of tax advantages. The main advantages are that dividends, charges and annual interest payable between group members may be payable without accounting for ACT/income tax, and that ACT may be "surrendered" between group members. These advantages are described in detail below.

Group income, charges and annual interest

Dividends payable by a 51% subsidiary either to its parent or to a fellow 51% subsidiary may be paid without accounting for ACT. Such dividends are known as "group income". Note that :

(a) The two companies involved must elect jointly that dividends should be paid in this way. The election will not normally come into force until 3 months after the date of this election.

(b) Group income is *not* FII and so cannot be used by the receiving company to frank its own dividend payments. The effect of the election is therefore to reduce the ACT payable by one group company but, at a later stage, to increase the ACT payable by another group company. This provides a cashflow advantage to the group.

(c) The election may be revoked at any time and can also be set aside for any specified dividend. The election might be set aside for an individual dividend if the paying company has FII of its own which can be used to frank the dividend payment.

(d) Dividends which are (or which could have been) the subject of a group income election are *not* included in the "profits" of the receiving company for small companies relief purposes.

Similarly, an election may be made for charges and annual interest payable between a 51% subsidiary and its parent (in either direction) or from one 51% subsidiary to a fellow 51% subsidiary to be paid without accounting for income tax. This election may also be revoked at any time but cannot be set aside for individual payments. (A payment of "annual interest" is a payment of interest from which income tax would normally be deducted i.e. interest relating to a loan relationship).

EXAMPLE 3

Hold Ltd owns 60% of the ordinary share capital of Sub Ltd. The companies have elected jointly that dividends payable from Sub Ltd to Hold Ltd should be paid without accounting for ACT. Both companies make up their annual accounts to 31 March. During the year to 31 March 1998, the following dividends are paid :

	£	
Sub Ltd	50,000	paid 1 July 1997
Hold Ltd	400,000	paid 1 January 1998

(a) Compute the ACT payable for the year by each company (assuming that neither company receives any FII).

(b) Show how this would differ if the group income election had not been made.

SOLUTION

(a) 40% of the dividend paid by Sub Ltd (£20,000) is to the minority shareholders and will attract ACT. The amount payable by 14 October 1997 is £20,000 x 20/80 = £5,000.

The £30,000 dividend received by Hold Ltd from Sub Ltd is group income (not FII) and cannot be used to frank Hold Ltd's dividend payment. ACT on this payment, payable 14 April 1998, is £400,000 x 20/80 = £100,000.

(b) Without a group income election, Sub Ltd will pay ACT on its whole dividend payment. The amount due on 14 October 1997 is £50,000 x 20/80 = £12,500.

The dividend received by Hold Ltd now ranks as FII. ACT payable by Hold Ltd on 14 April 1998 is therefore (£400,000 - £30,000) x 20/80 = £92,500.

Note that, in both cases, the total ACT payable is £105,000 but the group obtains a cashflow benefit from making the group income election.

Surrender of ACT

A parent company which has paid ACT in relation to a CAP may "surrender" all or part of that ACT to a 51% subsidiary. The effect of this surrender is that the surrendered ACT is treated as if it had been paid not by the parent company but by the subsidiary company instead. Note that :

(a) The parent company may surrender any of its ACT, not just its surplus ACT.

(b) The subsidiary company must have been a 51% subsidiary of the parent company throughout the whole of the parent company's CAP.

(c) The surrendered ACT is treated in most respects as if it had been paid by the subsidiary company. However, if the subsidiary cannot make full use of the surrendered ACT in the CAP to which it relates, the surplus *cannot* be carried back to earlier CAP's. Such a surplus is carried forward and may be used in future CAP's, so long as the subsidiary company remains a 51% subsidiary of the parent company.

(d) If, in a given CAP, the subsidiary company has ACT of its own, as well as ACT surrendered to it by its parent, the surrendered ACT is relieved *before* the subsidiary's own ACT. This order of set-off benefits the subsidiary, since any of its own ACT which cannot be relieved may then be carried back to earlier CAP's (whereas surplus surrendered ACT can only be carried forward).

(e) Any amount of money paid to the parent by the subsidiary in exchange for the surrendered ACT is ignored for tax purposes so long as the amount of the payment does not exceed the amount of the surrendered ACT.

(f) A subsidiary company cannot surrender ACT to its parent company or to a fellow subsidiary. The only permissible surrender is from parent to subsidiary.

EXAMPLE 4

Upper Ltd has 9 wholly-owned subsidiaries, of which Lower Ltd is one. Both companies prepare accounts to 31 March each year. In the year to 31 March 1998, the two companies have the following results :

	Upper Ltd	*Lower Ltd*
	£	£
Trading profits	800,000	220,000
Group income (from Lower Ltd)	100,000	-
Group income (from other subsidiaries)	320,000	-
Dividends received from non-group companies	40,000	-
Dividends paid	750,000	100,000

Elections have been made for all dividends payable within the group to be paid without accounting for ACT. Assuming that Upper Ltd surrenders any surplus ACT to Lower Ltd, compute each company's corporation tax liability for the year.

SOLUTION

Upper Ltd has chargeable profits of £800,000 and profits for SCR purposes of £850,000 (£800,000 + £40,000 x 100/80). Since the small company limits are shared between 10 companies, the upper limit per company is only £150,000 so Upper Ltd must pay corporation tax at the full rate of 33%. Similarly, Lower Ltd must pay corporation tax at 33% on its chargeable profits of £220,000. The computation is as follows :

		Upper Ltd	*Lower Ltd*
		£	£
Chargeable profits		800,000	220,000
Corporation tax @ 33%		264,000	72,600
Less : Lower of :			
(a) ACT payable for the year : 20/80 x (£750,000 - £40,000)	177,500		
(b) Maximum ACT set-off : 20% x £800,000	160,000	160,000	
Surplus ACT surrendered	17,500		17,500
Mainstream corporation tax payable		104,000	55,100

75% groups

Company A is a "75% subsidiary" of Company B if all of the following conditions are satisfied :

(a) Both companies are resident in the UK, and

(b) Company B owns, either directly or indirectly, at least 75% of Company A's ordinary share capital (ignoring any shares held indirectly through a non-UK resident company), and

(c) Company B is entitled to at least 75% of the profits available to Company A's ordinary shareholders, and

(d) Company B would be entitled to at least 75% of the assets available to Company A's ordinary shareholders if Company A were wound-up.

Two companies are said to be "members of a 75% group" if one is a 75% subsidiary of the other, or if they are both 75% subsidiaries of a third company. By definition, the members of a 75% group are associated companies and are also members of a 51% group, with the tax implications described above. But the members of a 75% group benefit from two further tax reliefs. These are :

(a) the right to transfer trading losses and certain other items between group members ("group relief"), and

(b) the transfer of chargeable assets between group members in such a way that no chargeable gain arises on the transfer.

These reliefs are described in detail below.

Group relief

Group relief consists of the surrender of trading losses and/or certain other items by one member of a 75% group (the "surrendering company") to another member of the group (the "claimant company"). The items which may be surrendered are :

(a) trading losses (but not capital losses)

(b) net debits on non-trading loan relationships

(c) trade or non-trade charges in excess of profits for the CAP (i.e. profits *before* the deduction of losses or any other reliefs brought forward or carried back)

(d) excess management expenses of an investment company.

The surrender may be in whole or in part as best meets the requirements of the surrendering company and the claimant company. A group relief claim may be made in preference to any other loss relief claim, if desired. Note the following points :

(a) A surrender may be made from subsidiary to parent, from parent to subsidiary or from subsidiary to fellow subsidiary.

(b) Only current-period losses etc. are eligible for group relief and these must be set against profits of the claimant company for a *corresponding* CAP. If the CAP's of the surrendering company and the claimant company do not correspond exactly, group relief is available only in respect of the period of overlap between the two CAP's. The losses etc. of the surrendering company and the profits of the claimant company are time-apportioned so as to determine the amounts which fall into the overlap period.

(c) The amount surrendered to any one claimant company cannot exceed that claimant company's chargeable profits for the corresponding CAP, *after* the deduction of the claimant company's :

    (i) trading losses brought forward under Section 393(1), and

    (ii) net debits on non-trading loan relationships relieved against profits of the current period, and

    (iii) current-period trading losses which are relieved (or which could have been relieved) under S393A(1)(a), and

    (iv) charges for the CAP

    but *before* the deduction of trading losses carried back from a subsequent CAP under Section 393A(1)(b).

(d) A group relief claim must be made within 2 years of the end of the surrendering company's CAP.

(e) Any amount of money paid to the surrendering company by the claimant company as consideration for the surrendered items is ignored for tax purposes so long as the payment does not exceed the amount of the surrendered items.

EXAMPLE 5

Low Ltd is a wholly-owned subsidiary of High Ltd. Both companies prepare accounts to 31 March each year. Results for the year to 31 March 1998 are :

	High Ltd	*Low Ltd*
	£	£
Trading profit/(loss)	100,000	(180,000)
Chargeable gains	5,000	10,000
Trade charges	12,000	-

Show how the trading loss sustained by Low Ltd may be relieved.

SOLUTION

High Ltd has chargeable profits of £93,000 (£100,000 + £5,000 - £12,000). This sets an upper limit on the amount of group relief which may be claimed. The trading loss sustained by Low Ltd may be relieved in a number of ways. For example :

(a) The entire loss could be carried forward under S393(1).

(b) £10,000 of the loss could be relieved against the company's chargeable gains under S393A(1)(a) and the balance of £170,000 carried forward.

(c) The claim under S393A(1)(a) could be supplemented by a further claim under S393A(1)(b) to set the remaining £170,000 of the loss against the profits of Low Ltd for the previous 36 months.

(d) Group relief of anything up to £93,000 could be claimed and the balance of the loss then dealt with as above.

EXAMPLE 6

L Ltd prepares accounts annually to 31 March and is a 75% subsidiary of H Ltd, which prepares accounts annually to 31 December. Recent results are as follows :

	H Ltd	*L Ltd*
	£	£
Trading loss for year to 31 March 1997		(40,000)
Chargeable profits year to 31 December 1996	35,000	
Chargeable profits year to 31 December 1997	56,000	

Compute the amount of group relief that may be claimed.

SOLUTION

The CAP's of H Ltd and L Ltd do not correspond, so it is necessary to time-apportion profits and losses, as follows :

		1/4/96 - 31/12/96	*1/1/97 - 31/3/97*
		(275 days)	*(90 days)*
		£	£
(i)	H Ltd profit	26,370	13,808
(ii)	L Ltd loss	(30,137)	(9,863)

The group relief available in each period is the lower of (i) and (ii). Therefore, H Ltd may claim that group relief of £26,370 should be set against its 1996 profits and that group relief of £9,863 should be set against its 1997 profits. The remaining £3,767 of the loss is not eligible for group relief.

Using group relief effectively

Group relief should be used to ensure that trading losses are relieved as tax-effectively as possible and that the group's overall tax liability is minimised. Points to bear in mind are :

(a) Surrendering companies should surrender trading losses first to claimant companies which pay corporation tax at the marginal rate of 35.5%, then to claimant companies paying tax at 33% and only then to claimant companies paying tax at 23%.

(b) Claimant companies should consider claiming less than the full amount of capital allowances available for a CAP, so maximising the profits available for group relief set-off.

(c) A company with a trading loss should use the loss itself in a claim under S393A(1)(a) and S393A(1)(b), if this would save more tax than surrendering the loss to another group company.

Transfer of chargeable assets within a group

If a chargeable asset is transferred from one member of a 75% group to another, the transfer is deemed to have occurred at a value giving rise to neither a gain nor a loss. When an asset which has been transferred between group members in this way is finally disposed of outside the group, the chargeable gain arising on the disposal is then (in effect) calculated with reference to the original cost of the asset to the group.

The definition of a 75% group for this purpose is less rigorous than the definition given above in relation to group relief. A "capital gains group" consists of a "principal company", plus its 75% subsidiaries (as previously defined) plus the subsidiaries' 75% subsidiaries and so forth, subject to the overriding requirement that the principal company must have more than a 50% interest in each member of the group.

EXAMPLE 7

J Ltd owns 80% of the ordinary share capital of K Ltd, which owns 80% of the share capital of L Ltd, which owns 80% of the share capital of M Ltd, which owns 80% of the share capital of N Ltd. Which of these companies belongs to a capital gains group with J Ltd as the principal company ?

SOLUTION

At first sight, all five companies seem to belong to the capital gains group which has J Ltd at its head. However, J Ltd must have more than a 50% interest in each member of the group. J Ltd's actual interests in each member are as follows :

K Ltd	80%
L Ltd	80% x 80% = 64%
M Ltd	80% x 80% x 80% = 51.2%
N Ltd	80% x 80% x 80% x 80% = 40.96%

Therefore, N Ltd is not a member of this capital gains group.

Note that a chargeable gain may arise in relation to an intra-group transfer if a company has a chargeable asset transferred to it from another group member and then leaves the group within 6 years of the date of the transfer. The company leaving the group is deemed :

(a) to have sold the asset on the date of the intra-group transfer for its market value on that date (perhaps giving rise to a chargeable gain), and then

(b) to have immediately re-acquired the asset on the same date and for the same amount.

Any chargeable gain arising from this treatment is chargeable in the CAP in which the company leaves the group.

EXAMPLE 8

SubOne Ltd and SubTwo Ltd are members of a capital gains group. In January 1994, SubOne Ltd transferred a chargeable asset to SubTwo Ltd. The asset had originally cost £10,000 and its market value in January 1994 was £25,000. If the asset had been sold outside the group in January 1994, indexation allowance of £1,350 would have been available. In July 1997, SubTwo Ltd (which prepares accounts to 31 December each year) leaves the group. Calculate the chargeable gain arising on SubTwo Ltd's departure.

SOLUTION

SubTwo Ltd is deemed to have sold the asset for £25,000 in January 1994. This would have given rise to a chargeable gain of £13,650 (£25,000 - £10,000 - £1,350) so a chargeable gain of £13,650 arises in SubTwo Ltd's CAP for the year to 31 December 1997.

Roll-over relief for capital gains groups

For the purposes of roll-over relief on the replacement of a business asset (see Chapter 22), all the companies in a capital gains group are treated as a single company. This means that a gain arising on the disposal of a business asset by one member of a group can be rolled-over against the cost of a qualifying business asset acquired by any other member of that group.

It is important to note that the qualifying business asset against which a gain is rolled-over must be an asset which has been newly acquired *by the group as a whole.* It is not possible to roll-over a gain against an asset which has been acquired by one group member from another.

Capital losses

If a group member has capital losses, it is *not* possible to surrender those capital losses to another group member. This is in contrast to the treatment of trading losses, which can be surrendered between group members (see above). However, there is a way around this problem. Imagine that Company L and Company G are both members of a capital gains group, that Company L has capital losses and that Company G is about to dispose of an asset and realise a capital gain. Company L's capital losses can be set against this gain if the following procedure is adopted :

(a) Company G transfers the asset in question to Company L (giving rise to neither nor a loss).

(b) Company L then disposes of the asset. The disposal is now in Company L's name and therefore Company L's losses can be set against the gain arising on the disposal.

Pre-entry capital losses

A group which anticipates making disposals which will give rise to substantial capital gains might seek to shelter those gains by first acquiring a "capital loss company" i.e. a company which has substantial capital losses brought forward, or has assets which would realise substantial capital losses on disposal. The intention of such an acquisition would be to set these capital losses against the group's capital gains (by means of the procedure outlined above) and so reduce the group's overall corporation tax liability.

This tax-avoidance manoeuvre is prevented by TCGA 1992, which allows a group company's "pre-entry capital losses" to be set only against gains arising on the following types of disposal :

(a) disposals of assets which the company owned before it became a member of the group, and
(b) disposals of assets acquired by the company *from outside the group* since becoming a group member.

The "pre-entry capital losses" of a company are defined as :

(a) any capital losses incurred by the company before joining the group, and
(b) the pre-entry part of any capital losses incurred by the company after joining the group on the disposal of pre-entry assets.

When a company joins a group and subsequently disposes of a pre-entry asset at a loss, the pre-entry part of that loss is obtained by applying a formula to each item of allowable expenditure in the computation and then aggregating the results. The formula used is :

$$A \times \frac{B}{C} \times \frac{D}{E}$$

where : A = the total amount of the allowable loss

B = the amount of the item of allowable expenditure

C = the sum of the amounts of all the items of allowable expenditure

D = the length of time between the date of acquiring the asset (or 1 April 1982 if later) and the date of joining the group

E = the length of time between the date of acquiring the asset (or 1 April 1982 if later) and the date of disposal.

EXAMPLE 9

A company acquired a chargeable asset on 1 January 1988 at a cost of £200,000 and incurred enhancement expenditure of a further £50,000 on 1 January 1992. The company joined a capital gains group on 1 April 1997 and the asset was sold on 1 September 1997 for £130,000. Calculate the total loss arising on this disposal and the amount of the pre-entry loss (calculating to the nearest whole month).

SOLUTION

	£	£
Sale proceeds		130,000
Less : Cost	200,000	
Enhancement	50,000	250,000
Allowable loss		(120,000)

Notes :

(i) Indexation allowance is £nil, since indexation allowance cannot be used to increase a loss.

(ii) The asset was originally acquired 111 months before joining the group and 116 months before disposal. The enhancement expenditure was incurred 63 months before joining the group and 68 months before disposal.

(iii) The pre-entry loss is :

$$£120{,}000 \times \frac{£200{,}000}{£250{,}000} \times \frac{111}{116} + £120{,}000 \times \frac{£50{,}000}{£250{,}000} \times \frac{63}{68} = £114{,}097.$$

Pre-entry surplus ACT

In Chapter 25, it was stated that there are restrictions on the carry-forward of a company's surplus ACT when the ownership of the company changes and there is a major change in the nature of the company's business. Another restriction on the relief of surplus ACT arises when a company joins a group, but this time there is no need for there to be a major change in the nature of the company's business. The restriction is that the company's "pre-entry surplus ACT" cannot be set against the corporation tax due in relation to disposals of chargeable assets which :

(a) are acquired from other group members (on a no-gain, no-loss basis), and

(b) are disposed of within 3 years of the company joining the group.

This provision is intended to prevent groups from acquiring ACT-rich companies with the sole intention of using the surplus ACT to avoid paying corporation tax on the group's capital gains.

Consortia

A company is owned by a consortium (and is known as a "consortium company") if at least 75% of its ordinary share capital is owned by other UK resident companies (known as "consortium members"), each of which :

(a) owns at least 5% but less than 75% of the consortium company's ordinary share capital, and

(b) is entitled to at least 5% of the profits available to the consortium company's ordinary shareholders, and

(c) would be entitled to at least 5% of the assets available to the consortium company's ordinary shareholders on a winding-up.

A 90% subsidiary of a consortium company is also a consortium company.

Group relief for a consortium

Group relief (see above) is available in either direction between a consortium member and a consortium company, so long as the consortium company is either :

(a) a trading company, or

(b) a holding company, which (for this purpose) is one whose business consists wholly or mainly of holding shares in trading companies which are its 90% subsidiaries.

Note the following points :

(a) The relief available is restricted in proportion to the consortium member's shareholding in the consortium company. For instance, if CC Ltd is a consortium company and CM Ltd is a consortium member which owns x% of CC Ltd, CM Ltd may claim up to x% of CC Ltd's losses. Alternatively, CM Ltd may surrender to CC Ltd losses of up to x% of CC Ltd's profits.

(b) A group relief claim must be agreed by all the consortium members.

(c) The amount of a consortium company's trading loss which is available for group relief is the amount of the loss less any potential claim for loss relief under S393A(1)(a), whether or not such a claim is actually made.

EXAMPLE 10

The ordinary share capital of W Ltd (a UK trading company) is owned 30% by X Ltd, 25% by Y Ltd and 45% by Z Ltd. All companies are UK resident and prepare accounts to 31 March annually. Results for the year to 31 March 1998 are as follows :

	W Ltd	*X Ltd*	*Y Ltd*	*Z Ltd*
	£	£	£	£
Trading profit/(loss)	(62,000)	41,000	11,000	38,000
Chargeable gains	10,000	-	-	-

What are the maximum possible group relief claims which may be made ?

SOLUTION

The amount of W Ltd's loss which is available for group relief is £52,000 i.e. £62,000 less a potential S393A(1)(a) claim of £10,000 (whether or not that claim is actually made). This is shared between the consortium members in proportion to their shares in the consortium, as follows :

	X Ltd	*Y Ltd*	*Z Ltd*
	£	£	£
Share of W Ltd's available loss	15,600	13,000	23,400
Chargeable profits	41,000	11,000	38,000
Maximum group relief claim	15,600	11,000	23,400

Group income, charges & annual interest for a consortium

Dividends payable by a consortium company to a consortium member may, on election, be paid without accounting for ACT. Similarly, charges and annual interest payable by a consortium company to a consortium member may be paid without accounting for income tax.

Reorganisations

If a company transfers a trade to another company (or to an individual), this ranks as a cessation of that trade. Therefore, in normal circumstances, any unrelieved trading losses incurred before the date of the transfer cannot be carried forward under S393(1) and set against the subsequent profits of the transferred trade.

However, if a trade is transferred between two companies and at least 75% of the trade is (in effect) owned by the same persons both :

(a) at some time within the year before the date of the transfer, and

(b) at some time within the two years after the date of the transfer

the unrelieved trading losses of the transferor company may be carried forward and set against the future trading profits (from that same trade) of the transferee company. This "succession of trade" relief is applicable if, for instance, a company creates a new wholly-owned subsidiary and then transfers a trade to that subsidiary. Note the following points in relation to such a transfer :

(a) For capital allowances purposes, assets are transferred at their tax-written down values, with no balancing adjustments.

(b) Chargeable business assets are transferred to the transferee company on a no-gain, no-loss basis, so long as the transferor company receives no consideration for the assets.

(c) Only trading losses may be carried forward as described above. The relief does not extend to non-trading losses, capital losses, surplus ACT or surplus FII, none of which can be carried forward.

Summary

- Two companies are associated if one of the companies is under the control of the other, or if they are both under the control of a third party.
- The upper and lower limits for small companies relief purposes are shared equally between associated companies.

- Dividends payable by a 51% subsidiary either to its parent or to a fellow 51% subsidiary may be paid without accounting for ACT. Such dividends are known as "group income".
- Charges and annual interest payable between a 51% subsidiary and its parent (in either direction) or from one 51% subsidiary to a fellow 51% subsidiary may be paid without accounting for income tax.
- A parent company may surrender ACT to a 51% subsidiary.
- Trading losses and related items may be surrendered between members of a 75% group. This is known as "group relief".
- Chargeable assets may be transferred between members of a capital gains group without giving rise to a chargeable gain.
- Subject to certain conditions, group relief is available between consortium members and consortium companies.
- If a trade is transferred between two companies, the unrelieved trading losses of the transferor company may, if certain conditions are satisfied, be carried forward and set against the subsequent trading profits of the transferee company.

Exercises

29.1 Arm Ltd and Foot Ltd are both 100% subsidiaries of Head Ltd, which has no other subsidiaries. They are all UK resident. How will the relationship of the three companies affect the way in which they are taxed ?

29.2 Alpha Ltd is a wholly-owned subsidiary of Beta Ltd, which has two other wholly-owned subsidiaries (one of which is dormant). In the year to 31 March 1998, Alpha Ltd has the following results :

	£
Trading profits, less capital allowances	220,000
Bank deposit interest	6,000
UFII (gross)	4,000
Dividends received from non-group companies	24,000
Patent royalties paid (gross)	17,000

Compute the corporation tax liability for the year.

29.3 Gamma Ltd owns 85% of the ordinary share capital of Delta Ltd. An election has been made for dividends payable from Delta Ltd to Gamma Ltd to be paid without accounting for ACT. Both companies prepare accounts annually to 31 December and dividends are paid as follows in the year to 31 December 1997 :

	£	
Gamma Ltd	1,000,000	paid 1 February 1997
Delta Ltd	200,000	paid 12 July 1997

(a) Compute the ACT payable for the year by each company, assuming that neither company has any FII.

(b) Compute the ACT payable by each company if the group income election is set aside for the dividend paid on 12 July 1997.

29.4 Base Ltd is a wholly-owned subsidiary of Apex Ltd. Both companies prepare accounts annually to 31 March and the results for the year to 31 March 1998 are as follows :

	Apex Ltd	*Base Ltd*
	£	£
Trading profit/(loss)	120,000	(90,000)
Trading losses b/f under S393(1)	(42,000)	(19,000)
Schedule A income	7,000	3,000
Trade charges	12,000	4,000

Calculate the maximum group relief that may be claimed for the year by Apex Ltd.

29.5 A1 Ltd owns 90% of the ordinary share capital of A2 Ltd. A2 Ltd owns 80% of the ordinary share capital of A3 Ltd and 70% of the ordinary share capital of A4 Ltd. Which of these companies forms a capital gains group with A1 Ltd as its principal company ?

29.6 The ordinary share capital of PP Ltd (a UK trading company) is owned 32% by QQ Ltd, 35% by RR Ltd, 23% by SS Ltd. The remaining 10% is owned by various individuals, none of whom own more than 1%. All companies are UK resident and prepare accounts to 31 July annually. Results for the year to 31 July 1997 are as follows :

	PP Ltd	*QQ Ltd*	*RR Ltd*	*SS Ltd*
	£	£	£	£
Trading profit/(loss)	(96,000)	41,000	38,000	11,000
Chargeable gains	-	15,000	-	-
Schedule D Case III income	12,000	6,000	11,000	4,000
Trade charges	-	(3,000)	(2,000)	(1,000)

Compute the maximum possible group relief claims.

***29.7** T Ltd owns 90% of the ordinary share capital of B Ltd. Recent results for the two companies are as follows :

	T Ltd	*T Ltd*	*B Ltd*
	y/e 31/3/97	*y/e 31/3/98*	*y/e 30/11/97*
	£	£	£
Trading profit(loss)	190,000	130,000	(174,000)
Chargeable gains	25,000	13,000	8,000
Patent royalties paid (gross)	5,000	5,000	4,000

No dividends have been paid or received by either company in any of these CAP's and maximum group relief is claimed. Calculate the corporation tax payable by each company for each CAP, making and stating any necessary assumptions.

***29.8** Height Ltd has 4 wholly-owned subsidiaries. All companies in the group prepare accounts to 31 March each year. One of the subsidiaries is Depth Ltd, which has the following results :

	y/e 31/3/97	*y/e 31/3/98*
	£	£
Trading profit	110,000	140,000
Bank interest received	2,000	2,400
Charitable covenant paid (gross)	3,000	3,600
Dividend paid	40,000	20,000

No election has been made for dividends to be paid by Depth Ltd without accounting for ACT. In the year to 31 March 1998, Height Ltd surrendered ACT of £30,000 to Depth Ltd.

Calculate the mainstream corporation tax payable by Depth Ltd for each of the two years, assuming that any reliefs are taken at the earliest opportunity.

Review questions (Set C)

C1 Tolbooth Ltd is a small manufacturing company. It commenced trading on 1 April 1996 and prepared its first set of accounts for the 18 month period to 30 September 1997. As the accounting technician responsible for preparing the tax computation, you have extracted the following information from the audit file :

		£
(i)	Trading profits (before capital allowances)	390,000
(ii)	Rental income (unfurnished) : £20,000 per year received annually in advance on 30 September	
(iii)	Bank deposit interest received gross :	
	30 June 1996	2,000
	31 December 1996	3,000
	30 June 1997	15,000
(iv)	Plant and machinery was purchased on 30 June 1996, costing	100,000
(v)	Patent royalties (gross amounts) :	
	Paid 31 December 1996	5,000
	Paid 30 June 1997	5,000
	Accrued to 30 September 1997	2,500

Required :

(a) State how the first period of account to 30 September 1997 will be divided into chargeable accounting periods.

(b) Calculate the corporation tax due for each chargeable accounting period. *(AAT)*

C2 P Ltd is a company with various shareholdings in other UK companies. As a means of avoiding National Insurance Contributions, it pays regular dividends to its directors, who are the only shareholders. It is in receipt of periodic payments in respect of patent royalties and it pays debenture interest twice in each accounting period. The following is a list, in date order, of the various transactions of the above type during the year to 31 March 1998 (amounts are shown net) :

		£
10/4/97	Dividends received from UK companies	12,000
8/5/97	Dividends paid to directors	9,600
10/5/97	Patent royalties received	24,640
12/7/97	Debenture interest paid	36,000
15/8/97	Dividends paid to directors	40,000
30/8/97	Patent royalties received	15,400

		£
12/10/97	Dividends received from UK companies	4,800
16/11/97	Dividends received from UK companies	14,400
24/11/97	Debenture interest paid	32,000
30/11/97	Charitable covenant paid	9,240
15/1/98	Patent royalties received	21,560
30/1/98	Dividends paid to directors	19,200

The directors wish to have information on the cash inflows and outflows arising from the taxation associated with each transaction.

You are required :

To calculate, by means of quarterly settlement statements for both ACT/FII and income tax, the amounts which became payable and/or recoverable in each case, stating the date (or approximate date) concerned. *(CIMA)*

C3 Poynton Producers Ltd, who make up annual accounts to 30 September, purchased a new industrial building for £150,000 on 1 April 1991. The building was not in an enterprise zone and was bought into industrial use immediately. On 31 August 1993, production ceased and the building was leased to a national charity as a collection centre. Production in the factory re-commenced on 1 February 1995. On 1 April 1997 the building was sold to Sale Switches Ltd, who make up annual accounts to 31 December, for £140,000. It was brought into industrial use immediately.

You are required to calculate :

(a) the Industrial Buildings Allowances for all accounting periods when the building was owned by Poynton Producers Ltd

(b) the balancing adjustment on the sale of the building in 1997

(c) the Industrial Buildings Allowances claimable by Sale Switches Ltd in respect of the building in future years. *(ACCA)*

C4 During 1993, Mr J developed a revolutionary method of manufacturing portable phones. He patented the invention and formed a company, CP Ltd, to manufacture the product, at the same time allowing other firms to manufacture the phones under a royalty arrangement.

At first the business enjoyed modest success but a recession eventually caused the market for the products of CP Ltd to collapse, resulting in a substantial trading loss in 1996. On 1 January 1997, the company became involved solely in the manufacture of cardboard boxes and a very modest recovery took place. The results of the company since its formation are :

	y/e 31/12/94 £000	*y/e 31/12/95* £000	*y/e 31/12/96* £000	*y/e 31/12/97* £000
INCOME				
Adjusted trading profit	30	50	-	10
Adjusted trading loss	-	-	(170)	-
Schedule A	10	8	-	-
Bank interest	12	4	-	2
Capital gain	-	-	20	-
Patent royalties (gross)	10	10	5	4
CHARGES PAID (gross)				
Trade charges	-	8	8	2
Charitable covenant	1	1	1	1
DIVIDEND PAID (on 1/5/95)	-	28	-	-

You are required :

(a) To set out the assessments to corporation tax for each of the above accounting periods. You are to assume relief for the trading loss is claimed in full at the earliest opportunity. You should show the amounts, if any, available for carry forward at 31 December 1997.

(b) To advise the directors of the amounts of corporation tax which will be repayable as a result of the loss claim and of the amount of corporation tax payable for the accounting period to 31 December 1997. (*Note* : No patent royalties were received and no charges were paid in the first 3 months of the accounting period). *(CIMA)*

C5 Antietam Ltd makes up accounts to 31 March annually. Results for the 12 months to 31 March 1998 are as follows :

	£
Trading profits	170,000
Capital allowances	32,000
Unfurnished rental income	18,000
Patent royalties received (net)	21,560
Capital gains	6,400

The company has capital losses brought forward from previous accounting periods of £1,400 and paid a charitable covenant on 31 March 1998 of £15,400 net. It also received a dividend from ICI plc on 16 December 1997 of £12,800.

Required :

(a) Calculate the mainstream corporation tax liability of Antietam Ltd for the year to 31 March 1998.

(b) Recalculate the liability if you are told that the company has one subsidiary company. *(AAT)*

***C6** Undulating Uplands Ltd is a UK resident manufacturing company with no associated companies. It had always made up accounts to 30 November but decided to change the year end from November to February. The company's results for the period from 1 December 1996 to 28 February 1998 are summarised below :

	Notes	£
Adjusted trading profit		750,000
Dividends received from UK companies	1	40,000
Bank interest received	2,7	13,000
Building society interest received	3,7	8,400
Patent royalties received (gross amount)	4,8	20,000
Charitable covenant paid (gross amount)	5,8	16,000
Dividends paid	6	147,200
Capital allowances on plant and machinery	16	85,000

The following additional information is available :

1. Dividends were received from UK companies as follows :

	£
30/12/96	6,400
30/3/97	9,600
30/9/97	8,000
30/1/98	16,000

2. Bank interest was credited by Natland Bank plc as follows :

	£
21/12/96	4,900
20/6/97	3,600
21/12/97	4,500

3. Building society interest was credited by Northshires Building Society as follows :

	£
31/3/97	4,000
30/9/97	4,400

4. Patent royalties were received as follows :

	£
28/2/97	4,000
31/5/97	4,000
31/8/97	4,000
30/11/97	4,000
28/2/98	4,000

5. The charitable covenant was paid as follows :

	£
15/5/97	8,000
15/11/97	8,000

6. Dividends were paid as follows :

	£
20/1/97	99,200
26/5/97	35,200
20/1/98	12,800

7. The amounts shown for bank and building society interest received are the actual amounts received.
8. Income tax has been deducted from the patent royalties received and charitable covenant paid.
9. The company has claimed maximum set-off of advance corporation tax in all periods to 30 November 1996.
10. The company had no advance corporation tax to carry forward on 30 November 1996.
11. The company had surplus franked investment income of £7,000 on 1 December 1996.
12. The company had trading losses brought forward of £400,000 on 1 December 1996.
13. The company had capital losses brought forward of £15,000 on 1 December 1996.
14. On 1 September 1997, the company bought a factory which qualifies for Industrial Buildings Allowance from the original owner for £450,000. The factory was first brought into qualifying use by the original owner on 1 September 1982. It had then cost £250,000 and a 75% initial allowance had been claimed. It was not in an Enterprise Zone. There had been no non-qualifying use before 1 September 1997.
15. The company had purchased a new factory, which qualified for Industrial Buildings Allowance, on 1 January 1992 for £150,000. It was brought into use immediately. The factory was sold on 1 January 1998 for £350,000. An appropriate claim to minimise the chargeable capital gain is made. The building was not in an Enterprise Zone. (Assume RPI's of 135.6 in January 1992 and 158.3 in January 1998).
16. The capital allowances figure of £85,000 comprised :

	£
12 months to 30/11/97	55,000
3 months to 28/2/98	30,000

You are required :

To calculate the mainstream corporation tax payable for the chargeable accounting periods ended 28 February 1998 and to state when this is payable. *(ACCA)*

***C7** R Ltd is a small company engaged in the manufacture and distribution of plumbing equipment. Following a period of poor trading results, its taxable income in recent years has been approximately £180,000. Early in 1997 the directors estimated that the taxable profits would be £220,000 for each of the two years to 31 March 1998 and 1999.

In March 1997, the directors were considering the possibility of R Ltd acquiring a controlling interest in two other small companies in the same trade - S Ltd and T Ltd. The taxable profits of each of these companies for the two years above were estimated at £15,000 per annum.

You are required :

To advise the directors of the differing aggregate corporation tax liabilities which will arise if :

(i) the above plan is adopted

(ii) R Ltd acquires the businesses of S Ltd and T Ltd - taking over their assets, trades and workforces, but not acquiring a shareholding. S Ltd and T Ltd would be wound up. *(CIMA)*

***C8** On 1 August 1994 X Ltd granted a 20-year lease to Y Ltd on the following terms :

- An annual rental of £20,000, payable quarterly in advance on 1 August, 1 November, 1 February and 1 May each year.
- A premium of £80,000 payable by Y Ltd on 1 August 1994.

On 1 April 1997, Y Ltd intends sub-letting the premises to Z Ltd on the following terms :

- A term of 5 years, at the end of which Y Ltd will resume occupancy.
- An annual rental of £28,000, payable in advance each year on 1 April.
- A premium of £45,000 payable by Z Ltd on 1 April 1997.

You are required :

(a) To compute, for the year ended 31 March 1995, the amount assessed to corporation tax under Schedule A on X Ltd and the amount of the premium which Y Ltd may deduct in arriving at its trading profits chargeable to corporation tax. (Assume that both companies make up accounts annually to 31 March).

(b) To compute the amount assessed to corporation tax under Schedule A on Y Ltd for its year ended 31 March 1998.

(c) To comment briefly on the capital gains implications of the above transactions.

(CIMA)

***C9** Mr B has been production manager in a large engineering firm for several years, earning approximately £40,000 p.a. He has recently decided to start up his own business and seeks your advice on all of the differences, from a taxation point of view, between trading as a sole trader or as a limited company. It is possible that his wife will become involved in the running of the business.

He has estimated that during the first year, while the business is developing, it is unlikely that any profit will result. Indeed, it is possible that a loss will arise. Thereafter he anticipates that profits will rise rapidly to approximately £70,000 p.a. His living expenses amount to about £15,000 per year and initially this will be provided from his savings.

You are required :

To prepare a list of headings which would be contained in a report designed to highlight these differences. Under each heading, you should give a brief description of the difference between trading as a sole trader or as a company. You are not required to write the complete report. *(CIMA)*

***C10** HD Ltd owns 80% of the ordinary share capital of SD Ltd. These shares were acquired during 1984. Both companies are UK resident for tax purposes and neither has any other associated companies. Their most recent results have been :

	HD Ltd *y/e 31/12/97* £	*SD Ltd* *9 months to 31/3/98* £
INCOME		
Trading profit	890,000	-
Trading loss	-	102,000
Bank interest	6,000	4,000
Schedule A	2,000	8,000
Capital gains	-	20,000
Capital losses	15,000	-
Dividend from SD Ltd (under group income election)	24,000	-
Dividends from UK companies (gross figure)	-	40,000
CHARGES PAID		
Trade charge (gross figure)	4,000	5,000
DIVIDEND PAID	327,000	30,000

A group income election is in force.

You are required :

(a) To compute the corporation tax payable by each company for the above accounting periods, assuming that maximum group relief is claimed by HD Ltd.

(b) To advise the directors on a more tax-efficient treatment of the inter-company dividend.

(c) To suggest a more tax-efficient way in which HD Ltd might have arranged the sales of the assets which gave rise to the capital gains and losses shown above.

(CIMA)

PART 4
MISCELLANEOUS

Chapter 30

Value added tax

Introduction

This chapter is concerned with value added tax (VAT), which is an indirect tax charged on the supply of a wide variety of goods and services. The tax was introduced in 1973 but current legislation is to be found in the VAT Act 1994, as amended by subsequent Finance Acts. As stated in Chapter 1, VAT is administered by the Customs and Excise, not by the Inland Revenue.

The principle of VAT

The basic principle of VAT is that tax should be charged at each stage of the production and distribution process but that the total tax due should be borne by the final consumer of the product. This is achieved as follows :

(a) Traders who are registered for VAT (see below) are required to charge VAT on their sales and must account for this "output tax" to Customs and Excise, but

(b) such traders are allowed to recover from Customs and Excise the "input tax" which they pay to their own suppliers, so that

(c) in effect, registered traders suffer no VAT and the total VAT is borne by the consumer at the end of the distribution chain.

EXAMPLE 1

A Ltd owns a quarry. It extracts stone from this quarry and sells the stone to B Ltd for £10,000 plus VAT. B Ltd converts all the stone into paving slabs and sells these slabs to C Ltd for £18,000, plus VAT. C Ltd owns and runs a garden centre, where the slabs are sold to the general public for a total of £32,000, plus VAT. Show how VAT is charged and collected at each stage of this process. (Assume that VAT is to be calculated at 17.5% throughout).

SOLUTION

	Cost price before VAT	*Input tax*	*Selling price before VAT*	*Output tax*	*Paid to C & E*
	£	£	£	£	£
A Ltd	-	-	10,000	1,750	1,750
B Ltd	10,000	1,750	18,000	3,150	1,400
C Ltd	18,000	3,150	32,000	5,600	2,450
Total VAT charged					5,600

Note :

None of the three companies involved suffers any net VAT. In each case, the total of input tax paid to suppliers and the amount due to Customs and Excise is precisely equal to the output tax received from customers. The final consumers, who are unable to reclaim the VAT which they pay, bear the total VAT of £5,600.

Taxable persons

Formally, VAT is chargeable when a *taxable person* makes a *taxable supply* of goods or services in the course of business.

For VAT purposes, the term "person" can refer to an individual, a partnership or a company, as well as to any other body which is supplying goods or services in the course of business. There is no requirement that a profit motive should exist, merely that goods or services are supplied for a consideration, so the term "person" can also refer to a charity, a club, an association etc.

A *taxable person* is a person making taxable supplies who is, or who should be, registered for VAT. Persons must register if their turnover of taxable items exceeds a prescribed threshold and might register voluntarily even if their turnover is below the threshold (see later in this chapter).

A taxable person charges VAT to customers when supplying them with taxable items, must account for this output tax to the Customs and Excise and may reclaim the tax suffered on inputs. A person who is not a taxable person can neither charge VAT to customers nor reclaim input tax.

Taxable supplies

A *taxable supply* is any supply of goods or services in the UK other than a supply which is specifically exempted from VAT. The rate at which VAT is charged on a taxable supply may be either the standard rate (17.5%), the zero rate (0%) or the special rate (8%) which applies only to domestic fuel and power. The types of supply which are taxable at each of these rates and the types of supply which are exempted from VAT altogether are described later in this chapter.

Supply of goods

A supply of goods is deemed to occur when the ownership of goods passes from one person to another. In general, a supply of goods will fall within the scope of VAT only if it is made for a consideration (i.e. in return for money or payment in kind) but the following are also deemed to be supplies of goods for VAT purposes :

(a) gifts of business assets, other than gifts costing no more than £15 and gifts consisting of samples
(b) goods permanently taken out of a business for private use by the owner or an employee of the business, in respect of which input tax has been paid.

The sale of goods on hire purchase is deemed to be a supply of goods even though, strictly speaking, ownership of the goods does not transfer until the end of the hire purchase contract. VAT is charged on the cash price of the goods, not the hire purchase price.

Supply of services

Any supply which is made for a consideration but which is not a supply of goods is deemed to be a supply of services. However, a gift of services is not a taxable supply. The hiring of goods to a customer is a supply of services, not a supply of goods, since the ownership of the goods does not pass to the customer. A supply of services is also deemed to occur if the owner or an employee of a business :

(a) temporarily makes private use of goods owned by the business, in respect of which input tax has been paid, or
(b) makes private use of services which have been supplied to the business, in respect of which input tax has been paid.

By concession, the private use of a business motor car does not rank as a taxable supply.

Exempt supplies

A supply of goods or services is an exempt supply if it falls within one of twelve exemption groups. In summary, these exemption groups are as follows :

Group 1 The sale or lease of land and buildings, other than :

(i) the sale (or lease for more than 21 years) of new buildings or reconstructed listed buildings to be used for residential or charitable purposes (zero-rated)

(ii) the sale of new commercial buildings or of land to be used for their construction (standard-rated)

(iii) used commercial buildings, if the vendor has elected to treat the supply as taxable at the standard rate (the "option to tax", see below).

Group 2 Insurance

Group 3 Postal services provided by the Post Office

Group 4 Betting, gaming and lotteries

Group 5 Financial services (e.g. bank charges, stockbroking, underwriting)

Group 6 Education provided by schools, universities and further education colleges

Group 7 Health and welfare services

Group 8 Burial and cremation services

Group 9 Supplies made to members of trade unions and professional bodies in return for a membership subscription

Group 10 Entry fees paid to non-profit-making bodies for the right to enter sports competitions

Group 11 Disposals of works of art to approved bodies (e.g. the National Gallery)

Group 12 Fund-raising events organised by charities.

The implications of a supply of goods or services being an exempt supply are as follows :

(a) VAT cannot be charged on an exempt supply.

(b) A person who makes only exempt supplies cannot register for VAT, charges no output tax, is not a taxable person and, most importantly, cannot reclaim input tax.

(c) In effect, a person making only exempt supplies is in the same position as the final consumer at the end of a distribution chain.

It is this inability to reclaim input tax which might lead the vendor of a used commercial building to elect for the "option to tax" (see above). If the election is made, the vendor charges output tax on the sale or rent of the building, becomes a taxable person and may reclaim input tax. Of course, the buyer of the building will have to pay VAT, but if the buyer is also a taxable person then he or she will be able to reclaim the tax paid and therefore may not object to the arrangement.

Zero-rated supplies

Supplies which are made by a taxable person and which are not specifically exempted from VAT are taxed at the standard rate of 17.5% unless they consist of domestic fuel and power (taxed at 8%) or fall within one of sixteen zero-rated groups. These are listed below.

Group 1 Food, but certain luxury foods (e.g. chocolates) and food supplied in the course of catering are standard-rated

Group 2 Sewerage services and water (other than for industrial use)

Group 3 Books, newspapers, journals etc. (but stationery is standard-rated)

Group 4 Talking books, radios etc. for the blind

Group 5 The sale by builders of new buildings to be used for residential or charitable purposes and second-hand buildings which were previously non-residential but which have been converted for residential use. Zero-rating also applies to the amount payable by a tenant on the grant of a lease of more than 21 years on such a building.

Group 6 The sale by builders of substantially reconstructed "protected buildings" (i.e. listed buildings) to be used for residential or charitable purposes. As for Group 5, zero-rating also applies to leases of more than 21 years on such buildings.

Group 7 International services (e.g. making arrangements for services which are to be performed outside the European Union)

Group 8 Passenger transport, but pleasure transport and transport in vehicles seating less than 12 people (e.g. taxis) are standard-rated

Group 9 Certain caravans and houseboats

Group 10 Gold supplied by a central bank to another central bank or to a member of the London Gold Market

Group 11 Bank notes

Group 12 Drugs, medicines etc. prescribed by a medical practitioner

Group 13 Certain exports (see later in this chapter)

Group 14 Sales in tax-free shops

Group 15 Sale by a charity of donated goods, and certain supplies to a charity (e.g. advertising)

Group 16 Children's clothing and footwear and certain protective clothing (e.g. crash helmets).

The implications of a supply of goods or services being zero-rated are as follows :

(a) The supply is a taxable supply but the VAT due is calculated at 0% so, in effect, no tax is charged.

(b) A person who makes only zero-rated supplies is nonetheless making taxable supplies and must register as a taxable person if taxable turnover exceeds the prescribed threshold. Having registered (and this may be done voluntarily, even if taxable turnover is less than the threshold, as explained below) the person will then be able to reclaim all input tax paid.

The value of a supply

The "value" of a taxable supply is the amount on which the VAT charge is based and this is normally equal to the price (before VAT) charged by the supplier. For example, if a standard-rated supply is made at a price of £1,000, plus VAT at 17.5%, then the value of the supply is £1,000 and the total consideration given for the supply is £1,175.

The VAT component of the consideration (for standard-rated supplies) can be found by multiplying the consideration by the "VAT fraction" which is currently 17.5/117.5 = 7/47. Note the following points regarding the value of a supply :

(a) If a supply consists of a gift of business assets, the value of the supply is deemed to be the price (excluding VAT) which the person receiving the gift would have to pay to purchase goods identical in every respect to the goods concerned. This rule also applies if assets are taken permanently out of a business for private use by the owner or an employee of the business.

(b) If the owner or an employee temporarily makes private use of business assets, the value of the resulting supply of services is the cost of providing the services. This cost is based on the amount by which the assets have depreciated whilst being used for private purposes.

(c) If private use is made of services which have been supplied to the business, the value of the resulting supply of services is equal to an appropriate proportion of the value of the supply which was made to the business.

(d) If the consideration for a supply is paid in kind or if the supply is made to a connected person for less than market value, the value of the supply is taken to be the market value of the goods or services supplied.

EXAMPLE 2

(a) A standard-rated supply is made with a value of £180. Calculate the VAT charged and the total consideration for the supply.

(b) A standard-rated supply is made for a total consideration of £1,739. Calculate the VAT element and the value of the supply.

SOLUTION

(a) The VAT charged is £31.50 (£180 x 17.5%) and therefore the total consideration is £211.50.

(b) The VAT element is £259 (£1,739 x 7/47) and therefore the value of the supply is £1,480.

Cash discounts

If a customer is offered a cash discount in return for prompt payment, the value of the supply is the price charged by the supplier (before VAT), less the maximum cash discount which the customer might receive. This is the case whether or not the customer actually takes advantage of the discount.

Note that the VAT fraction cannot be used to calculate the VAT component of the consideration if a cash discount is offered but not taken.

EXAMPLE 3

A standard-rated supply is made at a price of £4,000, plus VAT. The customer is offered a 3% discount if payment is made within 30 days. Calculate the value of the supply and the VAT charged on the supply.

SOLUTION

The value of the supply is £3,880 (£4,000, less 3%) and the VAT charged is £679 (£3,880 x 17.5%). If the customer pays within 30 days, the consideration will be £4,559. If the customer pays after 30 days, the consideration will be £4,679 (£4,000 + £679).

Mixed supplies

A "mixed supply" occurs if a mixture of goods and/or services is invoiced together at a single inclusive price. If all of the items in the mixture are chargeable to VAT at the same rate, the value of the supply and the related output tax can be calculated in the usual way. Otherwise, it will be necessary to apportion the price charged between the various elements of the mixture in order to calculate the output tax due. There is no standard way of achieving this apportionment but the method used must be fair and justifiable.

EXAMPLE 4

A VAT-exclusive price of £320 is charged for a mixed supply of goods. The goods concerned consist of standard-rated goods which cost the supplier £141 (excluding VAT) and zero-rated goods which cost the supplier £19. Calculate the output tax due.

SOLUTION

The value of the supply represented by standard-rated goods is £320 x 141/160 i.e. £282. VAT at 17.5% of this figure gives £49.35. Therefore the total price charged should be £369.35.

Composite supplies

A "composite supply" occurs if a mixture of goods and/or services is supplied together in such a way that it is not possible to split the supply into its component parts. In this case, the supply as a whole must be considered in order to determine the rate of tax due (if any). For example, in the case of *Mander Laundries Ltd* (1973) it was held that the services of a launderette consist of a single, standard-rated supply of services, not a mixed supply of water, heat, hire of washing machines etc.

Registration

The total value of the taxable supplies made by a person in the course of a year is known as that person's "taxable turnover". A person whose taxable turnover exceeds the registration threshold (currently £48,000 per annum) *must* register with the Customs and Excise. Form VAT 1 is used for this purpose. A VAT registration number is then issued, which must be quoted on the person's tax invoices (see later in this chapter).

A person who is liable to register but who fails to do so is still a taxable person and is personally responsible for the output tax due in relation to supplies made since the date on which registration should have occurred.

When deciding whether the registration threshold has been exceeded, it is necessary to aggregate the taxable turnover from all of a person's business activities. The registration relates to the person, *not* to an individual business. It is important to bear in mind the definition of the word "person" for VAT purposes (see above) and to aggregate taxable supplies only if they are made by the same person.

EXAMPLE 5

(a) Jim is a sole trader with a taxable turnover of £42,000 p.a. Is he required to register with Customs & Excise ?

(b) Pearl and Dean are in partnership, operating a business with a taxable turnover of £60,000 p.a. Is anyone required to register ?

(c) Julia is a sole trader with a taxable turnover of £21,000 p.a. She is also in partnership with Julie, operating a business with a taxable turnover of £45,000 p.a. Is anyone required to register ?

SOLUTION

(a) No. Jim's taxable turnover does not exceed the registration threshold.

(b) Yes. The partnership of Pearl and Dean is one "person" for VAT purposes and has a taxable turnover exceeding the registration threshold. Therefore the partnership must register.

(c) No. Julia as a sole trader is one "person", whilst the partnership of Julia and Julie is another, quite separate, "person". Neither of these persons has a taxable turnover exceeding the registration threshold so neither of them is required to register.

Business splitting

"Business splitting" or "disaggregation" occurs when a business with a taxable turnover exceeding the registration threshold is divided into two or more smaller businesses, each operated by a different person and each with a taxable turnover not exceeding the registration threshold, in the hope of avoiding registration.

If this type of manoeuvre were successful, supplies could be made to customers without charging VAT and the administrative costs associated with making VAT returns and maintaining VAT records (see below) could be avoided. The only disadvantage would be that input tax could not be reclaimed but in the case of a business with mainly exempt or zero-rated inputs this disadvantage would be slight.

However, if a business has been split artificially, Customs and Excise have the power to direct that the persons conducting the split businesses should be treated as a single taxable person for VAT purposes. This direction may be made even if the split businesses have never been operated as a single unit, if Customs and Excise are satisfied that only one business really exists.

When to register

A person is required to register for VAT if, at the end of any month, the value of that person's taxable supplies for the year ended on the last day of the month exceeds £48,000. Customs and Excise must be notified within 30 days of the end of the relevant month and registration will usually take effect from the start of the following month. However, the person will not be required to register if Customs & Excise are satisfied that taxable turnover during the next 12 months will not exceed £46,000.

Registration is also required if, at any time, there are reasonable grounds for believing that taxable turnover during the next 30 days will exceed £48,000. In this case, Customs & Excise must be notified no later than the end of the 30-day period and registration takes effect from the beginning of that period.

For the purpose of deciding whether the registration threshold has been or will be exceeded, supplies consisting of the capital assets of a business are not included in taxable turnover. (But note that such supplies normally receive no special treatment, so that the sale of a fixed asset will be a taxable supply unless the asset falls into one of the exemption groups).

EXAMPLE 6

Kevin begins trading on 1 January 1996. Taxable turnover during the first 18 months of trading is as follows :

1996	£	*1997*	£
January	1,800	January	3,900
February	2,100	February	3,500
March	2,800	March	3,000
April	2,600	April	3,500
May	2,400	May	4,500
June	2,900	June	4,800
July	3,300		
August	3,500		
September	4,200		
October	5,500		
November	6,900		
December	6,200		

The turnover in January 1997 includes £2,000 relating to the sale of plant and machinery previously used in the trade. When (if at all) will Kevin be required to register for VAT ?

SOLUTION

At the end of each month, cumulative taxable turnover during the previous 12 months (or since the start of trade, if less) are as follows :

1996	£	*1997*	£
January	1,800	January	44,300
February	3,900	February	45,700
March	6,700	March	45,900
April	9,300	April	46,800
May	11,700	May	48,900
June	14,600	June	50,800
July	17,900		
August	21,400		
September	25,600		
October	31,100		
November	38,000		
December	44,200		

Notes :

(i) The cumulative figure at the end of January 1997 consists of the turnover for the months of February 1996 to January 1997 inclusive, less the £2,000 relating to the sale of plant and machinery.

(ii) The registration threshold is passed at the end of May 1997. Kevin must notify Customs & Excise of this fact by 30 June 1997 and registration will probably take effect as from 1 July 1997.

Voluntary registration

A person making taxable supplies which do not exceed the registration threshold may nonetheless register for VAT voluntarily. This enables the person concerned to recover input tax but means that output tax must be charged when taxable supplies are made to customers. However, if the supplies are all zero-rated, or consist of standard-rated supplies made wholly or mainly to customers who are themselves taxable persons, the fact that output tax must be charged will probably not deter customers.

Being registered for VAT will add to the administrative costs of running the business but this consideration may be outweighed by the benefit of being able to recover input tax.

EXAMPLE 7

Lindsey is not registered for VAT. In the year to 31 December 1997, she has inputs costing £10,000 plus VAT at 17.5%. Her outputs total £32,000.

(a) How much profit does she make for the year ?

(b) If she had registered for VAT voluntarily, how much profit would she have made for the year ?

(c) Does it matter whether the supplies that she makes are all :

  (i) zero-rated ?

  (ii) standard-rated supplies made to VAT-registered businesses ?

  (iii) standard-rated supplies made to the general public ?

SOLUTION

(a) Her profit is £20,250 (£32,000 - £11,750).

(b) If she had registered for VAT (and her outputs had remained at £32,000) she would have been able to reclaim her input tax, giving her a profit of £22,000 (£32,000 - £10,000).

(c) (i) If she makes only zero-rated supplies, voluntary registration has no effect on her selling prices and, therefore, no effect on her sales.

  (ii) If she makes only standard-rated supplies to VAT-registered businesses, her prices will increase by 17.5% but her customers will be able to reclaim the extra tax paid and so there will be no effect on her sales.

  (iii) If she makes only standard-rated supplies to the general public, increasing her prices by 17.5% may well entail a loss of custom. In these circumstances she may prefer not to register.

Exemption from registration

Customs and Excise may grant exemption from registration to a person making supplies which exceed the registration threshold, so long as these supplies are all zero-rated. Such an application might be made if the amount of input tax which could be reclaimed if the person concerned were registered is small when contrasted with the increased administrative costs associated with VAT registration.

Group registration

A group of associated companies (see Chapter 29) may apply for the group to be registered as a single taxable person, rather than each company in the group being registered individually. Group registration has the following consequences :

(a) The input tax suffered by the group as a whole is set against the output tax charged by the group as a whole.

(b) One of the companies in the group is nominated as the "representative member" and this company takes responsibility for submitting VAT returns and accounting for VAT on behalf of the entire group.

(c) Supplies between group members are not regarded as taxable supplies and are ignored for VAT purposes.

Deregistration

Deregistration may be either voluntary or compulsory :

(a) A registered person may deregister voluntarily if the Customs and Excise are satisfied that taxable turnover (excluding supplies of capital assets) will not exceed £46,000 in the next 12 months.

(b) Compulsory deregistration is triggered when a registered person entirely ceases to make taxable supplies. The person must notify Customs and Excise within 30 days that this has occurred and deregistration will normally take effect as from the date on which taxable supplies ceased.

    Deregistration is also compulsory on a change of legal status (e.g. when a sole trader admits a partner or when the business of a partnership is taken over by a company).

On deregistration, the person concerned is deemed to make a supply of all the assets of the business and output tax is charged accordingly. However, assets on which no input tax was incurred are excluded from this deemed supply and the output tax due is not collected if it does not exceed £250 in total. The deemed supply does *not* take place if the business is sold as a going concern to another taxable person.

Accounting for VAT

At regular intervals (usually quarterly) registered persons must submit a return to Customs and Excise, showing the input tax and output tax for the period covered by the return. Any excess of output tax over input tax is payable to Customs and Excise, whilst any excess of input tax over output tax is repayable by Customs and Excise. The return is made on form VAT 100 and must be submitted within one month of the end of the "tax period" to which it relates, together with any tax due.

Monthly accounting

A registered person making supplies which are wholly or mainly zero-rated will be entitled to a VAT repayment in most tax periods. Such a person may opt to submit VAT returns monthly rather than quarterly, so speeding up tax repayments at the expense of making twelve returns per year rather than four.

Annual accounting

A registered person making supplies which are wholly or mainly standard-rated will be required to make a payment of VAT in most tax periods. So long as taxable turnover does not exceed £300,000 p.a., such a person may opt to join the "annual accounting scheme" and submit only one VAT return per year. The scheme operates as follows :

(a) At the beginning of each year, Customs and Excise estimate the total VAT liability for the year (based on past experience).

(b) During the year the person makes nine interim payments to Customs and Excise, each equal to 10% of the estimated liability for the year. These payments must be made by direct debit and begin in the fourth month of the year.

(c) At the end of the year the annual return is submitted together with a tenth payment consisting of the balance of the VAT due for the year. The return and payment must be made within 2 months of the end of the year.

The scheme operates differently for businesses with a taxable turnover which does not exceed £100,000 p.a. Such businesses are not required to make any interim payments at all unless their estimated VAT liability for the year is £2,000 or more, in which case three quarterly interim payments are required, each equal to 20% of the estimated liability for the year.

Monthly payments on account

A registered person who makes quarterly returns and whose annual VAT liability exceeds £2,000,000 is obliged to make monthly payments on account to Customs and Excise. The first payment on account is due one month before the end of the quarter, the second payment is due at the end of the quarter and a balancing payment is due one month after the end of the quarter. Each of the two payments on account is usually calculated as 1/24th of the person's total VAT liability for the previous year.

The tax point

The date on which a supply is deemed to occur is known as the "tax point" of that supply. The tax point of a supply determines :

(a) for outputs, the tax period in which the output tax relating to that supply must be accounted for

(b) for inputs, the tax period in which the input tax relating to that supply may be reclaimed

(c) the rate of VAT applicable to the supply (if VAT rates change).

For a supply of goods the "basic tax point" is the date on which the goods are removed or made available to the customer. For a supply of services the basic tax point is the date on which the services are performed. However, the actual tax point of a supply will differ from the basic tax point in the following circumstances :

(a) If the supplier issues a tax invoice or receives payment for the supply on a date which is earlier than the basic tax point, then that date becomes the actual tax point.

(b) If the supplier issues a tax invoice within 14 days after the basic tax point, then the invoice date becomes the actual tax point.

Customs and Excise may extend the 14-day rule mentioned above if asked to do so by a registered person. For example, a person who normally issues invoices at the end of each month might request that the invoice date should always be used as the tax point, even though this date will be more than 14 days after the basic tax point for supplies made in the first half of the month.

Cash accounting

A registered person whose taxable turnover does not exceed £350,000 p.a., may opt to join the "cash accounting scheme". Registered persons who belong to this scheme account for output tax in the tax period in which *payment is received* from the customer and reclaim input tax in the tax period in which *payment is made* to the supplier. (The tax point is ignored when allocating inputs and outputs to tax periods).

Joining this scheme allows a registered person to delay the payment of output tax to Customs & Excise until the tax has actually been received from customers, which is of benefit if customers are given extended credit. The scheme also provides automatic relief for bad debts (see below). On the other hand, input tax cannot be reclaimed until that input tax has actually been paid to suppliers.

A registered person may not join the cash accounting scheme unless :

(a) the person's taxable turnover (excluding sales of capital items) is not expected to exceed £350,000 in the next 12 months, and

(b) the person's VAT returns are up to date, and

(c) all amounts of VAT due to be paid to Customs and Excise (including any penalties and interest) have in fact been paid, or the person has come to an arrangement for such payments to be made by instalments, and

(d) within the previous 12 months, the person has not been convicted of a VAT offence or assessed to a penalty for VAT evasion involving dishonest conduct.

If a registered person who operates the cash accounting scheme has taxable turnover exceeding £437,500 for any year ending on the last day of a tax period and taxable turnover exceeding £350,000 in the next year, then the person concerned must leave the scheme at the end of the second of these two years.

Tax invoices

If a taxable person makes a taxable supply to another taxable person, then a "tax invoice" must be issued. The purpose of this invoice is to provide documentary evidence of the transaction, so allowing the person receiving the supply to reclaim the input tax related to that supply. The required contents of a valid tax invoice are as follows :

(a) the invoice number and date

(b) the tax point

(c) the name, address and VAT registration number of the supplier

(d) the name and address of the customer

(e) the type of supply (e.g. sale, HP sale, hire etc.)

(f) for each invoice item, a description of the goods or services supplied

(g) for each description, the quantity of the goods or the extent of the services, the amount payable (before VAT) and the rate of VAT applicable.

(h) the total amount due, before VAT

(i) the rate of any cash discount available

(j) the total amount of VAT chargeable at each rate

(k) the total amount of VAT chargeable.

The issue of a tax invoice is optional if a supply is made to a customer who is not a taxable person.

Retailers are not required to issue a tax invoice unless asked for one by the customer and may then issue a less detailed tax invoice (so long as the consideration for the supply does not exceed £100). A less detailed tax invoice need show only the following information :

(a) the name, address and VAT registration number of the retailer
(b) the tax point
(c) a description of the goods or services supplied
(d) the total amount payable by the customer, including VAT
(e) the rate of tax applicable to the supply.

Accounting records

Every taxable person must keep such records as are required by Customs and Excise. The main records which must be kept are as follows :

(a) the usual business and accounting records (e.g. cashbooks, till rolls, paying-in slips, bank statements, purchases and sales books, orders and delivery notes, business correspondence, annual accounts etc.)
(b) a VAT account
(c) a copy of each tax invoice issued
(d) all tax invoices received
(e) documentation relating to imports and exports.

These records must be retained for at least 6 years and are open to inspection by Customs and Excise, who make regular "control visits" to all registered persons.

Bad debts

If a taxable person makes use of the cash accounting scheme, the output tax relating to a supply is not accounted for until the consideration for that supply has been received, and so automatic relief is given for bad debts.

But persons who do not use the cash accounting scheme might account for the output tax relating to a supply before the consideration for that supply is received and then find that a bad debt has occurred. In these circumstances, a claim may be made for a refund of the VAT lost, so long as :

(a) goods or services have been supplied for a consideration in money, and the related output tax has been accounted for to Customs and Excise, and
(b) the value of the supply was no more than its open market value, and
(c) the debt has been written off in the books of account, and
(d) at least 6 months have elapsed since the date that payment was due, and

(e) in the case of a supply of goods, the property in the goods has passed to the person to whom they were supplied.

Non-deductible input tax

In general, a taxable person can reclaim the input tax relating to a supply so long as the supply is evidenced by a tax invoice and the goods or services involved are for use in the person's business. However, input tax is not reclaimable on certain types of supply, even though the supply is received in the course of business. The main examples of such "non-deductible input tax" are :

(a) VAT on business entertaining, if the entertaining is not allowable under the rules of Schedule D Case I

(b) VAT on costs incurred by a company in relation to the provision of domestic accommodation for a director of the company.

(c) VAT on the purchase of motor cars, apart from :

 (i) new cars acquired by a car dealer, as stock in trade, or

 (ii) cars acquired for use by a driving school, self-drive car rental business or taxi business

 (iii) cars acquired *wholly* for business use (primarily for leasing purposes).

 However, if the VAT paid on the purchase of a motor car cannot be reclaimed, no VAT is chargeable when the car is sold, unless it is sold for more than its purchase price. In this case, VAT is chargeable only on the excess of the selling price over the purchase price.

The VAT on goods or services which are not used at all for business purposes cannot be reclaimed. If goods or services are used partly for business purposes and partly for private purposes, then there are two possible treatments. Either :

(a) the input tax relating to the supply is apportioned and the business element of the tax is then reclaimed, or

(b) the whole of the input tax relating to the supply is reclaimed, but output tax is then accounted for in relation to the private use of the goods or services involved.

Fuel for private motoring

If the owner or an employee of a business is provided with fuel for private motoring, then all of the input tax relating to purchases of fuel by the business is reclaimable, but output tax (in accordance with set scale charges) must be accounted for in relation to the supply of fuel for private use.

The scale charges referred to above are derived from the car fuel scale charges used for Schedule E purposes (see Chapter 7). Each scale figure is treated as the VAT-inclusive cost of private car fuel per annum. Therefore, for a person who accounts for VAT quarterly, the amount of output tax which must be accounted for each quarter is equal to the Schedule E scale charge, divided by 4 (rounded down to the nearest whole number) and multiplied by the VAT fraction (currently 7/47). This gives the following figures :

	Petrol engines	*Diesel engines*
	£	£
up to 1,400 cc	29.79	27.55
up to 2,000 cc	37.53	27.55
2,001 cc or more	55.40	35.00

Note the following points :

(a) These scale charges can be avoided if no input tax at all is reclaimed in relation to car fuel.

(b) The input tax suffered in relation to car repairs and maintenance is reclaimable in full (without any adjustment for private use) so long as the car is used for business purposes.

(c) Only 50% of the input tax relating to car leasing charges is reclaimable if there is any private use of the car.

EXAMPLE 8

Malcolm is self-employed and owns a 1,300 cc petrol-engined car which he uses for both business and private use. During the year to 31 March 1998, the total cost of the fuel used by the car (all paid for out of Malcolm's business bank account) is £944. Should Malcolm reclaim the input tax paid in relation to this fuel ?

SOLUTION

The input tax in question is £944 x 7/47 = £140.60. If this is reclaimed, Malcolm will have to account for output tax amounting to 4 x £29.79 = £119.16. This is less than £140.60 and so Malcolm should reclaim the input tax.

Partial exemption

As stated earlier in this chapter, a taxable person making wholly taxable supplies may reclaim all input tax suffered (with the exceptions listed above), whilst a person making wholly exempt supplies is not a taxable person and may reclaim no input tax at all.

A taxable person making partly taxable and partly exempt supplies is "partially exempt" and may reclaim only part of the input tax suffered. The amount of input tax which may be reclaimed by a partially exempt person is usually calculated as follows :

(a) Input tax suffered in relation to goods and services used exclusively for the purpose of making taxable supplies is "attributed to taxable supplies" and is reclaimable in full.

(b) Input tax suffered in relation to goods and services used exclusively for the purpose of making exempt supplies is "attributed to exempt supplies" and cannot be reclaimed at all.

(c) Input tax suffered in relation to goods and services used for the purpose of making both taxable and exempt supplies is "non-attributable" and may be partly reclaimed, according to the ratio of taxable supplies to total supplies, expressed as a percentage rounded up to the nearest whole number. When computing this ratio, certain supplies made by the taxable person are omitted from the calculation, including self-supplies (see below) and supplies consisting of the capital assets of the business.

Note also the following points :

(a) If the amount of input tax attributable to exempt supplies is less than £7,500 per annum (and does not exceed 50% of all input tax) then this input tax is treated as if it were attributable to taxable supplies and may be reclaimed.

(b) Subject to Customs and Excise approval, alternative methods may be used to calculate the proportion of non-attributable input tax which is reclaimable.

EXAMPLE 9

During the quarter to 31 March 1998, Nancy made supplies as follows :

	£
Standard-rated supplies (excluding VAT)	120,000
Zero-rated supplies	80,000
Exempt supplies	50,000

She suffered input tax as follows :

	£
Attributable to taxable supplies	7,500
Attributable to exempt supplies	8,500
Non-attributable	12,000

Compute the VAT payable to Customs and Excise for the quarter.

SOLUTION

	£	£
Output tax		
Standard-rated supplies £120,000 @ 17.5%		21,000
Zero-rated supplies £80,000 @ 0%		0
		21,000
Input tax		
Attributable to taxable supplies	7,500	
Non-attributable :		
$\frac{£120{,}000 + £80{,}000}{£120{,}000 + £80{,}000 + £50{,}000}$ = 80% x £12,000	9,600	17,100
Payable to Customs and Excise		3,900

Self-supply

A "self-supply" occurs when a person makes a supply to himself or herself. For example, a self-supply of stationery takes place if a business sets up its own printing works to provide the business with necessary stationery and other printed matter.

The Treasury is empowered to order that, for VAT purposes, self-supplied goods or services are regarded as both :

(a) a taxable supply made *by* the business, and

(b) a taxable supply made *to* the business.

The effect of such an order is that output tax must be accounted for in relation to the supply but that an equal amount of input tax is deemed to have been suffered. All or part of this input tax will be irrecoverable if the person concerned makes wholly exempt supplies or is partially exempt.

Imports and exports

The VAT treatment of imports and exports depends upon whether the transactions are between the UK and a country which is not a member of the European Union (EU), or between the UK and another EU member.

Imports to the UK from non-EU countries

VAT is charged on the import of goods from outside the EU (at the same rate as if the goods had been supplied in the UK) and must be paid by the person to whom the goods are supplied, whether or not that person is a taxable person. Note the following points :

(a) The VAT on imported goods is normally payable at the point of entry to the UK, but importers who are taxable persons may defer immediate payment and pay by direct debit once a month. Customs and Excise require a guarantee from an approved bank or insurance company before allowing importers to defer payments in this way.

(b) For importers who are taxable persons, the VAT due on postal imports with a value not exceeding £2,000 may be deferred until the VAT return is submitted for the tax period which includes the date of importation.

(c) The VAT suffered by taxable persons on imported goods may be treated as input tax.

If a taxable person receives any services from abroad (or if a non-taxable person receives certain types of services from abroad), the person receiving the services is treated as if he or she were the supplier and is required to account for output tax in relation to them. This is known as the "reverse charge" procedure. The VAT suffered by taxable persons on imported services as a consequence of this procedure may be treated as input tax.

Exports from the UK to non-EU countries

Exports of goods to non-EU countries are zero-rated. Exports of services are largely outside the scope of UK VAT, but those which are taxable are zero-rated.

Trade between EU countries

If a registered person in one EU country supplies goods to a registered person in another EU country (and the customer's VAT registration number is obtained and shown on the sales invoice) then :

(a) the supply is zero-rated in the country of origin (so that the supplier does not have to account for any output tax in relation to the supply)

(b) the customer must account for VAT on the "acquisition" at whatever rate is applicable to those goods in the destination country

(c) the VAT suffered by the customer may then be treated as input tax.

If the purchaser's VAT registration number is not known, or if the purchaser is not a registered person, the supplier will charge VAT at the rate applicable in the country of origin.

VAT schemes

VAT "schemes" exist in order to simplify the workings of the VAT system. The annual accounting scheme and the cash accounting scheme have already been described (see above). Other schemes include :

(a) the retail schemes

(b) the second-hand goods scheme

(c) the flat-rate scheme for farmers.

Retail schemes

Retailers are those who supply goods and services directly to the public. A retailer's sales will often consist of a very large number of relatively small transactions and in these circumstances it would sometimes be difficult and expensive to keep detailed records of each transaction for VAT purposes. In response to this problem, retail schemes have been devised which enable retailers to calculate their output tax in a fairly straightforward way. The main retail schemes (at present) are as follows :

Scheme A — A retailer making only standard-rated supplies may calculate the output tax for a tax period by multiplying gross takings for that period by the VAT fraction.

Scheme B — This scheme (and all of the remaining schemes) applies to retailers who make a mixture of standard-rated and zero-rated supplies. Such a retailer may estimate the turnover of zero-rated supplies, subtract this from total turnover and then apply the VAT fraction to the remainder so as to calculate output tax. The estimate of zero-rated turnover is based on the value of zero-rated purchases. This scheme cannot be used if zero-rated turnover exceeds 50% of taxable turnover or if annual taxable turnover (including VAT) exceeds £1 million.

Scheme C — Retailers with an annual taxable turnover (including VAT) of up to £125,000 may calculate the turnover of standard-rated supplies (and hence output tax) by applying a fixed mark-up (set according to trade classification) to the purchase cost of standard-rated items.

Scheme D — A retailer with an annual taxable turnover (including VAT) which does not exceed £1 million may apportion total turnover between standard-rated and zero-rated supplies in proportion to the purchase costs of such supplies.

Scheme E — Retailers using this scheme estimate the turnover of standard-rated supplies by applying expected selling prices to the purchase costs of such supplies. An adjustment is required in each tax period for opening and closing stocks.

Scheme F This scheme may be used if takings can be separated into standard-rated supplies and zero-rated supplies at the point of sale. The output tax due is found by applying the VAT fraction to the recorded sales of standard-rated items.

Scheme G This scheme is similar to Scheme D but there is no turnover limit and the output tax due is increased by one-eighth so as to allow for any difference between the profit margin on standard-rated supplies and the profit margin on zero-rated supplies. Entry to this scheme was closed on 1 October 1991.

Schemes H/J These schemes are based on an apportionment of total turnover on the basis of the expected selling prices of standard-rated and zero-rated items.

The growing use of information technology by large retailers (and by many small retailers) means that it is now much easier to record individual sales than it was when VAT was introduced in 1973. This means that the original rationale for the retail schemes has been diminished over the years. Accordingly, retailers may not use any of these schemes unless permitted to do so by Customs and Excise. Permission will be granted only if a retailer cannot reasonably be expected to account for VAT in the normal way, so that the use of a retail scheme is strictly necessary.

It is also important to note that *a number of changes to the retail schemes will be introduced between 1 July 1997 and 31 March 1998*. The main impact of the changes will be to simplify and reduce the number of schemes and to provide for individually agreed schemes for retailers with an annual taxable turnover exceeding £10 million.

Second-hand goods scheme

Until 1 January 1995, VAT was charged on the full value of goods sold second-hand unless the goods fell within the scope of one of a number of second-hand schemes. These schemes applied only to restricted categories of goods (e.g. motor cars and works of art). On 1 January 1995, however, the scope of the second-hand goods schemes was extended to cover virtually all second-hand goods. The second-hand goods scheme operates as follows :

(a) VAT is charged only on the seller's margin (i.e. the difference between purchase price and selling price).

(b) The seller's margin is deemed to be VAT-inclusive, so the tax due is calculated by multiplying this margin by the VAT fraction.

(c) The cost of any repairs made to the goods by the seller are ignored when establishing the amount of the seller's margin.

(d) No tax invoice is issued.

(e) The buyer of the goods cannot reclaim the input tax suffered, even if he or she is a taxable person.

The second-hand goods scheme is intended mainly for use by those who deal in second-hand goods and the scheme can be used only if certain conditions are satisfied. The main condition which must be met is that the person concerned must have acquired the goods either :

(a) on a supply on which no tax was chargeable (e.g. the goods were acquired from a non-taxable person), or

(b) on a supply from someone who also sold the goods under the second-hand scheme.

EXAMPLE 10

A dealer in second-hand antiques buys an antique table from a member of the public for £2,000, spends a further £500 on restoration work and then sells the table for £5,000. Compute the output tax which must be accounted for on the sale.

SOLUTION

The dealer's margin is £3,000, ignoring the restoration costs. The output tax due is therefore £3,000 x 7/47 = £446.81.

Flat-rate scheme for farmers

In general, a farmer making taxable supplies which exceed the registration threshold is liable to register for VAT in the normal way. Similarly, a farmer whose taxable supplies are below the threshold may register voluntarily. Since farmers make mainly zero-rated supplies, a farmer who is registered will usually receive regular repayments of input tax, at the expense of maintaining the necessary VAT records.

An alternative to registration is the "flat-rate scheme", which is available to farmers regardless of the size of their taxable turnover and which is intended to reduce the administrative costs associated with VAT registration. This scheme operates as follows :

(a) A farmer who is a member of the scheme does not register for VAT. This reduces administrative costs but deprives the farmer of the opportunity to reclaim input tax.

(b) In compensation, the farmer is allowed to add a flat-rate addition of 4% to his or her selling prices and to retain this addition.

(c) From the point of view of a taxable person buying goods from a flat-rate farmer, the flat-rate addition is treated as input tax and may be reclaimed, subject to the usual rules.

A farmer may not join this scheme if the total of the flat-rate additions which would be charged if the farmer were a member of the scheme exceeds the total amount of input tax which the farmer would otherwise be entitled to reclaim by £3,000 p.a. or more.

Administration of VAT

Overall responsibility for the VAT system rests with the Board of Commissioners of Customs and Excise. There is an administration directorate in London but the collection of VAT is dealt with by the VAT Central Unit in Southend. The main functions of the VAT Central Unit are :

(a) to issue VAT registration certificates

(b) to issue VAT return forms to registered persons and to receive the completed returns

(c) the collect the VAT due from registered persons and to make repayments of tax where necessary.

There is also a network of local VAT offices which deal with VAT enquiries and which are responsible for making regular "control visits" to registered persons in their area. The purpose of a control visit is to check the accuracy of the registered person's VAT returns and to ensure that the VAT system is being operated correctly.

VAT assessments

VAT is very largely a self-assessed tax and, in the normal course of events, it is not necessary to raise formal tax assessments. However, the Commissioners may issue such assessments if they believe that a taxable person has either failed to make a VAT return or has made an incorrect or incomplete return.

In normal circumstances, assessments may not be raised any later than 3 years after the end of the tax period to which they relate, but this time limit is extended to 20 years if the taxable person has behaved dishonestly or fraudulently. Any claim for a refund of overpaid tax must also be made within 3 years.

Appeals

A person who disagrees with a Customs & Excise decision may, within 30 days of the date of the document containing the disputed decision, either appeal to a VAT tribunal or ask a local VAT office to reconsider the decision. Note that :

(a) Appeals to a tribunal are permitted in relation to a wide variety of matters, but certain matters may not be the subject of an appeal.

(b) A VAT tribunal may award costs to the successful party.

(c) If either the Customs and Excise or the person concerned is dissatisfied with a tribunal decision, a dispute on a point of law may be referred to the High Court and beyond.

(d) If the local VAT office is asked to reconsider a decision, it may either confirm the decision (in which case the person concerned has 21 days in which to lodge an appeal with a VAT tribunal) or revise the decision (in which case the person concerned may still wish to appeal to a tribunal and may do so within 30 days).

Penalties, surcharges and interest

A wide variety of penalties may be exacted for non-compliance with VAT regulations. The main penalties are as follows :

(a) **Criminal fraud**. A person who attempts to evade tax in such a way that his or her conduct amounts to criminal fraud may, on a "summary" conviction obtained before a magistrate, be imprisoned for up to 6 months and/or fined up to £2,000 or three times the amount of tax evaded, whichever is the greater. If the conviction is "on indictment" (i.e. obtained before a jury), the maximum term of imprisonment is 7 years and there is no limit to the size of any fine.

(b) **Civil fraud**. A person who attempts to evade tax in such a way that his or her conduct amounts to civil fraud is liable to a maximum penalty equal to 100% of the amount of tax evaded.

(c) **Serious misdeclaration**. If a VAT return is made which seriously understates the VAT payable or seriously overstates the VAT repayable, a penalty may be exacted of up to 15% of the tax which would have been lost if the error in the return had not been detected. A misdeclaration is regarded as "serious" if the amount of tax which would have been lost is at least 30% of the "gross amount of tax" (i.e. the total of input tax and output tax) for the period in question, or £1,000,000, whichever is the lower.

(d) **Persistent misdeclaration**. Customs and Excise may issue a "penalty liability notice" to a taxable person if that person has made a "material inaccuracy" in a VAT return. A material inaccuracy is defined as one which, if undiscovered, would have resulted in a loss of tax equal to at least 10% of the gross amount of tax for the period in question, or £500,000, whichever is the lower. If the person concerned then makes at least two further material inaccuracies during the "penalty period" specified in the notice, a penalty may be exacted of up to 15% of the tax which would have been lost.

(e) **Late registration**. A taxable person who fails to notify Customs and Excise of liability to register (see earlier in this chapter), or makes late notification, is liable to a penalty. The penalty is calculated as a percentage of the amount of tax due between the date on which registration should have occurred and the date on which notification is eventually made. The percentage is 5% for a delay of up to 9 months, 10% for a delay of between 9 and 18 months and 15% for a delay of over 18 months. The minimum penalty is £50 in all cases.

(f) **Breaches of regulations.** A taxable person who fails to comply with sundry VAT regulations will receive a written warning from Customs and Excise. If non-compliance is continued, the person is liable on a first offence to a penalty of £5 per day until the breach is remedied. The penalty rises to £10 per day on a second offence within a period of two years and to £15 per day on a third or subsequent offence. The maximum penalty which may be exacted is equal to 100 times the daily rate and the minimum penalty is £50.

(g) **Default surcharge.** If a taxable person submits a late VAT return, or submits a return on time but makes late payment of the VAT due, then a default has occurred and Customs and Excise may issue a "surcharge liability notice", specifying a "surcharge period". If, within this period, the person concerned makes a further default, a default surcharge is levied, calculated as a percentage of the tax paid late. The surcharge percentage is 2% for the first default within the surcharge period, 5% for the second default, 10% for the third default and 15% for the fourth and any subsequent default. A surcharge period comes to an end only when no defaults have occurred for a continuous 12-month period.

In general, penalties may be mitigated (i.e. reduced or not charged at all) if the taxable person has a reasonable excuse for his or her conduct. Penalties may also be mitigated if the person concerned has voluntarily disclosed any non-compliance and has co-operated fully with Customs and Excise.

Interest

"Default interest" is charged on VAT which has been assessed (see above) or which could have been assessed but for the fact that payment was made before an assessment was raised. Such interest normally runs from the "reckonable date" to the date of payment, where the reckonable date is the date on which the tax should originally have been paid. Conversely, if a taxable person makes an overpayment of VAT as a result of an error on the part of Customs and Excise, that person is paid interest on the amount of tax which is subsequently refunded.

Repayment supplement

If a taxable person is entitled to a repayment of VAT for a tax period, this repayment is increased by a "repayment supplement" of 5% or £50, whichever is the greater, so long as :

(a) the return for the relevant tax period is submitted on time, and

(b) the amount stated to be repayable in the return is correct, or differs from the correct figure by no more than £250 or 5% of the correct figure, whichever is the greater, and

(c) Customs and Excise fail, within 30 days from the date on which the return was received, to issue written instructions for the repayment to be made.

Summary

- ► VAT is chargeable when a taxable person makes a taxable supply of goods or services in the course of business.
- ► A taxable person may be an individual, a partnership, a company, a charity, a club or an association.
- ► A taxable supply is any supply other than an exempt supply and may be standard-rated or zero-rated (except that domestic fuel and power is taxed at 8%).
- ► A person making taxable supplies which exceed the registration threshold must register with Customs and Excise. A person making taxable supplies which do not exceed the threshold may register voluntarily.
- ► VAT is normally accounted for quarterly but monthly accounting and annual accounting schemes exist. Input tax on certain items (e.g. entertaining) is not reclaimable.
- ► A person making a mixture of taxable supplies and exempt supplies is "partially exempt" and may reclaim only part of the input tax suffered.
- ► Special VAT schemes exist in relation to retailers, small businesses, farmers and second-hand goods.
- ► The VAT system is administered by Customs and Excise and various penalties may be exacted for non-compliance with VAT regulations.

Exercises

30.1 A standard-rated supply is made at a price of £340, plus VAT. Calculate the VAT chargeable and the consideration for the supply if :

(a) no discount is offered

(b) a 2% discount is offered for prompt payment and the customer takes advantage of this discount

(c) a 2% discount is offered for prompt payment and the customer does not take advantage of this discount.

30.2 In each of the following cases, is anyone required to register with Customs and Excise ? If so, who ?

(a) Lorna is a sole trader, making taxable supplies of £52,000 p.a.

(b) Mike owns two distinct businesses. One has a taxable turnover of £28,000 p.a. and the other has a taxable turnover of £35,000 p.a.

(c) Pat and Phil are in partnership. The taxable turnover of their business is £41,000. Phil also owns another business with a taxable turnover of £32,000 p.a.

(d) JS Ltd has a taxable turnover of £250,000 p.a. The company's shares are owned entirely by John Smith and his wife.

30.3 Rosemary owns a business which has an annual turnover (excluding any VAT) of £52,000. Describe her VAT position if :

(a) she makes wholly exempt supplies

(b) she makes wholly standard-rated supplies

(c) she makes wholly zero-rated supplies.

30.4 List the required contents of a valid VAT invoice.

30.5 Describe the main features of :

(a) the cash accounting scheme

(b) the annual accounting scheme.

30.6 Calculate the output tax which must be accounted for or the input tax which may be reclaimed by a taxable person in respect of each of the transactions below. All of the amounts shown exclude any VAT which may be applicable.

(a) the purchase of a book for £18.95

(b) the sale for £3,000 of a motor car which had been bought originally for £4,000 (the input tax paid when acquiring the car could not be reclaimed)

(c) the sale of a used commercial building for £200,000.

30.7 Sebastian is self-employed. He drives a 3,000cc petrol-engined car and charges the cost of all the petrol used to his business bank account. In the quarter to 31 March 1998 he drives 2,800 miles on business and 1,400 miles for private purposes. The VAT-inclusive cost of all the petrol bought in the quarter is £411. How should Sebastian deal with petrol in his VAT return for the quarter ?

***30.8** During the quarter to 31 August 1997, a taxable person makes the following supplies :

	£
Standard-rated supplies (including VAT)	319,600
Zero-rated supplies	88,000
Exempt supplies	440,000

Input tax for the quarter is £118,000, attributed as follows :

	%
Attributable to taxable supplies	35
Attributable to exempt supplies	40
Non-attributable	25

Compute the VAT payable to or reclaimable from Customs and Excise for the quarter.

***30.9** Tracey is a sole trader. She has the following transactions during the quarter to 30 November 1997 (all amounts shown are VAT-exclusive) :

	£
Sales to UK customers :	
Standard-rated	39,400
Zero-rated	12,600
Exports :	
To non-EU members	8,600
To EU members (all customers are VAT registered)	17,300
Purchases :	
Standard-rated	25,800
Zero-rated	6,200
Expenses :	
Wages and salaries	22,450
Car repairs	120
Insurances	260
Entertaining foreign customers	420
Other expenses (all standard-rated)	9,700
Capital transactions :	
Purchase of new plant and machinery	8,000
Purchase of motor van	12,000

Tracey drives a 1,800cc diesel-engined car and charges the cost of all the petrol used, whether for business or private motoring, to her business bank account. Calculate the amount of VAT due for the quarter.

Chapter 31

Inheritance tax

Introduction

This chapter provides a basic introduction to Inheritance tax (IHT). An IHT liability can arise in a number of ways but the events which most commonly trigger such a liability are the transfer of assets on the death of their owner and the gift of assets during the lifetime of their owner.

IHT was introduced in 1986 but was firmly based on its predecessor, Capital Transfer Tax. Current legislation is to be found in the Inheritance Tax Act 1984, originally the Capital Transfer Tax Act 1984, as amended by subsequent Finance Acts.

Chargeable transfers of value

The main situation in which a charge to IHT may arise is when a *transfer of value* of *chargeable property* is made by a *chargeable person.*

Transfers of value

A "transfer of value" occurs when a person (known as the "transferor") makes a "disposition" such that his or her estate is lower in value than it was before the disposition occurred. The value of a transfer is equal to the reduction in the value of the transferor's estate. If the transferor also pays the IHT in relation to the transfer, this further reduces the value of the estate, so that the total value of the transfer is then equal to the amount of the disposition plus the associated IHT.

A "disposition" is any disposal of property or an interest in property. The term includes disposals made during the lifetime of the transferor ("lifetime transfers") as well as disposals caused by the death of the transferor. However, certain dispositions are *not* regarded as transfers of value for IHT purposes. The most important exemptions are :

(a) dispositions without gratuitous intent (e.g. genuine commercial transactions which give rise to a loss and therefore a reduction in the value of the transferor's estate)

(b) dispositions made for the maintenance of the transferor's family, including spouses, children and dependant relatives

(c) gratuitous dispositions which constitute allowable expenditure for the purposes of income tax and corporation tax (e.g. payments made by an employer into a pension fund for the benefit of employees)

(d) dispositions caused by the fact that the transferor has been killed whilst on active service.

Chargeable property

All property is chargeable property unless specifically excluded from charge. The main exclusions are :

(a) property which is situated outside the UK and owned by a person who is "domiciled" outside the UK (see Chapter 32)

(b) reversionary interests in a trust or settlement (see below) unless acquired for a consideration.

Chargeable persons

An individual who is domiciled in the UK is a chargeable person and is liable to IHT in relation to all of his or her chargeable property, wherever in the world that property is situated. An individual who is not domiciled in the UK is liable to IHT only in relation to property situated in the UK. Note the following points :

(a) Husbands and wives are assessed to IHT independently.

(b) A partnership is not a chargeable person. The assets of a partnership are owned by the partners and each partner is liable to IHT in relation to his or her share of those assets.

(c) A company is not a chargeable person and cannot incur an IHT liability. In certain circumstances, however, the participators of a close company (see Chapter 28) may incur an IHT liability in relation to transfers of value made by the company.

(d) The life tenants of an interest in possession trust (see below) are regarded for IHT purposes as owning the assets of the trust, divided between them in proportion to their interests. The trust itself is not a chargeable person.

Exempt transfers

Certain transfers are wholly exempt from IHT. In other cases, an exemption may serve to reduce the value of a transfer for IHT purposes. The main exemptions are of three types :

(a) business and agricultural property reliefs (see later in this chapter)

(b) exemptions for transfers made to certain transferees (see below)

(c) exemptions available to the transferor (see below).

If more than one type of exemption applies to a given transfer, then the exemptions should be applied in the order given above.

Exemptions for transfers made to certain transferees

The following transfers are wholly exempt from IHT whether made on death or during the lifetime of the transferor :

(a) transfers to the transferor's spouse

(b) transfers to charities

(c) transfers to political parties

(d) transfers made for national purposes to certain national bodies (museums, libraries, art galleries etc.)

(e) transfers of eligible property made for the public benefit to non-profit making bodies.

Exemptions available to the transferor

The following exemptions are available in relation to lifetime transfers only :

(a) **Small gifts**. Gifts to individuals with a value of up to £250 per transferee per tax year (6 April to 5 April) are wholly exempt from IHT. This exemption cannot be used to exempt part of a gift which has a value exceeding £250.

(b) **Normal expenditure out of income**. Transfers which consist of "normal expenditure out of income" (e.g. birthday and Christmas presents) are wholly exempt from IHT. In order that a transfer should benefit from this exemption, the Inland Revenue must believe that the transfer :

   (i) is part of the normal expenditure of the transferor, and

   (ii) is made out of income rather than capital, and

   (iii) leaves the transferor sufficient income to maintain his or her usual standard of living.

(c) **Gifts in consideration of marriage**. Gifts made by a transferor to a bride or bridegroom in consideration of their marriage are exempt from IHT up to the following limits :

   (i) £5,000 if made by a parent of the bride or groom

   (ii) £2,500 if made by the grandparent or remoter ancestor of the bride or groom

   (iii) £2,500 if made by the bride to the groom or vice-versa

   (iv) £1,000 in any other case.

   The above exemptions are per transferor per marriage and can be used to exempt part of the value of larger gifts.

(d) **Annual exemption**. The first £3,000 of lifetime transfers made in any tax year is exempt from IHT. Note that :

   (i) if the total of the lifetime transfers made in a tax year exceeds £3,000 the exemption is set against the year's transfers in chronological order

   (ii) any unused part of the annual exemption may be carried forward to the following tax year (but no further) and set against the excess of that year's lifetime transfers over that year's annual exemption.

EXAMPLE 1

Tania makes no transfers during 1995/96. Her only transfers during 1996/97 and 1997/98 are as follows :

		£
1996/97		
June 1996	Gift to her son on his marriage	6,000
October 1996	Gift to her granddaughter	4,500
January 1997	Gift to Oxfam	10,000
March 1997	Gift to a friend	100
1997/98		
July 1997	Gift to her nephew	1,000
August 1997	Gift to her cousin	3,500

Calculate the value of each of the above transfers after deduction of all the relevant exemptions. (None of the gifts are regarded as normal expenditure out of income).

SOLUTION

(AE = Annual exemption)

	Value before AE	*AE for current year*	*AE for previous year*	*Value after AE*
	£	£	£	£
1996/97				
Gift to son on marriage (£6,000 - £5,000)	1,000	1,000	-	-
Gift to granddaughter	4,500	2,000	2,500	-
Gift to charity (exempt)	-	-	-	-
Gift to friend (exempt as a small gift)	-	-	-	-
	5,500	3,000	2,500	-
1997/98				
Gift to nephew	1,000	1,000		-
Gift to cousin	3,500	2,000		1,500
	4,500	3,000		1,500

Note :

£500 of the 1995/96 annual exemption remains unused but cannot be carried forward beyond 1996/97. The 1996/97 and 1997/98 annual exemptions are fully utilised.

Potentially exempt transfers (PET's)

If a lifetime transfer has not been wholly exempted from IHT as a result of the various exemptions described above, then the transfer will be either a "chargeable lifetime transfer" (which is charged to IHT immediately) or a "potentially exempt transfer" (which is subject to IHT only if the transferor dies within seven years of the date of the transfer).

A potentially exempt transfer (PET) is a lifetime transfer which is made by an individual to either :

(a) another individual, or

(b) a trust with an interest in possession, or

(c) an accumulation and maintenance trust, or

(d) a trust which is for the benefit of a person who is physically or mentally handicapped.

Most lifetime transfers are in fact PET's. The main example of a chargeable lifetime transfer is a transfer made to a discretionary trust.

Types of trust

The above definition of a PET makes reference to various types of trust. These were introduced briefly in Chapter 6 but are explained again below :

(a) A trust (or settlement) is an arrangement whereby property is held by persons known as trustees for the benefit of other persons known as beneficiaries.

(b) If one or more persons are entitled to the lifetime use of the trust property or to the income generated by the trust property, those persons are "life tenants" and the trust is a "trust with an interest in possession". A person whose interest will not take effect until some future event occurs (e.g. the death of a life tenant) is said to have a "reversionary interest".

(c) A trust with no interest in possession is known as a "discretionary trust".

(d) An accumulation and maintenance trust is a special instance of a discretionary trust, where the trustees may choose whether to accumulate the trust income or to pay it out for the maintenance of the beneficiaries, who must be under 25 years old.

EXAMPLE 2

Consider each of the following transfers (assuming in each case that the annual exemption for both the current year and the previous year have been set against earlier transfers) and classify each one as either an exempt transfer, a PET or a chargeable lifetime transfer.

(a) a gift of £10,000 made by a husband to his wife

(b) a gift of £20,000 made by a mother to her son on his marriage

(c) a gift of £50,000 made to a trust with an interest in possession

(d) a gift of £100,000 made to a discretionary trust.

SOLUTION

(a) wholly exempt (transfers between spouses are not chargeable)

(b) exempt £5,000 (made in consideration of marriage); PET £15,000

(c) PET

(d) chargeable lifetime transfer.

IHT payable on chargeable lifetime transfers

The amount of IHT payable on a chargeable lifetime transfer depends upon :

(a) the value of the transfer (less any relevant exemptions), which must be grossed up if the tax is paid by the transferor

(b) the rates of IHT in force on the date of the transfer

(c) the total (including the current transfer) of the gross chargeable lifetime transfers made during the seven years ending on the date of the current transfer.

Grossing up

IHT is chargeable on the *gross* value of a transfer i.e. the reduction in the value of the transferor's estate which the transfer has caused. If the transferee pays the tax due on a transfer, the gross value of the transfer is simply the amount received by the transferee (less any exemptions). However, if the tax due is paid by the transferor, the amount received by the transferee (less exemptions) is only the net value of the transfer, and this must be grossed up at the appropriate rate or rates to find the gross value.

In general, any capital gains tax payable by the transferor in relation to the transfer is ignored when calculating the reduction in value of the transferor's estate.

Rates of IHT applicable to chargeable lifetime transfers

The rates of IHT applicable to chargeable lifetime transfers made on or after 6 April 1997 are as follows :

Gross chargeable lifetime transfers for the 7 years to date	*Rate of tax*	*Grossing up fraction*
first £215,000	0%	nil
remainder after the first £215,000	20%	100/80

The rates of tax have remained at 0% and 20% for many years, but the threshold beyond which 20% tax is payable has changed from time to time. Recent values of the threshold have been :

Date of transfer	£
6 April 1990 to 5 April 1991	128,000
6 April 1991 to 9 March 1992	140,000
10 March 1992 to 5 April 1995	150,000
6 April 1995 to 5 April 1996	154,000
6 April 1996 to 5 April 1997	200,000

For each transfer, the calculation of the tax due involves the following steps :

(a) The total gross value of chargeable lifetime transfers made in the preceding seven years is brought forward.

(b) If the total brought forward has utilised the whole of the 0% band, tax is due at 20% on the gross value of the current transfer.

(c) If the total brought forward has not utilised the whole of the 0% band, the balance of the 0% band is set against the current transfer. If this does not absorb the whole of the transfer, tax is due at 20% on the gross value of the remainder.

EXAMPLE 3

On 1 July 1997, Violet makes a chargeable lifetime transfer (after deduction of relevant exemptions) of £40,000. Her only previous chargeable lifetime transfer was made in 1992 and had a gross value (i.e. the value after exemptions, grossed up if necessary) of £181,000. Calculate the IHT due if :

(a) the transferee agrees to pay the tax due
(b) the tax due is paid by Violet.

SOLUTION

The total of transfers brought forward is £181,000, leaving £34,000 of the nil band to set against the current transfer.

(a) If the transferee pays the tax, the gross value of the transfer is £40,000 and the IHT due is £34,000 x 0% + £6,000 @ 20% = £1,200.

(b) If Violet pays the tax, the net value of the transfer is £40,000. The gross value and the tax due are calculated as follows :

	Net	*Gross*	*Tax*
	£	£	£
£34,000 grossed up @ 0%	34,000	34,000	0
£6,000 grossed up @ 20%	6,000	7,500	1,500
Totals	40,000	41,500	1,500

The gross value of the transfer is £41,500 and the tax due is £1,500. The total of gross transfers for the seven years to 1 July 1997 is now £222,500.

IHT payable on death

The IHT payable on death consists of :

(a) additional tax on any chargeable lifetime transfers made by the deceased person during the previous seven years

(b) tax on any PET's made by the deceased person during the previous seven years (these PET's have now become chargeable by virtue of the death of the transferor)

(c) tax on the estate of the deceased person as at the date of death.

Tax on chargeable lifetime transfers and PET's

The tax payable on death in respect of the chargeable lifetime transfers and PET's made in the seven years prior to the date of death is calculated as follows :

(a) The transfers are considered in chronological order, with no distinction made between chargeable lifetime transfers and PET's.

(b) The gross value of each chargeable lifetime transfer remains as previously calculated. The gross value of a PET is simply the amount received by the transferee, less any relevant exemptions (since the tax due is always paid by the transferee).

(c) Tax is recalculated on the gross value of each transfer using the IHT bands and rates in force *on the date of death* and taking into account any other chargeable transfers made in the seven years preceding the transfer. The tax rates used are those applicable to transfers on death, *not* those used for chargeable lifetime transfers. For deaths occurring on or after 6 April 1997 the applicable rates are as follows :

Gross chargeable transfers for the 7 years to date	*Rate of tax*
first £215,000	0%
remainder after the first £215,000	40%

(d) The tax calculated at (c) for each transfer may then be reduced by *taper relief*, depending upon the number of years which have elapsed between the date of the transfer and the date of death. Taper relief is given as follows :

Period between transfer and death	*Percentage tax reduction*
3 years or less	0%
Over 3 but not more than 4 years	20%
Over 4 but not more than 5 years	40%
Over 5 but not more than 6 years	60%
Over 6 but not more than 7 years	80%

(e) Finally, for each transfer, any tax paid during the lifetime of the transferor is subtracted, leaving a balance of tax due on that transfer. This tax liability is the responsibility of the transferee. If the lifetime tax paid in relation to a transfer exceeds the liability on death, no further tax is due on that transfer but no repayment is given.

EXAMPLE 4

Wilson dies on 20 December 1997, having made only the following transfers during his lifetime :

		£
6 June 1987	Gift to daughter	50,000
4 May 1993	Gift to discretionary trust	400,000
11 June 1994	Gift to son on marriage	50,000

Calculate the IHT payable during Wilson's lifetime (if any) in relation to each of the above transfers, assuming that Wilson paid this tax himself. Also calculate the further IHT payable (if any) on Wilson's death.

SOLUTION

The value of each gift after deduction of exemptions is as follows :

		Value before AE	*AE for current year*	*AE for previous year*	*Value after AE*
		£	£	£	£
1987/88	Daughter	50,000	3,000	3,000	44,000
1993/94	Discretionary trust	400,000	3,000	3,000	394,000
1994/95	Son (£50,000 - £5,000)	45,000	3,000	-	42,000

Lifetime tax liability

The gifts to Wilson's son and daughter were PET's and gave rise to no immediate tax liability but the gift to the discretionary trust was a chargeable lifetime transfer. There were no such transfers during the preceding 7 years so the whole of the 0% band (£150,000 at that time) was set against the gift. The tax due was £61,000, calculated as follows :

	Net	*Gross*	*Tax*
	£	£	£
£150,000 grossed up @ 0%	150,000	150,000	0
£244,000 grossed up @ 20%	244,000	305,000	61,000
Totals	394,000	455,000	61,000

Tax liability on death

The June 1987 PET is more than 7 years old at the time of Wilson's death. This PET is exempt from tax and can be completely ignored for IHT purposes. The tax due on the other two transfers is calculated as follows :

(i) *Transfer made on 4 May 1993*

The gross value of this transfer is £455,000 and there were no chargeable transfers in the previous 7 years (5/5/86 - 3/5/93). The tax due at the death rates applicable on 20/12/97 is :

	£
£215,000 @ 0%	0
£240,000 @ 40%	96,000
	96,000
Less : Taper relief (4-5 years) @ 40%	38,400
	57,600
Less : Lifetime tax paid	61,000
IHT payable by transferee	nil

(ii) *Transfer made on 11 June 1994*

The gross value of this transfer is £42,000. Gross chargeable transfers in the previous 7 years (12/6/87 - 10/6/94) were £455,000, completely absorbing the 0% band. The tax due at the death rates applicable on 20/12/97 is :

	£
£42,000 @ 40%	16,800
Less : Taper relief (3-4 years) @ 20%	3,360
	13,440
Less : Lifetime tax paid	0
IHT payable by transferee	13,440

Tax on the deceased person's estate

IHT on the deceased's person's estate is calculated using the rates of tax applicable on death (see above). The calculation proceeds as follows :

(a) First, the 0% band is reduced by the total of gross chargeable transfers made in the preceding seven years, including any PET's made during that period.

(b) The remainder of the 0% band (if any) is then set against the value of the estate and tax at 40% is calculated on the balance.

(c) The tax due is divided by the value of the estate and the result (expressed as a percentage) is the "estate rate" i.e. the average rate of tax borne by the estate.

EXAMPLE 5

Toby dies on 2 March 1998, leaving an estate valued at £265,000. Calculate the IHT due on the estate if the total of the gross chargeable transfers made by Toby in the seven years prior to his death was :

(a) Nil (b) £70,000 (c) £221,000.

SOLUTION

(a) £215,000 @ 0% + £50,000 @ 40% = £20,000. (Estate rate 7.5%).

(b) £145,000 @ 0% + £120,000 @ 40% = £48,000. (Estate rate 18.1%).

(c) £265,000 @ 40% = £106,000. (Estate rate 40%).

Quick succession relief

Quick succession relief (QSR) is available if property which forms part of a deceased person's estate was transferred to that person within the previous 5 years and was charged to IHT at that time. The tax payable on the estate is reduced by an amount which depends upon the value of the original transfer and the amount of IHT paid on that transfer. The relief is calculated as :

$$\frac{\text{net value of original transfer}}{\text{gross value of original transfer}} \text{ x IHT paid on original transfer x QSR\%}$$

The QSR percentage depends upon the date of the original transfer, as follows :

Period between original transfer and death	*QSR percentage*
1 year or less	100%
Over 1 but not more than 2 years	80%
Over 2 but not more than 3 years	60%
Over 3 but not more than 4 years	40%
Over 4 but not more than 5 years	20%

Valuation

As stated at the beginning of this chapter, the value of a transfer for IHT purposes is equal to the reduction in value of the transferor's estate as a result of that transfer. In general, this is equivalent to the open market value of the transferred assets on the date of the transfer but it should not be assumed that this will always be the case. For instance, if the transferor disposes of :

(a) a single item from a matching set of such items, or

(b) a small number of shares in a company, sufficient to convert a majority shareholding into a minority shareholding

it is likely that the true reduction in value of the transferor's estate (and therefore the value of the transfer for IHT purposes) will exceed the market value of the transferred assets. This caveat aside, determining the market value of the transferred assets may in itself cause difficulty and special valuation rules are sometimes required. The most important of these rules are described below.

Listed shares

Shares which are listed on the Stock Exchange are valued at the *lower* of :

(a) the lower of the two prices quoted for those shares on the day of the transfer, plus one-quarter of the difference between the lower price and the higher price (the "quarter-up" rule) and,

(b) the average of the highest and lowest prices at which bargains have been marked on that day (if any).

If listed shares are transferred on a non-working day (for which no prices are available) the shares are valued as if transferred on the last working day before the date of the transfer or the first working day after it, whichever gives the lower figure.

Units in a unit trust are valued at the bid price (i.e. the buying price quoted by the trust manager) for the day of the transfer. If this is a non-working day the bid price for the last working day before the date of the transfer is used.

EXAMPLE 6

On 1 June 1997, Shirley gives 5,000 shares in Listed plc to her daughter. The shares are quoted at 189 - 197 on that day, with bargains marked at 190, 192 and 196 (all quoted prices are in pence). Calculate the market value of the shares for IHT purposes.

SOLUTION

The quarter-up rule gives 189 + 1/4 x (197 - 189) = 191. The average of the highest and lowest marked bargains is 193, so the shares are valued at 191p and the transfer has a market value of 5,000 x £1.91 = £9,550.

Overseas property

Property situated outside the UK is valued in the appropriate foreign currency. This value is then converted into sterling, using the exchange rate for the day of the transfer which gives the lowest sterling value.

Related property

When calculating the value of a transfer for IHT purposes, the existence of any "related property" may be taken into account. Related property consists of property which :

(a) is owned by the transferor's spouse, or

(b) is owned by a charity, political party etc. (or has been within the previous 5 years) as a result of an exempt transfer made by either spouse.

Under the related property rules, the property being transferred and the related property are valued together, as a whole, and then part of that value is apportioned to the property being transferred. These rules are intended to prevent taxpayers from avoiding IHT by fragmenting the ownership of an asset and will only be used if the valuation given by the related property rules is greater than the valuation that would have been calculated normally.

EXAMPLE 7

Roy owns 3,500 ordinary shares in R Ltd, an unlisted company which has an issued share capital of 10,000 ordinary shares. Roy's wife owns a further 1,600 shares. Shareholdings in R Ltd are valued as follows :

	£
500 shares	5,000
3,000 shares	33,000
3,500 shares	43,750
4,600 shares	64,400
5,100 shares	96,900

Roy now transfers 500 of his shares to a discretionary trust. Calculate the value of this transfer for IHT purposes.

SOLUTION

Ignoring related property, Roy's estate has reduced in value by £10,750 (£43,750 - £33,000) and this would normally be the value of the transfer. But taking related property into account, the value of the transfer is calculated as follows :

	£
Value of Roy's holding before the transfer (£96,900 x 3,500/5,100)	66,500
Value of Roy's holding after the transfer (£64,400 x 3,000/4,600)	42,000
Value of the transfer	24,500

Since £24,500 exceeds £10,750, the value of the transfer is £24,500.

Business property relief

Business property relief of either 100% or 50% is available in relation to a transfer which meets all of the following conditions :

(a) the property transferred consists of "relevant business property", and

(b) the business concerned is a "qualifying business" (non-profit making businesses and investment businesses do not qualify), and

(c) the property has been owned by the transferor for at least two years, or has replaced other relevant business property, such that the combined period of ownership of both the original and replacement property is at least two years out of the five years preceding the date of the transfer.

The main categories of "relevant business property", together with the applicable rates of relief are as follows :

		Rate of relief
(a)	The whole or part of a business (e.g. the business of a sole trader or an interest in a partnership)	100%
(b)	Shares in an unlisted company	100%
(c)	Shares in a listed company of which the transferor has control	50%
(d)	Land, buildings, plant and machinery used in the transferor's business (including partnerships and companies controlled by the transferor)	50%
(e)	Land, buildings, plant and machinery owned by a trust of which the transferor is a life tenant and used in the transferor's business	50%

No relief is given in relation to "excepted assets" i.e. assets which have not been used for business purposes throughout the two years prior to the transfer (or since they were acquired, if within the last two years) and which are not required for the future use of the business.

Agricultural property relief

Agricultural property relief of either 100% or 50% is available in relation to a transfer of "agricultural property" so long as that property has been either :

(a) occupied by the transferor and used for agricultural purposes throughout the two years preceding the transfer, or

(b) owned by the transferor throughout the seven years preceding the transfer and occupied by the transferor or someone else for agricultural purposes throughout those seven years.

For this purpose, "agricultural property" consists mainly of agricultural land and pasture, woodlands and associated buildings. Land managed according to the terms of certain wildlife habitat schemes (together with associated buildings) is also eligible for agricultural property relief. The rates of relief are :

(a) 100% if the transferor enjoys vacant possession of the property, or if :

   (i) the property is let on a tenancy starting on or after 1 September 1995, or

   (ii) the property is let on a tenancy starting before 1 September 1995 but the transferor has the right to obtain vacant possession within the following 24 months.

(b) 50% if let before 1 September 1995 and the transferor does not have the right to obtain vacant possession within the following 24 months.

These rates apply only to the "agricultural value" of the property i.e. the value that the property would have if it could only ever be used for agricultural purposes. No relief is available in respect of any extra value that the property might have by virtue of its development potential. If a property qualifies for both business property relief and agricultural property relief, then agricultural property relief is given first.

Administration of IHT

Inheritance tax is administered by the Capital Taxes Office (CTO) of the Inland Revenue. For chargeable lifetime transfers and transfers caused by the death of the transferor, an "account" must be delivered to this office, giving details of the transfers made and their value. Details of this procedure are as follows :

(a) **Chargeable lifetime transfers**. The transferor must notify CTO of a chargeable lifetime transfer within 12 months of the end of the month in which the transfer occurred. There is no requirement to notify CTO if the transfer is exempt or potentially exempt, or if the total value of transfers for the tax year to date does not exceed £10,000 and the total for the 7 years to date does not exceed £40,000.

(b) **Death**. The personal representatives of a deceased person and anyone who is liable to tax as a result of the death (e.g. the transferee of a PET made within the previous 7 years) must notify CTO within 12 months of the end of the month in which the death occurred. There is no requirement to notify CTO if :

  (i) the deceased person was domiciled in the UK, and

  (ii) the gross value of the estate does not exceed £180,000, and

  (iii) no more than £30,000 of the estate is situated outside the UK, and

  (iv) there have been no chargeable lifetime transfers (or PET's) made within the previous 7 years, other than transfers consisting of cash, listed shares or listed securities with a total gross value not exceeding £50,000.

Assessments and appeals

When a transfer gives rise to an IHT liability, the CTO issues a "notice of determination", showing the value of the transfer for IHT purposes and the amount of IHT payable. Appeals in writing, stating the grounds for the appeal, may be lodged within 30 days of the date of the notice. Such appeals are normally heard in the first instance by the Special Commissioners but may progress to the courts.

Payment of IHT

The IHT relating to a transfer is usually payable 6 months after the end of the month in which the transfer (or death) occurred. However, the tax on chargeable lifetime transfers made in roughly the first half of the tax year (6 April to 30 September) is not payable until 30 April in the following tax year.

It is notable that the tax on a transfer is usually due for payment well before the end of the 12-month period within which an account of the transfer must be delivered to the CTO. Since interest is charged on tax paid late, there is an incentive to deliver the account (and pay the tax due) on or before the due date of payment.

Summary

- ► The main occasion on which IHT is charged is when a transfer of value of chargeable property is made by a chargeable person. A transfer may be a lifetime transfer or a transfer made on death.
- ► The value of a transfer is equal to the reduction in value of the transferor's estate as a result of the transfer.
- ► Transfers made to certain transferees (e.g. spouses, charities, political parties) are exempt from IHT.
- ► Lifetime transfers comprising small gifts, gifts made out of income and gifts made on consideration of marriage are wholly or partly exempt from IHT. The first £3,000 of lifetime transfers made in any tax year is exempt from IHT.
- ► A potentially exempt transfer (PET) is not chargeable to IHT unless the transferor dies within 7 years.
- ► The value of a transfer for IHT purposes may be reduced by business property relief and/or agricultural property relief.
- ► The IHT on a transfer is normally payable six months after the end of the month in which the transfer took place.

Exercises

31.1 Phoebe made the following transfers during 1997/98 :

		£
12 April 1997	Gift to grandson	50
17 May 1997	Gift to her nephew on his marriage	3,000
3 August 1997	Gift to her husband	25,000
31 October 1997	Gift to a discretionary trust	10,000
1 January 1998	Gift to the Labour Party	5,000

None of the gifts are regarded as normal expenditure out of income. Phoebe made no transfers at all during 1996/97. Calculate the value of each of her 1997/98 transfers after deduction of all the available exemptions.

31.2 Classify each of the following lifetime transfers as either exempt, potentially exempt, or chargeable :

(a) a gift to an accumulation and maintenance trust

(b) a gift to the transferor's favourite charity

(c) a gift to a discretionary trust

(d) a gift to the transferor's grandfather

(e) a gift to a trust with an interest in possession.

31.3 On 5 December 1997, Nicholas makes a gift of £80,000 to a discretionary trust. His only previous chargeable lifetime transfers were in June 1988 (gross chargeable value £200,000) and July 1992 (gross chargeable value £171,000). Calculate the IHT payable and state the due date of payment :

(a) if the trustees pay the tax (b) if Nicholas pays the tax.

31.4 On 31 August 1992, Martha gave £500,000 to her daughter as a wedding present. On 1 June 1996 she gave a further £500,000 to a discretionary trust. Martha died on 1 January 1998, having made only these two transfers during her life.

(a) Calculate any lifetime tax due on each of the above transfers and state the due date of payment, assuming the Martha paid this tax herself.

(b) Calculate any further tax due on Martha's death in relation to these transfers and state the due date of payment.

31.5 On 29 June 1997, Hyacinth makes a transfer consisting of 1,000 shares in a listed company. The shares are quoted at 572 - 588 on that day, with bargains marked at 572, 577 and 578. Calculate the market value of the transfer for IHT purposes.

***31.6** On 12 November 1987, Hazel made a gross chargeable transfer to a discretionary trust of £161,000. On 1 April 1993 she gave £300,000 to her grandson. These were her only transfers. She died on 17 December 1997. Calculate the tax payable by her grandson as a result of Hazel's death.

***31.7** Tony died on 11 July 1997, leaving an estate valued at £500,000. He had made the following transfers during his lifetime :

		£
3/5/89	Gift to discretionary trust (tax paid by trustees)	100,000
1/7/90	Gift to daughter	250,000
1/8/90	Gift to son	250,000
10/6/94	Gift to discretionary trust (tax paid by Tony)	450,000

Calculate the tax payable as a result of Tony's death.

Chapter 32

Overseas aspects of taxation

Introduction

The main purpose of this final chapter is to consider the way in which the UK tax system deals with the overseas income and gains of UK resident individuals and companies. The treatment of non-residents with income or gains arising in the UK is also briefly considered.

The chapter begins by explaining the factors which affect an individual's UK tax status and then continues with a brief review of the overseas aspects of income tax, capital gains tax and inheritance tax. The UK tax status of companies and overseas aspects of corporation tax are dealt with towards the end of the chapter.

Residence, ordinary residence and domicile

The extent to which an individual is chargeable to UK tax depends entirely upon that individual's *residence*, *ordinary residence* and *domicile*. These key concepts are explained below. It should be noted that an individual's nationality is usually *not* an important factor when determining that individual's UK tax status.

Residence

The term "residence" is not clearly defined in statute law and therefore the meaning of the term has had to evolve from case law. Although most individuals are very obviously resident in one country, it is possible (for UK tax purposes at least) to be resident in more than one country for a given tax year or even to be resident in no country at all. The main circumstances in which an individual is normally deemed to be UK resident are as follows :

(a) An individual who is physically present in the UK for at least 183 days during a given tax year (excluding days of arrival or departure) is deemed to be resident in the UK for the whole of that tax year.

(b) An individual who is in the habit of making regular visits to the UK (averaging at least 91 days per tax year, excluding days spent in the UK because of circumstances beyond the individual's control e.g. illness) is usually regarded as UK resident. Two situations are possible :

   (i) An ex-resident who has now left the UK but who makes regular visits as described above is deemed to be UK resident for the whole of each tax year during which the visits continue.

   (ii) An individual who was not previously a UK resident but who begins making regular visits as described above is normally deemed to be UK resident with effect from the fifth year of the visits. However, if it is clear from the outset that the visits are going to be regular, the individual may be regarded as UK resident with effect from the first year of the visits.

Note that the concept of UK residence normally applies to whole tax years. An individual is deemed to be UK resident for the whole of a tax year or for none of it and it is not usually possible to apportion a tax year into periods of residence and non-residence. (The significance of this will become clear when the tax implications of residence and non-residence are described below). However, by concession, such apportionment is permitted in the following cases :

(a) in the year of arrival, if an individual comes to the UK in order to take up permanent residence or to work for at least two years

(b) in the year of departure, if an individual leaves the UK in order to take up permanent residence abroad

(c) in the years of departure and return, if an individual leaves the UK in order to take up employment abroad under a contract of employment for at least a whole tax year (in which case the individual concerned is normally regarded as being non-resident throughout the period of the contract, so long as UK visits during that period do not exceed 183 days in any one tax year or 91 days per year on average).

If a tax year is apportioned into periods of residence and non-residence, personal allowances are available in full for that year.

Ordinary residence

The term "ordinary residence" is also without a statutory definition. In general terms, an individual is ordinarily resident in the UK if he or she is habitually UK resident i.e. resident year after year. In a given tax year, it is quite possible to be resident but not ordinarily resident, or vice-versa.

An individual who is ordinarily resident in the UK but who is temporarily abroad during a given tax year (i.e. not present for at least 183 days but not absent for the entire tax year either) is deemed to be resident in the UK for the whole of that tax year.

EXAMPLE 1

(a) Pierre, who has lived in France for the whole of his life, arrives in the UK on 1 May 1997 and remains until 31 March 1998, when he returns permanently to France. What is his UK residence status for 1997/98 ?

(b) Peter, who has lived in the UK for the whole of his life, leaves the UK on 1 May 1997 and returns permanently on 31 March 1998. What is his UK residence status for 1997/98 ?

(c) Petra, who has lived in the UK for the whole of her life, leaves the UK on 1 April 1997 and returns permanently on 30 April 1998. What is her UK residence status for 1997/98 ?

SOLUTION

(a) Pierre is *resident* in 1997/98 (spending at least 183 days in the UK during the year) but he is *not ordinarily resident.*

(b) Peter does not spend at least 183 days in the UK during 1997/98. However, he does spend at least some time in the UK during the year and he is *ordinarily resident.* Therefore he is also *resident* for the year.

(c) Petra is *ordinarily resident.* However, she is absent from the UK for the whole of 1997/98 and therefore she is *not resident* for that year.

Domicile

An individual's domicile is the country in which the individual has his or her permanent home. Whilst it is possible to be resident in more than one country at a time, it is not possible to have more than one domicile at a time.

Individuals acquire a "domicile of origin" on birth. This is usually the domicile of the father or other person on whom the individual is dependent and is not necessarily the country of birth. Having reached the age of 16, an individual may then change domicile and acquire a "domicile of choice", but such a domicile can only be acquired by settling in the chosen country.

If an individual acquires a domicile of choice, that domicile is also acquired by anyone under the age of 16 who is dependent on that individual. A domicile acquired in this way is known as a "domicile of dependency".

Income tax - general rules

The general rules governing an individual's liability to UK income tax are as follows :

(a) Individuals who are *resident* in the UK for a tax year are liable to pay UK income tax on all of their income for that year, including both UK income and overseas income. Note that :

  (i) Income from an overseas employment is taxed under Schedule E, income from an overseas trade, profession or vocation is usually taxed under Schedule D Case I or II and other overseas income is taxed under Schedule D Cases IV and V.

  (ii) Personal allowances may be claimed by UK residents.

  (iii) The overseas income of a UK resident who is not domiciled in the UK is only subject to UK income tax to the extent that the income is remitted to the UK. This is known as the "remittance basis".

(b) Individuals who are *not resident* in the UK are liable to pay UK income tax on their UK income only. Note that :

  (i) The property income of non-residents is payable after deduction of basic rate income tax by the letting agent or tenant.

  (ii) Personal allowances may be claimed by certain non-residents, principally those who are citizens of either the European Economic Area or the Commonwealth (see Chapter 3).

(c) Interest on most UK Government securities and (by concession) interest on UK bank accounts is exempt from UK income tax if the recipient is *not ordinarily resident* in the UK.

(d) If a tax year is apportioned into a period of residence and a period of non-residence (see above) then the above rules apply to the two periods as if they were separate tax years.

These general rules are subject to a number of exceptions, depending on the type of income involved (as explained later in this chapter).

Double taxation relief (DTR)

The rules given above are likely to lead to a number of situations in which income is taxed twice. For example, the overseas income of a UK resident will be taxed in the UK and might also be taxed in the country in which the income arises (depending upon that country's taxation laws). Similarly, the UK income of a non-resident will be taxed in the UK and might also be taxed overseas.

In order to avoid this situation, the UK has made "double taxation agreements" with many overseas countries. A detailed description of double taxation agreements is beyond the scope of this book but, typically, the outcome of such an agreement might be that :

(a) Country X agrees to give a tax credit for any tax paid to Country Y when computing tax payable to itself (and vice-versa), or

(b) Country X agrees to exempt the residents of Country Y from paying tax on income arising in Country X (and vice-versa).

Unilateral double tax relief

In the absence of a double taxation agreement with the country from which a UK resident receives income, the UK tax system provides "unilateral double tax relief" for the foreign tax which has been suffered. The foreign income (received net of foreign tax) is grossed up and charged to UK income tax but the taxpayer is then given a tax credit equal to the lower of :

(a) the foreign tax suffered (the "withholding tax")

(b) the UK tax due.

If the foreign tax suffered exceeds the UK tax due, part of the foreign tax suffered will be unrelieved. For the purposes of unilateral relief, the foreign income is normally treated as the top slice of the taxpayer's income (so maximising the amount of relief given).

If a taxpayer has savings income, this (as usual) is treated as the top slice of the taxpayer's income when calculating the income tax due for the year before considering DTR. Foreign income is treated as the top slice of the taxpayer's income for DTR purposes only.

EXAMPLE 2

Vicky is single and has the following income in 1997/98 :

	£
Salary from UK employment	31,000
Rents from foreign property (net of 30% withholding tax)	3,500

Vicky is UK resident in 1997/98. Calculate her UK income tax liability for the year.

SOLUTION

	£
UK Salary (Schedule E)	31,000
Foreign rents (Schedule D Case V) £3,500 x 100/70	5,000
	36,000
Less : Personal allowance	4,045
Taxable income	31,955

	£
Income tax	
4,100 @ 20%	820.00
22,000 @ 23%	5,060.00
5,855 @ 40%	2,342.00
	8,222.00
Less : Double tax relief, lower of :	
(a) foreign tax (£1,500)	1,500.00
(b) UK tax on foreign income (40% x £5,000)	
UK tax liability	6,722.00

Income from employment

Schedule E is divided into three cases (Cases I, II and III) and the extent to which an individual's income from employment is charged to UK income tax depends upon which of these three cases is applicable. The circumstances in which each case applies are as follows :

Residence status	*Duties performed wholly or partly in the UK*		*Duties performed wholly outside the UK*
	UK duties	*Non-UK duties*	
Resident and ordinarily resident	Case I	Case I	Case I or III (see below)
Resident but not ordinarily resident	Case II	Case III	Case III
Not resident	Case II	Not liable	Not liable

Note :

In the case of an individual who is both resident and ordinarily resident in the UK, the emoluments earned for duties performed wholly outside the UK are assessed under Case I unless they are "foreign emoluments", which are assessed under Case III. Foreign emoluments are those earned from a non-resident employer by an individual who is not domiciled in the UK.

Schedule E basis of assessment

Schedule E Case I and II assessments are made on the receipts basis. Case III assessments, on the other hand, are made on the remittance basis. Therefore any emoluments which fall within the scope of Case III but are not remitted to the UK escape UK income tax altogether.

The 100% deduction

As shown in the above table, individuals who are both resident and ordinarily resident in the UK are normally assessed under Schedule E Case I on all their emoluments, whether their duties are performed in the UK or abroad. However, if the duties are performed wholly or partly outside the UK throughout a continuous "qualifying period" of 365 days or more, then a 100% deduction is given against all the emoluments earned during this period (including the emoluments relating to any work performed in the UK). In effect, the emoluments attributable to such a qualifying period are entirely exempt from UK income tax.

Note that the emoluments which are attributable to a qualifying period are those which are *earned* in that period, not necessarily those which are received in that period.

A "qualifying period" begins when an individual leaves the UK to work abroad and the period is treated as continuous even if the individual returns to the UK from time to time, so long as :

(a) no visit in the UK during the period lasts for more than 62 days, and

(b) on each day of return to the UK, the total number of days present in the UK since the qualifying period began is no more than one-sixth of the total length of the period so far.

If condition (a) is broken, the qualifying period ends immediately before the start of the offending UK visit. If condition (b) is broken, the qualifying period ends immediately before the start of the most recent UK visit.

An individual is deemed to be present in the UK on a given day if he or she is in the UK at midnight on that day. Therefore, a day of arrival in the UK counts as a day present in the UK, but a day of departure from the UK does not.

EXAMPLE 3

Robin is domiciled in the UK and has lived in the UK all his life. On 1 June 1997 he leaves to work in Australia and does not visit the UK again until he returns permanently on 31 July 1998.

(a) What is his residence status in 1997/98 ?

(b) To what extent are his Australian earnings subject to UK income tax ?

SOLUTION

(a) Robin is ordinarily resident in the UK and spends some time in the UK during 1997/98. Therefore he is resident for the year.

(b) As Robin is domiciled, resident and ordinarily resident in the UK he is normally taxed under Schedule E Case I on all of his earnings from employment, no matter where in the world his duties are performed. But the period from 1 June 1997 to 31 July 1998 is a qualifying period of at least 365 days. Therefore Robin's Australian earnings are not subject to UK tax.

EXAMPLE 4

Rachel is ordinarily resident in the UK and is employed by a UK company. On 1 October 1996 she is sent to work in the company's Rome office, returning permanently to the UK on 24 December 1997. Her visits to the UK during this period are as follows :

Arrived in the UK	*Returned to Italy*
23 December 1996	25 January 1997
11 October 1997	30 November 1997

To what extent (if at all) are her emoluments during this period exempt from UK income tax ?

SOLUTION

The first point to note is that Rachel's contract of employment does not cover a whole tax year and therefore she remains UK resident for tax purposes throughout. Her emoluments are assessed under Schedule E Case I but the 100% deduction will be available if she has a suitable qualifying period. Her periods of presence and absence may be summarised as follows :

	Days absent	*Days present*	*Cumulative days present*	*Cumulative total days*
1/10/96 to 22/12/96	83		0	83
23/12/96 to 24/1/97		33	33	116
25/1/97 to 10/10/97	259		33	375
11/10/97 to 29/11/97		50	83	425
30/11/97 to 23/12/97	24		83	449

The qualifying period begins on 1/10/96. No visit to the UK lasts for more than 62 days, so the first condition is satisfied throughout. Testing for the one-sixth condition on each return to the UK :

(i) On 23/12/96, zero does not exceed one-sixth of 83. The condition is satisfied.

(ii) On 11/10/97, 33 does not exceed one-sixth of 375. The condition is satisfied.

(iii) On 24/12/97, 83 does exceed one-sixth of 449. The condition is not satisfied and so the qualifying period comes to an end immediately before her most recent UK visit i.e. on 10/10/97.

The qualifying period lasts from 1/10/96 to 10/10/97, a total of 375 days. This is more than 365 days so the emoluments earned by Rachel during this 375-day period are exempt from UK income tax.

Travelling and subsistence expenses

If the duties of an employment are performed abroad and the employee is resident and ordinarily resident in the UK then, so long as the emoluments concerned are not "foreign emoluments" (see above), the following expenses are allowable deductions under Schedule E :

(a) where duties are performed wholly abroad :

  (i) the costs of travelling abroad at the start of the employment and travelling back to the UK at the end of it

  (ii) the costs of overseas board and lodging paid for or reimbursed by the employer (and assessable as emoluments)

(b) where duties are performed partly in the UK and partly abroad, travelling and subsistence expenses paid for or reimbursed by the employer (and assessable as emoluments) relating to :

  (i) travel by the employee between the UK and the overseas place of work

  (ii) travel by the employee's spouse and minor children, if the employee is working abroad for a continuous period of 60 days or more, but limited to two return journeys per person per tax year.

Similar deductions to those described at (b) above are available to non-UK domiciled individuals who are working in the UK but these deductions are available for only five years, beginning with the date of arrival in the UK.

Income from overseas businesses

The profits of a business carried on in the UK are taxed under Schedule D Case I (or Case II), whilst the profits of a business carried on overseas are taxed under Schedule D Case V. Note that :

(a) A business is deemed to be "carried on" in the country from which it is controlled, no matter where in the world the business activities actually take place. Therefore a business owned by a UK resident is usually deemed to be carried on in the UK and is taxed under Schedule D Case I, even if the business is conducted entirely overseas.

(b) In the case of a partnership, it is possible for a given partner to be UK resident whilst control of the partnership is located abroad. In this case, the UK resident partner would be assessed under Schedule D Case V.

(c) A business which is exercised in the UK by a non-resident is also assessed under Schedule D Case I, even though the business is controlled from abroad.

If the profits of a business are assessed under Schedule D Case V, the assessable profits are computed using the rules of Schedule D Case I. However, there are two significant differences between Case I and Case V :

(a) Case V trading losses may be relieved under Sections 385 and 388 in the same way as Case I losses, but relief under Sections 380 and 381 is available only against overseas trading income, overseas pensions and foreign emoluments.

(b) Case I income is UK income (always assessed in full) whilst Case V income is overseas income and is assessed only on the remittance basis for non-UK domiciled individuals (see above).

Travelling and subsistence expenses

So long as the profits of an overseas business are not taxed on the remittance basis, the following expenses are allowable deductions :

(a) expenses incurred by the proprietor of the business in travelling between the UK and the location of the overseas business (if wholly and exclusively for business purposes), and

(b) expenses relating to travel by the proprietor's spouse and minor children, if the proprietor is abroad for a continuous period of 60 days or more, but limited to two return journeys per person per tax year.

Income from overseas investments/possessions

Income from foreign *securities* (i.e. investments which yield interest, but not stocks and shares) is assessed under Schedule D Case IV. Income from foreign *possessions* is assessed under Schedule D Case V. Income assessed under Case V includes :

(a) rents from overseas property
(b) dividends from overseas companies
(c) overseas pensions and annuities
(d) profits of overseas trades (see above).

Note the following points :

(a) The basis of assessment for both Case IV and Case V is normally the same as that of Case III (see Chapter 6). However, as stated above, the profits of an overseas trade assessed under Case V are computed using the rules of Case I.

(b) As stated earlier in this chapter, the overseas income of a UK resident who is not domiciled in the UK is assessed on the "remittance basis".

(c) Savings income arising abroad which falls within the taxpayer's basic rate band is taxed at 20% (as is the case for UK savings income) unless the remittance basis applies, in which case such income is taxed at 23%.

(d) The tax due on foreign pensions and annuities is calculated on only 90% of the amount assessable in the tax year (unless the remittance basis applies, in which case the income is fully taxable).

Capital gains tax - general rules

The general rules which govern an individual's liability to UK capital gains tax (CGT) are as follows :

(a) Individuals who are resident or ordinarily resident in the UK for a tax year are liable to CGT on all disposals of chargeable assets occurring in that year, no matter where in the world the assets are situated. Double taxation relief (as described above for income tax) may be available.

(b) Individuals who are neither resident nor ordinarily resident in the UK are not liable to CGT at all, even in relation to disposals of assets situated in the UK.

There are two main exceptions to these general rules :

(a) A non-UK domiciled individual who is resident or ordinarily resident in the UK is fully liable to CGT on the disposal of assets situated in the UK but is liable to CGT on the remittance basis only in relation to disposals abroad.

(b) An individual who is neither resident nor ordinarily resident in the UK but who carries on a business in the UK is chargeable to CGT in relation to disposals of business assets situated in the UK.

Note also that a claim may be made to defer a CGT assessment relating to a disposal of overseas assets if it can be shown that the gain in question cannot be remitted to the UK because of either :

(a) the laws of the country in which the gain arises, or

(b) the actions of the government of that country, or

(c) the impossibility of obtaining foreign currency in that country.

Such a claim must be made by 31 January in the sixth year of assessment following the year in which the gain arises. If the conditions preventing remittance of the gain to the UK subsequently cease to exist, the gain becomes chargeable in the year in which this occurs.

Inheritance tax - general rules

An individual who is domiciled in the UK is liable to inheritance tax (IHT) in relation to all of his or her chargeable property, wherever in the world that property is situated. An individual who is not domiciled in the UK is liable to IHT only in relation to property situated in the UK.

The definition of "domicile" for IHT purposes is broader than the general definition given earlier in this chapter. An individual is treated as domiciled in the UK on the date of a transfer if that individual :

(a) was domiciled in the UK at any time within the previous 3 years, or

(b) was UK resident for at least 17 of the 20 tax years ending on 5 April at the end of the tax year in which the transfer takes place.

Corporation tax - general rules

A company's liability to UK corporation tax depends upon whether or not it is resident in the UK. A company is regarded as resident in the UK if it is incorporated in the UK or if its central management and control is situated in the UK. The general rules which govern a company's liability to UK corporation tax are as follows :

(a) A UK resident company is chargeable to UK corporation tax on all of its profits, no matter where in the world those profits are earned. The overseas income and gains of UK resident companies are taxed as follows :

  (i) The profits of a trade conducted through an overseas branch or agency but controlled in the UK are taxed under Schedule D Case I. Trading losses may be relieved in the usual way (see Chapter 27).

  (ii) The profits of a trade conducted through an overseas branch or agency which is controlled abroad are taxed under Schedule D Case V. Trading losses may only be carried forward and set against future profits of the same trade.

  (iii) Income from foreign investments is taxed under either Schedule D Case III (foreign securities) or Schedule D Case V (foreign possessions). Schedule D Case IV does not apply to companies. Dividends received from non-UK resident companies are not franked investment income.

  (iv) The gains arising on the disposal of overseas assets are chargeable gains and form part of the company's chargeable profits.

(b) A non UK resident company is chargeable to UK corporation tax only if it carries on a trade in the UK through a branch or agency, and then only on the following profits :

(i) the trading profits of the branch or agency
(ii) income from property in the possession of the branch or agency
(iii) chargeable gains arising from the disposal of assets used by the branch or agency.

A non UK resident company is not entitled to the small companies rate of corporation tax or to the marginal relief.

Overseas subsidiaries

As explained in Chapter 29, groups of companies enjoy a number of corporation tax reliefs, including (subject to certain conditions) :

(a) the payment of dividends and charges between group members without accounting for ACT or income tax
(b) the surrender of ACT between group members
(c) the transfer of trading losses between group members
(d) the transfer of chargeable assets between group members on a no-gain, no-loss basis.

But, as was also stated in Chapter 29, these reliefs are available only to UK resident companies and therefore none of them apply to an overseas subsidiary. However, an overseas subsidiary *does* count as an associated company for small company relief purposes.

Company migration

A UK resident company may wish to "migrate" overseas in order to escape paying UK corporation tax on its worldwide profits. This is only possible for companies which are incorporated outside the UK and involves moving the central management and control of the company from the UK to an overseas location. A company wishing to take this step must :

(a) notify the Inland Revenue of its intentions, specifying the date on which it intends to become non-resident, and
(b) give the Inland Revenue a statement of all the tax payable up to that date, specifying the arrangements which will be made to ensure that this tax is paid.

On the date that a company becomes non-resident it is deemed to make a disposal of all its assets at their market value on that date. This deemed disposal is likely to result in a sizeable chargeable gain, which is sometimes referred to as the "exit charge". However, this charge is not made in full in the following circumstances :

(a) If a company retains a branch or agency in the UK, the deemed disposal does not include assets which are situated in the UK and which are used for trade purposes by the branch or agency.

(b) If the company in question is, immediately on becoming non-resident, a 75% subsidiary of a UK resident company (the "principal company"), the gains arising in connection with the deemed disposal of the company's *foreign* assets may be postponed, so long as both companies make an election in writing to that effect. The postponed gains will crystallise if :

    (i) within the following 6 years, any of the foreign assets are disposed of, or

    (ii) at any time, the company concerned ceases to be a 75% subsidiary of the principal company, or

    (iii) at any time, the principal company ceases to be UK resident.

    Any gains which crystallise are chargeable on the principal company.

Controlled foreign companies (CFC'S)

A UK resident company which wishes to operate overseas may either :

(a) operate via an overseas branch or agency, or

(b) operate via a separate non-UK resident company which is under the control of the UK company.

Since the profits of a non-UK resident company are not generally chargeable to UK corporation tax, it would seem to be beneficial for a UK company to adopt the second of these alternatives, especially if the operation is carried on in a country with low tax rates. The overseas profits would not be subject to UK tax at all and could be accumulated in the overseas company. Admittedly, any dividends paid to the UK company would be taxed under Schedule D Case V but such dividends might be put off indefinitely or at least paid some time after the accounting year to which they relate, so delaying the Case V liability.

To prevent companies from avoiding tax in this way, the Inland Revenue may direct that the profits of a "controlled foreign company" (CFC) should be apportioned between their shareholders and that the profits which are apportioned to UK resident companies should be charged to UK corporation tax. A CFC is a company which :

(a) is resident overseas, but which

(b) is controlled by persons resident in the UK, and

(c) is subject to a level of taxation in the country in which it is resident which is less than 75% of the corresponding UK tax which would be due if the company were UK resident.

However, a CFC is excepted from the Inland Revenue direction for a given CAP if any of the following conditions are satisfied for that CAP :

(a) the CFC adopts an "acceptable distribution policy", which means that it has distributed at least 90% of its taxable profits within 18 months of the end of the CAP, or

(b) the profits of the CFC for the CAP do not exceed £20,000 per annum, or

(c) the CFC has a public quotation, at least 35% of its ordinary share capital is held by the public and its shares have been dealt in on a recognised stock exchange, or

(d) the CFC is engaged in certain exempt activities, or

(e) the Inland Revenue are convinced that the main reason for setting up the CFC was not to achieve a reduction in UK tax.

Double taxation relief for companies

As mentioned earlier, the UK has negotiated double taxation agreements with many countries. In the absence of such an agreement, a UK resident company receiving foreign income which has suffered foreign tax is given unilateral relief. This relief usually takes the form of a tax credit equal to the lower of the foreign tax suffered and the UK tax due on the foreign income.

EXAMPLE 5

In the year to 31 March 1998, a UK resident company had UK trading profits of £5,200,000 and received foreign dividends (net of 35% withholding tax) of £130,000. Compute the corporation tax liability for the year.

SOLUTION

	UK	*Overseas*	*Total*
	£	£	£
Sch D Case I	5,200,000		5,200,000
Sch D Case V £130,000 x 100/65		200,000	200,000
Chargeable profits	5,200,000	200,000	5,400,000
Corporation tax @ 33%	1,716,000	66,000	1,782,000
Less : Unilateral DTR		(66,000)	(66,000)
Corporation tax due	1,716,000	-	1,716,000

Note :

The unilateral relief given is restricted to the UK tax due on the foreign income. The remaining £4,000 (£70,000 - £66,000) of foreign tax paid is unrelieved.

Underlying DTR

If a UK resident company owns at least 10% of the voting power of an overseas company from which it receives a dividend, then an additional form of unilateral relief, known as "underlying double tax relief", is available. The idea of underlying DTR is to give relief for the foreign tax suffered on the profits out of which the dividend has been paid. Underlying relief is calculated by the formula :

$$\frac{D}{P} \times T$$

where : D = the gross dividend received

P = the profit available for distribution as shown in the accounts for the accounting period to which the dividend relates

T = the overseas tax actually paid on the profits of that period.

EXAMPLE 6

A UK resident company receives a dividend from an overseas company (in which it holds 15% of the voting power) of £10,500, net of 30% withholding tax. The profit and loss account of the overseas company for the year to which the dividend relates is as follows :

	£
Profit before tax	400,000
Less : Provision for taxation liability	150,000
Profits after tax	250,000
Dividends	100,000
Retained profits c/f	150,000

The actual tax liability of the overseas company for the year is finally agreed at £160,000. Compute the maximum unilateral double tax relief available in respect of the £10,500 dividend received.

SOLUTION

(i) D = £10,500 x 100/70 = £15,000. P = £250,000. T = £160,000

(ii) Withholding tax = £4,500

(iii) Underlying tax = $\frac{D}{P} \times T = \frac{£15,000}{£250,000} \times £160,000 = £9,600$

(iv) Maximum unilateral DTR = £4,500 + £9,600 = £14,100. The gross dividend is £24,600 (net £10,500 + tax £14,100).

Unilateral expense relief

A company may waive the right to claim unilateral "credit relief", as described above (i.e. where the double tax relief is given in the form of a tax credit) and opt instead for unilateral "expense relief". In this case, the company is assessed on the net foreign income, with the foreign tax deducted as if it were an expense. Expense relief may be attractive if, for example, the company has incurred a large trading loss and has no corporation tax liability against which to set a tax credit.

EXAMPLE 7

A UK resident company has a trading loss for the year to 31 March 1998 of £50,000. During the year, the company received a dividend from an overseas company of £12,000, net of 40% withholding tax. Show the corporation tax computation for the year if :

(a) unilateral credit relief is claimed (underlying relief is not available), or

(b) unilateral expense relief is claimed.

Note : The company will be claiming loss relief under S393A(1)(a).

SOLUTION

		Credit relief	*Expense relief*
		£	£
Schedule D Case I		0	0
Schedule D Case V :			
Gross dividend	20,000	20,000	
Foreign tax	8,000		12,000
		20,000	12,000
Less : S393A(1)(a) relief		(20,000)	(12,000)
Chargeable profits		0	0
Corporation tax @ 23%		0	0
Less : Unilateral credit relief :			
(Lower of £8,000 and £nil)		0	-
Corporation tax liability		0	0
Losses available for carry-back or carry-forward		30,000	38,000

Notes :

(i) No unilateral credit relief is available since the foreign dividend is absorbed by the S393A(1)(a) claim, leaving a UK tax liability of £nil.

(ii) The choice of expense relief increases by £8,000 the trading losses available for carry-back under S393A(1)(b) or carry-forward under S393(1).

Interaction of charges, loss reliefs and unilateral DTR

As explained in Chapters 23 and 27, a company's chargeable profits are reduced by the amount of any charges paid in the CAP and by the amount of any loss relief claimed under S393A(1). Normally, it is sufficient simply to subtract the charges and loss reliefs from total income without allocating these deductions to particular sources of income. However, if unilateral double tax relief is claimed, such an allocation must be made so that the amount of UK tax payable on the foreign income can then be computed.

Clearly, if any charges or losses are deemed to be set against the foreign income, this will have the effect of reducing the UK tax due on that foreign income and so reducing the maximum unilateral DTR available. Therefore charges and losses should be set first against UK income, then against foreign income. If a company has more than one source of foreign income, charges and losses should be set against foreign income which has suffered low rates of foreign tax in preference to foreign income which has suffered high rates of foreign tax.

Unilateral DTR and ACT

As explained in Chapter 25, the maximum amount of ACT which may be set against a company's corporation tax liability for a CAP is equal to the ACT which would be payable on a dividend equal to the chargeable profits for that CAP. If double tax relief is claimed, the maximum offset is further restricted to the amount of corporation tax payable on each source of income after DTR has been deducted.

EXAMPLE 8

In the year to 31 March 1998, a UK resident company had UK trading profits of £4,800,000 and received foreign dividends (net of 45% withholding tax) of £2,750,000. Charges of £1,000,000 (gross) were paid in the year and a dividend of £6,000,000 was paid on 1 January 1998. Compute the mainstream corporation tax liability for the year.

SOLUTION

	UK	*Overseas*	*Total*
	£	£	£
Schedule D Case I	4,800,000		4,800,000
Schedule D Case V			
£2,750,000 x 100/55		5,000,000	5,000,000
c/f	4,800,000	5,000,000	9,800,000

	UK	*Overseas*	*Total*
	£	£	£
b/f	4,800,000	5,000,000	9,800,000
Less : Charges	1,000,000	-	1,000,000
Chargeable profits	3,800,000	5,000,000	8,800,000
Corporation tax @ 33%	1,254,000	1,650,000	2,904,000
Less : Unilateral DTR		(1,650,000)	(1,650,000)
Corporation tax liability	1,254,000	-	1,254,000
Less : ACT set-off	760,000	-	760,000
MCT due 1 January 1999	494,000	-	494,000

Notes :

(i) The charges are set against the UK income so as to maximise double tax relief on the overseas income.

(ii) DTR is limited to the UK tax due on the overseas income. Foreign tax paid is £2,250,000, of which £600,000 remains unrelieved.

(iii) ACT set-off is restricted in the usual way but is also restricted to the corporation tax liability on each source of income after deduction of DTR. For the UK income, the first of these restrictions gives a maximum set-off of £760,000 (20% of £3,800,000). For the overseas income, the second of these restrictions gives a maximum set-off of £nil.

(iv) ACT paid for the year is £1,500,000 (£6,000,000 x 20/80), so there is surplus ACT of £740,000.

Foreign income dividends (FID's)

The above example illustrates the plight of many UK resident companies which derive a substantial proportion of their income from abroad. Surplus ACT is likely to be a regular occurrence for such companies and neither the carry-back nor the carry-forward provisions are likely to be of much help (since there will probably be surplus ACT in all of the previous 6 years and in all future years).

In order to assist such companies, the Foreign Income Dividend Scheme was introduced with effect from 1 July 1994. The main features of this scheme are as follows :

(a) A UK resident company may elect that a dividend paid during a CAP should be treated as a foreign income dividend (FID) and should be matched with foreign profits of the same CAP, the immediately previous CAP or subsequent CAP's.

(b) ACT is payable on a FID, but if a company both pays and receives FID's in a given CAP then ACT is payable only on the excess of FID's paid over FID's received.

(c) Any surplus ACT arising in respect of a FID paid out of foreign profits is repayable by the Inland Revenue.

(d) Shareholders receiving a FID are treated as if they have received a dividend net of 20% tax and no further tax is due in the 20% or 23% bands. However, the 20% which is regarded as having already been paid by deduction at source is not a normal tax credit and cannot be repaid if it exceeds the shareholder's tax liability on the dividend. Higher rate taxpayers are required to pay a further 20% in the usual way.

(e) A company which is an "international headquarters company" (IHC) may pay a FID without paying ACT. This provision is designed to make the UK an attractive base for large multinational companies. The definition of an IHC is complex but, broadly, a company qualifies as an IHC if at least 80% of the share capital is owned by non-residents and if each shareholder owns at least 5% of the share capital.

Summary

- ► An individual's liability to UK tax depends upon that individual's residence, ordinary residence and domicile.
- ► Individuals who are resident in the UK for a tax year are liable to UK income tax on their worldwide income for that year.
- ► Double taxation relief may be available if income is subject to both UK tax and overseas tax.
- ► Income from employment is taxed under the three cases of Schedule E. Case III assessments are made on the remittance basis only.
- ► A 100% deduction is available against all of the Schedule D Case I emoluments earned in a period of 365 days or more during which the employee works wholly or partly abroad, so long as certain conditions are satisfied.
- ► Income from an overseas trade which is controlled from the UK is assessed under Schedule D Case I.
- ► Individuals who are resident or ordinarily resident in the UK for a tax year are liable to UK CGT on their disposals throughout the world in that year.
- ► Individuals who are domiciled in the UK are liable to UK IHT. The definition of "domicile" for IHT purposes is broader than the general definition.

- UK resident companies are liable to UK corporation tax on their worldwide profits. Non-resident companies are chargeable only on the profits of a trade carried on in the UK through a branch or agency.
- The profits of a controlled foreign company may be apportioned between the controlling UK companies and assessed to UK corporation tax.
- In the absence of a double tax agreement, double tax relief for companies may take the form of credit relief, underlying tax relief or expense relief.
- The Foreign Income Dividend Scheme allows companies to pay dividends out of foreign income and to recover any surplus ACT which arises.

Exercises

32.1 Jean-Paul is a Canadian citizen. He owns a house in Canada and regards Canada as his home but he lives in London for nearly all of tax year 1997/98. His income for the year is derived from the following sources :

(a) a part-time employment with a UK company (the duties of which are performed entirely in London)

(b) a second part-time employment with a Belgian company (the duties of which are performed entirely in Brussels, which he visits on one day each month)

(c) dividends from stocks and shares held in Canada

(d) interest on a UK bank account.

To what extent is any of his income chargeable to UK income tax ?

32.2 Amy is domiciled in the UK and has lived in the UK all her life. On 1 January 1997 she leaves to work in Australia for three years. Explain her UK income tax status for tax years 1996/97 to 1999/00 inclusive.

32.3 Bryan is ordinarily resident in the UK. On 1 July 1996 he leaves the UK to take up work in Geneva, returning permanently to the UK on 31 October 1997. His visits to the UK during this period are as follows :

Arrived in the UK	*Returned to Geneva*
24 December 1996	3 January 1997
7 April 1997	27 May 1997
4 July 1997	31 July 1997

To what extent is his income from employment during this period chargeable to UK income tax ?

32.4 Cara is a UK resident. She receives a pension of £10,000 per annum from the Italian company for whom she used to work when she lived in Italy. Explain how the UK income tax system will treat this pension if Cara is :

(a) domiciled in the UK

(b) domiciled in Italy.

32.5 How would a UK resident company proceed if it wished to "migrate" overseas ? Why might this be a desirable step ?

32.6 Explain the term "controlled foreign company" (CFC). In what circumstances are the profits of a CFC chargeable to UK corporation tax ?

32.7 Brits Ltd is a UK resident company and has a trading profit of £120,000 for the year ended 31 March 1998. During the year, the company received a dividend from a wholly-owned overseas subsidiary of £57,400 (net of 18% withholding tax). The overseas company is liable to 50% overseas tax on all of its profits. Compute the corporation tax liability of Brits Ltd for the year.

***32.8** Donald is domiciled, resident and ordinarily resident in the UK. He has the following income in 1997/98 :

	£
UK trading profits	24,445
UK dividends	1,600
Income from foreign property (net of 45% withholding tax)	2,200

Donald claims only the personal allowance. Compute his income tax payable for 1997/98.

***32.9** X Ltd is a UK resident company with nineteen subsidiaries, one of which is situated abroad. In the year to 31 March 1998, X Ltd had the following results :

	£
UK trading profits	720,000
UK dividends received	40,000
UK chargeable gains	120,000
Dividend from overseas subsidiary (net of 30% withholding tax)	8,400
Charges paid (gross figure)	80,000
Dividend paid on 1 March 1998	840,000

The summarised profit and loss account of the overseas subsidiary (of which X Ltd owns 60% of the ordinary share capital) for the year to 31 March 1998 is as follows :

	£
Profit before tax	75,000
Less : Provision for taxation liability	25,000
Profits after tax	50,000
Dividends	20,000
Retained profits c/f	30,000

Calculate the mainstream corporation tax payable by X Ltd for the year.

Review questions (Set D)

D1 You have received a letter from the managing director of Wakem & Co. Ltd, a company making wholly standard rated supplies. Extracts from the letter are as follows :

"During the course of the last quarter, sales have been very good. In particular, we sold £30,000 worth of goods to St. Oggs Inc, an American company, and we also sold £20,000 worth of goods to Rappit Ltd in Scotland. Mr Jakin, the managing director of Rappit Ltd, drove a hard bargain and to secure the order we had to allow a 5% discount for prompt settlement. As we closed down the box manufacturing line, we sold off the machinery and made a useful £15,000. The electrical equipment remaining has been hired to Mudport Ltd for £1,000 per month. One piece of bad news is that Garum Furs plc has gone into liquidation owing us £14,000, though there is a possibility of recovering part of that amount in the liquidation."

Required :

Explain the significance for VAT purposes of the events described in this letter. *(AAT)*

D2 A Ltd is the holding company for a group of five companies. The relationships between the companies in the group are shown in the diagram below :

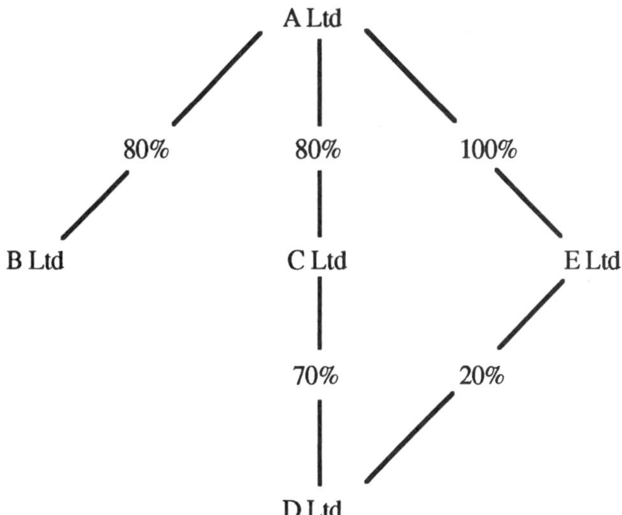

All of the companies are UK resident except for E Ltd which is resident in a country where the rate of tax is 5%. For the purposes of this question, E Ltd can be regarded as a

Controlled Foreign Company. All of the companies have an accounting year ended 31 March 1998 and their incomes/(losses) for the year were as follows :

	Schedule D Case I	*Bank interest*
	£	£
A Ltd	90,000	-
B Ltd	100,000	15,000
C Ltd	(90,000)	12,000
D Ltd	(25,000)	-
E Ltd	15,000	-

You are required :

(a) To identify the companies which are treated as associated companies.

(b) To identify the companies which form a group (or groups) for group relief purposes.

(c) To compute the MCT payable by each company, assuming that the most efficient use is made by the group of any trading losses.

(d) To advise the board of any steps it should take to minimise next year's corporation tax liabilities, given that D Ltd is expected to make a trading loss of approximately £100,000 and E Ltd will have chargeable profits of £30,000. *(CIMA)*

D3 Your company has a number of branches and subsidiaries trading outside the UK. The board is about to offer contracts to employees resident in the UK and working in UK locations which will allow them to transfer to foreign locations on a temporary basis, with all of their duties being performed outside the UK. There are two contracts being offered - one lasting nine months and one lasting eighteen months.

You are required :

To draft a report to the board on the taxation implications, for the employees, of each of the possible contracts. *(CIMA)*

D4 M Ltd, a UK resident trading company, owns 6% of the share capital of Z Inc and 8% of the share capital of X S.A. Neither of these companies is resident in the UK for tax purposes. In addition, M Ltd has a controlling interest in two UK resident companies - N Ltd and O Ltd. The following information relates to M Ltd's 12-month accounting period ended 31 March 1998 :

	£	£
INCOME		
Schedule D Case I trading profits		500,000
Schedule D Case V :		
Dividend from Z Inc, after deduction of 30% withholding tax	35,000	
Dividend from X S.A., after deduction of 5% withholding tax	38,000	73,000
CHARGE PAID		
Patent royalties (gross figure)		10,000
DIVIDEND PAID DURING THE YEAR		434,000

You are required :

To compute the MCT payable for the above period by M Ltd, showing clearly your treatment of ACT and the relief for double taxation. *(CIMA)*

***D5** David Deans started trading as a painter and decorator on 1 July 1997. He has notified you of his turnover each month which, up to November 1997, has been as follows :

	£
July 1997	5,000
August 1997	6,000
September 1997	7,000
October 1997	8,200
November 1997	9,000

In anticipation of a meeting with Mr Deans, you have received a letter from him, of which the following is an extract :

"In preparation for our meeting, I have some further information for you and some questions which I hope you will be able to answer for me. I anticipate that my turnover is likely to be £10,000 in December 1997 and £8,500 in January 1998. It must be reaching the time at which I need to be registered for VAT. Could you give me some idea of when this might be and whether I could delay it in order to improve my cash flow ?

Since starting business I have purchased substantial quantities of stock. Will I be able to recover any of the VAT I have paid ?

In June next year, I intend to buy a new van and a new car for the business. Their cost, including VAT, will be £14,000 and £8,000 respectively. I assume that I will be able to recover the VAT on both items. The van will be used wholly for business and the car both for business and private use. The firm will pay for all the petrol used by both vehicles.

As yet, I have not suffered any bad debts but as the business expands there is always the risk that they might arise. Are there any special VAT arrangements to deal with them ?"

Required :

Draft notes in preparation for the meeting with Mr Deans, responding to the queries which he has raised. *(AAT)*

***D6** Mrs Lammle, who is registered for VAT, has traded as a manufacturer of standard-rated items since 1 January 1990. She has decided to retire on 31 May 1998, her 65th birthday, and you are asked to finalise her tax position up to that date. You are provided with the following information :

(i) Mrs Lammle's first accounts covered the period to 31 May 1991. Since then, she has prepared accounts annually to 31 May. Recent profits, adjusted for tax purposes, have been agreed as :

	£
Year to 31 May 1996	48,000
Year to 31 May 1997	45,000

(ii) The last accounts will be for the year to 31 May 1998. Interim accounts have been prepared to 28 February 1998, revealing the following :

	£
Sales	100,200
Cost of sales	24,700
Gross profit	75,500
Expenses	29,000
Net profit	46,500

All of the above figures are net of VAT and contain no disallowable items for income tax purposes.

(iii) For the last three months to 31 May 1998 (which is also the last VAT quarter), you have extracted the following figures from the accounting records :

	£
Sales :	
To UK customers	30,652
To overseas customers	8,000
Materials purchased :	
Standard-rated	4,087
Zero-rated	2,000
Exempt	800
Expenses :	
General (all standard-rated)	6,130
Wages	7,000
Hire of machinery	613
Business bank charges	500
Entertaining overseas clients	400

All of the above include VAT if appropriate. All of Mrs Lammle's sales are made to order so there is no outstanding stock left at the date of cessation. All the general expenses are allowable for income tax purposes.

(iv) The tax written down value of the plant and machinery carried forward after capital allowances had been calculated for the year to 31 May 1997 was :

	£
Plant and machinery pool	12,375
Expensive car (with no private use)	5,250

No plant and machinery was acquired during the year to 31 May 1998.

(v) The business was sold as a going concern to a major competitor on 31 May 1998 (RPI 159.5). The items sold were :

	£
Freehold shop	200,000
Freehold workshop	130,000
Goodwill	180,000
Plant (no item worth more than £6,000)	25,000
Car	6,000

The shop and workshop were acquired on 1 January 1990 (RPI 119.5) for £30,000 and £27,000 respectively.

Required :

(a) Calculate the VAT due for the quarter to 31 May 1998.

(b) Calculate the final adjusted profit for the year to 31 May 1998, after deduction of capital allowances.

(c) Calculate Mrs Lammle's Schedule D Case I assessment for 1998/99, assuming that the Inland Revenue make no direction concerning the 1996/97 assessment.

(d) Calculate the chargeable gain assessable on the disposal of the business. *(AAT)*

***D7** The group structure below shows holdings in ordinary shares in other companies. All of the companies are UK resident except for O Inc which is foreign resident.

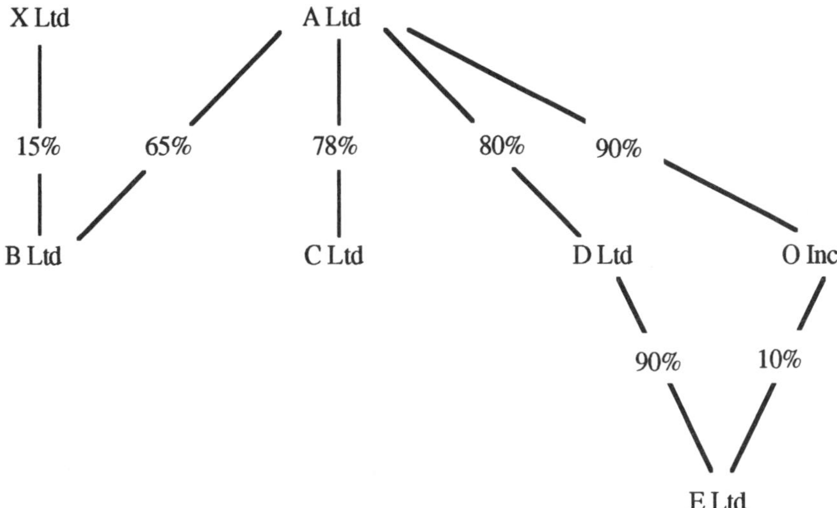

The results for each of the above companies for the accounting year ended 31 March 1998 are as follows :

		£			£
X Ltd	Loss	(40,000)	D Ltd	Profit	35,000
B Ltd	Profit	60,000	O Inc	Loss	(30,000)
A Ltd	Profit	103,000	E Ltd	Loss	(8,000)
C Ltd	Loss	(70,000)			

You are required :

(a) To identify the associated companies for small company rate purposes and to state the upper and lower thresholds for each of the companies shown.

(b) To identify any groups and consortia in the above structure qualifying for group relief.

(c) To compute the MCT payable by each company, assuming that loss relief has been claimed in the most efficient manner.

(d) To advise the directors of A Ltd on the weakness, from a tax point of view, of the existing structure. *(CIMA)*

***D8** You are the chief accountant of Z Ltd, a UK resident company, whose activities to date have been confined wholly to the UK. The company is about to acquire three UK resident subsidiaries and the members of the newly-formed group will engage, for the first time, in import and export activities (all with non-EU countries).

You are required :

To draft a brief report to the board on the VAT implications of the above changes.

(CIMA)

PART 5
ANSWERS

Answers to exercises

Chapter 2

2.1

(a) 4,100 @ 20% + 7,800 @ 23% = £2,614.00.

(b) 4,100 @ 20% + 22,000 @ 23% + 7,700 @ 40% = £8,960.00.

(c) 4,100 @ 20% + 22,000 @ 23% + 33,703 @ 40% = £19,361.20.

2.2

(a)

	Non-savings	Savings	Tax credits
	£	£	£
Schedule D Case I/II	18,920		
Dividends £720 x 100/80		900	180.00
Statutory total income	18,920	900	
Less : Personal allowance	4,045		
Taxable income	14,875	900	

Income tax due				
Lower rate band		4,100	@ 20%	820.00
Basic rate band	: Non-savings	10,775	@ 23%	2,478.25
	: Savings	900	@ 20%	180.00
		15,775		
Tax borne				3,478.25
Less : Tax credits				180.00
Tax payable				3,298.25

(b)

	Non-savings	Savings	Tax credits
	£	£	£
Schedule D Case I/II	18,880		
Bank interest £1,500 x 100/80		1,875	375.00
Dividends £8,000 x 100/80		10,000	2,000.00
Statutory total income	18,880	11,875	
Less : Personal allowance	4,045		
Taxable income	14,835	11,875	

Income tax due				
Lower rate band		4,100	@ 20%	820.00
Basic rate band	: Non-savings	10,735	@ 23%	2,469.05
	: Savings	11,265	@ 20%	2,253.00
Higher rate		610	@ 40%	244.00
		26,710		
Tax borne				5,786.05
Less : Tax credits				2,375.00
Tax payable				3,411.05

(c)

	Savings	*Tax credits*
	£	£
Dividends £24,800 x 100/80	31,000	6,200.00
Statutory total income	31,000	
Less : Personal allowance	4,045	
Taxable income	26,955	

Income tax due				
Lower rate band		4,100	@ 20%	820.00
Basic rate band	: Savings	22,000	@ 20%	4,400.00
Higher rate		855	@ 40%	342.00
		26,955		
Tax borne				5,562.00
Less : Tax credits				6,200.00
Tax refund due				(638.00)

2.3

(a) Income from employment is assessed under Schedule E. Rents received are assessed under Schedule A. NSB interest would normally be assessed under Schedule D Case III but ordinary account interest of less than £70 is exempt from income tax. Bank interest and dividends are taxed at source and not directly assessed under a Schedule or Case.

(b)

	Non-savings	*Savings*	*Tax credits*
	£	£	£
Schedule E	17,750		
Schedule A	12,000		
Bank interest £160 x 100/80		200	40.00
Dividends £200 x 100/80		250	50.00
Statutory total income	29,750	450	
Less : Personal allowance	4,045		
Taxable income	25,705	450	

Income tax due				
Lower rate band		4,100	@ 20%	820.00
Basic rate band	: Non-savings	21,605	@ 23%	4,969.15
	: Savings	395	@ 20%	79.00
Higher rate		55	@ 40%	22.00
		26,155		
Tax borne				5,890.15
Less : Tax credits				90.00
Tax payable				5,800.15

Note : Stephanie would also be given credit for any PAYE tax paid.

2.4

	Non-savings	*Savings*	*Tax credits*
	£	£	£
Schedule E	3,030		
Dividends £420 x 100/80		525	105.00
Statutory total income	3,030	525	
Less : Personal allowance	3,030	525	
Taxable income	0	0	

£490 of Ernest's personal allowance (£4,045 - £3,030 - £525) is unused. Tax borne is £nil and Ernest is entitled to a refund of the £105.00 tax credit.

Chapter 3

3.1

(a) No full tax months have passed since the start of the tax year, so the full MCA of £1,830 is available.

(b) Eight full tax months have passed since the start of the tax year, so the MCA is reduced to £1,830 x 4/12 = £610.

(c) Ten full tax months have passed since the start of the tax year, so the MCA is reduced to £3,185 x 2/12 = £531.

3.2

	(a)	(b)	(c)
	£	£	£
HUSBAND			
Statutory total income	11,420	3,500	4,380
Less : Personal allowance	4,045	3,500	4,045
Taxable income	7,375	0	335

Income tax

(a)	(b)	(c)				
4,100	0	335	@ 20%	820.00	0.00	67.00
3,275	0	0	@ 23%	753.25	0.00	0.00
7,375	0	335		1,573.25	0.00	67.00
Less : MCA £1,830 @ 15%				274.50		
MCA £1,830 x 8/12 @ 15% = £183.00 (all transferred to wife)					0.00	
MCA £1,830 @ 15% = £274.50 (£207.50 transferred to wife)						67.00
Tax borne				1,298.75	0.00	0.00

WIFE

Statutory total income	12,720	8,480	10,920
Less : Personal allowance	4,045	4,045	4,045
Taxable income	8,675	4,435	6,875

Income tax

(a)	(b)	(c)				
4,100	4,100	4,100	@ 20%	820.00	820.00	820.00
4,575	335	2,775	@ 23%	1,052.25	77.05	638.25
8,675	4,435	6,875		1,872.25	897.05	1,458.25
Less : WBA £1,830 @ 15%						(274.50)
MCA transferred from husband					(183.00)	(207.50)
Tax borne				1,872.25	714.05	976.25

3.3

(a) This taxpayer is in the 65-74 age group and is entitled to a PA of £5,220 for the year.

(b) This taxpayer is over 75 and has an STI which exceeds the limit by £1,000, giving a PA of £4,900 (£5,400 - 1/2 x £1,000).

(c) This taxpayer reaches the age of 65 during tax year 1997/98 and has an STI which exceeds the income limit by £3,600. This would give a PA of £3,420 (£5,220 - 1/2 x £3,600) but the allowance is never reduced to less than the PA for those aged under 65 so the taxpayer will claim £4,045.

3.4

(a) The husband is over 75 and therefore receives a PA of £5,400. His wife is over 65 but her STI exceeds the limit by £300, giving her a PA of £5,070 (£5,220 - 1/2 x £300). The MCA is £3,225 (which is not reduced at all, since the husband's STI does not exceed the income limit).

(b) The husband is over 65 but his STI exceeds the limit by £700, giving him a PA of £4,870 (£5,220 - 1/2 x £700). His wife is over 65 and is entitled to a PA of £5,220 (of which £1,720 is unused). An MCA of £3,185 is also available. This is not reduced at all since the reduction required because of the husband's STI has already been made in full against his PA.

(c) The husband is over 65 but his STI exceeds the limit by £4,560. Therefore he must lose a total of £2,280 in allowances. His own PA is first reduced from £5,220 to the minimum of £4,045 (a reduction of £1,175). The remaining £1,105 is deducted from the MCA of £3,185 giving an MCA of £2,080. His wife is under 65 and is therefore entitled to a PA of £4,045.

3.5

		Non-savings	*Savings*	*Tax credits*
		£	£	£
Pension (Schedule E)		4,380		
Bank interest £912 x 100/80			1,140	228.00
Statutory total income		4,380	1,140	
Less : Personal allowance (£5,400)		4,380	1,020	
Taxable income		0	120	
Income tax due				
120 @ 20%	24.00			
Less : Tax credits	228.00			
Refund due	(204.00)			

3.6

(a) PA £4,045, Blind person's allowance £1,280.

(b) PA £4,045, WBA £1,830, APA £1,830. Unused MCA may also be transferred to her.

(c) PA £4,045 (which is mostly unused).

(d) PA £4,045 (better than £5,220 - 1/2 x £9,400). There is no widower's bereavement allowance.

3.7

			Richard	*Patricia*	
			£	£	
Schedule D Case I/II			17,480		
BSI £1,600 x 100/80				2,000	(tax credit £400)
Less : Personal allowance			4,045	2,000	
Taxable income			13,435	0	
Income tax					
Richard	*Patricia*				
4,100	0	@ 20%	820.00	0.00	
9,335	0	@ 23%	2,147.05	0.00	
13,435	0		2,967.05	0.00	
Less : MCA £2,245 @ 15%			336.75		
Tax borne			2,630.30	0.00	
Less : Tax credits			0.00	400.00	
Tax payable (refunded)			2,630.30	(400.00)	

Notes :

(i) Patricia reaches 65 in the tax year so the age-related MCA can be claimed. Richard's STI exceeds the limit by £1,880 so the allowance is reduced to £2,245 (£3,185 - 1/2 x £1,880).

(ii) Patricia is entitled to a PA of £5,220 but can use only £2,000 of this. The remainder is lost.

Chapter 4

4.1

			£
Income			17,820
Less : Charges £192.50 x 100/77			250
Statutory total income			17,570
Less : Personal allowance			4,045
Taxable income			13,525
Income tax			
	4,100	@ 20%	820.00
	9,425	@ 23%	2,167.75
	13,525		
Tax borne			2,987.75
Add : Tax deducted from charge			57.50
Tax liability			3,045.25

4.2

				(a)	(b)
				£	£
Income				34,250	34,250
Less : Charges £1,232 x 100/77				1,600	
Statutory total income				32,650	34,250
Less : Personal allowance				4,045	4,045
Taxable income				28,605	30,205
Income tax					
	(a)	(b)			
	4,100	4,100	@ 20%	820.00	820.00
	22,000	22,000	@ 23%	5,060.00	5,060.00
	2,505	4,105	@ 40%	1,002.00	1,642.00
	28,605	30,205			
Tax borne				6,882.00	7,522.00
Add : Tax deducted from charge				368.00	
Tax liability				7,250.00	7,522.00

Paul's tax liability is reduced by £272 if he makes the charitable donation. The cost of the donation to him is therefore only £960 (payment £1,232 less reduction in tax liability £272). In effect, the gross donation of £1,600 is reduced by tax relief at 40% (£640), leaving £960 as the cost to Paul.

4.3

	£
Income	3,985
Less : Charges £19.25 x 100/77	25
Statutory total income	3,960
Less : Personal allowance (restricted)	3,960
Taxable income	nil
Income tax	
0 @ 20%	0.00
Add : Tax deducted from charge	5.75
Tax liability	5.75

4.4

(a) marginal rate (b) basic rate (23%) (c) 15% (d) 15%.

4.5

At present, tax relief on the deed of covenant is shared equally between husband and wife. Depending on how high their "high" salaries are it is possible that they are each receiving 40% tax relief on their half-share of the payment. If the wife's income drops virtually to zero she will in future receive no tax relief on her half-share of the payment and the tax system will claw back the tax relief deducted at source.

It is not possible simply to elect that payments made under a joint deed of covenant should be allocated entirely to the husband. As soon as possible, therefore, the couple should cancel the existing joint deed of covenant and make out a new one in the husband's name.

4.6

		£
Statutory total income		21,200
Less : Personal allowance		4,045
Taxable income		17,155
Income tax		
4,100	@ 20%	820.00
13,055	@ 23%	3,002.65
17,155		
		3,822.65
Less : MI £2,160 @ 15%		(324.00)
Less : MCA £1,830 @ 15%		(274.50)
Tax borne and tax liability		3,224.15

Tax relief on the mortgage interest is limited to the interest paid on the first £30,000 of the loan i.e. 7.2% of £30,000 = £2,160.

4.7

			Non-savings	*Savings*	*Tax credits*
			£	£	£
Schedule E			28,820		
Dividends £2,400 x 100/80				3,000	600.00
Statutory total income			28,820	3,000	
Less : Charge £77 x 100/77			100		
Taxable income			28,720	3,000	
Less : Personal allowance			4,045		
Taxable income			24,675	3,000	
Income tax due					
Lower rate band		4,100	@ 20%	820.00	
Basic rate band	: Non-savings	20,575	@ 23%	4,732.25	
	: Savings	1,425	@ 20%	285.00	
Higher rate		1,575	@ 40%	630.00	
		27,675			
				6,467.25	
Less : MCA 1,830 @ 15%				274.50	
Tax borne				6,192.75	
Add : Tax deducted from charge				23.00	
Tax liability				6,215.75	
Less : Tax credits				600.00	
Tax payable				5,615.75	

Note :

Geoffrey does not receive the additional personal allowance in respect of his children since he is married (unless, of course, his wife is incapacitated).

Chapter 5

5.1

The income assessable in 1997/98 (i.e. the income accrued for the year, calculated on a daily basis) is £4,104 (£4,000 x 270/365 + £4,400 x 95/365). The amount actually received is not relevant.

5.2

	£	£	£
Rents received £120 x 48			5,760
Less : Expenses allowed in full :			
Accountant's fee		35	
Repairs to furniture		50	
Apportioned expenses :			
Council tax	400		
Gardener's wages	520		
Insurance	230		
	$\frac{48}{52}$ x 1,150	1,062	
Wear and tear (see below)		539	1,686
Schedule A assessment			4,074

Note :

The wear and tear allowance is 10% of (£5,760 - (£400 x 48/52)) = £539.

5.3

(a) Premiums received in relation to the granting of long leases (i.e. leases of more than 50 years) are not assessable to income tax.

(b) £12,000 less (49 x 2% of £12,000) = £240.

(c) £12,000 less (19 x 2% of £12,000) = £7,440.

5.4

The premium assessed on Jasper's landlord is £12,300 i.e. £15,000 less (9 x 2% of £15,000). Therefore Jasper will be allowed an annual deduction from his trading profits of £1,230 for each of the 10 years of the lease.

5.5

All three flats pass the 140-day test. However, Flat 1 does not pass the 70-day test and so will not be regarded as a furnished holiday let unless it can be averaged with one or more of the other flats. Possible averaging claims are :

(a) Average Flat 1 with Flat 2. This is no use since the average number of days let is only 68.

(b) Average Flat 1 with Flat 3. This is no use since the average number of days let is only 69.

(c) Average Flat 1 with Flat 2 and Flat 3. This is beneficial since the average number of days let is 70.

Chapter 6

6.1

	Savings income	Tax credits	Tax due
	£	£	£
BSI £5,600 x 100/80	7,000	1,400.00	
Dividends £24,400 x 100/80	30,500	6,100.00	
Statutory total income	37,500	7,500.00	
Less : Personal allowance	4,045		
Taxable income	33,455		
Income tax			
Lower rate band	4,100	@ 20%	820.00
Basic rate band : Savings income	22,000	@ 20%	4,400.00
Higher rate	7,355	@ 40%	2,942.00
	33,455		
Tax borne			8,162.00
Less : Tax credits			7,500.00
Tax payable			662.00

6.2

	Non-savings	Savings	Tax credits
	£	£	£
Schedule E	4,786		
Bank interest £384 x 100/80		480	96.00
Dividends £520 x 100/80		650	130.00
Statutory total income	4,786	1,130	226.00
Less : Personal allowance (£5,400)	4,786	614	
Taxable income	0	516	

Income tax due	
516 @ 20%	103.20
Less : Tax credits	226.00
Refund due	(122.80)

Note :

The TESSA interest is not taxable since no capital has been withdrawn from the account.

6.3

The NSB ordinary account is an "older" source (income first arose before 6 April 1994) and is taxed on the transitional basis in 1996/97. The amount assessed is therefore £20 i.e. 50% of (£88 + £92), less first £70 exempt. In 1997/98, the current year basis applies, giving an assessment of £25.

The NSB investment account is a "newer" source (income first arose after 5 April 1994) and is taxed on the current year basis throughout. The amount assessed in 1996/97 is therefore £53 and the amount assessed in 1997/98 is £56.

Tony's Schedule D Case III assessment for 1996/97 is £73 (£20 + £53) and the 1997/98 assessment is £81 (£25 + £56).

6.4

See text.

6.5

	Non-savings	Savings	Tax credits
	£	£	£
Schedule E	6,670		
NSB investment a/c interest		52	
BSI £48 x 100/80		60	12.00
Statutory total income	6,670	112	12.00
Less : Personal allowance (75 or over)	5,400		
Taxable income	1,270	112	

Income tax due	
1,382 @ 20%	276.40
Less : WBA £1,830 @ 15%	274.50
Tax borne	1.90
Less : Tax credits	12.00
Refund due	(10.10)

Notes :

(a) The NSB ordinary account is an older source but is taxed on the current year basis as from 1997/98. The income is only £68, which is less than the exemption of £70, so there is no taxable income from this source in 1997/98.

(b) The NSB investment account is also taxed on the current year basis.

(c) Bernice reaches her 75th birthday during 1997/98 and is therefore entitled to the personal allowance of £5,400 for the year.

(d) Bernice is entitled to the WBA in both 1996/97 (the year in which she was widowed) and 1997/98.

Chapter 7

7.1

See text.

7.2

The basis of assessment for Schedule E is the receipts basis. The assessable income for 1997/98 is therefore £19,850 (£17,500 + £2,350).

7.3

(a) 15p per day would be exempt. The remaining £1.85 per day would be taxable.

(b) Free meals in the company canteen are exempt if available to all employees.

(c) Removal expenses of up to £8,000 are exempt if reasonable and incurred on first taking up an appointment or transferring to a new location.

(d) Long-service awards made in cash are taxable.

(e) A gift on marriage is exempt so long as reasonable in amount.

(f) The mileage allowance is exempt since it is less than the standard figure of 35p per mile for the first 4,000 miles in a car with this engine size. The employee has an allowable expense of £250 (2,500 @ 10p).

7.4

(a) Not allowable since not incurred in performing the duties of the employment.

(b) Allowable so long as necessarily incurred.

(c) Allowable if relevant to the employment.

(d) Allowable.

(e) Not allowable, even if worn only at the office. A suit provides warmth and decency and is therefore not purchased exclusively for the purposes of the employment.

(f) Not allowable since not incurred in performing the duties of the employment.

7.5

For the purpose of deciding Kim's classification it is necessary to take into account all emoluments (valued as if she were a P11D employee) and to ignore expenses other than superannuation contributions. This gives total emoluments of £9,450 (95% of £7,000 + £1,000 + £1,800) which exceeds £8,500 so Kim is a P11D employee.

7.6

Car benefit is £1,439 i.e. 35% of £18,500, less a two-thirds reduction for high business mileage and a further one-third reduction for a car over 4 years old at the end of the tax year. There is a further assessable fuel benefit of £940.

7.7

The SRP of £1,750 is exempt from income tax but reduces the usual £30,000 exemption for partially exempt payments to £28,250.

(a) £12,000 is less than £28,250 and therefore exempt from income tax.

(b) £29,000 exceeds £28,250 so the excess of £750 is taxable.

Chapter 8

8.1

Subject matter; length of ownership; frequency of transactions; supplementary work; reason for sale; motive.

8.2

Expenditure must be incurred wholly and exclusively for the purposes of the trade.

8.3

(a) allowable so long as the salary is commensurate with the work done

(b) not allowable under Schedule D Case I, but treated as a charge on income

(c) not allowable (capital expenditure)

(d) allowable so long as the diaries carry a prominent advertisement for the business

(e) allowable

(f) not allowable (fails the duality test)

(g) not allowable (related to capital expenditure)

(h) probably allowable as a trade subscription

(i) not allowable (food, drink or tobacco)

(j) allowable (relates directly to trading).

8.4

(a) add £45 (b) add £15 (c) no adjustment required.

8.5

(a) The allowable amount each year is given by :

$$£5{,}670 \times \frac{£12{,}000 + 1/2(£21{,}000 - £12{,}000)}{£21{,}000} = £4{,}455$$

The amount to be added back each year is therefore £1,215 (£5,670 - £4,455).

(b) The allowable amount each year is given by :

$$\frac{£15{,}000 - 14 \times 2\% \times £15{,}000}{15} = £720.$$

The amount to be added back each year is therefore £280 (£1,000 - £720).

8.6

	£	£
Net profit for the year		6,960
Add : *Disallowed expenditure* :		
Proprietor's salary	10,400	
Cost of new heating system	3,800	
Telephone (1/4th of £880)	220	
Motor expenses (1/5th of £3,250)	650	
Entertaining	520	
General provision for bad debts	200	
Loss on sale of fixed asset	70	
Depreciation	2,500	18,360
		25,320
Less : *Non-trading income* :		
Rents receivable	1,200	
Bank interest receivable	80	
Profit on sale of fixed assets	310	1,590
Adjusted profit for Schedule D Case I purposes		23,730

Chapter 9

9.1

(a) 1997/98 (b) 1997/98 (c) 1999/00 (d) 1998/99

9.2

(a)	1997/98	Actual	1/7/97 to 5/4/98
	1998/99	12 months to a/c date in year 2	1/7/97 to 30/6/98
	1999/00	CYB	y/e 30/6/99
	2000/01	CYB	y/e 30/6/00

There is an overlap period between 1 July 1997 and 5 April 1998.

(b)	1997/98	Actual	1/7/97 to 5/4/98
	1998/99	Actual	6/4/98 to 5/4/99
	1999/00	12 months to a/c date in year 3	1/5/98 to 30/4/99
	2000/01	CYB	y/e 30/4/00

There is an overlap period between 1 May 1998 and 5 April 1999.

(c)	1997/98	Actual	1/7/97 to 5/4/98
	1998/99	First 12 months	1/7/97 to 30/6/98
	1999/00	CYB	y/e 30/4/99
	2000/01	CYB	y/e 30/4/00

There is an overlap period between 1 July 1997 and 5 April 1998. There is another overlap period between 1 May 1998 and 30 June 1998.

9.3

				£
1996/97	Actual	1/1/97 to 5/4/97	£27,300 x 95/546	4,750
1997/98	Actual	6/4/97 to 5/4/98	£27,300 x 365/546	18,250
1998/99	12 months to a/c date in year 3	1/7/97 to 30/6/98	£27,300 x 365/546	18,250

Overlap period is 1/7/97 to 5/4/98 (279 days). Overlap profits are 279/546 x £27,300 = £13,950.

9.4

(a)	2000/01	CYB	y/e 31/1/01
	2001/02	CYB	y/e 31/1/02
	2002/03	End of previous basis period up to date of cessation	1/2/02 to 31/5/02
(b)	2000/01	CYB	y/e 31/1/01
	2001/02	CYB	y/e 31/1/02
	2002/03	End of previous basis period up to date of cessation	1/2/02 to 31/3/03
(c)	2001/02	CYB	y/e 31/1/02
	2002/03	12 months to normal a/c date	1/2/02 to 31/1/03
	2003/04	End of previous basis period up to date of cessation	1/2/03 to 30/4/03

9.5

Year	*Basis period*	*Workings*	*Assessment*
			£
1995/96	y/e 31/7/94		12,700
1996/97	24 months to 31/7/96	50% x (£21,500 + £14,300)	17,900
1997/98	y/e 31/7/97		15,900
1998/99	y/e 31/7/98	£12,800 - transitional overlap relief £10,803	1,997

Transitional overlap relief relates to the period between 1 August 1996 (the end of the 1996/97 basis period) and 5 April 1997 (248 days). The relief is £15,900 x 248/365 = £10,803.

Chapter 10

10.1

	Pool	*Expensive car*		*Allowances*
	£	£		£
1/1/97 - 31/1/98				
Additions (£12,000 + £6,000)	18,000	15,000		
Disposals	(1,500)			
	16,500			
WDA @ 25% x 396/365	4,475			4,475
WDA (restricted, £3,000 x 396/365)		3,255	x 60% =	1,953
WDV c/f	12,025	11,745		
Total allowances				6,428

The adjusted profit is now £35,372 (£41,800 - £6,428). Schedule D Case I assessments are :

Year	*Basis period*	*Workings*	*Assessment*
			£
1996/97	1/1/97 to 5/4/97	£35,372 x 95/396	8,486
1997/98	1/2/97 to 31/1/98	£35,372 x 365/396	32,603

Overlap period is the 64 days from 1/2/97 to 5/4/97. Overlap profits = £35,372 x 64/396 = £5,717.

10.2

	General Pool	*Cars pool*	*Allowances*
	£	£	£
y/e 31/3/98			
WDV b/f	2,700	7,600	
Additions	1,000	8,000	
	3,700	15,600	
Disposals (restrict to original cost)	(4,000)	(3,000)	
Balancing charge	(300)		(300)
		12,600	
WDA @ 25%		3,150	3,150
WDV c/f	0	9,450	

Total capital allowances are £2,850.

10.3

Norma's first accounting period covers 20 months and must be divided into two chargeable periods for capital allowances purposes. These are 1 November 1995 to 31 October 1996 and 1 November 1996 to 30 June 1997. The capital allowances computation is as follows :

	General Pool	*Cars Pool*	*Car bought 12/10/96 (40% private)*	*Car bought 31/3/98 (40% private)*	*Allowances*
	£	£	£	£	£
1/11/95 - 31/10/96					
Additions	27,400		8,800		
WDA @ 25%	6,850		2,200 x 60%		8,170
	20,550		6,600		
1/11/96 - 30/6/97					
Additions	4,600	7,200			
	25,150				
Disposals	(1,750)				
	23,400				
WDA @ 25% x 242/365	3,879	1,193	1,094 x 60%		5,728
	19,521	6,007	5,506		
Total allowances					13,898
y/e 30/6/98					
Additions	11,500			14,100	
	31,021				
Disposals	(1,500)		(6,300)		
	29,521				
Balancing charge			(794) x 60%		(476)
WDA @ 25%	7,380	1,502			8,882
WDA (restricted)				3,000 x 60%	1,800
WDV c/f	22,141	4,505		11,100	
Total allowances					10,206

Profits after deduction of capital allowances are £42,302 (£56,200 - £13,898) for the period from 1/11/95 to 30/6/97 and £49,694 (£59,900 - £10,206) for the year to 30 June 1998. The first four Schedule D Case I assessments are as follows :

Year	*Basis period*	*Workings*	*Assessment*
			£
1995/96	1/11/95 to 5/4/96	£42,302 x 156/607	10,872
1996/97	6/4/96 to 5/4/97	£42,302 x 365/607	25,437
1997/98	1/7/96 to 30/6/97	£42,302 x 365/607	25,437
1998/99	y/e 30/6/98		49,694

The overlap period is the 279 days from 1/7/96 to 5/4/97 and overlap profits are 279/607 x £42,302 = £19,444.

10.4

	Factory	*Allowances*
	£	£
y/e 30/6/97		
Cost	57,500	
WDA @ 4% of £57,500	2,300	2,300
WDV c/f	55,200	
y/e 30/6/98		
WDA @ 4% of £57,500	2,300	2,300
WDV c/f	52,900	

Note :

Subtracting the cost of the land (which does not attract IBA's) from the total cost of the factory leaves £80,000. The cost of the offices is more than 25% of £80,000 and so IBA's are available only on the cost excluding offices i.e. £57,500.

10.5

(a)

	Building	*Allowances*
	£	£
y/e 31/12/97,98,99,00,01,02 & 03		
Cost	45,000	
WDA @ 4% of £45,000 for 7 years	12,600	12,600
WDV c/f	32,400	
y/e 31/12/04		
Disposal value	30,000	
Balancing allowance	2,400	2,400

Note :

The building was not is use on 31/12/96 and therefore no IBA's are available for the year to 31/12/96.

(b) The residue of expenditure is £30,000 (£32,400 - £2,400). The tax life of the building ends on 31 December 2021, giving an unexpired life of 17 years 184 days on the date of the second-hand purchase by Maria. Maria may claim an annual WDA of £30,000/17.504 = £1,714.

Note that Maria's first accounting period (1/5/04 - 30/11/04) is only 214 days long, so she will receive IBA's for that period of only £1,714 x 214/365 = £1,005.

10.6

(a) Giles' allowances are :

		£
year to 31/3/97	£30,000 x 4%	1,200
year to 31/3/98	£30,000 x 4% x 183/365	602

Pam's allowances are :

1/5/97 to 31/12/97	£30,000 x 4% x 92/365	302
y/e 31/12/98 etc.	£30,000 x 4%	1,200

Note :

Pam will continue to receive WDA's of £1,200 per annum until the barn's WDV reaches zero.

(b) Giles' allowances in y/e 31/3/97 are £1,200, reducing the WDV of the building to £28,800. The building is sold for £35,000, but the disposal value is restricted to the original cost of £30,000, giving a balancing charge of £1,200 in y/e 31/3/98.

The tax life of the building began on 1 April 1996 (the first day of the chargeable period in which ABA's were first given) and ends on 31 March 2021, giving an unexpired life of 23 years and 182 days on the date of the second-hand purchase by Pam (23.499 years). The residue of expenditure is £30,000 (£28,800 + £1,200). Therefore Pam's annual WDA is calculated at £30,000/23.499 = £1,277. But Pam's first accounting period is only 245 days long, so she will receive ABA's for that period of only £1,277 x 245/365 = £857.

Chapter 11

11.1

(a) £nil.

(b) The loss will be carried forward indefinitely under S385 and set against the first available profits of the same trade.

(c) The loss may be set against the STI of 1997/98 and/or 1996/97.

11.2

	1997/98	*1998/99*	*1999/00*	*2000/01*
	£	£	£	£
Adjusted profits	-	4,710	6,210	14,810
Less : S385 relief	-	(4,710)	(6,210)	(7,940)
	-	-	-	6,870
Other income	5,000	5,000	5,000	5,000
Total income	5,000	5,000	5,000	11,870

11.3

(a) The Schedule D Case I assessments are :

Year	*Basis period*	*Workings*	*Assessment*
			£
1995/96	1/1/96 to 5/4/96	(£12,720 - £2,460) x 95/365	2,670
1996/97	1/1/96 to 31/12/96	£12,720 - £2,460	10,260
1997/98	y/e 31/12/97		nil

(b) The trading loss of 1997/98 is £9,800 (£7,680 + £2,120). A Section 380 claim could be made for 1997/98 or for 1996/97 or for both of these years :

(i) A claim for 1997/98 is pointless since there is no income in that year.

(ii) A claim for 1996/97 would reduce total income for that year to £460 (£10,260 - £9,800) and so eliminate the income tax liability for the year. Personal allowances would largely be wasted, but Marcus' wife may be able to use the MCA.

(iii) A claim for both years is pointless since a claim in 1997/98 is pointless.

The 1996/97 claim would be less wasteful if Marcus declined to claim any capital allowances in either of the first two years of trading. The 1996/97 assessment would become £12,720 and the 1997/98 loss would become £7,680. Claiming Section 380 relief in 1996/97 would then leave income of £5,040 for the year, which would absorb nearly all of the personal allowances.

11.4

The losses eligible for Section 381 relief are :

Year	*Basis period*	*Workings*	*Loss*	*Years for S381 claim*
			£	
1995/96	1/10/95 to 5/4/96	£(11,850) x 187/457	(4,849)	92/93-94/95
1996/97	1/1/96 to 31/12/96	£(11,850) x 365/457 - overlap		
		£(11,850) x 95/457	(7,001)	93/94-95/96
1997/98	y/e 31/12/97		(9,660)	94/95-96/97

If all possible Section 381 claims are made, total income is :

		1992/93	*1993/94*	*1994/95*	*1995/96*
		£	£	£	£
Schedule D Case I		-	-	-	nil
Other income		6,100	6,250	6,400	3,450
		6,100	6,250	6,400	3,450
Less : Section 381 relief :	1995/96 loss	(4,849)			
	1996/97 loss		(6,250)	(751)	
	1997/98 loss			(5,649)	(3,450)
Total income (after loss reliefs)		1,251	-	-	-

Notes :

(a) Personal allowances are totally wasted in 1993/94 to 1995/96 and partly wasted in 1992/93.

(b) The loss incurred in 1997/98 has been only partly relieved. The remaining £561 of the loss (£9,660 - £5,649 - £3,450) is eligible for S381 relief in 1996/97 but there is no income in this year against which to set the loss. The loss will be carried forward under S385.

Chapter 12

12.1

	Nickleby	*Copperfield*	*Drood*	*Total*
	£	£	£	£
1/1/97 - 31/3/97				
(£18,250 x 90/365 = £4,500)	1,500	1,500	1,500	4,500
1/4/97 - 31/12/97				
(£18,250 x 275/365 = £13,750)	2,750	5,500	5,500	13,750
Allocation of profit for the year	4,250	7,000	7,000	18,250

12.2

	Pickwick	*Snodgrass*	*Tupman*	*Total*
	£	£	£	£
Interest on capital	720	1,200	600	2,520
Salaries	8,000	-	8,000	16,000
Remainder (shared equally)	(1,340)	(1,340)	(1,340)	(4,020)
	7,380	(140)	7,260	14,500
Notional loss divided 7,380:7,260	(71)	140	(69)	-
Allocation of profit for the year	7,309	-	7,191	14,500

12.3

The allocation of profit for each accounting period is :

	Dodson	*Fogg*	*Jackson*	*Total*
	£	£	£	£
y/e 30/6/95 (shared equally)	8,500	8,500	-	17,000
y/e 30/6/96 (shared 5:4:1)	11,000	8,800	2,200	22,000
y/e 30/6/97 (shared 5:4:1)	14,500	11,600	2,900	29,000

The assessments on each partner are :

Dodson

Year	*Basis period*	*Workings*	*Assessment*
			£
1994/95	1/7/94 to 5/4/95	£8,500 x 279/365	6,497
1995/96	y/e 30/6/95		8,500
1996/97	y/e 30/6/96		11,000
1997/98	y/e 30/6/97		14,500

Fogg

Year	*Basis period*	*Workings*	*Assessment*
			£
1994/95	1/7/94 to 5/4/95	£8,500 x 279/365	6,497
1995/96	y/e 30/6/95		8,500
1996/97	y/e 30/6/96		8,800
1997/98	y/e 30/6/97		11,600

Jackson

Year	*Basis period*	*Workings*	*Assessment*
			£
1995/96	1/7/95 to 5/4/96	£2,200 x 279/365	1,682
1996/97	y/e 30/6/96		2,200
1997/98	y/e 30/6/97		2,900

Note

Dodson and Fogg each have overlap profits of £6,497. Jackson has overlap profits of £1,682.

12.4

(a) The trading profit of £23,490 for the year to 30 September 1996 is allocated Wardle £16,443, Jingle £4,698, Trotter £2,349. The trading profit of £27,310 for the year to 30 September 1997 is allocated Wardle £19,117, Jingle £5,462, Trotter £2,731. The Schedule D Case I assessments on each partner are :

	Wardle	*Jingle*	*Trotter*
	£	£	£
1995/96 (187/365 x y/e 30/9/96)	8,424	2,407	1,203
1996/97 (y/e 30/9/96)	16,443	4,698	2,349
1997/98 (y/e 30/9/97)	19,117	5,462	2,731

(b) The untaxed interest of £2,000 for the year to 30 September 1996 is allocated Wardle £1,400, Jingle £400, Trotter £200. The untaxed interest of £2,200 for the year to 30 September 1997 is allocated Wardle £1,540, Jingle £440, Trotter £220. The Schedule D Case III assessments on each partner are :

	Wardle	*Jingle*	*Trotter*
	£	£	£
1995/96 (187/365 x y/e 30/9/96)	717	205	102
1996/97 (y/e 30/9/96)	1,400	400	200
1997/98 (y/e 30/9/97)	1,540	440	220

(c) The taxed interest of £1,250 (gross) for the year to 30 September 1996 is allocated Wardle £875, Jingle £250, Trotter £125. The taxed interest of £1,360 (gross) for the year to 30 September 1997 is allocated Wardle £952, Jingle £272, Trotter £136. The amount assessed on each partner in 1996/97 is:

		£
Wardle	(£875 x 178/365 + £952 x 187/365)	914
Jingle	(£250 x 178/365 + £272 x 187/365)	261
Trotter	(£125 x 178/365 + £136 x 187/365)	131

Chapter 13

13.1

See text.

13.2

(a) 15% of £20,000 = £3,000.

(b) 15% of £84,000 = £12,600.

13.3

See text.

13.4

		£	£
Profits assessed under Schedule D Case I or II			22,450
Less :	Loss relief	1,200	
	Excess of trade charges over unearned income (£250 - £0)	250	1,450
Net relevant earnings for 1997/98			21,000

Karen was aged 60 at the start of 1997/98 so her allowable percentage is 35%. The maximum allowable personal pension premium which Karen could pay in 1997/98 is £7,350 (35% of £21,000).

13.5

Damon reaches his 36th birthday on 10 July 1996, so the allowable percentage of NRE is 17.5% in 1995/96 and 1996/97 and 20% in 1997/98.

In 1995/96, 17.5% of NRE is £3,010. The premiums paid of £2,500 are allowed in full and there is £510 of unused relief to carry forward (up to 2001/02).

In 1996/97, 17.5% of NRE is £3,220. The premiums paid of £2,600 are allowed in full and there is £620 of unused relief to carry forward (up to 2002/03).

In 1997/98, 20% of NRE is £1,120, so there are excess premiums of £1,480 in the year. The unused relief of £400 from 1990/91 is now too old to be used but £1,130 of the excess premiums can be relieved by using the unused relief from 1995/96 and 1996/97 (£510 + £620). The remaining £350 of excess premiums (£1,480 - £1,130) cannot be relieved in any way.

Chapter 14

14.1

(a) No POA's are required because the 1996/97 liability (less tax deducted at source) is less than £500. A balancing payment of £440 (£1,750 - £1,250 - £60) is payable on 31 January 1999.

(b) The amount paid by deduction at source in 1996/97 (£4,390) is less than 80% of the total liability for 1996/97 and the remainder of the liability (£2,340) exceeds £500, so POA's are required for 1997/98. A first POA of £1,170 (one-half of £2,340) is due on 31 January 1998 and a second POA of £1,170 is due on 31 July 1998. A balancing *repayment* of £605 (£6,580 - £4,810 - £35 - £2,340) will be made on 31 January 1999. Marie could have made a claim to pay reduced POA's for 1997/98 if she had known that the POA's based on her 1996/97 liability were likely to be excessive.

(c) No POA's are required because more than 80% of the 1996/97 liability was satisfied by deduction at source. A balancing payment of £3,600 (£16,110 - £12,370 - £140) is payable on 31 January 1999.

14.2

(a) Dorothy's balancing payment was not more than 28 days late so no surcharges are payable.

(b) The first POA of £12,000 was paid 27 days late, the second POA of £12,000 was paid 43 days late and the balancing payment of £4,000 was paid 21 days late. The interest payable is as follows :

	£
£12,000 x 8.5% x 27/365	75.45
£12,000 x 8.5% x 43/365	120.16
£4,000 x 8.5% x 21/365	19.56
	215.17

14.3

(a) Jabran notified the Inland Revenue of his chargeability to tax within the permitted six months and so incurs no penalty in relation to this notification.

(b) His completed tax return was due to be submitted to the Inland Revenue within 3 months of the issue date. He submitted the return late (but not more than 6 months late) and so incurs a fixed penalty of £100.

(c) The balancing payment was due 3 months after the issue date of the tax return. His payment was more than 28 days late and therefore he incurs a 5% surcharge.

(d) Interest is payable on the tax paid late and interest is payable on the surcharge if it is not paid within 30 days of the date of its imposition.

Chapter 15

15.1

(a) Primary : 2% x £62 + 10% x £16 = £2.84
Secondary : 3% x £78 = £2.34

(b) Primary : 2% x £62 + 10% x £116 = £12.84
Secondary : 7% x £178 = £12.46

(c) Primary : 2% x £62 + 10% x £403 = £41.54
Secondary : 10% x £475 = £47.50

(d) Primary : nil (earnings are less than the lower earnings limit)
Secondary : nil (earnings are less than the lower earnings limit)

(e) Primary : 2% x £269 + 10% x £144 = £19.78
Secondary : 3% x £413 = £12.39

(f) Primary : 2% x £269 + 10% x £1,746 = £179.98
Secondary : 10% x £2,500 = £250.

15.2

(a) Primary : 2% x £62 + 8.4% x £16 = £2.58
Secondary : 3% x £62 + 0% x £16 = £1.86

(b) Primary : 2% x £62 + 8.4% x £116 = £10.98
Secondary : 7% x £62 + 4% x £116 = £8.98

(c) Primary : 2% x £62 + 8.4% x £403 = £35.09
Secondary : 10% x £62 + 7% x £403 + 10% x £10 = £35.41

(d) Primary : nil (earnings are less than the lower earnings limit)
Secondary : nil (earnings are less than the lower earnings limit)

(e) Primary : 2% x £269 + 8.4% x £144 = £17.48
Secondary : 3% x £269 + 0% x £144 = £8.07

(f) Primary : 2% x £269 + 8.4% x £1,746 = £152.04
Secondary : 10% x £269 + 7% x £1,746 + 10% x £485 = £197.62.

15.3

Mark's profit for Class 2 purposes in 1997/98 is £5,589 (£6,890 x 239/365 + £3,120 x 126/365). This exceeds the small earnings exemption limit so Mark is liable to pay Class 2 contributions of £6.15 per week. His profit for Class 4 purposes in 1997/98 is £7,200 so Class 4 contributions of £11.40 are payable (6% x (£7,200 - £7,010)).

Chapter 16

16.1

(a) Companies are not chargeable persons, so the sale will not give rise to a CGT liability.

(b) Disposals between husband and wife who are living together are deemed to occur at a disposal value such that neither a gain nor a loss arises, therefore there will be no CGT liability on the gift.

(c) Gifts to charities are exempt from CGT.

(d) Charities are not chargeable persons, therefore disposals by charities do not give rise to a CGT liability.

(e) The sale is made in the course of trade. Therefore the profit arising will be subject not to CGT but to income tax under Schedule D Case I.

(f) The partnership is not a chargeable person but the partners are. Any CGT liability arising on the disposal of the leasehold property will be divided between them.

16.2

(a) Shares and securities are chargeable assets (apart from gilt-edged securities and certain corporate bonds).

(b) Gilt-edged securities are not chargeable assets.

(c) A table is a chattel. Chattels disposed of for £6,000 or more are chargeable assets.

(d) A chair is a chattel. Chattels disposed of for less than £6,000 are not chargeable assets.

(e) A taxpayer's principal private residence is not a chargeable asset.

(f) Motor cars are not chargeable assets.

16.3

(a) Net losses are £2,500. The annual exemption is lost and the CGT assessment is £nil.

(b) Net losses are £1,000. The annual exemption is lost and the CGT assessment is £nil.

(c) Net gains are £2,150. The unused part of the annual exemption (£4,350) is lost and the CGT assessment is £nil.

(d) Net gains are £8,450. The annual exemption of £6,500 is fully used and the CGT assessment is £1,950.

16.4

The CGT assessment is £3,400 (£9,900 - £6,500). Taxable income is £23,275 (£27,320 - £4,045), using the whole of the 20% band and £19,175 of the 23% band. This leaves £2,825 (£22,000 - £19,175) of the 23% band remaining. Therefore CGT is payable at 23% on the first £2,825 and 40% on the remaining £575, giving a CGT liability of £879.75.

16.5

(a) Net gains are £5,700. £800 of the annual exemption is lost and the CGT assessment is £nil. The losses brought forward of £4,800 remain unrelieved and are carried forward to 1998/99.

(b) Net gains are £7,100. This exceeds the annual exemption by £600, so £600 of the losses brought forward are relieved and the CGT assessment is £nil. The remaining £4,200 of the losses brought forward are carried forward to 1998/99.

(c) Net gains are £12,700. This exceeds the annual exemption by £6,200, so all of the losses brought forward are relieved and the CGT assessment is £1,400 (£6,200 - £4,800). There are no unrelieved losses to carry forward.

16.6

Net losses in 1997/98 are £14,200. The annual exemption is lost and the CGT assessment for the year is £nil. The net losses may be offset against the net gains of 1996/97, 1995/96 and 1994/95, in that order, to the extent that those net gains exceed the annual exemption. Relief available is £nil in 1996/97, £2,800 (£8,800 - £6,000) in 1995/96 and £6,500 (£12,300 - £5,800) in 1994/95. Total relief is £9,300. The remaining £4,900 of net losses in 1997/98 cannot be relieved at all.

16.7

31 January 1999.

Chapter 17

17.1

		£
Sale proceeds		62,000
Less : Incidental costs of disposal		3,100
		58,900
Less : Acquisition cost	35,000	
Enhancement expenditure	3,000	38,000
Unindexed gain		20,900
Less : Indexation allowance :		
(i) on acquisition cost		
$\frac{156.8 - 103.3}{103.3}$ = 0.518 x £35,000	18,130	
(ii) on enhancement expenditure		
$\frac{156.8 - 103.7}{103.7}$ = 0.512 x £3,000	1,536	19,666
Chargeable gain		1,234

(The repainting costs do not rank as enhancement expenditure).

17.2

	(a)	(b)	(c)
	£	£	£
Sale proceeds	4,950	4,350	5,380
Less : Deemed acquisition cost	4,500	4,500	4,500
Unindexed gain (loss)	450	(150)	880
Less : Indexation allowance			
$\frac{158.3 - 135.6}{135.6} = 0.167 \times £4,500 = £752$	450	nil	752
Chargeable gain (allowable loss)	nil	(150)	128

Notes :

(a) Indexation allowance is restricted to £450 to avoid converting an unindexed gain into a loss.

(b) There is an unindexed loss. Therefore the indexation allowance is restricted to £nil.

(c) The indexation allowance can be given in full.

17.3

	£
Sale proceeds (June 1997)	100,000
Less : Incidental costs of disposal	5,000
	95,000
Less : Part cost :	
$\frac{£100,000}{£100,000 + £500,000} \times £240,000$	(40,000)
Part incidental costs of acquisition :	
$\frac{£100,000}{£100,000 + £500,000} \times £12,000$	(2,000)
Unindexed gain	53,000
Less : Indexation allowance	
$\frac{156.2 - 134.1}{134.1} = 0.165 \times £42,000$	6,930
Chargeable gain	46,070

	£
Sale proceeds (January 1998)	520,000
Less : Remainder of cost (£240,000 - £40,000)	(200,000)
Remainder of costs of acquisition (£12,000 - £2,000)	(10,000)
Unindexed gain	310,000
Less : Indexation allowance	
$\frac{158.3 - 134.1}{134.1} = 0.180 \times £210,000$	37,800
Chargeable gain	272,200

17.4

(a)

	Original cost	Rebasing
	£	£
Sale proceeds	37,500	37,500
Less : Original cost	12,500	
Market value 31/3/82		10,000
Unindexed gain	25,000	27,500
Less : Indexation allowance		
$\frac{158.9 - 79.44}{79.44}$ = 1.000 x £12,500	12,500	12,500
Chargeable gain	12,500	15,000

The rebasing calculation gives the higher gain, so rebasing does not apply and the chargeable gain is £12,500.

(b)

	Original cost	Rebasing
	£	£
Sale proceeds	37,500	37,500
Less : Original cost	12,500	
Market value 31/3/82		15,000
Unindexed gain	25,000	22,500
Less : Indexation allowance		
$\frac{158.9 - 79.44}{79.44}$ = 1.000 x £15,000	15,000	15,000
Chargeable gain	10,000	7,500

The rebasing calculation gives the lower gain, so rebasing applies and the chargeable gain is £7,500.

17.5

(a)

	£
Deemed disposal proceeds	80
Less : Acquisition cost	6,000
Unindexed loss	(5,920)
Less : Indexation allowance	
$\frac{157.4 - 125.1}{125.1}$ = 0.258 x £6,000 = £1,548	nil
Allowable loss	(5,920)

(b)

	£
Disposal proceeds	120
Less : Deemed acquisition cost	80
Unindexed gain	40
Less : Indexation allowance	
$\frac{158.9 - 157.4}{157.4}$ = 0.010 x £80	1
Chargeable gain	39

17.6

(a)

	Original cost	*Rebasing*
	£	£
Sale proceeds	8,450	8,450
Less : Original cost	100	
Market value 31/3/82		8,500
Unindexed gain (loss)	8,350	(50)
Less : Indexation allowance		
$\frac{156.8 - 79.44}{79.44}$ = 0.974 x £8,500	8,279	nil
Chargeable gain (allowable loss)	71	(50)

One calculation gives a gain and the other gives a loss. So the situation is "no gain, no loss".

(b)

	Original cost	*Rebasing*
	£	£
Sale proceeds	8,450	8,450
Less : Original cost	100	
Market value 31/3/82		12,500
Unindexed gain (loss)	8,350	(4,050)
Less : Indexation allowance		
$\frac{156.8 - 79.44}{79.44}$ = 0.974 x £12,500 = £12,175	8,350	nil
Allowable loss	nil	(4,050)

The rebasing calculation gives the greater loss, therefore rebasing does not apply and the allowable loss is £nil.

Chapter 18

18.1

(a) Wasting chattel.
(b) Chattel.
(c) Wasting chattel.
(d) Wasting asset.
(e) Wasting asset.
(f) Wasting chattel.
(g) Chattel.

18.2

	£
Sale proceeds	7,200
Less : Incidental disposal costs	200
	7,000
Less : Acquisition cost	2,000
Unindexed gain	5,000
Less : Indexation allowance	
$\frac{157.4 - 115.5}{115.5} = 0.363 \times £2,000$	726
Chargeable gain	4,274

However, the chargeable gain is restricted to (£7,200 - £6,000) x 5/3 = £2,000.

18.3

	£
Sale proceeds (restricted)	6,000
Less : Deemed acquisition cost	50,000
Unindexed loss	(44,000)
Less : Indexation allowance	nil
Allowable loss	(44,000)

18.4

	£
Sale proceeds	25,000
Less : Part cost :	
$\frac{£25,000}{£25,000 + £85,000} \times 38,500$	8,750
Unindexed gain	16,250
Less : Indexation allowance	
$\frac{158.3 - 86.84}{86.84} = 0.823 \times £8,750$	7,201
Chargeable gain	9,049

The maximum chargeable gain is (£110,000 - £6,000) x 5/3 x 25/110 = £39,394. The actual gain is far less than this so the chargeable gain is £9,049.

18.5

	(a)	(b)
	£	£
Sale proceeds	60,000	35,000
Less : Acquisition cost	50,000	50,000
	10,000	(15,000)
Less : Available capital allowances	0	15,000
Unindexed gain/(loss)	10,000	0
Less : Indexation allowance		
$\frac{158.9 - 130.9}{130.9}$ = 0.214 x £50,000 = £10,700	10,000	0
Chargeable gain	nil	nil

18.6

	£
Sale proceeds	8,000
Less : Unexpired portion of cost $\frac{3}{5}$ x £10,000	6,000
Unindexed gain	2,000
Less : Indexation allowance	
$\frac{156.2 - 149.8}{149.8}$ = 0.043 x £6,000	258
Chargeable gain	1,742

18.7

When the lease was acquired it had a 25-year life (Sch 8 percentage 81.100%). On 31 March 1982 there were 23 years and 5 months remaining (Sch 8 percentage 78.055 + 1.567 x 5/12 = 78.708%). When it was assigned there were 8 years remaining (Sch 8 percentage = 39.399%). Therefore the computation is as follows :

	Original cost	*Rebasing*
	£	£
Sale proceeds	20,000	20,000
Less : Unexpired portion of cost		
$\frac{39.399}{81.100}$ x £12,500	6,073	
Unexpired portion of MV 31/3/82		
$\frac{39.399}{78.708}$ x £15,000		7,509
Unindexed gain	13,927	12,491

	Original cost	Rebasing
	£	£
Unindexed gain	13,927	12,491
Less : Indexation allowance		
$\frac{156.8 - 79.44}{79.44}$ = 0.974 x £7,509	7,314	7,314
Chargeable gain	6,613	5,177

The rebasing calculation gives the lower gain, so rebasing applies and the chargeable gain is £5,177.

Chapter 19

19.1

(a)	20 October 1997	200	(bought on same day)
	17 October 1997	50	(bought within previous 9 days)
(b)	17 October 1997	50	(FA1985 pool)
	4 August 1981	50	(1982 holding)
(c)	4 August 1981	950	(1982 holding)
	10 September 1962	250	(pre-6 April 1965)

19.2

	No. of shares	Cost	Indexed cost
		£	£
Bought 29 June 1982	1,000	3,000	3,000
Bought 5 May 1984	1,000	3,500	3,500
Add : Indexation to April 1985			
(a) $\frac{94.78 - 81.85}{81.85} = 0.158$			
0.158 x £3,000			474
(b) $\frac{94.78 - 88.97}{88.97} = 0.065$			
0.065 x £3,500			228
FA 1985 pool at 5 April 1985	2,000	6,500	7,202
Add : Indexation to August 1987			
$\frac{102.1 - 94.78}{94.78}$ x £7,202			556
			7,758
Bought 13 August 1987	1,350	6,500	6,500
FA 1985 pool at 13 August 1987	3,350	13,000	14,258
Add : Indexation to September 1990			
$\frac{129.3 - 102.1}{102.1}$ x £14,258			3,798
c/f	3,350	13,000	18,056

	No. of shares	Cost	Indexed cost
		£	£
b/f	3,350	13,000	18,056
Bought 7 September 1990	2,650	14,150	14,150
FA 1985 pool at 7 September 1990	6,000	27,150	32,206
Add : Indexation to October 1995			
$\frac{149.8 - 129.3}{129.3} \times £32,206$			5,106
Bought 4 October 1995	2,000	22,500	22,500
FA 1985 pool at 4 October 1995	8,000	49,650	59,812

19.3

FA 1985 pool at 4 October 1995	8,000	49,650	59,812
Add : Indexation to April 1997			
$\frac{155.6 - 149.8}{149.8} \times £59,812$			2,316
			62,128
Sold April 1997 (2,000/8,000th)	(2,000)	(12,413)	(15,532)
FA 1985 pool c/f	6,000	37,237	46,596

	(a)	(b)	(c)
	£	£	£
Sale proceeds	14,000	12,000	16,000
Less : Cost	12,413	12,413	12,413
Unindexed gain (loss)	1,587	(413)	3,587
Less : Indexation allowance			
(£15,532 - £12,413 = £3,119)	1,587	nil	3,119
Chargeable gain (allowable loss)	nil	(413)	468

19.4

The value of the 1982 holding is as follows :

	No. of shares	Cost
		£
Acquired 5 August 1978	300	2,400
Acquired 12 May 1980	200	1,700
Acquired 11 July 1981	250	2,000
	750	6,100
Sold August 1997 (150/750th)	(150)	(1,220)
1982 holding c/f	600	4,880

The calculation of the chargeable gain arising on the disposal is as follows :

	Original cost	Rebasing
	£	£
Sale proceeds	3,000	3,000
Less : Original cost	1,220	
Market value 31/3/82		1,500
Unindexed gain	1,780	1,500
Less : Indexation allowance		
$\frac{156.8 - 79.44}{79.44}$ = 0.974 x £1,500	1,461	1,461
Chargeable gain	319	39

The rebasing calculation gives the lower gain, so rebasing applies and the chargeable gain is £39.

19.5

FA 1985 pool :

	No. of shares	Cost	Indexed cost
		£	£
Bought 21 June 1990	10,000	9,000	9,000
Add : Indexation to March 1993			
$\frac{139.3 - 126.7}{126.7}$ x £9,000			895
			9,895
Bought 3 March 1993	10,000	11,000	11,000
FA 1985 pool at 3 March 1993	20,000	20,000	20,895
Add : Indexation to December 1997			
$\frac{158.0 - 139.3}{139.3}$ x £20,895			2,805
			23,700
Sold December 1997	(20,000)	(20,000)	(23,700)
FA 1985 pool c/f	nil	nil	nil

The chargeable gain on the disposal of the FA1985 pool is :

	£
Sale proceeds (20,000 @ £1.25)	25,000
Less : Cost	20,000
Unindexed gain	5,000
Less : Indexation allowance	
(£23,700 - £20,000)	3,700
Chargeable gain	1,300

1982 holding :

	No. of shares	*Cost*
		£
Bought 28 December 1980	10,000	5,000
Sold December 1997 (5,000/10,000th)	(5,000)	(2,500)
1982 holding c/f	5,000	2,500

The chargeable gain on the disposal from the 1982 holding is :

	Original cost	*Rebasing*
	£	£
Sale proceeds (5,000 @ £1.25)	6,250	6,250
Less : Original cost	2,500	
Market value 31/3/82		3,000
Unindexed gain	3,750	3,250
Less : Indexation allowance		
$\frac{158.0 - 79.44}{79.44}$ = 0.989 x £3,000	2,967	2,967
Chargeable gain	783	283

The chargeable gain is £283. The total chargeable gain is therefore £1,583 (£1,300 + £283).

19.6

The value of the 1982 holding is as follows :

	No. of shares	*Cost*
		£
Acquired 17 February 1963 (@ £9)	500	4,500
Acquired 8 January 1980	700	8,500
	1,200	13,000
Sold September 1997 (1,000/1,200th)	(1,000)	(10,833)
1982 holding c/f	200	2,167

The chargeable gain on the disposal is :

	Original cost	*Rebasing*
	£	£
Sale proceeds (1,000 @ £40)	40,000	40,000
Less : Original cost	10,833	
Market value 31/3/82 (1,000 @ £15)		15,000
Unindexed gain	29,167	25,000
Less : Indexation allowance		
$\frac{157.1 - 79.44}{79.44}$ = 0.978 x £15,000	14,670	14,670
Chargeable gain	14,497	10,330

The chargeable gain is £10,330.

19.7

1982 holding :

	No. of shares	*Cost*
		£
Acquired 8 January 1980	700	8,500
Sold September 1997	(700)	(8,500)
1982 holding c/f	nil	nil

The gain on the disposal of the 1982 holding is :

	Original cost	*Rebasing*
	£	£
Sale proceeds (700 @ £40)	28,000	28,000
Less : Original cost	8,500	
Market value 31/3/82 (700 @ £15)		10,500
Unindexed gain	19,500	17,500
Less : Indexation allowance		
$\frac{157.1 - 79.44}{79.44}$ = 0.978 x £10,500	10,269	10,269
Chargeable gain	9,231	7,231

The rebasing calculation gives the lower gain, so rebasing applies and the chargeable gain is £7,231.

Pre-6 April 1965 shares :

	Original cost	*MV 6/4/65*
	£	£
Sale proceeds (300 @ £40)	12,000	12,000
Less : Original cost (£4,000 x 300/500)	2,400	
Market value 6/4/65 (300 @ £9)		2,700
Unindexed gain	9,600	9,300
Less : Indexation allowance		
$\frac{157.1 - 79.44}{79.44}$ = 0.978		
0.978 x £4,500 (300 @ £15)	4,401	4,401
Chargeable gain	5,199	4,899

The lower gain is £4,899, which is then compared with the gain produced by rebasing i.e. :

	Rebasing
	£
Sale proceeds	12,000
Less : Market value 31/3/82 (300 @ £15)	4,500
Unindexed gain	7,500
Less : Indexation allowance	4,401
Chargeable gain	3,099

This is lower than £4,899 so rebasing applies and the chargeable gain is £3,099. The total gain is £7,231 + £3,099 = £10,330.

Chapter 20

20.1

1982 holding :

	No. of shares	*Cost*
		£
Acquired 17 February 1980	600	900
Bonus issue July 1997 (1 for 4)	150	nil
1982 holding c/f	750	900

FA1985 pool :

	No. of shares	*Cost*	*Indexed cost*
		£	£
Acquired 13 November 1988	200	400	400
Bonus issue July 1997 (1 for 4)	50	nil	nil
FA 1985 pool (indexed to Nov. 1988)	250	400	400

Revised market value at 31/3/82 is 4/5th of £1.70 = £1.36 per share.

20.2

FA1985 pool (250 shares sold) :

	No. of shares	*Cost*	*Indexed cost*
		£	£
b/f (indexed to Nov. 1988)	250	400	400
Add : Indexation to March 1998 $\frac{158.9 - 110.0}{110.0} \times £400$			178
			578
Sold March 1998	(250)	(400)	(578)
FA 1985 pool c/f	nil	nil	nil

The chargeable gain on the disposal of the FA1985 pool is :

	£
Sale proceeds (250 @ £4)	1,000
Less : Cost	400
Unindexed gain	600
Less : Indexation allowance (£578 - £400)	178
Chargeable gain	422

1982 holding (50 shares sold) :

	No. of shares	*Cost*
		£
b/f	750	900
Sold March 1998 (50/750th)	(50)	(60)
1982 holding c/f	700	840

The chargeable gain on the disposal from the 1982 holding is :

	Original cost	*Rebasing*
	£	£
Sale proceeds (50 @ £4)	200	200
Less : Original cost	60	
MV 31/3/82 (50 @ £1.36)		68
Unindexed gain	140	132
Less : Indexation allowance		
$\frac{158.9 - 79.44}{79.44}$ = 1.000 x £68	68	68
Chargeable gain	72	64

The rebasing calculation gives the lower gain, so rebasing applies and the chargeable gain is £64. The total gain on the entire disposal of 300 shares is £486 (£422 + £64).

20.3

The 1982 holding is :

	No. of shares	*Cost*
		£
Acquired 30 September 1979	2,000	1,200
Rights issue January 1998 (1 for 8)	250	250
1982 holding c/f	2,250	1,450

The FA1985 pool is :

	No. of shares	*Cost*	*Indexed cost*
		£	£
Acquired 1 December 1992	3,000	3,600	3,600
Add : Indexation to January 1998			
$\frac{158.3 - 139.2}{139.2}$ x £3,600			494
			4,094
Rights issue January 1998 (1 for 8)	375	375	375
FA 1985 pool c/f	3,375	3,975	4,469

20.4

FA1985 pool :

	No. of shares	Cost	Indexed cost
		£	£
b/f at January 1998	3,375	3,975	4,469
Add : Indexation to March 1998			
$\frac{158.9 - 158.3}{158.3}$ x £4,469			17
			4,486
Sold March 1998	(3,375)	(3,975)	(4,486)
FA 1985 pool c/f	nil	nil	nil

The chargeable gain on the disposal of the FA1985 pool is :

	£
Sale proceeds (3,375 @ £1.80)	6,075
Less : Cost	3,975
Unindexed gain	2,100
Less : Indexation allowance (£4,486 - £3,975)	511
Chargeable gain	1,589

1982 holding :

	No. of shares	Cost
		£
b/f	2,250	1,450
Sold March 1998	(2,250)	(1,450)
1982 holding c/f	nil	nil

The chargeable gain on the disposal of the 1982 holding is :

	Original cost	Rebasing
	£	£
Sale proceeds (2,250 @ £1.80)	4,050	4,050
Less : (i) *2,000 original shares* :		
Cost	(1,200)	
Market value 31/3/82 (2,000 @ £0.75)		(1,500)
(ii) *250 rights shares* :		
Cost	(250)	(250)
Unindexed gain c/f	2,600	2,300

	Original cost	Rebasing
	£	£
Unindexed gain b/f	2,600	2,300
Less : Indexation allowance :		
(i) *2,000 original shares* : $\frac{158.9 - 79.44}{79.44}$ = 1.000 x £1,500	(1,500)	(1,500)
(ii) *250 rights shares* : $\frac{158.9 - 158.3}{158.3}$ = 0.004 x £250	(1)	(1)
Chargeable gain	1,099	799

The rebasing calculation gives the lower gain, so rebasing applies and the chargeable gain is £799. The total gain on the entire disposal is £2,388 (£1,589 + £799).

20.5

The value of the part disposed of is £100 (100 @ £1) and the value of the part remaining is £150 (100 @ £1.50), so there has been a 100/250th part disposal. The FA1985 pool is :

	No. of shares	Cost	Indexed cost
		£	£
Bought November 1989	100	500	500
Add : Indexation to May 1997 $\frac{155.9 - 118.5}{118.5}$ x £500			158
			658
Distribution May 1997 (100/250th)	-	(200)	(263)
FA 1985 pool c/f	100	300	395

The computation of the allowable loss is :

	£
Disposal proceeds	100
Less : Part cost	(200)
Unindexed loss	(100)
Less : Indexation allowance (£263 - £200)	nil
Allowable loss	(100)

20.6

The value of Yolande's shares immediately prior to the sale of rights was £600. £25 is less than 5% of £600, so the sale of rights ranks as a small capital distribution. Assuming that the gain on this small capital distribution is rolled over, the FA1985 pool is :

	No. of shares	*Cost*	*Indexed cost*
		£	£
Bought January 1990	300	360	360
Add : Indexation to March 1993 $\frac{139.3 - 119.5}{119.5}$ x £360			60
			420
Distribution March 1993	-	(25)	(25)
	300	335	395
Add : Indexation to November 1997 $\frac{157.7 - 139.3}{139.3}$ x £395			52
			447
Sold November 1997	(300)	(335)	(447)
FA1985 pool c/f	nil	nil	nil

The chargeable gain on the disposal is :

	£
Sale proceeds	780
Less : Cost	335
Unindexed gain	445
Less : Indexation allowance (£447 - £335)	112
Chargeable gain	333

20.7

Walter received 6,400 shares worth £27,520, plus £2,000 in cash i.e. a total of £29,520. The amount received in cash is more than 5% of the total, so this does not rank as a small capital distribution. The FA1985 pool is :

	No. of shares	*Cost*	*Indexed cost*
		£	£
Bought (Oval plc) April 1993	4,000	23,400	23,400
Add : Indexation to Sept. 1997 $\frac{157.1 - 140.6}{140.6}$ x £23,400			2,746
			26,146
Sold Sept. 1997 (2,000/29,520th)	-	(1,585)	(1,771)
FA1985 pool after disposal	4,000	21,815	24,375
FA 1985 pool (Round plc) c/f	6,400	21,815	24,375

The chargeable gain on the disposal is :

	£
Disposal proceeds	2,000
Less : Cost	1,585
Unindexed gain	415
Less : Indexation allowance (£1,771 - £1,585)	186
Chargeable gain	229

Chapter 21

21.1

So long as Mohammed actually resides in both properties he may choose which is to be regarded as his PPR. Whichever property he bought and lived in first was automatically regarded as his PPR. After he bought the second property (and began residing in it) he could, if he wished, elect that this property should become his PPR for CGT purposes. He would do this if he thought that the gain arising on the disposal of the second property would exceed the gain arising on the disposal of the first property. The election would have to be made within 2 years of the date from which it is to take effect.

21.2

	Original cost	*Rebasing*
	£	£
Sale proceeds	58,000	58,000
Less : Original cost	18,000	
Market value 31/3/82		21,000
Unindexed gain	40,000	37,000
Less : Indexation allowance		
$\frac{157.7 - 79.44}{79.44}$ = 0.985 x £21,000	20,685	20,685
Gain before PPR exemption	19,315	16,315

The rebasing calculation gives the lower gain, so rebasing applies and the gain arising (before considering the PPR exemption) is £16,315. Considering each of the three cases individually :

(a) The house is not a chargeable asset and the disposal is exempt from CGT. The chargeable gain is therefore £nil.

(b) After 31 March 1982, Melanie owned the house for 15 years and 7 months (187 months) and was absent for 48 months. There is no indication that the absence was work-related and this absence exceeds the permissible maximum "absence for any reason" by 12 months. Therefore the PPR exemption is £16,315 x 175/187 = £15,268 and the chargeable gain is £16,315 x 12/187 = £1,047.

(c) Letting relief is available equal to the lowest of £1,047, £15,268 and £40,000 i.e. £1,047. This reduces the chargeable gain to £nil.

21.3

	£
Sale proceeds	172,000
Less : Acquisition cost	55,000
Unindexed gain	117,000
Less : Indexation allowance	
$\frac{158.9 - 86.67}{86.67}$ = 0.833 x £55,000	45,815
Gain before PPR exemption	71,185

Rupert's period of ownership (a total of 172 months) is broken down as follows :

(i)	1 November 1983 to 31 October 1987	48 months	Actual residence
(ii)	1 November 1987 to 31 October 1988	12 months	Working abroad
(iii)	1 November 1988 to 31 January 1989	3 months	Actual residence
(iv)	1 February 1989 to 30 April 1993	51 months	Working in UK
(v)	1 May 1993 to 31 May 1993	1 month	Actual residence
(vi)	1 June 1993 to 1 March 1998	57 months	Living with friend

Periods (i), (iii) and (v) are exempt (actual residence) and period (ii) is exempt (working abroad). Period (iv) exceeds the 4-year maximum allowable for working in the UK but the remaining 3 months of this period are exempt as part of the 36 months allowed for any reason. The last 36 months of ownership are exempt but the remaining 21 months of period (vi) cannot be exempt since they are not followed by a period of actual residence. The chargeable gain is :

	£
Total gain (as above)	71,185
Less : PPR exemption : £71,185 x 151/172	62,494
	8,691
Less : Letting relief (lowest of £8,691, £62,494 and £40,000)	8,691
Chargeable gain	nil

21.4

	£
Sale proceeds	75,000
Less : Acquisition cost	37,500
Unindexed gain	37,500
Less : Indexation allowance	
$\frac{156.8 - 89.94}{89.94}$ = 0.743 x £37,500	27,863
Gain before PPR exemption	9,637

Samantha owned the house for a total of 13 years (156 months). For 6 years (72 months) the house was used partly for business purposes. The computation of the chargeable gain is as follows :

	£	£
Total gain (as above)		9,637
Less : PPR exemption :		
£9,637 x 84/156	5,189	
£9,637 x 72/156 x 4/5	3,558	8,747
Chargeable gain		890

Chapter 22

22.1

The allowable expenditure in relation to the porcelain is £9,850 (£10,000 incurred March 1986, plus £3,850 incurred March 1992, less £4,000 received July 1992). The computation of the gain arising in March 1998 is :

	£	£
Sale proceeds		23,500
Less : Allowable expenditure		9,850
Unindexed gain		13,650
Less : Indexation allowance :		
(i) on original cost $\frac{158.6 - 96.73}{96.73}$ = 0.640 x £10,000	6,400	
(ii) on restoration costs $\frac{158.6 - 136.7}{136.7}$ = 0.160 x £3,850	616	
(iii) on compensation received $\frac{158.6 - 138.8}{138.8}$ = 0.143 x £4,000	(572)	6,444
Chargeable gain		7,206

22.2

The gain arising on the loss of the original necklace is as follows :

	£
Disposal proceeds	19,000
Less : Acquisition cost	13,500
Unindexed gain	5,500
Less : Indexation allowance	
$\frac{142.1 - 103.7}{103.7}$ = 0.370 x £13,500	4,995
Chargeable gain	505

The allowable cost of the new necklace is reduced to £18,995 (£19,500 - £505). The gain arising on its disposal is as follows :

		£
Disposal proceeds		22,000
Less : Deemed acquisition cost		18,995
Unindexed gain		3,005
Less : Indexation allowance		
$\frac{158.3 - 142.1}{142.1}$	= 0.114 x £18,995	2,165
Chargeable gain		840

22.3

The gain on the disposal of the original building is computed as follows :

		£
Sale proceeds		64,300
Less : Acquisition cost		50,000
Unindexed gain		14,300
Less : Indexation allowance		
$\frac{157.1 - 129.3}{129.3}$	= 0.215 x £50,000	10,750
Chargeable gain		3,550

(a) £2,500 of the sale proceeds have been retained. Therefore £2,500 of the gain is immediately chargeable. The remaining £1,050 may be rolled-over against the cost of the new building, reducing its allowable cost to £60,750 (£61,800 - £1,050).

(b) £5,000 of the sale proceeds have been retained. This exceeds the chargeable gain. Therefore the whole gain is immediately chargeable and no part of the gain may be rolled-over. The allowable cost of the new building is the full £59,300.

(c) The entire sale proceeds have been spent on a replacement building. Therefore none of the gain is immediately chargeable and the entire gain may be rolled-over against the cost of the new building, reducing its allowable cost to £63,250 (£66,800 - £3,550).

22.4

The gains which may be held-over are those relating to chargeable business assets i.e. the freehold (£23,500) and the goodwill (£40,000), totalling £63,500. Listed investments do not rank as a chargeable business asset, so the gain of £10,600 is immediately chargeable.

22.5

(a) The taxpayer is fully eligible for retirement relief. The first £250,000 is fully exempt and half of the remaining £300,000 is also exempt. Total retirement relief is £400,000 (£250,000 + £150,000), leaving a chargeable gain of £150,000.

(b) The taxpayer is entitled to a proportionate retirement relief based on 9 years of trading. The lower and upper limits are scaled down to £225,000 and £900,000 respectively. The first £225,000 is fully exempt and 50% relief will be granted on the gains lying between £225,000 and £900,000 (i.e. the next £675,000). Total retirement relief is £562,500 (£225,000 + £337,500), leaving a chargeable gain of £637,500.

(c) The taxpayer is entitled to a proportionate retirement relief based on 2 years of trading. The lower and upper limits are scaled down to £50,000 and £200,000 respectively. The first £50,000 is fully exempt and half of the remaining £150,000 is also exempt. Total retirement relief is £125,000 (£50,000 + £75,000), leaving a chargeable gain of £75,000.

Chapter 23

23.1

(a) The year to 30 November 1997 is a CAP.

(b) The period from 1 October 1996 to 31 July 1997 does not exceed 12 months and is a CAP.

(c) The period from 1 January 1998 to 31 January 1998 does not exceed 12 months and is a CAP.

(d) The 33 months to 31 August 1997 is divided into 3 CAP's. These are the 12 months to 30 November 1995, the 12 months to 30 November 1996 and the 9 months to 31 August 1997.

(e) The 18 months to 30 September 1997 is divided into 2 CAP's. These are the 12 months to 31 March 1997 and the 6 months to 30 September 1997.

23.2

(a) (i) The dividend received is franked investment income. It does not form part of the company's chargeable profits.

(ii) The debenture interest received is Schedule D Case III income (assuming that the debentures were acquired for non-trading purposes). The income tax of £320 (£1,280 x 20/80) suffered by deduction may be reclaimed, but the gross debenture interest accrued during the CAP is chargeable to corporation tax.

(iii) The income tax of £2,160 (£8,640 x 20/80) deducted at source from the debenture interest paid must be accounted for to the Inland Revenue, but the gross interest accrued during the CAP is allowed either as a trading expense in the company's Schedule D Case I computation or as a debit when computing the net credit or debit arising from non-trading loan relationships (depending on whether or not the loan is for trade purposes).

(b) All three items would normally be shown gross in the company's profit and loss account.

23.3

Companies receive bank interest gross. Therefore the £1,500 of bank interest received will be assessed under Schedule D Case III and will form part of the company's chargeable profits for the CAP in which it is received.

Assuming that the interest on Government securities is received net, the income tax of £375 (£1,500 x 20/80) suffered by deduction at source may be reclaimed. The gross amount of interest accrued for the CAP is a credit on a non-trading loan relationship (assuming that the securities were acquired for non-trading purposes) and will be aggregated with other debits and credits arising on non-trading loan relationships. Net credits are assessed under Schedule D Case III. Net debits may be relieved in various ways (see text).

23.4

The 17 months to 30 June 1997 will be divided into two CAP's. These are the 12 months to 31 January 1997 and the 5 months to 30 June 1997. The chargeable profits for each CAP are as follows :

	365 days to 31/1/97	150 days to 30/6/97
	£	£
Trading income (time apportioned)	301,214	123,786
Building society interest received	2,450	2,675
Rents, furnished (time apportioned)	6,386	2,624
Rents, unfurnished :		
Due 1/2/96, 1/5/96, 1/8/96, 1/11/96	12,000	
Due 1/2/97, 1/5/97		6,000
Chargeable gains	28,700	49,760
	350,750	184,845
Less : Charges on income	12,000	-
	338,750	184,845

Notes :

(a) The BSI (received gross by a company) is allocated according to the date received. The charges on income are allocated according to the date of payment. Accruals are ignored in both cases.

(b) The rents on unfurnished property are allocated according to the dates due.

(c) The chargeable gains are allocated according to the dates of the disposals. Even though the two disposals are on consecutive days, they fall into different CAP's.

23.5

The chargeable profits for the year to 31 March 1998 are as follows :

		£
Schedule D Case I		1,549,400
Schedule D Case III		
Bank deposit interest received (£43,800 + £44,670)	88,470	
Debenture interest receivable (£10,500 x 100/80)	13,125	101,595
Chargeable gains		531,000
		2,181,995
Less : Charges on income (£6,930 x 100/77)		9,000
Chargeable profits		2,172,995

23.6

	21 L/R	23 N/R	25 N/R	25 T/R	27 L/R	27 L/R
	£	£	£	£	£	£
Rent due :						
24 June 1997	500	25			625	
29 September 1997	500	25		750	625	
25 December 1997	500	25		750		
25 March 1998	500	25		750		650
c/f	2,000	100	0	2,250	1,250	650

	£	£	£	£	£	£
b/f	2,000	100	0	2,250	1,250	650
Less :						
Insurance	(200)	(120)		(150)		(125)
Rent collector's fees	(120)			(135)	(75)	(39)
Repairs whilst vacant						(154)
Repairs whilst let	(3,450)	(180)	(28)			(77)
Surplus/(loss)	(1,770)	(200)	(28)	1,965	1,175	255
Loss on Number 21	1,430				(1,175)	(255)
	(340)	(200)	(28)	1,965	0	0
	c/f	c/f				

The Schedule A assessment for the year to 31 March 1998 is £1,965.

Notes :

(i) The void period at Number 25 was not immediately preceded by a lease at full rent and so the repairs incurred during this period are not allowable.

(ii) The void period at Number 27 was immediately preceded and followed by a lease at full rent and so the repairs incurred during this period are allowable.

(iii) The loss incurred on Number 21 can be set against surpluses from other landlord's repairing leases in this or future CAP's. The only surpluses available in this CAP are those on Number 27 but these absorb only £1,430 of the loss, leaving £340 to be carried forward.

(iv) The loss on the nominal rent lease at Number 23 can only be relieved against future surpluses (if any) on the same lease. The loss on the nominal rent lease at Number 25 cannot be carried forward since the lease has terminated and is therefore unrelieved.

Chapter 24

24.1

FY96	1 July 1996 to 31 March 1997	£2,500,000 x 274/365 = £1,876,712
FY97	1 April 1997 to 30 June 1997	£2,500,000 x 91/365 = £623,288

24.2

(a) Profits are £287,500 (£267,000 + £16,400 x 100/80). This is less than the lower limit for FY97 of £300,000 so the small company rate applies and the corporation tax liability is £61,410 (23% x £267,000).

(b) Profits are £1,505,000 (£1,450,000 + £44,000 x 100/80). This exceeds the upper limit for FY97 of £1,500,000 so the full rate applies and the corporation tax liability is £478,500 (33% x £1,450,000).

(c) Profits and chargeable profits are both £10,000,000. Profits exceed the upper limit so the full rate applies and the corporation tax liability is £3,300,000 (33% x £10,000,000).

24.3

The company's profits are £577,000 (£536,000 + £32,800 x 100/80), a figure which lies between the lower limit and the upper limit for FY97. The chargeable profits (£536,000) are taxed at the full rate and marginal relief is available. The computation is as follows :

	£	
Corporation tax on £536,000 @ 33%	176,880.00	
Less : Marginal relief : $\frac{1}{40}$ x (£1,500,000 - £577,000) x $\frac{£536,000}{£577,000}$	21,435.35	
Corporation tax due	155,444.65	

24.4

The company has chargeable profits of £875,983 and profits of £908,783 (£875,983 + £32,800) for its CAP which falls partly into FY96 and partly into FY97. (Note that the FII figure was stated gross). Chargeable profits, profits, lower limits and upper limits are apportioned between the two FY's as follows :

	FY96 (1/3/97 to 31/3/97)	*FY97 (1/4/97 to 28/2/98)*
Chargeable	£875,983 x 31/365 = £74,399	£875,983 x 334/365 = £801,584
Profits	£908,783 x 31/365 = £77,184	£908,783 x 334/365 = £831,599
Lower limit	£300,000 x 31/365 = £25,479	£300,000 x 334/365 = £274,521
Upper limit	£1,500,000 x 31/365 = £127,397	£1,500,000 x 334/365 = £1,372,603

In both FY's, profits are between the lower and upper limits so marginal relief applies. The computation is :

FY96	£	£
Corporation tax on £74,399 @ 33%	24,551.67	
Less : Marginal relief : $\frac{9}{400}$ x (£127,397 - £77,184) x $\frac{£74,399}{£77,184}$	1,089.03	23,462.64
FY97		
Corporation tax on £801,584 @ 33%	264,522.72	
Less : Marginal relief : $\frac{1}{40}$ x (£1,372,603 - £831,599) x $\frac{£801,584}{£831,599}$	13,036.94	251,485.78
Corporation tax liability for the CAP		274,948.42

24.5

The due date of payment is 1 June 1997 (9 months and one day after 31 August 1996). The final payment of £46,500 was made on 3 October 1997, i.e. 124 days late. The interest due is :

$$£46,500 \times 6.25\% \times \frac{124}{365} = £987.33.$$

Chapter 25

25.1

(a) The dividend paid is 2,000,000 @ 7p = £140,000, so the ACT payable is £140,000 x 20/80 = £35,000. The franked payment is £175,000 (£140,000 + £35,000).

(b) The ACT is payable on 14 January 1998.

(c) The ACT paid of £35,000 will be offset against the corporation tax liability for the year to 31 December 1997 (due 1 October 1998).

(d) The amount of ACT would be the same, but the payment date would be 14 April 1998 and the offset would be against the corporation tax liability for the year to 31 December 1998 (due 1 October 1999).

25.2

1/12/96 to 31/12/96, 1/1/97 to 31/3/97, 1/4/97 to 30/6/97, 1/7/97 to 30/9/97, 1/10/97 to 30/11/97.

25.3

Dividend paid 1 June 1996 :

(a) ACT due is £160,000 x 20/80 = £40,000. The franked payment is £200,000 (£160,000 + £40,000).

(b) ACT is payable on 14 July 1996.

(c) The offset will be against the corporation tax liability for the year to 30 April 1997 (the year in which the dividend was paid).

Dividend paid 1 April 1997 :

(a) ACT due is £72,000 x 20/80 = £18,000. The franked payment is £90,000 (£72,000 + £18,000).

(b) ACT is payable on 14 May 1997 (14 days after the fifth return period of the year, covering the dates 1 April 1997 to 30 April 1997).

(c) The offset will be against the corporation tax liability for the year to 30 April 1997 (the year in which the dividend was paid).

25.4

Return period	*FP*	*FII*	*FP - FII*	*Cumulative FP - FII*	*ACT payable (repayable)*
	£	£	£	£	£
1/4/97 - 30/6/97		5,500	(5,500)	(5,500)	0.00
1/7/97 - 30/9/97	8,000		8,000	2,500	500.00
1/10/97 - 31/12/97	8,750	4,000	4,750	7,250	950.00
1/1/98 - 31/3/98		1,500	(1,500)	5,750	(300.00)
	16,750	11,000	5,750		1,150.00

Notes :

(i) In the first return period, FII exceeds FP's. The surplus FII is carried forward to the next return period but the tax credit of £1,100 (20% of £5,500) is not repayable to the company.

(ii) At the end of the second return period, FP's for the year to date exceed FII by £2,500. ACT is payable on this at 20% i.e. £500.

(iii) At the end of the third return period, FP's for the year to date exceed FII by £7,250. ACT is payable on this at 20% i.e. £1,450, less the £500 previously paid, giving £950.

(iv) At the end of the fourth return period, FP's for the year to date exceed FII by £5,750. ACT is payable on this at 20% i.e. £1,150. However, a total of £1,450 has already been paid in earlier return periods so a £300 refund is payable to the company.

25.5

The maximum ACT set-off is the ACT attributable to a franked payment of £24,000,000 i.e. 20% x £24,000,000 = £4,800,000. In other words, the company could pay a dividend of £19,200,000, giving rise to an ACT liability of £4,800,000 (£19,200,000 x 20/80) and all of this ACT could be offset against the company's corporation tax liability for the year.

25.6

ACT of £16,000 (£64,000 x 20/80) is attributable to the dividend. But the maximum ACT set-off for the year is 20% x £78,000 = £15,600 so there is surplus ACT of £400. The MCT due on 1 January 1999 is :

	£	£
Corporation tax liability (£78,000 @ 23%)		17,940
Less : Lower of :		
(a) ACT payable for the year	16,000	
(b) Maximum ACT set-off	15,600	15,600
MCT payable		2,340

Chapter 26

26.1

(a) payment made net of 20% income tax

(b) income received net of 20% income tax

(c) neither (dividends paid trigger payments of ACT)

(d) neither (dividends received are franked investment income)

(e) neither (interest paid to a UK bank is paid gross)

(f) neither (interest from a UK bank is received by companies gross).

26.2

Return period	*Tax deducted*	*Tax suffered*	*Tax deducted less tax suffered*	*Cumulative*	*Income tax payable (repayable)*
	£	£	£	£	£
1/4/97 - 30/6/97	4,000	2,300	1,700	1,700	1,700
1/10/97 - 31/12/97	4,000		4,000	5,700	4,000
1/1/98 - 31/3/98		1,300	(1,300)	4,400	(1,300)
	8,000	3,600	4,400		4,400

26.3

The income tax returns for the year are as follows :

Return period	*Tax deducted*	*Tax suffered*	*Tax deducted less tax suffered*	*Cumulative*	*Income tax payable (repayable)*
	£	£	£	£	£
1/4/97 - 30/6/97		70,000	(70,000)	(70,000)	0
1/7/97 - 30/9/97	90,000		90,000	20,000	20,000
1/1/98 - 31/3/98		70,000	(70,000)	(50,000)	(20,000)
	90,000	140,000	(50,000)		0

The company requires an income tax repayment of £50,000. This is made by means of a reduction in the MCT liability for the year, as follows :

	£
Corporation tax liability for the year (33% of £2,400,000)	792,000
Less : ACT paid (£420,000 x 20/80)	105,000
	687,000
Less : Income tax repayable	50,000
MCT payable 1 January 1999	637,000

Chapter 27

27.1

	y/e 31/5/95	*y/e 31/5/96*	*y/e 31/5/97*
	£	£	£
Schedule D Case I	-	23,800	11,500
Less : S393(1)/(9) relief	-	23,800	9,600
	-	0	1,900
Less : Non-trade charges	-	-	600
	-	0	1,300
Less : Trade charges	-	-	1,300
Chargeable profits	0	0	0
Trading losses and trade charges c/f	32,200	9,600	100
Non-trade charges unrelieved	400	500	-

27.2

	£
Schedule D Case I	-
Schedule A	10,200
Chargeable gains	540
c/f	10,740

	£
b/f	10,740
Less : S393A(1)(a) relief	7,300
	3,440
Less : Non-trade charges	3,440
	0
Less : Trade charges	0
Chargeable profits	0
Trade charges c/f	9,000
Non-trade charges unrelieved	560

27.3

The correct answer is (c). Under S393A(1)(a), trading losses may be relieved against total profits (including capital gains) of the CAP in which the loss was incurred.

27.4

		y/e 30/6/94	*y/e 30/6/95*	*y/e 30/6/96*	*y/e 30/6/97*
		£	£	£	£
Schedule D Case I		54,800	22,700	8,600	-
Capital gains		-	-	-	8,700
		54,800	22,700	8,600	8,700
Less : S393A(1)(a) relief		-	-	-	8,700
		54,800	22,700	8,600	0
Less : Trade charges		5,000	5,000	5,000	-
		49,800	17,700	3,600	0
Less : S393A(1)(b) relief	(1)			3,600	
	(2)		17,700		
	(3)	11,900			
		37,900	0	0	0
Less : Non-trade charges		1,000	-	-	-
Chargeable profits		36,900	0	0	0
Trade charges c/f		-	-	-	5,000
Non-trade charges unrelieved		-	1,000	1,000	1,000

27.5

The main effects of a S393A(1)(b) claim are as follows :

(a) Chargeable profits for the year to 31 March 1997 will be reduced to £600,000. This is beneath the upper limit for marginal relief purposes so the corporation tax due will be calculated at 33%, less marginal relief.

(b) The maximum ACT set-off for the year to 31 March 1997 will be reduced to 20% of £600,000 = £120,000. Since ACT of £125,000 has been paid for the year (one-quarter of £500,000), this will generate surplus ACT of £5,000.

(c) The corporation tax refund due for the year to 31 March 1997 will carry interest dating from 1 January 1998 (or the date on which the tax was originally paid, if later).

Chapter 28

28.1

(a), (d) and (e) are associates, (b) and (c) are not.

28.2

The top five shareholders are Sejanus (with Apicata) 1020 shares, Claudius (with Livia) 590 shares, Agrippa 300 shares, Cleopatra 300 shares and Tiberius 200 shares, totalling 2410 shares. So the company is not under the control of five or fewer shareholders.

Sejanus is ranked as a director (since he is a manager and, with his wife, owns 20.4% of the share capital). So the directors are Sejanus (with Apicata) 1020 shares, Claudius (with Livia) 590 shares, Agrippa 300 shares, Cleopatra 300 shares, Tiberius 200 shares and Gaius 200 shares, totalling 2610 shares. The company is under the control of its participator-directors and is therefore a close company.

28.3

(a) The director owns more than 5% of the company's share capital so the loan is taxable. The company must pay notional ACT of £3,000 by 1 January 1999 (unless the loan is repaid before then). Once paid, this tax is not refundable until 9 months after the end of the CAP in which the loan is repaid. The director will be subject to Schedule E income tax on loan interest calculated at the official rate.

(b) The director will be subject to Schedule E income tax on a benefit in kind of £1,500. But if the ticket had been given to a shareholder who was *not* a director or other employee, it would have been treated as a distribution. ACT of £375 would have been payable by the company and the shareholder would have been charged to income tax on a gross distribution of £1,875 (tax credit £375).

Chapter 29

29.1

(a) They are associated companies and so share the upper and lower limits for small companies relief purposes.

(b) They form a 51% group so Arm Ltd and Foot Ltd may pay dividends to Head Ltd without accounting for ACT. Charges and annual interest may be paid between any of the group members without accounting for income tax.

(c) Head Ltd may surrender ACT to Arm Ltd and/or Leg Ltd.

(d) They also form a 75% group so trading losses and related items may be surrendered by a group member to any other group member.

(e) Chargeable assets are transferred between the three companies without giving rise to a chargeable gain.

29.2

	£	
Trading profits, less capital allowances	220,000	
Bank deposit interest	6,000	
UFII	4,000	
Patent royalties	(17,000)	
Chargeable profits	213,000	
FII (£24,000 x 100/80)	30,000	
Profits for SCR purposes	243,000	
SCR lower limit (£300,000 x 1/3)	100,000	
SCR upper limit (£1,500,000 x 1/3)	500,000	
		£
Corporation tax on £213,000 @ 33%		70,290.00
Less : Marginal relief :		
$\frac{1}{40}$ x (£500,000 - £243,000) x $\frac{£213,000}{£243,000}$		5,631.79
Corporation tax due		64,658.21

Note :

The SCR limits are shared between Alpha Ltd, Beta Ltd and the other active subsidiary.

29.3

(a) (i) Delta Ltd will pay ACT of £200,000 x 15% x 20/80 = £7,500, due 14 October 1997.

(ii) Gamma Ltd will pay ACT of £1,000,000 x 20/80 = £250,000, due 14 April 1997.

(b) (i) Delta Ltd will pay ACT of £200,000 x 20/80 = £50,000, due 14 October 1997.

(ii) Gamma Ltd will pay £250,000 as before but will then be entitled to an ACT repayment of £200,000 x 85% x 20/80 = £42,500 for the return period to 30 September 1997.

29.4

Base Ltd has current year trading losses of £90,000 and excess charges of £1,000, giving a total of £91,000. But Apex Ltd has chargeable profits of only £73,000 (£120,000 - £42,000 + £7,000 - £12,000), so the maximum group relief that may be claimed is £73,000.

29.5

A1 Ltd owns at least 75% of A2 Ltd and A2 Ltd owns at least 75% of A3 Ltd, of which A1 Ltd (indirectly) owns more than 50%. Therefore A1 Ltd, A2 Ltd and A3 Ltd form a capital gains group. A2 Ltd does not own at least 75% of A4 Ltd, so A4 Ltd is not a member of the group, even though A1 Ltd does (indirectly) own more than 50% of its ordinary share capital.

29.6

The amount of PP Ltd's loss which is available for group relief is £84,000 i.e. £96,000 less a potential S393A(1)(a) claim of £12,000. This is shared between the consortium members as follows :

	QQ Ltd	*RR Ltd*	*SS Ltd*
	£	£	£
Share of PP Ltd's available loss	26,880	29,400	19,320
Chargeable profits	59,000	47,000	14,000
Maximum group relief claim	26,880	29,400	14,000

Chapter 30

30.1

(a) The value of the supply is £340, VAT charged is 17.5% x £340 = £59.50 and the consideration for the supply is £399.50.

(b) The value of the supply is £333.20 (£340, less 2%), VAT charged is 17.5% x £333.20 = £58.31 and the consideration for the supply is £391.51.

(c) VAT chargeable remains at £58.31 but the consideration for the supply is £398.31.

30.2

(a) Lorna must register since her taxable turnover exceeds the registration threshold.

(b) Mike must register since his aggregate taxable turnover exceeds the registration threshold.

(c) No-one need register. The partnership of "Pat and Phil" is not the same person as "Phil" so the turnover of the two businesses is not aggregated.

(d) The taxable "person" in this case is the company (not the shareholders) and therefore the company must register.

30.3

(a) She is not a taxable person, may not register for VAT and cannot reclaim input tax.

(b) She is a taxable person and must register for VAT. She must account for output tax and may reclaim input tax.

(c) She is a taxable person and must register for VAT unless granted an exemption by Customs and Excise. If she registers she may reclaim input tax. If she is granted exemption she will not be able to reclaim input tax but she will avoid the administrative burden associated with VAT registration.

30.4

See text.

30.5

See text.

30.6

(a) Books are zero-rated. No input tax has been paid and so none may be reclaimed.

(b) No output tax is chargeable if a second-hand car is sold for less than its original purchase price, so long as input tax paid when acquiring the car was not deductible.

(c) The supply of a used commercial building is exempt unless the seller has elected for the "option to tax". If this is the case, output tax of £200,000 @ 17.5% = £35,000 must be accounted for.

30.7

Input tax reclaimed is £411 x 7/47 = £61.21. Output tax of £55.40 (scale figure) must be accounted for.

Chapter 31

31.1

	Value before AE	*AE for 1997/98*	*AE for 1996/97*	*Value after AE*
	£	£	£	£
Gift to grandson (exempt as a small gift)	-	-	-	-
Gift on marriage (£3,000 - £1,000)	2,000	2,000	-	-
Gift to husband (spouse exemption)	-	-	-	-
Gift to discretionary trust	10,000	1,000	3,000	6,000
Gift to Labour Party (exempt)	-	-	-	-
	12,000	3,000	3,000	6,000

31.2

(a) PET (b) exempt (c) chargeable (d) PET (e) PET.

31.3

The total of transfers brought forward in the last 7 years is £171,000, leaving £44,000 of the nil band to set against the current transfer.

(a) If the trustees pay the tax, the gross value of the transfer is £80,000 and the IHT due is £44,000 x 0% + £36,000 @ 20% = £7,200, payable on 30 June 1998.

(b) If Nicholas pays the tax, the net value of the transfer is £80,000. The gross value and the tax due are as follows :

	Net	*Gross*	*Tax*
	£	£	£
£44,000 grossed up @ 0%	44,000	44,000	0
£36,000 grossed up @ 20%	36,000	45,000	9,000
Totals	80,000	89,000	9,000

The tax due is £9,000, payable on 30 June 1998.

31.4

The value of each gift after deduction of exemptions is as follows :

		Value before AE	*AE for current year*	*AE for previous year*	*Value after AE*
		£	£	£	£
1992/93	Daughter (£500,000 - £5,000)	495,000	3,000	3,000	489,000
1996/97	Discretionary trust	500,000	3,000	3,000	494,000

Lifetime tax liability

The gifts to Martha's daughter was a PET, so no lifetime tax was payable. The lifetime tax on the gift to the discretionary trust was £73,500, payable on 30 April 1997 and calculated as follows :

	Net	*Gross*	*Tax*
	£	£	£
£200,000 grossed up @ 0%	200,000	200,000	0
£294,000 grossed up @ 20%	294,000	367,500	73,500
Totals	494,000	567,500	73,500

Tax liability on death

(i) *Transfer made on 31 August 1992*

The gross value of this transfer is £489,000 and there were no chargeable transfers in the previous 7 years. Tax due at death rates applicable on 1/1/98 :

	£
£215,000 @ 0%	0
£274,000 @ 40%	109,600
	109,600
Less : Taper relief (5-6 years) @ 60%	65,760
	43,840
Less : Lifetime tax paid	0
IHT payable by daughter on 31 July 1998	43,840

(ii) *Transfer made on 1 June 1996*

The gross value of this transfer is £567,500 and gross chargeable transfers in the previous 7 years (2/6/89 - 31/5/96) were £489,000, which used the whole of the 0% band. Tax due at death rates applicable on 1/1/98 :

	£
£567,500 @ 40%	227,000
Less : Taper relief (0-3 years) @ 0%	0
	227,000
Less : Lifetime tax paid	73,500
IHT payable by trustees on 31 July 1998	153,500

31.5

The quarter-up rule gives 572 + 1/4 x (588 - 572) = 576. The average of the highest and lowest marked bargains is 575, so the shares are valued at 575p and the transfer has a market value of 1,000 x £5.75 = £5,750.

Chapter 32

32.1

Jean-Paul is a UK resident during 1997/98 but he is neither ordinarily resident nor domiciled in the UK. His UK income tax position is as follows :

(a) The emoluments of his UK employment are fully taxable under Schedule E Case II.

(b) The emoluments of his Belgian employment are assessed under Schedule E Case III but only on the remittance basis. This would be the case even if he were ordinarily resident in the UK (the "foreign emoluments" rule).

(c) The dividends on the Canadian shares are assessed under Schedule D Case V but only on the remittance basis.

(d) The UK bank interest is (by concession) exempt from UK income tax since Jean-Paul is not ordinarily resident in the UK.

(e) He may claim personal allowances for 1997/98.

32.2

Normally, a person is regarded as being either resident for the whole of a tax year or non-resident for the whole of that year, but a person who leaves the UK to take up employment abroad for at least an entire tax year (as Amy has done) is regarded as resident for the part of the tax year before the date of departure and non-resident thereafter. Amy's situation is therefore as follows :

(a) In 1996/97 she is resident until 31/12/96 and non-resident from 1/1/97. She will receive full personal allowances for 1996/97 to set against her income for that year. Her income for UK tax purposes after 31/12/96 will consist only of any income arising in the UK (e.g. rents from letting her house whilst away). Her Australian salary will not be subject to UK tax.

(b) In 1997/98 and 1998/99 she is non-resident. Her Australian salary will not be subject to UK tax and she will be taxed only on her UK income, if any. As a citizen of the European Economic Area, she is entitled to personal allowances.

(c) In 1999/00 she is resident from 1/1/00. She will receive full personal allowances for 1999/00 to set against her income for the year. Her income for UK tax purposes before 1/1/00 consists only of her UK income. Once again, her Australian salary will not be subject to UK tax.

However, if Amy visits the UK for 183 days or more in any one tax year she will be resident for that year and her worldwide income will be subject to UK income tax. Similarly, she will be regarded as resident if she visits the UK for 91 days or more per annum.

32.3

Bryan's contract of employment does not cover a whole tax year and so he is UK resident throughout. His employment income is assessed under Schedule D Case I. His periods of presence and absence are :

	Days absent	*Days present*	*Cumulative days present*	*Cumulative total days*
1/7/96 to 23/12/96	176		0	176
24/12/96 to 2/1/97		10	10	186
3/1/97 to 6/4/97	94		10	280
7/4/97 to 26/5/97		50	60	330
27/5/97 to 3/7/97	38		60	368

	Days absent	*Days present*	*Cumulative days present*	*Cumulative total days*
4/7/97 to 30/7/97		27	87	395
31/7/97 to 30/10/97	92		87	487

The qualifying period begins on 1/7/96. No visit to the UK lasts for more than 62 days. Testing for the one-sixth condition on each return to the UK :

(i) On 24/12/96, zero does not exceed one-sixth of 176. The condition is satisfied.

(ii) On 7/4/97, 10 does not exceed one-sixth of 280. The condition is satisfied.

(iii) On 4/7/97, 60 does not exceed one-sixth of 36. The condition is satisfied.

(iv) On 31/10/97, 87 does exceed one-sixth of 487, so the qualifying period comes to an end on 3/7/97.

The qualifying period lasts for 368 days. This is more than 365 days so the emoluments earned by Bryan during this 368-day period are exempt from UK income tax. The remaining emoluments are taxable.

32.4

(a) 90% of the pension is subject to UK income tax under Schedule D Case V.

(b) 100% of the amount of the pension remitted to the UK is subject to UK income tax under Schedule D Case V.

32.5

See text.

32.6

See text.

32.7

	UK	*Overseas*	*Total*
	£	£	£
Schedule D Case I	120,000		120,000
Schedule D Case V			
(£57,400 x 100/82 x 100/50)		140,000	140,000
Chargeable profits	120,000	140,000	260,000
Corporation tax @ 23%	27,600	32,200	59,800
Less : Unilateral DTR		(32,200)	(32,200)
Corporation tax due	27,600	-	27,600

Notes :

(i) Underlying tax relief is available since Brits Ltd owns at least 10% of the voting power of the overseas company.

(ii) The unilateral relief given is restricted to the UK tax due on the foreign income. The remaining £50,400 (£82,600 - £32,200) of foreign tax paid is unrelieved.

Answers to review questions

Set A

Question A1

(a)

	£
Car (35% of £19,500)	6,825
Fuel scale charge	1,010
Loan (6.75% of £5,250)	354
LV's (200 @ £4.85)	970
Nursery fees	2,000
	11,159

(b) (i) Drive an extra 100 miles per year on business and reduce the taxable car benefit by one-third, a reduction of £2,275.

(ii) If the £400 contribution is made towards the running costs of the car, not towards private fuel, it will reduce the taxable car benefit.

(iii) Reduce the loan to £5,000, so that no taxable benefit arises.

(iv) Take the canteen meals instead of LV's. No taxable benefit will arise.

(v) Transfer the son to the in-house nursery. No taxable benefit will arise.

These combined measures would reduce the taxable benefits by £5,999 (£2,275 + £400 + £354 + £970 + £2,000).

(c)

	Mr T	*Mrs T*
	£	£
Salary	50,000	14,000
Less : Pension contributions		840
		13,160
Benefit package	11,159	
BSI (x 100/80)	8,000	2,800
Dividends (x 100/80)	5,200	
	74,359	15,960
Less : PA	4,045	4,045
Taxable income	70,314	11,915

Income tax

Mr T	*Mrs T*			
4,100	4,100	@ 20%	820.00	820.00
22,000	5,015	@ 23%	5,060.00	1,153.45
	2,800	@ 20%		560.00
44,214		@ 40%	17,685.60	
70,314	11,915		23,565.60	2,533.45
Less : MCA £1,830 @ 15%			274.50	
Tax borne			23,291.10	2,533.45

Tax could be saved by switching investments from Mr T to Mrs T, so as to use the rest of her basic rate band (where savings income would be taxed at only 20%).

Question A2

1997/98

Abel and Zoe may each claim the personal allowance of £4,045. MCA is available of £1,678 (£1,830 x 11/12). This will be allocated to Abel unless an election is made by both spouses for the MCA to be allocated to Zoe or an election is made by Zoe for 50% of the MCA to be allocated to her. If either spouse has insufficient income to use his/her allocation of MCA, that spouse may elect that the unused amount should be transferred to the other spouse.

1998/99

Abel and Zoe may each claim the personal allowance of £4,045. The full MCA of £1,830 is available and this will be allocated as described above for 1997/98. Each spouse may claim the full APA of £1,830, but this will be reduced by any MCA also claimed by that spouse (ignoring any MCA which has been transferred between spouses because the other spouse's income is insufficient to use it). Abel makes maintenance payments to Zoe of £1,560 (£40 x 39 weeks) in the year and is entitled to tax relief in relation to these payments.

1999/00

Abel and Zoe may each claim the personal allowance of £4,045 and the APA of £1,830. No MCA is available. Abel's maintenance payments in the year total £2,340 (£40 x 39 weeks + £60 x 13 weeks) but he is entitled to tax relief on only £1,830 of these payments.

Question A3

Sarah was 36 years old at the start of 1989/90 and 44 years old at the start of 1997/98, so the applicable percentage in all years is 20%. Unused relief is therefore :

	£
1997/98	10,000
1996/97	6,000
1995/96	2,000
1994/95	1,800
1993/94	1,600
1992/93	1,400
1991/92	1,200
1990/91	1,000
1989/90	800

(i) Sarah should pay a premium in 1997/98 for 1997/98 of £10,000.

(ii) She should also pay a premium of £6,000 in 1997/98 and elect for this to be carried back to 1996/97, so using the 1996/97 relief. This election must be made by 31 January 1999.

(iii) Unused relief in the six years prior to 1996/97 (1990/91 to 1995/96) totals £9,000. Sarah should therefore pay a premium of £9,000 in 1997/98 and elect (by 31 January 1999) for this to be carried back to 1996/97, where it will be covered by the unused relief brought forward from the previous six years.

(iv) The total premium to be paid in 1997/98 is £25,000 (£10,000 + £6,000 + £9,000).

Question A4

(i) *Mr de Praet*

	1996/97	*1997/98*
	£	£
Schedule D Case I	20,000	nil
Schedule A	5,000	5,000
	25,000	5,000
Less : S380 relief	25,000	5,000
Statutory total income	nil	nil

Mr de Praet's own personal allowance is lost in both years. His wife can use a small part of the tax reduction relating to the MCA but most of this is lost as well. Tax savings are achieved at 20% and 23%. If the loss had been carried forward under S385, there would have been much less loss of personal allowances and tax savings would have been achieved at 40%.

(ii) Capital allowances of £4,600 (25% x £18,400) are available in the year to 30 June 1998. These increase the loss to £14,600. A Section 380 claim for 1997/98 will reduce total income to £1,400 (£16,000 - £14,600), so wasting personal allowances.

It would be better to restrict the capital allowances claim to £1,955. This reduces the S380 claim to £11,955, leaving total income of £4,045 which exactly absorbs the 1997/98 personal allowance. The unclaimed capital allowances increase the WDV carried forward and so result in higher capital allowances in future years.

Question A5

If the transactions are of a trading nature, then the profits made by the partnership of Bernard and Gerald will be charged to income tax in years 1997/98 and 1998/99 under Schedule D Case I. The "badges of trade" will be used to decide whether they are trading, as follows :

(a) *Subject matter.* It appears that the subject matter of the transaction is of a type normally associated with a trading venture, rather than of a type more normally associated with investments or personal consumption.

(b) *Frequency of transactions.* There was only one purchase but there were several sales. The fact that sales were made to a number of different garden centres gives the impression of trading.

(c) *Length of ownership.* This was a fairly short-term venture. Most of the barrels had been sold within 6 months and this again gives the impression of trading.

(d) *Supplementary work.* The barrels were sawn in half and Bernard and Gerald canvassed garden centres in the hope of finding customers. These activities constitute supplementary work and support the view that they were trading.

(e) *Motive*. It seems clear that the barrels were bought with only one view in mind - resale at a profit. This is a clear indicator of trading.

(f) *Acquisition*. The barrels were not inherited or gifted. They were purchased by Bernard and Gerald. This and all the other badges of trade combine to support the view that they were trading and are liable under Schedule D Case I.

Set B

Question B1

Scott Stockings Ltd is Angela's personal company since she has at least 5% of the voting rights. All chargeable assets are business assets (gilt-edged securities are not chargeable) so the full gain is eligible for retirement relief. Relief is given at 60% of maximum (based on lower of Angela's time as full-time working director and the time for which she has owned her shares). The assessable capital gain is :

		£
Chargeable gain as calculated		290,000
Less : Retirement relief :		
(i) basic relief (60% x £250,000)	150,000	
(ii) 50% x (£290,000 - £150,000)	70,000	220,000
		70,000
Less : Annual exemption		6,500
Assessable capital gain		63,500

Note :

Upper limit for 50% relief is 60% x £1,000,000 = £600,000.

Question B2

FA1985 pool :

	No. of shares	*Cost* £	*Indexed cost* £
Bought 1 April 1987	1,000	11,000	11,000
Add : Indexation to Sept. 1989 $\frac{116.6 - 101.8}{101.8} \times £11,000$			1,599
			12,599
Rights issue Sept. 1989 (1 for 2)	500	3,000	3,000
	1,500	14,000	15,599
Add : Indexation to August 1997 $\frac{156.8 - 116.6}{116.6} \times £15,599$			5,378
All sold 1 August 1997	1,500	14,000	20,977

Sale proceeds are £30,000 (£42,000 x 1,500/2,100), and therefore the chargeable gain is £9,023 (£30,000 - £20,977).

1982 holding :

	No. of shares	*Cost*
		£
Acquired 1 August 1978	600	7,200
Rights issue Sept. 1989 (1 for 2)	300	1,800
	900	9,000
Sold 1 August 1997 (600/900th)	600	6,000
1982 holding c/f	300	3,000

The gain arising on the disposal from the 1982 holding is :

	Original cost	*Rebasing*
	£	£
Sale proceeds (£42,000 x 600/2,100)	12,000	12,000
Less : (i) *400 original shares* :		
Cost (£7,200 x 400/600)	(4,800)	
Market value 31/3/82 (400 @ £8)		(3,200)
(ii) *200 rights shares* :		
Cost (£200 @ £6)	(1,200)	(1,200)
Unindexed gain	6,000	7,600
Less : Indexation allowance :		
(i) *400 original shares* :		
$\frac{156.8 - 79.44}{79.44}$ = 0.974 x £4,800	(4,675)	(4,675)
(ii) *200 rights shares* :		
$\frac{156.8 - 116.6}{116.6}$ = 0.345 x £1,200	(414)	(414)
Chargeable gain	911	2,511

The lower gain is £911.

Total chargeable gain on entire disposal = £9,023 + £911 = £9,934.

Question B3

(i) The gain on the disposal of the building is :

	£
Sale proceeds	200,000
Less : Acquisition cost	100,000
Unindexed gain	100,000
Less : Indexation allowance	
$\frac{157.7 - 88.64}{88.64}$ = 0.779 x £100,000	77,900
	22,100
Less : "Held-over" gain	12,100
Chargeable gain	10,000

The chargeable gain is the amount not re-invested (£200,000 - £190,000).

(ii) The "held-over" gain of £12,100 is deferred until the earliest of :

a. disposal of the plant

b. December 2006 (10 years after the acquisition of the plant)

c. the date that the plant ceases to be used in the company's business.

Question B4

(a) *FA1985 pool* :

	No. of shares	*Cost*	*Indexed cost*
		£	£
Bought 25 March 1984	6,000	9,000	9,000
Add : Indexation to April 1985			
0.083 x £9,000			747
			9,747
Bonus issue June 1987 (1 for 3)	2,000	-	-
	8,000	9,000	9,747
Add : Indexation to April 1989			
0.206 x £9,747			2,008
	8,000	9,000	11,755
Bought 10 April 1989	7,000	14,000	14,000
	15,000	23,000	25,755
Add : Indexation to June 1997			
0.367 x £25,755			9,452
All sold 30 June 1997	15,000	23,000	35,207

Sale proceeds are £39,000 (£65,000 x 15,000/25,000), and therefore the chargeable gain is £3,793 (£39,000 - £35,207).

1982 holding :

	No. of shares	*Cost*
		£
Acquired 10 July 1979	12,000	12,000
Bonus issue Feb. 1981 (1 for 4)	3,000	-
Bonus issue June 1987 (1 for 3)	5,000	-
	20,000	12,000
Sold 30 June 1997	10,000	6,000
1982 holding c/f	10,000	6,000

The gain arising on the disposal from the 1982 holding is :

	Original cost	Rebasing
	£	£
Sale proceeds (£65,000 - £39,000)	26,000	26,000
Less : Cost	6,000	
MV 31/3/82		18,000
Unindexed gain	20,000	8,000
Less : Indexation allowance		
0.966 x £18,000 = £17,388	17,388	8,000
	2,612	nil

The lower gain is £nil. The total gain on the entire disposal is £3,793 + £nil = £3,793.

(b) In August 1988, £30,000 was not re-invested and was therefore immediately chargeable. The remaining £20,000 of the gain is chargeable in August 1997 when the plant is scrapped.

(c) (i) Gain on the painting is £1,692 (£7,500 - £3,000 - 0.936 x £3,000). This is restricted to 5/3 x (£7,500 - £6,000) = £2,500, so the chargeable gain is £1,692.

(ii) Chandelier is sold for less than £6,000 so not chargeable.

(iii) The two disposals are considered together, since the items form a set and are sold to connected persons. The gain is £724 (£8,000 - £4,000 - 0.819 x £4,000). This is restricted to 5/3 x (£8,000 - £6,000) = £3,333, so the chargeable gain is £724.

Question B5

(a) *Disposal of flat*

	Original cost	Rebasing
	£	£
Sale proceeds	71,000	71,000
Less : Incidental costs of disposal	2,000	2,000
	69,000	69,000
Less : Part cost :		
$\frac{£71,000}{£71,000 + £65,000}$ x £29,000	(15,140)	
Part market value 31/3/82 :		
$\frac{£71,000}{£71,000 + £65,000}$ x £40,000		(20,882)
Part conversion costs :		
$\frac{£71,000}{£71,000 + £65,000}$ x £18,000	(9,397)	(9,397)
Unindexed gain	44,463	38,721
Less : Indexation allowance		
$\frac{158.0 - 79.44}{79.44}$ = 0.989 x £20,882	(20,652)	(20,652)
$\frac{158.0 - 90.11}{90.11}$ = 0.753 x £9,397	(7,076)	(7,076)
Chargeable gain	16,735	10,993

The lower gain is £10,993.

Disposal of ICI shares

FA1985 pool :

	No. of shares	Cost	Indexed cost
		£	£
Bought December 1983	20,000	60,000	60,000
Add : Indexation to April 1985 $\frac{94.78 - 86.89}{86.89}$ = 0.091 x £60,000			5,460
			65,460
Add : Indexation to December 1997 $\frac{158.0 - 94.78}{94.78}$ x £65,460			43,663
All sold December 1997	20,000	60,000	109,123

The chargeable gain is £40,877 (£150,000 - £109,123) and the total gain on the flat and the shares is £51,870 (£10,993 + £40,877). After deducting the annual exemption for 1997/98, the chargeable gains for the year are £45,370. CGT due is (£26,100 - £20,000) @ 23% + £39,270 @ 40% = £17,111.00.

(b) Mr More should transfer the shares to Mrs More (at no gain, no loss). If she then disposes of them and realises the gain of £40,877, this will be entirely covered by her annual exemption and losses brought forward, so saving a substantial amount of CGT.

(c) *Disposal of shares in Hampton Ltd* :

	£		£
Sale proceeds :			
Freehold land	800,000		
Plant and machinery	60,000		
Investments	300,000		
Goodwill	280,000		
Net current assets	370,000		
	1,810,000		
Less : 10% discount	181,000		
	1,629,000	x 1/3 =	543,000
Less : Cost			40,000
			503,000
Less : Indexation allowance $\frac{159.8 - 79.44}{79.44}$ = 1.012 x £40,000			40,480
Chargeable gain			462,520

If the shares are sold in December 1998, Mr More will be over 50 and entitled to retirement relief, reducing the gain considerably. The computation is :

	£
Sale proceeds £1,810,000, less 15% x 1/3	512,833
Less : Cost	40,000
	472,833
Less : Indexation allowance	
$\frac{161.6 - 79.44}{79.44}$ = 1.034 x £40,000	41,360
Gain before retirement relief	431,473
Gain eligible for retirement relief :	
$\frac{£800{,}000 + £280{,}000}{£800{,}000 + £280{,}000 + £300{,}000}$ x £431,473	337,674
Less : Retirement relief : (£250,000 + 50% x £87,674)	293,837
	43,837
Add : Gain not eligible for retirement relief	93,799
Chargeable gain	137,636

Set C

Question C1

(a) The CAP's are the 12 months to 31 March 1997 and the 6 months to 30 September 1997.

(b)

	365 days to 31/3/97	*183 days to 30/9/97*
	£	£
Trading profits (time apportioned)	259,763	130,237
Less : Capital allowances :		
25% x £100,000	25,000	
25% x £75,000 x 183/365		9,401
Schedule D Case I	234,763	120,836
Schedule A	20,000	20,000
Schedule D Case III	5,000	15,000
	259,763	155,836
Less : Charges on income	5,000	5,000
Chargeable profits	254,763	150,836
Corporation tax @ 24%	61,143.12	
Corporation tax @ 33%		49,775.88
Less : 1/40 x (£752,055 - £150,836)		15,030.48
Corporation tax liability	61,143.12	34,745.40

Note : SCR upper limit for 2nd CAP is £1,500,000 x 183/365 = £752,055.

Question C2

Quarterly accounting for ACT/FII

Return period	*FP*	*FII*	*FP - FII*	*Cumulative FP - FII*	*ACT payable (repayable)*
	£	£	£	£	£
1/4/97 - 30/6/97	12,000	15,000	(3,000)	(3,000)	-
1/7/97 - 30/9/97	50,000	-	50,000	47,000	9,400
1/10/97 - 31/12/97	-	24,000	(24,000)	23,000	(4,800)
1/1/98 - 31/3/98	24,000	-	24,000	47,000	4,800
	86,000	39,000	47,000		9,400

£9,400 is payable on 14 October 1997. £4,800 will be repaid in (approximately) January 1998. £4,800 is payable on 14 April 1998.

Quarterly accounting for income tax

Return period	*Tax deducted*	*Tax suffered*	*Tax deducted less tax suffered*	*Cumulative*	*Income tax payable (repayable)*
	£	£	£	£	£
1/4/97 - 30/6/97	-	7,360	(7,360)	(7,360)	-
1/7/97 - 30/9/97	9,000	4,600	4,400	(2,960)	-
1/10/97 - 31/12/97	10,760	-	10,760	7,800	7,800
1/1/98 - 31/3/98	-	6,440	(6,440)	1,360	(6,440)
	19,760	18,400	1,360		1,360

£7,800 is payable on 14 January 1998, but £6,440 of this is repaid in (approximately) April 1998.

Question C3

(a) *Poynton Producers Ltd*

	£
Cost 1 April 1991	150,000
WDA for CAP to 30/9/91 (4%)	6,000
	144,000
WDA for CAP to 30/9/92	6,000
	138,000
Notional WDA's for 2 CAP's to 30/9/94	12,000
	126,000
WDA for CAP to 30/9/95	6,000
	120,000
WDA for CAP to 30/9/96	6,000
WDV at 30/9/96	114,000

(b) The net cost of the building is £10,000 (£150,000 - £140,000). The period of ownership is 6 years and the period of industrial use is 4 years and 212 days (4.581 years), so the adjusted net cost is £7,635 (£10,000 x 4.581 ÷ 6). The allowances actually given are £24,000, so the balancing charge is £16,365 (£24,000 - £7,635).

(c) The residue of expenditure after the sale is £130,365 (£114,000 + £16,365) and the remaining tax life of the building is 19 years. Sale Switches Ltd may claim an annual WDA of £6,861 (£130,365 x 1/19) for each of its 19 CAP's to 31 December 2015.

Question C4

(a)

	y/e 31/12/94	*y/e 31/12/95*	*y/e 31/12/96*	*y/e 31/12/97*
	£000	£000	£000	£000
Schedule D Case I	30	50	-	10
Schedule A	10	8	-	-
Schedule D Case III	12	4	-	2
Capital gain	-	-	20	-
UFII	10	10	5	4
	62	72	25	16
Less : S393A(1)(a) relief	-	-	25	-
	62	72	-	16
Less : Trade charges	-	8	-	2
	62	64	-	14
Less : S393A(1)(b) relief	62	64	-	-
	-	-	-	14
Less : Non-trade charges	-	-	-	1
Chargeable profits	-	-	-	13
Non-trade charges unrelieved	1	1	1	-

The unrelieved trading losses, including trade charges, are £27,000. These cannot be carried forward to the year ended 31 December 1997, since the trade has changed from manufacturing telephones to manufacturing cardboard boxes.

(b) (i) Corporation tax repaid for the year to 31/12/94 is £15,250 i.e. 25% x (£62,000 - £1,000).

(ii) Corporation tax repaid for the year to 31/12/95 is £8,750. This is equal to the original liability for the year of £15,750 i.e. 25% x (£64,000 - £1,000), less ACT of £7,000 (£28,000 x 1/4). The £7,000 of ACT becomes surplus ACT.

(iii) The corporation tax due for the year to 31 December 1997 is :

	£
90/365 x £13,000 @ 24% + 275/365 x £13,000 @ 23%	3,022
Less : Surplus ACT b/f (maximum set-off 20% x £13,000)	2,600
	422
Less : Excess of income tax suffered over income tax deducted	230
	192

Question C5

(a)

	£
Trading profits	170,000
Less : Capital allowances	32,000
Schedule D Case I	138,000
Schedule A	18,000
UFII £21,560 x 100/77	28,000
Capital gains £6,400 - £1,400	5,000
	189,000
Less : Charges on income £15,400 x 100/77	20,000
Chargeable profits	169,000
Corporation tax @ 23%	38,870
Less : Excess of income tax suffered over income tax deducted from payments	1,840
MCT due 1 January 1999	37,030

(b) If the company has one subsidiary, the limits for the small companies rate are divided by 2. The lower limit becomes £150,000 and the upper limit becomes £750,000. The company's profits, including grossed-up FII, are £185,000 (£169,000 + £12,800 x 100/80). Corporation tax is due as follows :

	£
£169,000 @ 33%	55,770.00
Less : $\frac{1}{40}$ x (£750,000 - £185,000) x $\frac{£169,000}{£185,000}$	12,903.38
	42,866.62

Set D

Question D1

(i) The sale to St Oggs Inc is an export to a non-EU country and is zero-rated, even though the goods in question are normally standard-rated. Customs and Excise may require documentary evidence that the goods have actually been exported.

(ii) Scotland is not outside the UK so the sale to Rappit Ltd is not an export and the supply is standard rated. The value of the supply is £19,000 (£20,000 less 5%) and the related output tax is £3,325 (17.5% of £19,000). This is the case whether or not Rappit Ltd takes advantage of the discount offered.

(iii) The sale of the machinery is a taxable supply of goods, even though the machinery was a fixed asset rather than stock in trade.

(iv) The hire of electrical equipment is a taxable supply of services.

(v) Unless Wakem & Co. Ltd operates the cash accounting scheme, output tax relating to supplies of goods to Garum Furs plc will have been paid over to Customs and Excise at the end of the quarters in which the supplies took place. This VAT can be recovered from

Customs and Excise so long as at least 6 months have elapsed since the date of supply and Wakem & Co. Ltd has written off the debt in its books. If part-payment is eventually received from the liquidator, part of the recovered VAT will be repayable to Customs and Excise.

Question D2

(a) A Ltd controls B Ltd, C Ltd, D Ltd and E Ltd, so all five companies are associated companies.

(b) A Ltd controls 75% or more of B Ltd and C Ltd and so these three companies form a 75% group for group relief purposes. E Ltd is not UK resident and so cannot belong to the group. A Ltd owns a total of 76% of D Ltd but 20% of this is owned indirectly via a non-resident company. The remaining 56% is not sufficient for D Ltd to be regarded as part of the group.

(c) The profits of E Ltd (a CFC) do not exceed £20,000, so there is no allocation of E Ltd's profits to A Ltd. The profits of £15,000 are not chargeable to UK corporation tax at all.

Both A Ltd and B Ltd will pay tax at the marginal rate of 35.5% unless their chargeable profits are reduced to the lower limit of £60,000 (£300,000 x 1/5th). Therefore the most efficient use of C Ltd's trading loss is to use it to reduce the profits of A Ltd and B Ltd to £60,000 each and then to set the remainder of the loss against C Ltd's own Schedule D Case III income. The MCT payable by each company is as follows :

	A Ltd	*B Ltd*	*C Ltd*	*D Ltd*	*E Ltd*
	£	£	£	£	£
Schedule D Case I	90,000	100,000	-	-	-
Schedule D Case III	-	15,000	12,000	-	-
	90,000	115,000	12,000	-	-
Less : Group relief	30,000	55,000	-	-	-
S393A(1)(a)	-	-	5,000	-	-
Chargeable profits	60,000	60,000	7,000	-	-
Tax @ 23%	13,800	13,800	1,610	-	-

(d) If E Ltd has profits exceeding £20,000, as seems likely next year, these profits will be allocated to A Ltd (since E Ltd is a CFC) and assessed to UK corporation tax. This can only be avoided if E Ltd adopts an "acceptable distribution policy", which will involve paying at least 90% of its profits to A Ltd. This 90% would then be subject to UK corporation tax but the remaining 10% would escape UK tax.

As regards D Ltd's losses, it would be helpful if these losses could form the subject of a group relief claim. This means that D Ltd should be brought into the group in some way. Two possibilities are :

(i) E Ltd transfers its shares in D Ltd to A Ltd. This transfer may have tax implications in the country in which E Ltd is resident.

(ii) E Ltd becomes UK resident by transferring its central management and control to the UK. This would have the desired effect but E Ltd's profits would then be fully chargeable to UK corporation tax.

Question D3

The report should make the following points :

(a) Employees on a 9-month contract will not be absent from the UK for a whole tax year and so, for tax purposes, these employees will be both resident and ordinarily resident in the UK throughout the 9 months. Their earnings whilst working abroad will be fully assessable to UK income tax under Schedule E Case I.

(b) Employees on an 18-month contract which includes an entire tax year will be treated as non-resident for the duration of the contract. Their earnings from duties performed overseas (and any other foreign income) will not be subject to UK income tax. As non-residents, they will also not be liable to UK capital gains tax. They will, however, be liable to UK income tax on any income arising in the UK (e.g. rents from letting their homes whilst working abroad).

(c) Employees on an 18-month contract which does not include an entire tax year will be treated as both resident and ordinarily resident in the UK throughout the 18 months. Their overseas earnings will therefore be assessed under Schedule E Case I, but a 100% deduction will be available if there is a qualifying period of at least 365 days (see Chapter 32).

Question D4

	UK income	*Income from Z Inc*	*Income from X S.A.*	*Total*
	£	£	£	£
Schedule D Case I	500,000	-	-	500,000
Schedule D Case V	-	50,000	40,000	90,000
	500,000	50,000	40,000	590,000
<u>Less</u> : Charges	10,000	-	-	10,000
Chargeable profits	490,000	50,000	40,000	580,000

M Ltd, N Ltd and O Ltd are associated companies, so the upper and lower limits are divided between them. Each company has an upper limit of £500,000 and a lower limit of £100,000. M Ltd's chargeable profits are £580,000, so tax is due at 33%.

	UK income	*Income from Z Inc*	*Income from X S.A.*	*Total*
	£	£	£	£
Corporation tax at 33%	161,700	16,500	13,200	191,400
<u>Less</u> : DTR	-	15,000	2,000	17,000
	161,700	1,500	11,200	174,400
<u>Less</u> : ACT	98,000	1,500	8,000	107,500
MCT due 1/1/99	63,700	-	3,200	66,900

Notes:

(a) Maximum ACT set-off is :

(i) UK income, 20% x £490,000 = £98,000

(ii) Income from Z Inc, 20% of £50,000 = £10,000, restricted to £1,500

(iii) Income from X S.A., 20% of £40,000 = £8,000.

(b) Surplus ACT is £1,000 (£434,000 x 1/4, less £107,500).

Index